བོད་རང་སྐྱོང་ལྗོངས་ཡིག་ཚགས་ཁང་གིས་རྩོམ་སྒྲིག་བྱས།

西藏自治區檔案館編

COMPILED BY
THE ARCHIVES OF THE TIBET AUTONOMOUS REGION


# བོད་ཀྱི་ལོ་རྒྱུས་ཡིག་ཚགས་གཅེས་བསྡུས།།

# 西藏歷史檔案薈粹

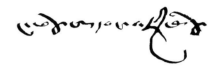

# A COLLECTION OF HISTORICAL ARCHIVES OF TIBET


རིག་དངོས་དཔེ་སྐྲུན་ཁང་ནས་དཔེ་བསྐྲུན་བྱས།

文 物 出 版 社

CULTURAL RELICS PUBLISHING HOUSE

བོད་མི་རིགས་ཀྱི་ཕུལ་དུ་བྱུང་བའི་ལོ་རྒྱུས་རིག་གནས་ནི་ཀྲུང་ཧྭ་མི་རིགས་
ཀྱི་རིག་གནས་གཏེར་མཛོད་ནང་གི་གལ་ཆེའི་གྲུབ་ཆ་ཞིག་ཡིན།

ཅང་ཙེ་མིང་ནས་༡༩༩༠ལོའི་ཟླ་བ་༧ཚེས་༢༥

ཉིན་བོད་ལྗོངས་ལོ་རྒྱུས་ཡིག་ཚགས་ཁང་དུ་བྲིས།

The splendid historical culture of the Tibetan nationality is an important component part of the cultural treasure–house of the Chinese nation.

Jiang Zemin

July 25, 1990

Tibet Historical Archives

藏民族優秀的歷史文化是中華民族文化寶庫中的重要組成部分

江澤民

一九九〇年七月廿五日

於西藏歷史檔案館

Authentic documents, Historical witnesses.

Li Tieying

བཀའ་གཏན་ཡིག་རིགས། ལོ་རྒྱུས་ཀྱི་བདེན་དཔང་།

ལི་ཐེ་དབྱིང་ནས།

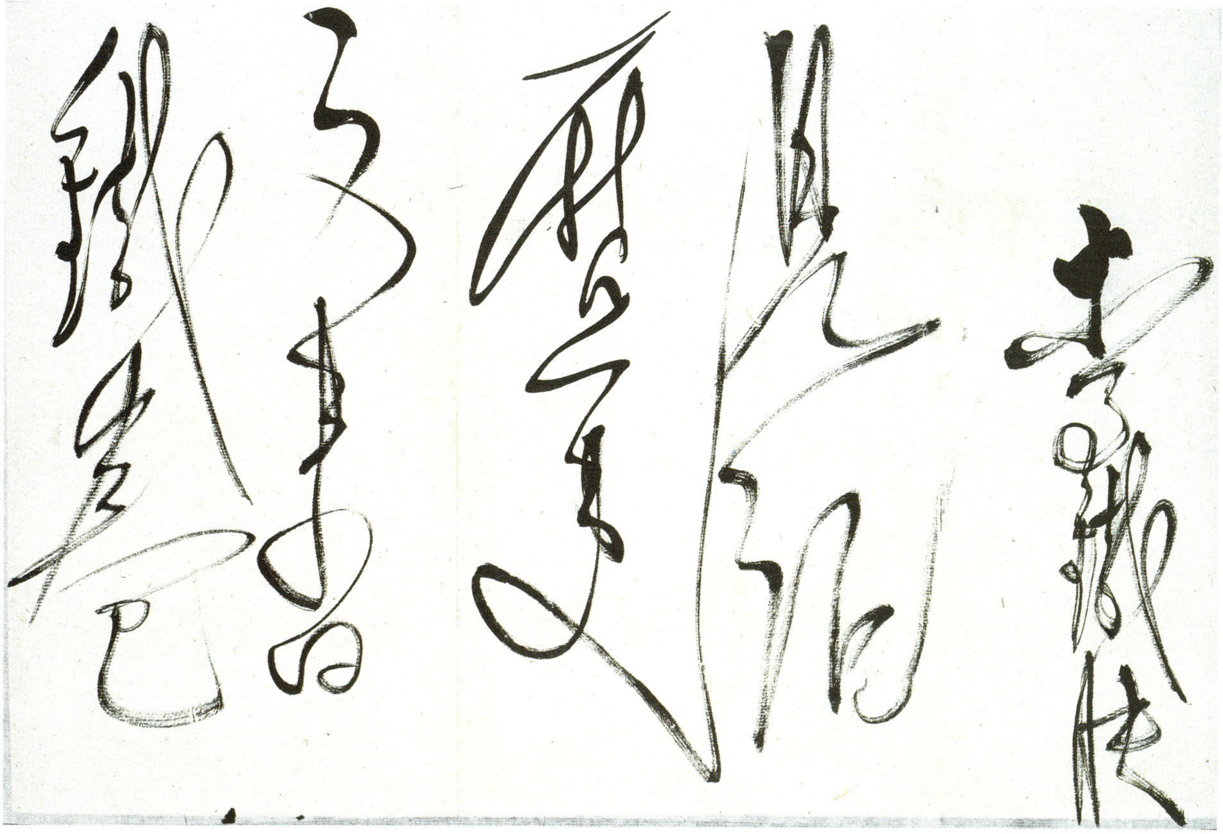

《བོད་ཀྱི་ལོ་རྒྱུས་ཡིག་ཚགས་གཅེས་བསྡུས》རྩོམ་སྒྲིག་ཨུ་ཡོན་ལྷན་ཁང་།

སྤྱི་ཁྱབ་རྩོམ་སྒྲིག་པ། སྒྲོལ་དཀར།
ཞའོ་ཧོད་ཡོན།
འོད་ཟེར།

རྩོམ་སྒྲིག་ཨུ་ཡོན། རྭ་སྒྲེང་ཡེ་ཤེས་ཚུལ་ཁྲིམས།
ལི་གོ་ཆིང་།
བྱམས་པ་དཔལ་འབྱོར།
ངག་དབང་ཆོས་དར།
ཚེ་རིང་རྒྱལ་པོ།
བློ་བཟང་རྒྱལ་མཚན།

《西藏歷史檔案薈粹》 編輯委員會

總編 卓 嘎
蕭懷遠
唯 賽

委員 熱振·益西楚臣
李國清
强巴班覺
阿旺曲達
次仁杰保
洛桑更參

The Editorial Committee of
*A Collection of Historical Archives of Tibet*

Chief editor: Sgrolkar
Xiao Huaiyuan
Vodzer

Members: Yeshes Tshulkhrim
Li Guoqing
Byampa Palbyor
Ngagwang Chosdar
Tshering Gyalpo
Lozang Gyaltshan

# དཀར་ཆག



## ཡོན་རྒྱལ་རབས་ཀྱི་ཡིག་ཚགས།

༡༢. ཀུན་དགའ་རྒྱལ་མཚན་དཔལ་བཟང་པོ་ཏི་ཤྲི་ནས་ཡེ་ཤེས་ཀུན་དགའ་ལ་བསྩལ་པའི་བཀའ་ཡིག

༡༣. ཐ་ཨི་རྒྱལ་ཡུམ་ནས་སྐུ་ཞང་གྲགས་པ་རྒྱལ་མཚན་ལ་བསྩལ་པའི་བཀའ་ཡིག

༡༤. ཧི་ཤན་རྗོད་ཉིང་ཕང་ནས་ཞ་ལུ་དགོན་ལ་བསྩལ་པའི་བཀའ།

༡༥. རིང་ཟླ་ལུ་སྲོན་ལྷི་སིའི་མི་དཔོན་གྱི་གཏམ།

༡༦. རྒྱལ་ཁབ་ཁག་གི་གྲྭ་བཙུན་རྣམས་འགོ་འཛིན་བྱས་ཏེ་སངས་རྒྱས་བསྟན་པ་སྤེལ་བའི་ཏཱ་དབེན་ཏི་ཤྲིའི་

ཐམ་ཀ

༡༧. ཏི་ཤྲི་སངས་རྒྱས་དཔལ་གྱི་ཐམ་ཀ

༡༨. གོ་ཤྲིའི་ཐམ་ཀ

༡༩. རྒྱལ་བསྟན་འགོ་གཙོ་ཏཱ་དབེན་གོ་ཤྲིའི་ཐམ་ཀ

༢༠. དབང་བསྒྱུར་གོ་ཤྲིའི་ཐམ་ཀ

༢༡. ཨིས་མྣར་གམ་དམག་འབངས་ཁྲི་དཔོན་ཁང་གི་ཐམ་ཀ

༢༢. པེ་ལན་ཕང་གི་ཐམ་ཀ

## མིང་རྒྱལ་རབས་ཀྱི་ཡིག་ཚགས།

༢༣. གོང་མ་ཧུང་ཝུས་ཆོས་ཀུན་སྐྱབས་ལ་བསྩལ་པའི་བཀའ་ལུང་།

༢༤. གོང་མ་ཡུན་ལོས་བླ་མ་ཀརྨ་པ་ལ་བསྩལ་པའི་འཕྲིན་ཡིག

༢༥. གོང་མ་ཡུན་ལོས་སོ་པ་ལྷ་བཙན་སྐྱབས་ལ་བསྩལ་པའི་བཀའ་ལུང་།

༢༦. གོང་མ་ཡུན་ལོས་བཀའ་བཞི་བ་བསོད་ནམས་མགོན་ལ་བསྩལ་པའི་བཀའ་ལུང་།

༢༧. གོང་མ་ཤོན་དས་ཀརྨ་པ་ལ་བསྩལ་པའི་བཀའ་ལུང་།

༢༨. གོང་མ་ཅིང་ཐོང་གིས་བླ་མ་ཀརྨ་པ་ལ་བསྩལ་པའི་བཀའ་ལུང་།

༢༩. གོང་མ་ཆིང་ཧྭས་ནམ་མཁའ་བཀྲ་ཤིས་རྒྱལ་མཚན་དཔལ་བཟང་པོ་ལ་བསྩལ་པའི་བཀའ་ལུང་།

༣༠. གོང་མ་ཆིང་ཧྭས་ཀརྨ་པ་ལ་བསྩལ་པའི་བཀའ་ལུང་།

༣༡. དེ་བཞིན་གཤེགས་པ་རིན་པོ་ཆེ་ཆོས་རྒྱལ་གྱི་ཐམ་ཀ

༣༢. བདེན་པ་མངོན་པར་རྟོགས་པའི་ཐེག་ཆེན་ཆོས་ཀྱི་རྒྱལ་པོའི་ཐམ་ཀ

༣༣. འབྲི་གུང་ཁྲི་དཔོན་ཁང་གི་ཐམ་ཀ

## ཆིང་རྒྱལ་རབས་ཀྱི་ཡིག་ཚགས།

༣༤. གོང་མ་ཤུན་ཀྲིས་པཎ་ཆེན་རིན་པོ་ཆེ་ལ་བསྩལ་བའི་བཀའ།

༣༥. གོང་མ་ཤུན་ཀྲིས་ཏཱ་ལའི་བླ་མར་བསྩལ་བའི་བཀའ།

༣༦. གོང་མ་བདེ་སྐྱིད་ཀྱིས་པཎ་ཆེན་སྐུ་ཕྲེང་ལྔ་པ་ལ་ཚོ་ལོ་དང་འཇའ་ས་བསྩལ་བའི་བཀའ་ལུང་།

༣༧. གོང་མ་བདེ་སྐྱིད་ཀྱིས་ཧྲུན་གར་བའི་འབྲུག་ཐེང་བདེ་འཛགས་སུ་བཏང་བའི་བྱས་རྗེས་ཡོད་མཁན་ལ་གོ་མིང་དང་བྱ་དགའ་གནང་བའི་དོན་དུ་ཚོག་ཐུ་ལ་བསྩལ་བའི་བཀའ་ལུང་།

༣༨. གོང་མ་བདེ་སྐྱིད་ཀྱིས་སངས་རྒྱས་ཀྱི་བསྟན་པ་དར་རྒྱས་སུ་གཏོང་དགོས་པའི་དོན་དུ་ཏཱ་ལའི་བླ་མ་སྐུ་ཕྲེང་དྲུག་པར་བསྩལ་བའི་བཀའ་ལུང་།

༣༩. གོང་མ་བདེ་སྐྱིད་ཀྱིས་ལེགས་སྐྱེས་ཕུལ་བར་གསོལ་རས་གནང་བའི་དོན་དུ་ཏཱ་ལའི་བླ་མ་སྐུ་ཕྲེང་དྲུག་པ་ལ་བསྩལ་བའི་བཀའ་ལུང་།

༤༠. གོང་མ་ཡུང་ཅིང་གིས་ཚོ་ལོ་དང་གསེར་གྱི་ཐམ་ཀ་གནང་བའི་དོན་དུ་ཏཱ་ལའི་བླ་མ་སྐུ་ཕྲེང་དྲུག་པ་ལ་བསྩལ་བའི་བཀའ་ལུང་།

༤༡. གོང་མ་ཡུང་ཅིང་གིས་ཁང་ཆེན་པ་ནས་བོད་དོན་ཐག་གཅོད་དགོས་པའི་དོན་དུ་ཏཱ་ལའི་བླ་མར་བསྩལ་བའི་བཀའ་ལུང་།

༤༢. གོང་མ་ལྷ་སྐྱོང་གིས་ཏཱ་ལའི་བླ་མའི་ཡང་སྲིད་གསེར་ཁྲིར་མངའ་གསོལ་སོགས་ཀྱི་དོན་དུ་པཎ་ཆེན་རིན་པོ་ཆེར་བསྩལ་བའི་བཀའ་ལུང་།

༤༣. གོང་མ་ལྷ་སྐྱོང་གིས་གསེར་ཁྲིར་མངའ་གསོལ་གྱི་དོན་དུ་ཏཱ་ལའི་བླ་མར་བསྩལ་བའི་བཀའ་ལུང་།

༤༤. དགའ་ལྡན་ཁྲི་པ་ཨེར་ཏེ་ནི་ནོ་མིན་ཧན་སོགས་ཀྱིས་བཀའ་བློན་ཚད་གསབ་ཀྱི་དོན་དུ་བོད་བཞུགས་ཨམ་བན་ལ་བཏང་བའི་ཡི་གེ

༤༥. བཀའ་བློན་ཐུན་མོང་གིས་དགའ་ལྡན་ཁྲི་པ་ནོ་མིན་ཧན་ལ་ཕུལ་བའི་ཡི་གེ

༤༦. ཁྲིན་དུའི་ཅང་ཅུན་ཨོ་དེ་སོགས་ཀྱིས་བོད་དམག་སྦྱོང་བརྡར་གྱི་དོན་དུ་བཀའ་སློབ་བསྟན་འཛིན་དཔལ་འབྱོར་སོགས་ལ་བཏང་བའི་བསྒྲགས་ཡིག

༤༧. གོང་མ་ལྷ་སྐྱོང་གིས་ཏཱ་ལའི་སྤྱན་ཟླ་སོགས་ཀྱི་ལས་གནས་གཞན་དུ་བསྒྱུར་པའི་སྐོར་ལ་ཏཱ་ལའི་བླ་མར་བསྩལ་པའི་བཀའ་ལུང་།

༤༨. བོད་བཞུགས་ལས་དོན་སློབ་ཆེན་སུང་ཡུན་སོགས་ཀྱིས་བོད་འབངས་གནས་སྡོ་དང་ཁྲལ་རིགས་སོགས་ཀྱི་དོན་དུ་བཀྲས་ལྷུན་བླ་བྲང་ལ་སྤྲད་པའི་ལག་ཁྱེར་རྩ་ཚིག

༤༩. བོད་བཞུགས་ཨམ་བན་སུང་ཡུན་སོགས་ཀྱིས་གཙང་གི་མི་སེར་རྣམས་བདེ་བར་གནས་པ་དང་ཁྲལ་རིགས་སོགས་ཀྱི་སྐོར་བཀྲམས་པའི་རྩ་ཚིག

༥༠. གོང་མའི་བཀའ་འབྲེལ་ལུགས་སྲོལ་གསར་འཛུགས་ཀྱི་དོན་ཚན་ཉེར་དགུ

༥༡. རྗེ་དྲུང་རྟོ་ཐོག་ཐུ་དང་བཀའ་བློན་ཐུབ་མོང་གིས་མདའ་དཔོན་ཁ་སྐོང་བྱེད་རྒྱུའི་སྐོར་བོད་བཞུགས་ཨམ་བན་ལ་བཏང་བའི་ཡི་གེ།

༥༢. བོད་བཞུགས་ཨམ་བན་ཡུ་ཉིང་སོགས་ཀྱིས་སྤྱི་ཁྱབ་མཁན་པོ་ཁ་སྐོང་བྱེད་རྒྱུའི་སྐོར་རྗེ་དྲུང་རྟོ་ཐོག་ཐུ་ལ་བཏང་བའི་ཡི་གེ

༥༣. གོང་མ་བརྟགས་སྟོན་གྱིས་ཏཱ་ལའི་བླ་མའི་ཡང་སྲིད་ངོས་འཛིན་བྱུང་བའི་དོན་དུ་པཎ་ཆེན་རིན་པོ་ཆེར་བསྩལ་པའི་བཀའ་ལུང་།

༥༤. བོད་བཞུགས་ཨམ་བན་ཝུན་པེ་སོགས་ཀྱིས་རག་རྩིབས་པ་སོགས་གནས་སྤར་དང་བསྐོ་བཞག་བྱེད་རྒྱུའི་དོན་དུ་བཀའ་བློན་རྣམས་ལ་བཏང་བའི་ཡི་གེ

༥༥. གོང་མ་བརྟགས་སྟོན་གྱིས་ལེགས་སྐྱེས་ཕུལ་བར་གསོལ་རས་གནང་བའི་དོན་དུ་ཏཱ་ལའི་བླ་མར་བསྩལ་པའི་བཀའ་ལུང་།

༥༦. བོད་བཞུགས་ཨམ་བན་ཤེས་མིང་སོགས་ཀྱིས་མདའ་དཔོན་ཁ་སྐོང་བྱེད་རྒྱུའི་སྐོར་དེ་མོ་རྟོ་ཐོག་ཐུ་ལ་བཏང་བའི་ཡི་གེ

༥༧. གོང་མ་བརྟགས་སྟོན་གྱིས་ཏཱ་ལའི་བླ་མ་ཞིང་བརྗེས་རྗེས་འབྲེལ་ཡོད་ལས་དོན་སྐོར་ངག་དབང་འཇམ་དཔལ་ཚུལ་ཁྲིམས་ལ་བསྩལ་པའི་བཀའ་ལུང་།

༥༨. གོང་མ་སྲིད་གསལ་གྱིས་ཏཱ་ལའི་བླ་མ་ཞིང་བརྗེས་རྗེས་གནས་སྐབས་སྲིད་སྐྱོང་བསྐོ་དགོས་སྐོར་ངག་དབང་འཇམ་དཔལ་ཚུལ་ཁྲིམས་ལ་བསྩལ་བའི་བཀའ་ལུང་།

༥༩. གོང་མ་སྲིད་གསལ་གྱིས་ལེགས་སྐྱེས་ཕུལ་བར་གསོལ་རས་གནང་བའི་དོན་དུ་ཏཱ་ལའི་བླ་མར་བསྩལ་བའི་བཀའ་ལུང་།

༦༠. བོད་བཞུགས་ཨམ་བན་ཧུའི་ཤན་སོགས་ཀྱིས་རྭ་སྒྲེང་དགོན་པའི་ཏཱ་བླ་མ་ཁ་སྐོང་བྱེད་རྒྱུའི་སྐོར་ཇོ་མིན་ཧན་ལ་བཏང་བའི་ཡི་གེ

༦༡. གོང་མ་སྲིད་གསལ་གྱིས་མི་སྣ་བཏང་སྟེ་གསེར་བུམ་དཀྲུགས་པ་དང་གསེར་ཁྲིར་མངའ་གསོལ་སྐོར་ཏཱ་ལའི་བླ་མའི་ཡང་སྲིད་ལ་བསྩལ་བའི་བཀའ་ལུང་།

༦༢. ལྷ་སར་སྡོད་པའི་དམག་སྒར་གྱི་ཤུ་སྤྲིས་ནས་བཀའ་བློན་དང་མདའ་དཔོན་སོགས་ནུས་ཤུགས་བཏོན་མཁན་གྱི་དཔོན་རིགས་འོས་སྦྱོར་བྱེད་རྒྱུའི་སྐོར་གྱི་ཞུ་ཡིག

༦༣. གོང་མ་ཀུན་ཁྱབ་འཕེལ་རྒྱས་ཀྱིས་ཏཱ་ལའི་བླ་མའི་ཡང་སྲིད་སྐུ་ན་ཕྲ་སྐབས་གནས་སྐབས་རིང་སྲིད་སྐྱོང་བསྐོ་དགོས་སྐོར་རྭ་སྒྲེང་བླ་མར་བསྩལ་བའི་བཀའ་ལུང་།

༦༤. གོང་མ་ཀུན་ཁྱབ་འཕེལ་རྒྱས་ཀྱིས་གསེར་ཁྲིར་མངའ་གསོལ་སྐོར་ཏཱ་ལའི་བླ་མར་བསྩལ་བའི་བཀའ་ལུང་།

༦༥. ཛེ་དྲུང་ཏོ་ཐོག་ཐུ་དང་བཀའ་བློན་ཐུན་མོང་ནས་བོད་ཀྱི་དཔོན་རིགས་ཁ་སྐོང་བྱེད་རྒྱུའི་སྐོར་བོད་བཞུགས་ཨམ་བན་ལ་བཏང་བའི་ཡི་གེ

༦༦. གོང་མ་ཀོང་ཞུ་ནས་གསེར་ཁྲིར་མངའ་གསོལ་སྐོར་ཏཱ་ལའི་བླ་མའི་ཡང་སྲིད་ལ་བསྩལ་བའི་བཀའ་ལུང་།

༦༧. བོད་བཞུགས་ཨམ་བན་ཧྲིན་ཐེ་ནས་དཔོན་རིགས་ཁ་སྐོང་དང་ལས་གནས་སྤོ་རྒྱུའི་སྐོར་དེ་མོ་ཏོ་ཐོག་ཐུ་ལ་བཏང་བའི་ཡི་གེ

༦༨. བོད་བཞུགས་ཨམ་བན་ཧྲིན་ཐེ་དང་དེ་མོ་ཏོ་ཐོག་ཐུ་ནས་དངུལ་ལོར་འགྲོ་རྒྱུག་སྐོར་བཀྲམས་པའི་རྩ་ཚིག

༦༩. བོད་བཞུགས་ཨམ་བན་ཀྲང་དབྱིན་ཐང་སོགས་ཀྱིས་བོད་དུ་ལམ་གཏེར་སོགས་ལས་ཁུངས་འཛུགས་རྒྱུའི་སྐོར་བཀྲམས་པའི་བསྐོ་བཞག་གི་ཡི་གེ

༧༠. བོད་བཞུགས་ཨམ་བན་ལེན་ཡུས་ནས་ཚྭ་ཁྲལ་བསྡུ་རྒྱུའི་སྐོར་བཀྲམས་པའི་རྩ་ཚིག

༧༡. གོང་མ་ཡུང་ཅིང་ནས་ཏཱ་ལའི་བླ་མ་སྐུ་ཕྲེང་བདུན་པར་བསྩལ་བའི་གསེར་གྱི་ཐམ་ཀ

༧༢. གོང་མ་ལྷ་སྐྱོང་གིས་ཏཱ་ལའི་བླ་མ་སྐུ་ཕྲེང་བརྒྱད་པ་ལ་བསྩལ་པའི་ཚོ་ལོ་དང་གཡང་ཏིའི་འཇའ་ས།

༧༣. གོང་མ་ལྷ་སྐྱོང་གིས་ཕོ་བྲང་པོ་ཏ་ལར་བསྩལ་པའི་ཕྱག་བྲིས་ཕྱག་བསྟར་མའི་པན་ཡིག

༧༤. གོང་མ་སྲིད་གསལ་གྱིས་ཏཱ་ལའི་བླ་མ་སྐུ་ཕྲེང་བཅུ་གཅིག་པ་ལ་བསྩལ་པའི་ཚོ་ལོ་དང་གསེར་གྱི་འཇའ་ས།

༧༥. གོང་མ་སྲིད་གསལ་གྱིས་སྨིན་གྲོལ་གླིང་ལ་བསྩལ་པའི་ཕྱག་བྲིས་ཕྱག་བསྟར་མའི་པན་ཡིག

༧༦. གོང་མ་ཐུང་ཀྲི་ནས་བཀྲ་ཤིས་ལྷུན་པོ་དགོན་པར་བསྩལ་པའི་ཕྱག་བྲིས་ཕྱག་བསྟར་མའི་པན་ཡིག

༧༧. རྒྱལ་ཡུམ་ཚི་ཤིས་ཐའི་ཧུས་ཏཱ་ལའི་བླ་མ་སྐུ་ཕྲེང་བཅུ་གསུམ་པར་བསྩལ་པའི་ཕྱག་བྲིས་ཕྱག་བསྟར་མའི་རི་མོ།

༧༨. གོང་མ་ཀོང་ཞུའི་འདྲ་པར།

༧༩. རྒྱལ་ཡུམ་ཚི་ཤིས་ཐའི་ཧུའི་འདྲ་པར།

## མིང་གོའི་ཡིག་ཚགས།

༨༠. མིང་གོའི་གནས་སྐབས་ཀྱི་ཙུང་ཐུང་ཆེན་པོས་བོད་སོག་གཅིག་སྒྱུར་ཆབ་སྲིད་ལེགས་བཅོས་ལྷན་ཚོགས་བཙུགས་པར་ཚོག་མཆན་བཀོད་པའི་དོན་དུ་བསྩལ་པའི་བཀའ།

༨༡. ཅང་ཀྲུང་ཀྲིན་ནས་ཏཱ་ལའི་བླ་མ་ལ་ཕུལ་བའི་འཕྲིན་ཡིག

༨༢. གོ་མིང་སྲིད་གཞུང་གིས་ཏཱ་ལའི་བླ་མ་ལ་བསྩལ་པའི་ཚོ་ལོ།

༨༣. གོ་མིང་སྲིད་གཞུང་གིས་པཎ་ཆེན་ཨེར་ཏི་ནི་ལ་མཚན་སྙན་གསོལ་བའི་དོན་དུ་བསྩལ་པའི་བཀའ།

༨༤. གོ་མིང་སྲིད་གཞུང་གིས་པཎ་ཆེན་ཨེར་ཏི་ནི་ལ་གཟེངས་བསྟོད་གནང་བའི་བཀའ།

༨༥. ཧྲོང་མའོ་སུང་གིས་ཏཱ་ལའི་བླ་མའི་ཡང་སྲིད་འཚོལ་རྒྱུའི་དོན་དུ་རྭ་སྒྲེང་སོགས་ལ་བཏང་བའི་ཏ་ར།

༨༦. པཎ་ཆེན་ཨེར་ཏི་ནི་སྐུ་ཕྲེང་དགུ་པའི་ཞལ་ཆེམས།

༨༧. གོ་མིང་སྲིད་གཞུང་གིས་ཝུ་ཀྲུང་ཞིན་ཆེད་དུ་མངགས་ནས་རྭ་སྒྲེང་དང་མཉམ་དུ་ཏཱ་ལའི་བླ་མ་འཁྲུངས་པའི་ལས་དོན་གྱི་གཙོ་འགན་འཁུར་དགོས་སྐོར་བསྩལ་པའི་བཀའ།

༨༨. གོ་མིང་སྲིད་གཞུང་གིས་ཝུ་ཀྲུང་ཞིན་ཆེད་དུ་མངགས་ནས་རྭ་སྒྲེང་དང་མཉམ་དུ་ཏཱ་ལའི་བླ་མ་འཁྲུངས་པའི་ལས་དོན་གྱི་གཙོ་འགན་འཁུར་དགོས་སྐོར་སྲིད་འཛིན་ཁང་ལ་བསྩལ་པའི་བཀའ།

༨༩. གོ་མིང་སྲིད་གཞུང་གིས་ལྷ་མོ་དོན་གྲུབ་མཆོག་ཏཱ་ལའི་བླ་མ་སྐུ་ཕྲེང་བཅུ་བཞི་པར་ངོས་འཛིན་བྱུང་བའི་དོན་དུ་བཏང་བའི་བཀའ།

༩༠. ཏེ་ཁྲིན་ཞན་གྱིས་ལྷ་མོ་དོན་གྲུབ་ཏཱ་ལའི་བླ་མ་སྐུ་ཕྲེང་བཅུ་བཞི་པར་ངོས་འཛིན་བྱུང་བའི་དོན་དུ་རྭ་སྒྲེང་ལ་བཏང་བའི་རྗེས་འབྲེལ་ཞུ་བའི་ཏར།

༩༡. ཝུ་ཀྲུང་ཤིན་གྱིས་ཏཱ་ལའི་བླ་མ་གསེར་ཁྲིར་མངའ་གསོལ་སྐོར་གོ་མིང་སྲིད་གཞུང་གི་ཀྲུའུ་ཞི་སོགས་ལ་བཏང་བའི་ཏར།

༩༢. ལྷ་མོ་དོན་གྲུབ་མཆོག་ནས་རང་ཉིད་ཏཱ་ལའི་བླ་མ་སྐུ་ཕྲེང་བཅུ་བཞི་པར་ངོས་འཛིན་བྱས་པར་གོ་མིང་སྲིད་གཞུང་ལ་བཏང་བའི་འཕྲིན་ལན།

༩༣. ཐུབ་བསྟན་བཟང་པོ་ལ་བསྩལ་པའི་གོ་མིང་ཚོགས་ཆེན་གྱི་འཐུས་མིའི་ལག་ཁྱེར།

༩༤. བོད་སོག་ཨུ་ཡོན་ལྷན་ཁང་གིས་པཎ་ཆེན་ཨེར་ཏེ་ནིའི་ཡང་སྲིད་གསེར་ཁྲིར་མངའ་གསོལ་བྱེད་རྒྱུའི་སྐོར་བཀའ་ཤག་ལ་བཏང་བའི་ཏར།

༩༥. ཙུང་ཐུང་ཁང་གིས་པཎ་ཆེན་ཨེར་ཏེ་ནི་སྐུ་ཕྲེང་བཅུ་པས་ཕུལ་བའི་ཐུགས་རྗེ་ཆེ་ཞུས་པའི་ཏར་སྐོར་བོད་སོག་ཨུ་ཡོན་ལྷན་ཁང་ལ་བཏང་བའི་ཡི་གེ

༩༦. རྒྱལ་ཁབ་རོགས་བྱེད་འགྲོ་བ་ཀུན་འདུལ་བསམ་གཏན་གྱི་སློབ་དཔོན་རྭ་སྒྲེང་ཧོ་ཐོག་ཐུའི་ཐམ་ཀ

## ཀྲུང་ཧྭ་མི་དམངས་སྤྱི་མཐུན་རྒྱལ་ཁབ་ཀྱི་ཡིག་ཚགས།

༩༧. ཏཱ་ལའི་བླ་མས་ཞི་བའི་གྲོས་མོལ་བྱེད་རྒྱུའི་སྐོར་སྲིད་སྐྱོང་ལས་ཚབ་ལ་བསྩལ་པའི་བཀའ།

༩༨. ཀྲུང་ཧྭ་མི་དམངས་སྤྱི་མཐུན་རྒྱལ་ཁབ་ཚབ་མདོ་ས་ཁུལ་མི་དམངས་བཅིངས་འགྲོལ་ཨུ་ཡོན་ལྷན་ཁང་གི་ཐ་ཚིག

༩༩. ལྷོ་ནུབ་དམག་སྲིད་ཨུ་ཡོན་ལྷན་ཁང་དང་ཀྲུང་གོ་མི་དམངས་བཅིངས་འགྲོལ་དམག་ལྷོ་ནུབ་དམག་ཁུལ་ཁང་གི་ཐ་ཚིག

༡༠༠. ཀྲུང་དབྱང་མི་དམངས་སྲིད་གཞུང་དང་བོད་ཀྱི་ས་གནས་སྲིད་གཞུང་གཉིས་བོད་ཞི་བས་བཅིངས་འགྲོལ་འབྱུང་ཐབས་སྐོར་གྱི་གྲོས་མཐུན།

༡༠༡. ཏཱ་ལའི་བླ་མ་སྐུ་ཕྲེང་བཅུ་བཞི་པས་གྲོས་མཐུན་ཐྲུང་བར་བརྩི་བཀུར་ཞུ་བའི་དོན་དུ་ཀྲུའུ་ཞི་མའོ་ཙེ་ཏུང་ལ་ཕུལ་བའི་ཏར།

༡༠༢. ཀྲུའུ་ཞི་མའོ་ཙེ་ཏུང་ནས་ཏཱ་ལའི་བླ་མ་ལ་བཏང་བའི་ཏར་ལན།

༡༠༣. ཀྲུའུ་ཞི་མའོ་ཙེ་ཏུང་ནས་ཏཱ་ལའི་བླ་མ་ལ་བཏང་བའི་འཕྲིན་ཡིག

༡༠༤. ཙུང་ལི་ཀྲུའུ་ཨེན་ལེ་ནས་ཏཱ་ལའི་བླ་མ་ལ་བཏང་བའི་འཕྲིན་ཡིག

༡༠༥. ཨུ་ཡོན་ཀྲང་ལིའུ་ཧྲོ་ཆི་ནས་ཏཱ་ལའི་བླ་མ་ལ་བཏང་བའི་འཕྲིན་ཡིག

༡༠༦. ཀྲུའུ་ཞི་གཞོན་པ་ཀྲུའུ་ཏེ་ནས་ཏཱ་ལའི་བླ་མ་ལ་བཏང་བའི་འཕྲིན་ཡིག

༡༠༧. ཏཱ་ལའི་བླ་མ་སྐུ་ཕྲེང་བཅུ་བཞི་པས་ཀྲུའུ་ཞི་མའོ་ཙེ་ཏུང་ལ་བསྟོད་པའི་སྙན་ཚིག

མཇུག་བྱང་།

# 目　　錄



## 元朝檔案

## 明朝檔案



## 清朝檔案

## 民國檔案

## 中華人民共和國檔案

# CONTENTS



## Yuan Dynasty Archives

## Ming Dynasty Archives



## Qing Dynasty Archives

## Archives from the Period of the Republic of China

## Archives from the Period Following the Founding of the People's Republic of China

# འགོ་བརྗོད།

༄༅། །ཀྲུང་གོ་ནི་ལོ་རྒྱུས་ཡུན་རིང་ལྡན་ཞིང་། ས་ཁྱོན་རྒྱ་ཆེ་བ། མི་རིགས་མང་བའི་རྒྱལ་ཁབ་ཅིག་ཡིན། བོད་མི་རིགས་ཀྲུང་ཧྭ་མི་རིགས་ཀྱི་ཁྲིམ་ཚང་ཆེན་པོའི་ཁོངས་མི་ཞིག་ཏུ་གྱུར་པ་དེ་ནི་ཡུན་རིང་ལོ་རྒྱུས་འཕེལ་རྒྱས་ཀྱི་འབྲས་བུ་ཞིག་ཡིན།

ལོ་ངོ་སྟོང་ཕྲག་གཅིག་ལྷག་ཙམ་གྱི་སྔ་རོལ་ནས་ཐང་གོང་མ་ཚང་གི་སྲས་མོ་འོན་ཤིང་ཀོང་ཇོ་བོད་ཀྱི་བཙན་པོ་སྲོང་བཙན་སྒམ་པོའི་ཁབ་ཏུ་བཞེས་པ་ནས་བཟུང་བོད་དང་ཀྲུང་ཡོན་ས་ཁུལ་གྱི་མི་རིགས་དབར་དཔལ་འབྱོར་དང་། རིག་གནས་སོགས་ཀྱི་ཐད་རྒྱ་ཆེ་ཞིང་གཏིང་ཟབ་པའི་འབྲེལ་བ་བྱུང་ཡོད། དུས་རབས་བཅུ་གསུམ་པའི་དུས་དཀྱིལ་ལ་སོག་པོ་མི་རིགས་འབུར་དུ་ཐོན་ཏེ་ཡོན་རྒྱལ་རབས་གསར་འཛུགས་བྱས་པ་དང་ཕྱོགས་མཚུངས་བོད་ཀྱི་ས་ཆ་ཡང་ཧྭ་དབྱིན་གོང་མའི་རྒྱལ་ཁབ་ཀྱི་མངའ་ཁོངས་སུ་ཚུད་པ་རེད། དུས་དེ་ནས་བཟུང་སྟེ་ཀྲུང་ཧྭ་མི་དམངས་སྤྱི་མཐུན་རྒྱལ་ཁབ་དབུ་བརྙེས་བར་ལོ་ངོ་བདུན་བརྒྱ་ལྷག་ཙམ་རིང་བོད་ས་གནས་འདི་ཉིད་ཀྲུང་གོའི་སྲིད་འཛིན་གྱི་ཁྲབ་ཁོངས་ཤིག་ཡིན་པར་བརྟེན་ཐོག་མཐའ་བར་གསུམ་དུ་ཀྲུང་དབྱང་སྲིད་གཞུང་གིས་བདག་འཛིན་བྱེད་མུས་རེད།

དེབ་འདི་ནང་སྤྱི་ལོ་༡༣༧༧ལོ་ནས་སྤྱི་ལོ་༡༩༥༨བར་གྱི་བོད་ཡིག སོག་ཡིག རྒྱ་ཡིག མཉྫུའི་ཡི་གེ་སོགས་རིན་ཐང་ཧ་ཅང་ཆེ་བའི་ཡིག་ཚགས་དཔྱད་ཡིག་དང་རིག་དངོས་བཅས་བརྒྱ་ལྷག་ཙམ་བསྡུས་ཡོད། དེའི་ནང་ཆེས་མང་ཆེ་བ་ནི་བོད་རང་སྐྱོང་ལྗོངས་ཡིག་ཚགས་ཁང་གིས་ཉར་ཚགས་བྱས་པའི་ཡིག་ཚགས་ནང་གི་དེ་སྔ་ཁྲབ་བསྒྲགས་བྱས་མ་མྱོང་བའི་རྩ་ཆེའི་དངོས་ནོར་ཡིན། གྲངས་འབོར་ངོས་ནས་བཤད་ན། བོད་ཀྱི་ལོ་རྒྱུས་ཡིག་ཚགས་ནོར་བུའི་བང་མཛོད་ནང་གི་ཨོག་ལྷེ་འགའ་ཤས་ལྷ་བུ་ཞིག་ཡིན་ཙང་འདི་དག་ནི་མིའི་རིགས་ཀྱི་ལོ་རྒྱུས་འགྱུལ་སྐྱོད་ཀྱི་ཟིན་ཐོ་ངོ་མ་ཡིན་སྟབས། བོད་འདི་ཉིད་ཀྲུང་གོའི་མངའ་ཁོངས་ཤིག་ཡིན་པར་ར་སྤྲོད་གསལ་པོ་བྱེད་ཐུབ།

ཡིག་ཚགས་མ་ཡིག་གི་པར་ལེན་ཡིག་ཆ་དང་། བོད། རྒྱ། དབྱིན་གསུམ་གྱི་ཡིག་རིགས་བསྒྱུར་ཡིག་ཚུད་པའི་དེབ་འདི་ནི་ནང་དོན་ཕུན་སུམ་ཚོགས་ལ་པར་རིས་དང་ཡི་གེ་གཉིས་ལྡན་གཞན་དང་མི་འདྲ་བའི་ཁྱད་ཆོས་ཡོད་པར་བརྟེན་རྒྱལ་ཁབ་ཕྱི་ནང་གི་རྒྱ་ཆེའི་ཞློག་པ་པོར་ལོ་རྒྱུས་དང་། སྒྱུ་རྩལ། རིག་གཞུང་ཞིབ་འཇུག་བྱ་རྒྱུ་བཅས་ལ་རིན་ཐང་ཧ་ཅང་ཆེན་པོ་ལྡན་ཡོད། གཞན་ཡང་དེབ་འདིའི་རྩོམ་སྒྲུར་གྱི་ལས་ཀའི་ཐད་དུས་རབས་འགའ་ཞིག་བགྲལ་བའི་བོད། རྒྱ། སོག མན། དབྱིན་སོགས་ཡིག་རིགས་མི་འདྲ་བ་མང་པོའི་ཡི་གེ་ཕར

ཚུར་སྒྱུར་རྒྱུའི་དཀའ་ཚེགས་ཆེ་བའི་ལས་འགན་འཁུར་དགོས་བྱུང་བ་དང་ཕྱོགས་མཚུངས་རྩོམ་སྒྱུར་གྱི་དུས་ཚོད་ཐུང་བ། ང་ཚོའི་ཆུ་ཚད་མི་འདང་བ་བཅས་ཀྱི་རྐྱེན་གྱིས་མ་འགྲིག་ས་ཡོད་པ་ནི་གཡོལ་ཐབས་མེད་པས་ཀློག་པ་པོ་སྤྱི་དང་ལྷག་པར་དུ་ཕྱོགས་སོ་སོའི་རིགས་གཅིག་མཁས་པ་དང་མཁས་དབང་རྣམས་ནས་སྒྲ་གསང་མེད་པའི་མཛུབ་སྟོན་དང་ནོར་བཅོས་མཛད་རྒྱུའི་རེ་འདུན་ཞུའོ། །

«བོད་ཀྱི་ལོ་རྒྱུས་ཡིག་ཚགས་གཅེས་བཏུས»རྩོམ་སྒྲིག་ཨུ་ཡོན་ལྷན་ཁང་གིས་

སྤྱི་ལོ་༡༩༩༩ ལོའི་ཟླ་བ་བཅུ་པར་ལྷ་ལྡན་དུ་བྲིས་པའོ། །

# 序　　言

中國是個歷史悠久、幅員遼闊、民族衆多的國家。藏民族成爲中華民族大家庭的一員，是長期歷史發展的結果。

自一千多年前，唐室文成公主出嫁給吐蕃贊普松贊干布以來，吐蕃和中原民族就在經濟、文化等方面有了廣泛而密切的聯系。到公元十三世紀中葉，隨着蒙古民族的崛起和元朝的建立，吐蕃疆土歸入大元帝國的版圖。從那時起直到中華人民共和國成立後的今天，七百餘年間，西藏地方作爲中國的一個行政區域，始終處於中央政府的統轄之下。

本書刊載了從公元1277年至1956年百餘份藏文、蒙文、漢文、滿文等十分寶貴的檔案文獻和文物，其中絶大部分係未曾公布過的西藏自治區檔案館的館藏珍品。論其數量，雖猶如西藏歷史檔案寶庫中的幾頁紙，但是它們作爲人類歷史活動的真實記錄，也足資證明西藏是中國領土的一部分。

本書包含檔案原件的影印件與藏、漢、英三種文字的譯文，内容豐富，圖文並茂，别具特色，對國内外廣大讀者均具有很高的史料價值、藝術價值和學術研究價值。另一方面，由於本書包容了跨幾個世紀的藏、蒙、漢、滿、英等多種文字，對譯工作十分艱難，加上編譯時間短和我們水平有限，不妥之處在所難免。望讀者及各方專家、學者不吝賜教，加以指正。

《西藏歷史檔案薈粹》編輯委員會

公元1994年10月書於拉薩

# FOREWORD

China is an ancient, vast and multi–national country and as part of the Chinese nation, the Tibetan people's role has developed through history.

Over a thousand years ago, the marriage of Princess Wencheng from the Tang Dynasty royal family and King Songzan Gambo of Tubo (ancient name of Tibet) marked the beginning of the close relationship between the Tubo people and the people of the central areas of China in the economic, cultural and other fields. During the mid–13th century, with the rise of the Mongolian nationality and the founding of the Yuan Dynasty, Tubo became part of the Yuan Empire. From that time to the present era of the People's Republic of China, a period spanning over 700 years, Tibet has remained an administrative division under a central Chinese government.

This book contains more than 100 documents written in Tibetan, Mongolian, Chinese and Manchu which come from archives dating to the period between 1277 and 1956. Most are in the Archives of the Tibet Autonomous Region and have never before been made public. Those published here represent just a small part of the archives of Tibetan history, but they are a faithful record of human history and capable of adequately verifying the fact that Tibet is a part of China's territory.

This book features photocopies of the originals and translations of these documents in Tibetan, Chinese and English. It is an informative book, with coordinated photos and articles, and an invaluable resource for the study of Tibetan history, art and other subjects. Nevertheless, due to the fact that the material covers a period of seven centuries, and because of the difficulties of working through several languages and the constraints of time and knowledge, there may be imperfections in the book. We shall be grateful for any comments you might have.

Editorial Staff
October 1994
Lhasa

# ཀློག་སྟངས།

དང་པོ། དེབ་འདིས་པར་ལེན་ཡིག་ཆ་དང་བོད་རྒྱ་དབྱིན་གྱི་སྒྱུར་ཡིག་ལྡན་ཅིག་ཏུ་བསྒྲིགས་ཏེ་ཡིག་ཚགས་མ་ཡིག་གི་རྣམ་པ་དང་། ཡིག་རིགས། ནང་དོན་བཅས་ཇི་མ་ཇི་བཞིན་གྱི་སྒོ་ནས་ཀློག་པ་པོའི་སྤྱན་ལམ་དུ་ཕུལ་ཏེ་ངོ་སྤྲོད་བྱས་ཡོད།

གཉིས་པ། དེབ་འདིའི་ནང་བརྟན་པའི་ཡིག་ཚགས་སྒྱུར་ཡིག་གི་ཁ་བྱང་དང་སྤྱི་ལོའི་ལོ་ཚིགས་ཚང་མ་རྩོམ་སྒྱུར་པས་སྒྲིག་སྦྱོར་བྱས་པ་དང་། དེབ་འདིར་བཀོད་པའི་ཡིག་ཚགས་མཚན་འགྲེལ་ཡི་གེའི་ནང་གསལ་བའི་འཇལ་བྱེད་ཚང་མ་ལི་སྨི་ཡིན།

གསུམ་པ། དེབ་འདིའི་པར་ལེན་ཡིག་ཆའི་མ་ཡིག་བོད་ཡིག་གམ་རྒྱ་ཡིག་ཡིན་ཞོ། དབྱིན་ཡིག་ལ་ཕབ་བསྒྱུར་བྱས་པ་ཕུད། བོད་ཡིག་གམ་རྒྱ་ཡིག་ཁ་བྱང་མ་གཏོགས་བྲིས་མེད། པར་ལེན་ཡིག་ཆ་རེ་གཉིས་བོད་ཡིག་གམ་རྒྱ་ཡིག་གི་ཡིག་གཟུགས་ངོས་འཛིན་བྱེད་དཀའ་བ་ཡིན་ཞོ། བོད་ཡིག་གམ་རྒྱ་ཡིག་གི་བཤུས་ཡིག་བཀོད་ཡོད། དེ་མིན་ཡིག་ཆ་འགའ་རེའི་ནང་དོན་ཡིག་ཚོགས་མང་ཞིང་བསྐྱར་བཟློས་བྱས་པའི་རྐྱེན་གྱིས་ཚིག་ཚོགས་ཇེ་ཉུང་དུ་གཏོང་ཆེད། རྟགས་འདི་འདྲ་[ ]ནང་དུ་ནང་དོན་རགས་བསྡུས་ཤིག་མཚམས་སྦྱོར་བྱས་ཡོད།

བཞི་པ། དེབ་འདིར་ཡོན་རྒྱལ་རབས་སྐབས་ཀྱི་ཡིག་ཚགས་རྒྱལ་པོའི་ལུང་། གསེར་ཡིག་ལུང་གི་བྱང་བུ། ཏེ་ཤྲིའི་གཏམ། གོང་མའི་བཙུན་མོ་དང་སྲས་ཀྱི་བཀའ། སློན་ལྷི་སེའི་མི་དཔོན་གྱི་བསྒྲགས་ཡིག་སོགས་ཀྱི་གོ་རིམ་ལྟར་བསྒྲིགས་ཡོད། རྒྱལ་རབས་གཞན་གྱི་ཡིག་ཚགས་རྣམས་དུས་ཚོད་སྔ་ཕྱི་ལྟར་བསྒྲིགས་ཡོད།

ལྔ་པ། དེབ་འདིའི་ནང་གི་ཡིག་ཚགས་ཡིག་འབྲུ་ཧྲུལ་ཆད་དུ་སོང་བ་རྣམས་ལ་མཚོན་རྟགས………[ ] འདི་འདྲ་བརྒྱབ་ཡོད་ལ་མཚོན་རྟགས་ནང་གསལ་བཤད་ཀྱང་རགས་ཙམ་བྱས་ཡོད།

དྲུག་པ། དེབ་འདིར་གསལ་བའི་ཡིག་ཚགས་མི་འདྲ་བའི་ནང་གི་མི་མིང་དང་། ས་མིང་གཅིག་པའི་བོད་ཡིག་དང་རྒྱ་ཡིག་གི་སྒྲ་བསྒྱུར་རྣམས་རྩ་བའི་ཆ་ནས་ལོ་རྒྱུས་ཐོག་གི་ཡིག་སྒྱུར་གོམས་གཤིས་རང་སོར་བཞག་ཡོད་སྟབས་དུས་སྐབས་སོ་སོའི་ཡི་གེ་བེད་སྤྱོད་གཏོང་ཚུལ་མི་འདྲ་བ་རེ་གཉིས་ཡོད།

བདུན་པ། དེབ་འདིའི་ནང་གི་བོད་ཡིག་གི་མི་མིང་དང་། ས་མིང་སོགས་ཀྱི་དབྱིན་ཇིའི་སྒྲ་བསྒྱུར་རྣམས་རྩ་བའི་ཆ་ནས་བོད་ཡིག་སྦྱོར་ཀློག་གི་ཆོས་ཉིད་ལྟར་ལ་ཏིང་ཡི་གེས་བོད་ཡིག་གི་ཚབ་བྱས་ཏེ་བྲིས་ཡོད་པ་མ་ཟད། ཀློག་བདེ་ཡོང་ཆེད་བོད་ཡིག་གི་ཐུ་ཡོད་མགོ་ཅན་དང་སྔོན་འཇུག ཡང་འཇུག་བཅས་མང་ཆེ་བ་སྐབས་འཕྲལ་གྱི་གནས་བབ་དང་བསྟུན་ཏེ་དོར་ཡོད། བོད་ཡིག་གི་གསལ་བྱེད་སུམ་བཅུའི་ཚབ་ཏུ་ལ་ཏིང་ཡི་གེ ka kha ga ng ca cha ja nya ta tha da na pa pha ba ma tsa tsha dza wa zha za va ya ra la sha sa ha a བཅས་བཀོད་ཡོད་པ་དང་། དབྱངས་ཡིག་བཞི་ཡི་ཚབ་ཏུ་ལ་ཏིང་ཡི་གེ i u e o བཅས་བཀོད་ཡོད།

# 凡　　例

一、本書以影印件與藏、漢、英譯文爲一體，向讀者原原本本地展示、介紹所載檔案原件的形式、文種和内容。

二、本書所載檔案的標題和譯文中的公元紀年，均由編譯者所加。本書收錄檔案説明文字中標注的尺寸均以厘米爲單位。

三、本書影印件的原有文字是藏文或漢文時，除有英文譯文外，藏文或漢文僅列標題。個別影印件藏文或漢文字跡難以辨認的，附以藏文或漢文的錄文。此外，個別檔案文字繁複，爲壓縮篇幅，只在符號［ ］内作内容概略介紹。

四、本書元代檔案按皇帝聖旨、金字聖牌、帝師法旨、皇太后懿旨、皇太子令旨、宣慰司官員文告等類別順序編排，其它朝代檔案均按時間先後編排。

五、本書檔案文字缺損部分，以符號……表示，并在符號［ ］内略加注明。

六、本書不同檔案中同一人名或地名的藏、漢文譯音，原則保留歷史上翻譯習慣，各個時代用字時有不同。

七、本書藏文人名、地名等的英文譯音，基本上按藏文拼音規律，用拉丁藏文代字轉寫。並且，爲了便於閱讀，原藏文固有的上加字、前加字和又後加字多數酌情删去。藏文三十個字母的拉丁代字爲 ka kha ga ng ca cha ja nya ta tha da na pa pha ba ma tsa tsha dza wa zha za va ya ra la sha sa ha a，四個母音的拉丁代字爲i u e o。

# EXPLANATORY NOTES

1. This book features the form, language and content of the original archives, comprising photoprints and translations in Tibetan, Chinese and English.

2. The title and date of the Christian Era for each piece of translation are provided by the editor and translator. The size is indicated in terms of cm. in the explanations made for the archives.

3. If the original text of a photoprint is in Tibetan or Chinese, an English translation is provided together with a title in Tibetan or Chinese. In a few photoprints where some of the Tibetan or Chinese words are indiscernible, a printed version in Tibetan or Chinese is prepared for easier reading. Besides, a brief account is given within the mark [ ] to avoid redundancy or repetition wherever it exists in the text of a few archives.

4. Archives of the Yuan Dynasty are arranged in the following order: imperial edicts, an imperial plate bearing words raised with gold, decrees from imperial tutors, decrees from an emperor's mother and a prince, a proclamation issued by the Pacification Commissioners Office, etc. The archives of other dynasties are in chronological order.

5. Missing words in archives are indicated by [ ] with a brief note contained within.

6. Chinese and Tibetan transliterations of the same Tibetan person or place follow the transliterations used historically, and characters may differ from dynasty to dynasty.

7. By and large, the English transliterations of Tibetan persons or places are based on Tibetan spelling and transformed into Latin letters in lieu of Tibetan let-

ters. For easy reading, the prefixes, suffixes and the elements fixed above words in the Tibetan language have been omitted whenever possible. The Latin letters used in lieu of the 30 Tibetan letters are: ka, kha, ga, ng, ca, cha, ja, nya, ta, tha, da, na, pa, pha, ba, ma, tsa, tsha, dza, wa, zha, za, va, ya, ra, la, sha, sa, ha, a. The four vowels are: i, u, e, o.

## ཡོན་རྒྱལ་རྒྱལ་རབས་སྐབས་ཀྱི་ཡིག་ཚགས།

འདིར་འདེམས་བཀོད་བྱས་པའི་ཧོར་ཡིག་གསར་པའི་སོག་སྐད་ཀྱི་རྒྱལ་པོའི་ལུང་དང་བོད་ཡིག་ཏི་ཤྲིའི་གཏམ། རྒྱལ་པོའི་བཙུན་མོ་དང་རྒྱལ་སྲས་ཀྱི་བཀའ། སྭོན་ལྷི་སིའི་མི་དཔོན་གྱི་གཏམ། ཐམ་ཀ་སོགས་ཀྱི་ནང་དོན་ནི་རྒྱལ་པོས་ཐད་ཀར་བོད་ཀྱི་ས་ཆའི་ཆུའུ་ཐའུ་སིའི་མི་དཔོན་དང་ཁྲི་དཔོན་བསྐོ་བཞག་བྱས་པ་དང་ཏི་ཤྲིས་སྟོང་དཔོན་བསྐོ་བཞག་བྱས་པ། བོད་ཀྱི་ནང་པ་སངས་རྒྱས་ཀྱི་དགོན་པ་དང་ས་གནས་འགོ་དཔོན་གྱི་ཁེ་དབང་ལ་སྲུང་སྐྱོབ་བྱས་པ་སོགས་དང་འབྲེལ་བ་ཡོད་པ་རེད།

## 元朝檔案

所載八思巴文蒙古語皇帝聖旨、藏文皇帝帝師法旨，還有皇太后懿旨、皇太子令旨、宣慰司官員文告、官印等，內容涉及皇帝直接任命吐蕃地方招討使和萬户長、帝師任命千户長以及保護吐蕃佛教寺廟和地方頭人權利等。

## Yuan Dynasty Archives

Reproduced here are imperial edicts written in the script created by Phags–pa for the Mongolian language and decrees in Tibetan issued by imperial tutors. Other historical documents include decrees issued by an empress dowager and a crown prince, a proclamation made by the Pacification Commissioners Office in Tibet and impressions of official seals. These edicts and decrees were issued to appoint governor–generals, heads of *wanhu* (ten thousand households) or*qianhu*(a thousand households) in Tibet and to protect the rights of the Buddhist monasteries and local chiefs in Tibet.

# སེ་ཆེན་རྒྱལ་པོས་ལྷ་རྗེ་སེང་གེ་དཔལ་ལ་བསྩལ་པའི་ལུང་།
# 薛禪皇帝頒給拉潔・僧格貝的聖旨
# Edict Issued to Lharje Senggedpal by Emperor Sechen

230 × 55.8

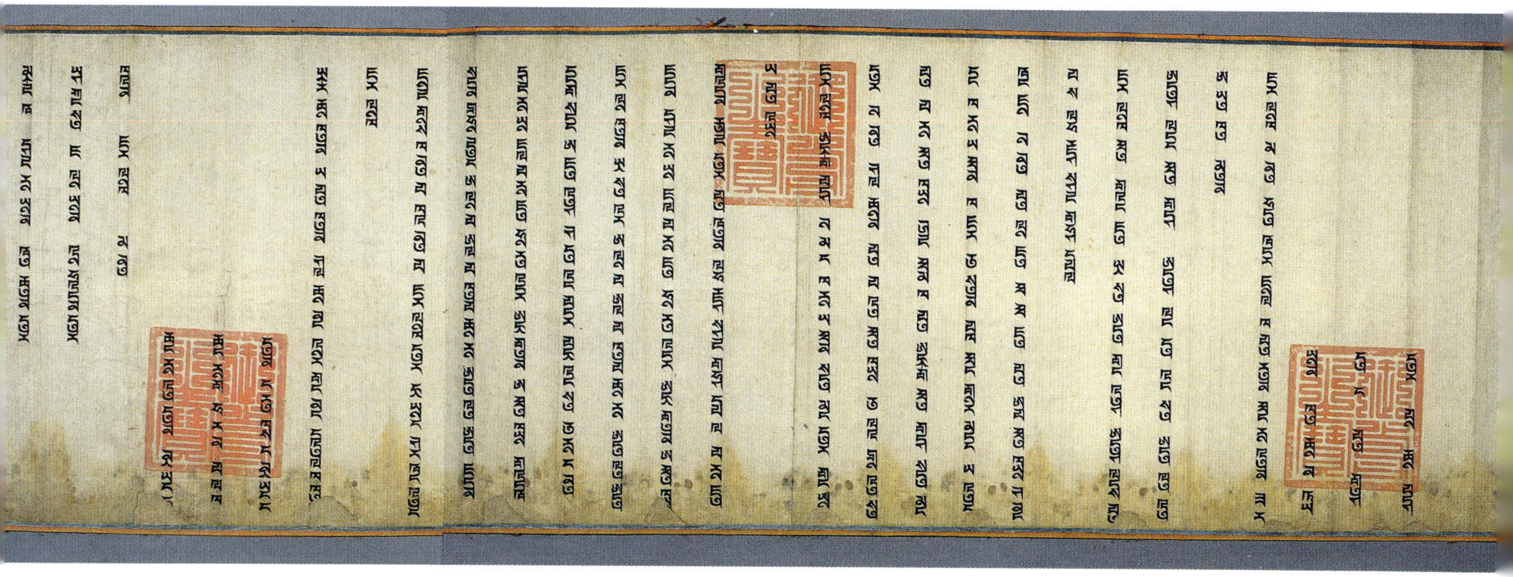

1 - 1

༄༅། །ཚེ་རིང་གནམ་གྱི་སྟོབས་ལ་བརྟེན་པ་དང་བསོད་ནམས་ཆེན་པོའི་དཔལ་གྱིས་སྐྱོང་བའི་རྒྱལ་པོའི་ལུང་།

དམག་དཔོན། དམག་མི། མཁར་གྱི་ད་ར་ཁ་ཆེ། མི་དཔོན། འགྲུལ་བྱེད་པ། མི་སྡེ་རྣམས་ལ་སྙན་བ།

ཇིང་གིར་རྒྱལ་པོ། ཧ་གན་རྒྱལ་པོ་བཅས་ཀྱི་ལུང་དུ་ཧྭ་ཤང་། ཨེར་ཁེ་ཨུན། སེན་ཤྲིང་རྣམས་ནས་ཁྲལ་ཅི་ཡང་འཇལ་མི་དགོས་པ་དང་གནམ་ལ་སྨོན་ལམ་འདེབས། སྐྱབས་འཇུག་ཞུ་ཞེས་འཁོད་ཡོད་པས། སྔར་གྱི་ལུང་བཞིན་ཁྲལ་ཅི་ཡང་འཇལ་མི་དགོས་པ་དང་། གནམ་ལ་སྨོན་ལམ་འདེབས། སྐྱབས་འཇུག་ཞུར་བཅུག་བཟླས་ནས་ཪོང་གི་ལྷ་རྗེ་སེང་གེ་དཔལ་ལ་འཛིན་རྒྱུའི་ལུང་བྱིན་པ་ཡིན། ཁོ་རང་ལ་དབང་བའི་དགོན་པ་དང་ཁང་གཞིས་སུ་འཆར་མ་འབབ། ཟ་མ་ཨུ་ལག་མ་ལེན། ཚང་དམ་ཁ་མ་ལེན། དགོན་པར་བདག་པའི་ས། ཆུ། ཤིང་། ཐོ་འཐག་བྱེད་མཆིག་སོགས་མ་འཕྲོག མ་འཐེན། འདི་པས་ཀྱང་འཛིན་རྒྱུའི་ལུང་ཡོད་ཟེར་ནས་ཁྲིམས་དང་འགལ་བའི་བྱ་བ་མ་བྱེད། བྱས་ན་མི་སྐྲག་པ་ཨེ་ཡིན།

གླང་ལོ(སྤྱི་ལོ་༡༢༧༧—༡༢༨༩)ཟླ་བ་དང་པོའི་ཚེས་སུམ་ཅུ་ཉིན་ཏའི་ཏུར་བྲིས་པའི་ལུང་། །

བོད་རང་སྐྱོང་ལྗོངས་རིག་དངོས་ཪ་དམ་ཡུ་ཡོན་ལྷན་ཁང་དུ་ཉར་ཚགས་བྱས་ཡོད།

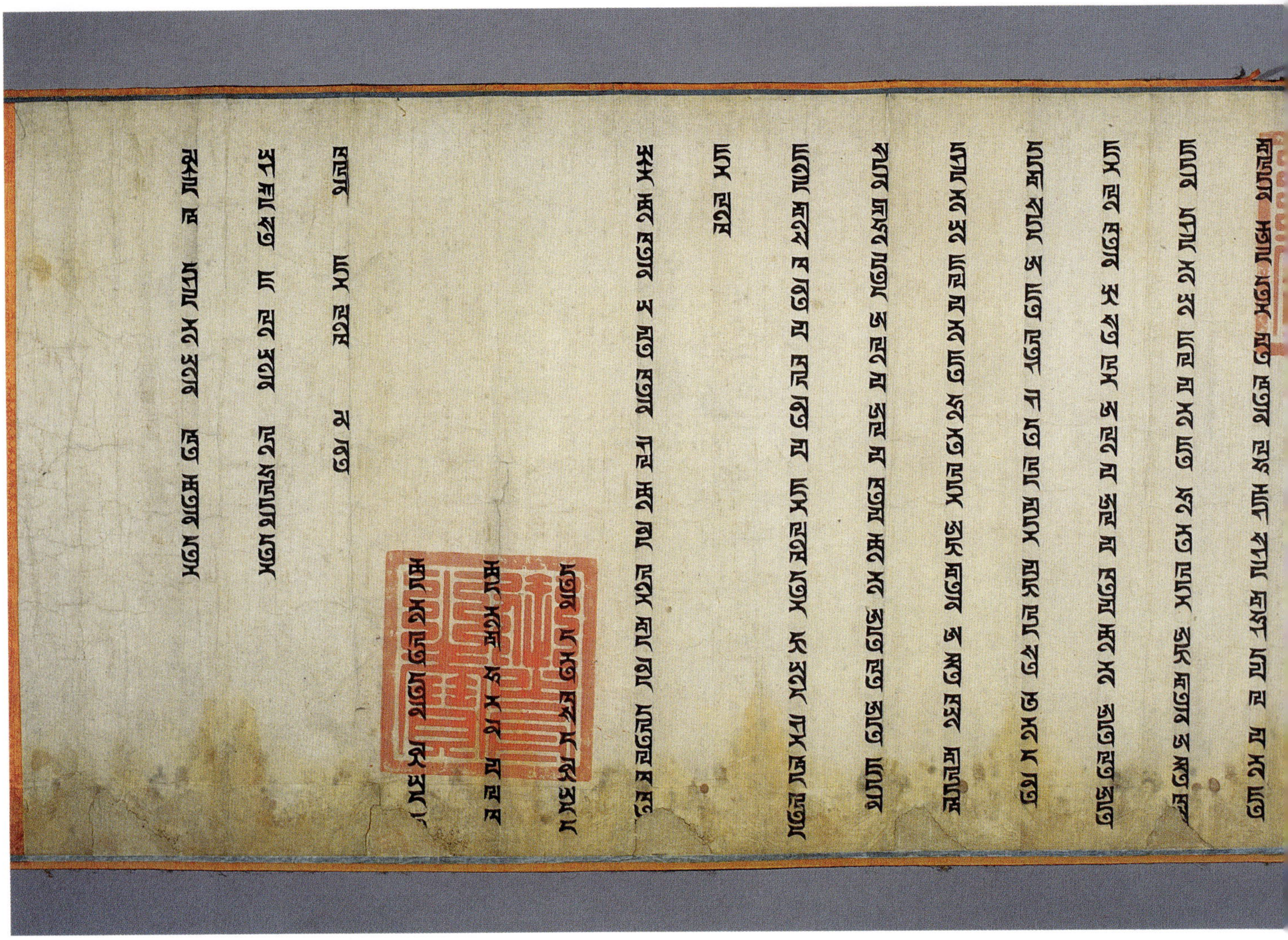

1 - 2

靠長生天的氣力，托大福蔭的護助，皇帝聖旨。

向軍官們、士兵們、城子達魯花赤們、官員們、來往的使臣們、百姓們宣諭：

成吉思汗、哈罕（窩闊台）皇帝聖旨裏説道：“和尚們、也里可溫們、先生們不承擔任何差發，禱告上天保佑。”玆按以前的聖旨，不承擔任何差發，禱告上天保佑，向絨地的拉潔·僧格貝頒發了所持的聖旨，在他的寺院、房舍裏，使臣不得下榻；不得向他們索取鋪馬、祇應；不得徵收地税、商税；不得搶奪寺院所屬土地、河流、園林、碾磨等。他也不得因持有聖旨而做無理的事。如做，他豈不怕?

聖旨，牛年（公元1277年或1289年）正月三十寫於大都。

西藏自治區文物管理委員會藏

The edict of the Emperor, who rules with the assistance of the great power and protection of everlasting Heaven.

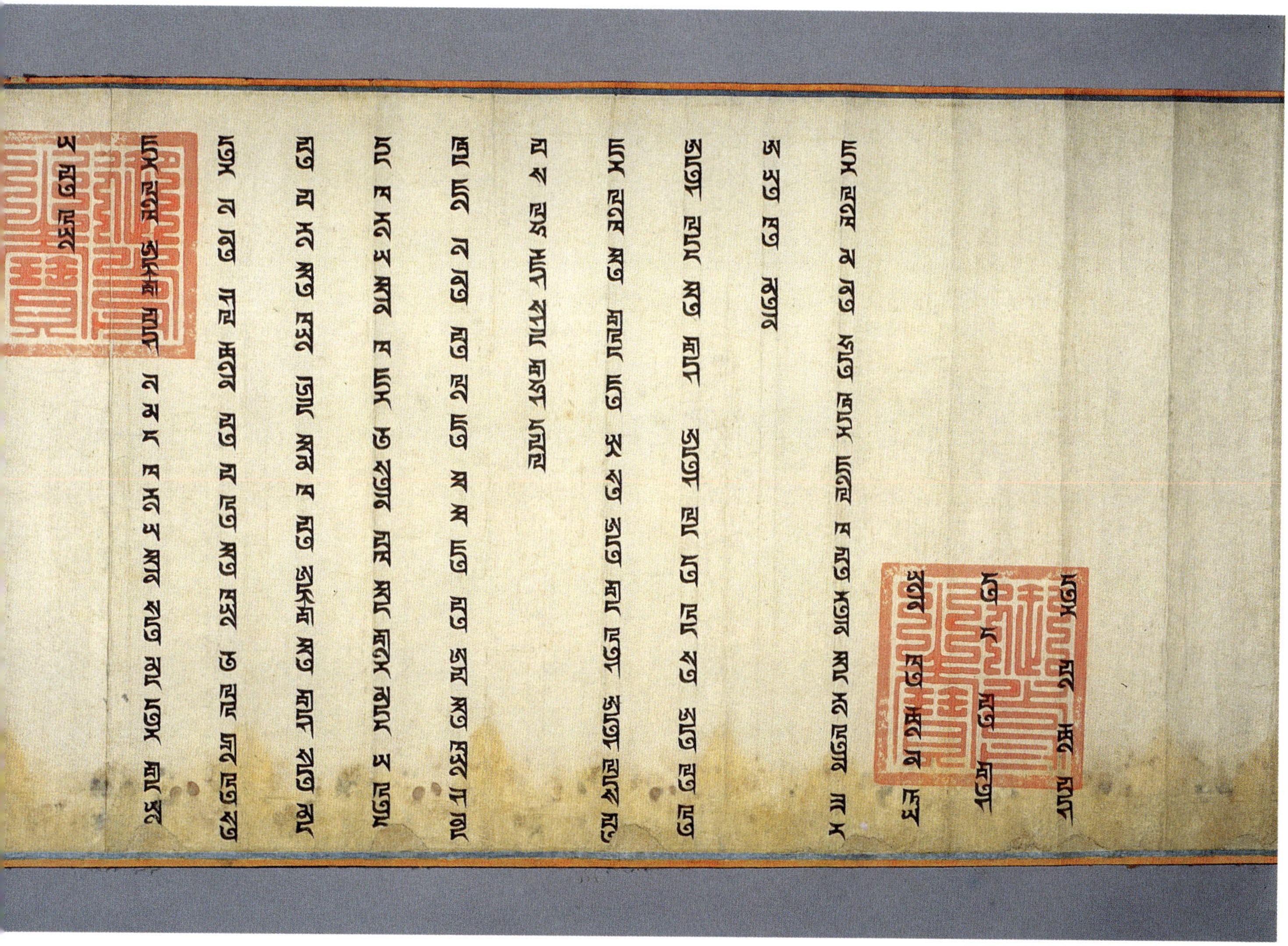

1 - 3

Make the following known to all military officers and men, Darakhaches and other officials, government messengers in transit and commoners:

Genghis Khan and Emperor Okholde stated in their edicts, "Buddhist, Christian and Taoist priests are exempt from all corvée. They invoke the blessing of Heaven upon us." This edict to reiterate that statement is hereby issued to Lharje Senggedpal from Ron for him to keep. Government messengers in transit shall not stay in his monasteries or other buildings or demand free horse service or provisions from him. No taxes shall be levied on land and trade in the area. Land, rivers, forests and millstones belonging to his monasteries shall not be infringed upon. Likewise Lharje Senggedpal is not allowed to abuse the rights I grant him in this edict. Dare he risk punishment by doing anything unreasonable?

Written in Dadu on the 30th day of the 1st month of the Year of the Ox (1277 or 1289)

Preserved by the Historical Relics Administration of the Tibet Autonomous Region.

# 2

## ཡེ་སུན་ཐེ་མུར་རྒྱལ་པོས་རི་བོ་ཆེ་དགོན་པའི་གྲྭ་པ་རྣམས་ལ་བསྩལ་པའི་ལུང་།

## 也孫鐵木兒皇帝頒給類烏齊寺和尚們的聖旨

## Edict Issued to the Monks of the Riboche Monastery by Emperor Yesun Themur

283 × 56.3

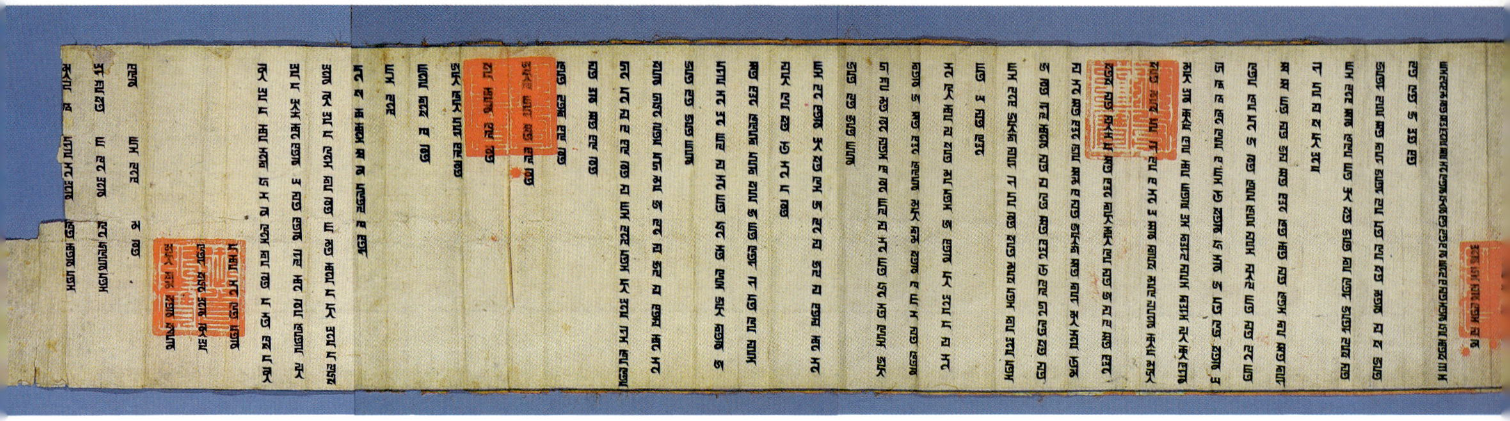

2 - 1

༄༅། །ཚེ་རིང་གནམ་གྱི་སྟོབས་ལ་བརྟེན་པ་དང་བསོད་ནམས་ཆེན་པོའི་དཔལ་གྱིས་སྐྱོང་བའི་རྒྱལ་པོའི་ལུང་།

མདོ་ཁམས་ཀྱི་སྟོན་ལྷི་སིའི་མི་དཔོན། དམག་དཔོན། དམག་མི། མི་སྡེའི་ད་ར་ཁ་ཆེ། མི་དཔོན། འགྲུལ་བྱེད་པ། ཁྱུང་པོའི་མི་དཔོན། མི་སྡེའི་འཇའ་སོ་ཆེ། ཧྭ་ཤང་། ལྷ་སྡེ། འགྲོག་སྡེ་རྣམས་ལ་བློ་བ།

ཛིང་གིར་རྒྱལ་པོ། ཨོ་ཁོ་དེའི་རྒྱལ་པོ། སེ་ཆེན་རྒྱལ་པོ། ཨོལ་ཛེའི་ཐུ་རྒྱལ་པོ། ཁུ་ལུག་རྒྱལ་པོ། བུ་ཡན་ཐུ་རྒྱལ་པོ། ཤི་དི་པ་ལ་རྒྱལ་པོ་བཅས་ཀྱི་ལུང་དུ་ཧྭ་ཤང་། ཨེར་ཁེ་ཝུན། སིན་ཤིང་། ད་ཤི་མན་རྣམས་ནས་ཁྲལ་ཅི་ཡང་འཇལ་མི་དགོས་པ་དང་། གནམ་ལ་སྨོན་ལམ་འདེབས། སྐྱབས་འཇུག་ཞུ་ཞིས་འཁོད་ཡོད་པས། སྔར་གྱི་ལུང་བཞིན་ཁྲལ་ཅི་ཡང་འཇལ་མི་དགོས་པ་དང་། སངས་རྒྱས་ཤཱཀྱ་མུ་ནེ་ལ་སྨོན་ལམ་འདེབས། སྐྱབས་འཇུག་ཞུར་བཅུག་བཞླས་ནས་མདོ་ཁམས་རི་བོ་ཆེ་དགོན་པའི་གྲྭ་པ་རྣམས་ལ་འཛིན་རྒྱུའི་ལུང་བྱིན་པ་ཡིན། འདི་པ་རྣམས་ལ་དབང་བའི་དགོན་པ་དང་ཁང་གཞིས་སུ་འཚོར་མ་འབབ། ཟ་མ་ཝུ་ལག་མ་ལེན། ཚང་དམ་ཁ་མ་ལེན། འདི་པ་རྣམས་ལ་མཛོ་ཧྲ་གསན་པ་དང་ཇོན་རྒྱག་ཏུ་མ་བཅུག མི་སུ་ཞིག་ཡིན་རུང་དགོན་པར་བདག་པའི་གངས་མདའ་ཕན་ཚོད། མཚོ་མདོ་ཡན་ཚོད། ཉང་ཆེ་ཆུང་། ཡར། གཡེལ་པེར། གཡེར་པོ། ཚོ་ཉེན། ཚ་བ་ཁ་སོགས་ཀྱི་ས། ཆུ། མི། ཕྱུགས་སོགས་ཅི་དང་ཅི་ཡིན་པ་རྣམས་མ་འཕྲོག མ་འཐེན། ཤེ་མོང་མ་བཙོང་། གྲྭ་པ་རྣམས་ནས་ཀྱང་འཛིན་རྒྱུའི་ལུང་ཡོད་ཟེར་ནས་ཁྲིམས་དང་འགལ་བའི་བྱ་བ་མ་བྱེད། བྱས་ན་མི་སྐྲག་པ་ཨེ་ཡིན།

ཐའི་ཏིང་ཁྲི་ལོ་དང་པོ་བྱི་ལོ (སྤྱི་ལོ་༡༣༣༤) ཟླ་བ་གསུམ་པའི་ཚེས་བཅུ་གསུམ་ཉིན་ཏའི་ཏུར་བྲིས་པའི་ལུང་།

བོད་རང་སྐྱོང་ལྗོངས་ཡིག་ཚགས་ཁང་དུ་ཉར་ཚགས་བྱས་ཡོད།

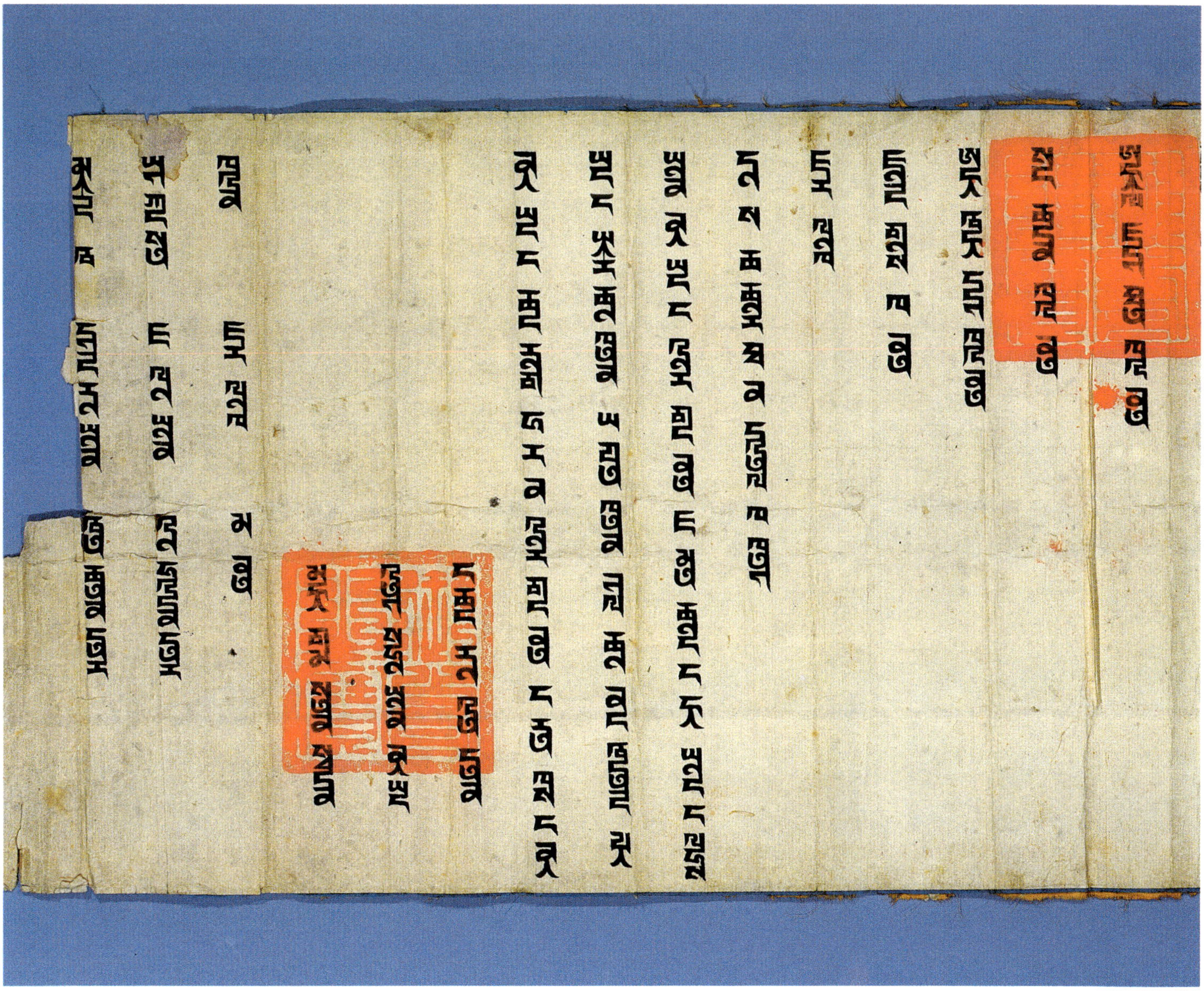

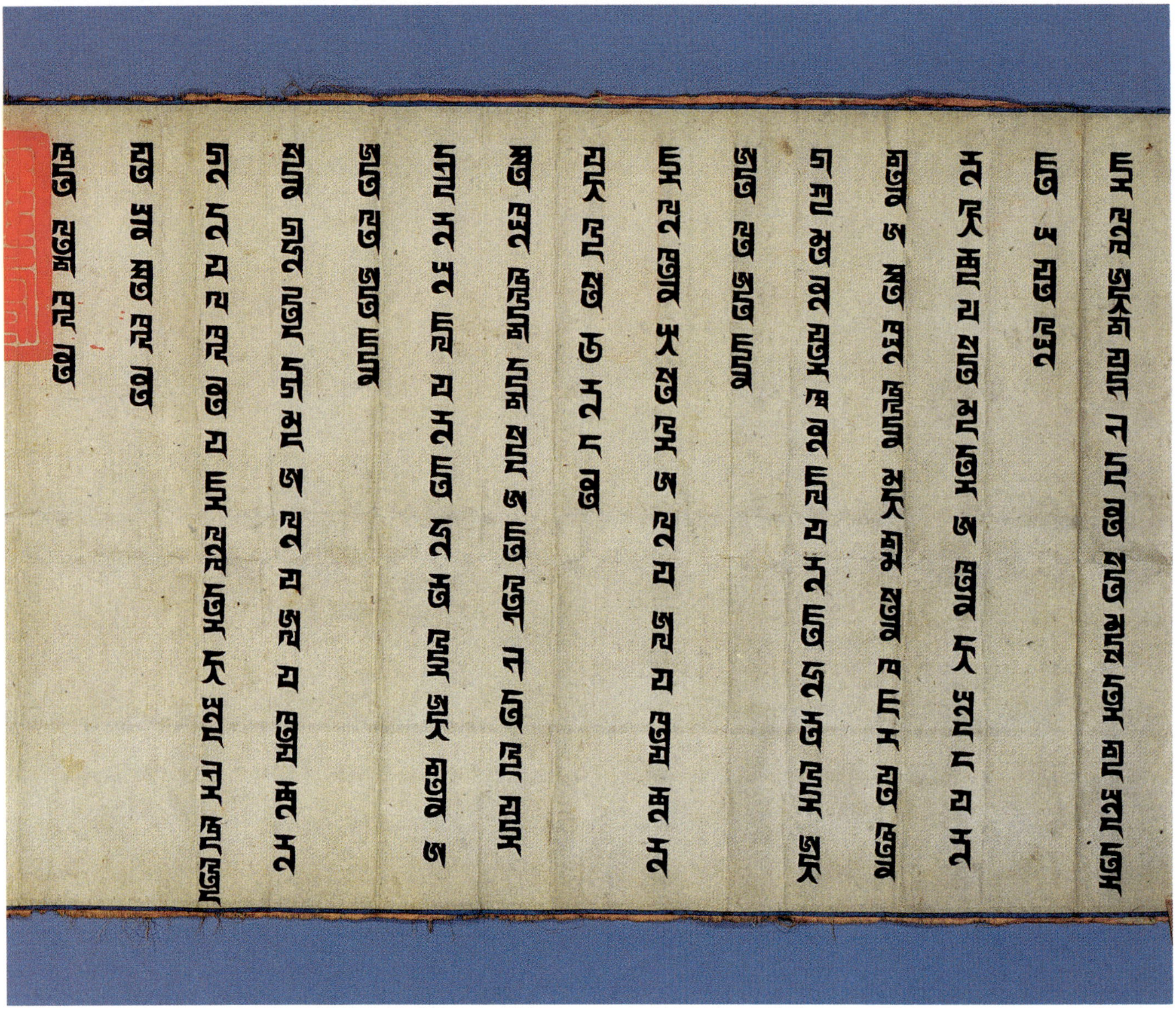

2 - 3

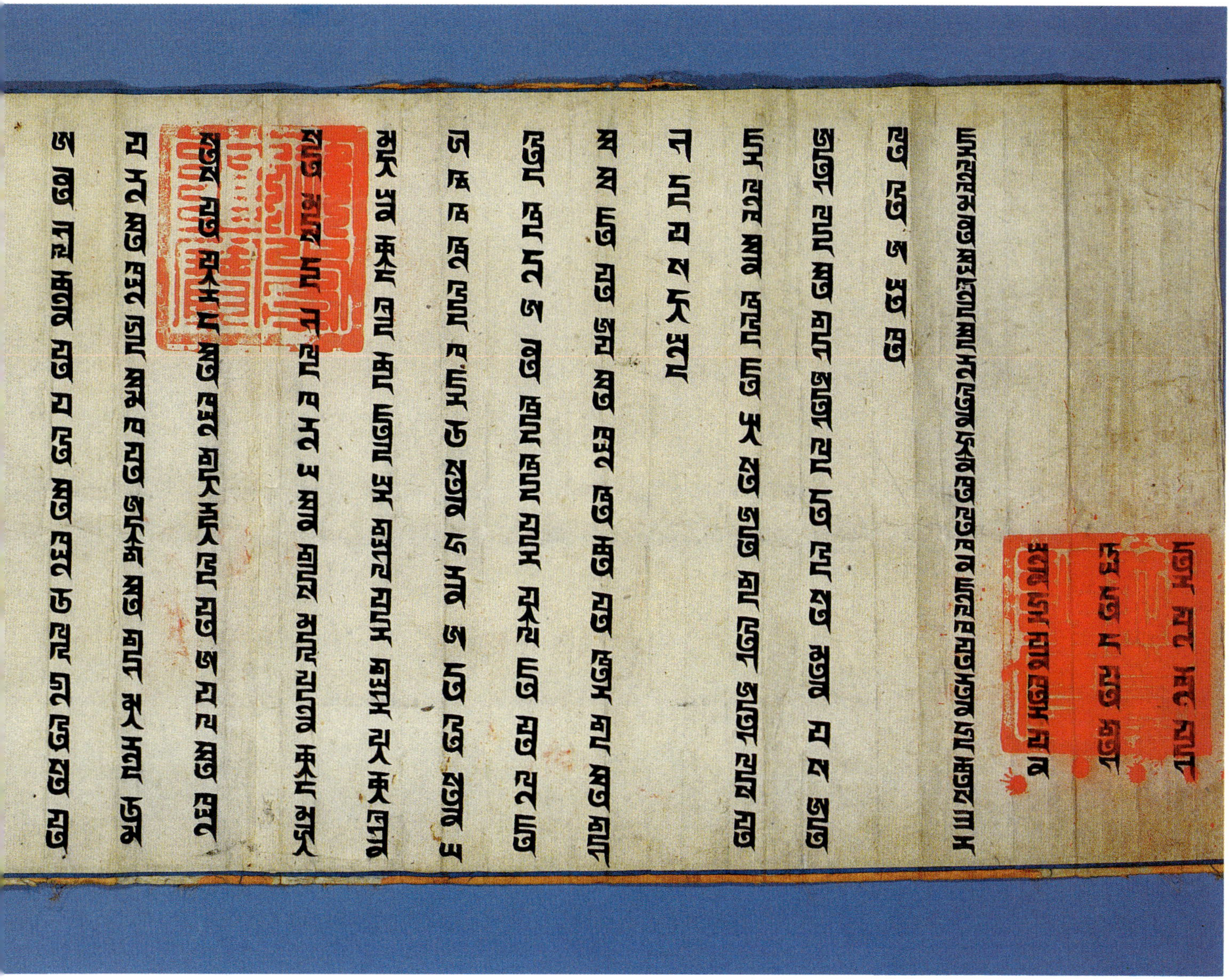

2 - 4

靠長生天的氣力，托大福蔭的護助，皇帝聖旨。

向朵甘思宣慰司官員們、軍官們、士兵們、百姓的達魯花赤們和官員們、來往使臣們、瓊布的官員們、百姓的站赤們、和尚們、寺院部衆們、駐帳房百姓們宣諭：

成吉思汗、窩闊台皇帝、薛禪皇帝、完者篤皇帝、曲律皇帝、普顏篤皇帝、碩德八剌皇帝聖旨裏説道："和尚們、先生們、答什蠻們不承擔任何差發，禱告上天保佑。"兹按以前的聖旨，不承擔任何差發，禱告釋迦牟尼佛保佑，向朵甘思類烏齊寺的和尚們頒發了所持的聖旨，在他們的寺院、房舍裏，使臣不得下榻；不得向他們索取鋪馬、祇應；不得徵收地税、商税；不得在他們那裏飼養牛馬和獵獸；任何人不得搶奪寺院所屬崗達以下措木多以上大小娘、亞爾、葉貝、葉布、却年、察瓦卡等地方的土地、河流、人口、頭匹等；不得對他們使用暴力，和尚們也不得因持有聖旨而做無理的事。如做，他豈不怕？

聖旨，泰定元年鼠年（公元1324年）三月十三日寫於大都。

西藏自治區檔案館藏

The edict of the Emperor, who rules with the assistance of the great power and protection of everlasting Heaven.

Make the following known to all officials of the Pacification Commissioners Office in Dokham, military officers and men, Darakhaches and other officials, government messengers in transit, officials of Khungpo, officials in charge of postal stations, monks and monastic staffs as well as herdsmen:

Genghis Khan and Emperors Okholde, Sechen, Oljevithu, Khulug, Buyanthu and Shidibala stated in their edicts, "Buddhist, Christian, Taoist and Islamic priests are exempt from all corvée. They invoke the blessing of Heaven upon us." This edict to reiterate that statement is hereby issued to the monks of the Riboche Monastery for them to keep. They invoke the blessing of Sakyamuni upon us. Government messengers in transit shall not stay in their monastery or other buildings or demand free horse service or provisions from them. No taxes shall be levied on land and trade in the area. Grazing and hunting in the area are not allowed. Monastic land, rivers, commoners and livestock in Greater and Lesser Nyang, Yar, Yelber, Yelpo, Chonyan and Tshawakha, which lie below Gangmdav and above Tshomdo, shall not be infringed upon and violence against monks is prohibited. Likewise the monks are not allowed to abuse the rights I grant them in this edict. Dare they risk punishment by doing anything unreasonable?

Written in Dadu on the 13th day of the 3rd month of the 1st year of Taiding (1324), the Year of the Rat

Preserved by the Archives of the Tibet Autonomous Region.

# ཡེ་སུན་ཐེ་མུར་རྒྱལ་པོས་བཀྲ་ཤིས་དན་གྱི་གྲྭ་པ་རྣམས་ལ་བསྩལ་བའི་ལུང་།
# 也孫鐵木兒皇帝頒給札西丹寺和尚們的聖旨
# Edict Issued to the Monks of the Krashisdan Monastery by Emperor Yesun Themur

234 × 57.3

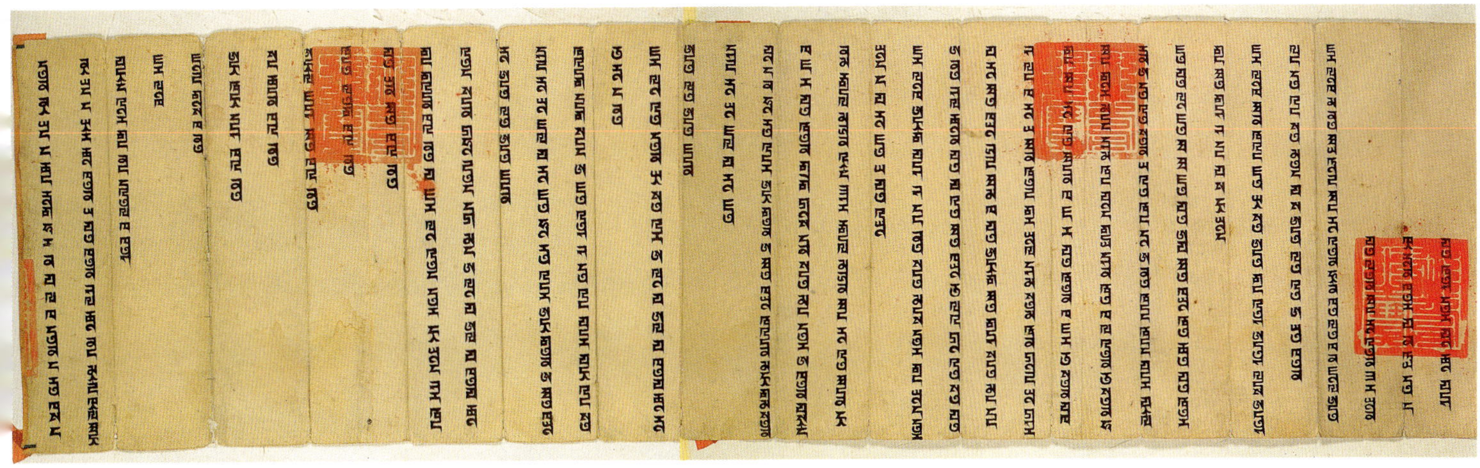

3－1

……[མགོའི་ཡི་གེ་རྒྱལ་ཆད་དུ་སོང་འདུག]དཔོན། དམག་མི། མཁར་གྱི་ད་ར་ཁ་ཆེ། མི་དཔོན། འགྲུལ་བྱེད་པ། སོག་པོད་མི་སྡེ་རྣམས་ལ་སྒྲོ་བ།

ཇིང་གིར་རྒྱལ་པོ། ཨོ་ཁོ་དེའི་རྒྱལ་པོ། སེ་ཆེན་རྒྱལ་པོ། ཨོལ་ཇེའི་ཐུ་རྒྱལ་པོ། གུ་ལུག་རྒྱལ་པོ། བུ་ཡན་ཐུ་རྒྱལ་པོ། གེ་གན་རྒྱལ་པོ་བཅས་ཀྱི་ལུང་དུ་ཧྭ་ཤང་། ཨེར་ཁེ་ཨུན། སྲིན་ཤིང་། ད་ཤི་མན་རྣམས་ནས་ཁྲལ་ཅི་ཡང་འཇལ་མི་དགོས་པ་དང་། གནམ་ལ་སྨོན་ལམ་འདེབས། སྐྱབས་འཇུག་ཞུ་ཞེས་འཁོད་ཡོད་པས། སྔར་གྱི་ལུང་བཞིན་ཁྲལ་ཅི་ཡང་འཇལ་མི་དགོས་པ་དང་། གནམ་ལ་སྨོན་ལམ་བཏབ་སྟེ་ངེད་ཚོར་སྐྱབས་འཇུག་ཞུར་བཅུག་བཟླས་ནས་མདོ་ཁམས་བཀྲ་ཤིས་དན་གྱི་བསོད་ནམས་རྒྱལ་མཚན་དང་འོད་ཟེར་རྒྱལ་མཚན་གྱིས་གཙོས་པའི་གྲྭ་པ་རྣམས་ལ་འཛིན་རྒྱུའི་ལུང་བྱིན་པ་ཡིན། འདི་པ་རྣམས་ལ་དབང་བའི་དགོན་པ་དང་ཁང་གཞིས་སུ་འཚོར་མ་འབབ། ཟ་མ་ཨུ་ལག་མ་ལེན། ཚང་དམ་ཁ་མ་ལེན། མི་སུ་ཞིག་ཡིན་རུང་དགོན་པར་བདག་པའི་གངས་དཀར། ཡིད་སྟོན། སུམ་ཐན། ཤིང་ཡི། ཤིར་གེ་སོགས་ཀྱི་ས། ཆུ། ཤིང་། སྤྱི་འཐག་བྱེད་མཆིག འགྲུལ་ཁང་། གདན། གཏེ་མའི་མཛོད། ཁྲུས་ཁང་། མི་ཕྱུགས་སོགས་ཅི་དང་ཅི་ཡིན་པ་རྣམས་མ་འཕྲོག མ་འཐེན། ཤེ་མོང་མ་བཙོང་། འདི་པ་རྣམས་ནས་ཀྱང་འཛིན་རྒྱུའི་ལུང་ཡོད་ཟེར་ནས་ཁྲིམས་དང་འགལ་བའི་བྱ་བ་བྱས་ན་མི་སྐྲག་པ་ཨེ་ཡིན། །

ཐའི་ཧིང་ཁྲི་ལོ་དང་པོ་བྱི་ལོ(སྤྱི་ལོ་༡༣༢༤)ཟླ་བ་བཅུ་པའི་ཚེས་ཉི་ཤུ་གསུམ་ཉིན་ཏའི་ཏུར་བྲིས་པའི་ལུང་།

བོད་རང་སྐྱོང་ལྗོངས་ཡིག་ཚགས་ཁང་དུ་ཉར་ཚགས་བྱས་ཡོད།

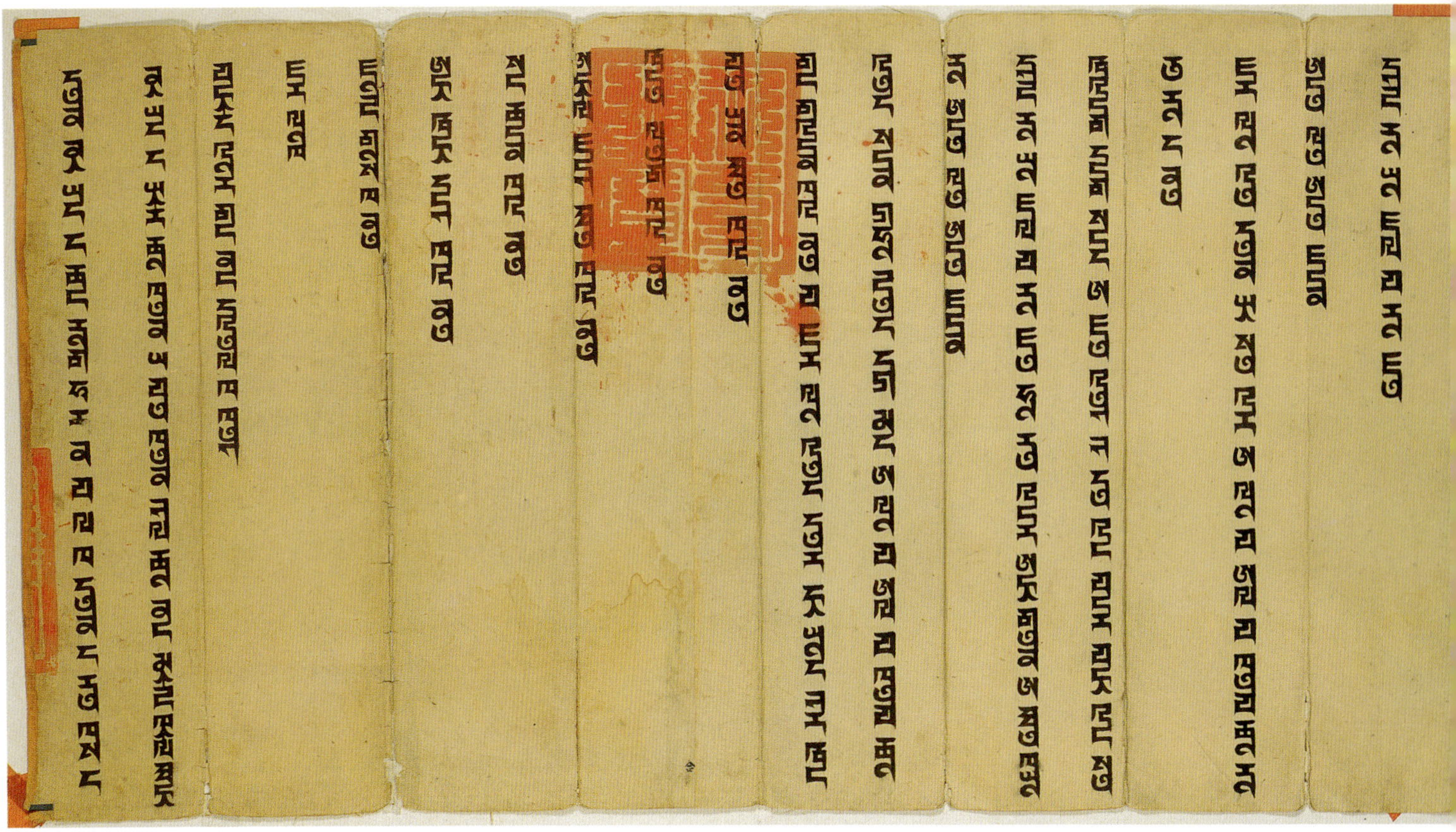

3-2

3-3

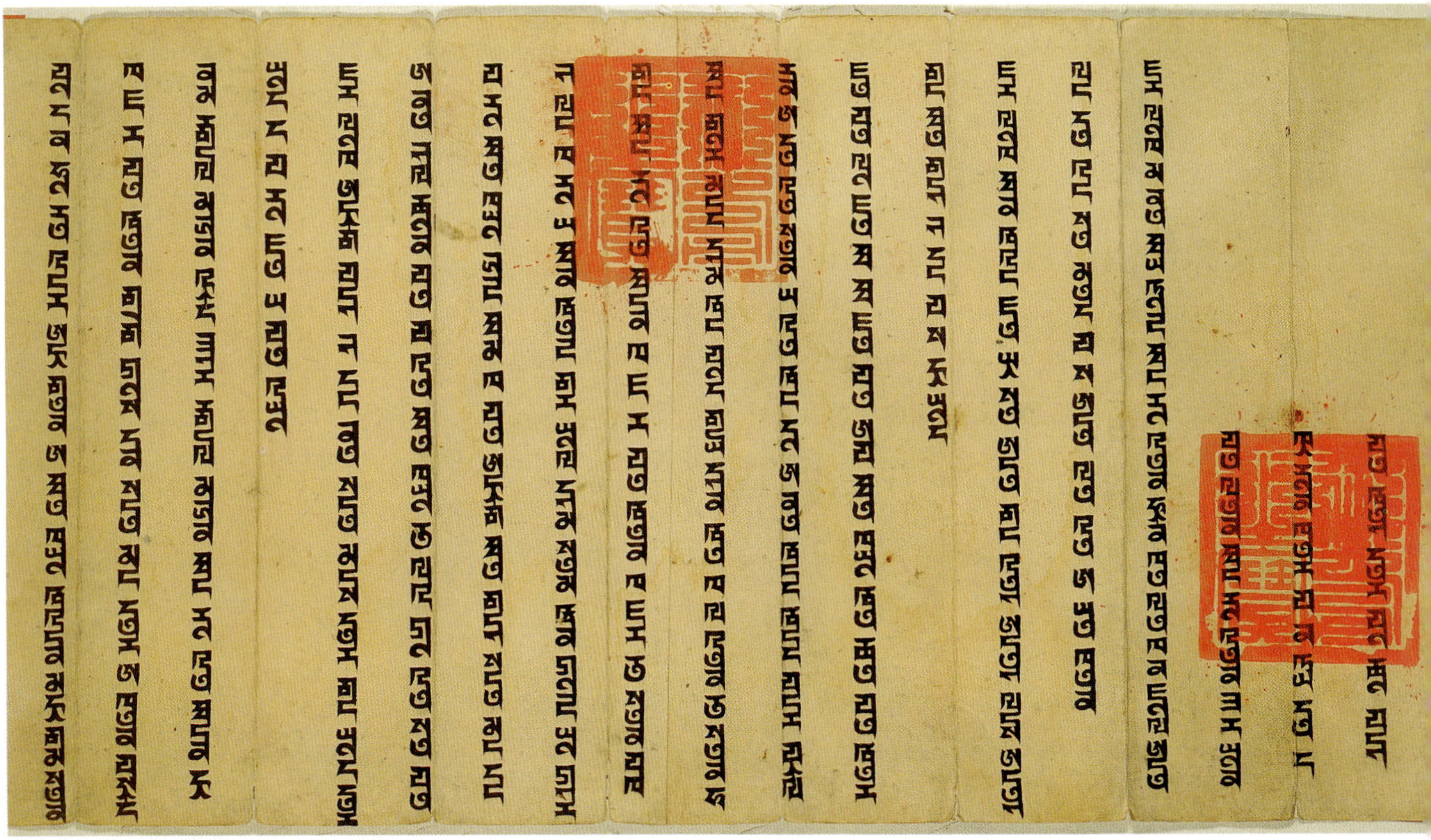

……［起首語部缺損］　官們、士兵們、城子達魯花赤們、官員們、來往使臣們、蒙古和吐蕃百姓們宣諭：

成吉思汗、窩闊台皇帝、薛禪皇帝、完者篤皇帝、曲律皇帝、普顏篤皇帝、格堅皇帝聖旨裏説道："和尚們、也里可溫們、先生們、答什蠻們不承擔任何差發，禱告上天保佑。"兹按以前的聖旨，不承擔任何差發，禱告上天保佑我們，向朵甘思札西丹寺的索南堅贊和斡節兒堅贊爲首的和尚們頒發了所持的聖旨。在他們的寺院、房舍裏，使臣不得下榻；不得向他們索取鋪馬、祗應；不得徵收地税、商税；任何人不得搶奪寺院所屬孔噶爾、義店、松萬、盛義、希爾格等地的土地、河流、園林、碾磨、店舍、鋪席、解典庫、浴堂、人口、頭匹等；不得對他們使用暴力，如果他們因持有聖旨而做無理的事，他豈不怕?

聖旨，泰定元年鼠年（公元1324年）十月二十三日寫於大都。

西藏自治區檔案館藏

[The first paragraph of the edict is missing.]

Make the following known to all military officers and men, Darakhaches and other officials, government messengers in transit and Mongolian and Tibetan commoners:

Genghis Khan and Emperors Okholde, Sechen, Oljevithu, Khulug, Buyanthu and Gegen stated in their edicts, "Buddhist, Christian, Taoist and Islamic priests are exempt from all corvée. They invoke the blessing of Heaven upon us." This edict to reiterate that statement is hereby issued to the monks of the Krashisdan Monastery in Dokham headed by Bsodnam Gyaltshan and Vodzer Gyaltshan for them to keep. Government messengers in transit shall not stay in their monastery or other buildings or demand free horse service or provisions from them. No taxes shall be levied on land and trade in the area. Monastic land, rivers, forests, millstones, shops, mattresses, pawnshops, bathrooms, commoners and livestock in Khunggar, Yilden, Sumwan, Shingyi and Sherge shall not be infringed upon and violence against them is prohibited. The monks are not allowed to abuse the rights I grant them in this edict. Dare they risk punishment by doing anything unreasonable?

Written in Dadu on the 23rd day of the 10th month of the 1st year of Taiding (1324), the Year of the Rat

Preserved by the Archives of the Tibet Autonomous Region.

# 4

## ཡེ་སུན་ཐེ་མུར་རྒྱལ་པོས་འོད་ཟེར་རྒྱལ་མཚན་ལ་བསྩལ་བའི་ལུང་།

## 也孫鐵木兒皇帝頒給斡節兒堅贊的聖旨

## Edict Issued by Emperor Yesun Themur to Vodzer Gyaltshan

108 × 59

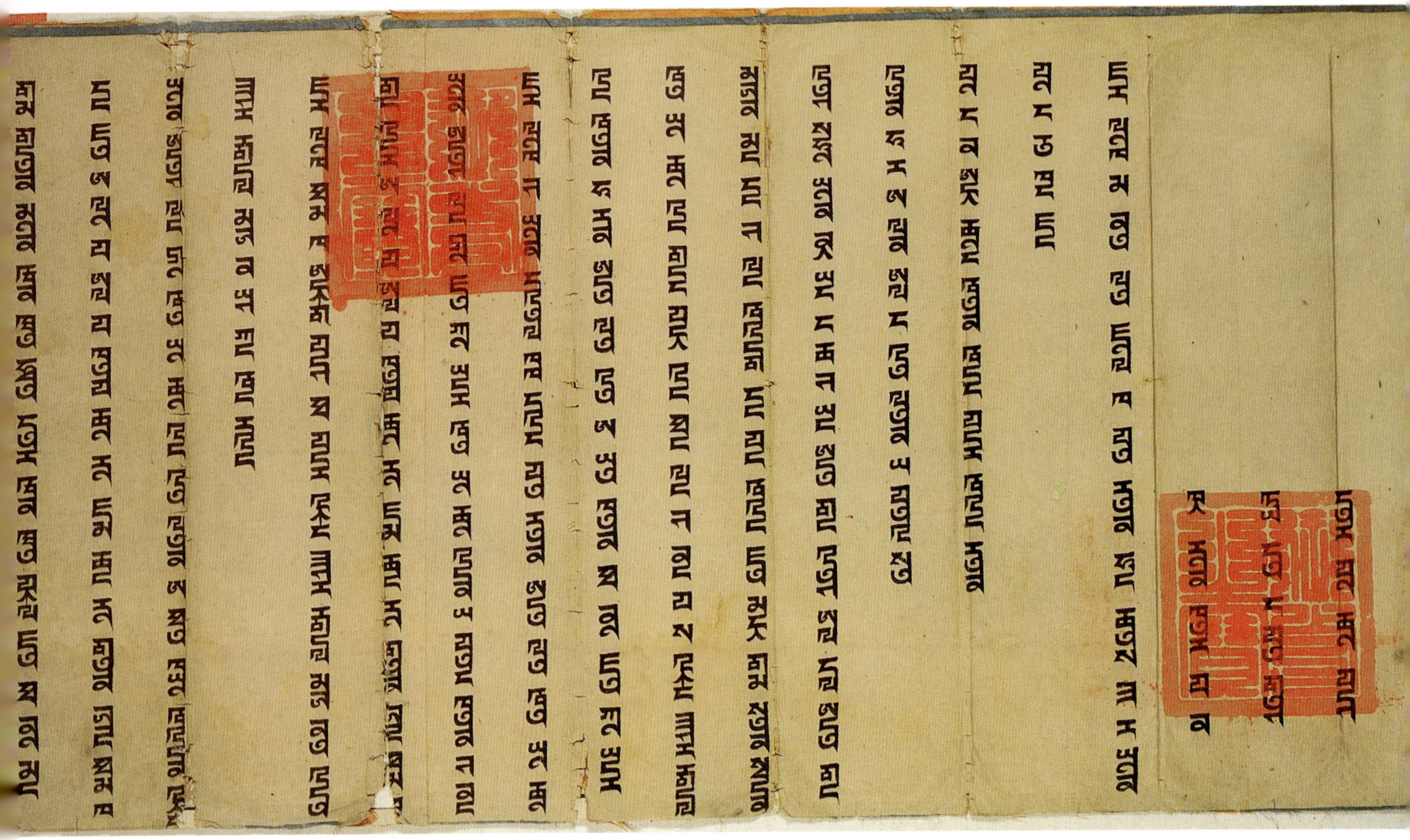

……[མདུན་གྱི་ཡིག་ཚིགས་ཕྱེད་ཙམ་རྡུལ་ཆད་དུ་སོང་འདུག]ཁམས་ཀྱི་དམག་དང་མི་སྡེའི་ཁྲི་དཔོན་ཁང་གི་ཁྲི་དཔོན་ལ་བསྐོས་ཏེ་ཁྱེད་རྣམས་ཀྱི་འགོ་བྱེད། ཁྲལ་རིགས་འཇའ་མོ་ཆེ་དང་དམག་གི་ཚང་དམ་ཁ་སོགས་ཀྱི་བྱ་བ་སྒྲུབ་ཏུ་བཅུག་པ་ཡིན་བཟླས་ནས་འོད་ཟེར་རྒྱལ་མཚན་ལ་བྱང་བུ་ཆེ་བ་དང་ལུང་བྱིན་པ་ཡིན། ཁྱེད་རྣམས་ནས་འོད་ཟེར་རྒྱལ་མཚན་གྱི་ངག་ལ་ཉན་ལ་ཁྲལ་རིགས་འཇའ་མོ་ཆེ་དང་དམག་གི་ཚང་དམ་ཁ་སོགས་ཀྱི་བྱ་བ་དུས་ལ་སླེབས་པར་སྒྲུབས། འདི་སྐད་བཟླས་བཞིན་མཐའ་དག་མ་བསྒྲུབས་པ་ཡོད་ན་མི་སྐྲག་པ་ཨེ་ཡིན། གལ་སྲིད་ཁྱེད་རྣམས་ནས་མཐའ་དག་བསྒྲུབས་ཡོད་པ་དང་འོད་ཟེར་རྒྱལ་མཚན་ནས་མདོ་ཁམས་ཀྱི་སྭོན་ཞྭི་སིའི་མི་དཔོན་དང་གྲོས་མ་བྱས་པར་རང་གི་དབང་ཤེད་ལ་བརྟེན་ནས་ཉེས་པ་མེད་པར་ཉེས་པ་ལེན་ན་ངེད་ཚོར་ཡར་ཞུས་ལ། ཅ་ར་བྱེད་དུ་འཇུག་རྒྱུའི་ཐག་གཅོད་ངེད་ཚོས་བྱ་རྒྱུ་ཡིན།

འབྲུག་ལོ(སྤྱི་ལོ་༡༣༢༨)ཟླ་བ་གསུམ་པའི་ཚེས་ཉི་ཤུ་གསུམ་ཉིན་ཏའི་ཏུར་བྲིས་པའི་ལུང་།

བོད་རང་སྐྱོང་ལྗོངས་ཡིག་ཚགས་ཁང་དུ་ཉར་ཚགས་བྱས་ཡོད།

……［前半部缺損］　任　［缺損］　甘軍民萬户府萬户，管領你們監督完成一切差發、站户、軍户的地税、商税等方面的事宜，爲此給斡節兒堅贊頒發了大牌和璽書。你們務必遵照斡節兒堅贊的話，認真完成一切差發、站户、軍户的地税、商税方面的事宜。聖旨如此宣諭了，不完全執行的人，難道不怕嗎？如果你們完全執行了，而斡節兒堅贊依仗其權，未經與朵甘思宣慰司官員商議，處罰無辜的人，要上奏我們。如何處置，由我們決定。

聖旨，龍年（公元1328年）三月二十三日寫於大都。

西藏自治區檔案館藏

[The first part of the edict is missing.]

I have appointed [missing] head of Smarkham *wanhu* (ten thousand households) to supervise your work of requisitioning all sorts of corvée and collecting land and trade taxes for the maintenance of postal stations and the army and have therefore conferred upon him documents of appointment affixed with my seal. You must fulfil your work in all earnest in accordance with his instructions. Dare you risk punishment by not following my edict? Report to us if you have fully implemented my edict, but Vodzer Gyaltshan abuses his power by punishing innocent persons without consulting officials from the Pacification Commissioners Office in Dokham. We shall decide how to punish him.

Written in Dadu on the 23rd day of the 3rd month of the Year of the Dragon (1328)

Preserved by the Archives of the Tibet Autonomous Region.

# 5

## ཐོ་གན་ཐེ་མུར་རྒྱལ་པོས་དཀོན་ཅོག་བཟང་པོ་སོགས་ལ་བསྩལ་པའི་ལུང་།

## 妥歡帖睦爾皇帝頒給貢覺桑布等的聖旨

## Edict Issued by Emperor Thogan Themur to Koncog Zangpo and Others

338 × 57

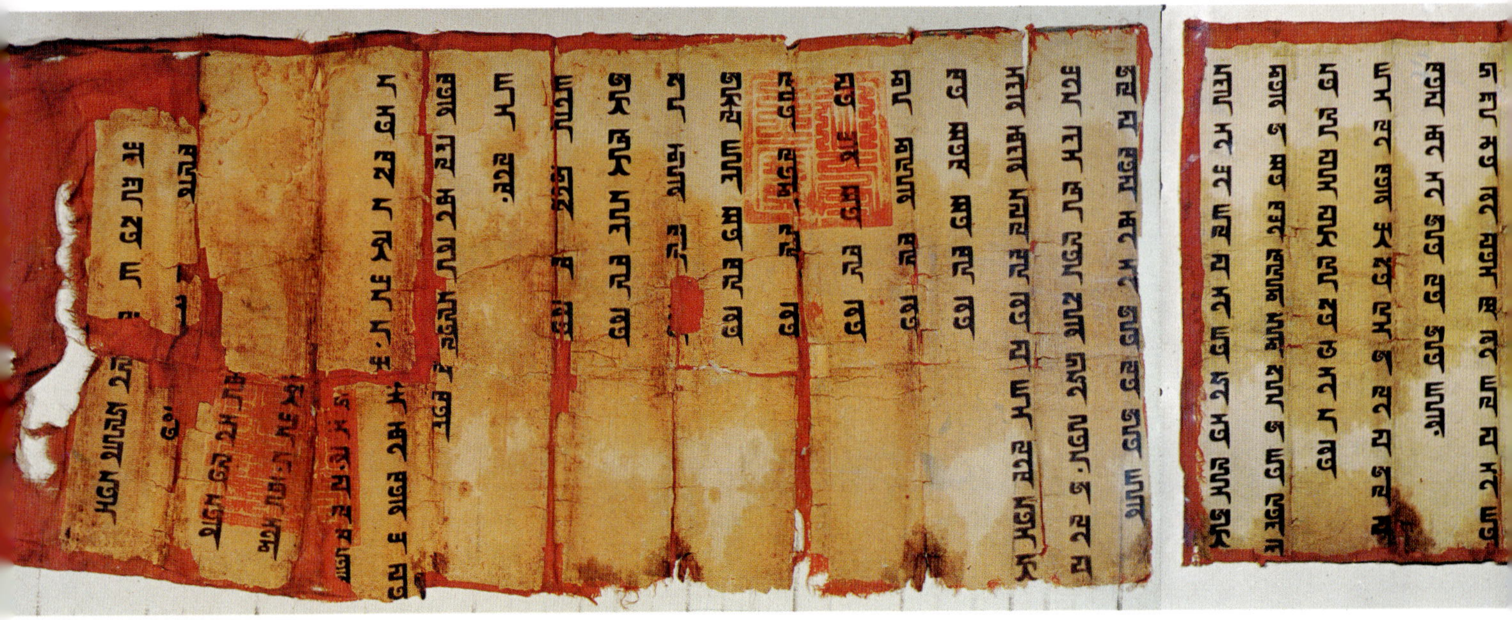

[ཚིག་མགོ་སྟེ“ཚེ་རིང་གནམ་གྱི་སྟོབས་ལ་བརྟེན་པ་དང་”ཞེས་རྒྱལ་ཆད་དུ་སོང་འདུག]བསོད་ནམས་ཆེན་པོའི་དཔལ་གྱིས་སྐྱོང་བའི་རྒྱལ་པོའི་ལུང་།

དམག་དཔོན་དང་དམག་མི། མཁར་གྱི་ད་ར་ཁ་ཆེ། མི་དཔོན། འགྲུལ་བྱེད་པ་རྣམས་ལ་ཐོས་བ།

ཛིང་གིར་རྒྱལ་པོ། ཨོ་ཁོ་དེའི་རྒྱལ་པོ། སེ་ཆེན་རྒྱལ་པོ། ཨོལ་ཛེའི་བུ་རྒྱལ་པོ། ཁུ་ལུག་རྒྱལ་པོ། བུ་ཡན་བུ་རྒྱལ་པོ། གེ་གེན་རྒྱལ་པོ། ཏུ་ཐུ་ཐུ་རྒྱལ་པོ་རིན་ཆེན་དཔལ་རྒྱལ་པོ་བཅས་ཀྱི་ལུང་དུ་ཏྲ་ཤང་། ཨེར་ཁེ་ཝུན། སེན་ཤྲིང་རྣམས་ནས་ཁྲལ་ཅི་ཡང་འཇལ་མི་དགོས་པ་དང་། གནམ་ལ་སྨོན་ལམ་འདེབས། སྐྱབས་འཇུག་ཞུ་ཞེས་འཁོད་ཡོད་པས། སྔར་གྱི་ལུང་བཞིན་ཁྲལ་ཅི་ཡང་འཇལ་མི་དགོས་པ་དང་། སངས་རྒྱས་ཤཱཀྱ་མུ་ནི་ལ་སྨོན་ལམ་འདེབས། སྐྱབས་འཇུག་ཞུར་བཅུག་བཟླས་ནས་གཙང་གི་ཀུན་དགའ་ཆོས་དགོན་དཀོན་ཅོག་བཟང་པོར་དབང་བའི་བྲིན་སྐལ་སྒོ་རིན་ཆེན་པི་ལོ་པ། ལུང་སྐབ་པི་ལྷ་ཛེ་རོང་ག་བ། གྲོང་གསར་བན་ཚན་གབ་སྒོ་སོགས་ཀྱི་གཞིས་ཀ་འཛོག་པ་རྣམས་ལ་འཛིན་རྒྱུའི་ལུང་བྱིན་པ་ཡིན། ཁོ་ཚོའི་དགོན་པ་དང་། གཞིས་ཀ ཁང་པའི་ནང་འགྲུལ་བྱེད་པས་འཚེར་མ་འབབ། ཟ་མ་ཝུ་ལག་མ་ལེན། ཚང་དམ་ཁ་མ་ལེན། མི་སུ་ཞིག་ཡིན་རུང་དགོན་པར་བདག་པའི་ས། ཆུ། ཤིང་། ཕྱི་འཐག་བྱེད་མཆིག འགྲུལ་ཁང་། གདན། གཏེ་མའི་མཛོད། ཁྲུས་ཁང་། མི་ཕྱུགས་སོགས་ཅི་དང་ཅི་ཡིན་པ་རྣམས་མ་འཕྲོག མ་འཐེན། ཤེ་མོང་མ་བཙོང་། འདི་པ་རྣམས་ནས་ཀྱང་འཛིན་རྒྱུའི་ལུང་ཡོད་ཟེར་ནས་ཁྲིམས་དང་འགལ་བའི་བྱ་བ་མ་བྱེད། བྱས་ན་མི་སྐྲག་པ་ཨེ་ཡིན།

ཛི་ཛིང་ཁྲི་ལོ་ལྔ་པ་བྱ་ལོ(སྤྱི་ལོ་༡༣༤༥)ཟླ་བ་དང་པོའི་ཚེས་ཉི་ཤུ་བདུན་ཉིན་ཏའི་ཏུར་བྲིས་པའི་ལུང་།

བོད་རང་སྐྱོང་ལྗོངས་གཞིས་རྩེ་ས་ཁུལ་ཡིག་ཚགས་ཁང་དུ་ཉར་ཚགས་བྱས་ཡོད།

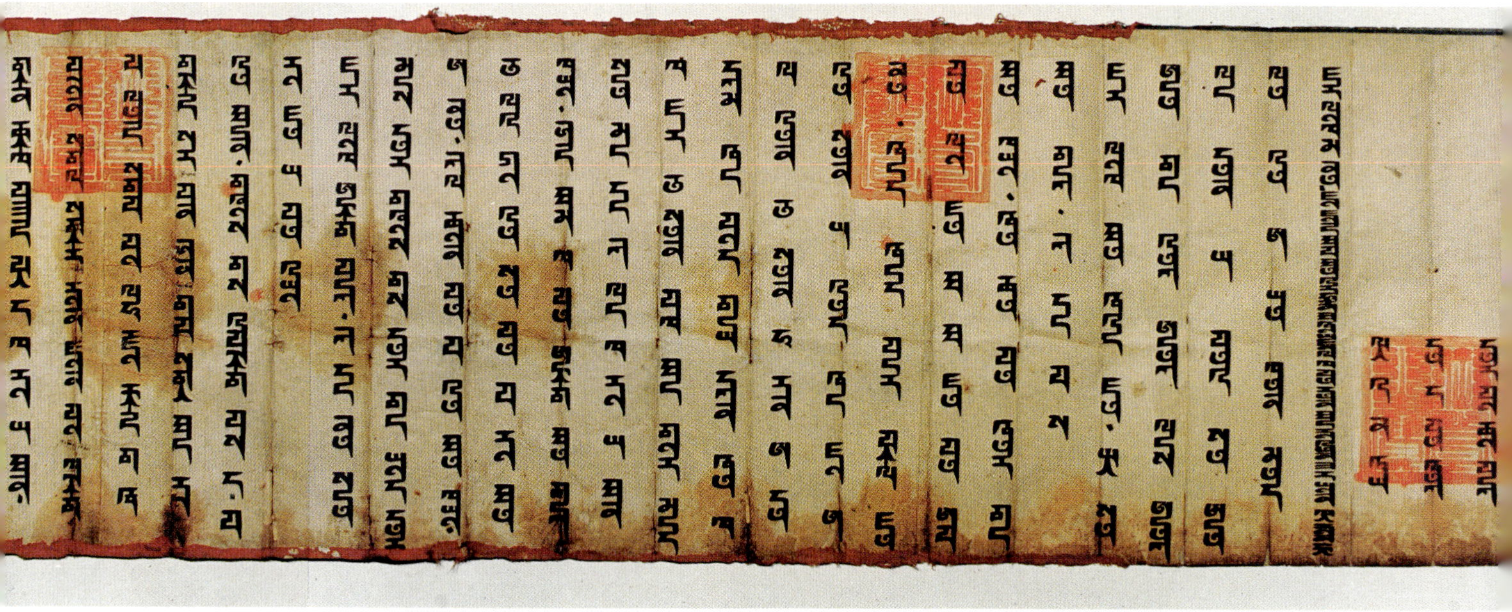

［首句"靠長生天的氣力"缺損］，托大福蔭護助，皇帝聖旨。

向軍官們、士兵們、城子達魯花赤們、往來使臣們宣諭：

成吉思汗、窩闊台皇帝、薛禪皇帝、完者篤皇帝、曲律皇帝、普顏篤皇帝、格堅皇帝、護都篤皇帝、懿璘質班皇帝聖旨裏說："和尚們、也里可溫們、道人們不承擔任何差發，禱告上天保佑。"今按以前的聖旨，不承擔任何差發，禱告釋迦牟尼佛保佑，向藏的公哥曲寺貢覺桑布管轄的真格廓仁青比羅巴、隆嘎、比拉吉絨卡瓦、仲薩班贊嘎廓等溪卡牧人頒發了所持的聖旨。在他們的寺廟、溪卡、房舍裏，使臣不得下榻，不得索取鋪馬、祗應；不得徵收地稅、商稅。凡屬寺廟的土地、河流、園林、碾磨、店舍、鋪席、解典庫、浴堂、人畜等一切，任何人均不得搶奪徵用，不得使用暴力。他們也不得因持有聖旨而做違法之事。如做，他們豈不怕？

聖旨，至正五年鷄年（公元1345年）正月二十七日寫於大都。

西藏日喀則地區檔案館藏

[The first sentence of the edict is missing.] The edict of the Emperor, who rules with the assistance of the great power and protection of everlasting Heaven.

Make the following known to all military officers and men, Darakhaches and other officials and government messengers in transit:

Genghis Khan and Emperors Okholde, Sechen, Oljevithu, Khulug, Buyanthu, Gegen, Huthuthu and Richepal stated in their edicts, "Buddhist, Christian and Taoist priests are exempt from all corvée. They invoke the blessing of Heaven upon us." This edict reiterates that statement and they are exempt from all corvée, but they should invoke the blessing of Sakyamuni upon us. This edict is hereby issued to the *zhiskha* herdsmen of Bringalgorinchenbilopa, Lunggabilhajerunggawa and Grongsarbantsanggabgo under the jurisdiction of Koncog Zangpo of Tsang's Kungavchos Monastey for them to keep. Government messengers in transit shall not stay in their monastery, *zhiskhas* and other buildings or demand free horse service or provisions from them. No taxes should be levied on land and trade in the area. All their monastic land, rivers, forests, millstones, shops, mattresses, pawnshops, bathrooms, commoners and livestock should not be infringed upon and violence against them is prohibited. Likewise, they are not allowed to abuse the rights I grant them in this edict. Dare they risk punishment by doing anything unreasonable?

Written in Dadu on the 27th day of the 1st month of the 5th year of Zhizheng (1345), the Year of the Cock

Preserved by the Xigaze Prefectural Archives of Tibet.

# ཛོ་གན་ཐེ་མུར་རྒྱལ་པོས་ཡོན་ཏན་རྒྱལ་མཚན་ལ་བསྩལ་བའི་ལུང་།

# 妥歡帖睦爾皇帝頒給雲丹堅贊的聖旨

# Edict Issued by Emperor Thogan Themur to Yontan Gyaltshan

273 × 58.6

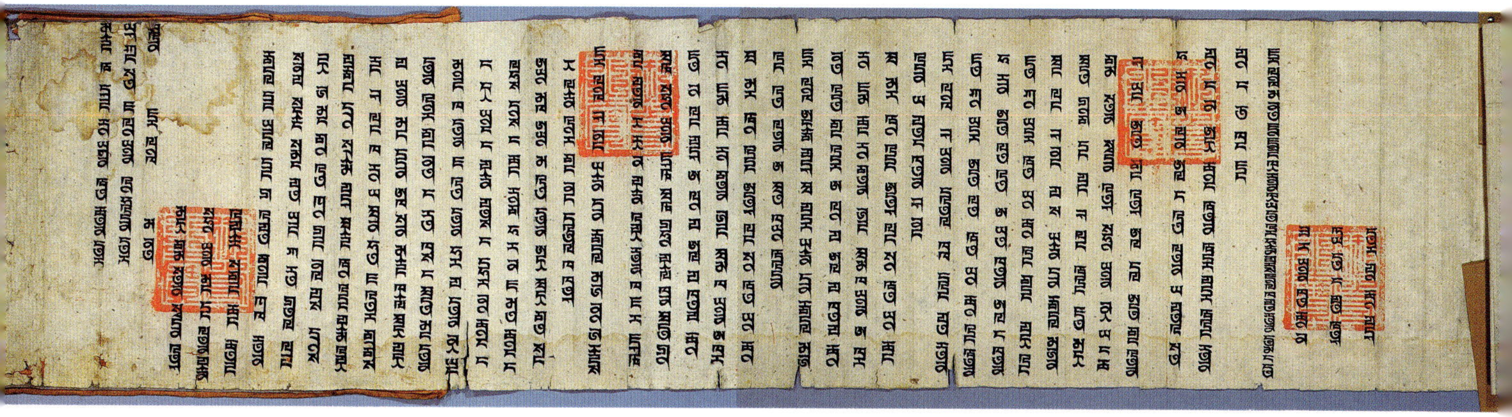

6 - 1

༄༅། །ཚེ་རིང་གནམ་གྱི་སྟོབས་ལ་བརྟེན་པ་དང་བསོད་ནམས་ཆེན་པོའི་དཔལ་གྱིས་སྐྱོང་བའི་རྒྱལ་པོའི་ལུང་།

མདོ་ཁམས་ཀྱི་སྟོན་ལྷི་སི་ལ་གཏོགས་པའི་སྤྱི་འཁོར་སྣང་ཆེ་ཆུང་། རྒྱལ་ཐང་། ཡངས་ཐང་། ཤ་འབྲུ་གིང་། ཉག་རོང་། ལབ་སྟོད་སྨད། བུ་ཡང་ག ཙུ་ཤུལ། ལང་སྟོ། མཚལ་སྨད། གེའུ། ཉི་ཤངས། ནལ་བས། དྲིལ་བཀེ། དྲུ་སྲོམ། བོད་ཐོང་སོགས་སྤྱི་འཁོར་ཁོངས་ཀྱི་ཐུར་གྲགས་པའི་མངའ་འོག་གི་སོག་བོད་མི་སྡེའི་ད་ར་ཁ་ཆེ། ཁྲི་དཔོན། སྟོང་དཔོན། བརྒྱ་དཔོན། བཅུ་དཔོན། བན་དེ། བོན་པོ། གྲྭ་པ། བཙུན་མ། ལྷ་སྡེ། དམག་མི། འཇའ་མོ་ཆེ། ཡུལ་དཔོན། མི་སྡེ་རྣམས་ལ་སྒྲོ་བ།

ཡོན་ཏན་རྒྱལ་མཚན་ལ་ཚ་ཨོང་གེབ་སྤྱི་འཁོར་ས་ཁུལ་གྱི་ཆའུ་ཐུའུ་སིའི་མི་དཔོན་བསྐོས་ཏེ་ཁྲལ་རིགས། འཇའ་མོ་ཆེ། དམག་གི་ཚང་དམ་ཁ་ལེན་པ་སོགས་ཀྱི་བྱ་བ་སྒྲུབ་ཕྱིར་དོ་དམ་བྱེད་དུ་བཅུག་པའི་ལུང་བྱིན་པ་ཡིན། ཁྱེད་རྣམས་ནས་ཡོན་ཏན་རྒྱལ་མཚན་གྱི་ངག་ལ་ཉན་ལ་ཁྲལ་རིགས། འཇའ་མོ་ཆེ། དམག་གི་ཚང་དམ་ཁ་སོགས་བྱ་བ་རྣམས་དུས་ལ་སླེབས་པར་སྒྲུབས། འདི་སྐད་བཟླས་ཤིང་མཐའ་དག་མ་བསྒྲུབས་པ་ཡོད་ན་མི་སྐྲག་པ་ཨེ་ཡིན། ཙ་ར་བྱེད་པར་མི་སྐྲག་པ་ཨེ་ཡིན། མཐའ་དག་བསྒྲུབས་པ་ཡིན་ན་ཡོན་ཏན་རྒྱལ་མཚན་གྱིས་བཀའ་མངགས་ཡོད་ཟེར་ནས་མདོ་ཁམས་ཀྱི་སྟོན་ལྷི་སིའི་མི་དཔོན་དང་གྲོས་མ་བྱས་པར་ཉེས་པ་མེད་པར་ཉེས་པ་ལེན་ཚེ་ངེད་ཚོར་ཡར་ཞུས་ལ། ཙ་ར་བྱེད་དུ་བཅུག་རྒྱུའི་ཐག་གཅོད་ངེད་ཚོས་བྱ་རྒྱུ་ཡིན།

ཛོ་ཛིང་ཁྲི་ལོ་ཉི་ཤུ་རྩ་གཉིས་སྟག་ལོ（སྤྱི་ལོ་༡༣༤༣）ཟླ་བ་གཉིས་པའི་ཚེས་སུམ་ཅུ་ཉིན་ཏའི་ཏུར་བྲིས་པའི་ལུང་།

བོད་རང་སྐྱོང་ལྗོངས་ཡིག་ཚགས་ཁང་དུ་ཉར་ཚགས་བྱས་ཡོད།

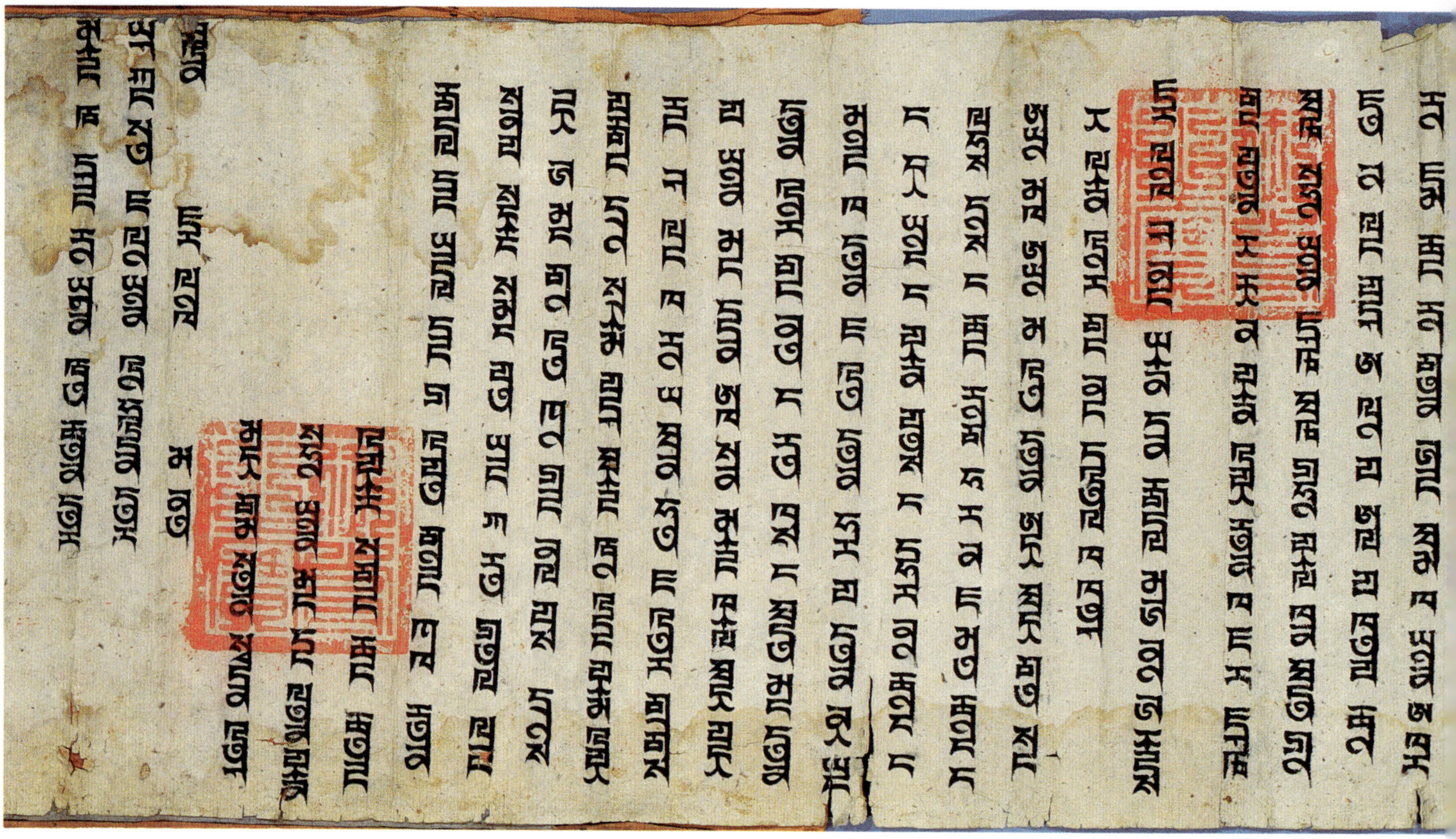

6 - 2

6 - 3

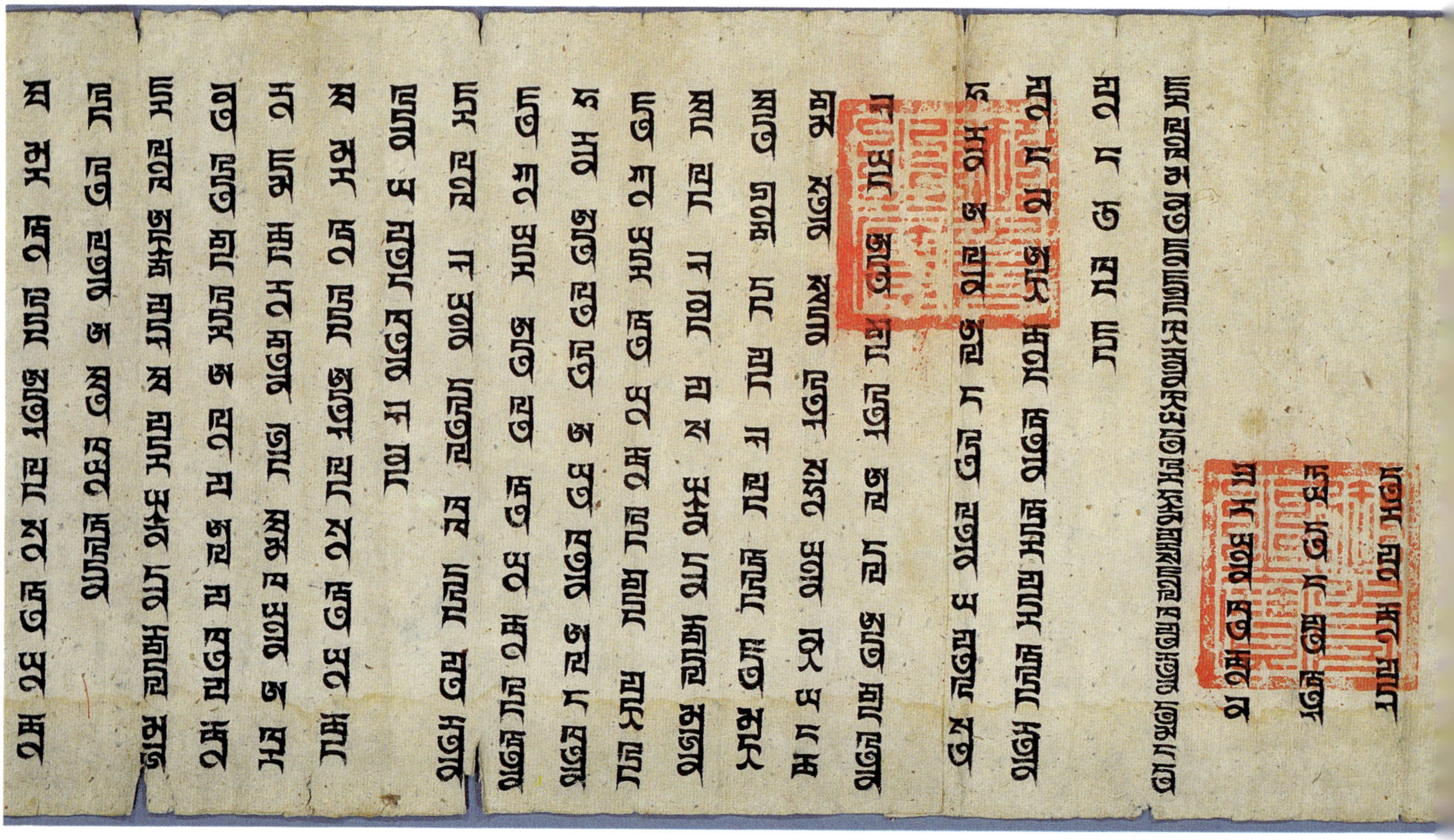

靠長生天的氣力，托大福蔭的護助，皇帝聖旨。

向朵甘思宣慰司所轄大小奔不兒亦思剛、建塘、洋塘、夏布更、聶隆、上下拉波、卜央噶、如須、郎翁、擦麥、給烏、尼香、那巴、直格、直松、白通等奔不所屬原由札巴掌管下的蒙古吐蕃百姓的達魯花赤們，萬户、千户、百户、什户的官員們，和尚們，苯教徒們，僧尼們，寺院部衆們，士兵們，站赤們，諸部落頭領們，百姓們宣諭：

茲委任雲丹堅贊爲察翁格奔不地方招討司的招討使，以監督完成一切差發、站户、軍户地税、商税的徵收等諸項事宜，特頒發了聖旨。你們務必遵照雲丹堅贊的命令，完成一切差發、站户、軍户地税、商税的徵收等諸項事宜。聖旨如此宣諭了，不完全執行的人難道不怕嗎? 又不怕處罰嗎? 如果完全執行了，而雲丹堅贊依仗對他的委托，未經與朵甘思宣慰司官員商議，處罰無辜的人，要上奏我們。如何處置，由我們決定。

聖旨，至正二十二年虎年（公元1362年）二月三十日寫於大都。

西藏自治區檔案館藏

The edict of the Emperor, who rules with the assistance of the great power and protection of everlasting Heaven.

Make the following known to all Mongolian and Tibetan Darakhaches, heads of *wanhu* (ten thousand households), *qianhu* (a thousand households), *baihu* (a hundred households) and *shihu*(ten households), believers in Bon, Buddhist monks and nuns, monastic staffs, soldiers, officials in charge of postal stations, tribal chiefs and commoners in Greater and Lesser Povborsgang, Gyalthang, Yangthang, Shabuging, Nyagrong, Upper and Lower Snab, Buyangka, Rushul, Langngo, Tshasmad, Giu, Nyishang, Nalpa, Drisge, Drisrom and Bethong in the area of Povbor, which was originally ruled by Gragpa and is now under the administration of the Dokham Pacification Commissioners Office:

This edict empowers Yontan Gyaltshan governor of Povbor in the area of Tshaonggib to supervise the work of requisitioning all corvée and collecting land and trade taxes for the maintenance of postal stations and the army. You must fulfil your work in accordance with his instructions. Dare you risk punishment by not following my edict? Report to us if you have fully implemented my edict, but Yontan Gyaltshan abuses his power by punishing innocent persons without consulting officials from the Dokham Pacification Commissioners Office. We shall decide how to punish him.

Written in Dadu on the 30th day of the 2nd month of the 22nd year of Zhizheng (1362), the Year of the Tiger

Preserved by the Archives of the Tibet Autonomous Region.

# 7

## ཧོར་ཡིག་གསར་པའི་སོག་སྐད་ཀྱི་རྒྱལ་པོའི་ལུང་གི་གསེར་ཡིག་གི་བྱང་བུ།

## 八思巴文蒙古語金字聖牌

## An Iron Plate of Authority

རྒྱུ་ལྕགས། གསེར་ཡིག དབྱིབས་སྒོར་མོ། ཐོར་ཅོག་ཙེ་རིས་ཅི་པ་ཏ། ལུགས་མ་འདོགས་ལུང་ཅན། ཚངས་ཐིག་རིང་ཚད་ལི་སྨི་༡༡.༥། རྒྱབ་མདུན་གྱི་ཡི་གེ་ཕྱིར་འབུར་བ།

དེའི་ནང་དོན་ཚེ་རིང་གནམ་གྱི་སྟོབས་ལ་བརྟེན་ནས་དབང་ཐོབ་པའི་རྒྱལ་པོའི་ལུང་། མི་སུ་ཞིག་ཡིན་རུང་བཀའ་ལ་མ་ཉན་ན་ཅར་བྱེད་དུ་བཏུག་རྒྱུ་ཡིན་ཞེས་འཁོད་འདུག

བྱང་བུ་འདི་ནི་ད་བར་མཐོང་རྒྱུ་བྱུང་བའི་ཧོར་ཡིག་གསར་པའི་སོག་སྐད་ཀྱི་རྒྱལ་པོའི་ལུང་གི་གསེར་ཡིག་གི་བྱང་བུ་གཅིག་བུ་རེད།

བཀྲ་ཤིས་ལྷུན་པོ་དགོན་དུ་ཉར་ཚགས་བྱས་ཡོད།

鐵質，金字，圓形，直徑11.5厘米，頂有蹋鼻獸圖樣，並有圓環供佩戴，正背兩面陽文："靠長生天的氣力，皇帝聖旨，誰若不從，即要問罪！"

此爲迄今所見唯一的八思巴文蒙古語金字聖牌。

扎什倫布寺藏

Made of iron and 11.5 cm. in diameter, the round plate has the motif of a snub-nosed animal with a ring on the top. It bears Mongolian words in the Phags-pa script raised with gold on both sides. The words read, "Anyone who disobeys the edicts issued by the Emperor, who rules with the assistance of the great power of everlasting Heaven, will be punished."

This plate is the only one of its kind found in China.

Preserved by Tashilhunpo Monastery.

# 8

## རིན་ཆེན་རྒྱལ་མཚན་ཏི་ཤྲི་ནས་སློབ་དཔོན་འཁོན་སྟོན་དང་སློབ་དཔོན་རིན་ཆེན་དཔལ་བཟང་པོར་བསྩལ་པའི་བཀའ་ཡིག

## 仁欽堅贊帝師頒給昆頓師長和仁欽貝桑布師長的法旨

## Decree Issued to High Priests Khonton and Rinchen Palzangpo by Imperial Tutor Rinchen Gyaltshan

138.6 × 64.5

བོད་རང་སྐྱོང་ལྗོངས་ཡིག་ཚགས་ཁང་དུ་ཉར་ཚགས་བྱས་ཡོད།

遵奉皇帝聖旨。

仁欽堅贊帝師法旨。

向烏思藏地方宣撫司官員、軍官、士兵、地方守官、法官、税官、過往官吏、站赤、牛馬飼養員、胥吏、地方頭人、百姓曉諭：

昆頓師長和仁欽貝桑布師長所屬埃巴地方寺廟溪卡、供法溪卡的僧人、施主、徒弟們聽講佛法，爲皇帝祈禱，安分守規。遵奉皇帝聖旨，對其擁有的耕地、溪卡、土地、河流、草場等，不得搶奪；不得在寺廟下榻；不得徵收地税、商税；不得以借貸、離間等爲口實，惹事生非；不得飼養牛馬；不得將農具和馱驢作抵押；不得攫奪羊群；不得派馱馬支烏拉；不得使用暴力。特頒發了執持的法旨。若見法旨仍倒行逆施，則必加懲罰。爾等亦不得做違法之事。

龍年（公元1304年）二月二十四日書於大都皇宮御花園。

西藏自治區檔案館藏

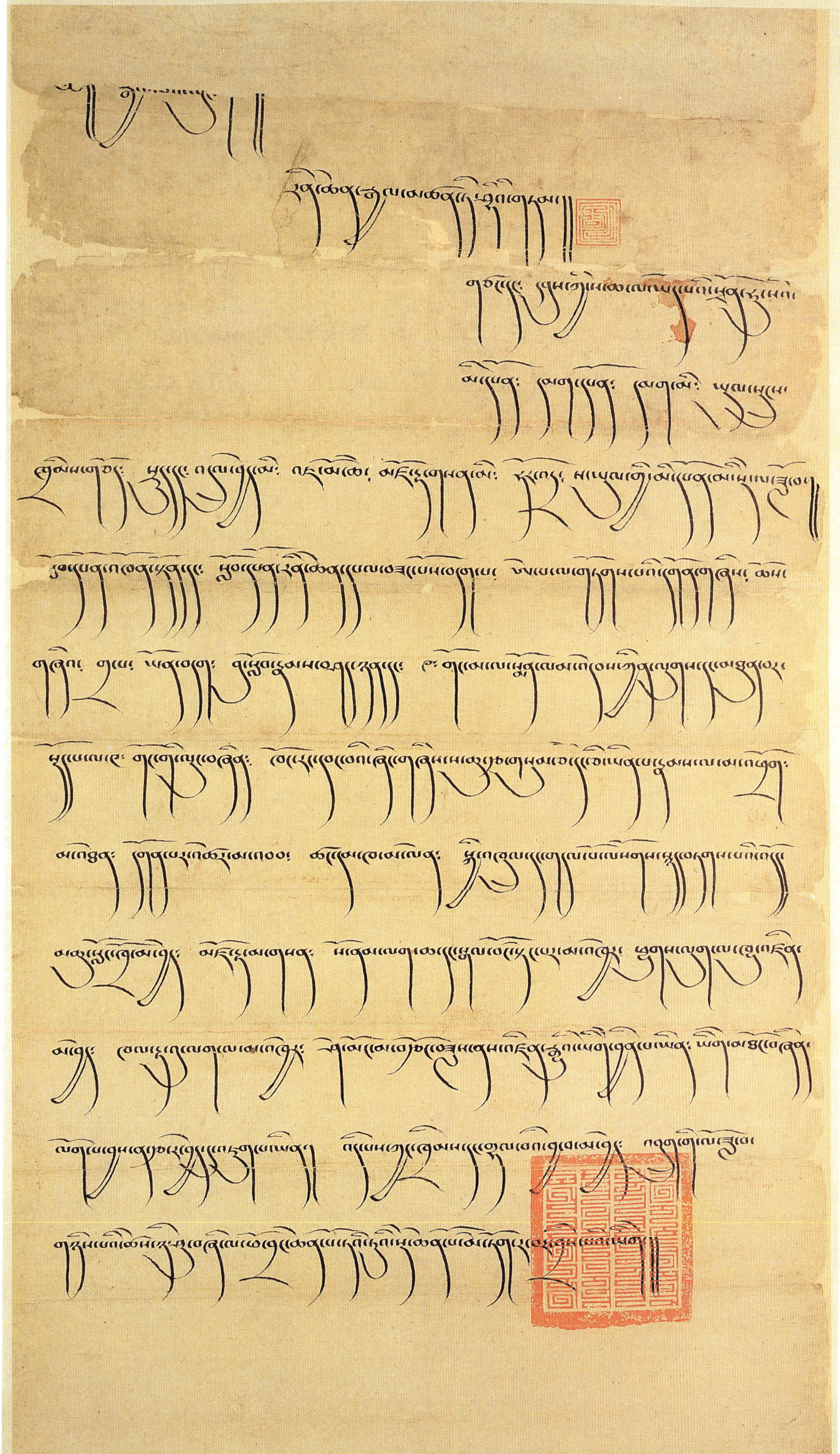

The decree of Imperial Tutor Rinchen Gyaltshan issued by order of the Emperor.

Make the following known to all officials of the Pacification Commissioners General Office in Dbustsang, military officers and men, local garrison commanders, judges, tax collectors, government messengers in transit, officials in charge of postal stations, stockmen, petty officials, tribal chiefs and commoners:

Buddhist monks and their patrons and followers in the monastic *zhiskhas* and in the *zhiskhas* which provide services for religious activities in Epa under the administration of high priests Khonton and Rinchen Palzangpo who study and preach Buddhism pray for the Emperor and abide by the law. In accordance with imperial edicts, the fields, *zhiskhas,* land, rivers and pastures belonging to them shall not be infringed upon. Government messengers shall not stay in their monasteries. No taxes shall be levied on land and trade. No person is allowed to stir up trouble by demanding loans from them or sowing discord. Grazing in their pastures is prohibited. Their farm tools and draught donkeys shall not be seized as security and their sheep shall not be taken by force. Levies of horse service and other corvée duties shall not be imposed upon them. Violence against them is not allowed. Offenders shall be punished. Likewise, monks are not allowed to abuse the rights I grant them in this decree or do anything that runs counter to the law.

Written in the palace garden in Dadu on the 24th day of the 2nd month of the Year of the Dragon (1304)

Preserved by the Archives of the Tibet Autonomous Region.

# སངས་རྒྱས་དཔལ་ཏི་ཤྲི་ནས་རིན་ཆེན་སྒང་པར་བསྩལ་པའི་བཀའ་ཡིག
# 桑杰貝帝師頒給仁欽崗巴的法旨
# Decree Issued to Rinchen Gangpa by Imperial Tutor Sanggyaspal

138.6×64.5

བོད་རང་སྐྱོང་ལྗོངས་རིག་དངོས་དོ་དམ་ཨུ་ཡོན་ལྷན་ཁང་དུ་ཉར་ཚགས་བྱས་ཡོད།

……［起首語損缺］ 官員、軍官、士兵、法官、天使、地方官員、地方守官、譯師、站赤、税官、過往官吏、百姓曉諭：

對仁欽崗巴所屬古窮和期供瑪吉的溪卡、恰崗、格頂、邦熱、托噶拜莎等不得增派差役；不得索取祇應、鋪馬；不得在溪卡、房舍下榻；不得飼養牛馬；不得攫奪羊群；不得將農具和馱驢作抵押；對其原有的人口、財産、耕田、土地、河流、草場等一切，不得搶奪；不得借故惹事生非。使其安居樂業。特頒發了執持的法旨。若見法旨仍倒行逆施，一經上奏，嚴加懲處。爾等亦不得因持有法旨而做違法之事。

猴年（公元1308年）閏十一月二十五日書於大都皇宮。

西藏自治區文物管理委員會藏

[The first part of the decree is missing.] ... officials, military officers and men, judges, imperial envoys, local officials and garrison commanders, interpreters, officials in charge of postal stations, tax collectors, government messengers in transit and commoners:

No additional corvée duties shall be imposed on the *zhiskhas* which provide services in the worship of Macig or on Byagang, Dgesdeng, Bangral and Thukapesar located in the area of Gurchung under the administration of Rinchen Gangpa. No person is allowed to demand free horse service or provisions from these places or to stay in the monastic *zhiskhas* or buildings. Grazing in these places is prohibited. Their sheep shall not be taken by force and their farm tools and draught donkeys shall not be seized as security. The inhabitants and their property as well as the farmland, land, rivers and pastures shall not be infringed upon. To enable the inhabitants to live and work in peace, no person is allowed to stir up trouble on any pretext. Those who continue their wrongdoing after they have seen this decree shall be punished severely as soon as they are informed on. Likewise, the inhabitants of these places are not allowed to abuse the rights I grant them in this decree or to do anything that runs counter to the law.

Written in the Imperial Palace in Dadu on the 25th day of the 11th (leap) month of the Year of the Monkey (1308)

Preserved by the Historical Relics Administration of the Tibet Autonomous Region.

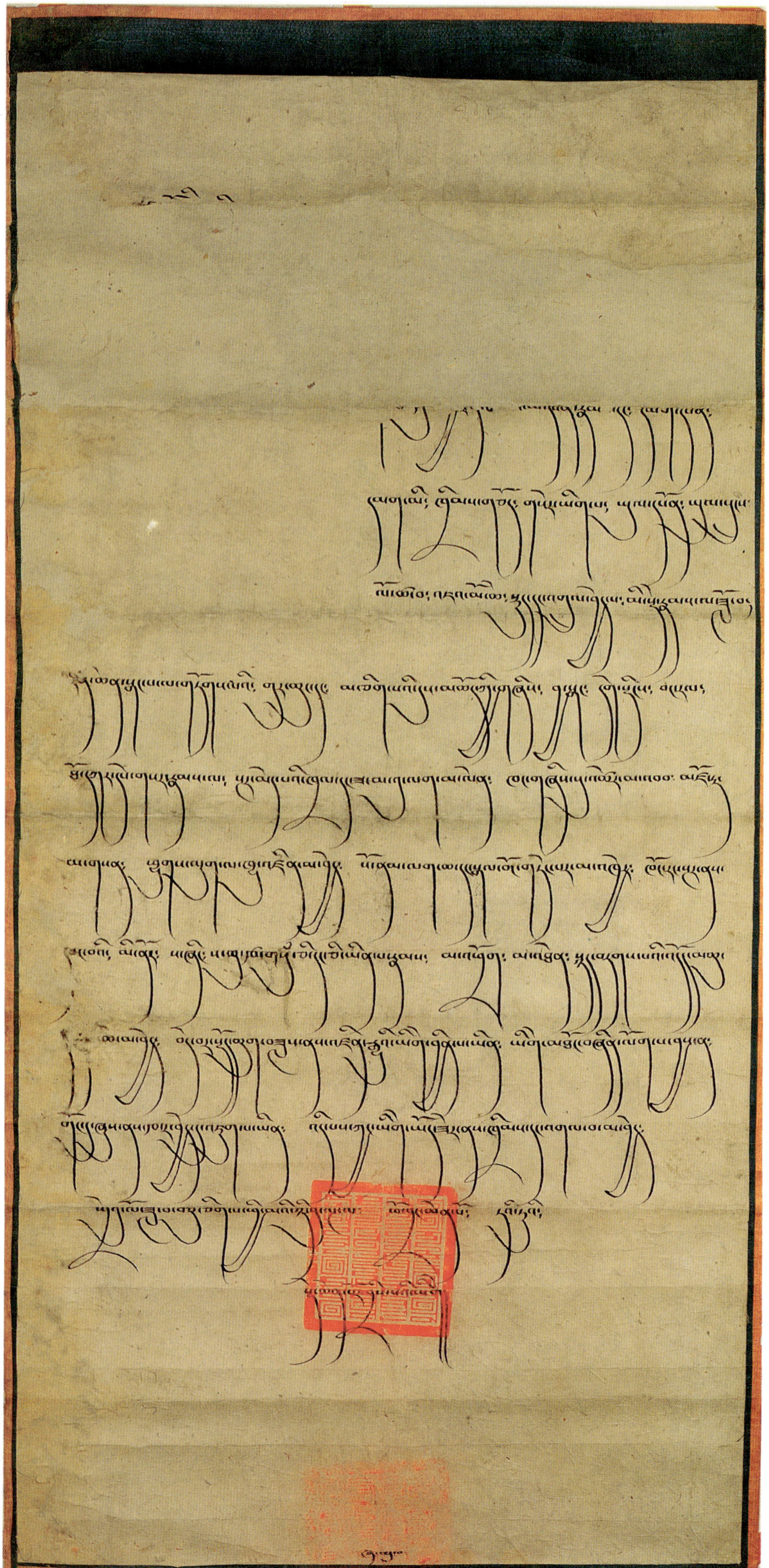

10

# ཀུན་དགའ་བློ་གྲོས་རྒྱལ་མཚན་དཔལ་བཟང་པོ་ཏི་ཤྲཱི་ནས་སློབ་དཔོན་རིན་ཆེན་མགོན་ལ་བསྩལ་པའི་བཀའ་ཡིག

# 貢噶羅追堅贊貝桑布帝師頒給仁欽貢師長的法旨

# Decree Issued to High Priest Rinchengon by Imperial Tutor Kungav Blogros Gyaltshan

94.3 × 54.5

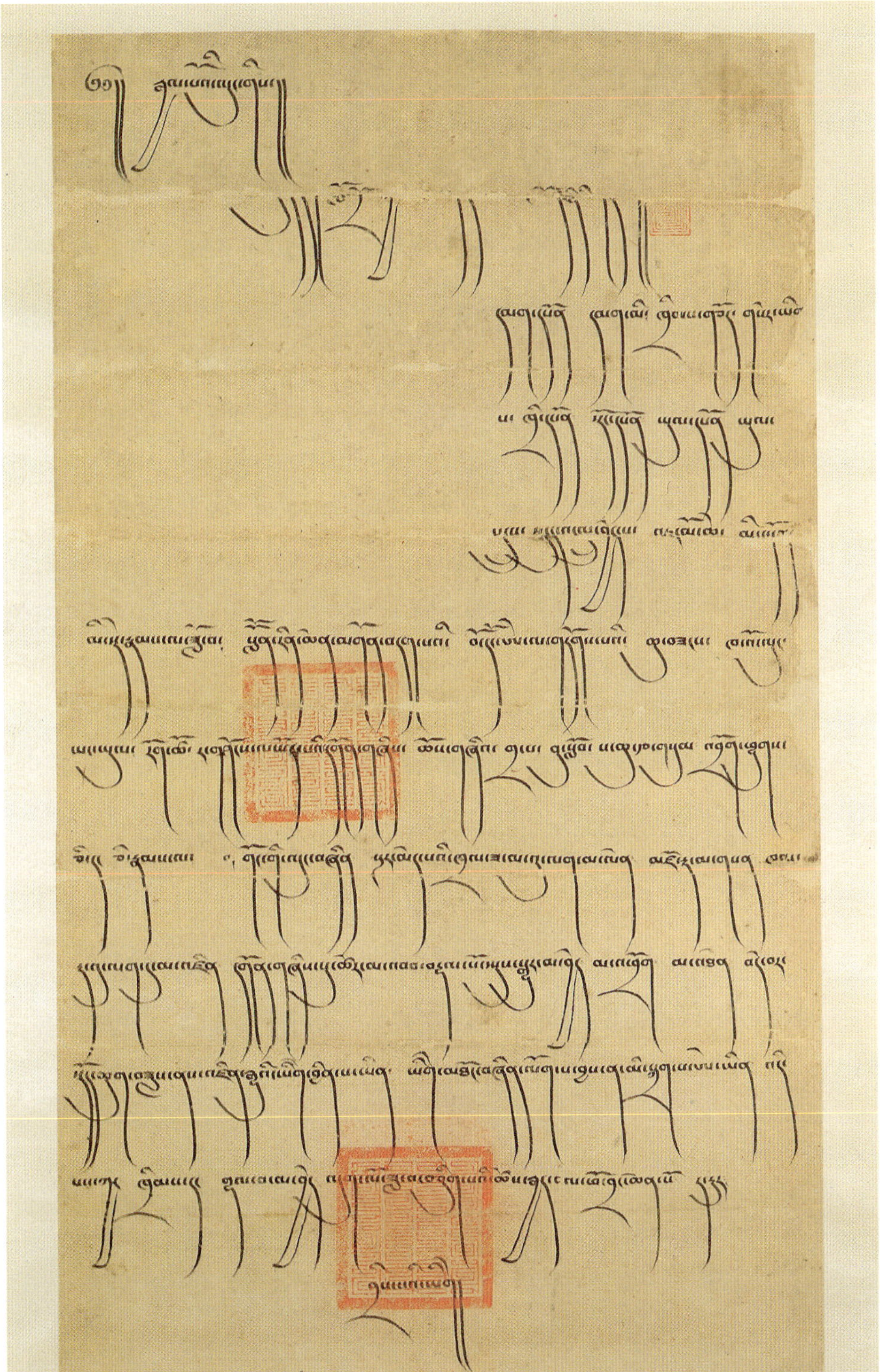

བོད་རང་སྐྱོང་ལྗོངས་ཡིག་ཚགས་ཁང་དུ་ཉར་ཚགས་བྱས་ཡོད།

遵奉皇帝聖旨。

貢噶羅追堅贊貝桑布帝師法旨。

向軍官、士兵、法官、天使、萬户長、千户長、地方官員、地方守官、税官、過往官吏、站赤、頭人、百姓曉諭：

對仁欽貢師長所屬珀東埃地方的曲桑、卡沃龍、央玉、若錯、熱雄的寺廟溪卡，供法溪卡的僧人、徒弟、土地、河流、草場、牧場、牲畜等一切，遵奉皇帝聖旨，不得增派差役；不得索取祇應、鋪馬；不得飼養牛馬；不得派馱馬支烏拉；不得在寺廟溪卡下榻；不得挑撥離間；不得搶奪；使之安居樂業。特頒發了執持的法旨。若見法旨仍倒行逆施，豈不畏懼。爾等亦不得做違法之事。

羊年（公元1319年）十一月初八書於大都皇宮。

西藏自治區檔案館藏

The decree of Imperial Tutor Kungav Blogros Gyaltshan issued by order of the Emperor.

Make the following known to all military officers and men, judges, imperial envoys, heads of *wanhu* and *qianhu,* local officials and garrison commanders, tax collectors, government messengers in transit, officials in charge of postal stations, tribal chiefs and commoners:

The monastic *zhiskhas* and the *zhiskhas* which provide services in religious activities and the monks and their followers as well as the land, rivers, pastures, grasslands and livestock belonging to them at Chubzang, Khaolung, Yangyul, Rogmtsho and Rashong in the Bodonge area are all under the administration of high priest Rinchengon. In accordance with imperial edicts, to enable the inhabitants in these places to live and work in peace, no additional corvée duties shall be imposed on them. Nobody shall demand free horse service or provisions from them. Grazing in their territory is not allowed. Nobody shall stay in the monastic *zhiskhas.* Sowing discord and robbery are prohibited. Offenders shall be punished. Likewise monks and their followers are not allowed to abuse the rights I grant them in this decree to do anything that runs counter to the law.

Written in the Imperial Palace in Dadu on the 8th day of the 11th month of the Year of the Sheep (1319)

Preserved by the Archives of the Tibet Autonomous Region.

# ཀུན་དགའ་བློ་གྲོས་རྒྱལ་མཚན་དཔལ་བཟང་པོ་ཏི་ཤྲི་ནས་དབང་རྒྱལ་ལ་བསྩལ་པའི་བཀའ་ཤོག

# 貢噶羅追堅贊貝桑布帝師頒給旺杰的法旨

# Decree Issued by Imperial Tutor Kungav Blogros Gyaltshan to Wanggyal

96 × 57

བོད་རང་སྐྱོང་ལྗོངས་ཡིག་ཚགས་ཁང་དུ་ཉར་ཚགས་བྱས་ཡོད།

遵奉皇帝聖旨。

貢噶羅追堅贊貝桑布帝師法旨。

向朵甘思宣慰司官員、招討司官員、地方守官、茺之百户長、什户長、百姓曉諭：

堅贊扎曾受皇帝聖旨和歷輩喇嘛法旨，被任命爲爾茺之千户長。今令其子旺杰承襲父職，任茺之千户長。爾哲察、仲察、尚强、卡布、甲娘、索諾、尚拉、瑪拉等百姓歷來居住於注册在茺之吉多、奔娘、若參，諸項公務，須遵照旺杰所言，及時辦理，此地百姓，若有被他人乘隙佔有者，由宣慰使和地方官員、地方守官勸其退還。如是曉諭，若有違犯，豈不畏懼。旺杰本人亦須盡力撫養爾所轄百姓，勤奮辦事。

鷄年（公元1321年）二月二十五日書於大都皇宮。

西藏自治區檔案館藏

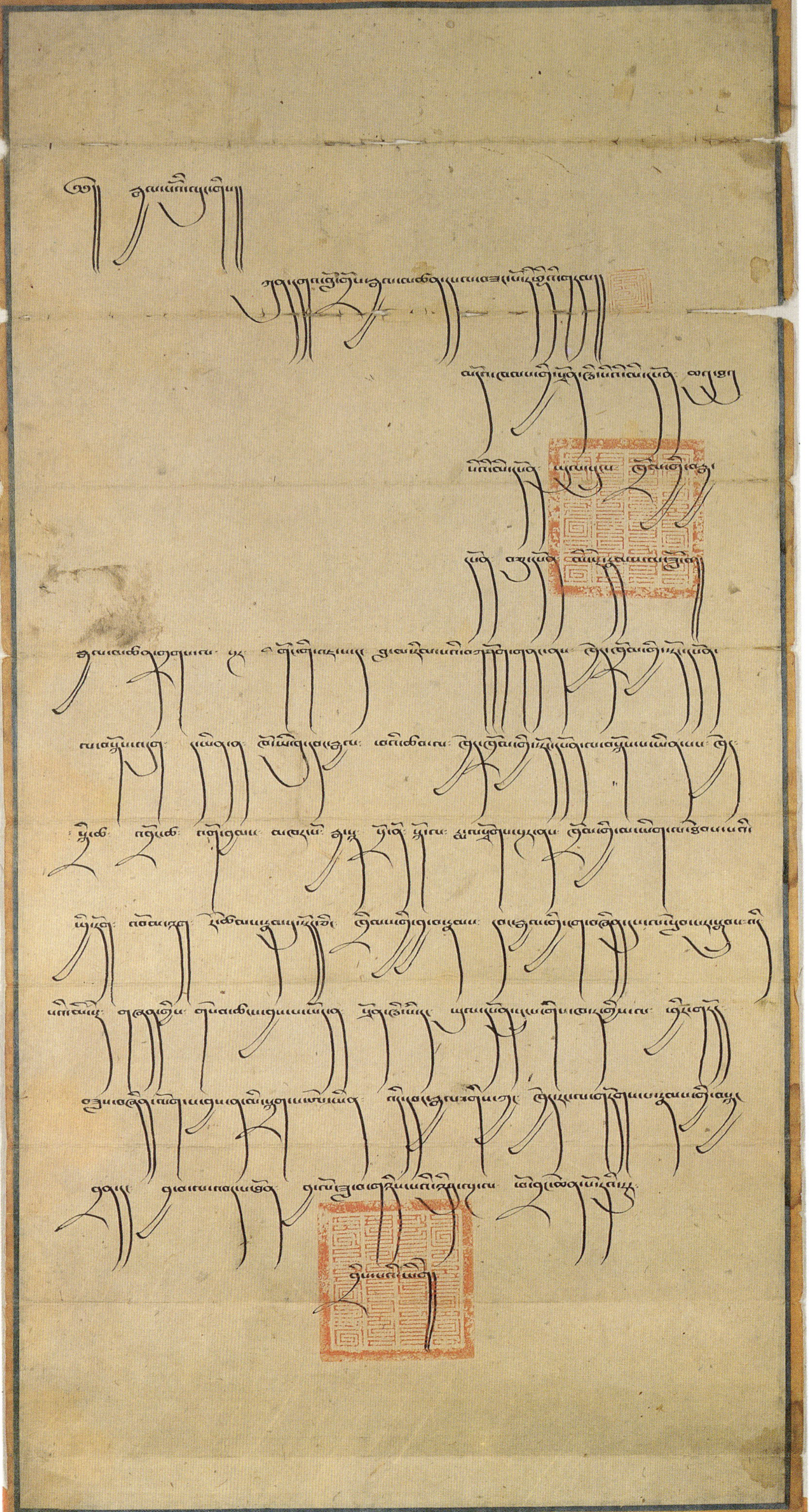

The decree from Imperial Tutor Kungav Blogros Gyaltshan issued by order of the Emperor.

Make the following known to all officials of the Pacification Commissioners Office in Dokham and the Office of the Governor–General of Dokham, local garrison officers, heads of *baihu* and *shihu* and commoners in Khrom:

Gyaltshangrag was assigned to the post of the head of *qianhu* of Khrom by the Emperor and ruling lamas. This decree is to appoint Wanggyal, his son, to succeed him as head of *qianhu* of Khrom. People from Gritsha, Brongtsha, Gobyam, Mkharpo, Rgyasnya, Srono, Skola and Rmala, who are permanent residents in Spyitog, Vbomnyag and Rotsham under the jurisdiction of Khrom, shall do all the work assigned to them without delay in accordance with Wanggyal's instructions. Should anyone avail himself of loopholes to take possession of commoners of these places, Pacification Commissioners and local officials and garrison officers are to persuade those involved to give them up. Violation of this decree is punishable. As head of *qianhu,* Wanggyal must work diligently and take good care of the people in his charge.

Written in the Imperial Palace of Dadu on the 25th day of the 2nd month of the Year of the Cock (1321)

Preserved by the Archives of the Tibet Autonomous Region.

# ཀུན་དགའ་རྒྱལ་མཚན་དཔལ་བཟང་པོ་ཏི་ཤྲི་ནས་ཡེ་ཤེས་ཀུན་དགའ་ལ་བསྩལ་པའི་བཀའ་ཡིག
# 貢噶堅贊貝桑布帝師頒給益西貢噶的法旨
# Decree Issued to Yeshes Kungav by Imperial Tutor Kungav Gyaltshan Palzapo

96 × 57

བོད་རང་སྐྱོང་ལྗོངས་ཡིག་ཚགས་ཁང་དུ་ཉར་ཚགས་བྱས་ཡོད།

遵奉皇帝聖旨。

貢噶堅贊貝桑布帝師法旨。

向西夏魯所轄百姓和然薩、瑪、賈、門卓、如參、然索、且林、江然、岩、卓等地百姓之千户長、百户長、什户長曉諭：

遵奉皇帝頒給益西貢噶的詔書和金册，已令爾等知曉，吾亦已任命。爾等須聽從其言，凡以軍事、驛站、地税、商税爲主的諸項公務，均得及時辦理，特此曉諭。若有違犯，必加懲處。同樣，爾益西貢噶若依仗法旨，未經與宣慰司官員們商議而做懲罰無辜或侵害百姓等違法之事，豈不畏懼。

牛年（公元1337年）四月十一日書於大都皇宫御花園。

西藏自治區檔案館藏

The decree of Imperial Tutor Kungav Gyaltshan Palzapo by order of the Emperor.

Make the following known to all heads of *qianhu, baihu* and *shihu* and commoners in Rasa, Mag, Lcag, Monjo, Rutsham, Rasog, Byegling, Lcangra, Yan and Sgrol in the area of western Zhalu:

I have made known to you the edict and the gold–leaf album of appointment given to Yeshes Kungav by the Emperor. You shall handle matters concerning military affairs, postal stations and land and trade tax collection without delay in accordance with his instructions. Anyone who violates my decree shall be punished. Likewise, Yeshes Kungav is not allowed to abuse the rights I grant him in this decree to punish innocent persons without consulting the Pacification Commissioners or to do anything harmful to his people. Dare he risk punishment by doing anything that runs counter to the law?

Written in the palace garden in Dadu on the 11th day of the 4th month of the Year of the Ox (1337)

Preserved by the Archives of the Tibet Autonomous Region.

# ཐ་དེ་རྒྱལ་ཡུམ་ནས་སྐུ་ཞང་གྲགས་པ་རྒྱལ་མཚན་ལ་བསྩལ་པའི་བཀའ་ཡིག
# 答吉皇太后頒給古香・札巴堅贊的懿旨
# Decree Issued to Skuzhang Gragpa Gyaltshan by Empress Dowager Daji

236.6 × 56.6

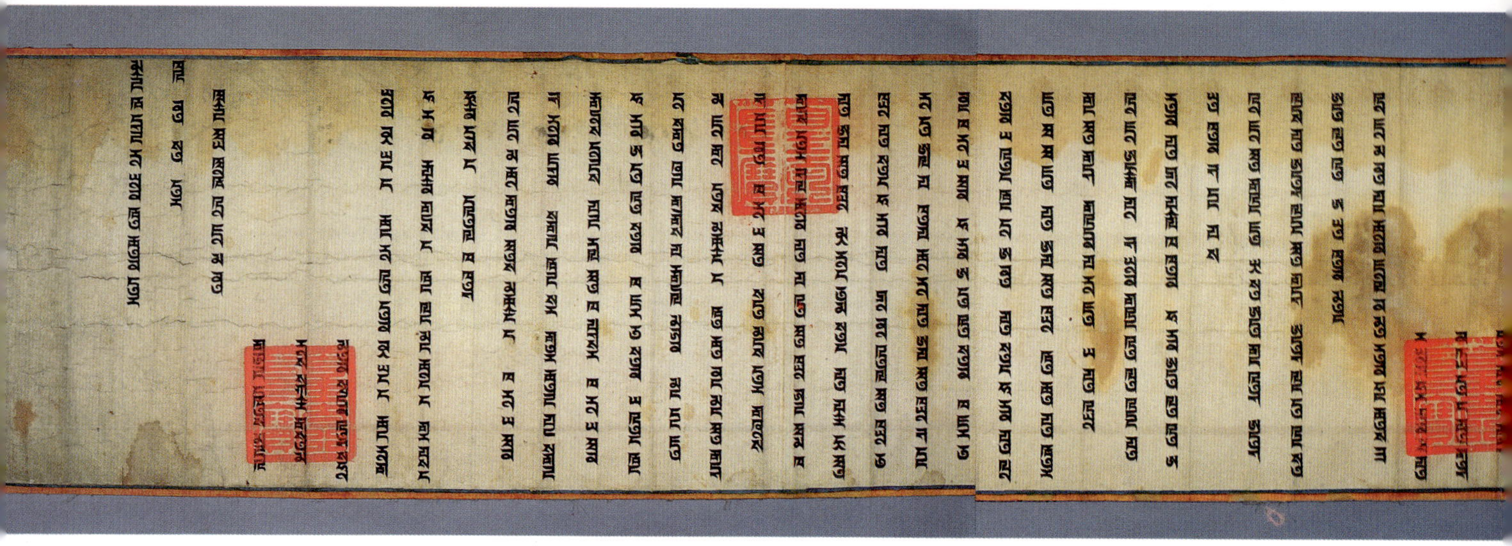

13－1

༄༅། །ཚེ་རིང་གནམ་གྱི་སྟོབས་ལ་བརྟེན་པ་དང་རྒྱལ་པོའི་བསོད་ནམས་ཀྱི་དཔལ་གྱིས་སྐྱོང་བའི་རྒྱལ་ཡུམ་གྱི་བཀའ།

དབུས་གཙང་མངའ་རིས་སྐོར་གསུམ་གྱི་སྟོན་ཕྱི་སིའི་མི་དཔོན། དམག་དཔོན། དམག་མི། ཡུལ་དཔོན། ཕོ་ཉ་བ། སྐྱར་པ། ཏོར་འདྲ་རྣམས་ལ་སྒོ་བ།

སྐུ་ཞང་གྲགས་པ་རྒྱལ་མཚན་ལ་མ་ཅིག་དུས་མཆོད་དུ་གཏོགས་པའི་རིན་ཆེན་སྒང་། ཁང་གསར། གུར་ཆུང་། བྱ་སྒང་། དགེ་སྡིངས། བང་རལ། ཐོ་དཀར་པོ་གསར་བཅས་ཀྱི་མི། ཕྱུགས། ས། ཆུ་སོགས་ཀྱི་བདག་གཉེར་དང་མ་ཅིག་དུས་མཆོད་ཀྱི་རོགས་བྱེད་དུ་བཅུག་པ་ཡིན། ཁོ་རྣམས་ལ་དབང་བའི་དགོན་གཞིས་སུ་འཚེར་མ་འབབ། ཚང་དམ་ཁ་མ་ལེན། མཛོ་ཧྲ་མ་གསན། མི་གཞན་གྱིས་ཁེ་ངོགས་མ་ཟ། ཐྲར་གྱི་ཁྲལ་ཆད་གསབ་མ་བྱེད། མི་གཞན་གྱིས་ཁོ་རྣམས་ལ་བདག་པའི་མི་ཕྱུགས་ས་ཆུ་མ་འཕྲོག མ་འཐེན། ཤེ་མོང་མ་བཙོང་བཟླས་ནས་བཀའ་ཡིག་ཕྱིན་པ་ཡིན། བཟླས་བཞིན་ལོག་པ་བྱས་ན་མི་སྐྲག་པ་ཨེ་ཡིན། འདི་པ་རྣམས་ནས་ཀྱང་འཛིན་རྒྱུའི་བཀའ་ཡིག་ཡོད་ཟེར་ནས་ཁྲིམས་དང་འགལ་བའི་བྱ་བ་མ་བྱེད། བྱས་ན་མི་སྐྲག་པ་ཨེ་ཡིན།

སྤྲེལ་ལོ（སྤྱི་ལོ་༡༣༢༠）ཟླ་བ་དགུ་པའི་ཚེས་བཅོ་ལྔ་ཉིན་ཏའི་ཏུར་བྲིས་པའི་བཀའ།

བོད་རང་སྐྱོང་ལྗོངས་རིག་དངོས་དོ་དམ་ཨུ་ཡོན་ལྷན་ཁང་དུ་ཉར་ཚགས་བྱས་ཡོད།

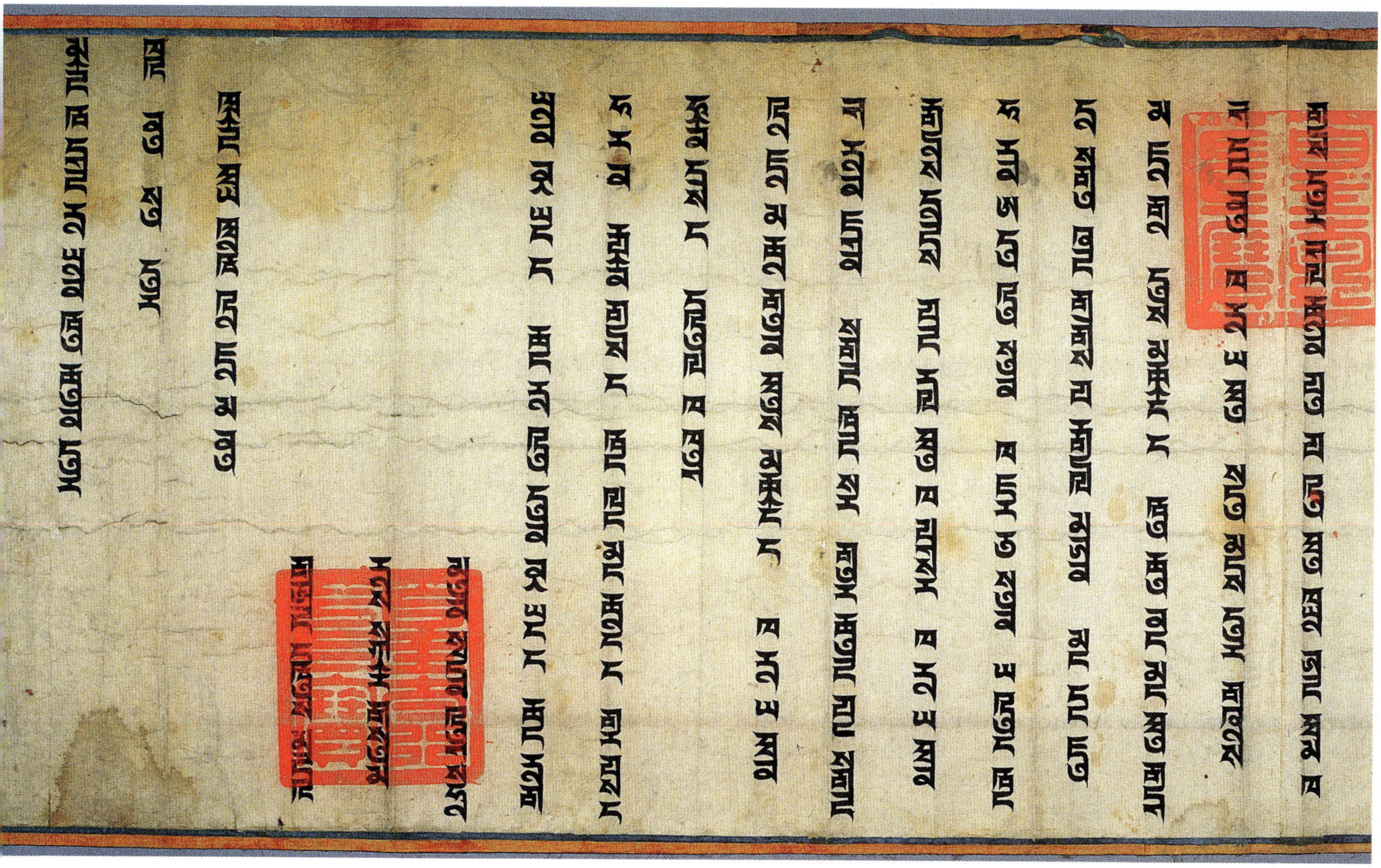

13-2

13-3

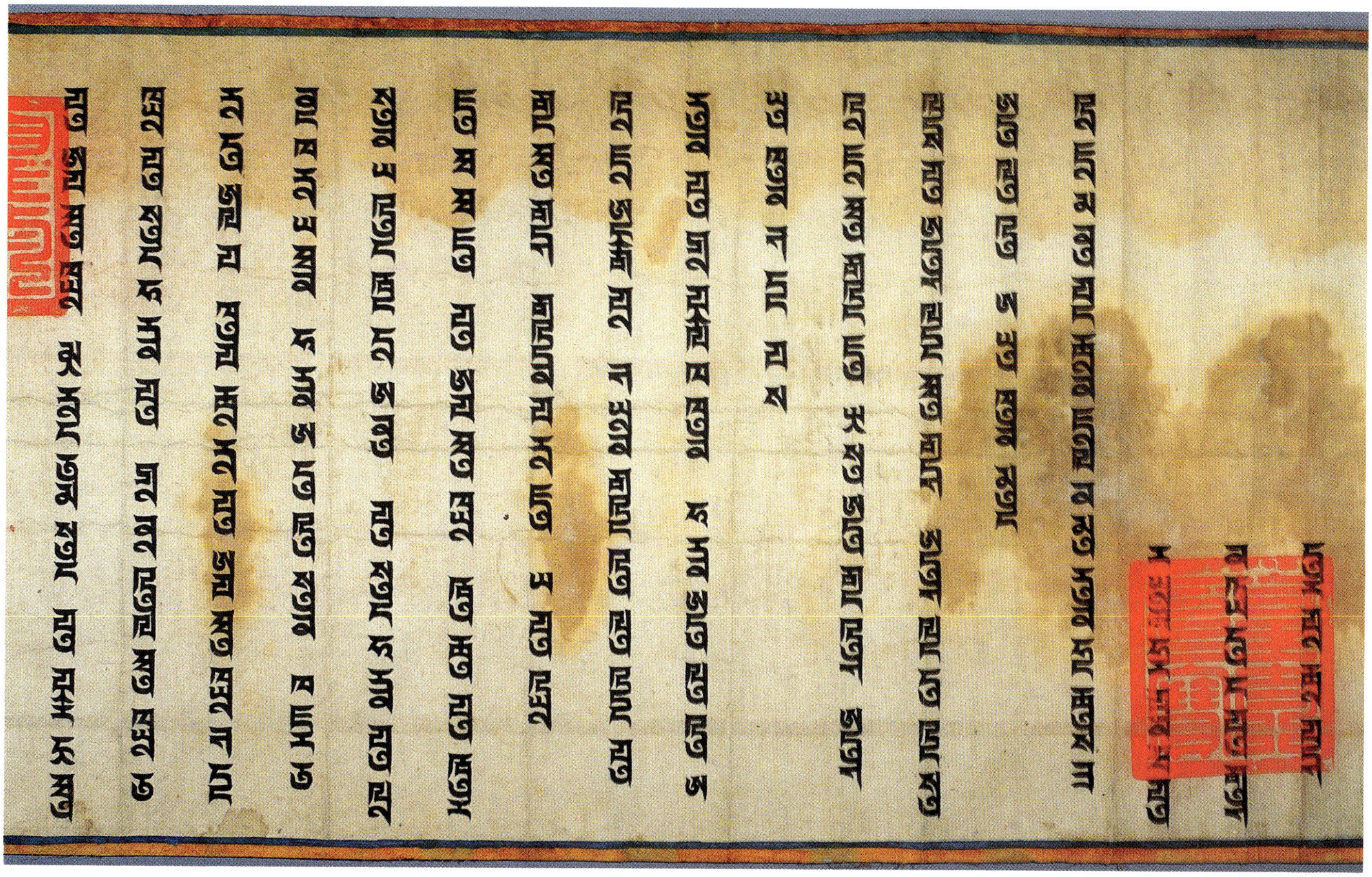

靠長生天的氣力，托皇帝福蔭，皇太后懿旨。

向烏思藏納里速古魯孫三圍宣慰司官員們、軍官們、士兵們、俗官們、譯員們、營官們、胥吏們宣諭：

麻吉期供所屬仁欽崗、康薩、古爾穹、甲崗、結丁、邦熱、土噶貝薩所屬人口、頭匹、土地、河流等，應由古香·札巴堅贊進行管理，并對麻吉期供提供幫助。在他們所屬的寺院、莊園裏，使臣不得下榻；不得向他們徵收地稅、商稅；在他們那裏不得飼養牛馬；他人不得圖利；不得補收以前的差發；不得搶奪他們所屬人口、頭匹、土地、河流等；不得對他們使用暴力。爲此頒發了所持的懿旨。如此宣諭了，違者豈不怕？他們也不得因持有懿旨而做無理的事。如做，他們豈不怕？

懿旨，猴年（公元1320年）九月十五日書於大都。

西藏自治區文物管理委員會藏

The decree of the Empress Dowager, who governs with the assistance of the great power of everlasting Heaven and the protection of the ruling Emperor.

Make the following known to all officials of the Pacification Commissioners Office, military officers and men, lay officials, interpreters, officials in charge of barracks and other petty officials of the three tribes in Ngavriskorsum, Dbustsang:

Rinchengang, Khanggsar, Gurchung, Byagang, Dgesdeng, Bangral and Thukapesar and their inhabitants, livestock, land and rivers shall be put under the administration of Skuzhang Gragpa Gyaltshan and he shall render assistance to the religious activities conducted periodically in the worship of Macig. Government messengers in transit shall not stay in their monasteries or manorial estates. No taxes shall be levied on their land and trade. Grazing in these locations is not allowed. Others shall not gain any profit there. The inhabitants shall be relieved of their corvée debts. Monastic commoners, livestock, land and rivers shall not be infringed upon and violence against them is prohibited. Those who violate this decree shall be punished. Aren't they afraid of this? Likewise monks are not allowed to abuse the rights I grant them in this decree. Dare they risk punishment by doing anything unreasonable?

Written in Dadu on the 15th day of the 9th month of the Year of the Monkey (1320)

Preserved by the Archives of the Tibet Autonomous Region.

# ཧེ་ཤན་ཧོད་ཞིང་ཤང་ནས་ཞ་ལུ་དགོན་པར་བསྩལ་བའི་བཀའ།

# 海山懷寧王頒給夏魯寺的令旨

# Order Issued to the Zhalu Monastery by Heshan, Prince of Huaining

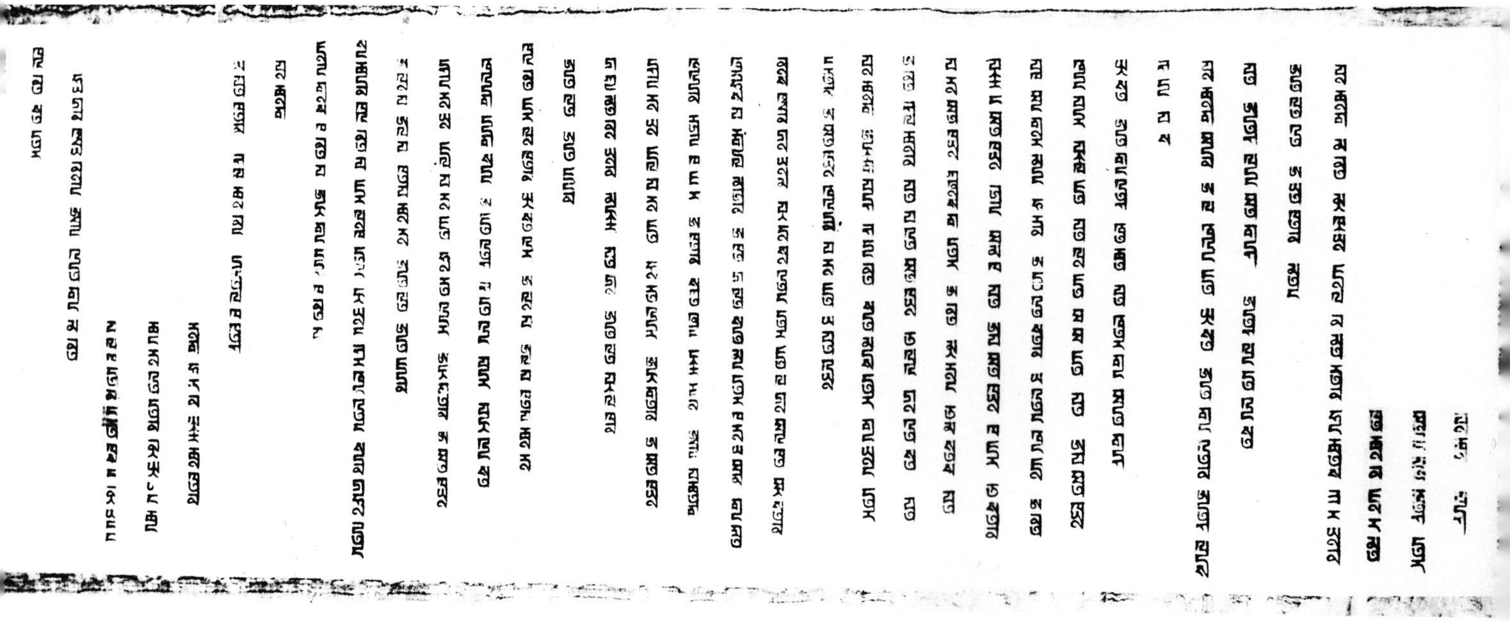

༄༅། །ཚེ་རིང་གནམ་གྱི་སྟོབས་ལ་བརྟེན་པ་དང་རྒྱལ་པོའི་བསོད་ནམས་ཀྱི་དཔལ་གྱིས་སྐྱོང་བའི་ཧེ་ཤན་ཧོད་ཞིང་ཤང་གི་བཀའ།

མཁར་གྱི་ད་ར་ཁ་ཆེ། མི་དཔོན། དམག་དཔོན། དམག་མི། འགྲུལ་བྱེད་པ་རྣམས་ལ་ཟློ་བ།

ཛིང་གིར་རྒྱལ་པོ། ཨོ་ཁོ་དེའི་རྒྱལ་པོ། སེ་ཆེན་རྒྱལ་པོ་བཅས་ཀྱི་ལུང་དུ་ཏྭ་ཤང་། ཨེར་ཁེ་ཝུན། སེན་ཤིང་རྣམས་ནས་ཁྲལ་ཅི་ཡང་འཇལ་མི་དགོས་པ་དང་། གནམ་ལ་སྨོན་ལམ་འདེབས། སྐྱབས་འཇུག་ཞུ་ཞེས་འཁོད་ཡོད་པས། རྒྱལ་པོའི་ལུང་བཞིན་ཁྲལ་ཅི་ཡང་འཇལ་མི་དགོས་པ་དང་ཤཱཀྱ་མུ་ནེའི་བསྟན་ཆོས་གཞིར་བཟུང་སྟེ་གནམ་ལ་སྨོན་ལམ་འདེབས། སྐྱབས་འཇུག་ཞུར་བཅུག་བཞག་ནས་གཙང་གི་སྐུ་ཞང་རྡོ་རྗེ་དབང་ཕྱུག་གྲགས་པ་རྒྱལ་མཚན་གནས་ས་ཞ་ལུ་དགོན་པའི་འཕགས་པ་སྤྱན་རས་གཟིགས་སྐུ་མདུན་གྱི་མཆོད་མེའི་མར་འབུལ་དགོས་དོན་དུ་བཀའ་བྱིན་པ་ཡིན། ཁོ་རྣམས་ཀྱི་དགོན་པ་དང་ཁང་པར་འགྲུལ་བྱེད་པས་འཚེར་མ་འབབ། ཁོ་རྣམས་རྟ་ནས་ཟ་མ་འུ་ལག་མ་ལེན། ཁོ་རྣམས་ཀྱི་གཞིས་ཀ་ནང་མཛོ་རྟ་མ་གསན། ཚང་དམ་ཁ་མ་ལེན། མི་སུ་ཞིག་ཡིན་རུང་ཁོ་རྣམས་ཀྱིས། ཆུ། ཞིང་། མི། ཕྱུགས་སོགས་མ་འཕྲོག མ་འཐེན། ཤེ་

སྲོང་མ་བཙོང་། འདི་པ་རྣམས་ནས་ཀྱང་འཛིན་རྒྱུའི་བཀའ་ཡིག་ཡོད་ཟེར་ནས་ཁྲིམས་དང་འགལ་བའི་བྱ་བ་མ་བྱེད། བྱས་ན་མི་སྐྲག་པ་ཨེ་ཡིན།

སྦྲུལ་ལོ(སྤྱི་ལོ་༡༣༠༥)ཟླ་བ་དགུ་པའི་ཚེས་སུམ་ཅུ་ཉིན་ཛི་ར་སྨུ་ཐུར་བྲིས་པའི་བཀའ།

བོད་རང་སྐྱོང་ལྗོངས་རིག་དངོས་དོ་དམ་ཨུ་ཡོན་ལྷན་ཁང་དུ་ཉར་ཚགས་བྱས་ཡོད།

靠長生天的氣力，托皇帝的福蔭，海山懷寧王令旨。

向城子達魯花赤們、官員們、軍官們、士兵們、往來的使臣們宣諭：

成吉思汗、窩闊台皇帝、薛禪皇帝聖旨裏説道："和尚們、也里可温們、先生們不承擔任何差發、禱告上天保佑。"兹按皇帝聖旨，不承擔任何差發，遵循釋迦牟尼教法，同時禱告上天保佑，爲後藏古香·多吉旺曲札巴堅贊所在夏魯寺聖觀世音佛燈供油事，頒發了令旨。在他們的寺院房舍裏，使臣不得下榻；不得向他們索取鋪馬、祗應；不得在他們的莊園里飼養牛馬；不得徵收地税、商税；任何人不得搶奪他們的土地、河流、園林、碾磨、人口、頭匹等；不得使用暴力，他們也不得因持有令旨而做無理的事，如做，豈不怕?

令旨，蛇年（公元1305年）九月三十日書於吉拉木圖。

西藏自治區文物管理委員會藏

The order of Heshan, Prince of Huaining, who governs with the assistance of the great power of everlasting Heaven and the protection of the Emperor.

Make the following known to all Darakhaches and other officials, military officers and men and government messengers in transit:

Genghis Khan and Emperors Okholde and Sechen stated in their edicts, "Buddhist, Christian and Taoist priests are exempt from all corvée. They invoke the blessing of Heaven upon us." This order is to reiterate that statement and to ensure lamp oil supplies for the worship of Avalokitesvara in the Zhalu Monastery in Lower Tibet under the charge of Skuzhang Rdorje Wangphyug Gragpa Gyaltshan. Government messengers in transit shall not stay in their monastery and other buildings or demand free horse service or provisions from them. Grazing in their manorial estates is prohibited. No taxes shall be levied on land and trade. Monastic land, rivers, forests, millstones, commoners and livestock shall not be infringed upon. Violence against monks is not allowed. Likewise the monks of the monastery shall not abuse the rights I grant them in this order. Dare they risk punishment by doing anything unreasonable?

Written in Jiramutu on the 30th day of the 9th month of the Year of the Snake (1305)

Preserved by the Historical Relics Administration of the Tibet Autonomous Region.

# རྡིང་ཟླ་ལུ་སྲོན་ལྷི་སིའི་མི་དཔོན་གྱི་གཏམ།
# 丁沙魯宣慰司官員文告
# Proclamation Issued by the Pacification Commissioners Office in Rdingzalu

35×18

བོད་རང་སྐྱོང་ལྗོངས་ཡིག་ཚགས་ཁང་དུ་ཉར་ཚགས་བྱས་ཡོད།

遵奉皇帝聖旨。

丁沙魯宣慰司都元帥府官員文告。

向軍官、士兵、法官、税官、過往僧俗官吏、大小站赤、牛馬飼養員、地方官員、百姓曉諭：

據稱，堪欽·索南扎巴所轄桑木耶白溪、錄布、堅達、康達等供法溪卡，歷來與兵役、户差等差役毫不相關。若確實如此，則爾等一概不得對其進行任何勒索，并須承侍供法溪卡。若違犯此文告，必加懲處。

兔年十月二十七日書

西藏自治區檔案館藏

The proclamation issued by the Pacification Commissioners Office by order of the Emperor.

All military officers and men, judges, tax collectors, monk and lay officials, officials in charge of postal stations and sub-stations, stockmen, local officials and commoners:

It is reported that the *zhiskhas* which provide services for religious activities at Bsamyaspegzhi, Lhudpu, Lcagmdav and Khamdav under the administration of Khanchen Sodnamgragpa have long been exempt from military service and all corvée duties. If this is true, you shall not force such duties on these *zhiskhas*. Instead, you should render assistance to them. Offenders shall be punished.

Written on the 27th day of the 10th month of the Year of the Hare

Preserved by the Shannan Prefectural Archives of Tibet.

# རྒྱལ་ཁབ་ཁག་གི་གྲྭ་བཙུན་རྣམས་འགོ་འཛིན་བྱས་ཏེ་སངས་རྒྱས་བསྟན་པ་སྤེལ་བའི་ཏཱ་དབེན་ཏི་ཤྲིའི་ཐམ་ཀ

# 大元帝師統領諸國僧尼中興釋教之印

# The Seal of the Imperial Tutor of the Great Yuan Dynasty, Leader of Monks and Nuns in All States Undergoing a Revival of Buddhism

16 - 1

16 - 2

16-3

རྒྱ་གཡང་ཏེ། དབྱིབས་གྲུ་བཞི། མཐའི་རིང་ཚད་ལི་སྨི་༩.༦

བོད་རང་སྐྱོང་ལྗོངས་རིག་དངོས་དོ་དམ་ཨུ་ཡོན་ལྷན་ཁང་དུ་ཉར་ཚགས་བྱས་ཡོད།

玉質，邊長9.6厘米。

西藏自治區文物管理委員會藏

A 9.6 cm. by 9.6 cm. jade seal.

Preserved by the Historical Relics Administration of the Tibet Autonomous Region.

# ཏི་ཤྲི་སངས་རྒྱས་དཔལ་གྱི་ཐམ་ཀ
# “桑杰貝帝師”印
# The Seal of Imperial Tutor Sanggyaspal

17 - 1

17-2

རྒྱ་གཡང་ཏེ། དབྱིབས་གྲུ་བཞི། མཐའི་རིང་ཚད་ལི་སྨི༨.༧
བོད་རང་སྐྱོང་ལྗོངས་རིག་དངོས་དོ་དམ་ཨུ་ཡོན་ལྷན་ཁང་དུ་ཉར་ཚགས་བྱས་ཡོད།

玉質，邊長8.7厘米。
西藏自治區文物管理委員會藏

An 8.7 cm. by 8.7 cm. jade seal.
Preserved by the Historical Relics Administration of the Tibet Autonomous Region.

# ཀོ་ཤྲིའི་ཐམ་ཀ
# 國師之印
# The Seal of the State Tutor

18 - 1

18 - 2

18－3

རྒྱ་གཡང་ཏེ། དབྱིབས་གྲུ་བཞི། མཐའི་རིང་ཚད་ལི་སྨི་༡༠.༩
བོད་རང་སྐྱོང་ལྗོངས་རིག་དངོས་དོ་དམ་ཨུ་ཡོན་ལྷན་ཁང་དུ་ཉར་ཚགས་བྱས་ཡོད།

玉質，邊長10.9厘米。

西藏自治區文物管理委員會藏

A 10.9 cm. by 10.9 cm. jade seal.

Preserved by the Historical Relics Administration of the Tibet Autonomous Region.

## རྒྱལ་བསྟན་འགོ་གཙོ་ཏཱ་དབེན་གོ་ཤྲིའི་ཐམ་ཀ།
## “統領釋教大元國師”印
## The Seal of the State Tutor of the Great Yuan Dynasty, Leader of the Buddhist Faith

19-1

19-2

19-3

རྒྱ་གཡང་ཏེ།   དབྱིབས་གྲུ་བཞི།   མཐའི་རིང་ཚད་ལི་སྨི་༡༡
བོད་རང་སྐྱོང་ལྗོངས་རིག་དངོས་དོ་དམ་ཨུ་ཡོན་ལྷན་ཁང་དུ་ཉར་ཚགས་བྱས་ཡོད།

玉質，邊長11厘米。

西藏自治區文物管理委員會藏

A 11 cm. by 11 cm. jade seal.

Preserved by the Historical Relics Administration of the Tibet Autonomous Region.

# དབང་བསྐུར་གོ་ཤྲིའི་ཐམ་ཀ
# 灌頂國師之印
# The Seal of the State Initiation Master

20 - 1

20 - 2

20 - 3

རྒྱ་གཡང་ཏེ། དབྱིབས་གྲུ་བཞི། མཐའི་རིང་ཚད་ལི་སྨི་༡༠.༤

བོད་རང་སྐྱོང་ལྗོངས་རིག་དངོས་དོ་དམ་ཨུ་ཡོན་ལྷན་ཁང་དུ་ཉར་ཚགས་བྱས་ཡོད།

玉質，邊長10.4厘米。

西藏自治區文物管理委員會藏

A 10.4 cm. by 10.4 cm. jade seal.

Preserved by the Historical Relics Administration of the Tibet Autonomous Region.

# ཨིས་སྨར་གམ་དམག་འབངས་ཁྲི་དཔོན་ཁང་གི་ཐམ་ཀ
# 亦思麻兒甘軍民萬户府印
# The Seal of Smarkham *Wanhu*

21－1

21－2

21－3

རྒྱ་ཟངས།　དབྱིབས་གྲུ་བཞི།　མཐའི་རིང་ཚད་ལི་སྨི་༨.༥
བོད་རང་སྐྱོང་ལྗོངས་རིག་དངོས་དོ་དམ་ཨུ་ཡོན་ལྷན་ཁང་དུ་ཉར་ཚགས་བྱས་ཡོད།

銅質，邊長8.5厘米。

西藏自治區文物管理委員會藏

An 8.5 cm. by 8.5 cm. copper seal.

Preserved by the Historical Relics Administration of the Tibet Autonomous Region.

# པེ་ལན་ཝང་གི་ཐམ་ཀ
# 白蘭王印
# The Seal of Prince Bailan

22 - 1

22 - 2

22－3

རྒྱ་ཟངས། དབྱིབས་གྲུ་བཞི། མཐའི་རིང་ཚད་ལི་སྨི་༡༡.༣
བོད་རང་སྐྱོང་ལྗོངས་རིག་དངོས་དོ་དམ་ཨུ་ཡོན་ལྷན་ཁང་དུ་ཉར་ཚགས་བྱས་ཡོད།

銅質，鎏金，邊長11.3厘米。

西藏自治區文物管理委員會藏

An 11.3 cm. by 11.3 cm. gilt–copper seal.

Preserved by the Historical Relics Administration of the Tibet Autonomous Region.

# མིང་རྒྱལ་རབས་ཀྱི་ཡིག་ཚགས།

གཤམ་གསལ་གྱི་ཡིག་ཚགས་ནི་མིང་རྒྱལ་རབས་ཀྱིས་ཡོན་རྒྱལ་རབས་ཀྱི་ལམ་ལུགས་རྒྱུན་འཛིན་གྱིས་བོད་ས་གནས་བདག་འཛིན་བྱས་པ་དང་། མི་འདྲ་བ་ཞིག་ལ་ཡོན་རྒྱལ་རབས་ཀྱིས་ས་སྐྱར་རྒྱབ་སྐྱོར་བྱས་པ་དེ་གཙོ་བོ་བཀའ་བརྒྱུད་པར་རྒྱབ་སྐྱོར་བྱས་པར་བསྒྱུར་པ་དང་དུས་མཚུངས་ཚོ་ལོ་མང་པོ་བསྐལ་པ། རྟེན་འབུལ་གནང་སྐྱེས་སོགས་དམིགས་བསལ་གྱི་སྲིད་ཇུས་ལག་བསྟར་བྱས་པ་མཚོན་ཐུབ།

# 明朝檔案

所載檔案反映了明襲元制，行使對吐蕃地方的主權。不同的是改元朝支持薩迦派爲主要支持噶舉派，並採取了“多封衆建”、“朝貢賞賜”等特殊政策。

# Ming Dynasty Archives

The Ming Dynasty archives reproduced here show that after it replaced the Yuan regime, the Ming court continued to exercise China's sovereignty over Tibet. The difference in policy towaru Tibet between the two is that the Yuan supported the Sakya–pa Sect while the Ming fostered the Kagyu–pa Sect. The Ming also adopted the special policy of creating as many fiefdoms as possible in Tibet and bestowing honorific titles and rewards upon those who paid tribute to the court.

# གོང་མ་ཧུང་ཝུས་ཆོས་ཀུན་སྐྱབས་ལ་བསྩལ་བའི་བཀའ་ལུང་།
# 洪武皇帝頒給搠思公失監的聖旨
# Edict Issued to Hrogskunrgyal by Emperor Hongwu

244 × 35

23 - 1

༄༅། །གནམ་ལ་གུས་པའི་སྟོབས་ལ་བརྟེན་ནས་རྒྱལ་པོའི་ལུང་། རྒྱལ་པོ་ངོས་ཀྱིས་གནམ་འོག་འདི་ལ་ས་ཕྱོགས་ཀུན་ནས་སྐྱབས་འཚོལ་དུ་ཡོང་བཞིན་ཡིན་ན་ཚང་མར་ལུགས་དང་མཐུན་པའི་སྟེ་ལེན་བྱེད་ཅིང་དཔོན་ལ་ཡང་བསྐོ་བ་ཡིན། ཆོས་ཀུན་སྐྱབས་ཁྱོད་ཡུན་རིང་པོ་ཞིག་ལ་ནུབ་ཕྱོགས་ས་ཁུལ་དུ་སྡོད་སྐབས་ངོས་ཀྱི་སྙན་གྲགས་དང་ཟིལ་ཤུགས་ཐོས་ཏེ་བསམ་དོན་ཡིད་བཞིན་དུ་བསྒྲུབས་པར་མ་ཟད། མཐའ་མཚམས་ཀྱི་མངའ་ཁོངས་ལ་སྲུང་སྐྱོབ་བྱས་སྟབས། ངོས་ཀྱིས་གཟིགས་བསྟོད་དུ་ད་ཧྭ་ཨོ་ལེ་སི་དམག་དམངས་ཡོན་ཧྲེ་ཁང་བཙུགས་ནས་ཁྱོད་ལ་ཡོན་ཧྲེའི་གོ་གནས་སྤྲད། ཁྱོད་ཀྱིས་ཀྱང་སྟོབས་ཤུགས་གང་ཡོད་བརྟོན་ཏེ་ཁྲིམས་ལུགས་བརྩི་སྲུང་དང་། མངའ་འོག་རྣམས་སྐྱོང་བ། མཐའ་མཚམས་བདེ་འཇགས་འོང་བར་བཙུག་ན། ངོས་ཀྱིས་གོ་གནས་བསྐོ་བཞག་བྱས་པའི་དགོངས་པ་དང་མཐུན། དེའི་ཕྱིར་ཧྲེ་ཡོན་དམག་དཔོན་ཨོ་ལེ་སི་དམག་དམངས་ཡོན་ཧྲེ་ཁང་གི་ཡོན་ཧྲེ་ཆོས་ཀུན་སྐྱབས་ལ་བཀའ་འདི་བསྩལ། དེ་ལྟར་སྒྲུབས་ཤིག

ཧུང་ཝུ་ཁྲི་ལོ་དྲུག་པ ( སྤྱི་ལོ་༡༣༧༣ ) ཟླ་བ་གཉིས་པར།

བོད་རང་སྐྱོང་ལྗོངས་ཡིག་ཚགས་ཁང་དུ་ཉར་ཚགས་བྱས་ཡོད།

西藏自治區檔案館藏

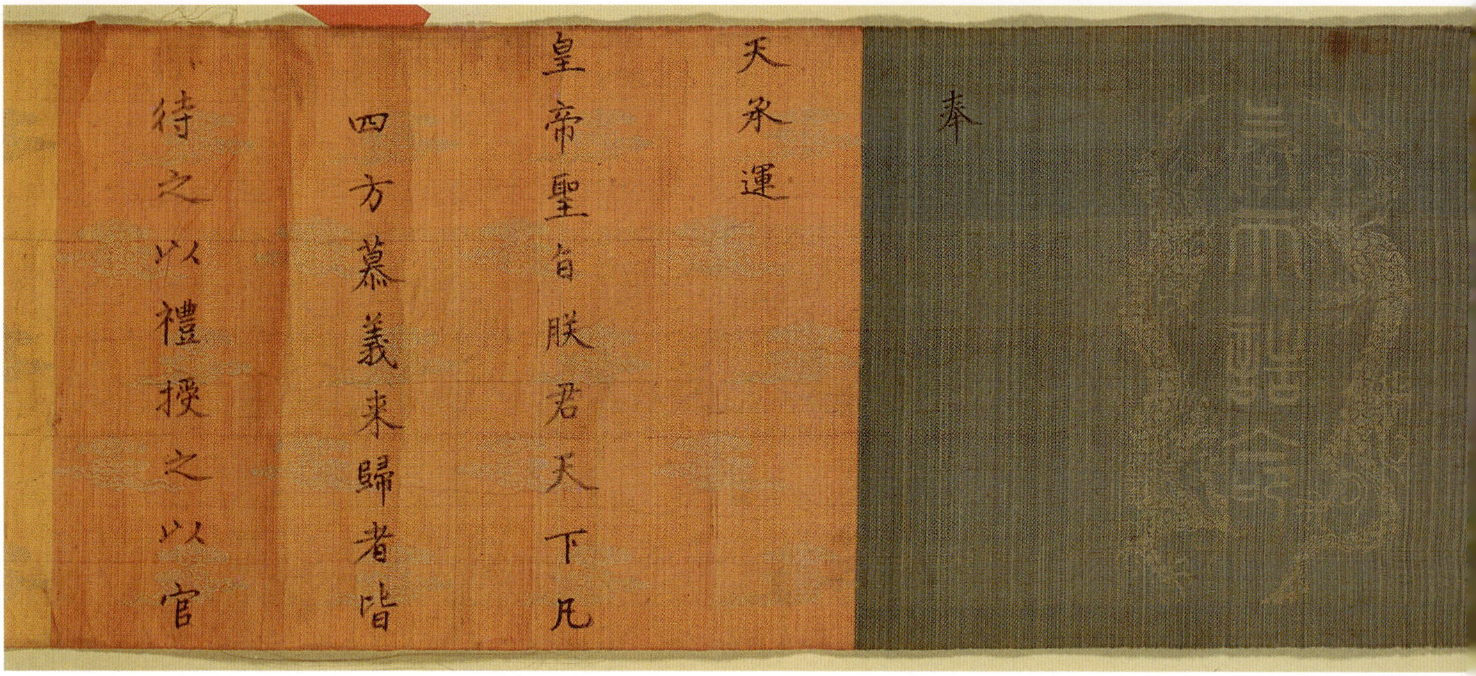
奉
天承運
皇帝聖旨朕君天下凡
四方慕義來歸者皆
待之以禮授之以官

23 - 2

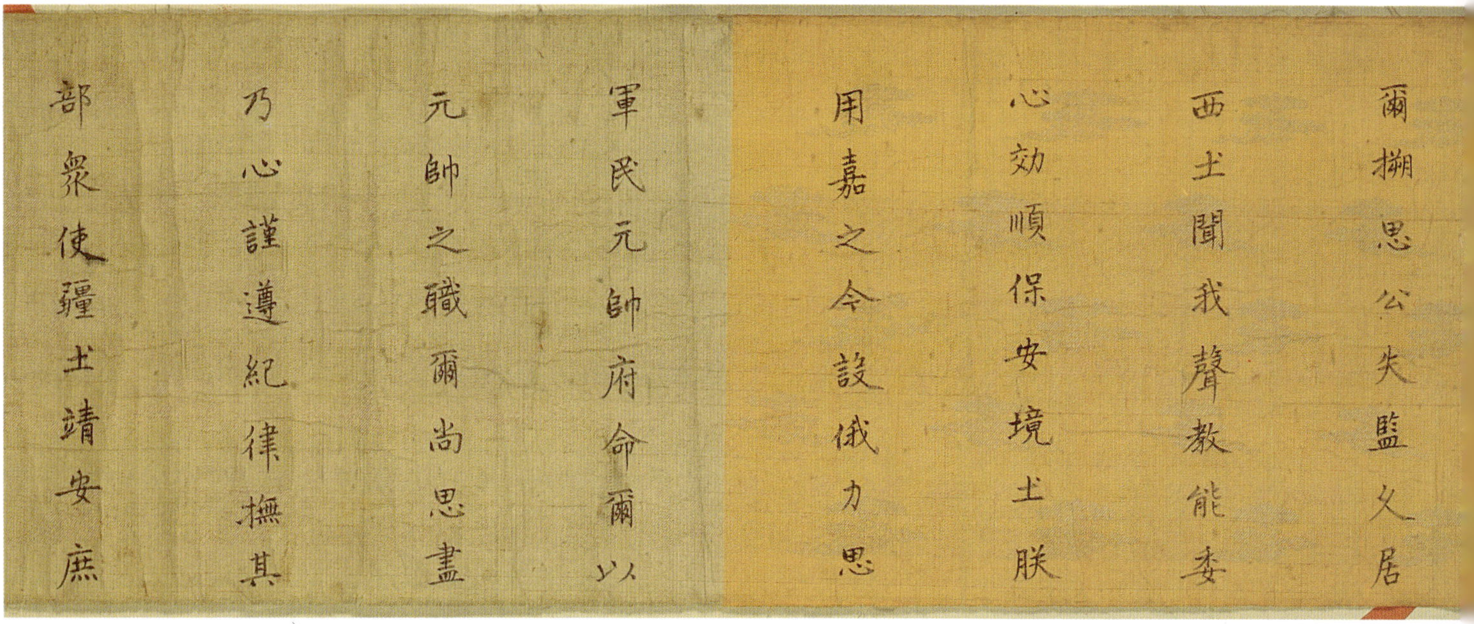
爾搠思公失監久居
西土聞我聲教能委
心効順保安境土朕
用嘉之今設俄力思
軍民元帥府命爾以
元帥之職爾尚思盡
乃心謹遵紀律撫其
部衆使疆土靖安庶

23 - 3

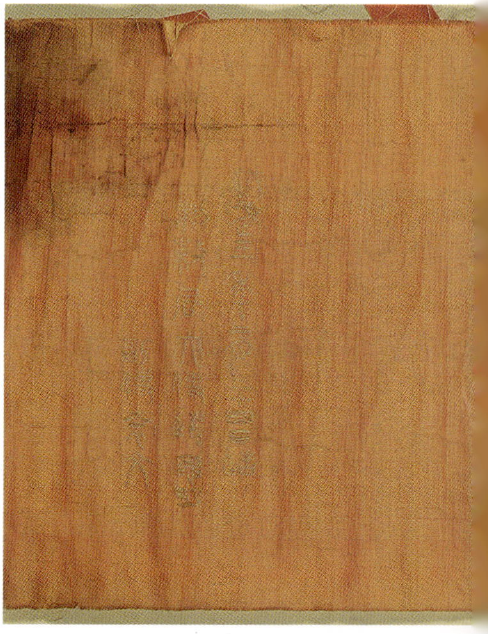

23 - 4

The edict from the Emperor, who rules the country by the mandate of Heaven,proclaims the following:

I, the sovereign of the Empire, treat people from all corners of the Empire who love righteousness and pledge allegiance to the court with courtesy and assign them official posts. I have learned with great pleasure that you, Hrogskunrgyal, who live in the Western Regions, inspired by my power and reputation, are loyal to the court and are capable of safeguarding the territory in your charge. The Office of the Governor–General of Olisi has just been established. I, therefore, appoint you head of the office with the title of Huaiyuan General, believing that you are most qualified for the post. I expect you to be even more conscientious in your work than in the past, to comply with discipline and to care for your men so that security and peace in your region can be guaranteed.

[Numeral for the day is missing in the original document] of the 2nd month of the 6th year of Hongwu (1373)

Preserved by the Archives of the Tibet Autonomous Region.

副朕委任之意可懷
遠將軍俄力思軍民
元帥府元帥宜令搠
思公失監准此
洪武六年二月　日

# གོང་མ་ཡུང་ལོས་བླ་མ་ཀརྨ་པ་ལ་བསྐུལ་པའི་འཕྲིན་ཡིག
# 永樂皇帝給尚師哈立麻的書信
# Letter to Lama Karmaba from Emperor Yongle

184×49

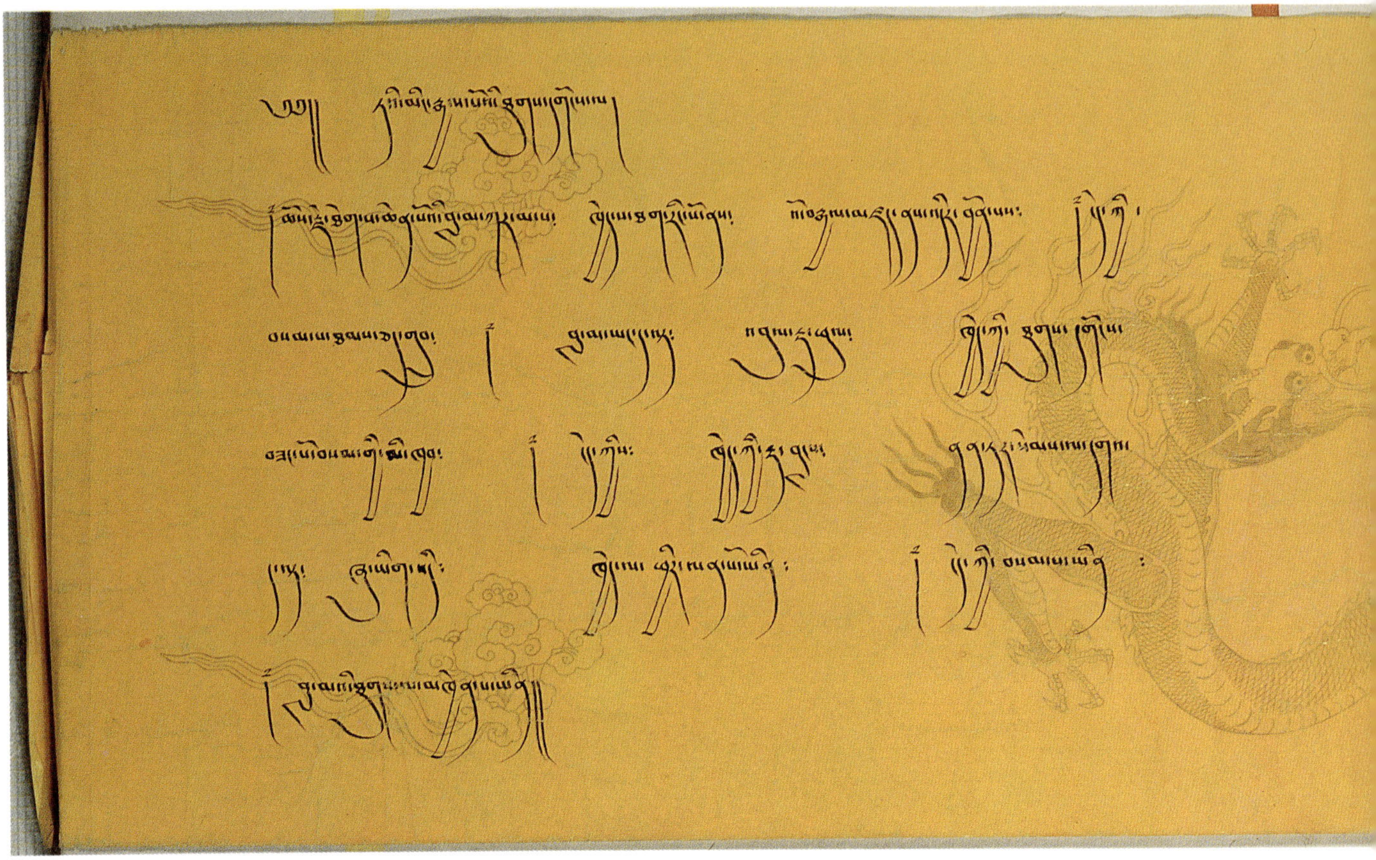

བོད་རང་སྐྱོང་ལྗོངས་ཡིག་ཚགས་ཁང་དུ་ཉར་ཚགས་བྱས་ཡོད།

西藏自治區檔案館藏

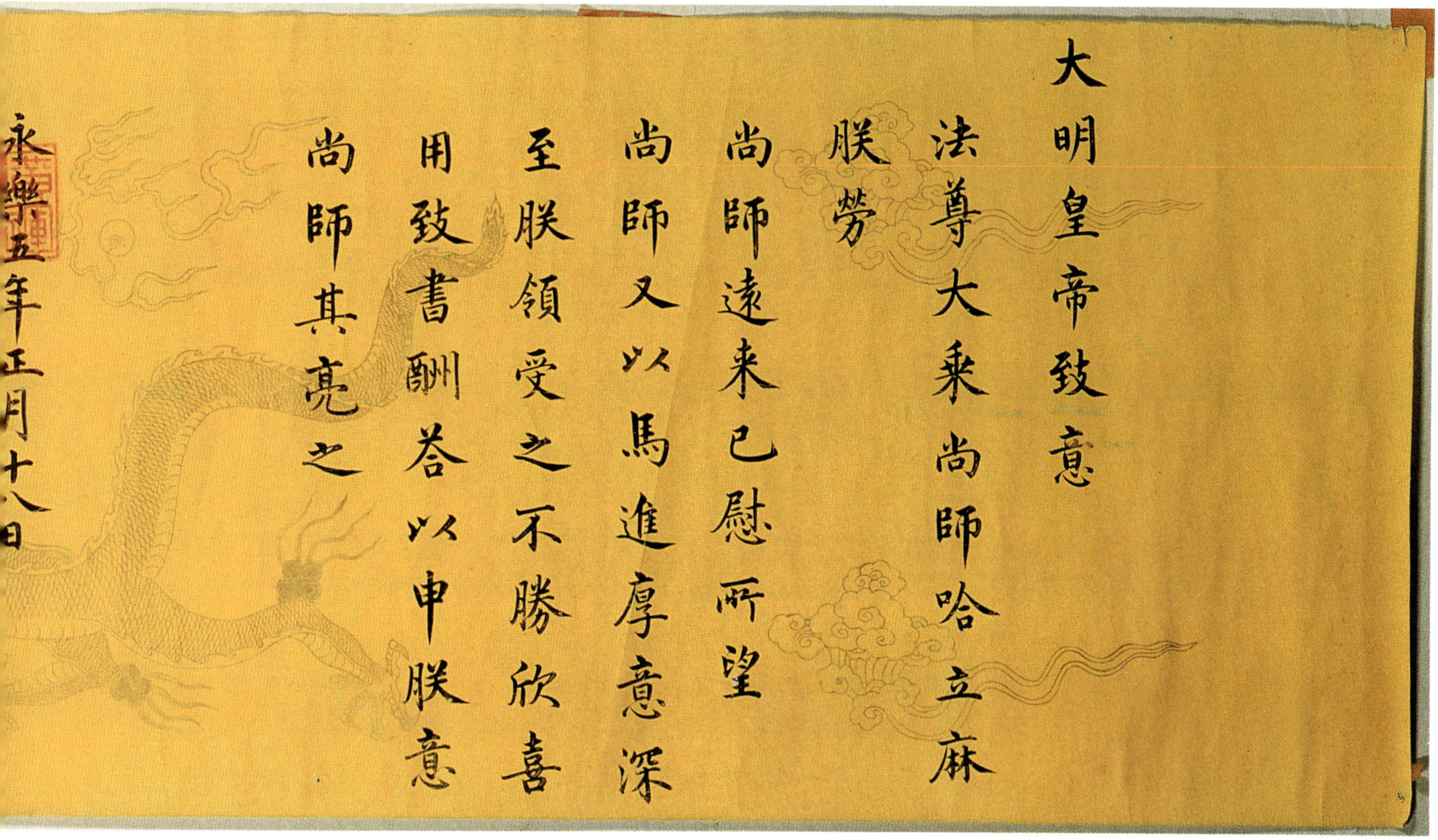
大明皇帝致意
法尊大乘尚師哈立麻
朕勞
尚師遠来已慰所望
尚師又以馬進厚意深
至朕領受之不勝欣喜
用致書酬荅以申朕意
尚師其亮之
永樂五年正月十八日

I, the Emperor of the Great Ming Empire, give my best regards to Karmaba, Lama of Mahayana Buddhism.

I am deeply satisfied that you have come here despite the long distance. I have accepted your generous present of horses with great pleasure. Please accept my thanks.

The 18th day of the 1st month of the 5th year of Yongle (1407)

Preserved by the Archives of the Tibet Autonomous Region.

# 25

## གོང་མ་ཡུན་ལོས་སོ་པ་ལྷ་བཙན་སྐྱབས་ལ་བསྩལ་པའི་བཀའ་ལུང་།

## 永樂皇帝頒給剌昝肖的敕諭

## Edict Issued to Lhatshangkyab by Emperor Yongle

400 × 32

25 - 1

༄༅། །རྒྱལ་པོའི་ལུང་གིས་གནམ་ས་ཆེ་བ་ནི་བཀབ་བརྟེག་མ་ཁྱབ་པ་མེད་ཅིང་བར་ན་ཡོད་པའི་དངོས་པོ་སྣ་ཚོགས་བདེ་བ། རྒྱལ་པོའི་ལུགས་ནི། ཉེ་རིང་མེད་པ་སྐྱོང་ན་རྒྱལ་ཁམས་ཐམས་ཅད་འཇགས་ཞིང་། ལས་དཀའ་དང་ཡོང་སྤྱོད་བསྐོས་ནའང་རང་རང་གིས་བྱ་བ་བཞིན་དུ་བསྐོས་པ་ཡིན། དེ་ལྟར་ན་མིའི་ལུགས་དང་མཐུན་ཅིང་བཀའ་དྲིན་ཆེ་བ་ཡིན་ནོ། །ཁྱོད་སོ་པ་མགོ་དཔོན་ལྷ་ཚང་སྐྱབས། སྔ་མོར་སངས་རྒྱས་ཀྱི་བསྟན་པ་ལ་དད་པ། ཐེག་པ་ཆེན་པོའི་དོན་རྟོགས་ཅིང་། སེམས་རྣམ་པར་དག་པ་གཙོར་བྱས། བྱམས་སྙིང་རྗེ་ལ་བརྟེན་ནས་གཞན་ལ་འདུལ་བ། གནམ་གྱི་ལུགས་ལ་གུས་པ་དང་མཐུན་པ། གོང་ལ་སེམས་བཟང་པོ་བསམ་ནས་བཀུར་སྟི་བྱས། ཡང་དག་པའི་ཞེ་སོང་ཕྱུང་ནས། སྔ་ཕྱིར་ཁྱད་པར་མེད་པ། དེའི་ཡོན་ཏན་ཡོད་པའི་དོན་ལ། བསྟོད་ར་བྱས་པ་ཡིན། ད་ལྟ་ནན་གྱིས་ཁྱོད་ལ་སི་ཐུའི་མིང་དང་ལས་དཀའ་བསྐོས་ནས། ཁྱོད་སངས་རྒྱས་ཀྱི་བསྟན་པ་ལ་ལྷག་པར་བརྩོན་འགྲུབ་བྱས་པ་དང་། སེམས་བཟང་པོ་བརྟན་པོར་བཟུང་ནས། བཀའ་དྲིན་དང་མཐུན་པ་དད་གུས་ཀྱིས།

ཡུན་ལོའི་ཁྲི་ལོ་བཅུ་གཅིག་པ (སྤྱི་ལོ་༡༤༡༣) ཟླ་བ་གཉིས་པའི་ཚེས་དགུ་གི་ཉིན།

བོད་རང་སྐྱོང་ལྗོངས་ཡིག་ཚགས་ཁང་དུ་ཉར་ཚགས་བྱས་ཡོད།

奉天承運皇帝制曰：

天地之大包含覆載而萬物亨，帝王之道懷柔撫綏而天下治。故命官錫爵，各因其宜，所以順人情而廣恩澤也。爾鎖巴頭目剌昝肖早從佛教，悟解真乘，以清淨而爲宗，以慈悲而化導，敬順天道，尊仰朝廷，竭誠奉職，始終一致，爰申寵命，用示褒榮，茲特授爾爲司徒，益加精進，肆揚闡於宗風；懋篤忠誠，永膺承於恩典。欽哉。

永樂十一年（公元1413年）二月初九日

西藏自治區檔案館藏

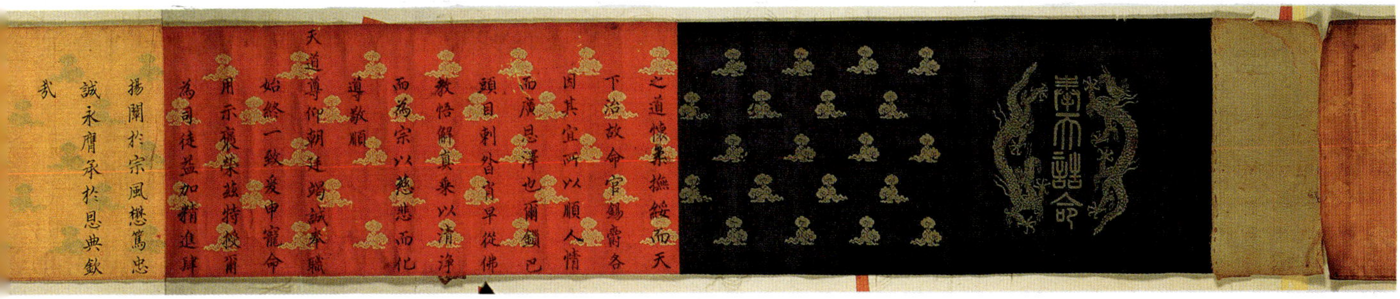


The edict from the Emperor, who rules the country by the mandate of Heaven, proclaims the following:

All things of the universe owe their prosperity to the benevolence of boundless Heaven and Earth. A country owes its peace and order to the good government of its ruler, who governs with restraint and kindness, bestowing honours and titles upon those who deserve them and extending his affection to as many people as possible. You, Lhatshangkyab, chieftain of Sopa, deserve high praise from the court because you are a pious Buddhist with a good understanding of the Buddhist doctrine, who abides by religious discipline, enlightens the masses with compassion, respects the will of Heaven, honours the court and has a good sense of responsibility. I, therefore, grant you the title of *situ*. I hope that you will redouble your efforts to cultivate virtue and to carry the religion forward and remain loyal to the court for ever.

The 9th day of the 2nd month of the 11th year of Yongle (1413)

Preserved by the Archives of the Tibet Autonomous Region.

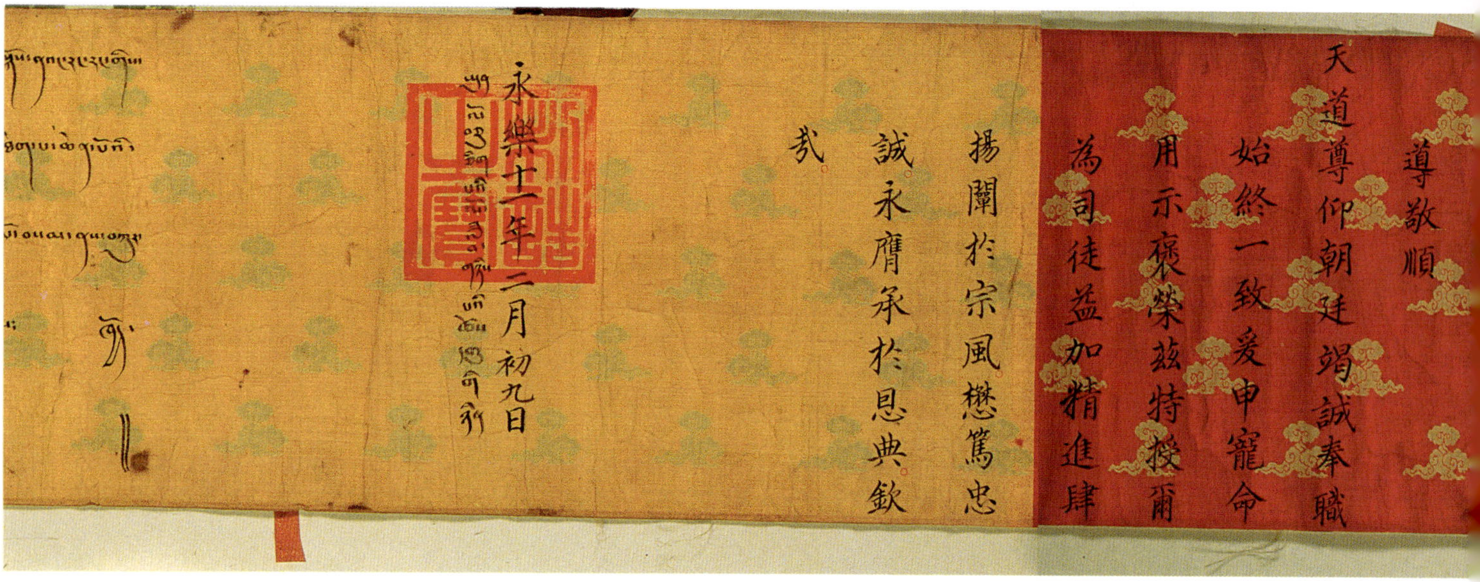
導敬順
天道尊仰朝廷竭誠奉職
始終一致爰申寵命
用示褒榮茲特授爾
為司徒益加精進肆
揚闡於宗風懋篤忠
誠永膺承於恩典欽
哉
永樂十一年二月初九日

25－2

25－3

永樂七年 月 日誥

奉天誥命
之道懷柔撫綏而天
下治故命官錫爵各
因其宜所以順人情
而廣恩澤也爾鎖巴
頭目刺昝肖早從佛

# 26

## གོང་མ་ཡུན་ལོས་བཀའ་བཞི་པ་བསོད་ནམས་མགོན་ལ་བསྩལ་པའི་བཀའ་ལུང་།

## 永樂皇帝頒給高日斡瑣南觀的敕諭

## Edict Issued to Kavzhiba by Emperor Yongle

185.7×49

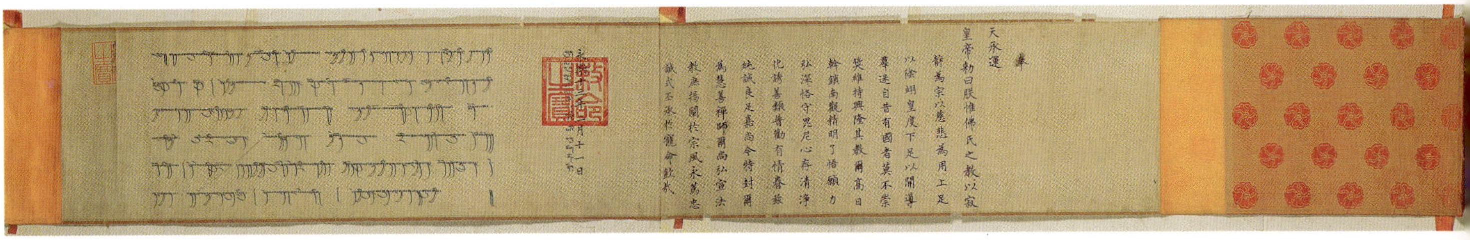

26－1

བོད་རང་སྐྱོང་ལྗོངས་ཡིག་ཚགས་ཁང་དུ་ཉར་ཚགས་བྱས་ཡོད།

西藏自治區檔案館藏

The edict from the Emperor, who rules the country by the mandate of Heaven, proclaims the following:

I believe that Buddhist teachings which stress calmness and compassion benefit rulers above and rid the masses below of their ignorance. Accordingly, rulers of the past all supported and fostered this religion. I have learned with great pleasure that you, Kavzhiba, are a man with profound knowledge of the Buddhist faith, one who strictly observes Buddhist discipline, is cleansed of all mundane desires and spreads the Buddhist faith to transform the masses. I, therefore, bestow upon you the title of Master of Wisdom and Kindness. It is my hope that you will continue to disseminate the teachings of Buddha and be loyal to the court.

The 11th day of the 2nd month of the 13th year of Yongle (1415)

Preserved by the Archives of the Tibet Autonomous Region.

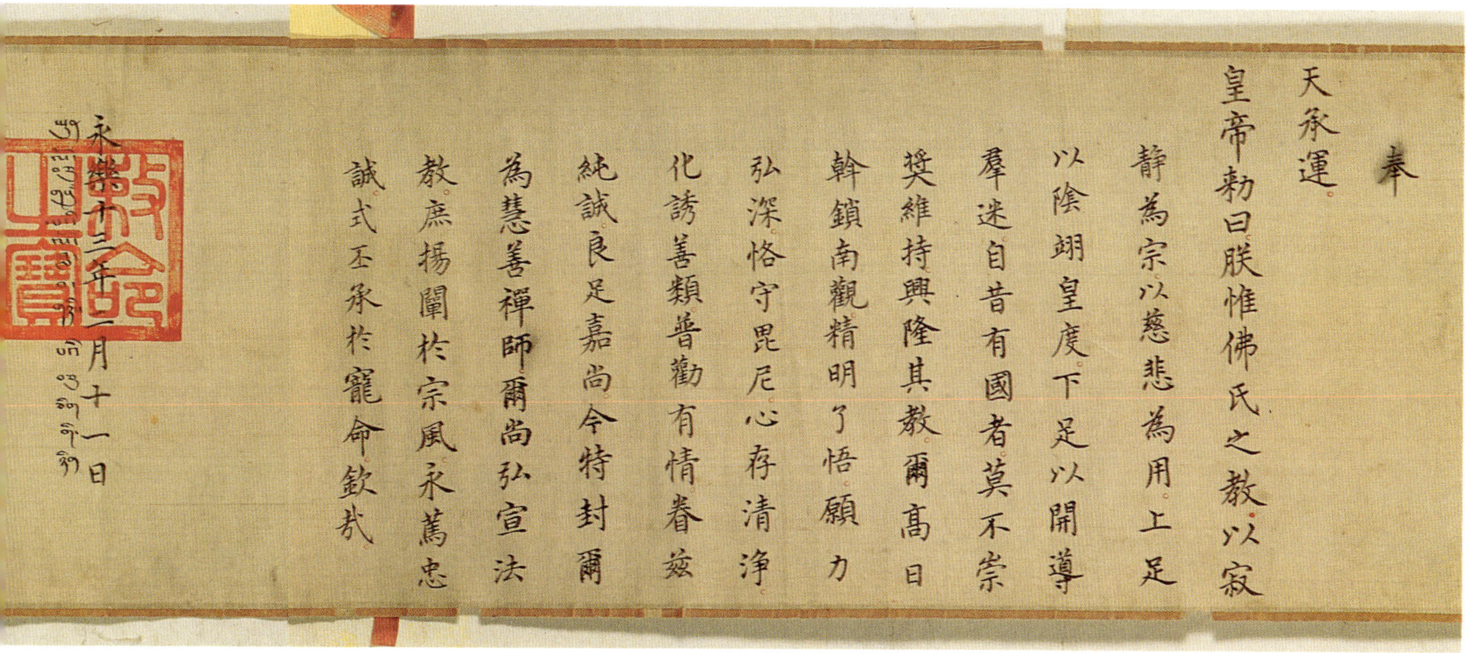

奉
天承運
皇帝勅曰朕惟佛氏之教以寂
靜為宗以慈悲為用上足
以陰翊皇度下足以開導
羣迷自昔有國者莫不崇
奬維持興隆其教爾高日
斡鎖南觀精明了悟願力
弘深恪守毘尼心存清淨
化誘善類普勸有情眷茲
純誠良足嘉尚今特封爾
為慧善禪師爾尚弘宣法
教庶揚闡於宗風永篤忠
誠式丕承於寵命欽哉
永樂十三年一月十一日

26－2

26－3

# གོང་མ་ཤོན་དེས་ཀརྨ་པ་ལ་བསྩལ་པའི་བཀའ་ལུང་།
# 宣德皇帝頒給葛里麻的敕諭
# Edict Issued to Karmaba by Emperor Xuande

285×32.5

27－1

བོད་རང་སྐྱོང་ལྗོངས་ཡིག་ཚགས་ཁང་དུ་ཉར་ཚགས་བྱས་ཡོད།

西藏自治區檔案館藏

The edict from the Emperor, who rules the country by the mandate of Heaven, proclaims the following:

The teaching of Buddha protects and helps the sovereign above and transforms the masses below. It is the regular practice for the court to commend and reward Buddhist priests for their praiseworthy religious attainments. You, Karmaba, have always abided by religious discipline, devoted yourself to purifying your mind and learned the doctrine of Buddha. For this you deserve high praises from the court. I, therefore, bestow upon you the title of Master of Wisdom and Benevolence. It is my hope that you will continue to carry forward the religion and to perpetuate the light of benevolence in extensive regions.

The 22nd day of the 1st month of the 2nd year of Xuande (1427)

Preserved by the Archives of the Tibet Autonomous Region.

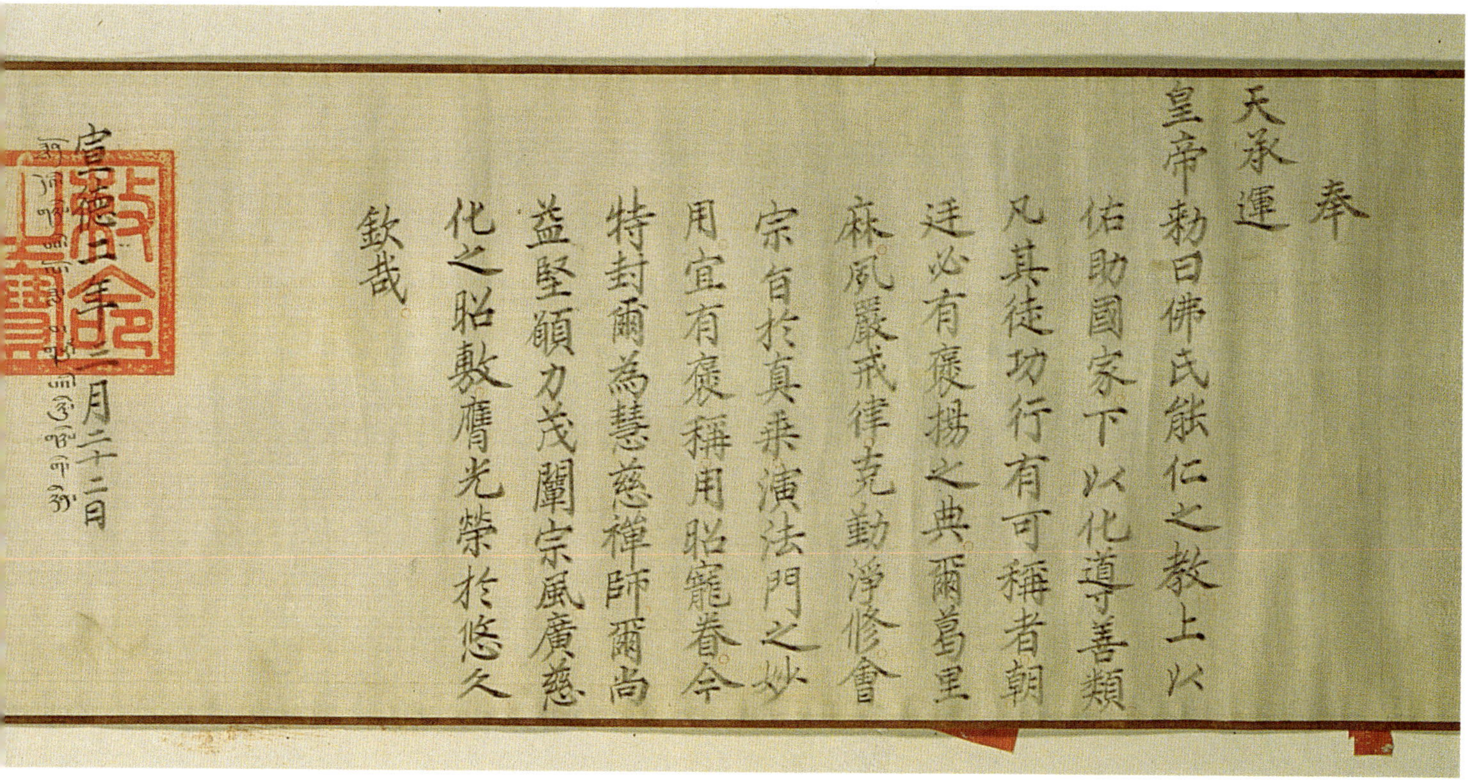

奉
天承運
皇帝勑曰佛氏能仁之教上以
佑助國家下以化導善類
凡其徒功行有可稱者朝
廷必有褒揚之典爾葛里
麻風嚴戒律克勤淨修會
宗旨於真乘演法門之妙
用宜有褒稱用昭寵眷今
特封爾為慧慈禪師爾尚
益堅願力茂闡宗風廣慈
化之昭敷膺光榮於悠久
欽哉
宣德二年二月二十二日

27－2

27－3

# གོང་མ་ཅིང་ཐོང་གིས་བླ་མ་ཀརྨ་པ་ལ་བསྩལ་བའི་བཀའ་ལུང་།

# 正統皇帝頒給尚師哈立麻巴的敕諭

# Edict Issued to Lama Karmaba by Emperor Zhengtong

110 × 37

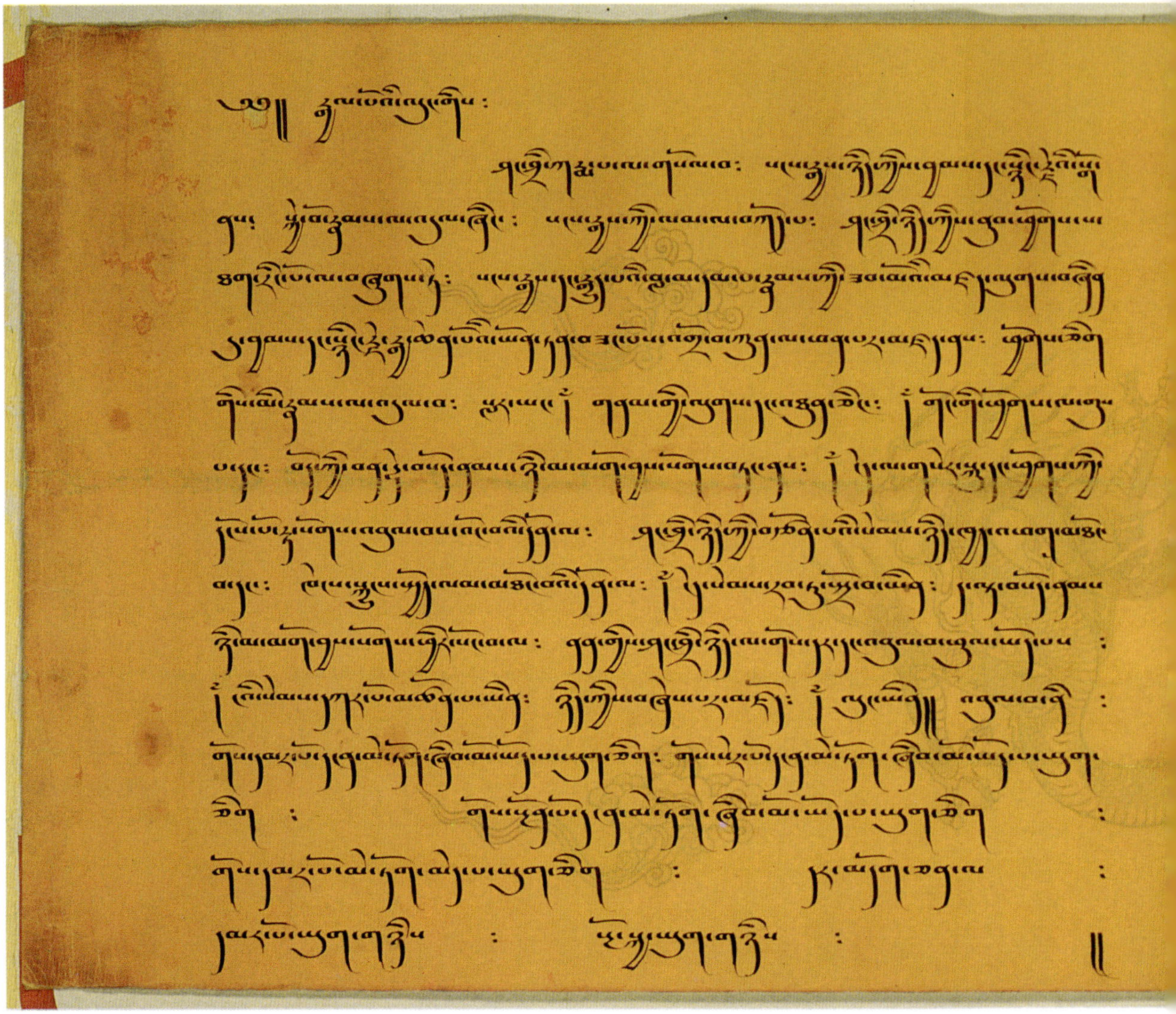

皇帝勅諭尚師哈立麻巴

佛氏以慈悲之道化人爲善皈依正覺尚師遠處西域得佛祖之真傳闡仁慈之功用開導衆類教行一方而能敬順

天道尊事朝廷遣番僧鎖南泥麻等以佛像并馬匹方物来貢于以見尚師效勤愈篤修職益虔朕用嘉之茲鎖南泥麻等回特賜尚師綵幣表裏用答至意其欽承之故諭

頒賜

紵絲

暗細花紅一匹　暗細花黃一匹

暗細花青一匹　素紅一匹

綵絹

紅二匹　藍二匹

正統十年六月初四日

བོད་རང་སྐྱོང་ལྗོངས་ཡིག་ཚགས་ཁང་དུ་ཉར་ཚགས་བྱས་ཡོད།

西藏自治區檔案館藏

The edict from the Emperor to Lama Karmaba proclaims the following:

Out of compassion the Lord Buddha taught people to be good and persuaded them to embrace his doctrine. You, who live in the remote Western Regions, have inherited the true doctrine of Buddha. I am deeply impressed not only by the compassion with which you preach among the people in your region for their enlightenment but also by your respect for the wishes of Heaven and your devotion to the court. I am very pleased that you have sent Sodnam Nyima and other Tibetan monks here bringing with them Buddhist images, horses and other local specialties as tribute to the court. This is yet another indication of your increasing devotion and sincerity toward the court. Taking the opportunity of Sodnam Nyima's return home, I entrust him with the following as my gifts for you:

A bolt of red silk with small, veiled flower patterns, a bolt of yellow silk with small, veiled flower patterns, a bolt of blue silk with small, veiled flower patterns, a bolt of red silk, two bolts of patterned red silk and two bolts of patterned blue silk.

The 4th day of the 6th month of the 10th year of Zhengtong (1445)

Preserved by the Archives of the Tibet Autonomous Region.

# གོང་མ་ཆེང་ཧྭས་ནམ་མཁའ་བཀྲ་ཤིས་རྒྱལ་མཚན་དཔལ་བཟང་པོ་ལ་བསྩལ་པའི་བཀའ་ལུང་།

# 成化皇帝頒給南葛箚失堅參叭藏卜的敕諭

# Edict Issued by Emperor Chenghua to Namkhav Krashis Gyaltshan Palzhangpo

411×25

བོད་རང་སྐྱོང་ལྗོངས་རིག་དངོས་དོ་དམ་ཨུ་ཡོན་ལྷན་ཁང་དུ་ཉར་ཚགས་བྱས་ཡོད།

奉天承運皇帝制曰：

佛氏之道以清浄爲宗，以慈悲爲用，上以翊贊皇度，下以開悟群迷，其徒有能承其教者，必有褒嘉之命。爾南葛箚失堅參叭藏卜乃已故輔教王南葛堅參巴藏卜之子，夙承梵教，恪守毗尼，化誘善類，良足嘉尚。爾父既没，今特命爾代輔教王之職。爾尚宣揚法教，丕闡宗風，永篤忠誠，式副寵命。欽哉。

成化五年（公元1469年）四月

西藏自治區檔案館藏

The edict from the Emperor, who rules the country by the mandate of Heaven, proclaims the following:

Buddhism, which attaches great importance to purity and compassion, benefits rulers above and rids the masses below of ignorance. The court has never failed to commend and reward Buddhist followers who have inherited the doctrine of the religion. I am very pleased that you Namkhav Krashis Gyaltshan Palzhangpo, son of the late Assistant Prince of the Doctrine Namkhav Gyaltshan Palzhangpo, are a true follower of Buddhism, one who strictly observes religious discipline and preaches enlightenment to the masses. Since your father is no more, I, therefore, appoint you to succeed him as Assistant Prince of the Doctrine. I hope that you will continue to disseminate Buddhist teachings and be loyal to the court.

The 4th month of the 5th year of Chenghua (1469)

Preserved by the Archives of the Tibet Autonomous Region.

29－1

29－2

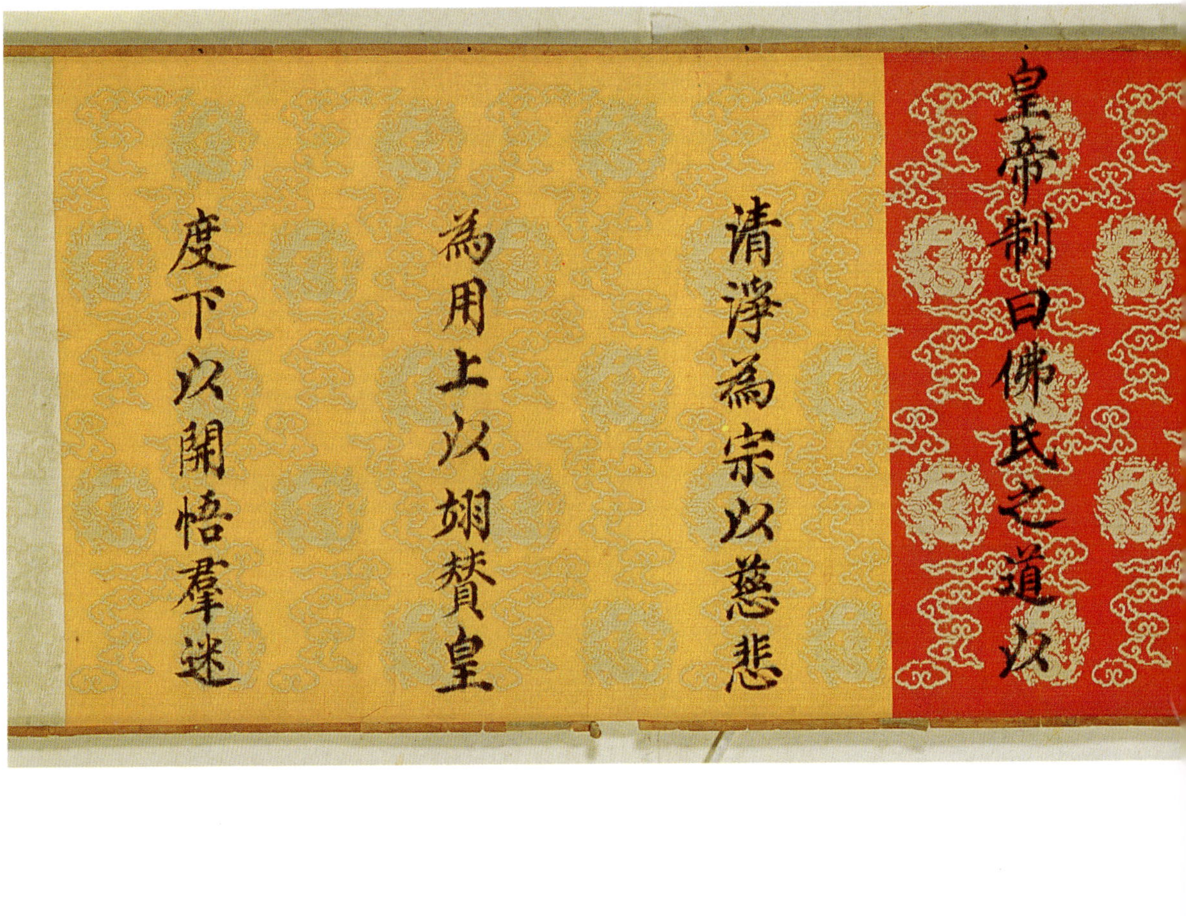

奉天誥命
奉
天承運
皇帝制曰佛氏之道以
清淨為宗以慈悲
為用上以翊贊皇
度下以開悟群迷
其徒有能承其教
者必有褒嘉之命
尔南葛剌失堅參
叭藏卜乃巴致輔
教王南葛堅參巴
藏卜之子夙承梵
代輔教王之職亦
尚宣揚法教丕闡
宗風秉篤忠誠式
副寵命欽哉

奉天誥命
奉

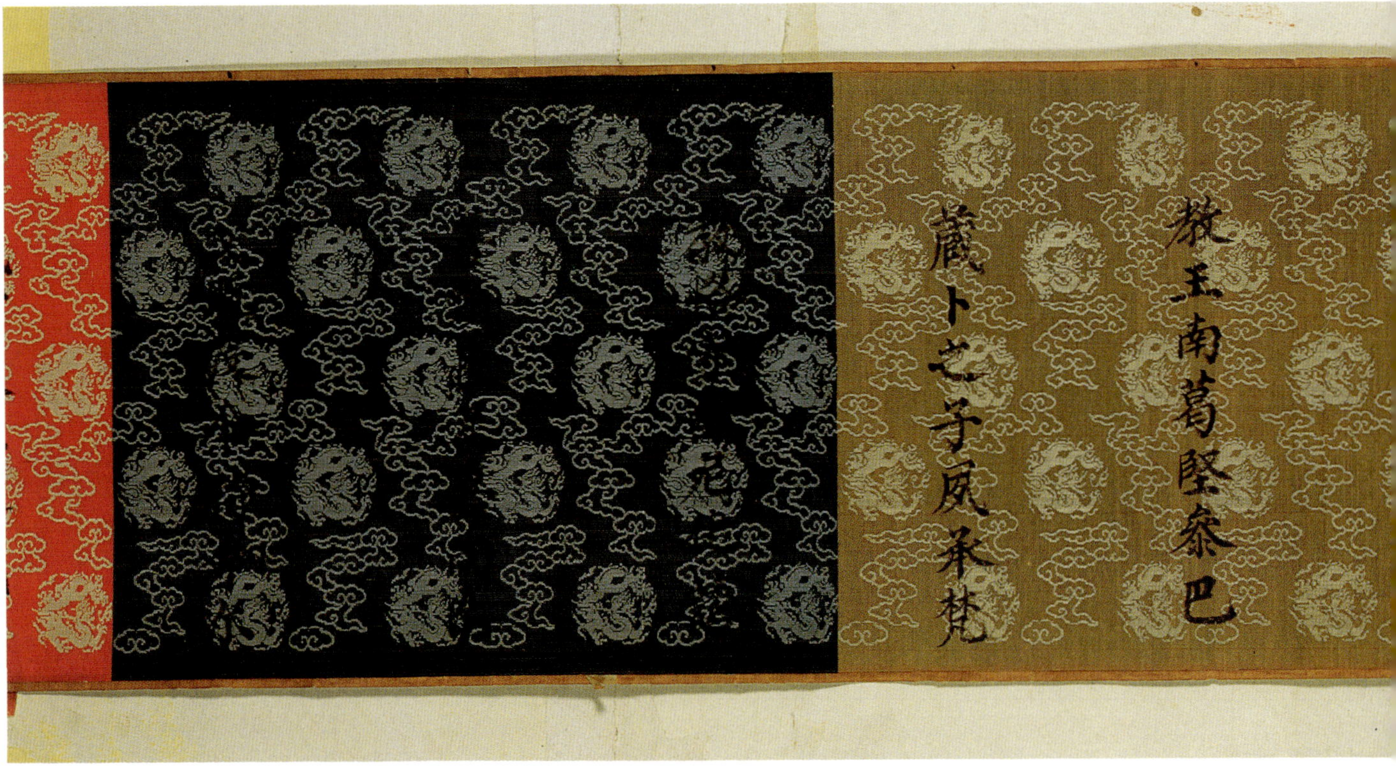


29 - 3

29 - 4

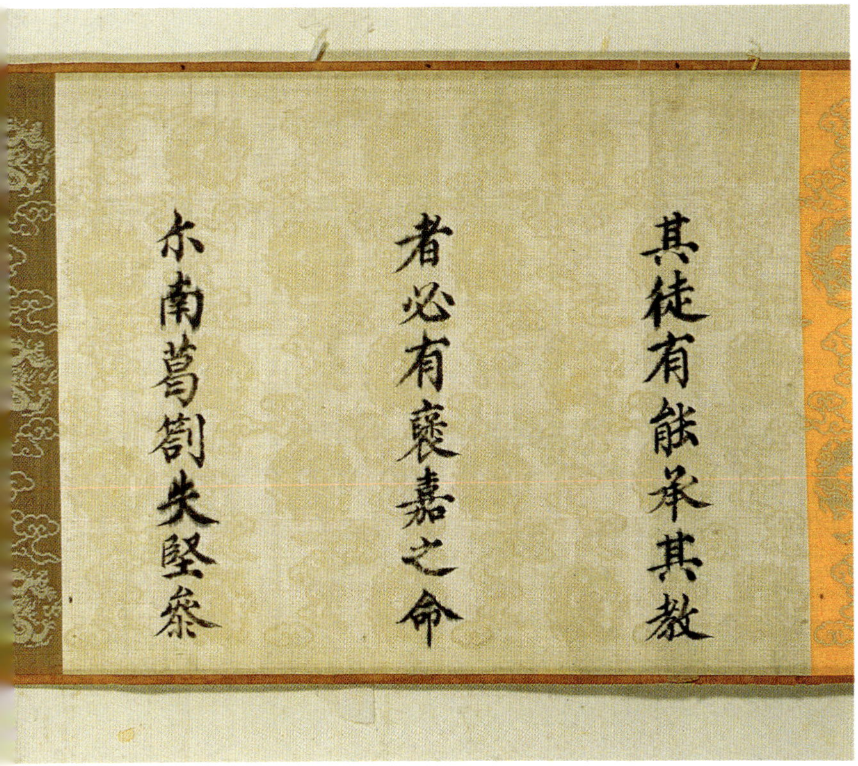


29 - 5

29-6

29 - 7

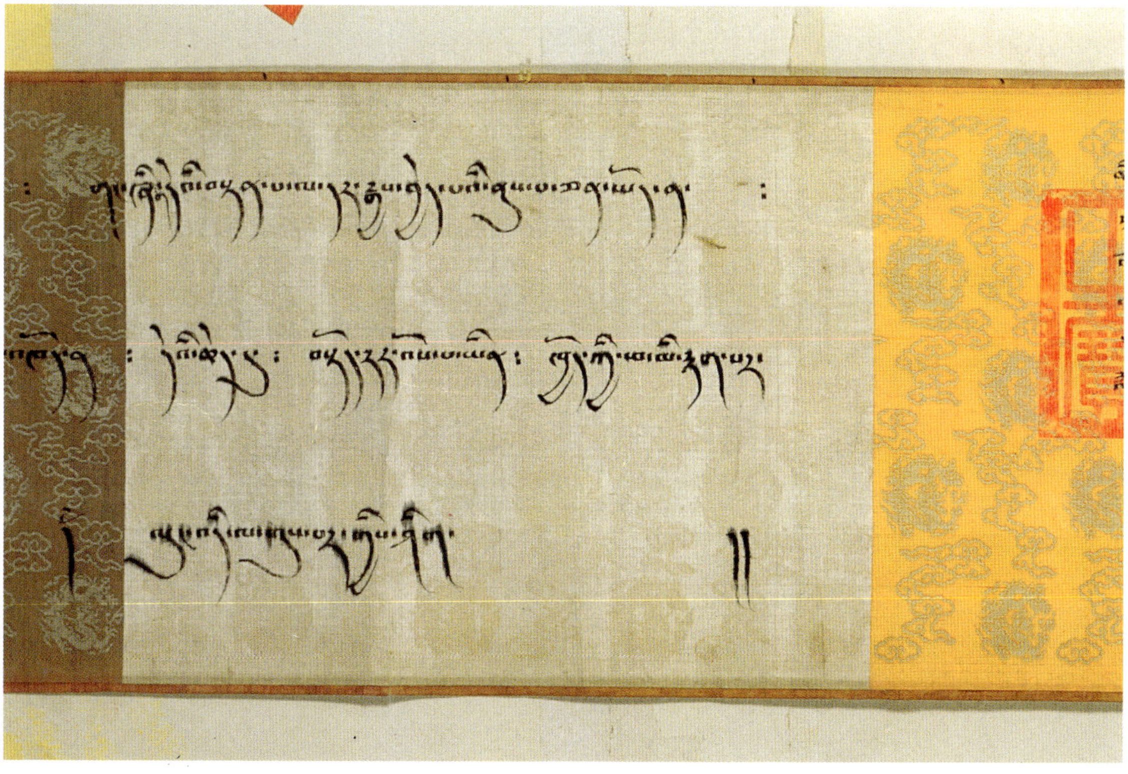

# 30

## གོང་མ་ཆིང་ཧྭས་ཀརྨ་པ་ལ་བསྩལ་བའི་བཀའ་ལུང་།

## 成化皇帝頒給葛哩麻巴的敕諭

## Edict Issued to Karmaba by Emperor Chenghua

116 × 50

皇帝勅諭烏思藏如来大寶法王葛哩麻巴
等尔能敬順
天道尊事朝廷恪修職貢愈久愈虔兹復
遣使以方物来進誠意可嘉使回特賜
尔綵幣表裏以示褒答至可領之故諭
回賜
如来大寶法王葛哩麻巴
紵絲
素青二匹　素紅二匹
綵絹
藍二匹　紅二匹
國師班卓端竹
紵絲
素青一匹　素紅一匹
綵絹
藍一匹　紅一匹
都指揮頭目班覺兒言千
紵絲
素紅一匹
綵絹
藍一匹

བོད་རང་སྐྱོང་ལྗོངས་ཡིག་ཚགས་ཁང་དུ་ཉར་ཚགས་བྱས་ཡོད།

西藏自治區檔案館藏

The edict from the Emperor to Karmaba, the Tathagata Great Treasure Prince of Dharma of Dbustsang, and others proclaims the following:

I am pleased that out of respect for the wishes of Heaven you have honoured the court with ever–increasing devotion. I am equally pleased that you have again sent envoys here bringing with them local specialties as tribute to the court. Taking the opportunity of your envoys′ return home, I am sending you the following gifts in return. I expect you to accept them upon their arrival.

Two bolts of pure blue silk, two bolts of pure red silk, two bolts of patterned blue silk and two bolts of patterned red silk for Karmaba, the Tathagata Great Treasure Prince of Dharma; a bolt of pure blue silk, a bolt of pure red silk, a bolt of patterned blue silk and a bolt of patterned red silk for State Tutor Palbyor Dongrub; and a bolt of pure red silk and a bolt of patterned blue silk for Governor–General Palbyor Gyaltshan.

The 13th day of the 7th month of the 22nd year of Chenghua (1486)

Preserved by the Archives of the Tibet Autonomous Region.

# དེ་བཞིན་གཤེགས་པ་རིན་པོ་ཆེ་ཆོས་རྒྱལ་གྱི་ཐམ་ཀ
# 如來大寶法王之印
# The Seal of the Tathagata Great Treasure Prince of Dharma

31－1

31－2

རྒྱ་གཡང་ཏེ། མཐའི་རིང་ཚད་ལི་སྨི་༡༢.༨

བོད་རང་སྐྱོང་ལྗོངས་རིག་དངོས་དོ་དམ་ཨུ་ཡོན་ལྷན་ཁང་དུ་ཉར་ཚགས་བྱས་ཡོད།

玉質，邊長12.8厘米。

西藏自治區文物管理委員會藏

A 12.8 cm. by 12.8 cm. jade seal.

Preserved by the Historical Relics Administration of the Tibet Autonomous Region.

# བདེན་པ་མངོན་པར་རྟོགས་པའི་ཐེག་ཆེན་ཆོས་ཀྱི་རྒྱལ་པོའི་ཐམ་ཀ
# 正覺大乘法王之印
# The Seal of the Enlightened, Great Vehicle Prince of Dharma

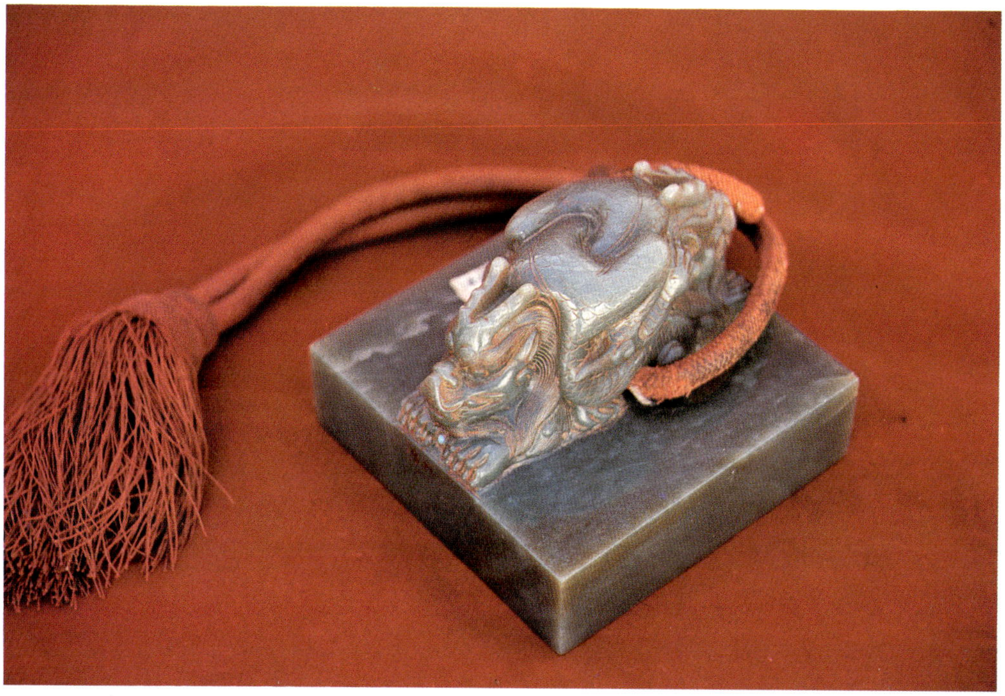

32 - 1

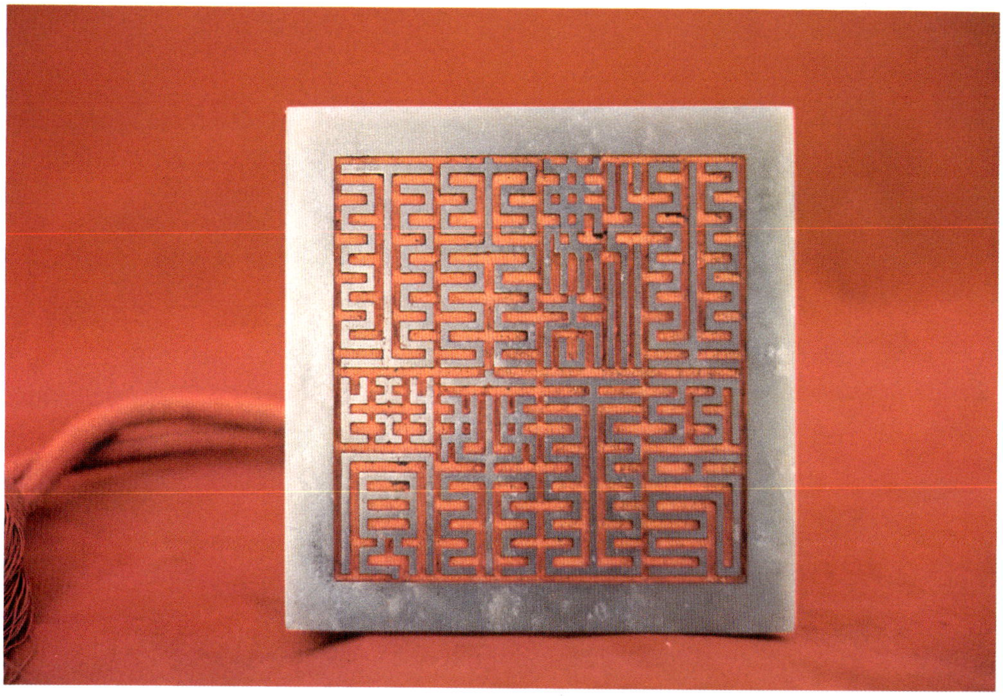

32 - 2

32 - 3

རྒྱ་གཡང་ཏི།  དབྱིབས་གྲུ་བཞི།  མཐའི་རིང་ཚད་ལི་སྨི་༡༢.༨

བོད་རང་སྐྱོང་ལྗོངས་རིག་དངོས་དོ་དམ་ཨུ་ཡོན་ལྷན་ཁང་དུ་ཉར་ཚགས་བྱས་ཡོད།

玉質，邊長12.8厘米。

西藏自治區文物管理委員會藏

A 12.8 cm. by 12.8 cm. jade seal.

Preserved by the Historical Relics Administration of the Tibet Autonomous Region.

# འབྲི་གུང་ཁྲི་དཔོན་ཁང་གི་ཐམ་ཀ
# 必力公萬户府印
# The Seal of the Vbrigung *Wanhu* Office.

33 - 1

33 - 2

རྒྱུ་ཟངས།  དབྱིབས་གྲུ་བཞི།  མཐའི་རིང་ཚད་ལི་སྨི་༨. ༢
བོད་རང་སྐྱོང་ལྗོངས་རིག་དངོས་དོ་དམ་ཨུ་ཡོན་ལྷན་ཁང་དུ་ཉར་ཚགས་བྱས་ཡོད།

銅質，邊長8.2厘米。

西藏自治區文物管理委員會藏

An 8.2 cm. by 8.2 cm. copper seal.

Preserved by the Historical Relics Administration of the Tibet Autonomous Region.

# ཆིང་རྒྱལ་རབས་ཀྱི་ཡིག་ཚགས།

གཤམ་གསལ་གྱི་བོད་ཡིག་དང་། མཇུའི་ཡི་གེ སོག་ཡིག རྒྱ་ཡིག་སོགས་ཡིག་རིགས་ཀྱི་གོང་མའི་གསེར་ཡིག་དང་། སྒྲིག་སྲོལ་སྣ་ཚོགས། རྩ་ཚིག་སོགས་ལས་མཇུའི་སྲིད་གཞུང་གིས་ཡོན་དང་མིང་རྒྱལ་རབས་ཀྱི་བོད་ས་གནས་ལ་གཅིག་གྱུར་བདག་འཛིན་བྱས་པའི་ལམ་ལུགས་རྒྱུད་འཛིན་བྱས་པ་མ་ཟད། གོང་གང་མདུན་སྤོས་ཀྱིས་ཆབ་སྲིད་དང་། དཔལ་འབྱོར། དམག་དོན། མི་དོན། ཕྱི་འབྲེལ། ཆོས་ལུགས། རིག་གནས་སོགས་ཕྱོགས་གང་ཅིའི་ཐད་ནས་བོད་ས་གནས་སུ་དབང་བསྒྱུར་ཤུགས་ཆེན་བྱས་ཡོད་པ་མཐོང་ཐུབ།

# 清朝檔案

通過所載藏文、滿文、蒙文、漢文等文種的皇帝聖旨和各種章程、告示等，不難看出，清朝政府不僅繼承了元、明統管吐蕃的制度，而且進一步在政治、經濟、軍事、人事、外交、宗教、文化等各方面加强了對烏思藏（即西藏）地方的統治。

# Qing Dynasty Archives

From the emperors' decrees, regulations and notices in the Tibetan, Manchu, Mongolian and Han languages cited below it is not difficult to see that the Qing Government not only inherited the system of administration of Tibet set up by the Yuan and Ming dynasties, but further strengthened its rule of Tibet with respect to politics, the economy, military affairs, personnel, diplomacy, religion and culture.

# གོང་མ་ཤུན་ཙིས་པཎ་ཆེན་རིན་པོ་ཆེ་ལ་བསྩལ་བའི་བཀའ།

# 順治皇帝頒給班禪活佛的聖旨

# Emperor Shunzhi's Decree to Living Buddha Panchen

187 × 49.3

༄༅། །ཚེ་རིང་གནམ་གྱི་ཤེ་མོང་གིས་དུ་ལྷ་ཡོངས་ཀྱི་བདག་པོ་ཧུང་ཏིའི་བཀའ། པཎ་ཆེན་ཧོ་ཐོག་ཐུ་སྤྲུལ་པའི་སྐུར་གུས་འདུད་ཞུ། ཧོ་ཐོག་ཐུ་གང་ཉིད་བདེ་བར་བཞུགས་པ་གཞིར་བཅས། ངོས་སོགས་བདེ་བར་མཆིས། སྐྱེ་རྒུ་སྐྱོང་བའི་ཆེད་དུ། འབྲུག་ལོའི་སྟོན་ཟླ་བདུན་པའི་ནང་ལ་ཏཱ་ལའི་བླ་མ་དང་ཐུག་ཕྲད་བྱ་རྒྱུའི་རེ་སྒུག་ཞུ་བཞིན་ཡོད། གདན་ཞུའི་པོ་ཉ་མངགས་ཐེན་པས་བླ་མ་ཁྱེད་ནས་ཏཱ་ལའི་བླ་མར་ལམ་དུ་ཆས་རོགས་ཞུ་འཚལ།

གདན་ཞུའི་པོ་ཉ་ནི་བློ་བཟང་དགེ་བཤེས་དང་། རྡོ་རྗེ་དར་ཧན་ནོ་ཡན། ཁྲ་ཀན་དགེ་སློང་། ཤེས་རབ་དགེ་སློང་། མཁས་གྲུབ་དགེ་སློང་དང་སྔོན་དུ་མངགས་པ་ཚེ་རིང་བཅས་ཡོད།

བཀའ་དང་མཉམ་དུ་གསོལ་རས་ལ། གསེར་གྱི་ཇ་མདོང་གཅིག གསེར་སྡེར་གཅིག གསེར་སྲང་བརྒྱ་ཐམ་པ། དངུལ་སྲང་ཉིས་སྟོང་། གོས་ཡུག་བརྒྱ་བཅས་བསྩལ། །

ཤུན་ཙི་ཁྲི་ལོ་བརྒྱད་པའི (སྤྱི་ལོ་༡༦༥༡) ཟླ་བ་བཞི་པའི་ཚེས་གཉིས་ཉིན།

བོད་རང་སྐྱོང་ལྗོངས་ཡིག་ཚགས་ཁང་དུ་ཉར་ཚགས་བྱས་ཡོད།

奉天承運皇帝聖旨。

向班禪呼圖克圖活佛致意。想必呼圖克圖處平安。朕等安好。爲助佑衆生，期待於龍年孟秋月與達賴喇嘛會晤。今派去邀請使者。望喇嘛爾敦請達賴喇嘛啟程。

邀請使者有：羅卜藏古西、道爾吉達爾罕諾彥、察干格隆、席喇卜格隆、克珠格隆及先遣者次仁。

隨敕賞賜：金茶筒一個、金盤一個、金一百兩、銀二千兩、緞一百匹。

順治八年（公元1651年）四月初二

西藏自治區檔案館藏

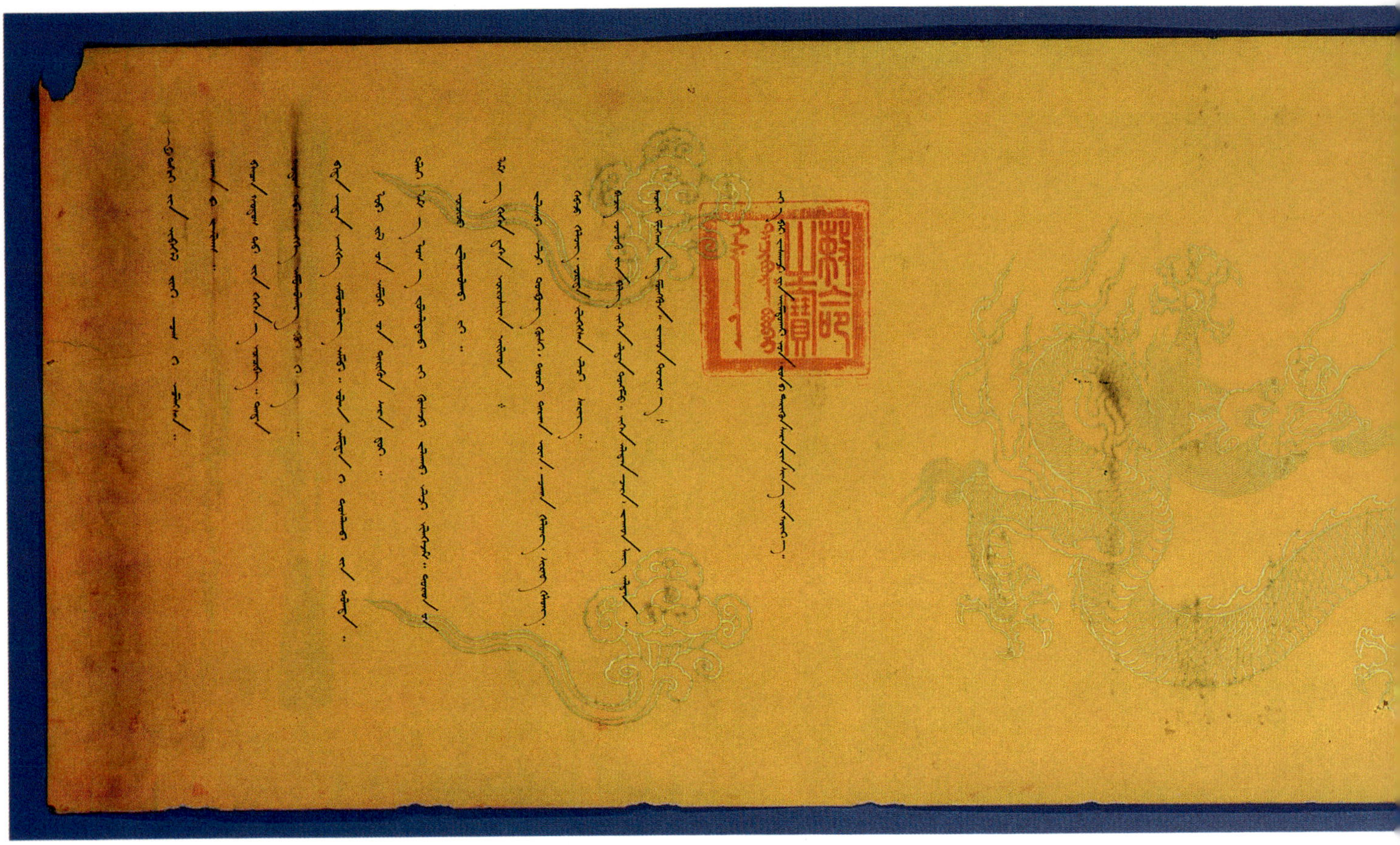

Decree from His Majesty the Emperor, who reigns by the mandate of Heaven.

Greetings to the Living Buddha Panchen. I believe all is well with you. I am also well. I look forward to meeting the Dalai Lama in the early autumn of the Year of the Dragon in the interest of all living beings. Envoys have been sent to extend a cordial invitation to him. I hope you will urge the Dalai Lama to make the journey soon.

Our envoys include: Tobzang Kushis, Rdorje Dargan Noyan, Tshagan Gelong, Gelong Shesrab and Gelong Khasgrub, in addition to our advance member Tshering.

I am presenting you with a gold vessel for tea leaves, a gold tray, 100 *liang* [1 *liang* = 31.25 grammes] of gold, 2,000 *liang* of silver and 100 rolls of satin.

The 2nd day of the 4th month of the 8th year of Shunzhi (1651)

Preserved by the Archives of the Tibet Autonomous Region.

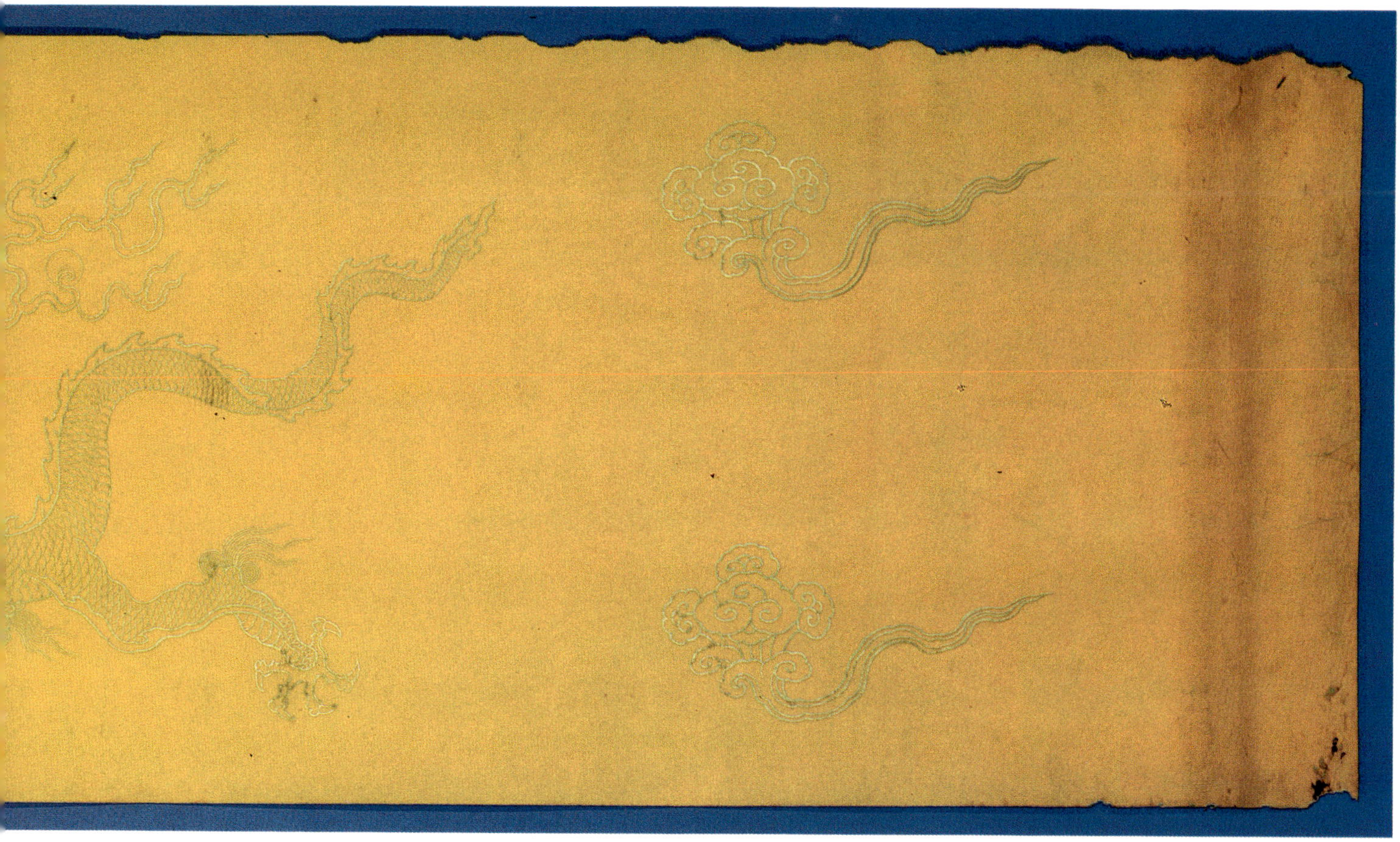

# གོང་མ་ཤུན་ཅིས་ཏཱ་ལའི་བླ་མར་བསྩལ་བའི་བཀའ།
# 順治皇帝給達賴喇嘛的敕諭
# Emperor Shunzhi's Decree to the Dalai Lama

80 × 63

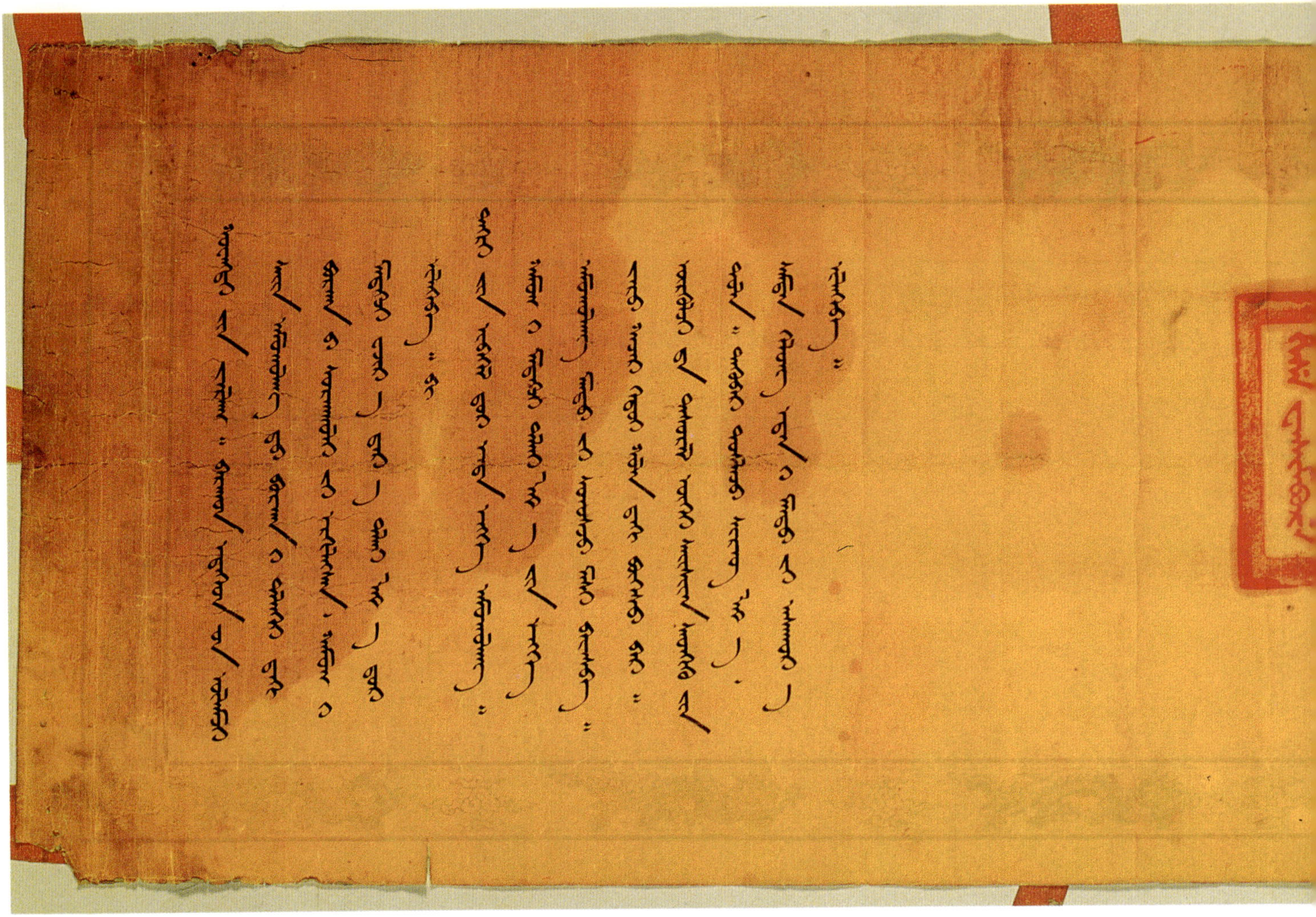

35 - 1

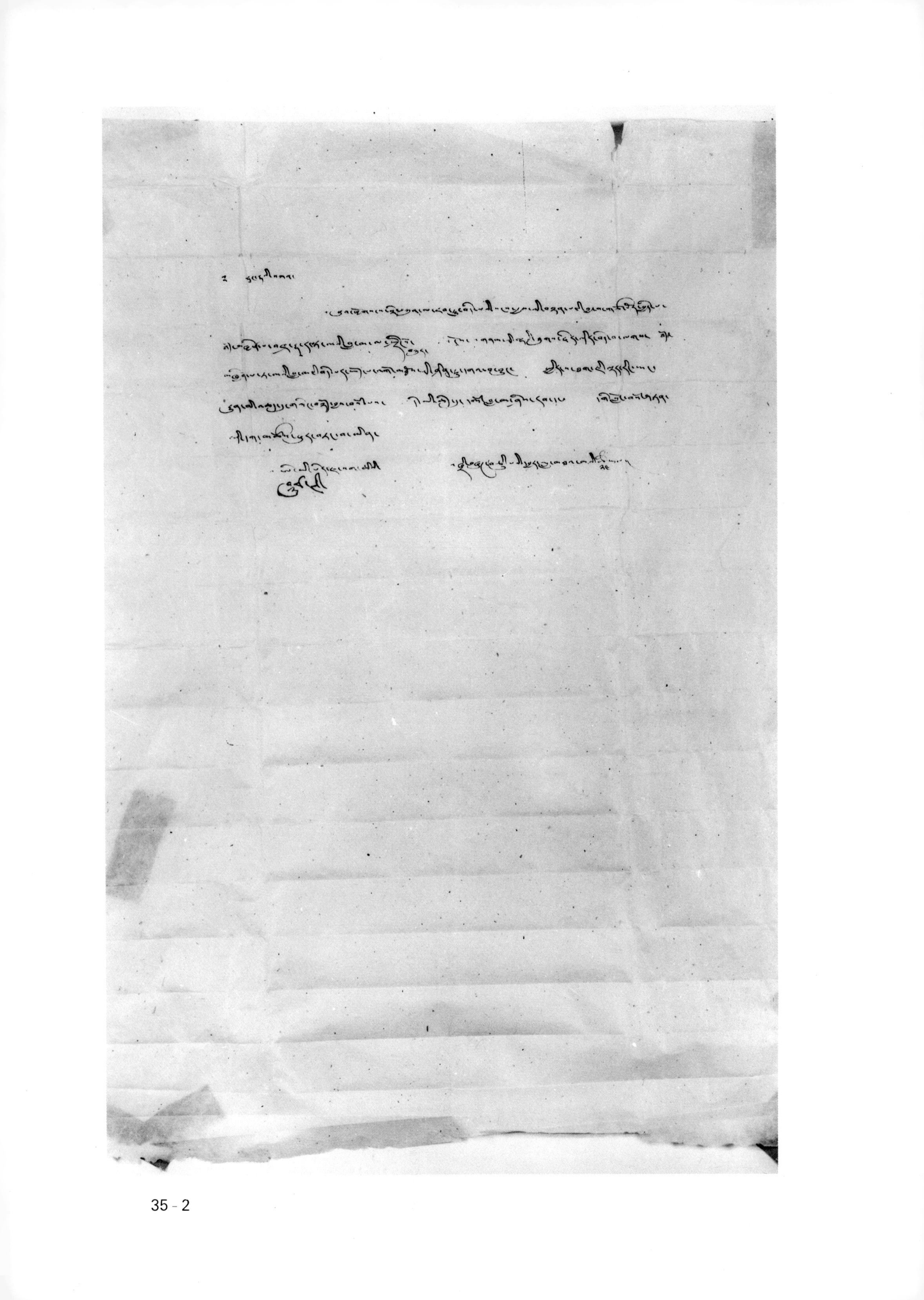

[illegible]

[illegible]

[illegible]

[illegible]

[illegible]

[illegible]

[illegible]　　　　[illegible]

[illegible]

བོད་རང་སྐྱོང་ལྗོངས་ཡིག་ཚགས་ཁང་དུ་ཉར་ཚགས་བྱས་ཡོད།

皇帝敕諭西天大善自在佛所領釋教普通瓦赤喇呾喇達賴喇嘛：

朕荷天眷佑，海宇敉寧，喜聞普通達賴喇嘛爾身體安康，朕甚感慰悦。道途雖遥，嘉悦靡間。兹特遣西繞喇嘛、桑木旦比丘往問佳履。

順治十四年（公元1657年）六月二十四日

西藏自治區檔案館藏

His Majesty the Emperor sends this decree to the Dalai Lama, the All-Knowing, *Jingang* Buddha of Great Benevolence and Comfort of the Western Paradise, Who Commands All Buddhist Sects:

By the grace of Heaven, we are at peace all over the Empire. I am pleased to know that you, the Dalai Lama, are in good health. Despite the great distance that separates us, I am extremely glad to hear this. I am sending Shesrab Blama and Gelong Samtan with my regards.

The 24th day of the 6th month of the 14th year of Shunzhi (1657)

Preserved by the Archives of the Tibet Autonomous Region.

# གོང་མ་བདེ་སྐྱིད་ཀྱིས་པཎ་ཆེན་སྐུ་ཕྲེང་ལྔ་པ་ལ་ཆོ་ལོ་དང་འཇའ་ས་བསྩལ་བའི་བཀའ་ལུང་།

# 康熙皇帝册封五世班禪的諭旨

# Emperor Kangxi's Decree Conferring Title on the 5th Living Buddha Panchen

300 × 79

བོད་རང་སྐྱོང་ལྗོངས་ཡིག་ཚགས་ཁང་དུ་ཉར་ཚགས་བྱས་ཡོད།

奉天承運皇帝制曰：

朕公平待衆，以慈悲撫治天下。對恪守戒律，遵守清規，精勤修道之人，向以褒嘉，并賜官封號。爾自前生以來，恪遵戒律，善意行進，弘揚正法，今又依照禮儀，虔誠進貢，以表耿耿忠心，故朕特賜印册，封爾爲班禪額爾德尼，主持札什倫布寺及其所屬寺院、寺屬溪卡，他人不得侵佔爭奪，使其永久安居。爾亦須堅持梵行，弘揚正法，教育僧衆及弟子，做到取捨無誤，精勤修行。

康熙五十二年（公元1713年）正月二十二日

西藏自治區檔案館藏

His Majesty the Emperor, who reigns by the mandate of Heaven, decrees:

I treat all with equality and rule the Empire with benevolence. I have always conferred honours and granted official posts and titles to those who abide by the commandments of Buddhism, observe the monastic rules and study the doctrines assiduously. In your former life you scrupulously abided by the commandments, proceeded with caution and expounded the Buddhist law. Today, in accordance with protocol, you are again reverently presenting tribute in expression of your loyalty to the throne. I hereby confer on you the title of Panchen Erdeni and present you with the seal and sealed certificate that go with it. You may now preside over the Tashilhunpo Monastery, all other monasteries under its jurisdiction and their manorial estates. No one shall be allowed to forcibly occupy or seize them and the monks are to be allowed to live there in eternal peace. You should also continue to observe the Buddhist tenets, spread the Buddhist law and educate the monks and disciples so that all will behave properly and work diligently at self-perfection.

The 22nd day of the 1st month of the 52nd year of Kangxi (1713)

Preserved by the Archives of the Tibet Autonomous Region.

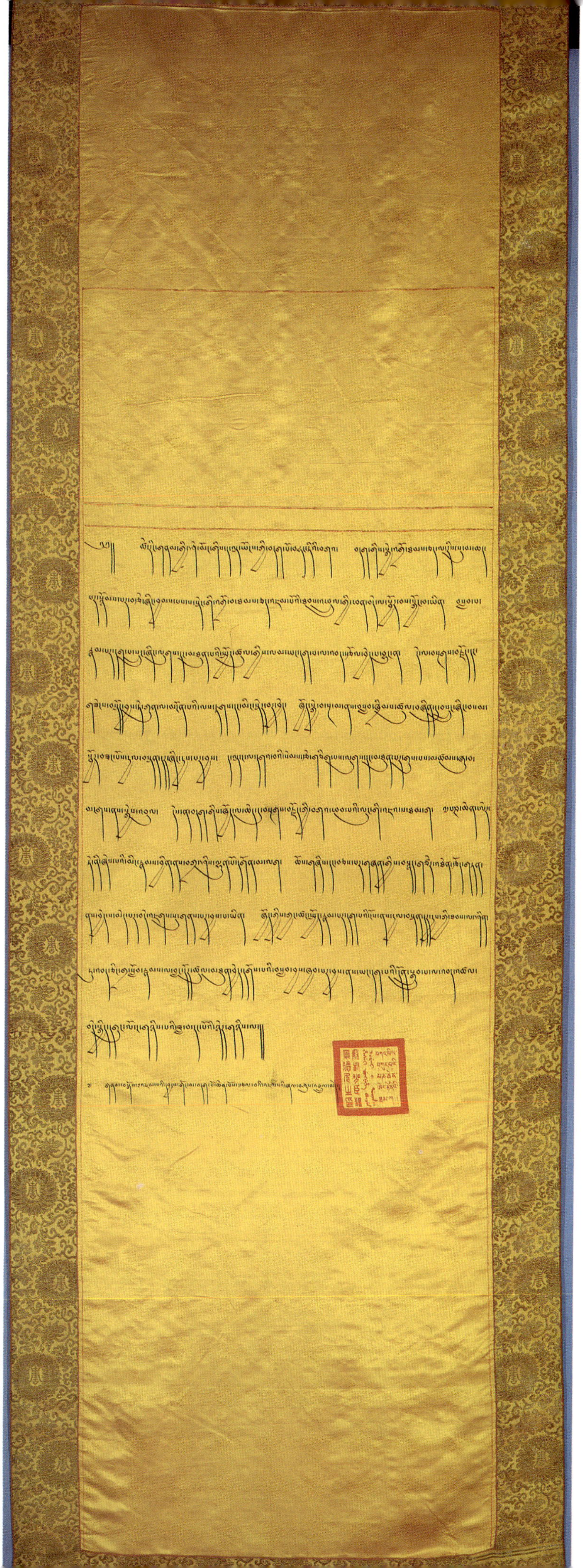

# གོང་མ་བདེ་སྐྱིད་ཀྱིས་ཇུན་གར་བའི་འཁྲུག་ཞིང་བདེ་འཇགས་སུ་བཏང་བའི་བྱས་རྗེས་ཡོད་མཁན་ལ་གོ་མིང་དང་བྱ་དགའ་གནང་བའི་དོན་དུ་ཆོག་ཐུ་ལ་བསྩལ་བའི་བཀའ་ལུང་།

# 康熙皇帝爲平定準噶爾有功封賞事給綽克托的敕諭

# Emperor Kangxi′s Decree to Chogthu Rewarding Him for Service Rendered During the Suppression of the Jungarian Rebellion

400 × 32

37 - 1

༄༅། །ཚེ་རིང་གནམ་གྱི་ཤེ་མོང་གིས། འཛིན་མའི་ཁྱོན་ལ་གནས་པའི་སྐྱེ་དགུ་རྣམས་ཕན་བདེས་སྐྱོང་བའི་ཀྲུང་ཧྲིའི་བཀའ། བདག་གིས་ཕྱི་ནང་གི་སྐྱེ་འགྲོ་མཐའ་དག་རིས་སུ་མ་ཆད་པར་སྐྱོང་ཞིང་། བརྩེ་བས་ལེགས་ལམ་དུ་སྒྱུར་བ་ལ་བསམ་པ་རྣམ་དག་གིས་བདག་གི་བསླབ་བྱ་ཉན་ཅིང་། སྔོན་པོའི་བསམ་སྦྱོར་ཚུལ་མཐུན་ལ་བརྩོན་པ་རྣམས། ཇི་ལྟར་ས་ཐག་རིང་ཞིང་ཡུལ་མཐར་གནས་ཀྱང་། ཕྱི་དང་ནང་ཞེས་རིས་སུ་མི་གཅོད་པར་བསྐྱམས་པས་བརྩེ་ཞིང་སྐྱོང་བ་ཡིན། གནམ་དང་སའི་བར་གྱི་འགྲོ་བ་རྣམས་སྐྱོང་ཤིང་སྐྱོང་བ་གནམ་སའི་གནས་ཚུལ་ཡིན་པ་ལྟར། བསམ་པ་རྣམ་དག་གིས་མགོ་གཏོད་བྱས་པ་རྣམས་ལ་གཟེང་བསྟོད་དང་ཆེད་འདོན་བྱེད་པ་ས་སྐྱོང་སྤྱིའི་ལུགས་ཡིན་པས་ན། ད་ལྟ་བདག་གིས་གནམ་སའི་ཚུལ་དང་མཐུན་པར། རྒྱལ་ཁྲིམས་དང་བྱ་དགའ་སྐྱོང་བ་ལ། བདག་གི་བསླབ་བྱར་ཚུལ་བཞིན་ཉན་པ། དགྲ་འཇོམས་དམག་ལས་ལ་འབད་རྩོལ་གྱིས་བརྩོན་པ་རྣམས་ལ་ལུང་ལས་དང་། ཆེད་འདོན་གནང་ཆ་གྱ་ནོམ་པ་སྩོལ་བ་ཡིན་པས་ན་ཆོག་ཐུ་ཁྱོད་ཐཱ་མ་ཏཱ་ལའི་བླ་མའི་མི་སྡེ། ཤ་རའི་གོལ་ཤྲི་ཐའི་ཇི་ཡིན་པ་ལ། སྔོན་ལམ་ལོག་པར་ཞུགས་པའི་ཇུང་གར་གྱི་ཚེ་དབང་རབ་བརྟན་གྱིས། དོན་མེད་ཀྱི་རྐུན་དམག་ལྷ་སར་བཏང་ནས། བསྟན་པ་བཤིག་ཅིང་། བོད་འབང་རྣམས་སྡུག་བཅུག་པར། ཆོག་ཐུ་ཁྱོད་རྐུན་དམག་གི་དབང་དུ་མ་སོང་བར། ཚེ་རིང་དོན་གྲུབ་ཀྱིས་ཁྱོད་རང་ལ་ཏ་དང་ནོར་ལུག་སོགས་ཀྱི་ཁྲལ་ལེན་པར་མི་ལྔ་བཏང་བ་ཐམས་ཅད་བསད། ཙང་ཇུན་ཨེ་རིན་ཐའི་སོགས་ལ་ཆས་ཀ་བསྐྱེལ་བར་ཁྱོད་རང་གི་བུ་ཨོར་ཁེ་ཇའི་ཚང་བཏང་བ་རྐུན་དམག་གིས་བསད་

ནས། ཁྱོད་ལ་གནོད་པའི་མི་སྡེ་ཐམས་ཅད་ཀུན་དམག་གིས་འཕྲོག་བཅོམ་བྱས་ནས་གཏོར་ནའང་། ཁྱོད་རང་གིས་ལུས་སྲོག་ལ་མ་ལྟོས་པར་ཀུན་དམག་ཚོ་དང་། སྔ་མོ་ནས་ད་ལྟའི་བར་དུ་རྒོལ་བ་སོགས་བྱེད་རང་གིས་སྙིང་ཐག་པའི་སྒོ་ནས་འབད་རྩོལ་འདི་བཞིན་བྱས་པ་རྣམས། ཅང་ཧྲུན་དབང་ཆེན་པོས་ཞུས་པར་བརྟེན། བཀའ་དྲིན་ཆེན་པོའི་བདག་རྐྱེན་གྱིས་ཁྱོད་ལ་ཚད་ལས་འདས་པའི་རིམ་པ་དང་པོའི་ཐའི་ཇི་བཞག་པ་ཡིན་པས། འདི་ཕྱིན་ཆད་སུ་གང་གི་ཐད་ནས་ཀྱང་ཁྱོད་ལ་གནོད་འཚེ་བྱས་མི་ཆོག་གཤིས། ད་ལའི་བླ་མར་ཁྲལ་གྱི་ལས་དང་བྱ་བ་གང་ལའང་སྔར་ལུགས་ལྟར་བྱེད་པ་ལས། སྔར་ལུགས་དང་མི་མཐུན་པའི་བྱ་བ་ཅི་ཡང་བྱས་མི་ཆོག་ཞིང་། ཁྱོད་རང་གི་རིགས་རྒྱུད་ལ་ཡང་རྒྱུན་མི་འཆད་པར་ཕན་པའི་བཀའ་དྲིན་ཆེན་པོའི་བདག་རྐྱེན་གྱིས། བཀའ་ཤོག་བསྩལ་བ་ཡིན་པས། ཁྱོད་ངའི་བཀའ་ལས་མི་མདའ་ཞིང་། ངའི་བཀའ་དྲིན་བདག་རྐྱེན་ནམ་ཡང་མ་བརྗེད་པར་རྒྱལ་ཁྲིམས་དང་མཐུན་པའི་བྱ་བར་ལེགས་པས་བརྩོན་ན། བཀའ་དྲིན་བདག་རྐྱེན་འདིས་ཁྱོད་རང་གི་ཕ་མེས་དང་། རིགས་རྒྱུད་ལ་ཡང་ལེགས་ཚོགས་སུ་འགྱུར་ལ་མ་ངེས་པའི་རྒྱལ་ཁྲིམས་དང་འགལ་བ་བྱུང་བའམ། བྱ་བ་རྣམས་སྔར་ལུགས་དང་མི་མཐུན་པའི་འགྲོ་འདུག་སྟིང་པོ་བྱུང་ན། ཁྱོད་རང་ལ་གང་ཅི་ནས་མི་ལེགས་ཤིང་། ཐའི་ཇིའི་ཚོ་ལོ་ཡང་བླང་ནས་རྒྱལ་ཁམས་སྤྱི་ཁྲབ་ལ་ཡོད་པའི་ཁྲིམས་ལུགས་དང་མཐུན་པ་ངེས་པར་བྱེད་པ་ཡིན།

བདེ་སྐྱིད་རྒྱལ་པོ་དགུང་ལོ་དྲུག་ཅུ་པའི་ཟླ་༩ཚེས་༨ལ།

བོད་རང་སྐྱོང་ལྗོངས་ཡིག་ཚགས་ཁང་དུ་ཉར་ཚགས་བྱས་ཡོད།

37－2

奉天承運皇帝詔曰：

朕總領天下，撫馭中外，凡效忠歸化、能盡臣義者，雖邊陲絶域，亦一視同仁，不念中外二致也，覆載萬物者乃天地之心，忠誠歸順者得享榮華，此乃帝王之尊例也。朕仰體天地之心，宣恩治政，凡歸順之兵卓有功績者，必封賞爵秩，施以鴻恩。綽克托爾原係土伯特部達賴喇嘛所屬錫喇古勒之台吉，準噶爾策妄喇布坦反叛，派兵潛入拉薩，毀滅宗教，擾害土伯特部，綽克托爾不隨賊，車凌敦多布由爾處科斂馬牛羊只，爾將五名逆賊均斬殺之；爲將軍

額倫特等解送廪餼時，爾子額爾克宰桑被賊戕害，爾之屬民被掠散，捨命御賊，始終抗敵。爾此功績，殊堪嘉獎，大將軍奏陳情由，特施恩將爾表彰，封爲頭等台吉。嗣後，不受任何人侵擾，向達賴喇嘛當差辦事，仍照舊例而行，絲毫不可更改前例，永頒旌敕，世襲罔替。爾不違朕旨，永不負朕恩，遵守法度，敬順而行，則恩及父祖，福延子孫；若違法度，擅改舊例，胡亂而行，則斷爾生計，革爾台吉名號。國法俱在，凡事務遵法度。

康熙六十年（公元1721年）四月初六

西藏自治區檔案館藏

37 - 3

His Majesty the Emperor, who reigns by the mandate of Heaven, decrees:

As the Emperor of the Empire and beyond I accord equal and fair treatment to all who pledge allegiance to me and acknowledge my rule, even to those who reside in the distant border areas. It is the will of heaven and earth to support and maintain all living things and it is the Emperor's honourable practice to ensure that those who come over to my side and pledge their loyalty to me enjoy honour and prosperity. In complying with the will of heaven and

earth and to demonstrate the magnanimity of my administration, I grant titles and bestow great favour on warriors who come over to my side and render outstanding service. You, Chogthu, were a *taiji* of the Bod tribe in Sharigola under the jurisdiction of the Dalai Lama. When the Jungarian rebels instigated rebellion, secretly sending troops to the Lhasa area to destroy the religion and harass the Bod tribe, you did not join the rebels, but instead you killed five of them when Tshering Dongrub came to collect sheep, cattle and horses as taxes from your tribe. While delivering grain and fodder to General Erenthivi, your son Erkhed Sitshang

37 - 4

was murdered by the bandits. The people of your tribe were scattered, many losing their lives while fighting the bandits. All the while you resisted the rebels and stood firm against the enemy. You truly deserve commending for such a distinguished record. Since General Erenthivi has petitioned the throne on this matter, I am hereby giving you a citation and conferring on you the title of *taiji,* 1st class. Henceforth, you shall not suffer harassment from anyone and shall work for the Dalai Lama as before without the slightest change. This title shall be conferred on your descendants from generation to generation without interruption. As long as you never go against my orders or become ungrateful for my graciousness and abide by the

law and obediently perform your duties, this honour shall be extended to your forefathers as well as to your sons and grandsons. If you violate the law, diverge from the time–honoured practice without authorization or become unruly in your conduct, I shall cut off your means of livelihood and recall your title of *taiji*. You have the law of the state to go by in conducting all your affairs.

The 6th day of the 4th month of the 60th year of Kangxi (1721)

Preserved by the Archives of the Tibet Autonomous Region.

# གོང་མ་བདེ་སྐྱིད་ཀྱིས་སངས་རྒྱས་ཀྱི་བསྟན་པ་དར་རྒྱས་སུ་གཏོང་དགོས་པའི་དོན་དུ་ དྲུ་ལའི་བླ་མ་སྐུ་ཕྲེང་དྲུག་པར་བསྐུལ་བའི་བཀའ་ཤོག།

# 康熙皇帝爲降諭興佛教事給六世達賴喇嘛的咨文

# Emperor Kangxi's Communication to the 6th Dalai Lama Concerning the Decree for the Promotion of Buddhism

162 × 83

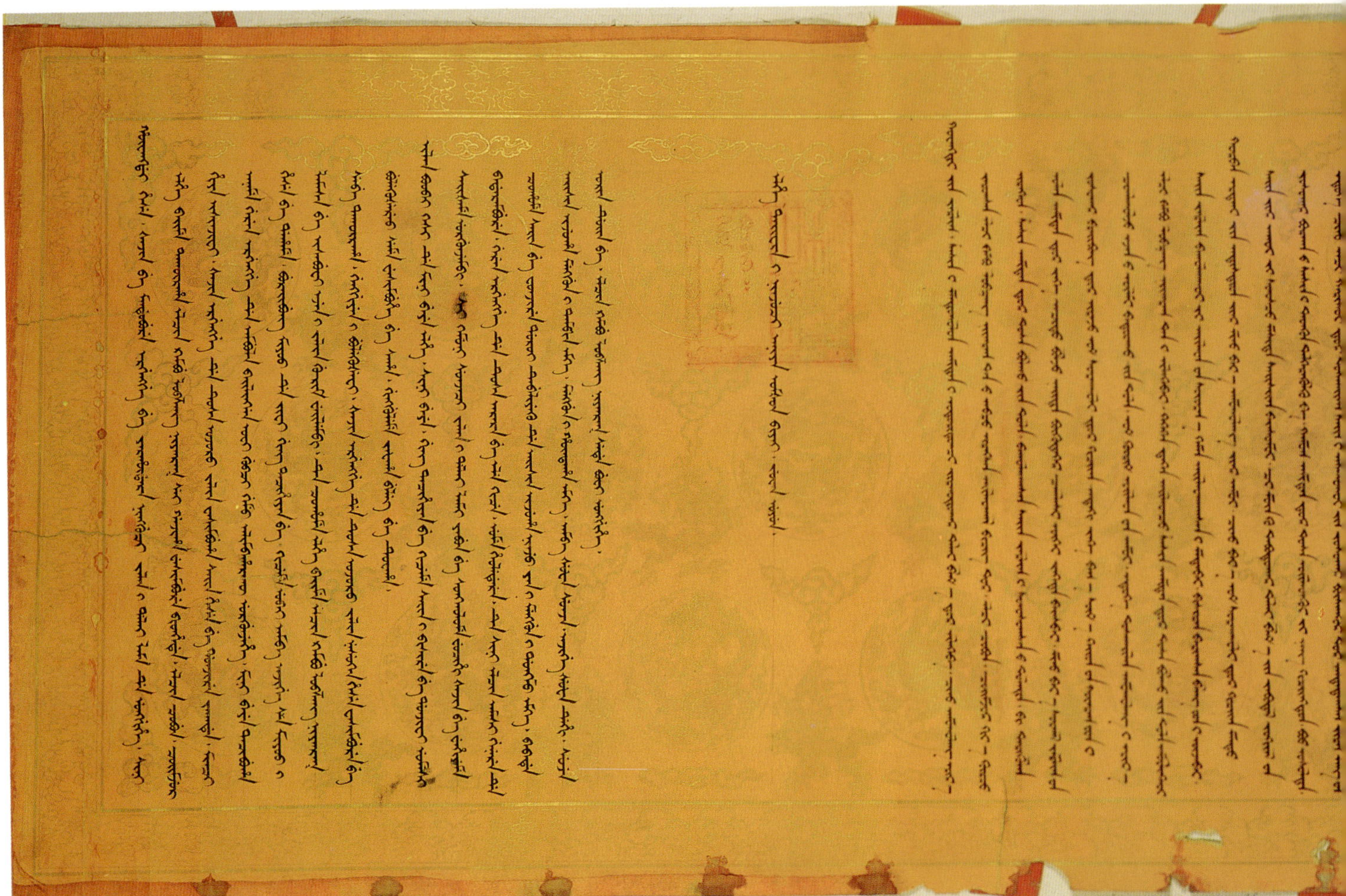

38 - 1

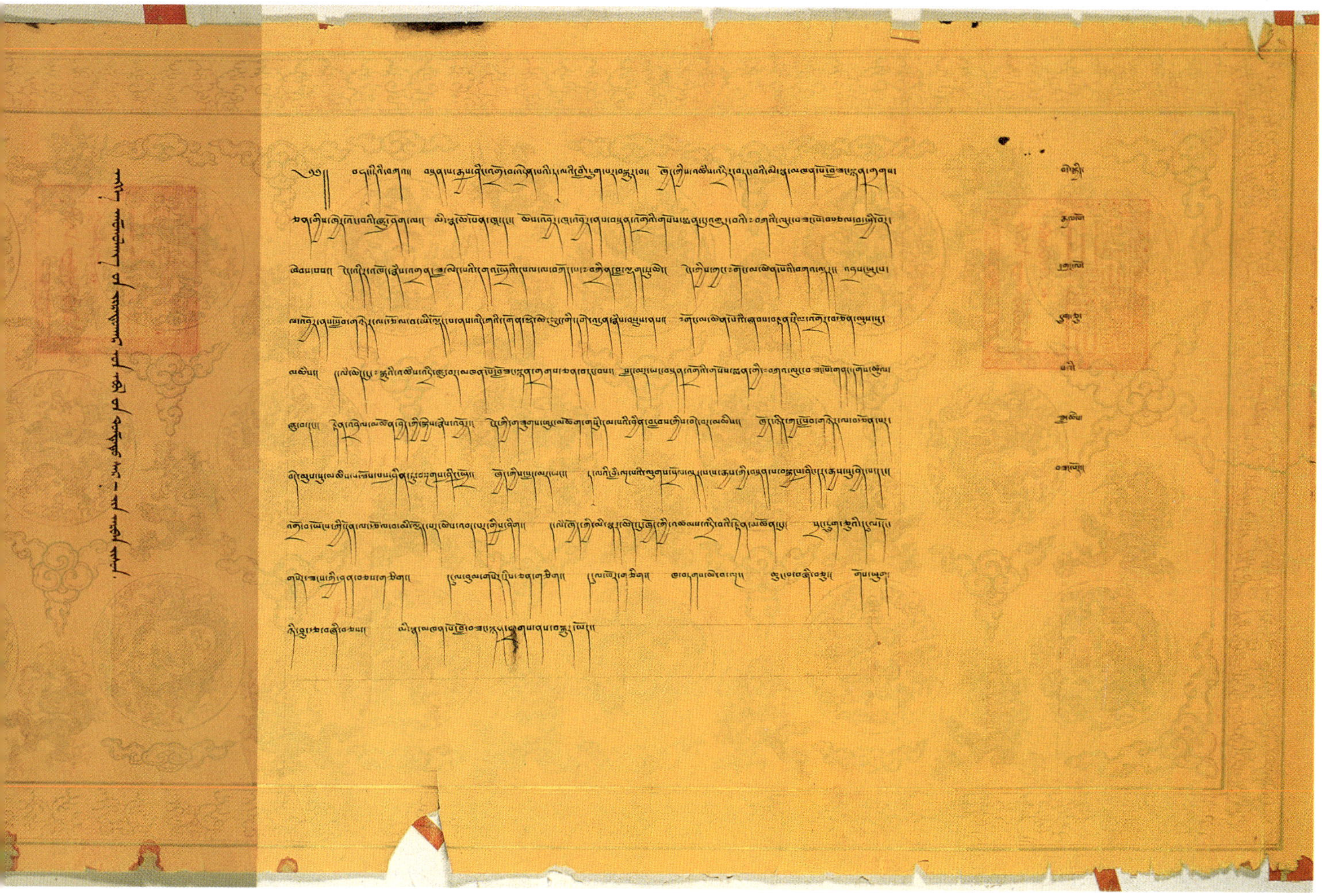

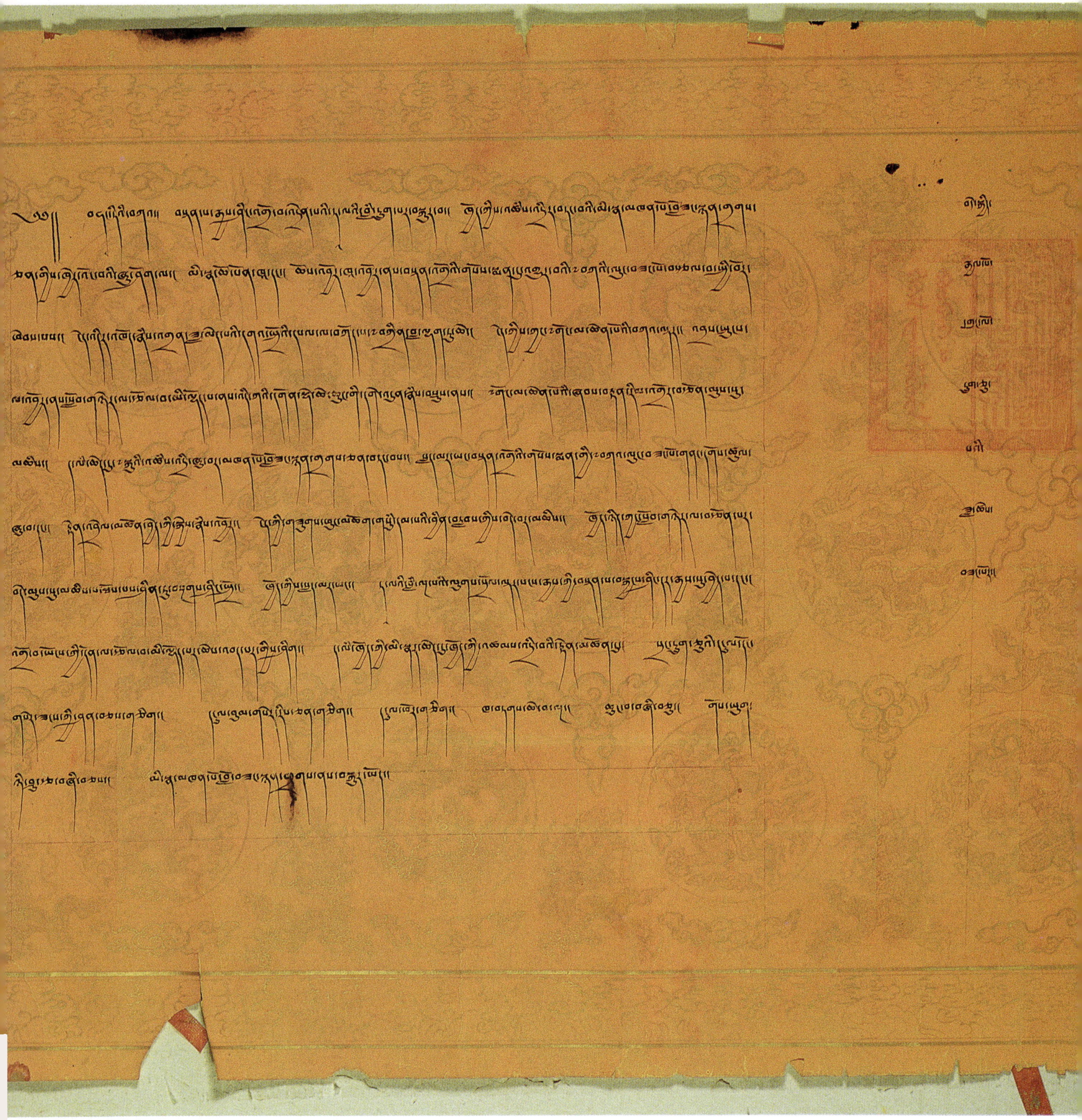

38 - 2

བོད་རང་སྐྱོང་ལྗོངས་ཡིག་ཚགས་ཁང་དུ་ཉར་ཚགས་བྱས་ཡོད།

皇帝敕諭：

咨行闡揚釋教、普度衆生六世達賴喇嘛。據爾派遣請安使者堪布洛桑年扎等所携呈文內稱：使者却奔、群覺侍衛到來後，聞爲興扶釋教、普濟群生而降仁旨，由我推及，於衆生廣施恩惠，所有人等，不勝欣悦。我親遵諭旨，來到哲蚌寺，勤習經藝，召集本地大小寺廟之喇嘛，爲聖主祈禱，今特遣使者堪布洛桑年扎請安，伏乞明鑒，懇請爲興扶釋教、普濟群生而降仁旨等因。朕覽呈文，并謹閱進貢禮品。仰蒙三寶之恩佑，朕體安康。聞爾親習經藝，身體健壯，朕甚嘉悦。爾應效法五世達賴喇嘛之行，闡揚釋教，普度衆生，勿得怠惰。今爾使返回，特致問候之禮，隨賞鍍金六十兩重銀茶桶一個、鍍金銀瓶一個、銀碗一隻、大哈達五條、小哈達四十條、綢緞二十四匹，交付爾使堪布洛桑年扎携回。

康熙六十年（公元1721年）十一月十九日

西藏自治區檔案館藏

The Emperor's edict to the 6th Dalai Lama, promoter of Buddhism and comforter of all living beings:

The petition presented to me by your envoy Khanpo Lozang Nyangrag, who has been sent by you to pay your respects to me, reads: "When my envoys Chospon and Chosbyor, aides—de—camp, arrived here, I learned that Your Majesty has issued a gracious edict for the promotion of Buddhism and the comfort of all living beings and that I have been requested to carry out your instructions and show graciousness to all under heaven. The people are overjoyed. In compliance with the imperial decree, I have come to the Braspus Monastery to study Buddhist scriptures and call together the lamas from all the large and small monasteries in the area to pray for the well—being of the Imperial Master. I am sending my envoy Khanpo Lozang Nyangrag to pay my respects to you and humbly beg Your Majesty to again send us a gracious decree for the promotion of Buddhism, the relief of the people , etc." I have read your petition and reviewed the list of tribute articles. By the grace of the Triratna, I am in good health, and I am pleased to know that you are well and applying yourself to the study of Buddhist scriptures. You should promote Buddhism and work ceaselessly to bring comfort to the people, taking the 5th Dalai Lama as your model. I am sending you my regards with your envoy and present you with a 60—*liang* gold— plated silver vessel for tea leaves, a gold—plated silver vase, a silver bowl, five large and 40 small hatas as well as 24 rolls of silk, which your envoy Khanpo Lozang Nyangrag is bringing back with him.

The 19th day of the 11th month of the 60th year of Kangxi (1721)

Preserved by the Archives of the Tibet Autonomous Region.

# གོང་མ་བདེ་སྐྱིད་ཀྱིས་ཞིགས་སྐྱེས་ཕུལ་བར་གསོལ་རས་གནང་བའི་དོན་དུ་ཏཱ་ལའི་བླ་མ་སྐུ་ཕྲེང་དྲུག་པ་ལ་བསྩལ་པའི་བཀའ་ལུང་།

# 康熙皇帝爲貢賞事給六世達賴喇嘛的敕諭

# Emperor Kangxi's Decree to the 6th Dalai Lama on Rewarding Him with Gifts

162×83

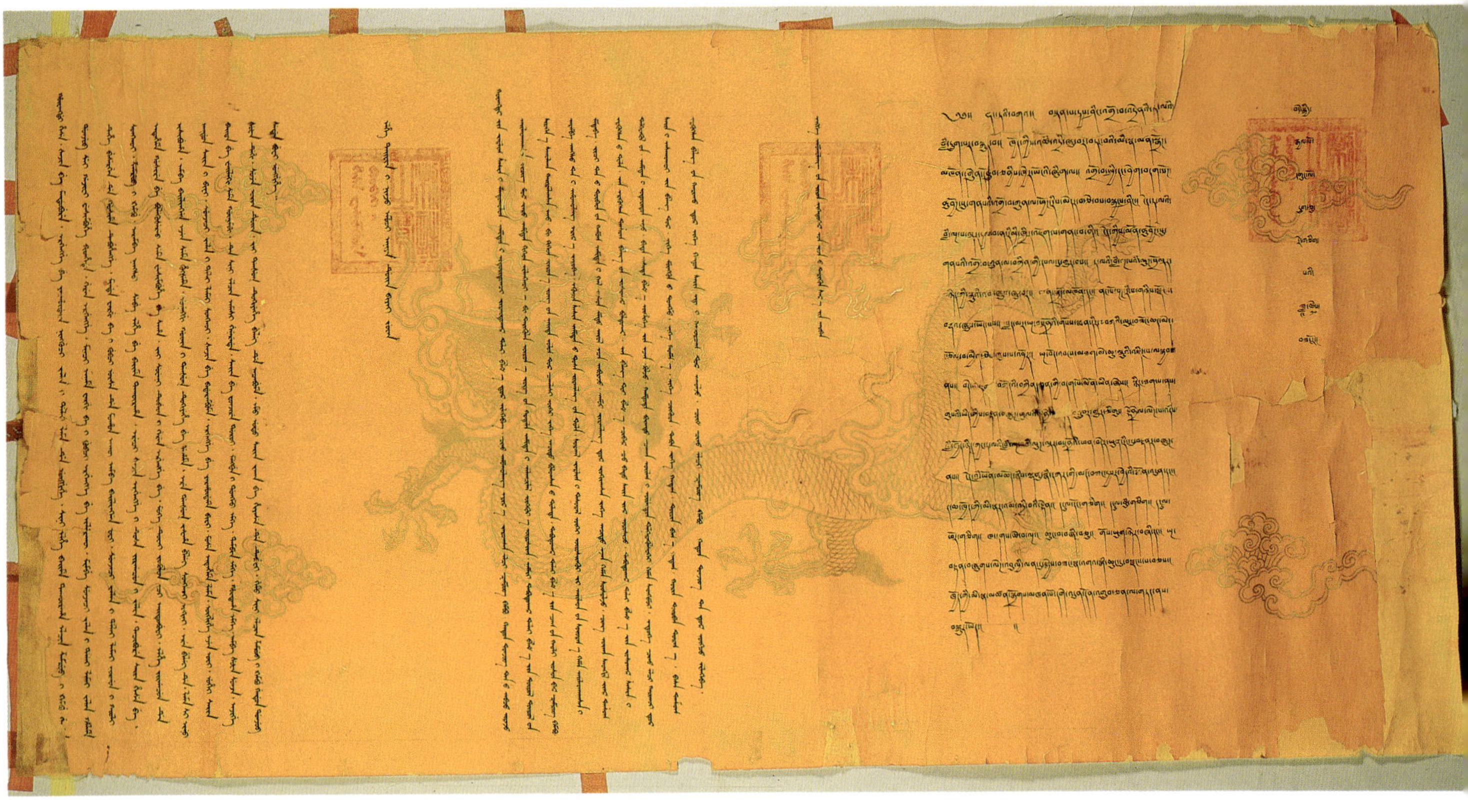

39－1

བོད་རང་སྐྱོང་ལྗོངས་ཡིག་ཚགས་ཁང་དུ་ཉར་ཚགས་བྱས་ཡོད།

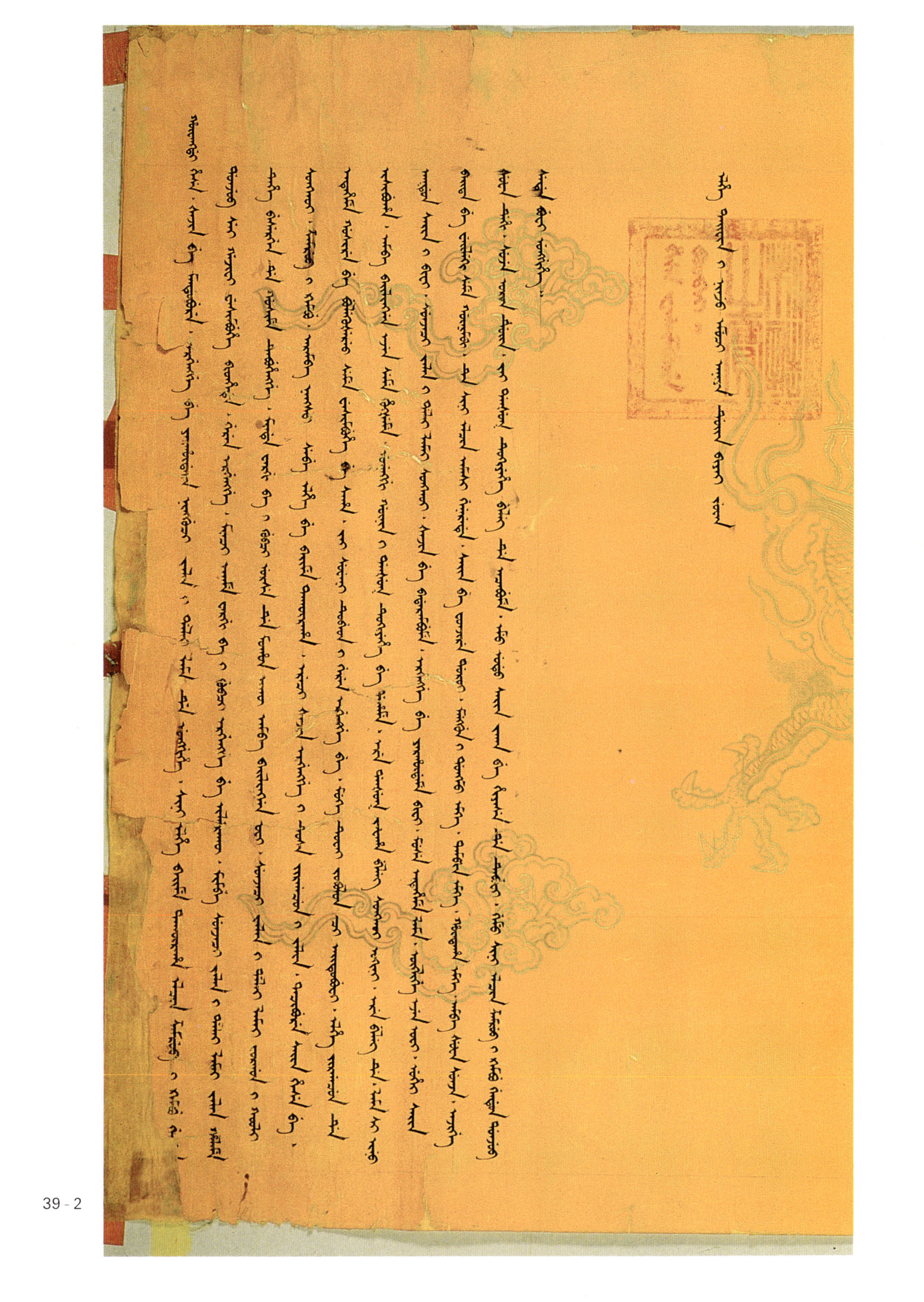

[illegible]

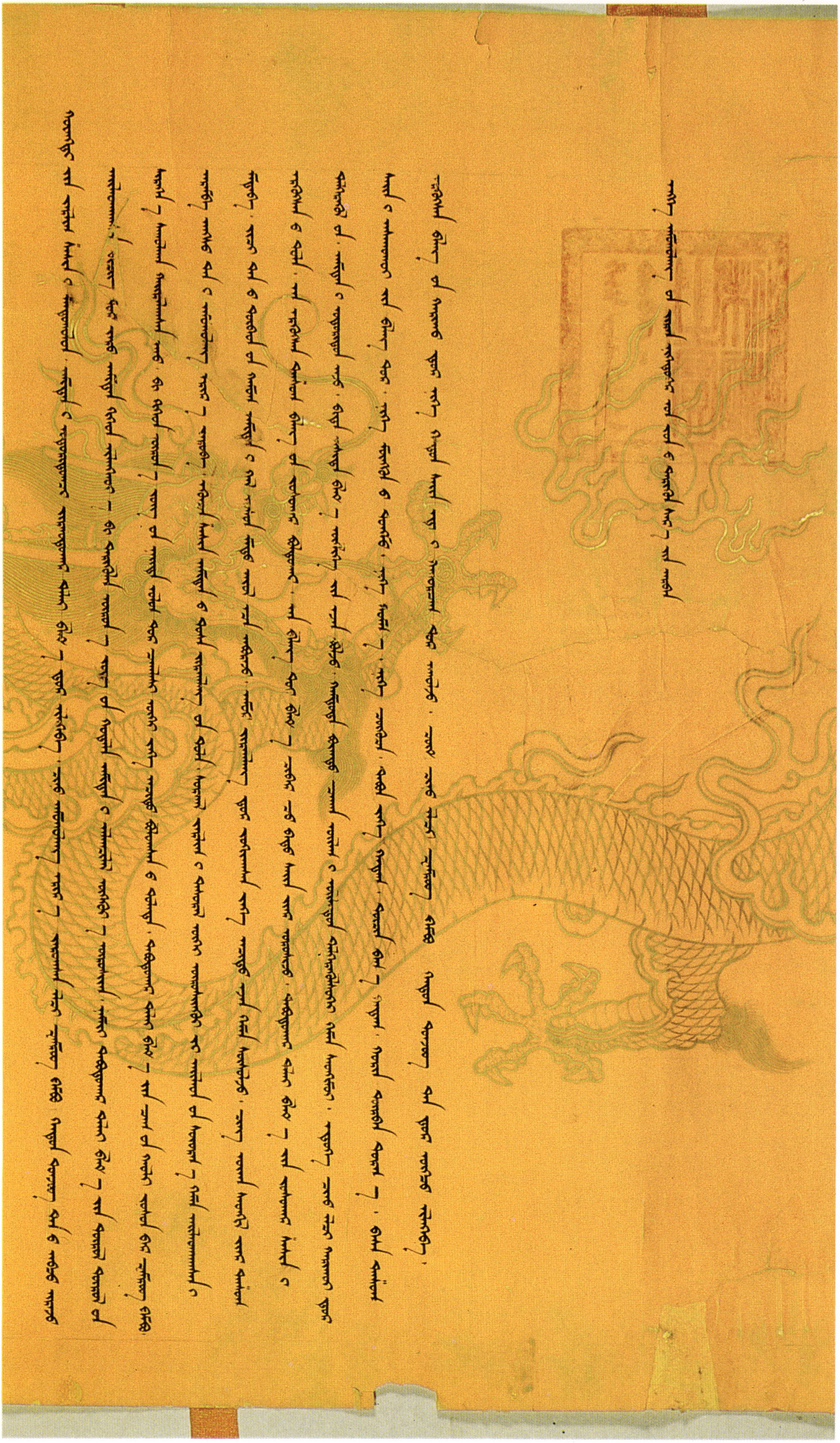

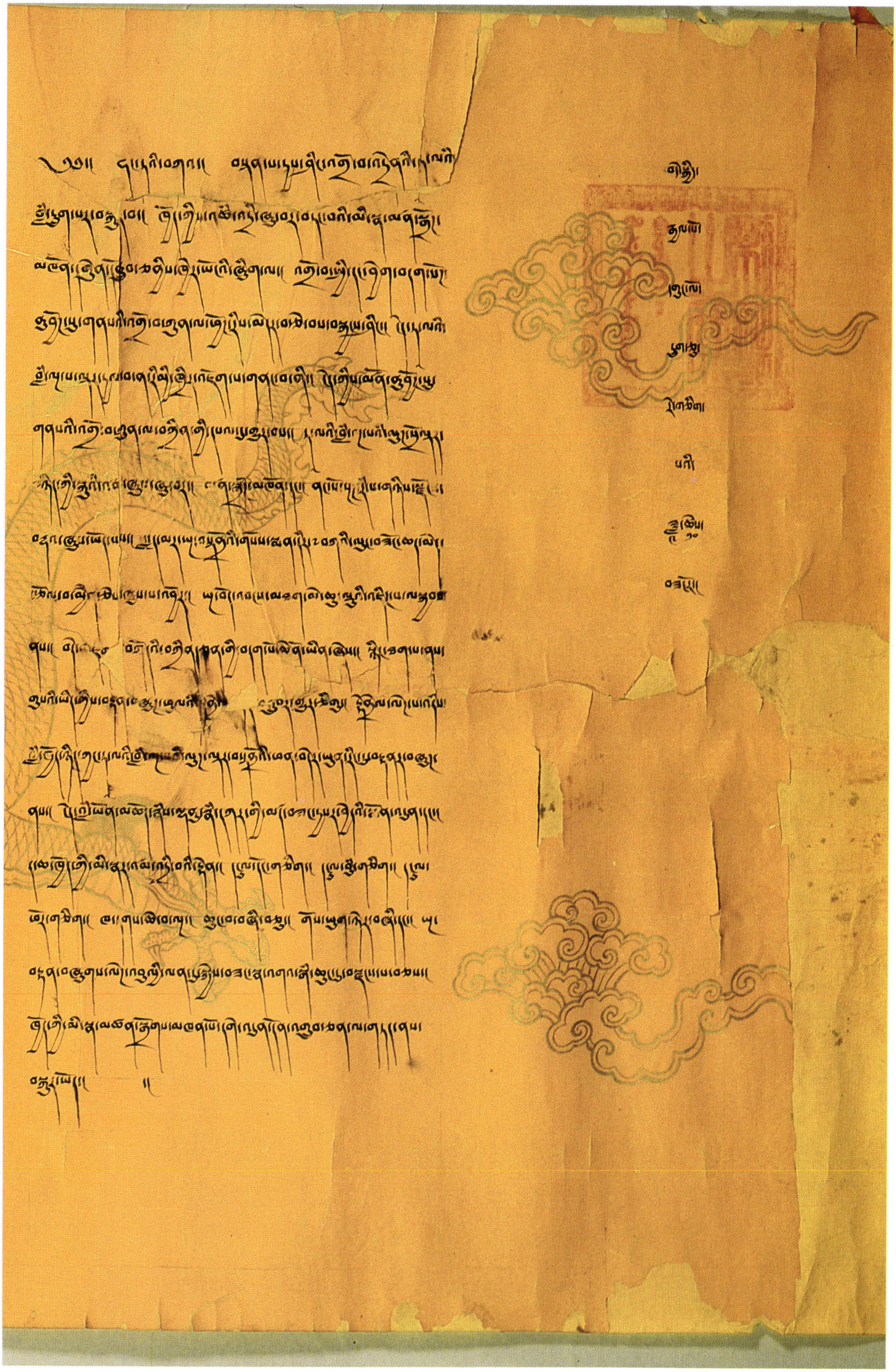

皇帝敕諭：

咨行闡揚釋教、普度衆生六世達賴喇嘛。爾遣請安使者贊卓堪布根敦敦珠等所携奏文內稱：不分衆生或由我推恩之西地群生，使我坐五世達賴喇嘛轉世之坐床，聖上施於我及西地衆民無疆鴻恩，故照五世達賴喇嘛之規例，派遣贊卓堪布、阿讓巴囊蘇等請安，爲闡揚釋教、普度衆生，懇請仁鑒，頒降訓諭等因，朕覽奏矣。再者，又稱將爾土伯特衆民，解救於水深火熱之苦難中，得以安居樂業，感戴大恩主，既然忠心敬獻丹書克，照此進呈丹書克之禮而行。進此禮物，喇嘛爾亦健在，惟期照五世達賴喇嘛弘揚釋教、普度衆生，我等各自永爲喇嘛、君主，共修善事。今爾使返回，致以問候之禮，隨賞銀茶桶一個、銀瓶一個、銀碗一隻、大哈達五條、小哈達四十條、綢緞二十四匹。再者，仰合敬獻丹書克之禮，將數件吉物裝匣交付爾使贊卓堪布根敦敦珠等携回。

康熙六十一年（公元1722年）四月十日

西藏自治區檔案館藏

His Majesty the Emperor's decree to the 6th Dalai Lama, promoter of Buddhism and comforter of all living beings:

The petition submitted by your envoy Tshangyog Khanpo Dgedun Dongrub and others, who you sent to pay your respects to me, reads: "In recognition of the boundless benevolence which Your Majesty has showered on me and the people in Tibet, putting me on the throne once held by the Dalai Lama in his 5th incarnation, I have sent envoys Tshangyog Khanpo and Sngagram Panangso to pay my respects, following the example set by the 5th Dalai Lama. I am submitting this petition to Your Majesty's notice to entreat you to send the instructions for the promotion of Buddhism, the comfort of all living beings, etc." I have read your petition. In addition, you also said that you are grateful to the great Imperial Saviour for relieving the Bod people from their abominable suffering, enabling them to live in peace. Since you have submitted a *danshuke* with sincerity and according to protocol and you are in good health as well, I look forward to your following the example of the 5th Dalai Lama in promoting Buddhism and comforting all living beings. You and I shall always remain lama and sovereign and together we shall perform good deeds. I have asked your envoys to give my regards on their return and present to you a silver vessel for tea leaves, a silver vase, a silver bowl, five large and 40 small *hatas* and 24 rolls of silk. I have also packed a few amulets in a box for your envoys to bring back to you, in return for your presentation of a *danshuke*.

The 10th day of the 4th month of the 61st year of Kangxi (1722)

Preserved by the Archives of the Tibet Autonomous Region.

# གོང་མ་ཡུང་ཅིང་གིས་ཆོ་ལོ་དང་གསེར་གྱི་ཐམ་ཀ་གནང་བའི་དོན་དུ་ཏཱ་ལའི་བླ་མ་སྐུ་ཕྲེང་དྲུག་པ་ལ་བསྩལ་བའི་བཀའ་ལུང་།

# 雍正皇帝爲加封賞賜印册事給六世達賴喇嘛的敕諭

# Emperor Yongzheng's Decree to the 6th Dalai Lama Presenting Him with the Title, Seal and Certificate

166 × 100

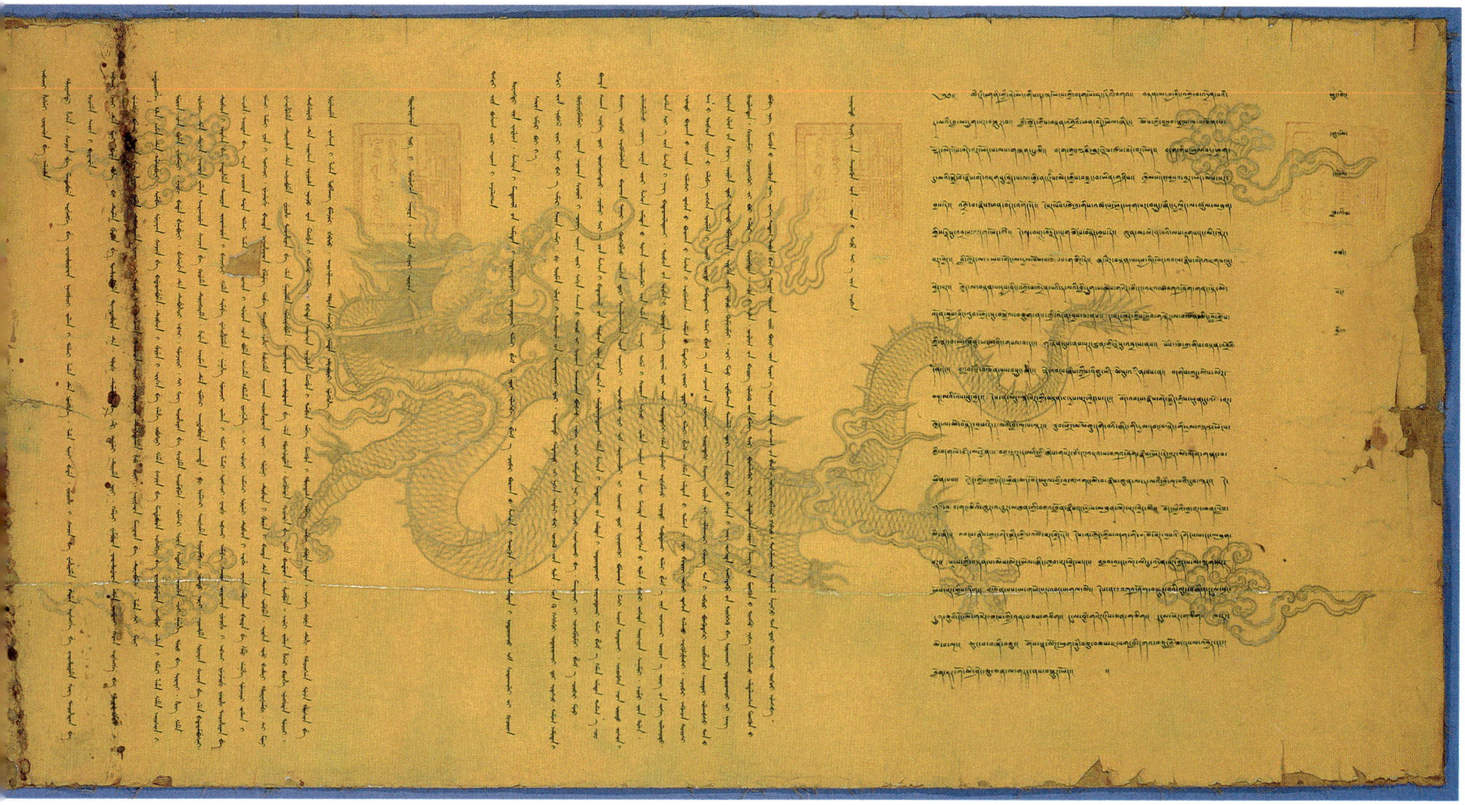

40 - 1

བོད་རང་སྐྱོང་ལྗོངས་ཡིག་ཚགས་ཁང་དུ་ཉར་ཚགས་བྱས་ཡོད།

奉天承運皇帝詔曰：

咨行闡揚釋教、普度衆生六世達賴喇嘛。喇嘛爾親奉佛法，普度衆生，勤習經藝，善哉。仰蒙皇天眷佑，朕體安康。朕撫馭萬邦，不分中外，一視同仁，信奉教化，養育衆生，篤誠信守賢德，凛遵王道，則務旌表封贈，以示嘉奬。喇嘛爾受皇考之仁恩，令爾弘揚黄教，俾土伯特衆民安居，封爲闡揚釋教、普度衆生六世達賴喇嘛，賜以金印册文，送往本地坐床以

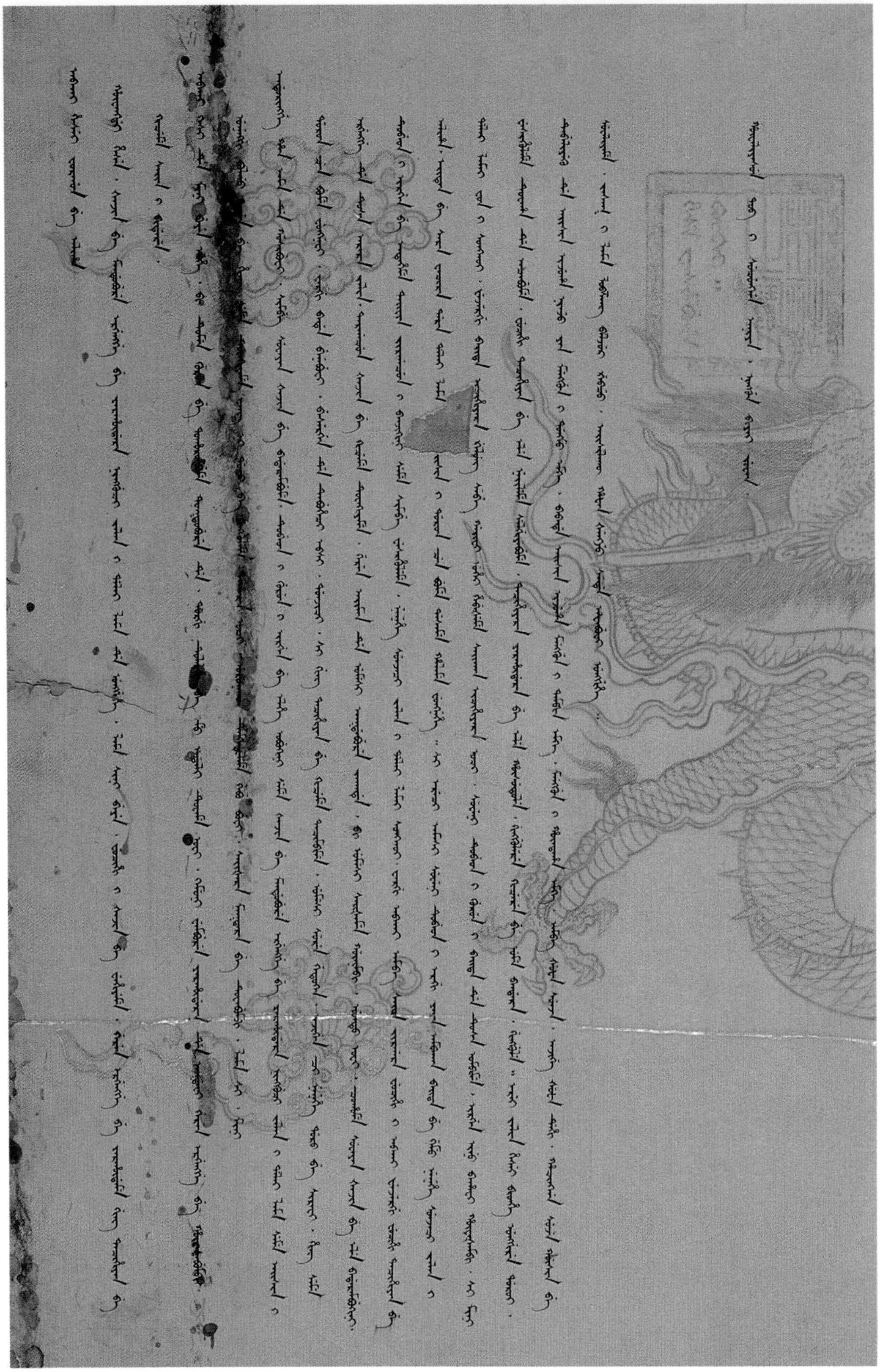

來，據聞，爾勤習經典，人甚聰慧，自幼承襲先道，虔誠爲民造福，嚴守戒律，信賴各部，朕甚嘉悦。故此，特爲崇揚黄教，俾土伯特衆民永遠安居樂業，將爾按照前五世達賴喇嘛之例，再行改封，尊爲西天大善自在佛所領天下釋教普通瓦赤喇呾喇達賴喇嘛，賜以金印册文。爾嗣後於土伯特所有大事，均照前五世達賴喇嘛之例，率辦理事務之噶倫等，共同協商，妥善辦理，則於爾土伯特部事務大有裨益，民有所養。爾仰副朕尊崇之意，宣揚佛法，

40－3

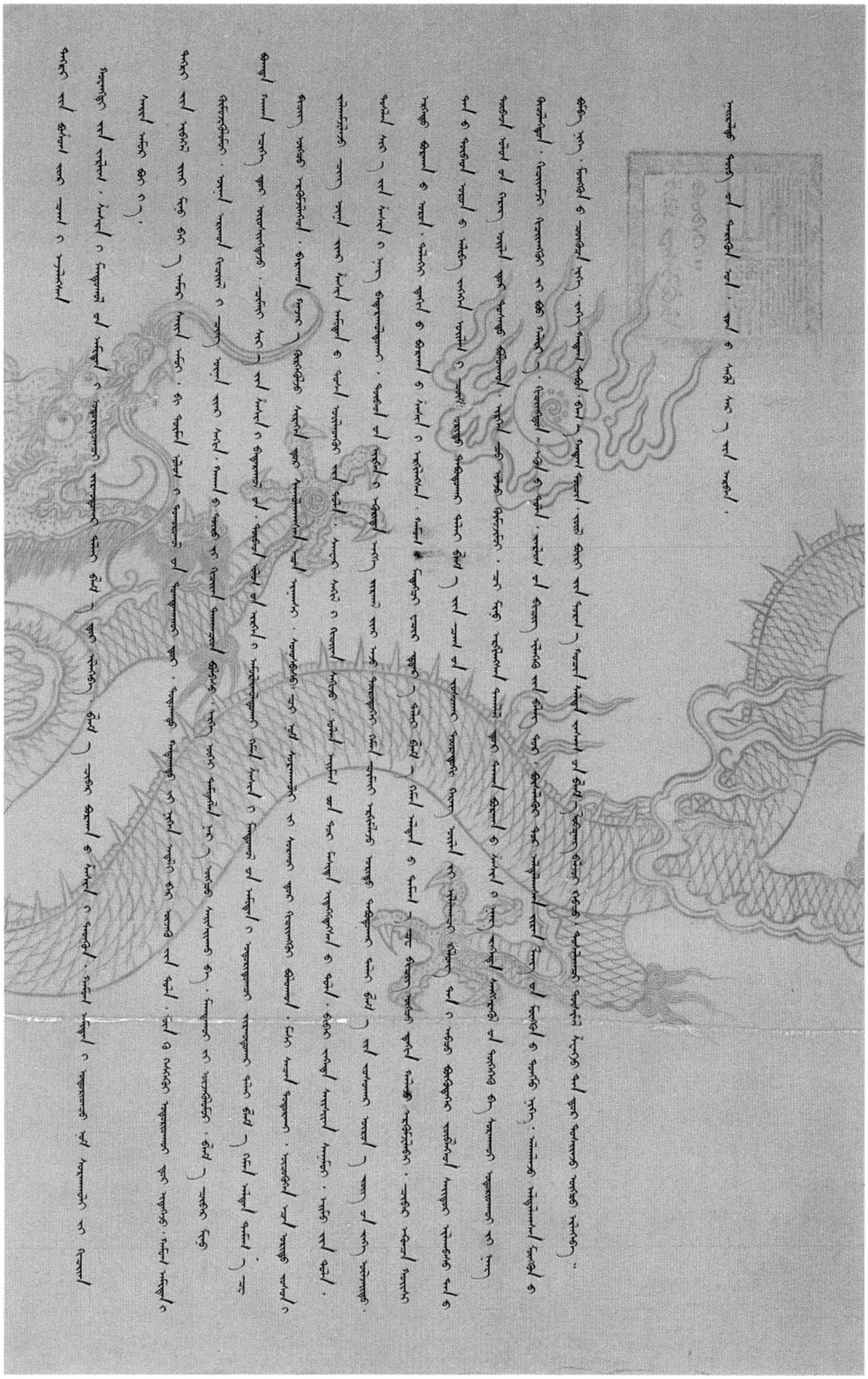

致力訓導，勤謹勿怠。慎之。爲此隨敕賞爾鍍金六十兩重銀茶桶一個、鍍金銀瓶一個、銀碗一隻、大哈達五條、小哈達四十條、各色綢緞三十匹，一併交付扎薩克喇嘛嘎布楚、羅卜藏巴勒珠爾、扎爾固齊升柱等携回。

雍正元年（公元1723年）六月十日

西藏自治區檔案館藏

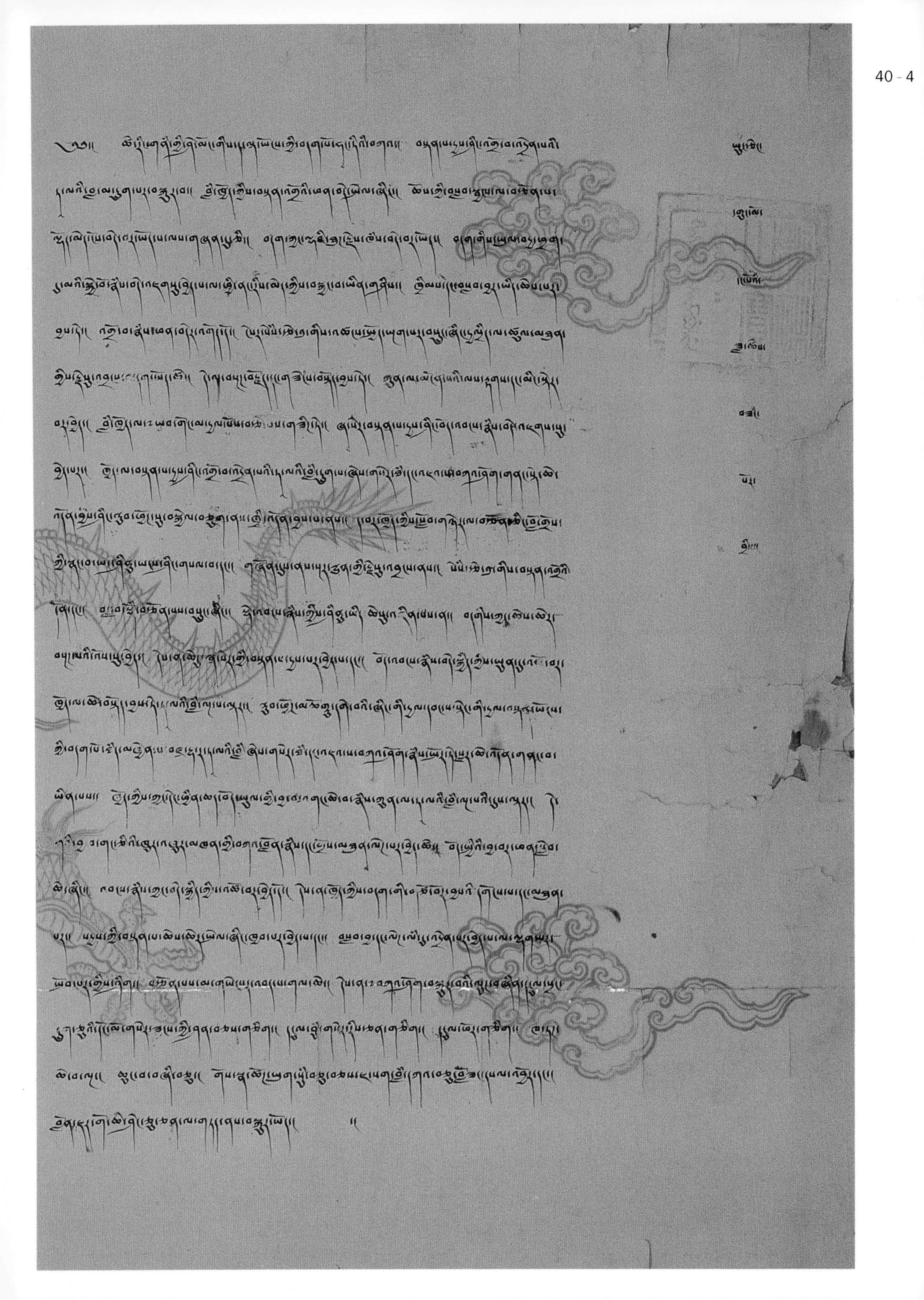

[illegible]

His Majesty the Emperor, who reigns by the mandate of Heaven, decrees:

To the 6th Dalai Lama, promoter of Buddhism and comforter of all living beings. You are to be commended for honouring the precepts of Buddha, comforting all living beings and applying yourself diligently to the study of the Buddhist scriptures. By the grace of Heaven, I am in good health. As the sovereign who rules the Empire, according equal treatment to all both inside and outside the Empire, I confer honour and titles on people to encourage those who follow the Buddhist teachings, feed all living beings, show themselves to be honest, obedient and virtuous, and strictly follow the laws of the country. Through the graciousness of my imperial father, you were requested to expound the Yellow Sect of Lamaism so that the Bod people could live in peace. Since the title of the 6th Dalai Lama, promoter of Buddhism and comforter of all living beings was conferred on you and you were presented with the golden seal and the sealed certificate and sent to be enthroned in Lhasa, I have learned with pleasure that you are intelligent and have been applying yourself to the study of Buddhist classics, that you have been adhering to the teaching of your former master from boyhood and have been working devoutly for the good of the people, and that you have been observing the rules and regulations and remaining faithful to all the tribes. Because of all this and in order to promote the Yellow Sect of Lamaism so that the Bod people may live in eternal peace, I have, in line with the precedent set by the late 5th Dalai Lama, conferred on you the honourable title of Dalai Lama, the All–Knowing, the Buddha of Great Benevolence and Freedom of the Mind of the Western Paradise Who Commands All Buddhist Sects Under Heaven, and presented you with the golden seal and the sealed certificate. From now on you should consult with the government ministers working under you on all important matters related to Bod and handle them carefully following the example set by the late 5th Dalai Lama. This will prove of great benefit to the affairs of the Bod tribe and the well–being of the people. You should live up to my trust, working ceaselessly to propagate Buddhist doctrines and enlighten the people. Be careful and prudent. With this decree I am presenting to you a 60–*liang* gold–plated silver tea vessel, a gold–plated silver vase, a silver bowl, five large and 40 small *hatas*, and 30 rolls of assorted silk, to be brought back by Dsasag Blamakacu, Bolozang Palbyor, Jrgoche Shengcu, etc.

The 10th day of the 6th month of the 1st year of Yongzheng (1723)

Preserved by the Archives of the Tibet Autonomous Region.

# གོང་མ་ཡུང་ཅིང་གིས་ཁང་ཆེན་པ་ནས་བོད་དོན་ཐག་གཅོད་དགོས་པའི་དོན་དུ་ཏཱ་ལའི་བླ་མར་བསྩལ་པའི་བཀའ་ལུང་།

# 雍正皇帝爲指派康濟鼐辦理藏務事給達賴喇嘛的敕諭

# Emperor Yongzheng's Decree to the Dalai Lama on the Appointment of Khangchennas to Administrator of Tibetan Affairs

174×110

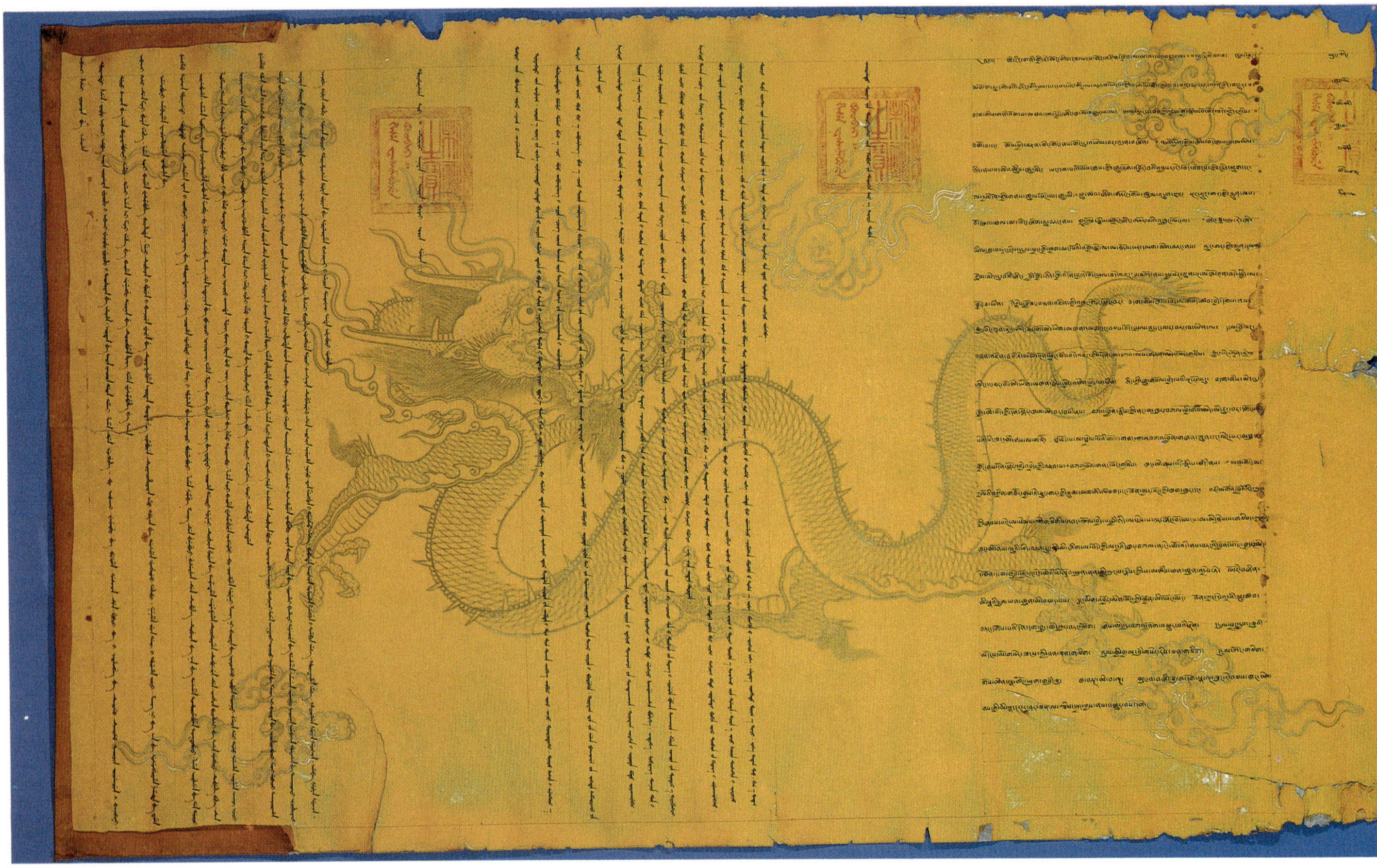

41－1

བོད་རང་སྐྱོང་ལྗོངས་ཡིག་ཚགས་ཁང་དུ་ཉར་ཚགས་བྱས་ཡོད།

41-2

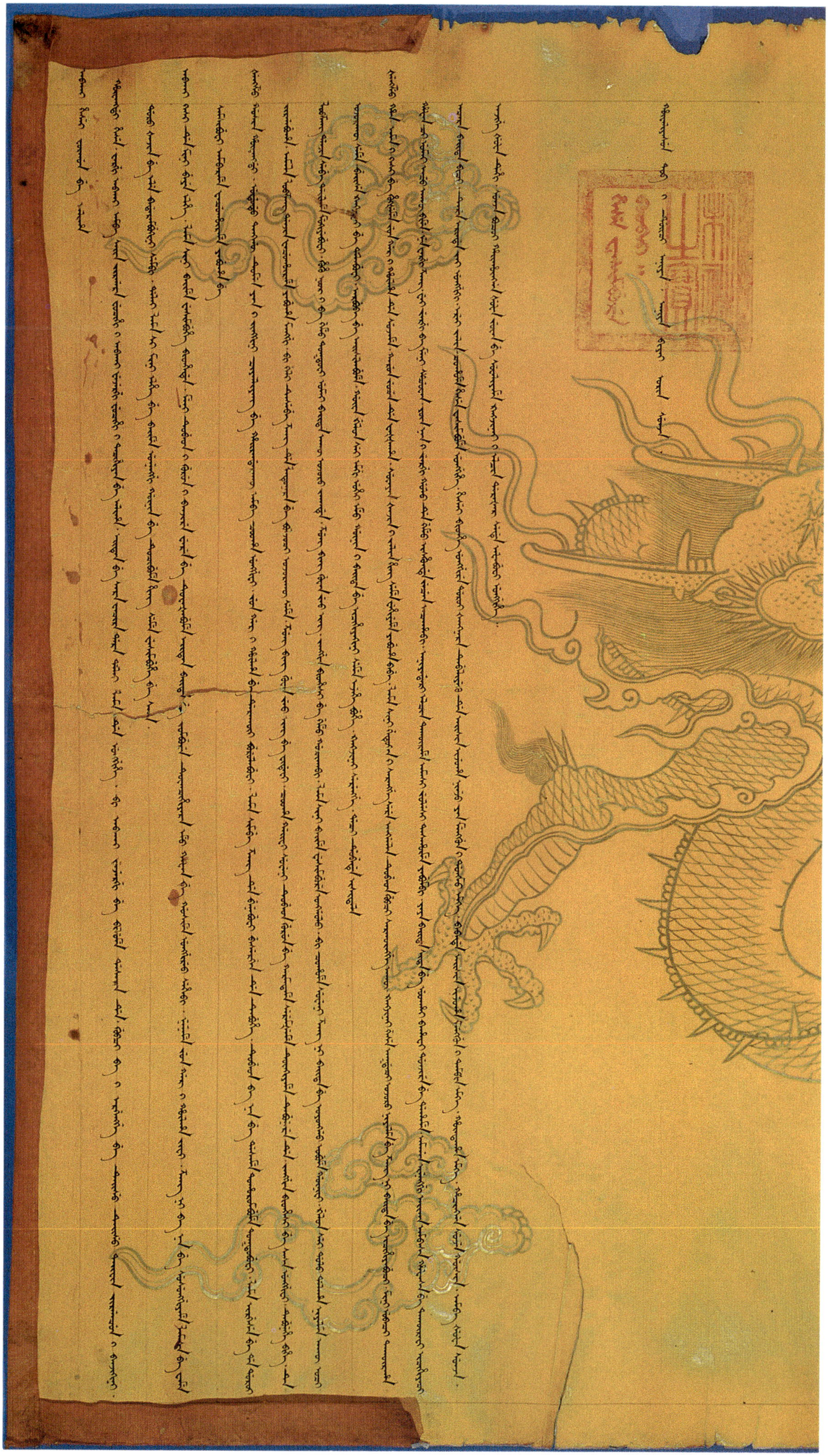

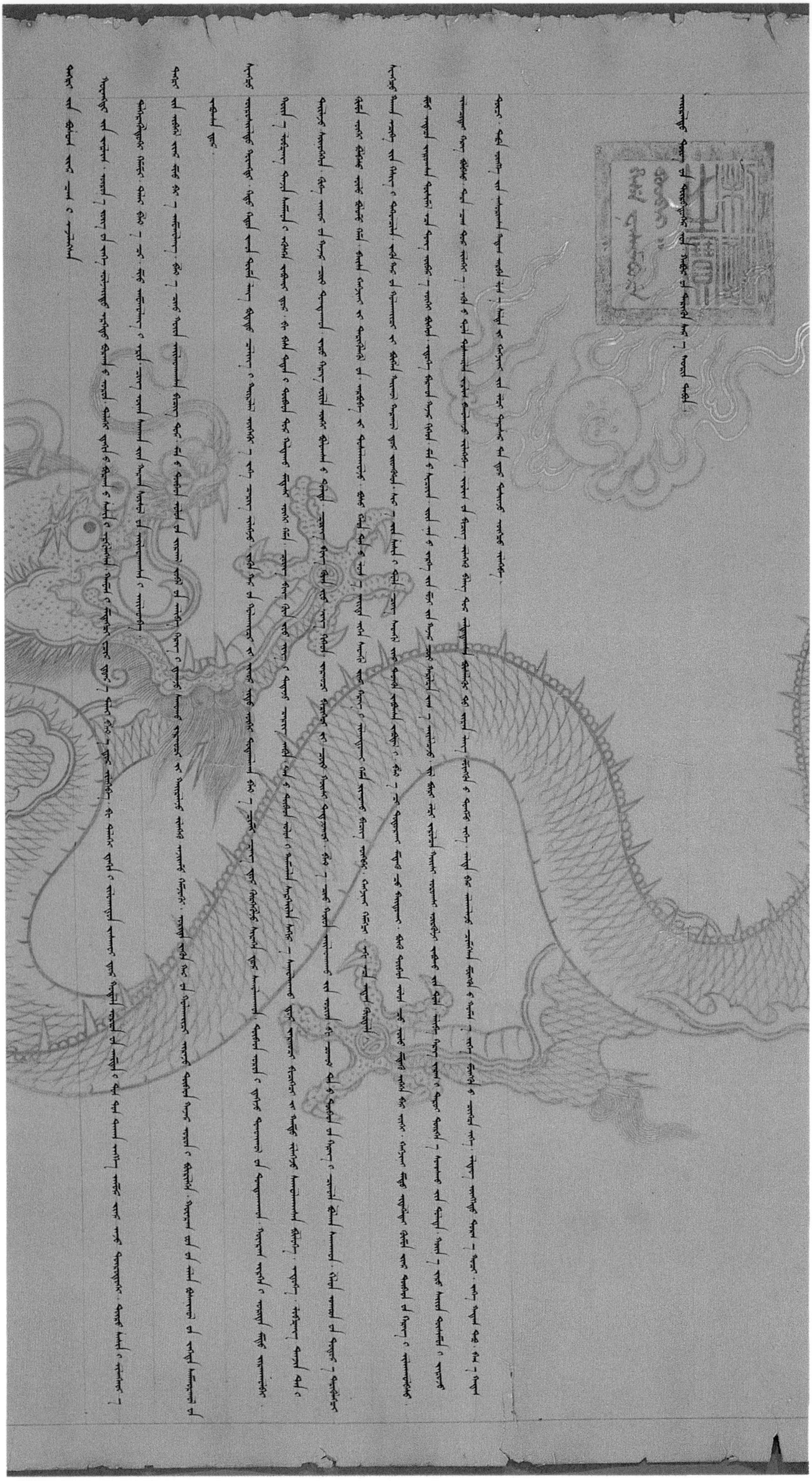

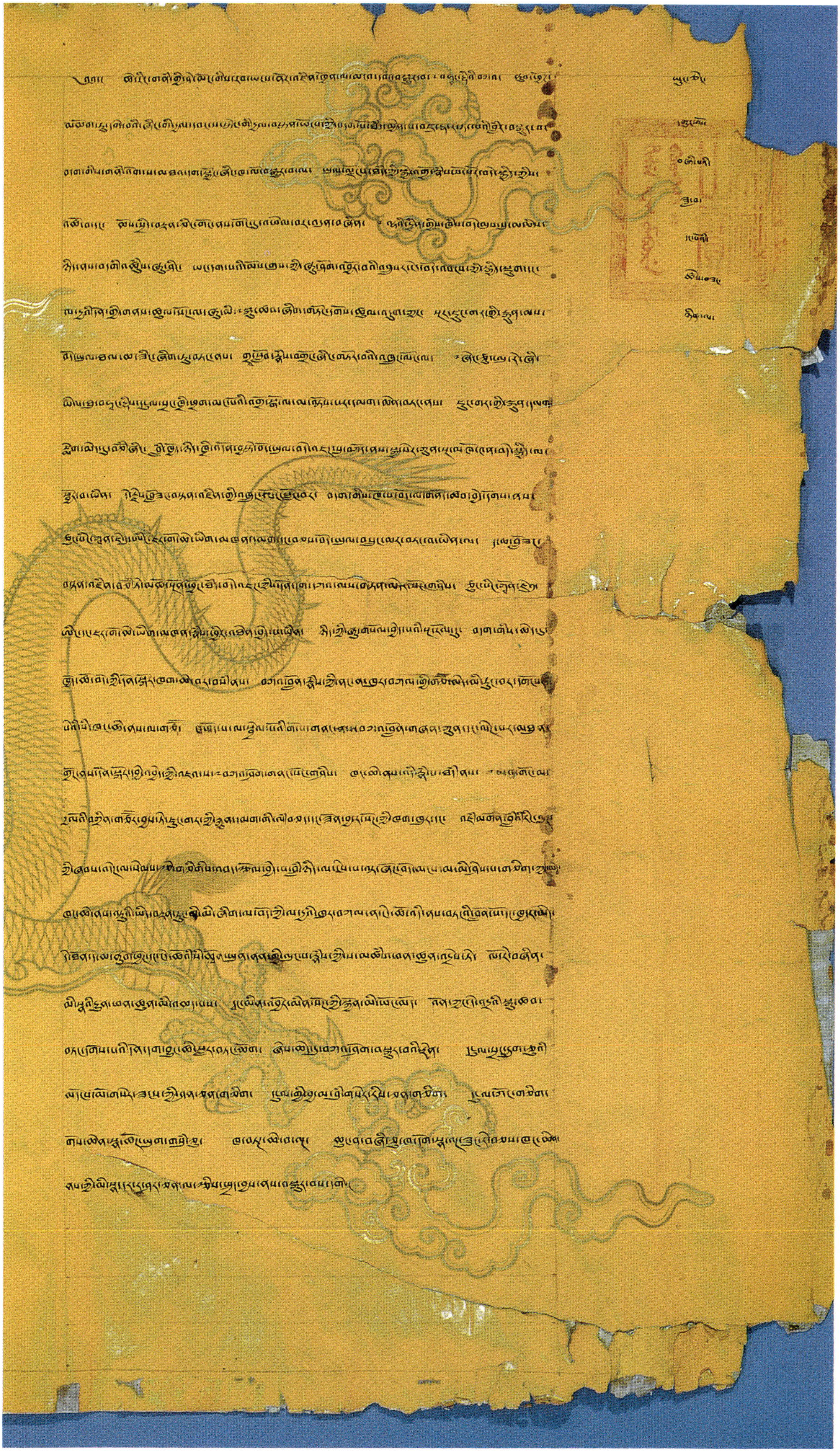

奉天承運皇帝詔曰：

諭西天大善自在佛所領天下釋教普通瓦赤喇呾喇達賴喇嘛。朕撫馭天下，惟期率土之民，各安生業，推興政教。達賴喇嘛爾上奏表請安，以示忠悃，朕覽奏。仰蒙皇天眷佑，朕體安康。據喇嘛爾奏請文書內稱：懇請派遣官員一名，以照護我土伯特部生計，教正所有事務等情。前準噶爾逆賊前來，殘害藏地，虐殺驅散喇嘛，肆行作亂，聖祖仁皇帝不惜耗費數百萬兩正項錢糧，派遣大軍全殲準噶爾賊兵後，將喇嘛爾送往藏地坐床，治理土伯特地方，俾僧俗照常安居。後羅卜藏丹津叛亂，朕又恐其侵擾藏地，不可逆料，曾調遣總兵官周瑛率兵駐守爾土伯特部，以資防衛，并派章京、筆帖式同駐，今已剿滅羅卜藏丹津，平定青海，已無事矣。故將總兵官周瑛、扎爾固齊、筆帖式均已撤回。喇嘛爾奏請之前，朕特降敕，念爾藏務爲要，因噶倫內不可無爲首之人，以康濟鼐爲首，輔佐阿爾布巴，與其他噶倫同心協力辦事等因。康濟鼐始終感戴聖祖皇考之恩，抵禦準噶爾賊，效力邊卡，爲黃教虔誠興扶之事，不僅喇嘛爾明知，即全土伯特亦無不知也。使康濟鼐般可信覽之人辦理藏務，與由朕處派遣之官員並無異，而今西地藏、衛與我川、滇等省均互相接界，每年遣使者往來不絕，凡事即可得聞。後日若有應派遣大臣官員辦理之事，彼時再派。爲此特降諭。隨敕賞賜爾鍍金六十兩重銀茶桶一個、鍍金鵝頸銀花瓶一個、銀燈一盞、各色綢緞三十匹、大哈達五條、小哈達四十條、五色哈達一條，一併交付康濟鼐使者達拉沙爾攜回。

雍正四年（公元1726年）正月二十五日

西藏自治區檔案館藏

His Majesty the Emperor, who reigns by the mandate of Heaven, decrees:

This is to instruct the Dalai Lama, the All–Knowing, the Buddha of Great Benevolence and Freedom of the Mind of the Western Paradise Who Commands All Buddhist Sects Under Heaven. As the sovereign who rules the Empire, I look forward to the people throughout the country living in peace, improving the political situation and promoting Buddhism. You, the Dalai Lama, have sent me a petition paying your respects and showing your loyalty. I have read your petition. By the grace of Heaven I am in good health. In your petition you requested that an official be sent to protect and preserve the well–being of the Bod people, handle all affairs properly, etc. When the Jungarian rebels raided Tibet, murdered and dispersed the lamas and indulged in wanton destruction, my imperial father did not hesitate to spend several million *liang* of silver, sending an expedition to exterminate the Jungarian rebels. Afterwards, you, the Dalai Lama, were sent to Lhasa to be enthroned and to administer the area, so that both the monks and the lay people could live in peace. Later, when Blozang Tandsin led a rebellion, I feared that the bandits would harass Lhasa, so I sent Commander Zhou Ying to garrison the Bod tribe to provide protection. Zhang Jing and Yigkhan were also sent. With the annihilation of Blozang Tandsin and the pacification of Qinghai peace has now returned. Therefore Commander Zhou Ying, Jrgoche and Yigkhan were recalled. However, in view of the importance of Tibetan affairs, and as the government ministers stand in need of a leader, before your petition arrived I issued a decree sending Khangchennas to assist Ngaphodpa to work with the other government ministers. Khangchennas, who has always been grateful to our imperial father, fought the Jungarian rebels and devoted himself to the defence of the border area and the promotion of the Yellow Sect of Lamaism, which is well known to you and everyone else in Bod. A man as respected as Khangchennas can administer Tibetan affairs as well as any officer sent by me. Upper and Lower Tibet share common borders with Sichuan and Yunnan provinces and envoys are frequently exchanged between them each year, so information can be easily exchanged. Other officials and ministers shall be sent whenever needed in the future. With this decree I am sending you a 60–*liang* gold–plated silver vessel for tea leaves, a gold– plated goose–necked silver vase, a silver lantern, 30 rolls of assorted silk, five large and 40 small *hatas* and a five–coloured *hata,* to be brought back by Khangchennas′ envoy Darrashar.

The 25th day of the 1st month of the 4th year of Yongzheng (1726)

Preserved by the Archives of the Tibet Autonomous Region.

# གོང་མ་ཆྱན་ལུང་གིས་ཏཱ་ལའི་བླ་མའི་ཡང་སྲིད་གསེར་ཁྲི་མངའ་གསོལ་སོགས་ཀྱི་དོན་དུ་པཎ་ཆེན་རིན་པོ་ཆེར་བསྩལ་བའི་བཀའ་ལུང་།

# 乾隆皇帝爲達賴喇嘛靈童坐床等事給班禪活佛的敕諭

# Emperor Qianlong's Decree to Living Buddha Panchen on the Enthronement of the Holy Child Dalai Lama and Other Matters

300 × 92

42 - 1

བོད་རང་སྐྱོང་ལྗོངས་ཡིག་ཚགས་ཁང་དུ་ཉར་ཚགས་བྱས་ཡོད།

奉天承運皇帝詔曰：

諭班禪額爾德尼。朕臨御大統，撫馭天下，率土之民，各安生業，推興政教。喇嘛爾闡揚釋教，普度衆生，興扶政教。仰蒙皇天眷佑，朕體安康。前第穆呼圖克圖將達賴喇嘛之呼畢勒罕延至聶塘寺居住，朕曾降諭恐呼畢勒罕年幼，畏懼見人，尚未熟諳經卷，俟達賴喇嘛長成後再見人則不畏懼矣等因。今據喇嘛爾、第穆呼圖克圖奏請，達賴喇嘛之呼畢勒罕今已長大成人，不畏懼見人，請迎至布達拉宮坐床等情。呼畢勒罕坐床乃一盛大喜事，故朕特派遣喀爾喀親王銜車布登扎布、副都統富精、阿嘉呼圖克圖、頭等侍衛富凌阿等，與爾等會合，擇一吉日，共同看視呼畢勒罕坐床。達賴喇嘛雖已坐床，班禪額爾德尼爾親奉佛法、利濟群生已年久矣，爾宜於達賴喇嘛之學習，善加教導，務照前世達賴喇嘛崇揚黃教［原文缺失］……隨敕賞爾［原文缺失］……黃緞四匹、片金緞一匹、紅緞二匹、大哈達五條、小哈達十條［原文缺失］……

乾隆二十七年（公元1762年）正月

西藏自治區檔案館藏

His Majesty the Emperor, who reigns by the mandate of Heaven, decrees:

These are the instructions to the Panchen Erdeni. I sit on the throne and rule the Empire allowing the people throughout the land to live in peace, improve the political situation and promote Buddhism. You, the Panchen Lama, also expound Buddhism, comfort all living beings, work to improve the political situation and promote Buddhism. By the grace of Heaven I am in good health. Some time ago, when Living Buddha Demo extended an invitation to the child Dalai Lama to reside in the Nyethang Monastery, I issued a decree containing instructions to the effect that, since he was so young, the child would be shy in the presence of strangers and would not be familiar with the scriptures, but that he would lose his shyness when he grew up. Now you, the Panchen Lama, and Living Buddha Demo have delivered a petition stating that the child Dalai Lama has grown up and is no longer shy when meeting people. Therefore, you have asked permission to extend an invitation to him to come to the Potala Palace to be enthroned. The enthronement of the Holy Child is a grand occasion, so I am sending Khalha Prince, Tshertankyab, deputy banner commander Fu Jing, Living Buddha Askya and imperial bodyguard 1st–class Hulunga to join you. You are to pick an auspicious day and jointly preside over the enthronement ceremony. Even after the Dalai Lama has been enthroned, you, the Panchen Erdeni, having for many years embraced the Buddhist faith and aided the people, should work to direct the child Dalai Lama's study so that he may follow the example of the Dalai Lama of the last incarnation in promoting the Yellow Sect of Lamaism... [missing in the original] with this decree I am presenting you with... [missing in the original] four rolls of yellow satin, a roll of gold–flake satin, two rolls of red satin, five large and 10 small *hatas*... [missing in the original]...

The 1st month of the 27th year of Qianlong (1762)

Preserved by the Archives of the Tibet Autonomous Region.

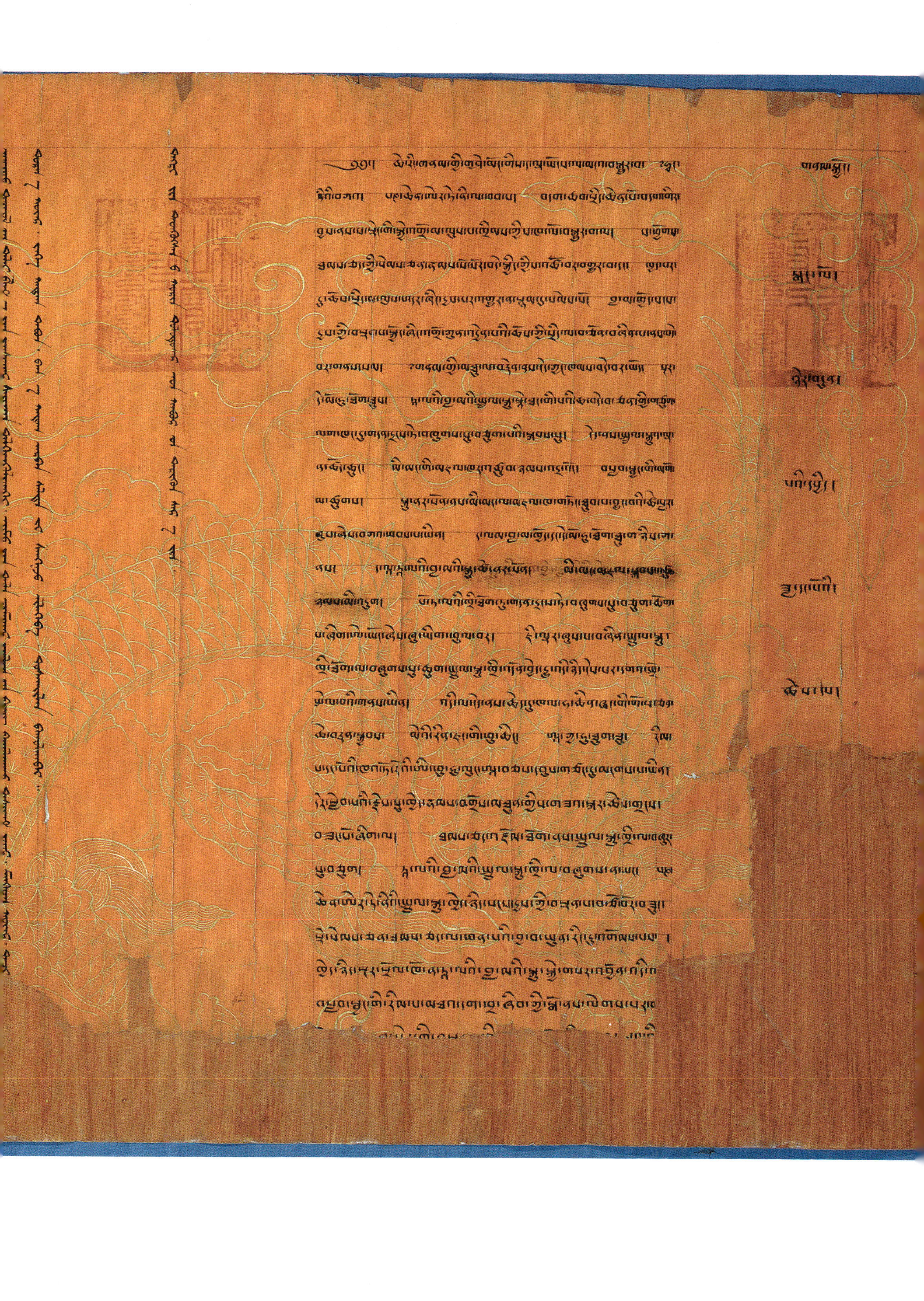

༄༅། །ཨོཾ་སྭསྟི། [illegible]

[illegible]

# 43

## གོང་མ་ལྷ་སྐྱོང་གིས་གསེར་ཁྲི་མངའ་གསོལ་གྱི་དོན་དུ་དྷ་ལའི་བླ་མར་བསྩལ་བའི་བཀའ་ལུང་།

## 乾隆皇帝爲坐床事給達賴喇嘛靈童的敕諭

## Emperor Qianlong's Decree to the Holy Child Dalai Lama Allowing Him to Take the Throne

150 × 82

43 - 1

བོད་རང་སྐྱོང་ལྗོངས་ཡིག་ཚགས་ཁང་དུ་ཉར་ཚགས་བྱས་ཡོད།

奉天承運皇帝詔曰：

諭達賴喇嘛之呼畢勒罕。朕撫馭天下，以其率土之民，各安生業，推興政教。前世達賴喇嘛弘揚釋教、普度衆生。今班禪額爾德尼、第穆呼圖克圖等奏請爾於布達拉宮坐床等因。故此朕特派遣喀爾喀親王銜車布登扎布等，看視爾於布達拉宮坐床。惟呼畢勒罕甚年少，尚未熟諳經卷，此間務必勤習經卷，仍照前世達賴喇嘛鑽研佛訓，闡揚黄教，勿違朕遵奉黄教之至意。隨敕賞爾純花大佛像掛圖一軸、哈達一條、裝净水銀花瓶一個、銀脚玉耳碗一隻、銀壇場一座、珐琅八瑞相八吉物各一份、西洋寶石轉輪一對、深藍玻璃五供一份、通人冠一頂、袈裟一件、七經衣一件、五經裙一條、經墊一塊、緊身服一件、腰帶一條、披單一塊、巾束一副、珍珠十四顆裝飾之腰帶二條，黄緞貂皮襖面一件、珊瑚佛珠一串、銀桶一個、銀茶壺一把、小銀茶碗一只、黄緞手支棍靠背坐褥一套、黄花大荷包一對、綉花小荷包四對、深藍玉如意一支、玉扁方花瓶一個、碧玉酒瓶一個、華蓋頂幔一副、金邊珐琅器皿一雙、珐琅寶瓶一個、四花瓣型珐琅器皿一個、珐郎油燈一盞、珐琅大小碗各一對、珐琅盤一雙、珐郎大器皿一對、搪瓷盆一個、搪瓷桶一對、搪

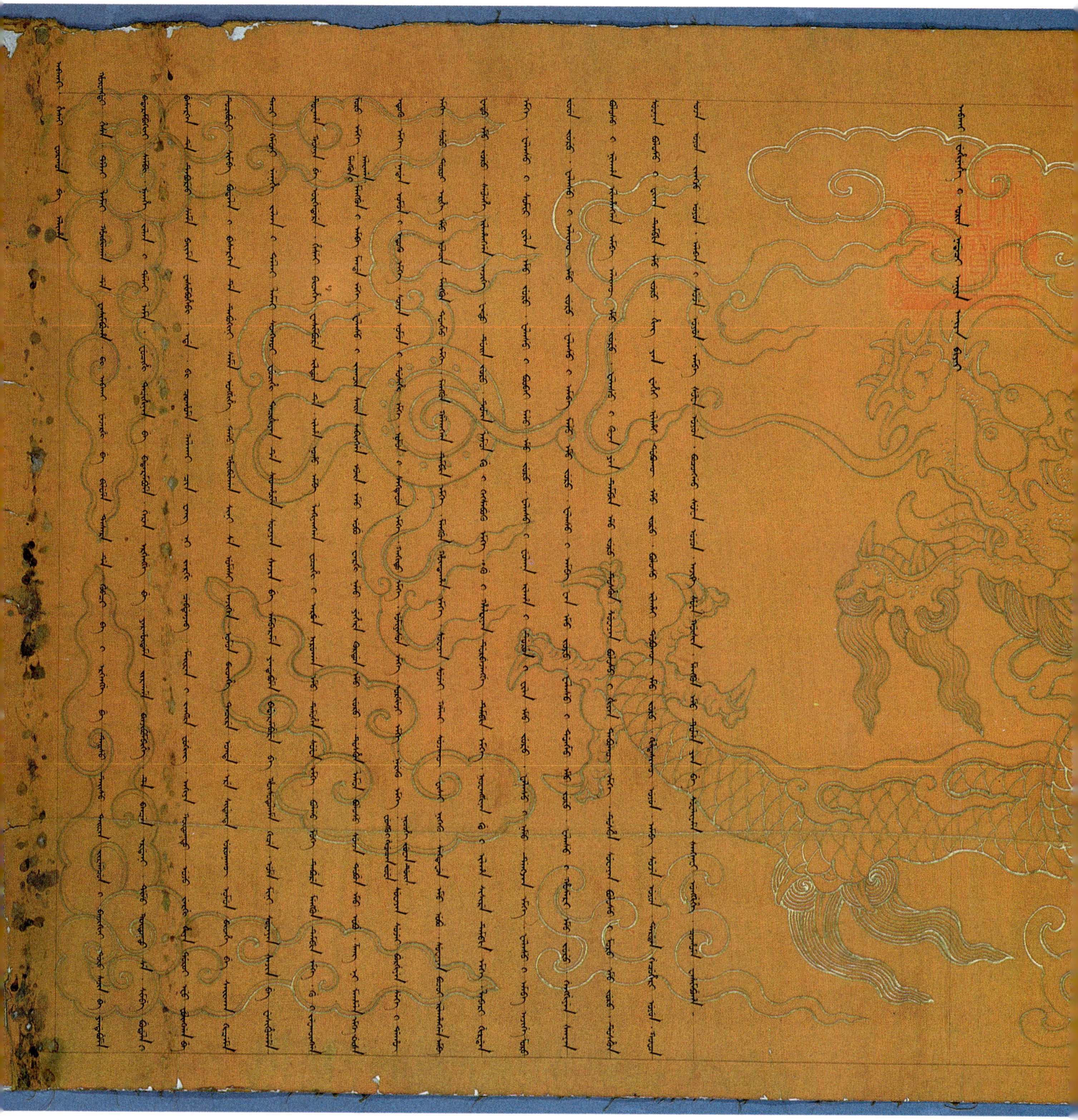

43－2

瓷開闢盒一個、白玻璃磨花大器皿一對、珐琅長頸小水瓶一對、暗黄玻璃香燈一盞、暗黄玻璃碗一隻、暗黄玻璃橄欖花瓶一對、寶石花酒瓶一對、玻璃花酒瓶一對、片金緞九匹、大緞九匹、銅錢花緞九匹、彭緞九匹、漳絨九匹、普通緞九匹、大哈達九條、各色哈達九條、小哈達三十條、銀一萬

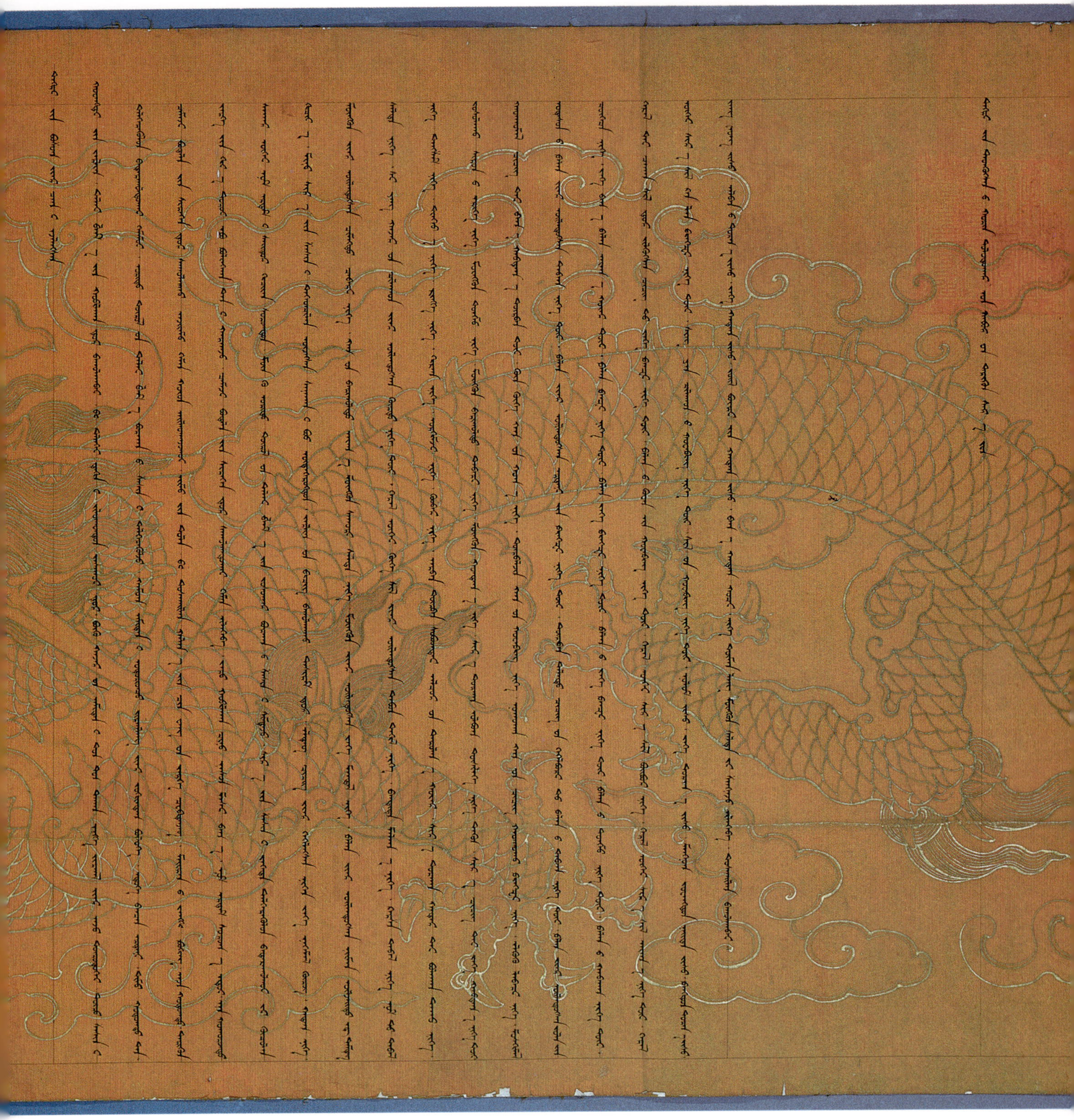

43 - 3

兩，一併交送。特諭。

乾隆二十七年（公元1762年）正月

西藏自治區檔案館藏

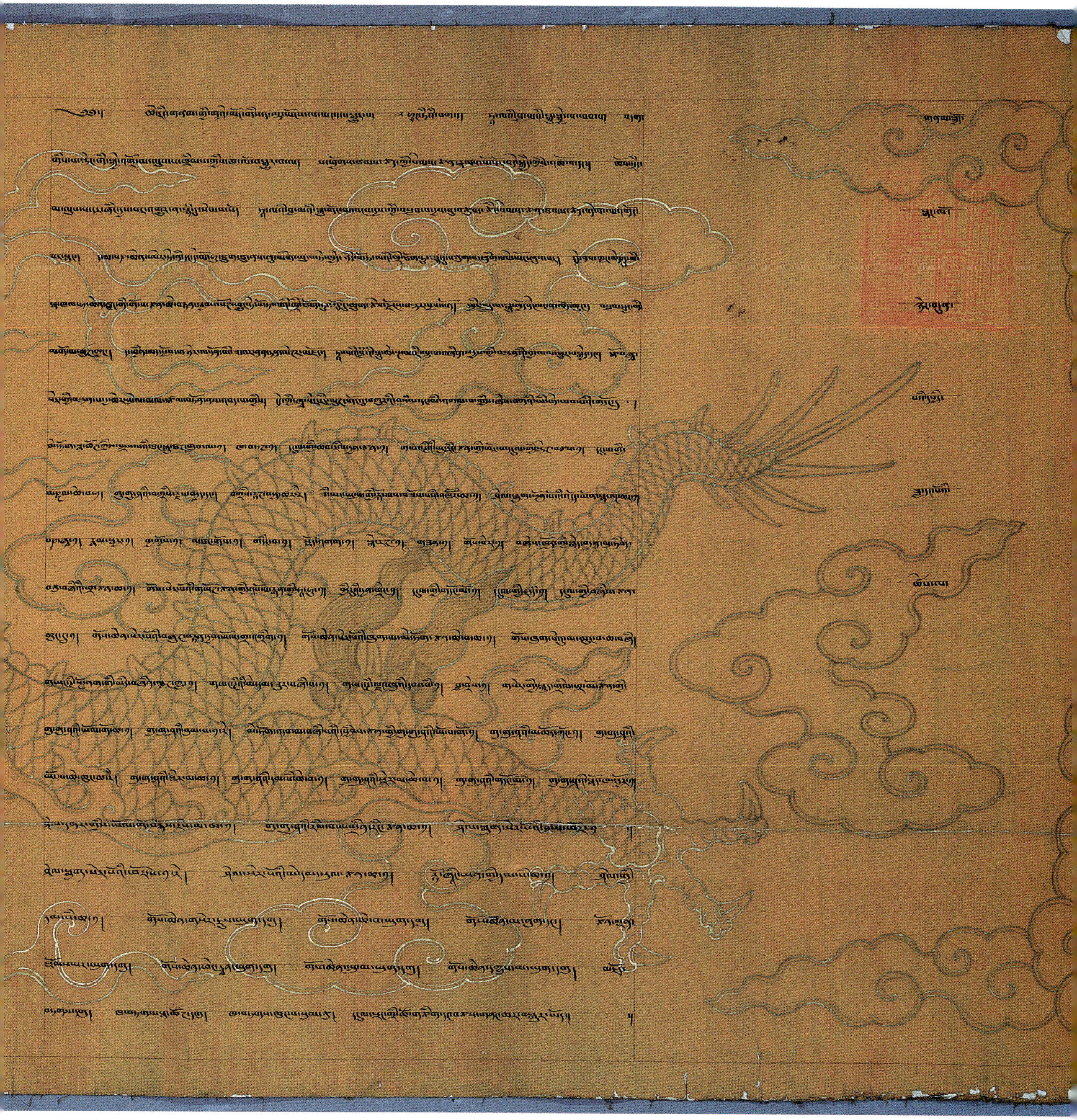

43 - 4

His Majesty the Emperor, who reigns by the mandate of Heaven, decrees:

These are the instructions to the child Dalai Lama. I rule the Empire allowing people all over the country to live in peace, improve the political situation and promote Buddhism. The

Dalai Lama of the last incarnation promoted Buddhism and comforted all living beings. The Panchen Erdeni and Living Buddha Demo have petitioned me for permission to have you enthroned in the Potala Palace. I am sending Khalha Prince Tshertankyab and others to preside over your enthronement in the Potala Palace. Since you are still young and have not become familiar with the scriptures yet, you must work diligently to become familiar with the scriptures and follow the example of the Dalai Lama of the last incarnation in studying the Buddhist doctrines and expounding the Yellow Sect, which you should keep in mind is my earnest wish. With this mandate I am presenting you with a hanging scroll depicting the Buddha with a floral background, a *hata,* a silver vase for holding holy water, a bowl with jade handles and silver base, a silver mandala, a set each of eight auspicious enamel images and amulets, a pair of prayer wheels studded with Western precious stones, a set of the five articles for worship of dark blue glass, a peaked crown, a *kasaya,* a *qijing* robe, a *wujing* apron, a scripture–cushion, a close–fitting garment, a girdle, a shawl, a pair of scarves, two belts studded with 14 pearls, a yellow satin coat lined with marten fur, a chaplet of coral beads, a silver container, a silver tea pot, a small silver tea bowl, a set of yellow satin cushions with wooden frames, a pair of pouches embroidered with yellow flowers, four pairs of small embroidered pouches, a pair of dark blue jade *ruyi,* a jade vase with rectangular top, an emerald wine decanter, a pair of decorated canopies, a pair of gold–rimmed enamelware containers, an enamelware flask, a 4–petal style enamelware container, an enamelware oil lamp, one pair of large and one pair of small enamelware bowls, a pair of enamelware plates, a pair of large enamelware containers, an enamelware basin, a pair of enamelware pails, an enamelware box, a pair of large clear ground glass containers, a pair of small long–necked enamelware flagons, a dark yellow glass fragrance lantern, a dark yellow glass bowl, a pair of dark yellow olive–shaped glass vases, a pair of wine decanters decorated with precious stones, a pair of glass wine decanters, nine rolls of gold–flake satin, nine rolls of brocade, nine rolls of satin with coin design, nine rolls of *peng* satin, nine rolls of *zhang* velvet, nine rolls of plain satin, nine large and 30 small *hatas,* nine assorted *hatas,* and 10,000 *liang* of silver, to be delivered all together. This is the end of the instructions.

The 1st month of the 27th year of Qianlong (1762)

Preserved by the Archives of the Tibet Autonomous Region.

44

# དགའ་ལྡན་ཁྲི་པ་ཨེར་ཏི་ནི་ནོ་མིན་ཧན་སོགས་ཀྱིས་བཀའ་བློན་ཆད་གསབ་ཀྱི་དོན་དུ་བོད་བཞུགས་ཨམ་བན་ལ་བཏང་བའི་ཞུ་ཡིག

# 噶丹赤巴額爾德尼諾門汗等爲補任噶倫事報駐藏大臣呈文

# Petition from Gavldan Khripa Ertini Nominhan and Others to the Resident Ministers in Tibet Concerning the Filling of a Government Minister Vacancy

104×54

བོད་རང་སྐྱོང་ལྗོངས་ཡིག་ཚགས་ཁང་དུ་ཉར་ཚགས་བྱས་ཡོད།

諸駐藏大臣：

爲噶倫札薩大汗堪布格桑丹增郎杰辭去噶倫之職補缺一事，依照皇帝所發第十三條佈告內開：由熟識黃教喇嘛內選噶倫後，册頒札薩克大喇嘛封誥，如與其它噶倫一起共事，有益於僧俗民衆。如此慣例，永久不變，故按傳統，由達賴喇嘛內侍僧人中選任噶倫爲好。

仲譯格桑朗杰之舅司膳札巴塔葉曾經多年負責前輩達賴喇嘛司膳工作，忠心耿耿。對此，前輩達賴喇嘛十分賞識，爲出色大司膳堪布之一。其侄仲譯格桑朗杰年滿四十三歲，自幼皈依佛門，善識教義。自年幼時起前輩達賴喇嘛即十分賞識，文秘人員中，此人知識淵博，後來第穆呼圖克圖任其爲達賴喇嘛之司膳堪布和秘書，此人辦事富有經驗，故此輩達賴喇嘛也十分賞識。至今他擔任內侍大堪布及秘書、司膳堪布等職，辦理一切大小事務，始終忠心耿耿，刻苦正直，精通文、算等項知識，沉着機智，能遵行一切。因此大汗堪布格桑丹增朗杰辭去噶倫之職，請求將仲譯格桑朗杰補此噶倫任缺。請予批示，祈請明鑒。此上所述非常重要，吾噶丹赤巴額爾德尼經過詳查，並與噶倫公班智達等經過權衡，共同商定呈上此文，望駐藏大臣將此轉奏。

噶丹赤巴額爾德尼諾門汗暨全體噶倫共禀。

土狗年（公元1778年）九月

西藏自治區檔案館藏

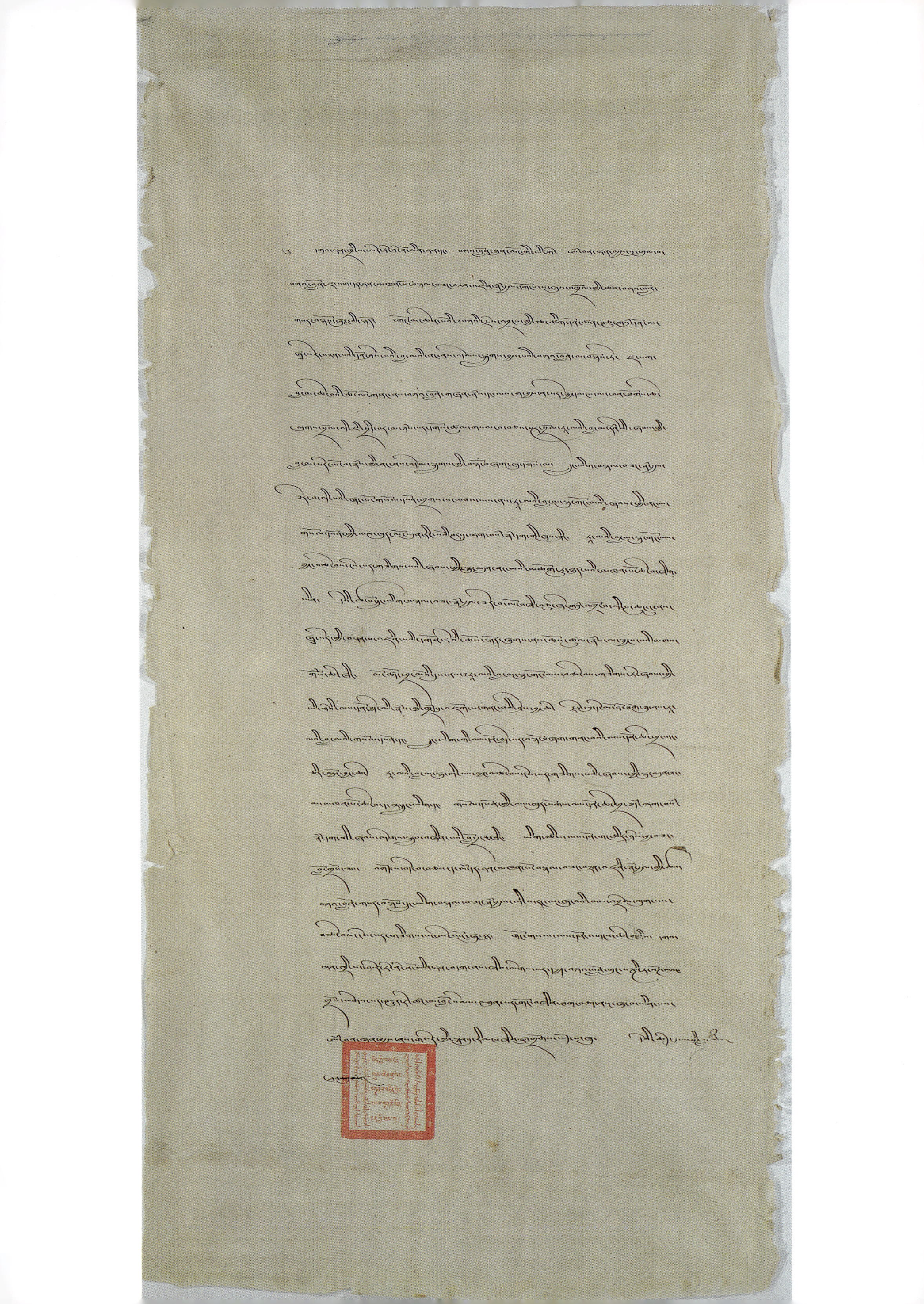

[illegible]

Resident Ministers in Tibet,

Concerning the filling of the vacancy of a government minister caused by the resignation of Minister Dsasag Darhand Khanpo Kalzang Tandsin Namgyail: According to Article 13 of the proclamation issued by His Majesty the Emperor, the post of a government minister is to be filled by a lama selected from among those who are familiar with the Yellow Sect of Lamaism, and the title and certificate are to be presented by Dsasag Blamakacu. A candidate who can work together with the other government ministers will prove of benefit to both the monks and the public at large. This practice shall remain unchanged for ever. Traditionally, it has seemed best to pick a candidate from among the Dalai Lama's attendant monks to serve as a government minister.

Gragpa Thavyas, uncle of Kalzang Namgyal, formerly served for many years as a caterer for the Dalai Lama of the last incarnation. His loyalty won the appreciation of the former Dalai Lama and he has been one of the outstanding Grand Khanpos in charge of catering affairs. His nephew Kalzang Namgyal, now 43, has embraced Buddhism from boyhood and is well acquainted with its doctrines. As a boy, he was held in high regard by the former Dalai Lama and later became a learned member of his secretarial staff. He was appointed by Living Buddha Demo as a Khanpo in charge of catering affairs and secretary for the Dalai Lama. He has a great store of working experience and is also highly regarded by the present Dalai Lama. Currently he is serving as the attendant Grand Khanpo, secretary and Khanpo in charge of catering affairs, handling matters great and small. He is loyal, hardworking, honest, well versed in literature and mathematics, cool-headed and resourceful, and faithfully follows all instructions. Now that Minister Dsasag Darhand Khanpo Kalzang Tandsin Namgyail has resigned from his post, we recommend that the vacancy be filled by Kalzang Namgyal. Please review this matter and send your instructions. The above is very important and I, Gavldan Khripa Ertini, have made a detailed investigation of this matter, discussing it and comparing my conclusions with Minister Gungpan Trita and others before arriving at the above solution which we now submit to you in this petition. We entreat the Resident Ministers in Tibet to submit this to His Majesty.

Submitted by Gavldan Khripa Ertini Nominhan and all the government ministers.

The Year of the Earth Dog (September 1778)

Preserved by the Archives of the Tibet Autonomous Region.

# བཀའ་བློན་ཁྲུན་མོང་གིས་ཁྲི་ཆེན་ནོ་མིན་ཧན་ལ་ཕུལ་བའི་ཞུ་ཡིག
# 衆噶倫致噶丹赤巴諾門汗函
# Letter from the Government Ministers to Gavldan Khripa Nominhan

68 × 49.2

བོད་རང་སྐྱོང་ལྗོངས་ཡིག་ཚགས་ཁང་དུ་ཉར་ཚགས་བྱས་ཡོད།

無數衆生和佛教的救主噶丹赤巴諾門汗惠鑒：

謹呈。值此良辰吉日，集一切佛陀之智、悲、力爲一體的人主之三密相好——閃耀着侍奉文殊大皇帝而利濟衆生之吉祥光輝的貴體安好? 派遣扎薩克喇嘛送來之印信，業已拜悉，實感恩不盡。包括天界在內衆生之至高無上的普通達賴喇嘛之相好光芒四射，我等衆人亦均健康，勤勉效力於公務。在此呈述如下，誠如閣下印信內開，受妖魔唆使之教敵廓爾喀人陸續侵佔了尼泊爾三部、南方之熱卡、札布曾等地以及西方諸侯國，確屬貪得無厭。儘管西藏和廓爾喀自第五世達賴喇嘛起便存在友好關係，但彼等全然不顧及此，竟以銀幣章喀和有關規定爲借口，自去年六月末以來，派兵侵佔聶拉木、吉隆、薩嘎等與尼泊爾接壤地帶，大軍壓境，兵臨協嘎，顯示邊夷之野蠻，妒恨吉祥幸福政教合一的噶丹波章。爲此，我方已調派衛、藏、塔、貢地區軍隊，同盤踞於協嘎、薩嘎之廓爾喀兵作戰，以色拉、哲蚌、甘丹三寺爲首各教派亦進行了阻攔敵人的禳災大法事。特別是文殊大皇帝仁愛西藏，陸續派遣將軍、提督等官員，率漢、滿、嘉戎等大軍前來協嘎。消息傳出，敵人震驚，盤踞於此之廓爾喀軍已紛紛退却。至於軍餉一事，欽遵大皇帝聖旨和閣下印照指令，此次派遣官兵喇嘛，純屬爲西藏之利益，爲酬報此無量功德，達賴喇嘛的內外管家府由閣下此間從衛藏各宗溪收納之倉儲浄糧中支撥二萬三千藏斗，並從各牧區調撥食用牛羊，獻作軍餉，均未收款。此事去年業經二位大臣具折奏報，奉文殊大皇帝閱批："達賴喇嘛所言極是，惟從庫內支撥物資應付銀兩，以用於善事。欽此。"今後我等仍須籌集軍餉，衛藏貴族及僧俗民衆亦願交納五萬藏斗糧食。此事業已上報，因二位大臣公務繁冗，不知呈報閣下之文是否已送至貴處。蒙文殊大皇帝無比仁恤西藏民衆、關懷佛教，派來大軍，故我等定能滅除佛教之敵人廓爾喀人。惟西藏地狹勢弱，對官兵軍餉之解運，能否妥善辦理，尚有疑慮。邊陲生計均賴互市貿易，爲西藏、尼泊爾雙方邊民利益計，已於札什倫布和薩迦，雙邊簽訂了和約。在吉隆，雙方貴族亦已會晤，事態有所緩解，惟願衆官兵不日即可返歸。對此，閣下有何賜教? 我衆噶倫等全體官吏員役均願爲達賴喇嘛盡心效力，願與邊疆內地之佛業衆生、與普通達賴喇嘛師徒、與對佛教和衆生功德無量之文殊大皇帝同心同德。請閣下銘記西藏乃佛教之聖地，勿爲邪惡所動搖，仍以慈悲爲懷，經常來信指教。祝閣下爲佛教和衆生安樂、健康長壽，請遵照文殊大皇帝之旨意，爲推興佛教和衆生偉業，對我等臣民作慈悲的佑助。

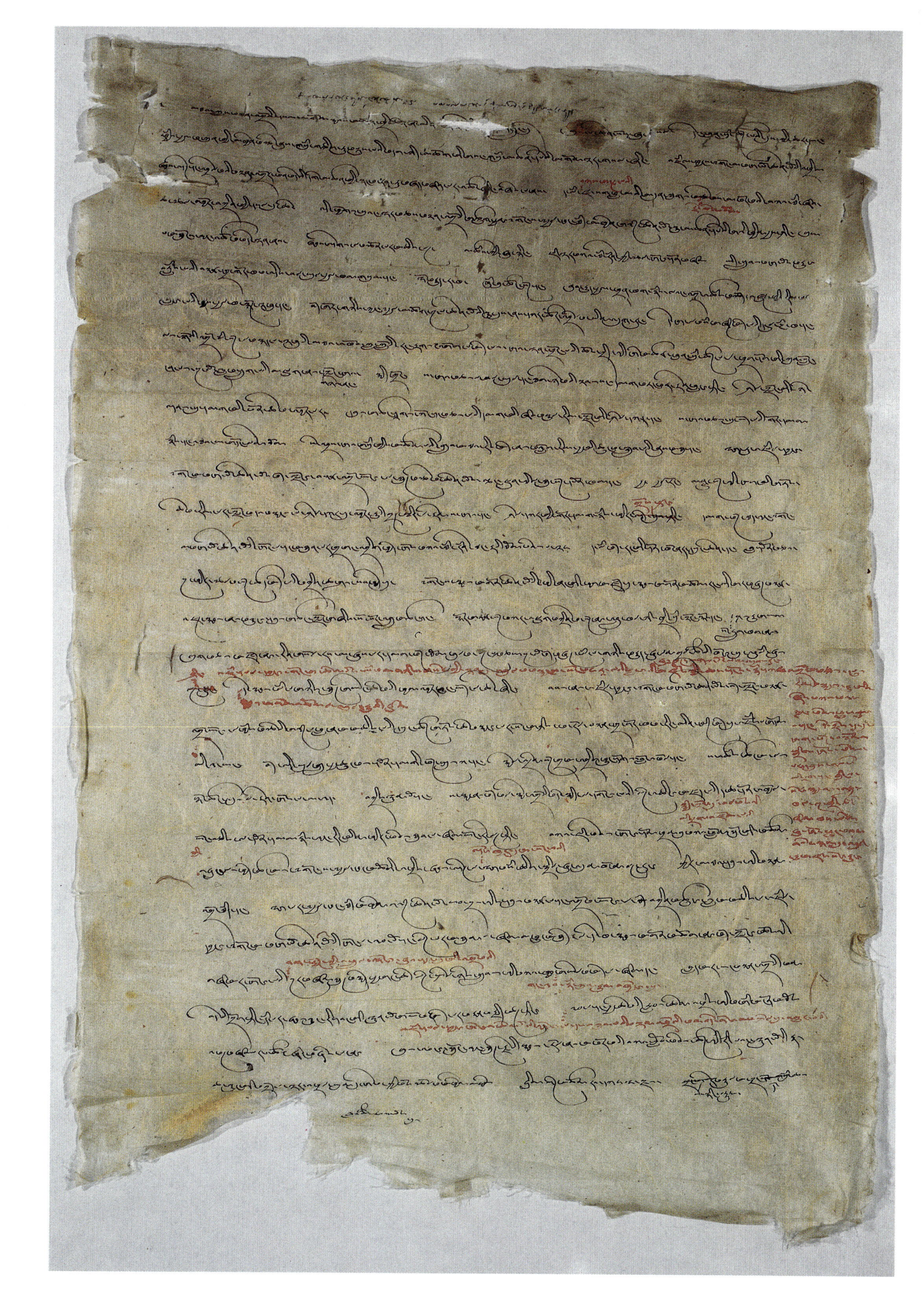

此獻潔白哈達一條、純金二兩。

西藏自治區檔案館藏

Gavldan Khripa Nominhan, Saviour of Buddhism and the Multitudes of Living Beings, kindly read the following:

On this auspicious day we wish you well, noble person who embodies the intelligence, benevolence and power of Lord Buddha and radiates with the auspicious glory that comes from serving His Majesty the Emperor and being good to all living beings. We are deeply grateful for the letter you sent through Dsasag Lama. Concerned with the well–being of all living beings in heaven and on earth, the boundless, all–knowing Dalai Lama brilliantly shines in all directions and we are in good health and diligently working hard in the public interest. For this reason we beg to state as follows. Just as Your Excellency's letter has made clear, the Gurkhas, enemies of our religion, acting under the devil's spell, have successively invaded and occupied the three regions of Nepal as well as Rakha and Khumbutsong in the south, in addition to some dukedoms and principalities to the west, showing insatiable greed. They are oblivious to the fact that friendly relations between Tibet and Gurkha have existed since the time of the 5th Dalai Lama. Using the matter of the Tibetan silver coin and the relevant stipulations as an excuse, since the end of the sixth month last year they have been sending troops to occupy Nyalam, Gyirong and Saga which adjoin Nepal as a large enemy force advances on the border and closes in on Xegar, showing the barbarity of the foreigners across the border in their enmity against the Tibetan government, which represents the auspicious and happy union of politics and religion. As a result, we dispatched troops from Upper and Lower Tibet, and from the Ta and Gong areas to battle the Gurkha soldiers that were entrenched in Xegar and Saga. In the meantime, the religious sects in the monasteries headed by the Ser, Braspus and Dgav monasteries also worked to restrain the enemy and prevent calamity. Of special importance were the generals and commanders with their Han, Manchu and Jiarong troops sent to Xegar by His Majesty the Emperor out of his kindness and concern for Tibet. When the news reached the enemy, the Gurkhas, they became frightened and rapidly retreated. As for the matter of supplies for the army, in compliance with His Majesty the Emperor's holy edict and Your Excellency's instructions which stated that the despatching of troops and lamas was solely for the benefit of Tibet, the Dalai Lama, to repay such boundless benevolence, has ordered his internal and external affairs stewards to set aside 23,000 Tibetan *dous* (1 Tibetan *dou* is equivalent to 14 kilogrammes) of grain from county and manorial granaries in Upper and Lower Tibet and gather cattle and sheep from every range area to provide for the army, with no money to be paid for any of this. This matter was reported to the throne by the Resident Ministers in Tibet last year whereupon His Majesty the Emperor issued these instructions. "The Dalai Lama is perfectly correct in saying that supplies and money should be allocated from the treasury for good causes." In the days to come, we shall still need to amass supplies for the army, for which the nobles, monks and civilians in Upper and Lower Tibet have already pledged to supply 50,000 Tibetan *dous* of grain. Although this matter has been reported to you, we cannot be certain that the document has come to Your Excellency's attention, because the two ministers are so busy with public affairs. Thanks to His Majesty the Emperor's benevolence and kindness towards the Tibetan multitudes, his concern for Buddhism, and his sending of the army, we shall certainly be able to annihilate the Gurkhas, enemies of Buddhism. However, considering that Tibet is weak and the land area is small, it is still not certain that the delivery of pay and supplies for the officers and soldiers can be handled properly. People in the border areas depend on trade for a living, so in the interests of both the Tibetan and Nepalese people in the border areas, a peace treaty was concluded between the two sides at Tashilhunpo and Sa'gya. Nobles from both sides have also met in Gyirong, easing the situation and we hope the officers and soldiers will be able to go home soon. What would be Your Excellency's instructions concerning this matter? We government ministers and all the other officials and their staffs have pledged to serve the Dalai Lama and work wholeheartedly for the Buddhist followers in the border areas and other areas, for the Dalai Lama and his disciples, as well as for His Majesty the Emperor, who has lavished his boundless benevolence on Buddhism and all living beings. Please keep in mind, Your Excellency, that Tibet is a sacred land of Buddhism. Do not be tempted by evil but be always motivated by benevolence and write often for our advice. For the sake of Buddhism and the peace and happiness of all living beings, we wish Your Excellency good health and a long life. We also hope that you will follow His Majesty the Emperor's orders and continue your benevolent protection and assistance to us, both officials and civilians, for the great task of the promotion of Buddhism and the benefit of all living beings.

We present you with a pure white *hata* and two *liang* of pure gold.

Preserved by the Archives of the Tibet Autonomous Region.

# ཁྲིན་ཏུའི་ཅང་ཅུན་ཨོ་ཧེ་སོགས་ཀྱིས་བོད་དམག་སྦྱོང་བརྡར་གྱི་དོན་དུ་བཀའ་བློན་བསྟན་འཛིན་དཔལ་འབྱོར་སོགས་ལ་བཏང་བའི་བསྒྲགས་ཡིག

# 成都將軍鄂輝等爲操練藏兵事曉諭噶布倫丹津班珠爾等

# Explicit Instructions from General E Hui of Chengdu to Government Minister Tandsin Palbyor Concerning the Training of Tibetan Soldiers

240 × 24.2

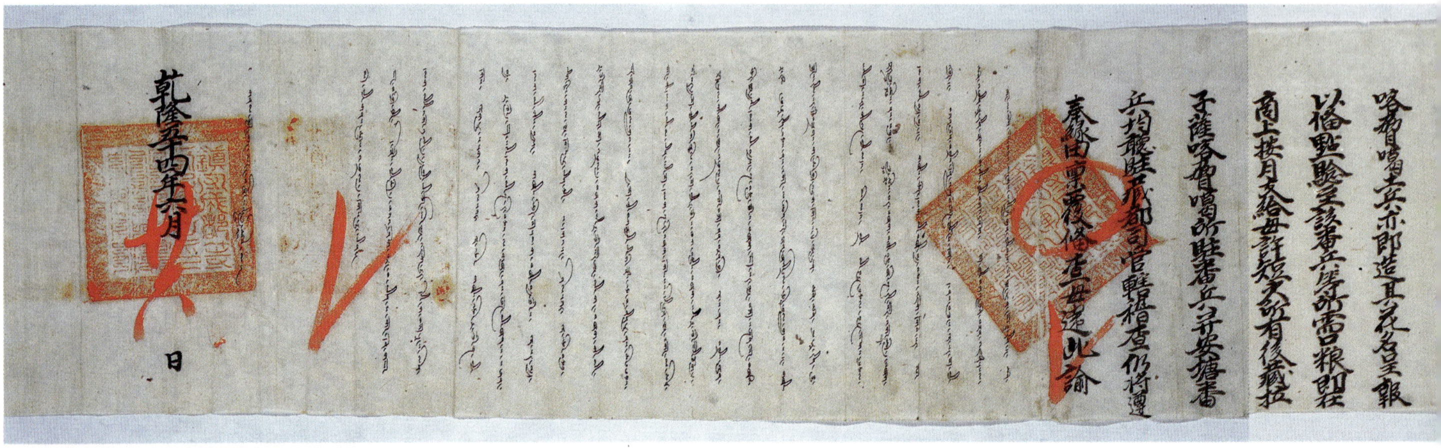
喀布倫噶兵亦即造具花名呈報
以憑點驗其該番兵等所需糧餉
商上按月支給毋許短欠所有後藏拉
子薩喀會噶所駐番兵亦要擄番
兵均飭駐藏都司官轄稽查仍將遵
奏緣由專覆備查毋違此諭
乾隆五十四年六月 日

46－1

General E in Charge of Chengdu and Surrounding Area in Sichuan by Imperial Order and Senior Officer in Command of Military Affairs of Sichuan and Councillor–Minister Cheng by Imperial Order hereby instruct government minister Tandsin Palbyor and others as follows:

It is hereby noted that according to the "Programme for Improved Administration of Tibet", every year after the autumn harvest, from the latter half of the 9th month to the end of the 10th month, the 800 Tibetan soldiers to be transferred to Bod from Upper Tibet and the 400 Tibetan soldiers to be transferred to Bod from Lower Tibet should be assembled for training for these 40 days or so after which they are to be sent back to their villages to live in peace. This matter has been reported by the two of us, together with His Excellencies Shu, Ba and Pu, in a petition to His Majesty the Emperor and duly recorded. In accordance with this, when we, General E and Councillor Cheng, arrived at Tashilhunpo, we personally drilled the guards stationed in the green–banner camp and ordered them to repair the barracks properly. There are 12 posts located between Lower and Upper Tibet, and every post should have a *tang*, or subpost, to be manned by four or five local people to be responsible for the delivery

བོད་རང་སྐྱོང་ལྗོངས་ཡིག་ཚགས་ཁང་དུ་ཉར་ཚགས་བྱས་ཡོད།

西藏自治區檔案館藏

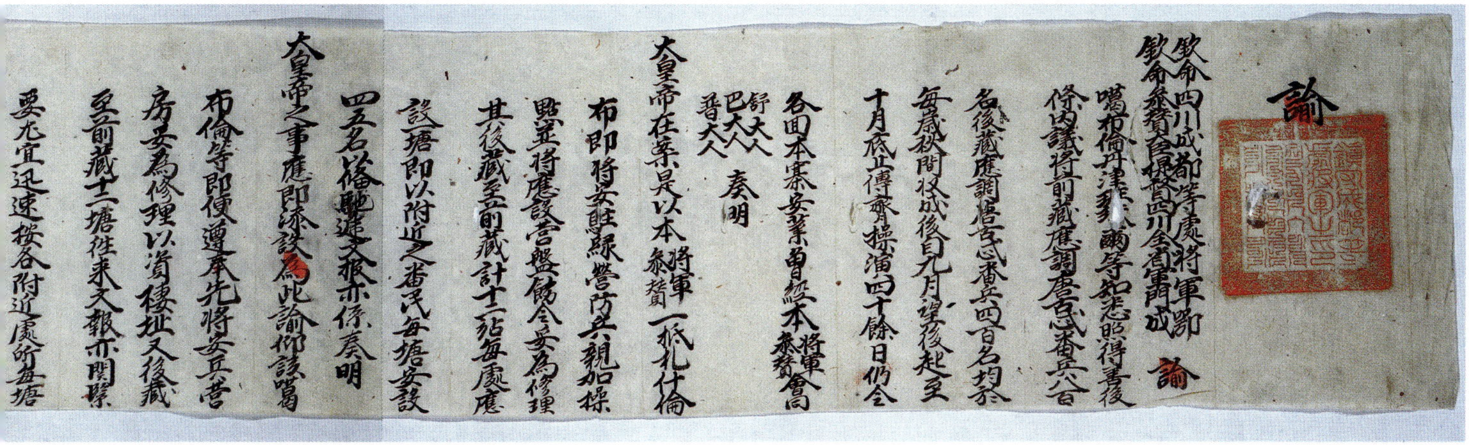

of messages and documents. This matter should also be reported in a petition to His Majesty the Emperor and the subposts should be set up forthwith, for which we are sending these instructions. We expect the government minister and others concerned to faithfully comply with this directive and first repair the barracks to provide proper accommodation for the soldiers. Since the reports and documents to be carried between the 12 subposts from Lower to Upper Tibet will be of great importance, the subposts should be set up promptly with the four or five couriers for each subpost quickly chosen from among the residents of the area and a list of the couriers submitted for the files. Local soldiers from Sakar should be stationed at Lhaze and a list of them prepared and submitted for examination. Their monthly rations should be provided using funds from the Treasury regularly and without fail or cutbacks. All Tibetan soldiers stationed in Lhaze and Sakar in Lower Tibet as well as those stationed at the subposts are to be supervised by the commander of the green–banner troops stationed in Tibet. Report back on how you have fulfilled the instructions for reference. Do not disobey these orders.

The 26th day of the 6th month of the 54th year of Qianlong (1789)

Preserved by the Archives of the Tibet Autonomous Region.

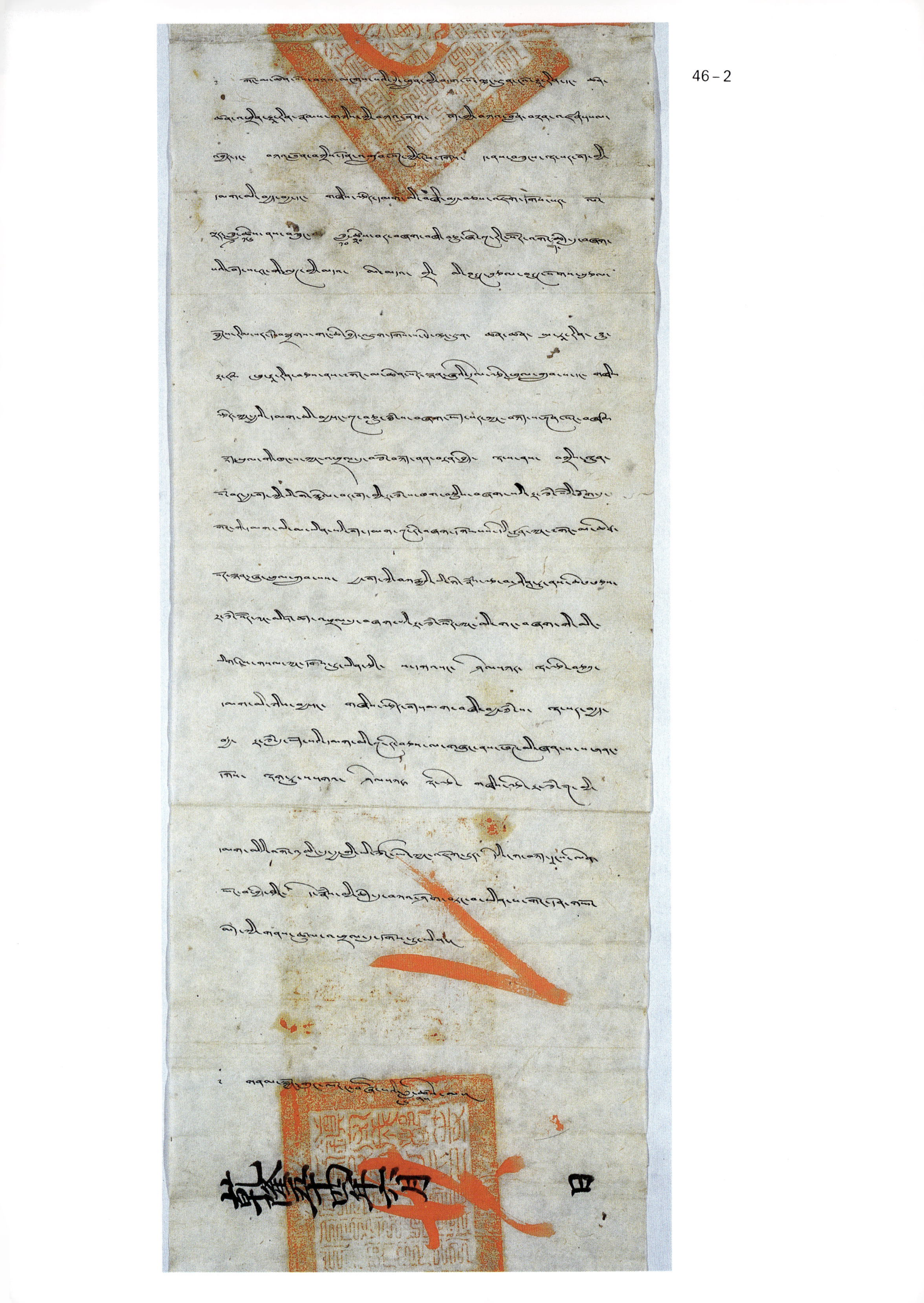

乾隆[illegible][illegible]年四 日

# གོང་མ་ལྷ་སྐྱོང་གིས་ཏཱ་ལའི་སྤྱན་སྔ་སོགས་ཀྱི་ལས་གནས་གཞན་དུ་བསྒྱུར་བའི་སྐོར་ཏཱ་ལའི་བླ་མར་བསྩལ་བའི་བཀའ་ལུང་།

# 乾隆皇帝爲調離達賴兄弟等人事給達賴喇嘛的敕諭

# Emperor Qianlong's Decree to the Dalai Lama Concerning the Transfer of His Brother

47－1

བོད་རང་སྐྱོང་ལྗོངས་ཡིག་ཚགས་ཁང་དུ་ཉར་ཚགས་བྱས་ཡོད།

奉天承運皇帝詔曰：

諭達賴喇嘛。朕統馭萬邦，撫治天下，以期率土衆民，各安生業，推興政教。喇嘛爾仰體朕意，弘揚黃教，勤習經卷，忠心耿耿，誠如前世達賴喇嘛一體盡意，崇佑佛法，闡揚經訓，祝禱三寶，朕甚嘉悅。今喇嘛爾特遣使，慶賀朕八十大壽，忠心奏獻丹書克，朕覽奏，內心甚悅。惟喇嘛爾兄弟、商卓特巴等欺瞞爾，肆行作弊，衆民齊怨，因於喇嘛爾甚無益處，朕將爾兄弟、商卓特巴等均召來京城。喇嘛爾嗣後惟遠避小人，崇佑佛法，勤習經訓，好自爲之。喇嘛爾乃黃教之衆望所歸，大喇嘛務勤習所有經卷，推興前世達賴喇嘛之舊道，造福衆生，闡揚佛教，以副朕尊崇黃教之至意。益加鑽研經卷，勉之勿怠。今爾使返回，降敕問候爾好，隨敕賞爾鍍金銀茶桶一個、鍍金銀瓶一個、供燈一盞、各色綢緞三十匹、大哈達五條、小哈達四十條、面子薄綾十條；又增賞玉佛一尊、鈴杵一套、玉如意一支、雲母石念珠一串、綉花黃緞龍袍一件、玉器一件、珐琅瓶一對、珐琅盤一隻、玻璃瓶一對、玻璃盤一對、玳瑁飯盒一對、黃龍蟒緞二匹、黃妝緞二匹、大荷包一對、小荷包三對、靠褥一套，一併交付爾使堪布等携回。特諭。

乾隆五十五年（公元1790年）九月十六日

西藏自治區檔案館藏

His Majesty the Emperor, who reigns by the mandate of Heaven, decrees: instructions for the Dalai Lama. I rule the Empire allowing the people all over the land to live in peace, improve the political situation and promote the religion. Honouring my wishes, you, the Dalai Lama, have been promoting the Yellow Sect of Lamaism, applying yourself to the study of the scriptures and demonstrating your loyalty. I am very glad to learn that, like the Dalai Lama of the last incarnation, you have devoted yourself to espousing the Buddhist principles, expounding the Buddhist doctrines and invoking the blessing of the Triratna. Today you have sent an envoy to celebrate my 80th birthday and present a *danshuke* to me. I was very pleased upon reading your petition. But your brother and Phyagdsod have been deceiving you, indulging in unbridled corruption and causing resentment among the people. As this is not in the least beneficial for you, I am summoning your brother and Phyagdsod to the capital. In future you should strictly avoid persons of low repute, cherish and protect the Buddhist doctrines and apply yourself to studying the Buddhist principles. It is all up to you. As the popular leader of the Yellow Sect of Lamaism, you should apply yourself to the study of all the Buddhist scriptures, carry forward the traditional principles upheld by the Dalai Lama of the last incarnation, be good to all living beings and promote Buddhism, thus living up to my earnest wish to honour the Yellow Sect. You should work harder than ever to study the Buddhist scriptures intensively and tirelessly. With your envoy going back to Tibet, I am sending you my greetings and this decree together with a gold–plated silver container for tea leaves, a gold–plated silver vase, a ritual lantern, 30 rolls of assorted silk, five large and 40 small *hatas* and 10 damask silk covers. In addition, I am presenting you with a jade figure of Buddha, a set of bells and sticks, a jade *ruyi,* a chaplet of mica beads, an embroidered dragon–patterned robe of yellow satin, a jade object, a pair of enamelware bottles, an enamelware tray, a pair of glass bottles, a pair of glass trays, a pair of hawksbill turtle cooked food containers, two rolls of yellow dragon and python–patterned satin, two rolls of yellow satin, a pair of large pouches, three pairs of small pouches and a set of padded mattresses, all to be carried back by your envoy. This is the end of the instructions.

The 16th day of the 9th month of the 55th year of Qianlong (1790)

Preserved by the Archives of the Tibet Autonomous Region.

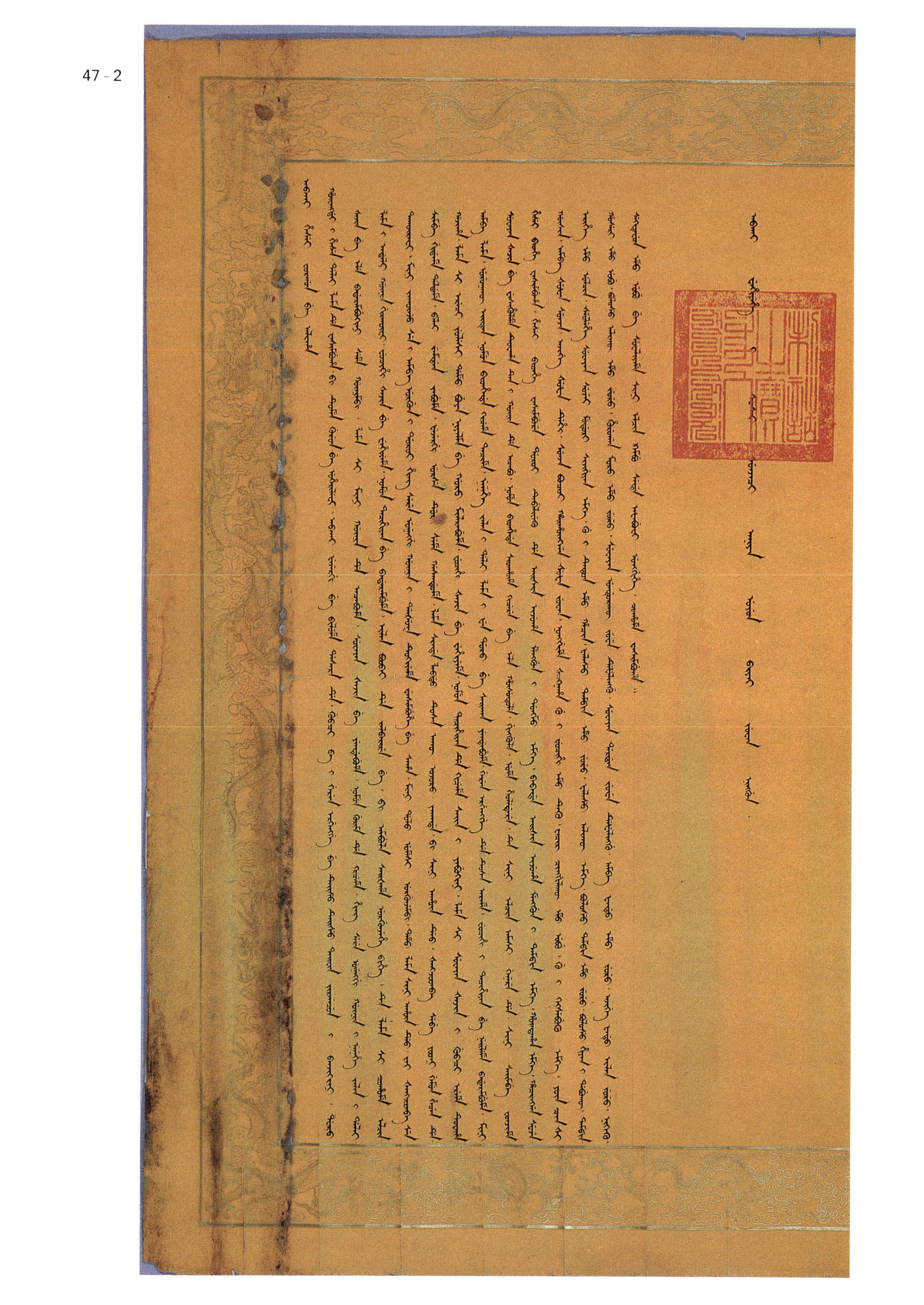

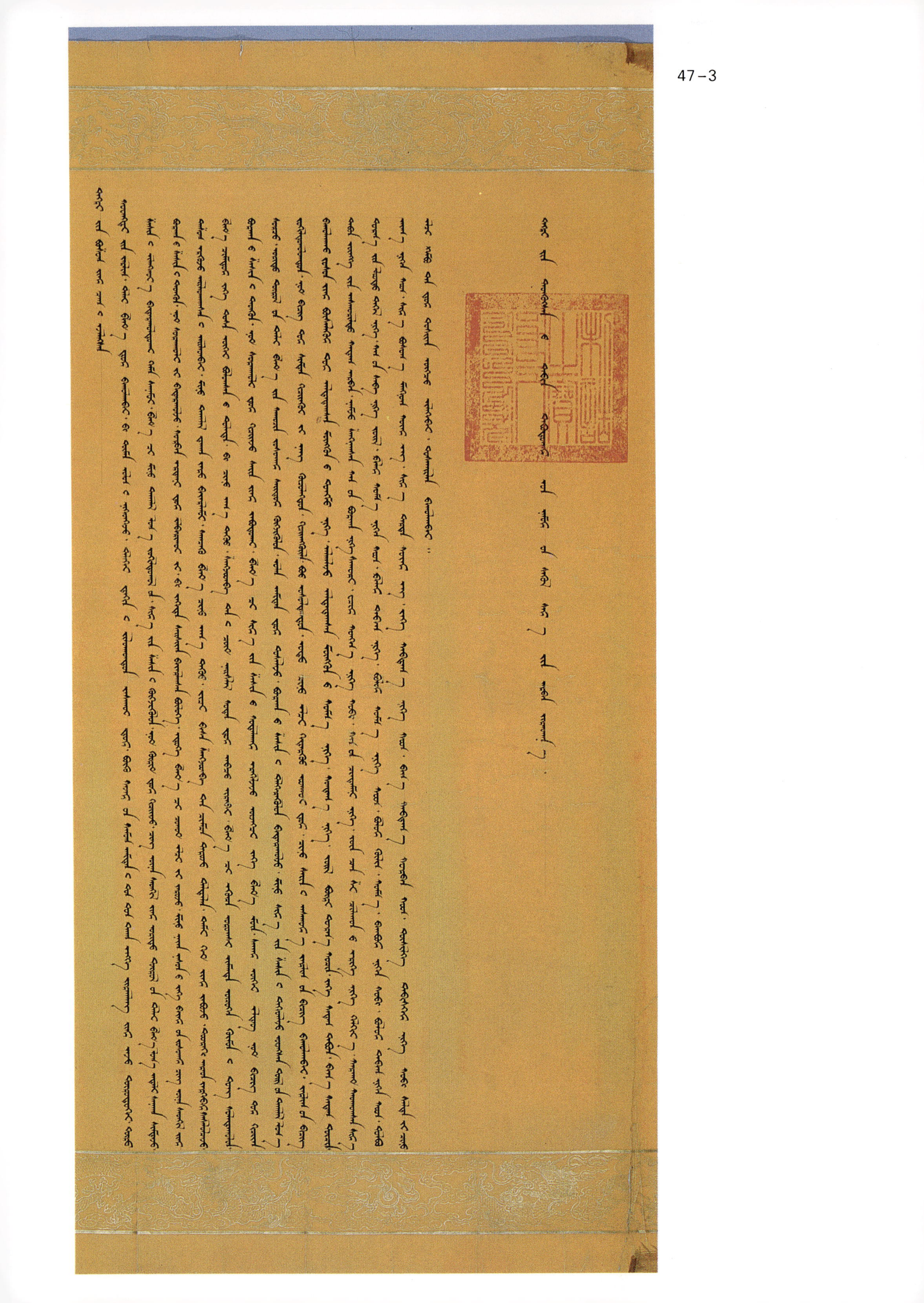

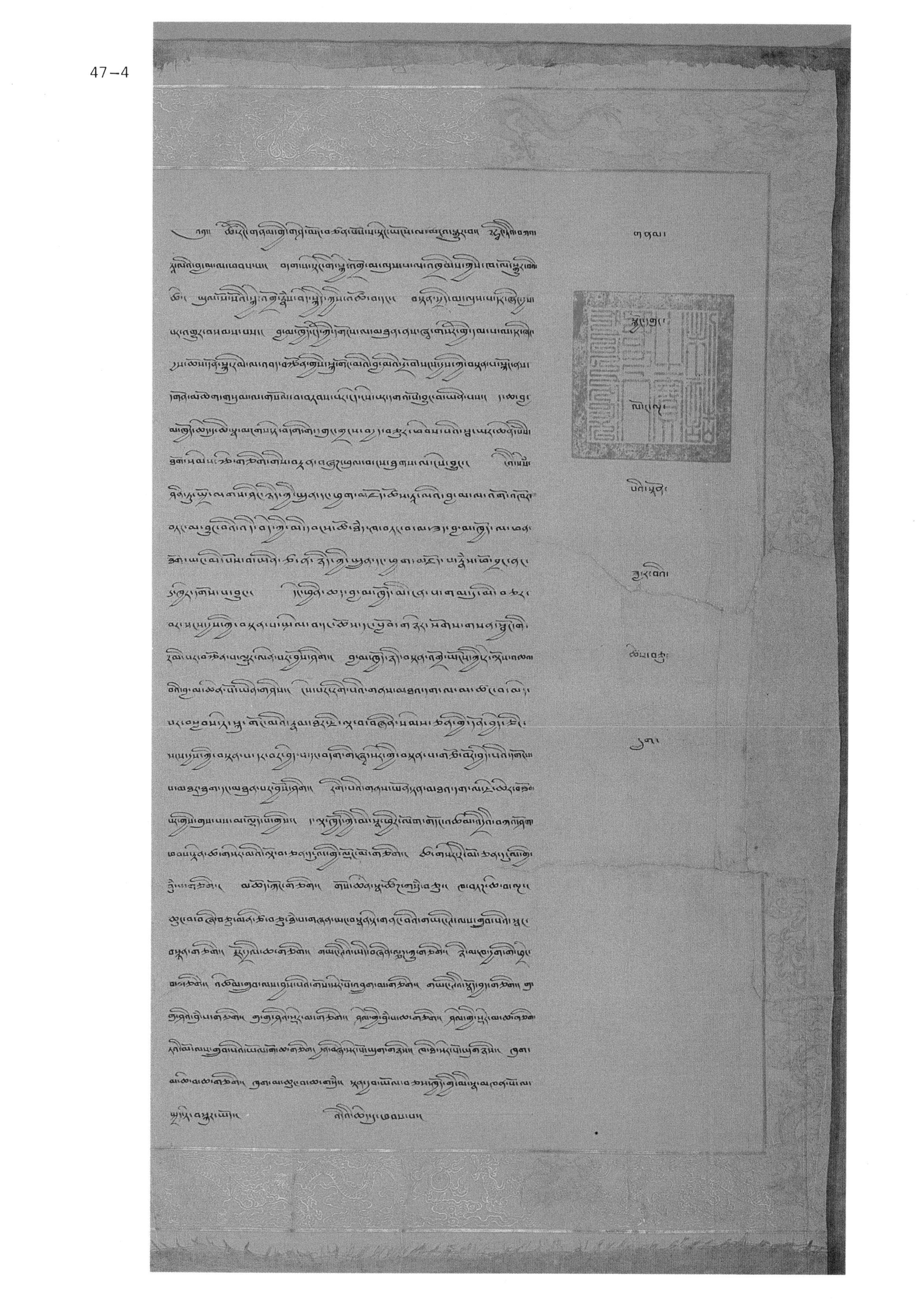

47-4

[illegible]

# བོད་བཞུགས་ལས་དོན་བློན་ཆེན་སུང་ཡུན་སོགས་ཀྱིས་བོད་འབངས་གནས་སྤོ་དང་ཁྲལ་རིགས་སོགས་ཀྱི་དོན་དུ་བཀྲས་ལྷུན་བླ་བྲང་ལ་སྤྲད་པའི་ལག་ཁྱེར་རྩ་ཆིག

# 駐藏辦事大臣松筠等爲藏民遷移及應差等事給後藏商上的印照

# Certificate Issued by the Resident Minister in Tibet Song Yun and Others to the Office of Administration in Lower Tibet Concerning the Migration of Tibetan People and the Performance of Their Corvée and Other Services

124 × 60

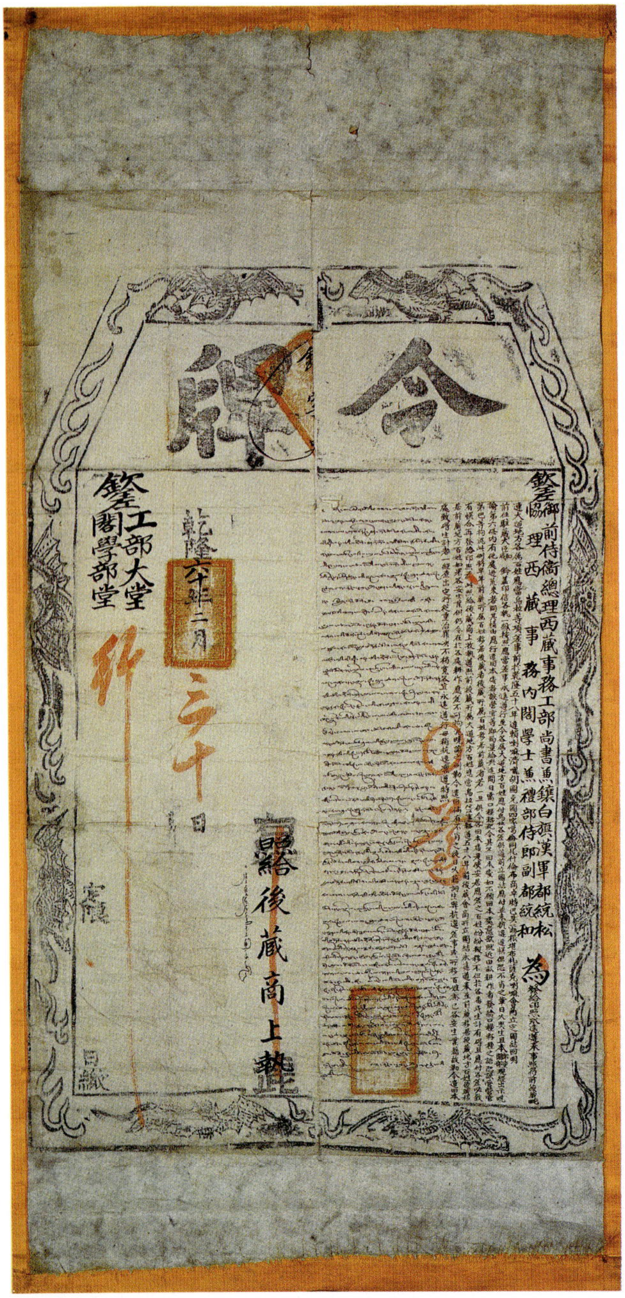


48－1

བོད་རང་སྐྱོང་ལྗོངས་ཡིག་ཚགས་ཁང་དུ་ཉར་ཚགས་བྱས་ཡོད།

西藏自治區檔案館藏

Song, Imperial Bodyguard Working in the Overall Management of Tibetan Affairs by Imperial Order, Minister of Works, and Han Commander of the White–Bordered Banner and He, Assistant in Command of Tibetan Affairs, Executive Secretary to the Cabinet, Vice–Minister of Rites and Deputy Commander issue the following certificate:

It is hereby noted that in the 58th year of Qianlong, the Dalai Lama, Living Buddha Rjedrung, the four government ministers and Phyagdsod,

Khanpo Mergan and Dsasag Lama of Tashilhunpo reached an agreement and produced a signed pledge through consultation, countersigned by the former Resident Ministers, He and Cheng, concerning the corvée and other services to be provided by people who live along the main road running through Upper and Lower Tibet. A copy of this document, which lists tasks to be performed in perpetuity, was given to each of the signers. Since then, people living along the main road have been performing these services as outlined in the pledge. There have been no instances of defying orders or delaying the work. However, to prevent dishonest people from availing themselves of certain loopholes in the future, a notice has been promulgated by the ministry and cabinet. The 6th article of this notice states that refugees fleeing from famine in other places should be interviewed to determine their situation, and then sent back to where they came from. The refugee camp directors should issue appropriate daily rations of *zanba* (roasted barley flour) for them to eat on the way and order them to return to their home villages. Those who are unwilling to return but wish to farm nearby fields should be given rations and seeds. There is a danger, however, that camp directors and *dipas,* strictly interpreting this article, may order those who have moved into an area long ago, moving from Upper Tibet to Lower Tibet or vice versa, to return to their places of origin. This would put people who are now living peacefully and providing corvée services back on the road, not only endangering these people's well–being, but also interrupting the performance of their services. In consideration of the above, another certificate is hereby being issued to the authorities in Lower Tibet instructing them to always adhere to the written pledge drawn up by the authorities of Upper and Lower Tibet through consultation in the 58th year of Qianlong, concerning the corvée required of the local people. People who have migrated from Upper Tibet to Lower Tibet, or vice versa, should be allowed to work the land and perform their corvee service in their current place of residence so long as they live in peace. They should not be rigidly ordered to return as dictated by the former instructions. Unworthy persons who create trouble by attempting to exploit the wording of this certificate and refuse to perform their corvée duties, or anyone that arbitrarily orders people who are living peacefully where they are to return to the area they came from, endangering their well–being, shall be punished severely without leniency when such cases are uncovered. These instructions should be followed by all in perpetuity and in every detail.

This certificate is issued to the Office of Administration in Lower Tibet for its records.

[Numeral for the day is missing in the original document] the 30th day of the 2nd month of the 60th year of Qianlong (1795)

Preserved by the Archives of the Tibet Autonomous Region.

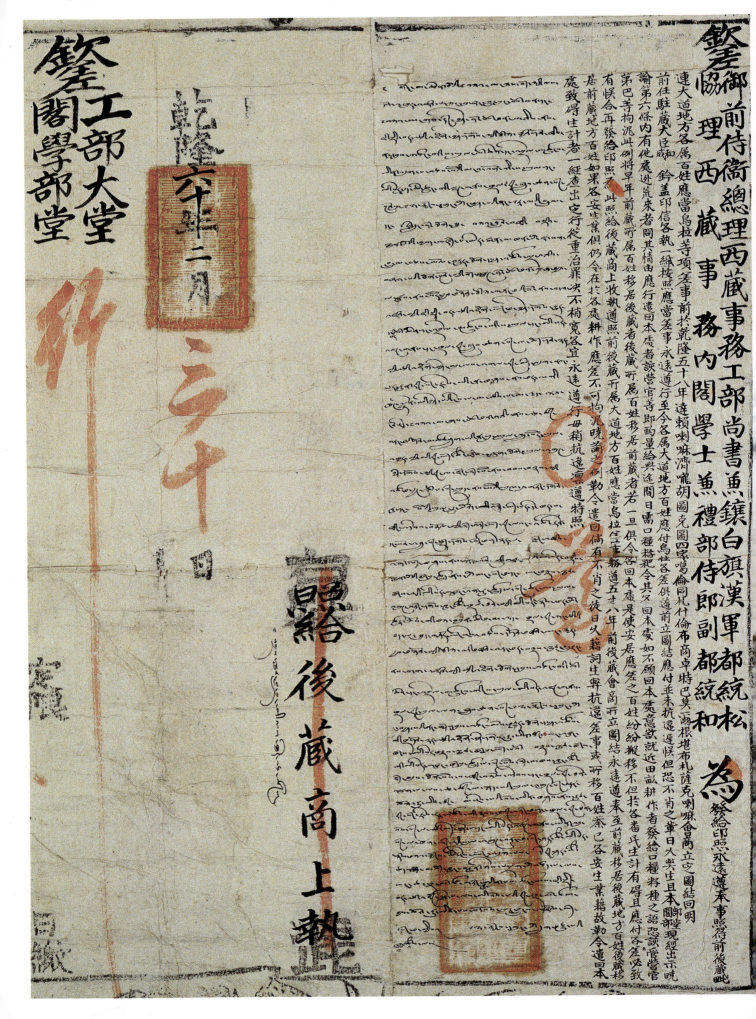

欽差御前侍衛總理西藏事務工部尚書兼鑲白旗漢軍都統松
欽差協理西藏事務內閣學士兼禮部侍郎副都統和 為

發給印照永遠遵奉事照得前後藏毗連大道地方各屬百姓應當烏拉等項差事前於乾隆五十八年達賴喇嘛濟嚨胡圖克圖四噶倫同扎什倫布商卓特巴莫爾根堪布扎薩克喇嘛會商立定圖結回明前任駐藏大臣和成 鈐蓋印信各執一紙按照應當差事永遠遵行至今各屬大道地方百姓應付烏拉各差俱遵前立圖結應付並未抗違遲悞但恐不肖之輩日久弊生且本閣部堂現經出示曉諭第六條內有他處逃荒來者問其情由應行遣回本處者該營官等即酌量給與途間日需口糧籽種令其仍回本處如不願回本處意欲就近田畝耕作者發給口糧籽種之語恐該營官第巴等拘泥此例將早年前藏所屬百姓移居後藏者後藏所屬百姓移居前藏者若一旦俱令各回本處是使安居應差之百姓紛紛搬移不但於各番民生計有碍且應付各差必致有悞合再發給印照為此照給後藏商上收執遵照前後藏所屬大道地方百姓應當烏拉等差事務遵五十八年前後藏會商所立圖結永遠遵奉至前藏移居後藏地方百姓及後藏移居前藏地方百姓如果各安生業俱仍令在於各處耕作應差不可拘泥曉諭之例勒令遣回倘有不肖之徒日久藉詞生弊抗違差事或所移百姓素已各安生業藉故勒令遣回本處致碍生計者一經查出定行從重治罪決不稍寬各宜永遠遵行毋稍抗違凛遵特照

右照給後藏商上收執

乾隆六十年二月 二十 日

欽差工部大堂
欽差內閣學部堂

行

# བོད་བཞུགས་ཨམ་བན་སུང་ཡུན་སོགས་ཀྱིས་གཙང་གི་མི་སེར་རྣམས་བདེ་བར་གནས་པ་དང་ཁྲལ་རིགས་སོགས་ཀྱི་སྐོར་བཀྲམས་པའི་རྩ་ཚིག

# 駐藏大臣松筠等爲曉諭後藏百姓安居當差等事發布告示

# Notice Issued by the Resident Minister in Tibet, Song Yun, Directing the People in Lower Tibet to Live in Peace and Perform Their Public Duties

105 × 78

བོད་རང་སྐྱོང་ལྗོངས་ཡིག་ཚགས་ཁང་དུ་ཉར་ཚགས་བྱས་ཡོད།

西藏自治區檔案館藏

Song, Imperial Bodyguard by Imperial Order, Minister of Works and Han Commander of the White-Bordered Banner in General Command of Tibetan Affairs, and He, Executive Secretary of the Cabinet by Imperial Order, Vice Minister of Rites, and Vice Commander and Assistant for Tibetan Affairs, hereby issue the following instructions:

Extending His Majesty the Emperor's gracious kindness towards the Tibetan people, the Panchen Erdeni has granted the Bod people in Lower Tibet exemption from one half of their tax grain for the current year and forgiveness of all their grain and taxes in arrears. He has also ordered that a survey of jobless persons living in places under his jurisdiction be taken and rations issued to them. They should also be given *zanba* and *qingke* barley seed, so that they have something to eat and are also able to resume farming and begin repairing the ruined houses so that the local people who are destitute have places to dwell in and are able to live in peace in perpetuity. This is due to the graciousness of the Panchen Erdeni, long live His Maj-

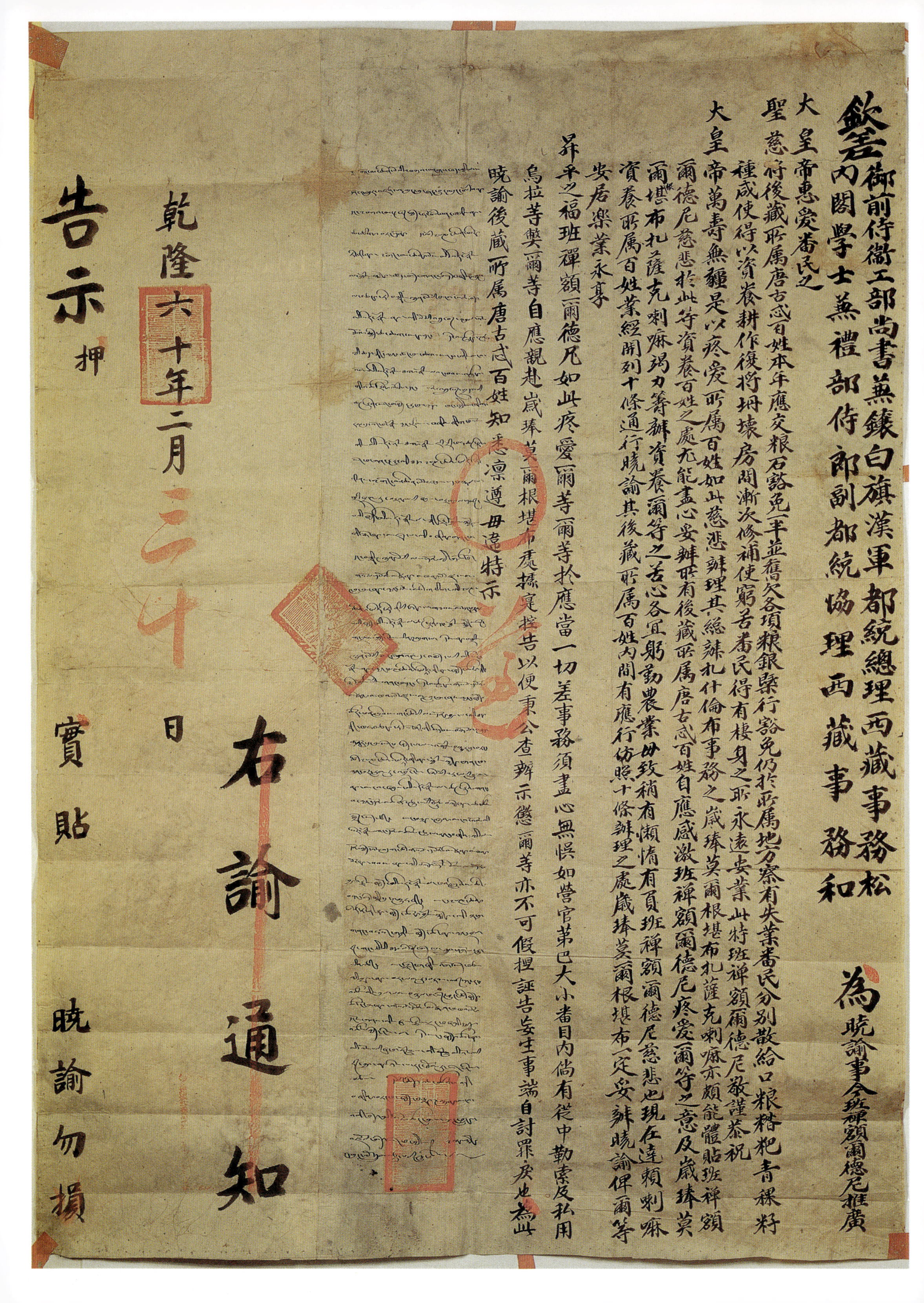

欽差御前侍衛工部尚書兼鑲白旗漢軍都統總理西藏事務松
內閣學士兼禮部侍郎副都統協理西藏事務和

為曉諭事今班禪額爾德尼推廣

大皇帝惠愛番民之
聖慈將後藏所屬唐古忒百姓本年應交粮石豁免一半並舊欠各項粮銀槩行豁免仍於所屬地方察有失業番民分別散給口粮籽種青稞籽種咸使得以資養耕作復將坍壞房間漸次修補使窮苦番民得有棲身之所永遠安業此特班禪額爾德尼敬謹恭祝
大皇帝萬壽無疆是以疼愛所屬百姓如此慈悲辦理其總辦札什倫布事務之歲琫莫爾根堪布札薩克喇嘛亦頗能體貼班禪額爾德尼慈悲於此等資養百姓之處尤能盡心妥辦所有後藏所屬唐古忒百姓自應感激班禪額爾德尼疼愛爾等之意及歲琫莫爾根堪布札薩克喇嘛竭力籌辦資養爾等之苦心各宜躬勤農業毋致稍有懶惰有負班禪額爾德尼慈悲也現在達賴喇嘛資養所屬百姓業經開列十條通行曉諭其後藏所屬百姓內間有應行仿照十條辦理之處歲琫莫爾根堪布一定妥辦曉諭俾爾等安居樂業永享
昇平之福班禪額爾德尼如此疼愛爾等爾等於應當一切差事務須盡心無誤如營官第巴大小番目內倘有從中勒索及私用烏拉等弊爾等自應覲赴歲琫莫爾根堪布處據實控告以便秉公查辦示懲爾等亦不可假捏誣告妄生事端自討罪戾也為此曉諭後藏所屬唐古忒百姓知悉凛遵毋違特示

右諭通知

乾隆六十年二月三十日

告示 押

實貼

曉諭勿損

esty the Emperor, who expressed his worry for the people. Khanpo Suibeng Mergan Dsasag Blamakacu, who is taking overall charge of affairs in Tashilhunpo, is sure to fully consider the Panchen Erdeni's graciousness and do his best to see to the well–being of the people. All the Bod people in Lower Tibet should, therefore, be thankful to the Panchen Erdeni for his good wishes, and to Khanpo Suibeng Mergan Dsasag Blamakacu for the great pains he takes to see your well–being, and relentlessly and tirelessly work on your farming. Do not do anything which would show that you are undeserving of the Panchen Erdeni's goodness. The Dalai Lama has promulgated ten provisions concerning the care of the people living in places under his jurisdiction. In areas of Lower Tibet covered by these provisions, Khanpo Suibeng Mergan will certainly carry them out well and widely publicize them so that you may live and work in peace and contentment for ever. You should therefore perform all your public duties conscientiously to show your gratitude for the Panchen Erdeni's great concern for you. Should any camp directors, *dipas,* or minor officials engage in abuses such as extortion or unlawful use of corvée labour, you should lodge complaints with the office of Khanpo Suibeng Mergan so that such malpractices may be investigated and dealt with impartially and the culprits punished according to law. On the other hand, you should not fabricate stories and make false charges or create disturbances, thereby courting trouble. For these reasons these directions are being made known to all the people in Bod in Lower Tibet, who must follow them to the letter. This is the end of the directions.

The 30th day of the 2nd month of the 60th year of Qianlong (1795)

After posting, these directions are not to be defaced in any way.

Preserved by the Archives of the Tibet Autonomous Region.

# 50

## གོང་མའི་བཀའ་འབྲེལ་ལུགས་སྲོལ་གསར་འཛུགས་ཀྱི་དོན་ཚན་ཉེར་དགུ

## 欽定二十九條章程

## The 29−Article Imperial Ordinance

359 × 53

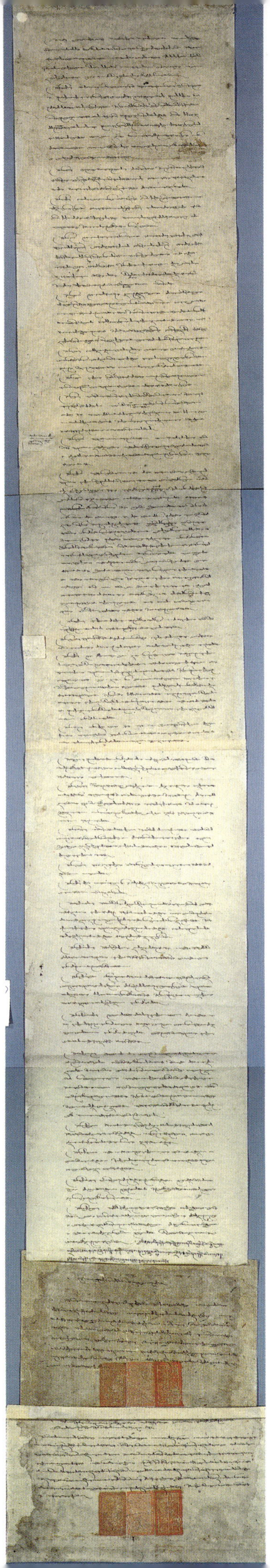

50 - 1

བོད་རང་སྐྱོང་ལྗོངས་ཡིག་ཚགས་ཁང་དུ་ཉར་ཚགས་བྱས་ཡོད།

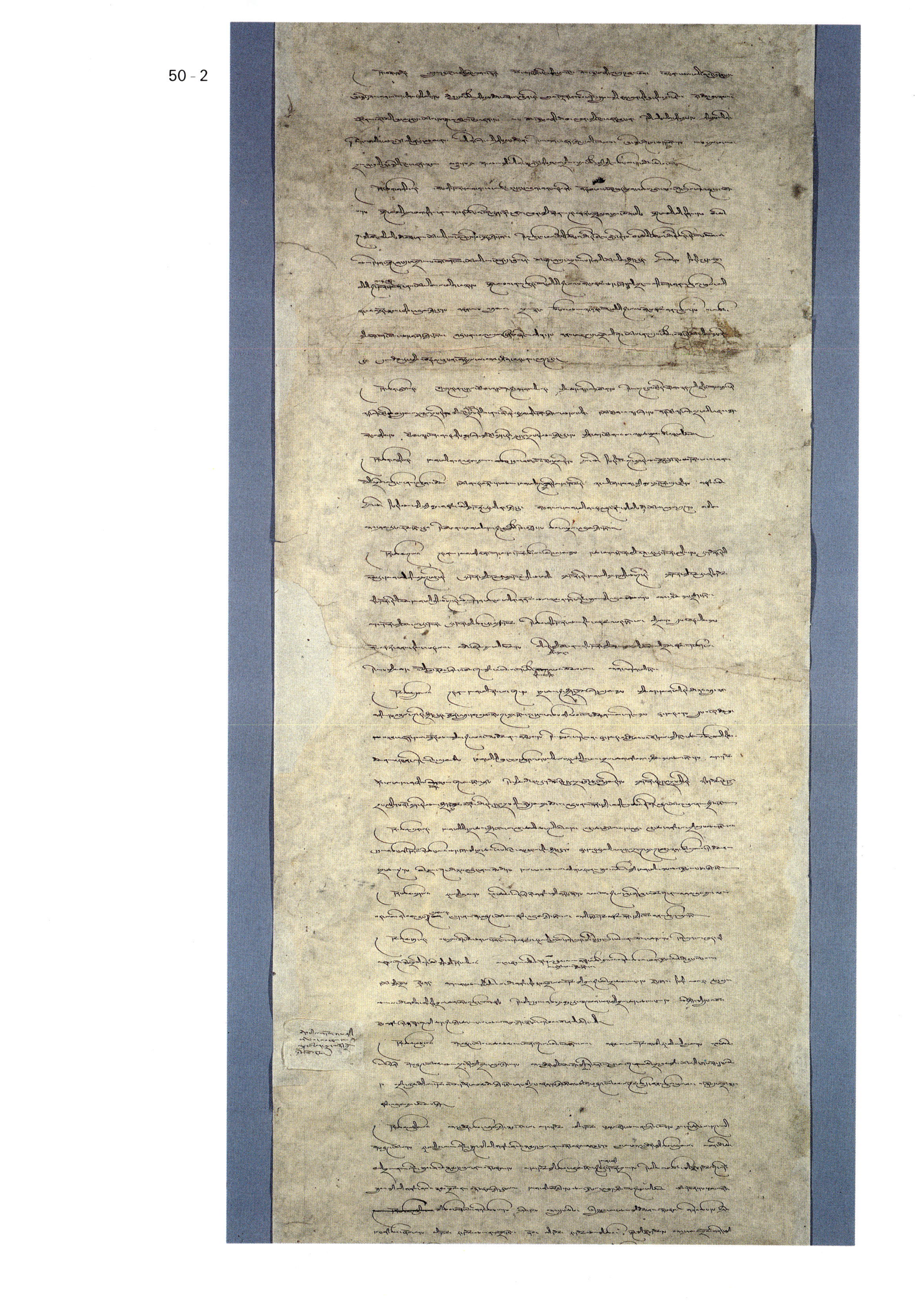

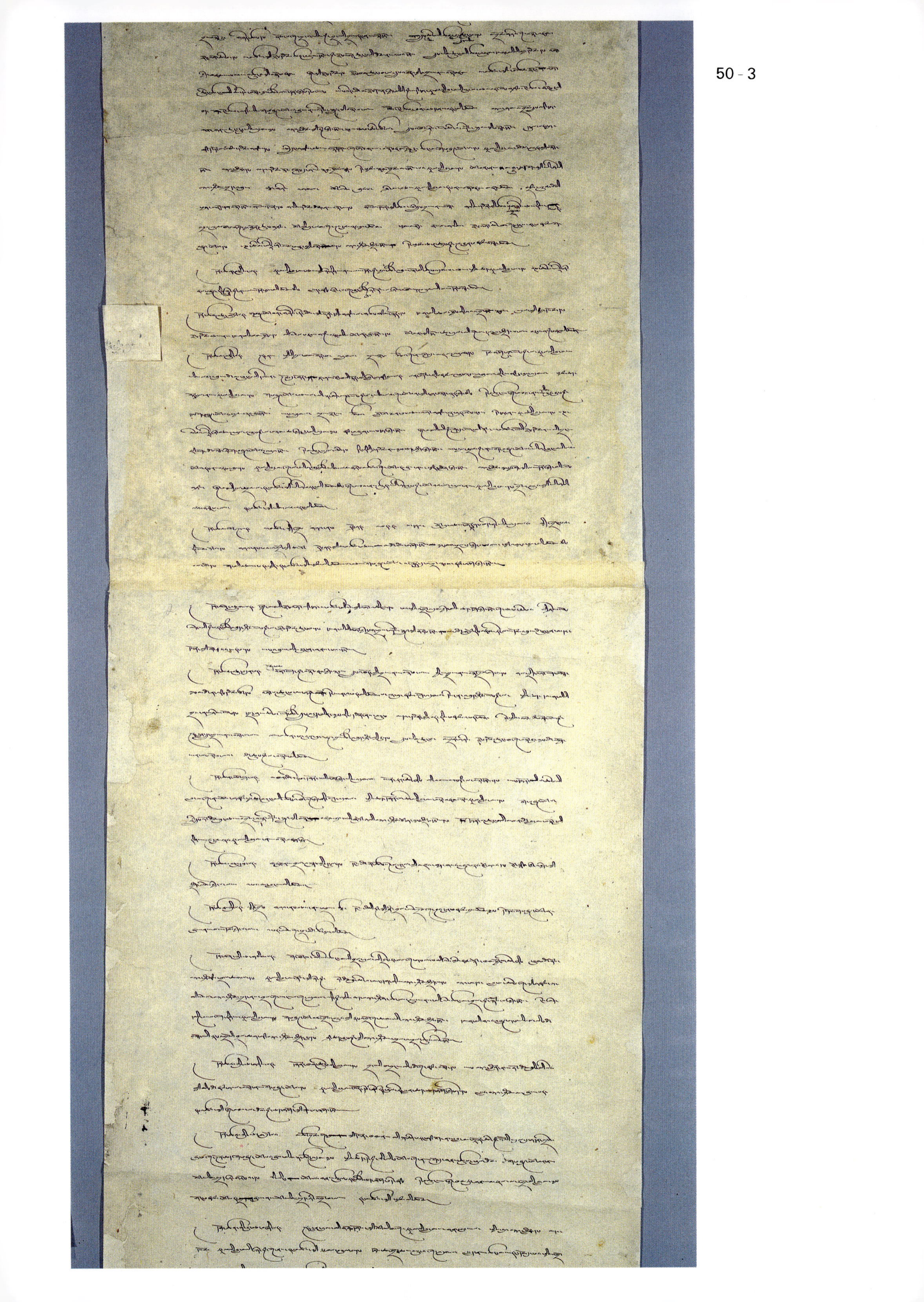

50 - 4

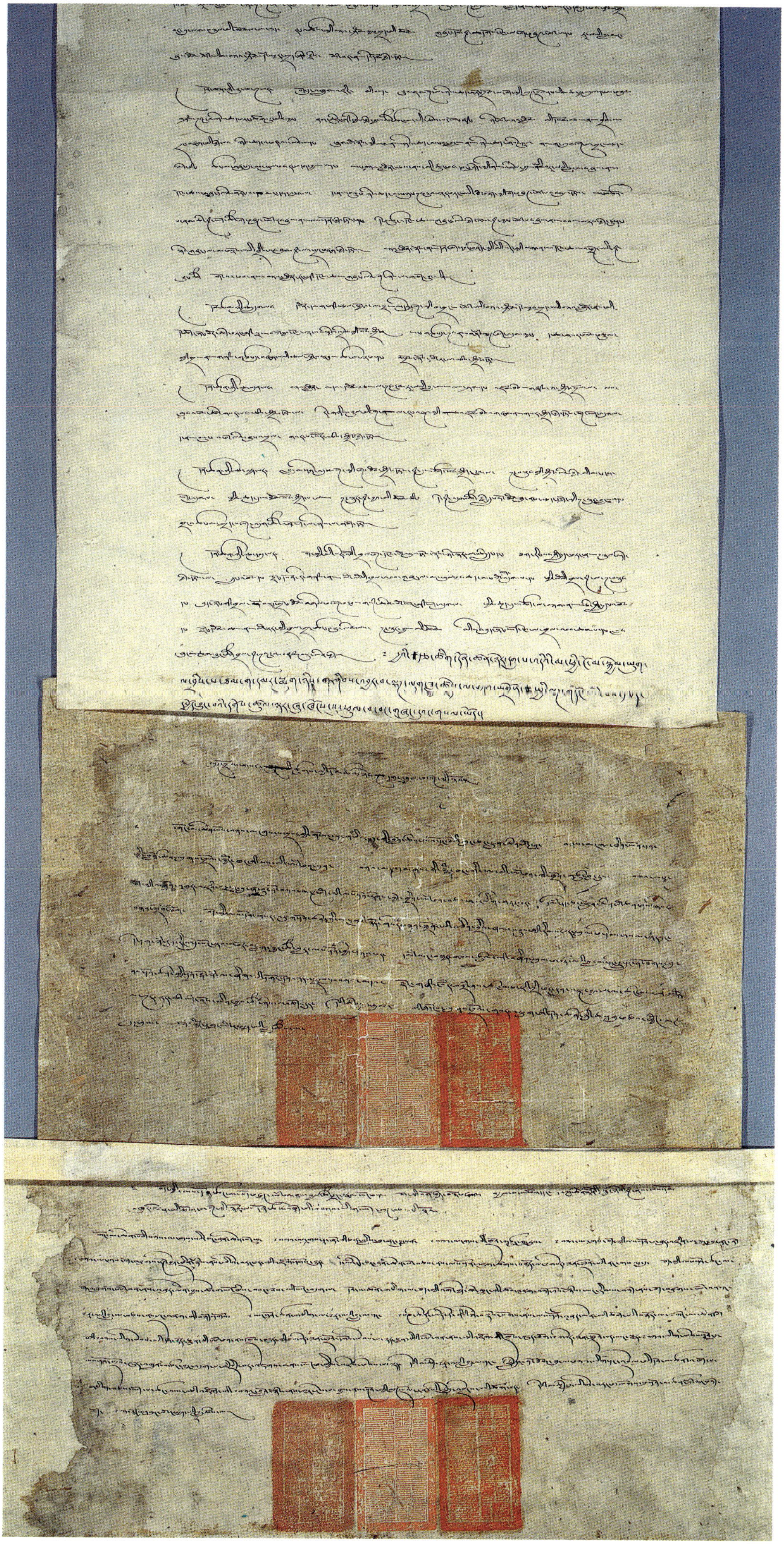

第一條　關於尋找活佛靈童事宜。經各方認真考查，並問卜於四大護法神之後，將在御賜金瓶内放入寫有擬定爲靈童者名字及出生年月的籤牌，選派學識淵博的喇嘛，祈禱七日後，由衆呼圖克圖會同駐藏大臣於釋迦牟尼佛像前認定。又若四位護法神認識一致，則將一有靈童名字之籤牌同一無名籤牌一併放入瓶内。若抽出無名籤牌，便不能認定之，需另外尋找。再者，認定達賴、班禪靈童時，須將其名以滿、漢、藏三體文字書於籤牌，如此則可取信於天下民衆。

第二條　欽派官兵進抵邊境，廓爾喀人已俯首投降，藏地獲得安寧。今後由鄰近國來拉薩之客商，須登記造册，呈報駐藏大臣衙門備案。尼泊爾客商每年可來三次，克什米爾客商每年可來一次，此等客商無論前往何地，須事先由該管頭領報請駐藏大臣衙門，按照該客商所經路線簽發路證，並於江孜和定日兩地新派官兵駐扎，此等客商經過時，須出具路證檢驗。對來藏之外人，須加調查，呈報人數，抵拉薩後，要接受檢查。由不丹、哲孟雄、宗巴等地來拉薩者，亦照上述辦法，由各邊地頭領進行調查。西藏政府派往尼泊爾修建三寶所依之人員或前往朝聖者，由駐藏大臣簽發路證，如有逾期不歸者，由駐藏大臣行文廓爾喀王，召回伊等。

第三條　西藏章喀，歷來摻假甚多，今後均須以純銀鑄造，並依舊制，每一章喀重一錢五分，六枚純銀章喀值一兩漢銀，漢銀一兩中含一錢銀子的鑄造費用。凡新製純銀章喀和尼泊爾純銀章喀，一律以上述比價爲標準。新舊摻假章喀，一律以八枚值漢銀一兩。今後所製新章喀，不得有絲毫摻假。

第四條　新建軍隊，在前後藏各駐一千名，江孜、定日各駐五百名，共三千名。每五百名兵員委任一代本管理，駐拉薩之藏軍總管由駐藏游擊擔任；駐日喀則、江孜、定日之軍隊總管由日喀則之駐藏都司擔任。上述新編軍隊之兵員，一份名册存駐藏大臣衙門，一份名册存噶廈，其中如因死亡等事産生缺額，即依名册補充。

第五條　關於軍官之職位，以前只有代本一職，此次在代本下設十二名如本，每一如本管轄二百五十名兵員。如本以下共設二十四名甲本，每一甲本管轄一百二十五名兵員。甲本以下設定本，每一定本管轄二十五名兵員。以上人員均挑選年青技優者充任，並發給令狀。代本由如本中升補，如本由甲本中升補，甲本由定本中升補，如此類推。即使貴族、俗官出身之軍職人員，亦須按照以上規定，逐級提升，不得越級提拔。按照舊例，一般不准平民擔任定本職務，今後一律依照其智勇技能逐級提升，不得阻礙。

第六條　以前兵丁不發糧餉和武器，今後每人每年應發糧食二石五斗，總共爲七千五百石，如此僅靠前後藏的收入不够支付，不足部分以夏瑪爾巴、仲巴呼圖克圖、丹增班覺爾的田産支付，如仍不足，即將夏瑪爾巴·洛桑江白的財産變賣支付，則足矣。另外，凡入伍兵員，由達賴喇嘛發給減免差役之執照。衆代本因已有代本溪卡，故無須另發薪餉。如本每人每年應發三十六兩銀子，甲本二十兩銀子，定本十四兩八錢，共計每年需二千六百兩銀子，由西藏政府交給駐藏大臣，分春秋兩季發給。

第七條　給軍人配備之武器，十分之五爲火槍，十分之三用弓箭，十分之二用刀矛，從前後藏各寺院物色收購，費用由夏瑪爾巴之牧場收入五百五十餘兩銀子中支付。由政府每年派人前往工布及邊壩制造武器火藥。兵丁亦須認真操練。

第八條　達賴喇嘛和班禪額爾德尼二人的收入，由其親屬和隨員等負責管理，恐有差錯及舞弊等情事，今後由駐藏大臣進行審核，按照聖旨，每年春秋二季各呈報一次。

第九條　像一切佛陀利濟衆生那般，達賴喇嘛來至僧衆中講經，尊重僧伽等，均係爲衆生之幸福，是對屬民的仁慈安撫，但受到盜賊之侵害，故此次決定蠲免吉仲、絨夏、聶拉木兩年的大小差税，蠲免宗嘎、定日、喀達、曲堆等地一年的差役，並蠲免前後藏各地鐵猪年所欠差役，減去孜雪的宗科、各宗溪頭領等所欠差役的一半，此一切均係爲了西藏之安寧。

第十條　駐藏大臣常設衙門中若有要事須到布達拉宫協商。其他諸項事務，由達賴喇嘛、班禪額爾德尼、駐藏大臣進行平等商議。以噶倫爲首在西藏任職之大小活佛等均須聽從駐藏大臣之指派。札什倫布之事務，有索本堪布公正辦理，凡事須先呈報駐藏大臣，以便出巡時查實。

第十一條　升補噶倫時，依軍代本、孜本、强佐之才能業績，由駐藏大臣和達賴喇嘛推選二人呈報任命；升補噶倫喇嘛時，從大堪布中推選呈報任命；升補代本時，從邊地宗本等推選二人呈報任命，軍官不可或缺，軍訓不可耽誤；升補孜本和强佐時，由業倉巴、審判官、噶厦大秘書、孜仲喇嘛中選任；升補業倉巴和審判官時，從雪巴、米本、達本中選任；升補達本時，從各級宗本及噶厦仲尼中選任；升補業倉巴和雪巴等僧官時，從僧人中選任；升補大秘書時，從小秘書和仲尼中選任；升補大宗宗本及邊地宗本時，從小宗宗本中選任；升補小秘書時，從軍隊的甲本等小頭目及其他合適人員中選任；邊地宗宗本及小宗宗本之缺額，由一般仲科中選任。將邊地等大小宗的宗本情況均予登記造册，以利於公務。以往僧官宗本因均屬達賴喇嘛之隨侍，故派其代理人前往，今後代理人均須報經駐藏大臣選定，不得擅自作主。噶厦的仲尼及秘書，雖官職較低，但其作爲噶倫之助手，不謂不重要，故須從仲科中挑選才能較强者充任之。管理造幣之人員，須委任孜本、孜仲各二名。以上所述委任事項均須由駐藏大臣和達賴喇嘛協商而定。除噶倫和代本須呈報任命外，其他人員之任命不必呈報，可由達賴喇嘛和駐藏大臣委任，並發給滿、漢、藏三體文字的委任狀。至於柴草、糌粑、帳篷、牧場的管理人員及侍衛等，可由達賴喇嘛自行委任。升補札什倫布的强佐時，從索本喇嘛和森本喇嘛中選任；升補索本時，從孜仲中選任；升補森本時，從仲尼中選任。如此逐級升任。札什倫布轄區較小，烏拉差役可按慣例辦理。强佐、索本、森本及大宗宗本等依照前藏之例，由駐藏大臣同班禪額爾德尼協商委任，並發令狀。其餘各小官吏，可照舊例委任。

第十二條　達賴喇嘛等人的親屬如果參政，多有不便，故達賴喇嘛和班禪額爾德尼在世時，其親屬不得參政。一旦圓寂，其親屬根據才能大小安排適當職務。

第十三條　二位駐藏大臣每年分春秋兩季輪流出巡後藏的軍訓校場。漢官和宗本等有無擾害軍民等事，須向駐藏大臣呈報。駐藏大臣所需烏拉等，均得付酬，不得虧欠。

第十四條　以往廓爾喀、不丹、哲孟雄、宗巴人等來西藏朝佛、進貢、辦事時，達賴喇嘛或有回覆不當之處，前如廓爾喀就章喀事進行交涉時，因回覆不當，致起戰端。今後廓爾喀方面特派使者面見達賴喇嘛和駐藏大臣時，其回文須按照駐藏大臣授意辦理。同樣，凡來自外方的書信，亦須呈報駐藏大臣過目。又，不丹、錫金、宗巴、洛保孟唐等藩屬，派人向達賴喇嘛和班禪額爾德尼朝貢時，雖不加阻撓，但須詳查。外方來藏人員，由各邊地宗宗本登記人數，呈報駐藏大臣，並由江孜和定日的漢官進行檢查。各藩屬國給駐藏大臣的信件，可由駐藏大臣自行回覆。給達賴喇嘛等之來信，如何回覆應報駐藏大臣酌定。噶倫乃辦理藏漢事務之官員，不得擅自與外方諸國通信。外方來信均應送交駐藏大臣會同達賴喇嘛協商之後，方可回覆，而不得擅自回覆。

第十五條　邊界的結仲、聶拉木、絨夏、喀爾達、薩嘎、昆布等地同廓爾喀接壤，須在結仲邊界之日索橋、聶拉木邊界之樟木橋、絨夏邊界等處速立界碑，不得遲誤。尼泊爾人和西藏人不可擅自越界出入。駐藏大臣出巡時加以檢查。

第十六條　邊地各宗之宗本既是邊民的頭目，又是來往行人的檢查者，所關甚要。如派才疏者任職，難免誤事，故須從精幹小宗本及軍隊頭目中選派；任滿三年後，如果勝任，可提升爲代本；不勝任者，予以降職。

第十七條　以往委任官吏時，均從仲科中選任，未有從民衆中委任之習慣，即便委任，也只能擔任定本以下小官吏，不能升任更高職務，此不妥也。今後非仲科出身之軍人，凡智勇雙全者，可從定本逐級提到代本等官職。一般情況下，仍依舊例從仲科中委任。但若幼子承襲父職，難免誤事，故此未滿十八歲者，不得委任爲小秘書、仲尼及小宗宗本等。

第十八條　堪布爲寺院之首領，應委任學識淵博、品德高尚者充任之。大寺院之喇嘛等佔有很多寺屬溪卡，經商牟利。今後委任大寺院之喇嘛，由達賴喇嘛、駐藏大臣、杰仲呼圖克圖等協商選定，並頒發加蓋三人印章之委任書。至於各小寺院堪布喇嘛之委任，仍依舊例由達賴喇嘛派任。

第十九條　政府所收税銀、實物交易等所用銀兩差價，均按新定規章，區别新舊章喀進行兑换，不得額外收取。

第二十條　結仲、聶拉木兩地抽收大米、食鹽、貨物等過境税仍依舊例收取，除非呈報駐藏大臣同意，不得增收絲毫税額。

第二十一條　西藏百姓支付烏拉等差役，一般貧苦百姓負擔苛重，而富家大户領得了免税執照，大呼圖克圖多有頒給達賴喇嘛親屬執照情事，噶倫、代本、大喇嘛等溪卡之百姓也因持有執照而負擔較輕。對此，今後收回所有執照，平均負擔差役。對需特殊優待者，經達賴喇嘛和駐藏大臣協商，發給免除差役之執照。對新招之兵員，根據名册一律發給免役執照，若有死亡者，須將所發免役執照收回。

第二十二條　各寺院的大小喇嘛和扎巴人數、名字，要詳造清册，呼圖克圖的屬民由噶倫造報花名册，駐藏大臣和達賴喇嘛各存一份，以便查核。以後若有不領護照而擅自越境者，一經查出，必加嚴懲。

第二十三條　以前青海等地官員派人來藏，迎請學識淵博的喇嘛時，有呈報或未呈報駐藏大臣等情況。今後必須通過西寧大臣行文西藏之後，由駐藏大臣發給路證，並行文駐西寧大臣，以便查考。到外方朝佛之喇嘛，亦須通過駐藏大臣領取護照，不得私自通行。

第二十四條　依照舊例，需支派烏拉時，其執照向由達賴喇嘛發給，噶倫、代本、達賴喇嘛之親屬，均有擅自支派差馬，收取食物等情事。今後因私往來時，一律不得支派烏拉，亦不得擅發執照；凡公務往來時，報經駐藏大臣和達賴喇嘛發給印照，沿途遵照執行。

第二十五條　對於鬥毆、殺人及盜掠等案之處罰，西藏的規則與内地不同，故今後不能按照舊規則處罰。按罪行輕重，區别懲處，方能取信於民。近來噶倫及米本不能秉公辦案，額外罰款，還將從富户所罰之大量金銀牛羊納入私囊，不交政府。噶倫中利用權勢，對於地位低下之人，任意加以罪名，呈報達賴喇嘛没收其財産者屢見不鮮。今後處罰多少，按例進行登記後呈送駐藏大臣，對罪大惡極之重犯，要報駐藏大臣處理。同時，需没收財物充公時，要請示大臣酌情處理。今後無論公私，如有訴訟事務，均須公正辦理。噶倫中如有依仗權勢無端搶佔民財者，則將其革職，没收其財産充公。

第二十六條　官兵操演所需彈藥等，由噶倫派精幹官員携帶駐藏大臣印照，前往工布地方製造，運至拉薩發給各部。以往後藏没有火炮，現從新造十三門火炮中調兩門給後藏，以便軍隊操練打靶時用，其餘均交與布達拉宫。

第二十七條　過去對噶倫及代本，達賴喇嘛照例撥給宅第莊園，卸任時移交新任者。但個别家屬等仍佔據不交，對此，又另撥與新任官宅第莊園。今後卸任時應一律移交給新任官。

第二十八條　依照舊例，應發給活佛及喇嘛之俸禄，均有定時，但近來發現多有提前發放情事。今後應按時發放，不得提前。杰仲呼圖克圖須加調查，如發現提前發放俸禄或未照數發放情事，要懲處其負責者。

第二十九條　西藏百姓應交納賦税，近處派孜仲前往催繳，遠處派雪仲前往催繳。個别仲科和宗本，將每年税收不交政府，致使欠款者甚多，還有提前催繳來年税收及將逃亡户之差役轉嫁常住户之情事，摧殘百姓，加重負擔。今後仲科及宗本等只准每年定時如數催收差税，不得提前催繳；對逃亡户之差役應予免除，俟該逃亡户返鄉後照舊承擔。

乾隆五十八年（公元1793年）二月

西藏自治區檔案館藏

Article 1　When the Holy Children of the reincarnated Living Buddhas have been located through careful investigations and their identities confirmed through the divination of the Four Guardians of Dharma, their names and dates of birth shall be recorded on ivory slips to be placed in a gold vase granted by His Majesty. This process shall be followed by a seven-day prayer session conducted by learned lamas. The reincarnations shall then be officially confirmed before the image of Sakyamuni by the Living Buddhas and the Resident Ministers in Tibet. If the Four Guardians of Dharma then agree on one boy, a blank slip shall be put in the vase in addition to the one bearing the name of the selected boy. If the blank slip is drawn, the soul of that boy shall not be recognized as the reincarnation of the Living Buddha, and a new candidate shall be sought. To win the people's trust, the reincarnations of the Dalai Lama and the Panchen Erdeni shall be confirmed in this manner, inscribing the names of the boy candidates in the Manchu, Han and Tibetan languages.

Article 2　Tibet has again become peaceful after His Majesty sent troops to the border region and the Gurkhas surrendered. Traders from neighbouring countries may therefore be allowed to come to Lhasa to stay and do business as usual provided that they abide by the law. Traders from neighbouring nations and Kashmir shall have their names reported to the Office of the Resident Ministers in Tibet for the record. Nepalese traders are allowed to come to Tibet three times a year and those from Kashmir, once a year. These traders, whatever their destinations, must have travel permits issued by the Office of the Resident Ministers at the request of their respective tribal chiefs, showing the specific routes they are to take. Two checkpoints are to be set up, one at Gyangze and the other at Tingri; traders passing through these points shall produce their travel permits for inspection. Foreigners who wish to travel to Lhasa shall be subject to investigation and their names are to be reported to the Office of the Resident Ministers. When foreigners arrive in Lhasa, they must register and again be subjected to inspection. The same procedures apply to those from Bhutan, Sikkim and Drongpa who wish to travel to Lhasa. Persons sent by the Tibetan government to Nepal to construct Buddhist images or who go as pilgrims shall be issued travel permits by the Resident Ministers; if they fail to return by the prescribed time, the Resident Ministers shall notify the Gurkha king and order them to return.

Article 3 The Tibetan *tramka* (a silver coin) has long been known to contain a lot of impurities. Henceforth, coins shall be minted with pure silver. The new coins, like the old ones, shall weigh one and a half *qian* each and be convertible to Han silver money at the rate of six pure silver *tramka* to a one *liang* [Before 1949, One *jin* (500 grammes) = 16 *liang* (10 *liang* today), One *liang* = 10 *qian* = 31.25 grammes, One *qian* = 3.125 grammes]Han silver coin. One *liang* of Han silver coin contains nine *qian* of silver, the one *qian* difference going to pay for the cost of manufacture. Silver coins minted by the government of Tibet or Nepal that contain no impurities shall be converted at the exchange rate quoted above. All the old *tramka* plus newly minted *tramka* not up to standard shall be converted into Han silver at the rate of eight such coins to one *liang* of Han silver money, and henceforth no *tramka* containing any impurities are to be minted.

Article 4 A standing army of 3,000 men is to be amassed, 1,000 of which are to be stationed in Upper Tibet, 1,000 in Lower Tibet, 500 in Gyangze, and the other 500 in Tingri. Soldiers shall be put under the command of a *dapon* in groups of 500. The Tibetan troops stationed in Lhasa shall be put under the authority of a *youji* (army officer with the rank of lieutenant—colonel) and those in Xigaze, Gyangze and Tingri under the authority of a *tusi* (army officer one rank below *youji*) in Xigaze. Two muster rolls for the army shall be maintained, one for the Office of the Resident Ministers in Tibet and the other for the *Kashak* (the Tibetan cabinet), for use in filling vacancies as they arise due to death or other circumstances.

Article 5 The *dapon* of the new army shall have 12 officers with the rank of *rupon* under his command, each in charge of 250 men; each *rupon* shall have 24 officers with the rank of *gyapon* under his command, each in charge of 125 men; and each *gyapon* shall have five officers with the rank of *dingpon* under his command in charge of 25 men each. These officers shall be selected from promising young men and issued certificates. Vacancies in the ranks of the officers shall be filled by those from the next lower rank through promotion. Those in the army who come from aristocratic or secular officials' families, when promoted, shall rise one rank at a time, starting from the rank of *dingpon;* arbitrary promotions are prohibited. According to the old practice, *dingpon* was usually a rank inaccessible to soldiers recruited from the common people. Henceforth, these soldiers shall not suffer such discrimination. Instead, they shall receive promotion, one rank at a time, on the basis of their ability and performance.

Article 6 In the past, rank—and—file soldiers were neither paid nor provided with food rations or weapons. Henceforth, each of them shall be issued 2.5 hectolitres of grain each year as food rations. As the grain levies from Upper and Lower Tibet alone will not be enough to meet the need for the rations, which will total 7,500 hectolitres of grain, grain from the estates of Shamarpa, Living Buddha Drungpa and Tandsin Palbyor shall also be appropriated. If there is still not enough, the difference shall be met by the proceeds from the sale of Shamarpa Blozang Jampal's property. The enlisted men will be given papers exempting them from corvée by the Dalai Lama. The *dapons* shall not receive any pay, as they have been given estates by the Dalai Lama. The *rupons* shall each be paid 36 *liang* of silver each year, the *gyapons* 20 *liang* and the *dingpons* 14.8 *liang*. The total of 2,600 *liang* of silver required for this purpose shall be provided by the Tibetan government, with payment made by the Resident Ministers in spring and autumn.

Article 7 Fifty percent of the army's equipment is to consist of guns, 30 percent bows and arrows, and 20 percent swords and spears. The weapons may be purchased from the monasteries in Upper and Lower Tibet and paid for out of the more than 550 *liang* of silver from the income of Shamarpa's ranch. Weapons and ammunition shall be made in Gongbo and Banbar by men sent there each year by the Tibetan government. Regular drills shall be carried out for the soldiers.

Article 8 The income of the Dalai Lama and the Panchen Erdeni has been handled entirely by their relatives and attendants. Such an arrangement is prone to accounting errors and embezzlement. The Resident Ministers in Tibet have been authorized by His Majesty to make regular audits of their accounts and report the findings twice a year in spring and autumn.

Article 9 Like all Buddhas, who bless all living creatures, the Dalai Lama expounds the Buddhist sutras among the masses of monks and shows great reverence for the monasteries, bringing happiness to all living creatures and benevolence to the people. To relieve the people of their suffering at the hands of bandits, a decision has been made to exempt the inhabitants in Kyirong, Rongxar and Nyalam from all corvée services for two years. A one—year exemption is granted to those in Zongga, Tingri, Khada and Tshongdu. It has also been decided that all the inhabitants in Upper and Lower Tibet shall be forgiven all taxes in arrears accumulated prior to the Year of the Iron Hog, and that monk and lay officials of the government and heads of *dzongs* and *shis* shall have their corvée in arrears reduced by half. These decisions have been made to ensure peace and tranquillity in Tibet.

Article 10 The Permanent Office of the Resident Ministers in Tibet shall hold consultations with the Potala Palace if important matters arise. Other matters shall be decided by the Dalai Lama, the Panchen Erdeni and the Resident Ministers on equal footing. All those working under the government ministers, including the Living Buddhas, shall be subordinate to the Resident Ministers regardless of their position or rank. Solpon Khanpo shall take charge of the local affairs of Tashilhunpo and handle matters fairly. He shall report all important matters to the Resident Ministers so that the latter will be able to find out the truth when he visits Tashilhunpo on inspection tours.

Article 11 When a vacancy arises in the office of a government minister, candidates to fill the vacancy shall be selected from among the *dapons, tsepons* and *chanzods* on the basis of ability and performance as government officials. Two candidates prepared jointly by the Resident Ministers in Tibet and the Dalai Lama shall be submitted to His Majesty for selection and appointment. Candidates to fill a vacancy left by a lama minister are to be selected from among Grand Khanpos and their names submitted to the higher authorities for appointment. A position left vacant by a *dapon* shall be filled through promotion from the ranks of border region *dzongpons*. The successful candidate is to be selected from two candidates and approved by the higher authorities. No military officer's position shall be left vacant and military training shall be continuous. When a position of *tsepon* or *chanzod* becomes vacant, the vacancy shall be filled by a candidate selected from among the *nyertsangpas,* law—enforcement officers, the grand secretary of the *Kashak* or the *tsezong* lamas. A vacant position among the *nyertsangpas* or law—enforcement officials shall be filled by a candidate selected from among the *shodepas, mipons* or *tapons. Tapons* are to be selected from among the *dzongpons* of all levels and *dronnyers* of the *Kashak;* monk officials of the rank of *nyertsangpa* or *shodepa* from among lamaist monks; the grand secretary from among minor secretaries or *dronnyers; dzongpons* of large counties and frontier counties from among *dzongpons* of small counties; minor secretaries from among *gyapons* of the army and other appropriate persons; and *dzongpons* of frontier counties and small counties from among low–ranking functionaries. For better administration, a file shall be kept on the personal details of all *dzongpons*. In the past, all monk *dzongpons* came from among the attendants of the Dalai Lama and they had agents working on their behalf. Henceforth, agents shall be nominated and appointed by the Resident Ministers. The *dronnyers* and the minor secretaries of the *Kashak*, although low in position, are important persons, as they assist the government ministers in their work. Therefore, only capable persons selected from among lay officials should hold these positions. Two *tsepons* and two *tsezongs* shall be appointed to manage the mint. Except for government ministers and *dapons*, who are to be appointed by His Majesty, all officials may be appointed by common agreement of the Dalai Lama and the Resident Ministers in Tibet. All shall be issued authorization papers in the Manchu, Han and Tibetan languages. Managerial personnel and guards responsible for firewood, roasted barley flour, tents and pasturelands for the Dalai Lama may be appointed by the Dalai Lama himself. In Tashilhunpo, a vacancy in the position of *chanzod* shall be filled by the *solpon* lama or the *senpon* lama; in the position of *solpon*, by the *tsezong*; and in the position of *senpon*, by the *dronnyer*. The promotion of these officials shall proceed one rank at a time. As the area of Tashilhunpo is not large, the distribution of *ula* (corvée labour service) quotas may remain the same as before. The appointment and authorization papers for *chanzods*, *solpons*, *senpons* and *dzongpons* of large counties shall be the joint responsibility of the Resident Ministers in Tibet and the Panchen Erdeni, as is stipulated for Upper Tibet. Minor appointments may be made by the Panchen Erdeni as before.

Article 12 It would not be proper for those related to the Dalai Lama and the Panchen Erdeni to engage in politics. It is stipulated that while the Dalai Lama and the Panchen Erdeni live, all their relatives shall be barred from holding public office, and that when they have passed away, their surviving relatives shall be given work in the government compatible with their capabilities.

Article 13 Each spring and autumn the two Resident Ministers in Tibet shall take turns making official visits to various places in Lower Tibet to inspect the troops. They shall also investigate complaints concerning any misconduct of Han officials or *dzongpons* toward the armymen and civilians. The local people shall be paid in full for services they provide to the Resident Ministers on these inspection tours.

Article 14 Disputes between Tibet and the neighbouring countries of Gurkha, Bhutan, Sikkim and Drongpa have been caused by inappropriate responses from the Dalai Lama to missions from these countries regarding pilgrimages to Tibet, payment of tribute to Tibet or the handling of affairs concerning Tibet and its neighbours. The war with the Gurkhas, for example, was the result of indiscretion on the part of Tibet in handling communications regarding the problem of silver coins. In future, all replies to Gurkha representatives who come to see the Dalai Lama or the Resident Ministers shall conform to the ministers' instructions. Correspondence from foreign countries to Tibet shall also be subject to censorship by the Resident Ministers. When the neighbouring countries of Bhutan, Sikkim, Drongpa and Lo Menthang send missions to pay tribute to the Dalai Lama and the Panchen Erdeni, the items of tribute shall be inspected carefully, but no objections shall be raised. The *dzongpons* of frontier counties shall keep a record of the number of foreigners coming into Tibet and report the figures to the Resident Ministers. Foreigners shall be inspected by the Han officials at Gyangze and Tingri. Letters from foreign countries to the Resident Ministers shall be handled by the ministers. Replies to letters from foreign countries written to the Dalai Lama and others shall be sent to the Resident Ministers for approval. As officials handling Tibetan and Han affairs, the government ministers are not allowed to carry on correspondence with foreign countries without authorization. Replies to letters from foreign countries addressed to them shall be subject to joint review by the Resident Ministers and the Dalai Lama, and the government ministers are not permitted to reply without authorization.

Article 15 Kyirong, Nyalam, Rongxar, Khada, Saga and Khumbu border on Gurkha territory; therefore, boundary markers are to be erected without delay by the Riban Bridge in Kyirong, by the Zham Bridge in Nyalam and at the border in Rongxar, to prevent Nepalese and Tibetans from illegally crossing the border. The Resident Ministers in Tibet shall check the boundary markers during their inspection tours of these places.

Article 16 The administration of the inhabitants of the border regions and the inspection of travelers passing through these areas are extremely important duties for the *dzongpons* of frontier counties. To avoid incompetence in these matters, the *dzongpons* of frontier counties shall be selected from among capable *dzongpons* of small counties and army officers. At the end of their three-year term of office, those who have successfully carried out their duties shall be eligible for promotion to the position of *dapon;* those found to be incompetent shall be demoted.

Article 17 In the past only the aristocrats of Tibet were allowed to hold government positions at or above the rank of *dapon,* while the common people were restricted to minor positions at or below the rank of *dingpon*. This is not proper. Henceforth, rank-and-file soldiers, regardless of their social status, may be promoted one rank at a time from *dingpon* up to *dapon,* if they prove themselves brave and resourceful. In general, government positions may be filled by aristocrats as before. However, young boys of the nobility who inherit their fathers' positions may not be competent to carry out the government work properly and, therefore, no one shall be appointed as a minor secretary, *dronnyer* or *dzongpon* of a small county until he reaches the age of 18.

Article 18 *Khanpos*, who serve as heads of monasteries, should be men of great learning and sound moral character. *Khanpos* of certain major monasteries own many estates and make money from commercial activities. Henceforth, the *khanpos* of all major monasteries shall be appointed through consultation by the Dalai Lama, the Resident Ministers and Living Buddha Kyirong and receive documents of authorization bearing their three seals. *Khanpos* for smaller monasteries shall be appointed by the Dalai Lama as before.

Article 19 Tax levied by the government and the difference of money in bartering shall be paid in the new or old *tramka* in accordance with the new regulations. Excessive levies are prohibited.

Article 20 The rates of transit duties on rice, salt and other items levied at Kyirong and Nyalam shall remain the same as before; the Tibetan government shall not increase these rates in the slightest without the approval of the Resident Ministers.

Article 21 The poor in Tibet are over—burdened with taxes and corvée while the rich and the relatives of the Dalai Lama have papers issued by the Grand Living Buddha exempting them from taxes and corvée. Those on the estates of the government ministers, *dapons* and Grand Lamas also hold such papers. All such papers shall be withdrawn to ensure equity in the distribution of corvée quotas. Only those who deserve exemption from corvée plus recruits for the army shall be eligible to hold these papers, which shall be issued jointly by the Dalai Lama and the Resident Ministers. When a soldier dies, his papers shall be rescinded.

Article 22 The Resident Ministers in Tibet and the Dalai Lama shall each be given a complete list of names of the Grand Lamas, lamas and *dragpas* of the monasteries and a list, to be prepared by the government ministers, of the inhabitants in the hamlets under the Living Buddhas throughout Tibet. Anyone caught crossing the border without a passport shall be punished.

Article 23 Missions sent from Qinghai carrying invitations for learned lamas to visit Qinghai sometimes informed the Resident Ministers in Tibet when they entered Tibet and sometimes not. Henceforth such missions must apply to the Resident Ministers in Tibet, going through the Resident Minister in Xining, for travel permits before they enter Tibet. Official messages shall be sent to the Resident Minister in Xining for examination. Lamas on pilgrimages outside Tibet must also have passports issued by the Resident Ministers in Tibet.

Article 24 Formerly, relatives of the government ministers, *dapons* and the Dalai Lama always made use of permits issued by the Dalai Lama entitling them to the use of corvée to transport food for private purposes. In future no one shall be allowed to use this free labour service when carrying out private business and no permits shall be issued without authorization for this purpose. Those traveling on government business shall require a permit bearing the seals of both the Resident Ministers in Tibet and the Dalai Lama.

Article 25 The regulations in Tibet for handling crimes such as fighting, murder and theft are different from those of the interior. To win the trust of the people, the old regulations shall be discontinued and future court decisions must be commensurate with the seriousness of the offence. Recent rulings made by the government ministers and the *mipons* have not only been unfair, but the fines were unreasonable and a lot of money, sheep and cattle turned over as fines from the rich went into their own pockets instead of being turned over to the government. Many of the government ministers have taken advantage of their power to confiscate the assets of people of low social standing on false charges, reporting their decisions only to the Dalai Lama. From now on, records of the amount of all fines shall be sent to the Resident Ministers in Tibet. The most serious crimes are to be handled by the Resident Ministers. The confiscation of an offender's property henceforth also requires the approval of the Resident Ministers. All lawsuits shall be handled impartially whether the parties involved are civilians or holders of public office. Government ministers found guilty of taking illegal possession of other people's property by abusing their power shall be dismissed from their posts and have their property confiscated.

Article 26 Ammunition needed for the exercises of the army shall be produced at Gongbo by highly trained officers sent by the government ministers and authorized by the Resident Ministers in Tibet. The ammunition shall be brought to Lhasa to be distributed to the troops. Two of the newly made 13 cannons shall be given to the troops in Lower Tibet, which never had cannons before, for target practice during training exercises. The remaining cannons shall be handed over to the Potala Palace.

Article 27 The government ministers and *dapons* were customarily given their official residences and estates by the Dalai Lama upon their appointment and turned them over to their successors when they left office. However, family members of some former government ministers and *dapons* held on to these places and other official residences and estates had to be allocated to the newly appointed government ministers and *dapons*. From now on, all outgoing government ministers and *dapons* shall turn over their residences and estates to their successors.

Article 28 The dates for the payment of salaries to the Living Buddhas and lamas have been stipulated. However, there have been many instances in recent years of advance payment of their salaries. Henceforth, no advance payment shall be allowed. Living Buddha Kyirong shall investigate this matter, and those responsible for advance or undue payment of salaries shall be disciplined.

Article 29 Monk officials are sent to nearby villages to collect taxes, and lay officials to distant villages. Recent investigation has uncovered embezzlement of tax money by some monk and lay officials as well as *dzongpons* every year, leading to accumulated arrears in government tax revenues. Cases of levies turned over a year in advance have also been found. In addition, corvée for runaway inhabitants were arbitrarily reassigned to those bound to their land. All this has added to the burden of the people and thus made life miserable for them. Henceforth, monk and lay officials as well as *dzongpons* shall collect only the taxes that fall due; collection in advance shall be prohibited. Runaway inhabitants shall be exempted from corvee, but they shall undertake it as usual after they have returned to their home villages.

The 2nd month of the 58th year of Qianlong (1793)

Preserved by the Archives of the Tibet Autonomous Region.

# རྗེ་དྲུང་ཧོ་ཐོག་ཐུ་དང་བཀའ་བློན་ཐུན་མོང་གིས་མདའ་དཔོན་ཁ་སྐོང་བྱེད་རྒྱུའི་སྐོར་བོད་བཞུགས་ཨམ་བན་ལ་བཏང་བའི་ཡི་གེ

# 濟隆呼圖克圖及諸噶倫爲補放代本事咨駐藏大臣文

# Communication from Living Buddha Rjedrung and Government Ministers to the Resident Ministers in Tibet Regarding the Filling of a *Dapon* Vacancy

61.7×49.5

བོད་རང་སྐྱོང་ལྗོངས་ཡིག་ཚགས་ཁང་དུ་ཉར་ཚགས་བྱས་ཡོད།

主持黄教之濟隆呼圖克圖與諸噶倫咨行欽差駐藏諸辦事大臣

爲四品官後藏代本江堅·次仁多吉病故出缺事。業經江孜守備陳玉顔及我等商量。五品官江孜如本白瑪旺杰德才兼備，年富力强，祖輩勞苦功高；定日如本杰布次仁年青有爲，才技優長，品貌與生計中等；日喀則如本諾增品貌與技能均優，生計中等。又據諸駐藏大臣來文内開：按照舊例裁定等因，若有適宜選拔之人可禀報，本人已與駐噶倫商量並擬從江孜、日喀則、定日等各如本當中選拔以上三名品貌端正、精明能幹的如本爲代本候選人。其他如本如江孜如本尼瑪與定日如本索朗達杰二位，品貌與生計一般，以上如本中選誰爲好，請諸駐藏大臣予以定奪。邊界宗堆中有適宜之人，但相距較遠，因邊界事務繁重而不能上報。

特呈。

西藏自治區檔案館藏

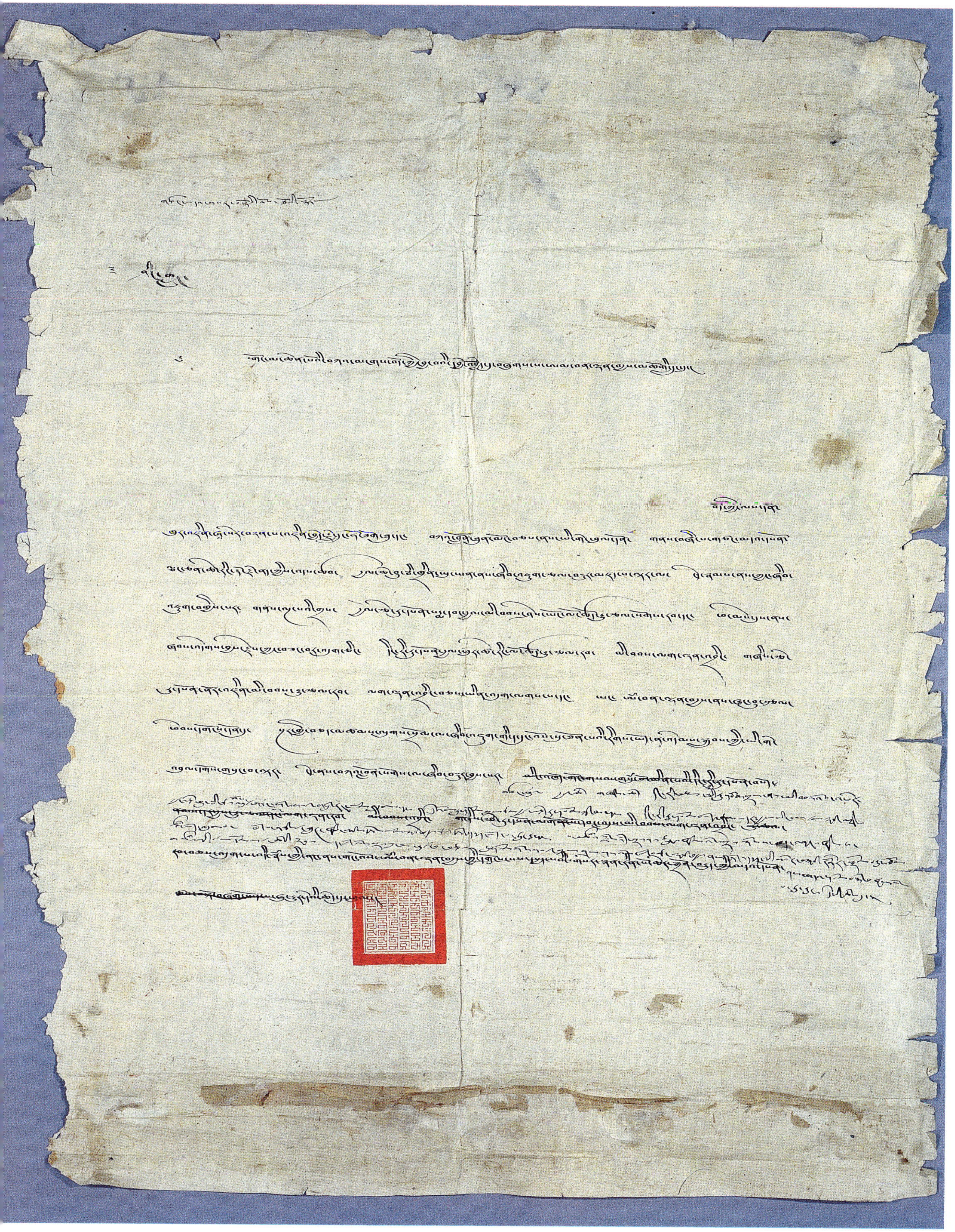

Living Buddha Rjedrung, who presides over the Yellow Sect, and the government ministers send this communication to the Resident Ministers in Tibet:

Concerning the filling of the vacancy caused by the death from illness of Lcangjian Shering, a 4th–ranking *dapon* in Lower Tibet. Chen Yuyan, garrison commander at Gyangze, has consulted with us, after which we decided on the following persons: Palma Wangyal, 5th–ranking *rupon* of Gyangze, who is young, able and morally sound, and whose forefathers were hard workers who made great contributions; Yalpo Shering, *rupon* of Tingri, who is young and shows promise, is technically skilled, and has an average appearance and occupation; and Nodsin, *rupon* of Xigaze, who has an excellent appearance and possesses ability and has an average occupation. The communication from the Resident Ministers in Tibet states that the names of any persons eligible for selection should be reported so that a decision can be made according to precedent. After consulting with the government ministers we have decided to select the three candidates mentioned above from among the *rupons* in Gyangze, Xigaze and Tingri and other eligible *rupons,* such as Nyima of Gyangze and Sonang Dayal of Tingri, who are average with respect to appearance and occupation. Please make the final decision as to who among the above is most eligible. Owing to the distance involved and the difficulties entailed in handling border affairs, persons suitable for selection among the *zongtuis* in the border area have not been reported.

Preserved by the Archives of the Tibet Autonomous Region.

# བོད་བཞུགས་ཨམ་བན་ཡུ་ཉིང་སོགས་ཀྱིས་སྤྱི་ཁྱབ་མཁན་པོ་ཁ་སྐོང་བྱེད་རྒྱུའི་སྐོར་རྗེ་དྲུང་ཧོ་ཐོག་ཐུ་ལ་བཏང་བའི་ཡི་གེ

# 駐藏大臣玉寧等爲補放基巧堪布事咨濟隆呼圖克圖文

# Communication from the Resident Minister in Tibet Yu Ning to Living Buddha Rjedrung Regarding the Filling of a Jiqiao Khanpo Vacancy

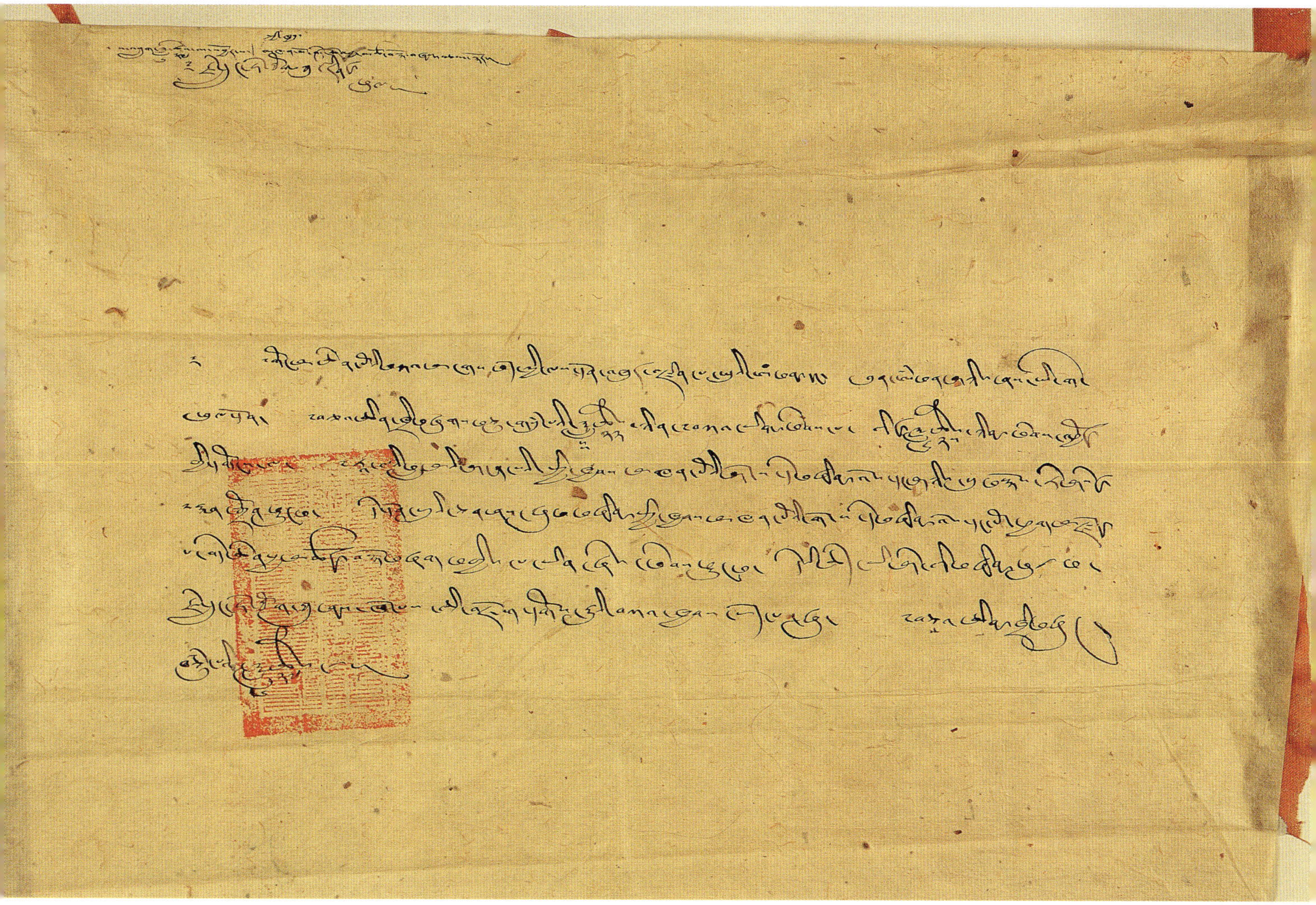

བོད་རང་སྐྱོང་ལྗོངས་ཡིག་ཚགས་ཁང་དུ་ཉར་ཚགས་བྱས་ཡོད།

欽差駐藏辦事大臣玉寧、文弼咨行：

嘉慶十三年閏五月二十二日來文，已於六月二十五日收悉。內開：補放達賴喇嘛的侍從基巧堪布之正選、備選名單已報等因。此據玉寧所禀，將正選人强佐德慶嘉措補基巧堪布之缺。請濟隆呼圖克圖下令遵行。特呈。

嘉慶十三年（公元1808年）六月二十七日

西藏自治區檔案館藏

The Resident Minister Yu Ning and Deputy Resident Minister Wen Bi in Tibet issue the following notice:

Your document of the 22nd day of the 5th month (leap month) of the 13th year of Jiaqing was received on the 25th day of the 6th month. It states that ″the list of main and alternate candidates for the vacancy of Jiqiao Khanpo, senior attendant to the Dalai Lama, is being submitted for approval, etc.″ In this regard, it is hereby decided that main candidate Yamtsho Tinchen Kyashog is to be appointed to fill the vacancy. Living Buddha Rjedrung is requested to give the order to carry this out.

The 27th day of the 6th month of the 13th year of Jiaqing (1808)

Preserved by the Archives of the Tibet Autonomous Region.

# གོང་མ་བཀྱགས་སྟོན་གྱིས་ཏཱ་ལའི་བླ་མའི་ཡང་སྲིད་ངོས་འཛིན་བྱུང་བའི་དོན་དུ་པཎ་ཆེན་རིན་པོ་ཆེར་བསྩལ་པའི་བཀའ་ལུང་།
# 嘉慶皇帝爲確立達賴喇嘛靈童事給班禪活佛的敕諭
# Emperor Jiaqing's Decree to Living Buddha Panchen Confirming the Status of the Holy Child Dalai Lama

162 × 95.5

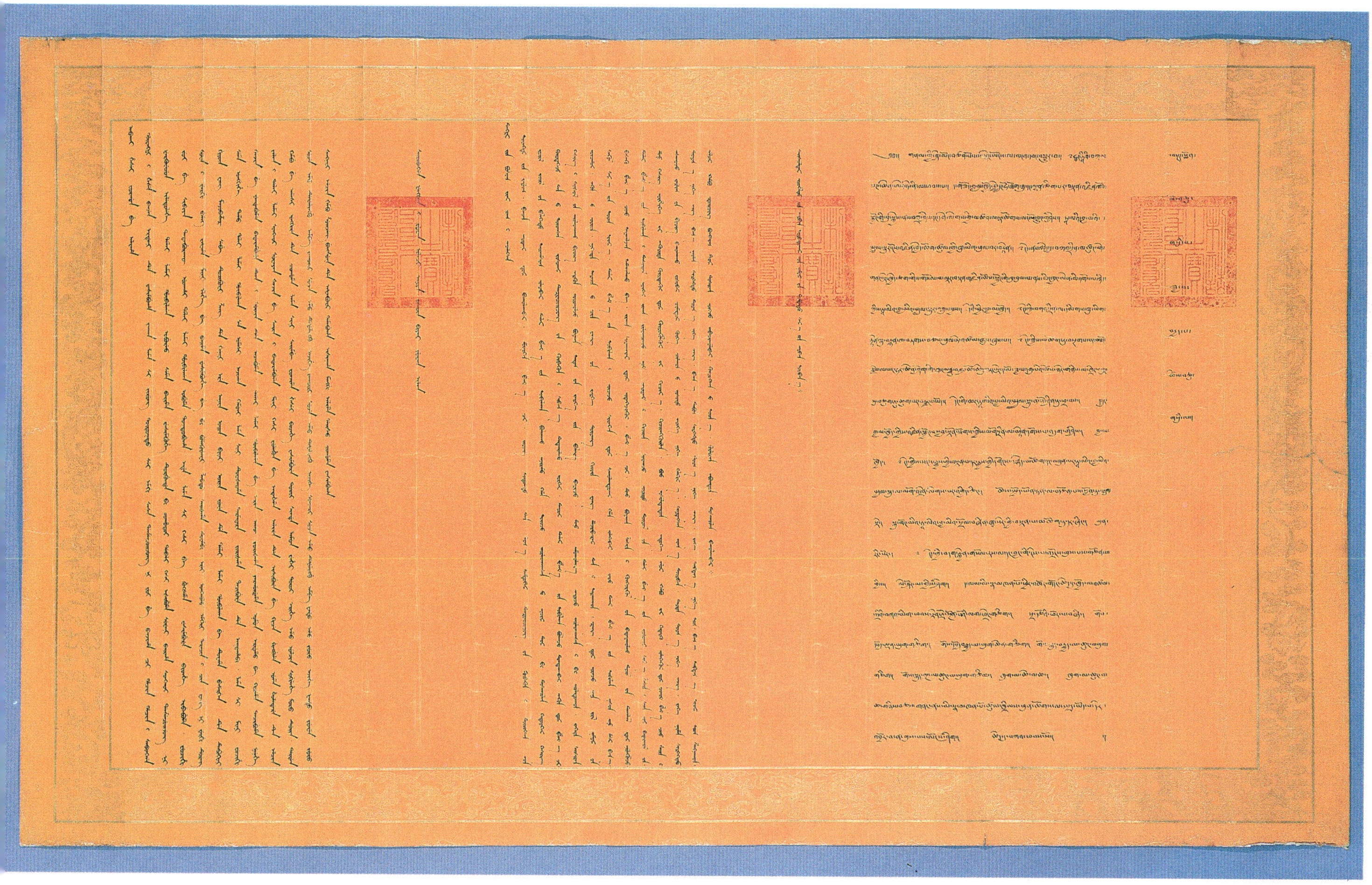

53 - 1

བོད་རང་སྐྱོང་ལྗོངས་ཡིག་ཚགས་ཁང་དུ་ཉར་ཚགས་བྱས་ཡོད།

奉天承運皇帝詔曰：

　　諭班禪額爾德尼。適才據喇嘛爾、濟隆呼圖克圖等共同奏請：丹增吹鍾之子自降生以來，多有吉祥佳兆，可作爲達賴喇嘛之呼畢勒罕等情。朕特逾格施恩照爾等所請將丹增吹鍾之子

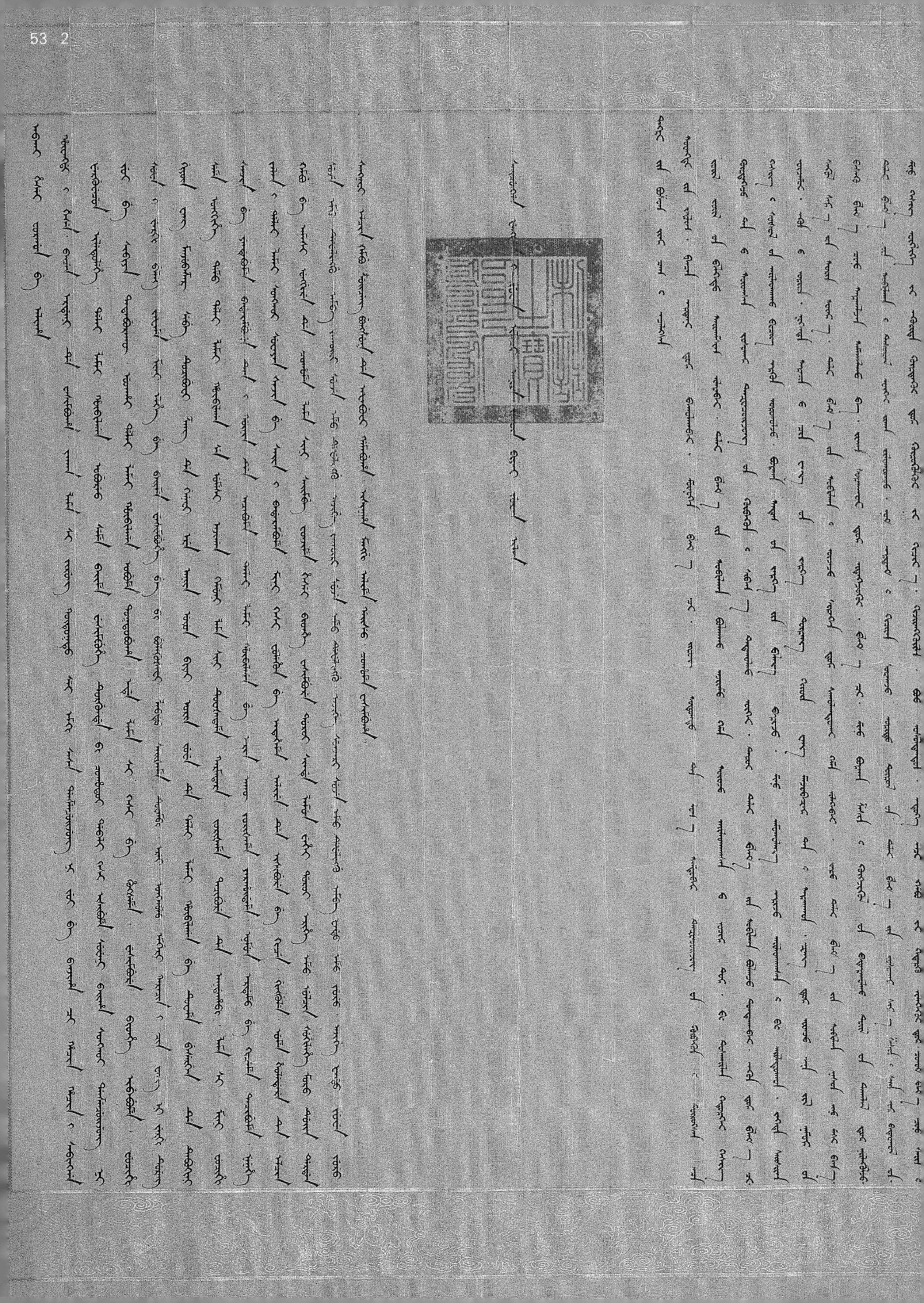

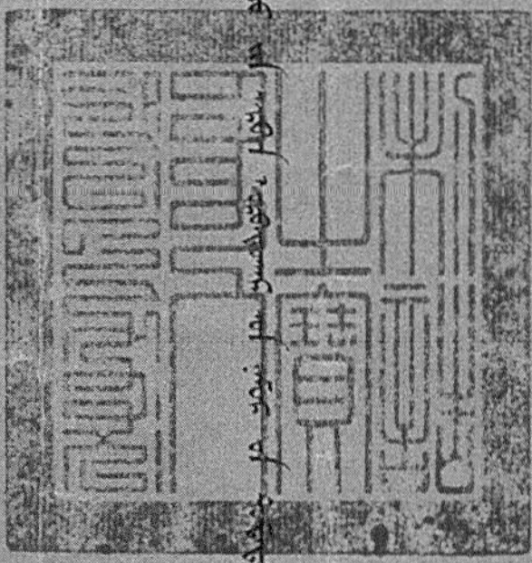

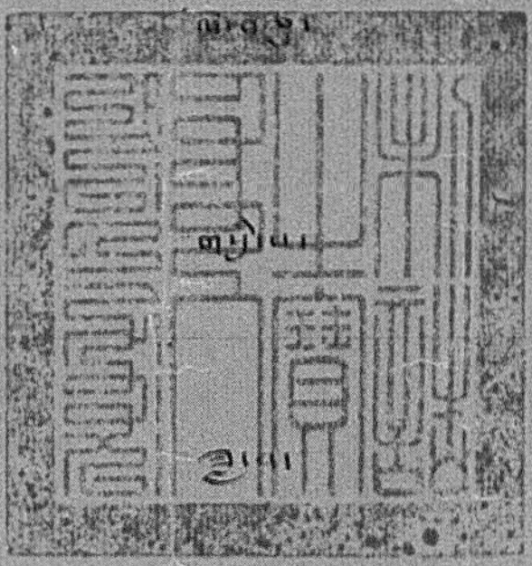

[illegible]

[illegible]

[illegible]

[illegible]

[illegible]

[illegible]

[illegible]

[illegible]

[illegible]

[illegible]

[illegible]

[illegible]

[illegible]

[illegible]

[illegible]

[illegible]

[illegible]

[illegible]

[illegible]

免予掣簽，即定爲達賴喇嘛之呼畢勒罕矣。故此喇嘛爾進奏表叩恩，恭獻佛尊哈達等禮物，並奏請朕安。朕覽之，甚爲嘉悦。此前已派遣喀喇沁親王銜杜楞郡王曼珠巴扎爾前往藏地，於今年九月二十二日看視達賴喇嘛之呼畢勒罕坐床。惟達賴喇嘛之呼畢勒罕甚年少，仍須喇嘛爾護佑指教，喇嘛爾仰副朕興扶佛教之至意，經常指導達賴喇嘛之呼畢勒罕，勤習經藝，以期照前世達賴喇嘛弘揚黄教，永沐朕恩。勉之勿怠。今使者堪布返回，特問候喇嘛爾好，隨敕賞爾藍寶石佛珠一串、漆碗四隻、妝緞一匹、大八絲緞一匹、小八絲緞一匹、小五絲緞一匹、大荷包一對、小荷包二對，交付使者堪布炊誠朋楚克携回。至時祗領。特諭。

嘉慶十三年（公元1808年）八月十三日

西藏自治區檔案館藏

His Majesty the Emperor, who reigns by the mandate of Heaven, decrees:

This is to instruct the Panchen Erdeni. You and Living Buddha Rjedrung have recently sent me a petition stating that the son of Tandsin Choskyong has been associated with auspicious signs since his birth, making him eligible to be considered as the possible reincarnation of the Dalai Lama. I have decided to diverge from the usual practice to grant your request, allowing the son of Tandsin Choskyong to be named the reincarnation of the Dalai Lama without going through the drawing of lots. For this you submitted a petition expressing deep gratitude, respectfully accompanied by gifts such as the statue of Buddha and the *hatas,* along with wishes for my good health. I was very pleased on reading your petition. Some time ago, I sent Manju Badacho, Dulong Jungwang who holds the title of Harchensho Giwang, to Tibet to preside over the enthronement of the child Dalai Lama on the 22nd day of the 9th month of this year. However, since the Dalai Lama is still young, he still needs your tutelage and guidance. To fulfil my sincere desire for the promotion of Buddhism, you need to give a great deal of guidance to the child Dalai Lama as he diligently studies the Buddhist scriptures, so that he will follow the example of the Dalai Lama of the last incarnation in promoting the Yellow Sect of Lamaism and enjoy my favour for ever, working tirelessly toward this end. As your envoy is going back, I am sending you my greetings and present you with a chaplet of sapphire beads, four lacquered bowls, a roll of *zhuang* satin, a roll of large *basi* satin, a roll of small *basi* satin, a roll of small *wusi* satin, a pair of large pouches and two pairs of small pouches, all of which your envoy Khanpo Tshulkhri Phuntshog is carrying back with him. This is the end of the instructions.

The 13th day of the 8th month of the 13th year of Jiaqing (1808)

Preserved by the Archives of the Tibet Autonomous Region.

54

# བོད་བཞུགས་ཨམ་བན་ཝུན་པེ་སོགས་ཀྱིས་རག་རྩིས་པ་སོགས་གནས་སྤར་དང་བསྐོ་བཞག་བྱེད་རྒྱུའི་སྐོར་བཀའ་བློན་རྣམས་ལ་བཏང་བའི་ཡི་གེ

# 駐藏大臣文弼等爲熱孜巴等人升調事咨諸噶倫文

# Resident Minister in Tibet Wen Bi's Communication to the Government Ministers Regarding the Promotion and Transfer of Ragtsispa and Others

64.4 × 56.2

བོད་རང་སྐྱོང་ལྗོངས་ཡིག་ཚགས་ཁང་དུ་ཉར་ཚགས་བྱས་ཡོད།

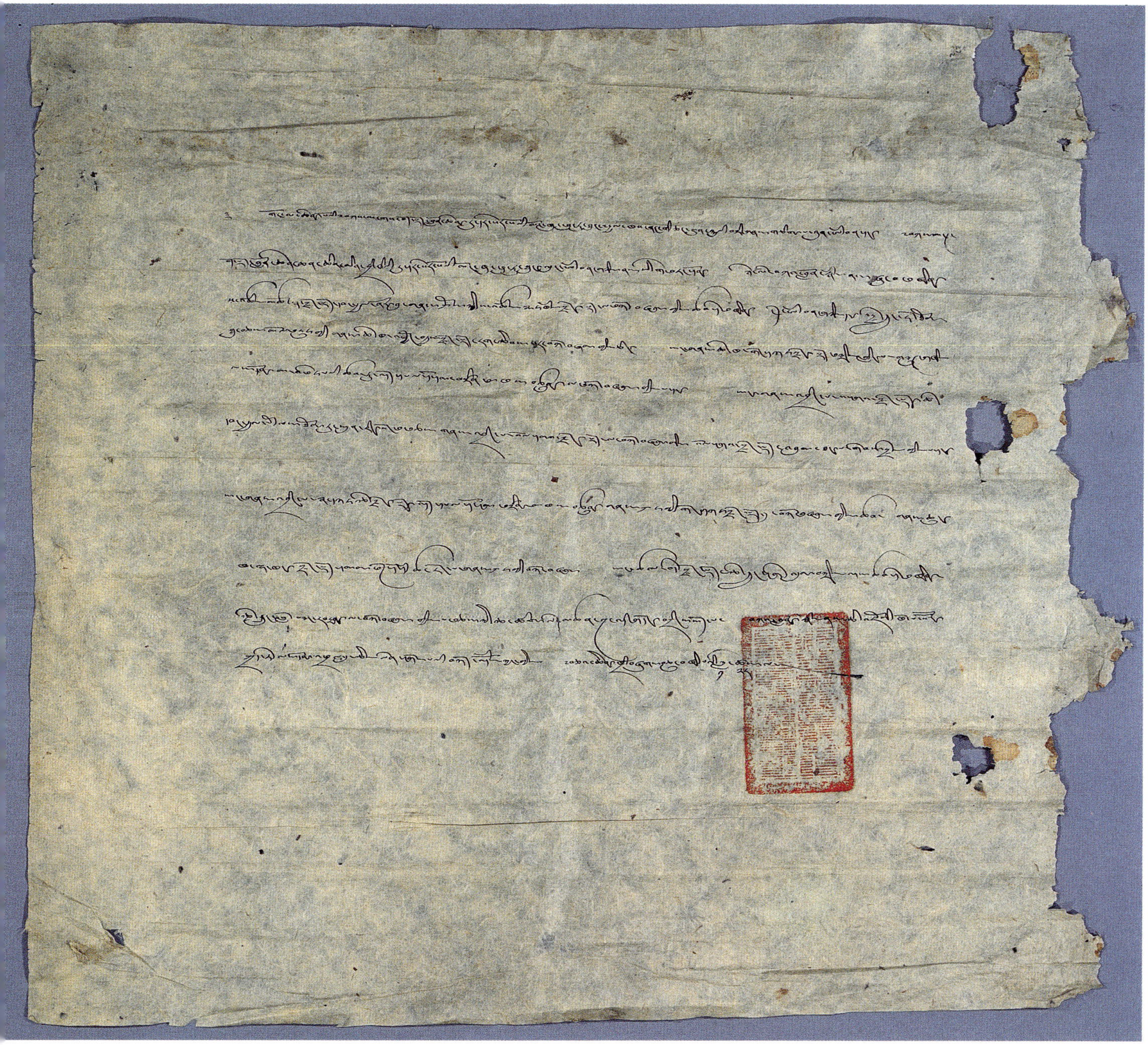

欽差駐藏辦事大臣鑲黄旗蒙古副都統、將軍銜大臣文弼，欽差駐藏大臣乾清門侍衛鑲黄旗蒙古副都統、大臣隆福咨行：

頃據諸噶倫呈稱：邊界宗措那宗堆旺杰羅布出任邊界芒康宗堆等因。經本大臣二人與濟隆呼圖克圖商議，由熱孜巴出任大宗窮結宗宗堆。大宗貢嘎宗堆扎西林巴因身體欠佳出缺，此缺補任堆白多旦丹增克尊。中等宗次旺杰布久任薩噶宗宗堆，應與現任維噶宗堆崩塘調換，分赴就職。中等宗浪卡子宗堆堆白多旦丹增克尊升任貢嘎宗堆。小宗拉康宗堆軍餉管事擦容升補其缺。采德宗堆孜仲更敦扎西因卒出缺，由孜仲洛桑熱旦補任。五張任職書均已發出，望諸噶倫遵行發給上述人員，並令火速赴任。

嘉慶十四年（公元1809年）正月二十八日

西藏自治區檔案館藏

Wen Bi, Resident Minister in Tibet by Imperial Order, Mongolian Vice–Commander of the Yellow–Bordered Banner and Minister with the Rank of General, and Long Fu, Resident Minister in Tibet by Imperial Order, Guard of Qianqing Gate, Mongolian Vice–Commander of the Yellow–Bordered Banner and Minister, issue the following communication:

The government ministers have just submitted a petition which states "Wanggyas Norbu, *zongtui* of Cona County on the border, is to be appointed *zongtui* of Markam County on the border, etc." After Living Buddha Rjedrung and we two discussed this matter, we decided that Ragtsispa should be appointed *zongtui* of the large county of Qonggyai. The post vacated because of health problems by Krashis Lingpa, *zongtui* of the large county of Gonggar, should be filled by Dodpal Dodam Tandsin Khasgrub. Tshewang Gyalpo, who has served as the *zongtui* of the medium–sized county of Saga for many years, should trade posts with Bumthang, who is currently the *zongtui* of Volgav County, and each should begin work on reaching his new destination. Dodpal Dodam Tandsin Khasgrub, *zongtui* of the medium–sized county of Nagarze, is being promoted to the *zongtui* of Gonggar County. His vacancy should be filled by Tsharong, officer in charge of soldiers' pay and provisions for the small county of Lhakhang. The vacancy caused by the death of Tsisdrung Gedun Krashis, *zongtui* of Dogde County, should be filled by Tsisdrung Blozang Rabtan. The five orders of appointment, which have already been sent out, should be properly executed by the government ministers distributing them to the above–mentioned personnel and ordering them to set out immediately for their posts.

The 28th day of the 1st month of the 14th year of Jiaqing (1809)

Preserved by the Archives of the Tibet Autonomous Region.

# གོང་མ་བཛྲགས་སྟོན་གྱིས་ལེགས་སྐྱེས་ཕུལ་བར་གསོལ་རས་གནང་བའི་དོན་དུ་ཏཱ་ལའི་བླ་མར་བསྩལ་བའི་བཀའ་ལུང་།

# 嘉慶皇帝爲貢賞事給達賴喇嘛的敕諭

# Emperor Jiaqing's Decree to the Dalai Lama on Presenting Him with Gifts

157×98.5

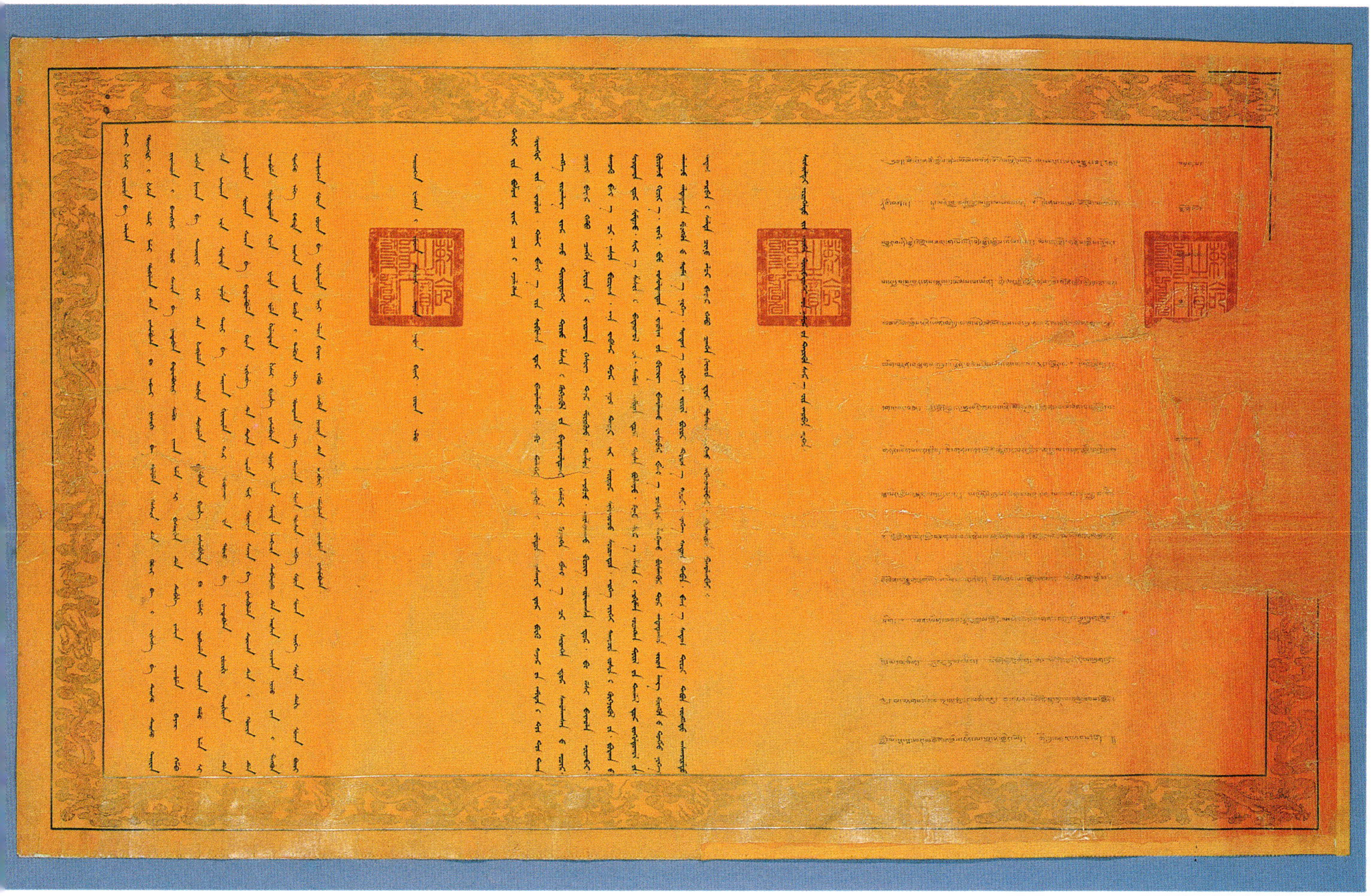

55－1

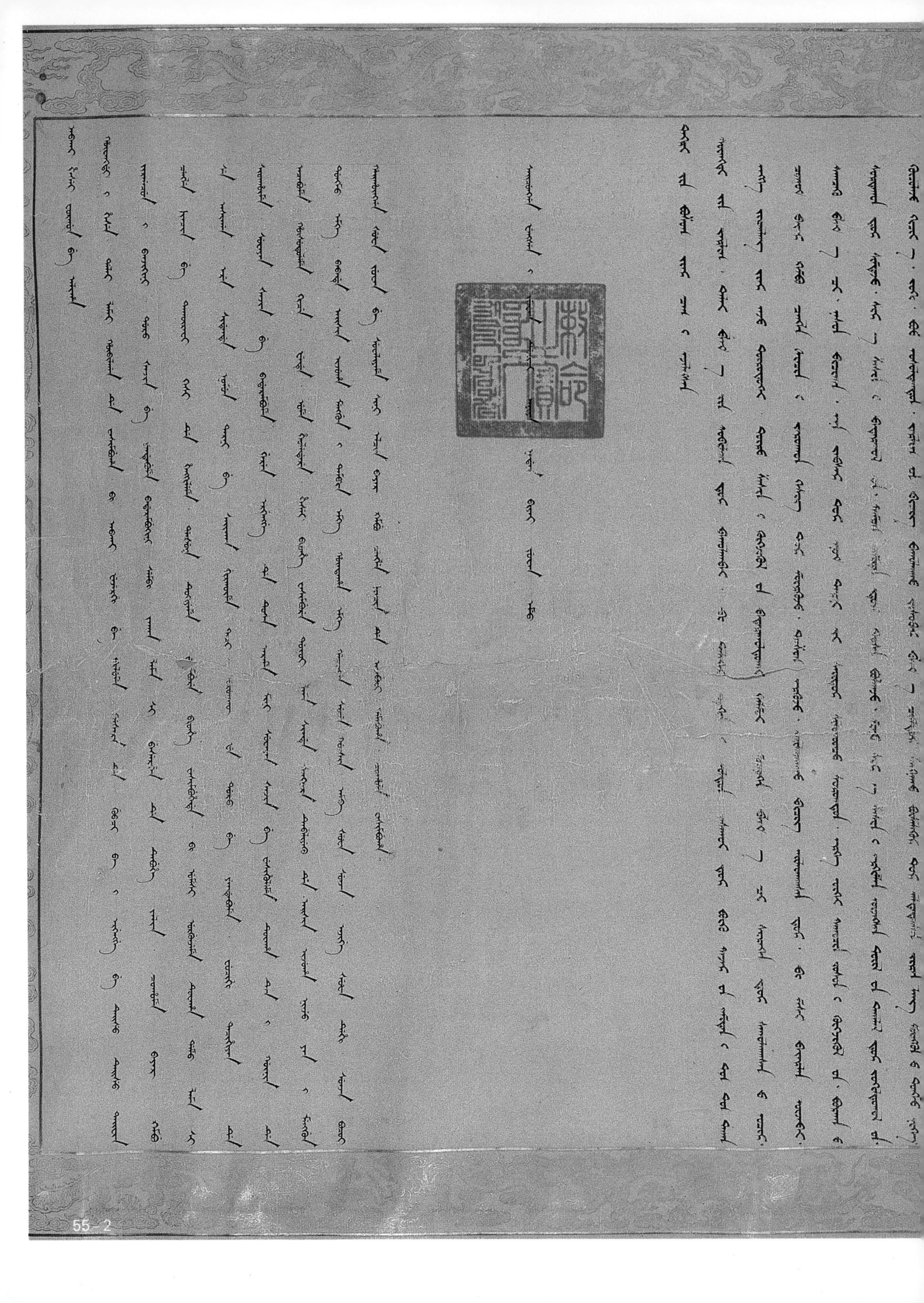

敕命之寶

敕命之寶
敕命之寶

བོད་རང་སྐྱོང་ལྗོངས་ཡིག་ཚགས་ཁང་དུ་ཉར་ཚགས་བྱས་ཡོད།

奉天承運皇帝詔曰：

諭達賴喇嘛之呼畢勒罕。朕撫馭天下，惟期率土之民，各安生業，推興政教。適才喇嘛爾爲坐床事特遣巴雅爾堪布成勒仁欽叩恩，敬獻丹書克，恭進奏表，朕均欣閱。惟喇嘛爾年少，此間須用心學習經咒，務興舊道，致力佛法，弘揚黃教，造福衆生，以期仰副朕尊崇黃教之至意，勿得怠惰。隨敕賞賜喇嘛爾鍍金六十兩重銀茶桶一個、銀瓶一個、酥油燈一盞、各色綢緞三十匹、大哈達五條、小哈達四十條、五色哈達十條，一併交付爾使巴雅爾堪布成勒仁欽携回。特諭。

嘉慶十四年（公元1809年）七月十一日

西藏自治區檔案館藏

His Majesty the Emperor, who reigns by the mandate of Heaven, decrees:

These are instructions to the Holy Child Dalai Lama. I rule the Empire allowing people all over the land to live in peace, improve the political situation and promote the religion. You, the Dalai Lama, have sent the Bayer Khanpo Phrinlas Rinchen to express deep gratitude on the occasion of your enthronement, respectfully present me with a *danshuke* and submit a petition. I was pleased on reading your petition. However, since you are still young, you must devote yourself to the study of Buddhist scriptures, promote the traditional way, work hard to study the precepts of Buddha, promote the Yellow Sect of Lamaism and help all living beings, so as to fulfil my earnest desire to honour the Yellow Sect by working tirelessly to attain this goal. With this decree I am sending you a 60–*liang* gold–plated silver container for tea leaves, a silver vase, a butter lamp, 30 rolls of assorted silk, five large and 40 small *hatas,* 10 five–coloured *hatas,* all with your envoy Bayer Khanpo Phrinlas Rinchen. This is the end of the instructions.

The 11th day of the 7th month of the 14th year of Jiaqing (1809)

Preserved by the Archives of the Tibet Autonomous Region.

# བོད་བཞུགས་ཨམ་བན་ཤིས་མིང་སོགས་ཀྱིས་མདའ་དཔོན་ཁ་སྐོང་བྱེད་རྒྱུའི་སྐོར་དེ་མོ་ཧོ་ཐོག་ཐུ་ལ་བཏང་བའི་ཡི་གེ

# 駐藏大臣喜明等爲補放代本事咨第穆呼圖克圖文

# Communication from the Resident Minister in Tibet Xi Ming to Living Buddha Demo Regarding the Filling of a *Dapon* Vacancy

58 × 33

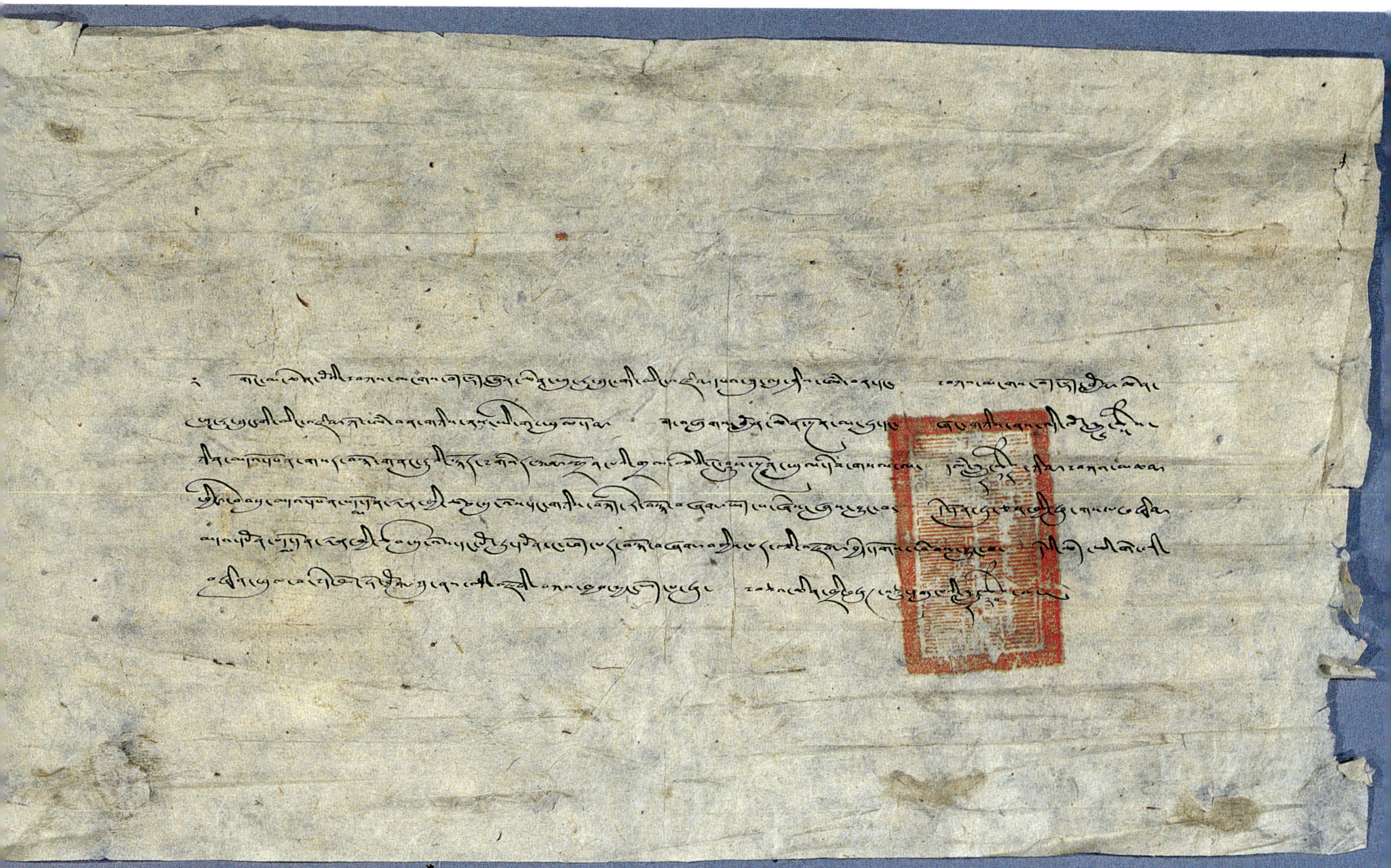

བོད་རང་སྐྱོང་ལྗོངས་ཡིག་ཚགས་ཁང་དུ་ཉར་ཚགས་བྱས་ཡོད།

欽差駐藏辦事大臣副都統喜明、駐藏大臣副都統珂什克咨開：

前駐藏大臣瑚圖禮、祥保二人今年六月五日就保薦代本之事所呈折子已抄出在案。八月十八日來文旁注內開：補代本白瑪頓旦之缺應擬正、擬陪等因。此據瑚圖禮所咨：將阿沛擬正，補代本白瑪頓旦之缺。請第穆呼圖克圖下令遵行。特呈。

嘉慶十九年（公元1814年）八月二十日

西藏自治區檔案館藏

Vice Commander Xi Ming, Resident Minister in Tibet by Imperial Order, and Vice Commander Keshike, Resident Minister in Tibet, issue the following notice:

A copy has been made for the record of the petition submitted by former Resident Ministers Hutuli and Xiang Bao on the 5th day of the 6th month of this year recommending a *dapon* candidate. Your communication of the 18th day of the 8th month states in a side note that ″one main and one alternate candidate should be recommended for the vacancy left by Padma Dondan, etc.″ In accordance with Hutuli′s petition, we have decided to make Ngapo the main candidate to fill the vacancy left by Padma Dondan. Living Buddha Demo is requested to issue the order to carry out this decision.

The 20th day of the 8th month of the 19th year of Jiaqing (1814)

Preserved by the Archives of the Tibet Autonomous Region.

# གོང་མ་བསྐྱགས་སྟོན་གྱིས་ཏཱ་ལའི་བླ་མ་ཞིང་བརྗེས་རྗེས་འབྲེལ་ཡོད་ལས་དོན་སྐོར་ངག་དབང་འཇམ་དཔལ་ཚུལ་ཁྲིམས་ལ་བསྩལ་བའི་བཀའ་ལུང་།

# 嘉慶皇帝爲達賴喇嘛圓寂後有關事務給阿旺强白楚臣的敕諭

# Emperor Jiaqing's Decree to Ungwang Jampal Tshulkhrim on Relevant Matters After the Demise of the Dalai Lama

271 × 70

57 - 1

བོད་རང་སྐྱོང་ལྗོངས་ཡིག་ཚགས་ཁང་དུ་ཉར་ཚགས་བྱས་ཡོད།

奉天承運皇帝詔曰：

諭噶爾丹錫勒圖薩瑪第巴克什之呼畢勒罕阿旺强白楚臣、衆寺之堪布喇嘛、四噶倫、衆代本第巴等。前達賴喇嘛圓寂之時，曾派遣第穆呼圖克圖總理達賴喇嘛商上事務。今達賴喇嘛之呼畢勒罕尚未出，第穆呼圖克圖又已圓寂，達賴喇嘛之呼畢勒罕出之前，若由一賢良大喇嘛爲首辦事，則於衛藏全境僧俗衆人方有裨益。阿旺强白楚臣誠實賢良，若令爾爲首辦理商上事務，則全藏僧俗衆民皆心悦誠服，故由駐藏辦事大臣處保奏，朕甚嘉悦。今施殊恩，賞爾爲厄爾德孟格諾門汗，並執掌印信，於達賴喇嘛之呼畢勒罕出之前，總理衛藏僧俗事務。阿旺强白楚臣爾惟效法第穆呼圖克圖，仰副朕憐愛天下衆生之至意，弘揚黄教，妥善辦理所有事務，俾衛藏僧俗衆人各享太平，安居樂業。再衆堪布、噶倫、代本、第巴等，爾等均應勤奮效力本職，共同輔佐阿旺强白楚臣，均如達賴喇嘛之呼畢勒罕在時一様，凡事皆與駐藏辦事大臣等權貴人物商定，照章行事，共勉勿怠。特諭。

嘉慶二十五年（公元1820年）二月初八

西藏自治區檔案館藏

His Majesty the Emperor, who reigns by the mandate of Heaven, decrees:

These are instructions for Gavldan Shirigethu Samatipagshivi Ungwang Jampal Tshulkhrim, the Khanpo lamas, the four government ministers, the *dapons* and the *dibas*. When the previous Dalai Lama left this world, I sent Living Buddha Demo to take overall charge of affairs in the district in which the Dalai Lama resided. At this time the child Dalai Lama has not made his appearance while Living Buddha Demo has also left this world. It would be beneficial for both the religious and secular sectors all over Tibet if an able and virtuous grand lama is appointed to supervise the administration of affairs prior to the emergence of the child Dalai Lama. Since you, Ungwang Jampal Tshulkhrim, are honest and virtuous, all the monks and lay people in Tibet should fully agree to your appointment to supervise the administration of affairs in the district. I am very pleased that the Office of the Resident Ministers in Tibet has petitioned the throne recommending you. Today I am granting this special favour of appointing you Ertimong Nomonhan to take charge of the seal and certificate, and to take full charge of the religious and secular affairs of Tibet pending the emergence of the child Dalai Lama. You, Ungwang Jampal Tshulkhrim, should follow the example of Living Buddha Demo, promoting the Yellow Sect of Lamaism and effectively handling all matters so that all the monks and common people in Tibet can live in peace, in order to fulfil my earnest desire for the good of all living beings. The Khanpos, government ministers, *dapons* and *dibas* should all perform their duties conscientiously and work together to assist Ungwang Jampal Tshulkhrim just as you will do for the child Dalai Lama when he emerges. You should consult influential persons such as the Resident Ministers in Tibet in all matters and obey the regulations, working tirelessly to carry out all the above. This is the end of the instructions.

The 8th day of the 2nd month of the 25th year of Jiaqing (1820)

Preserved by the Archives of the Tibet Autonomous Region.

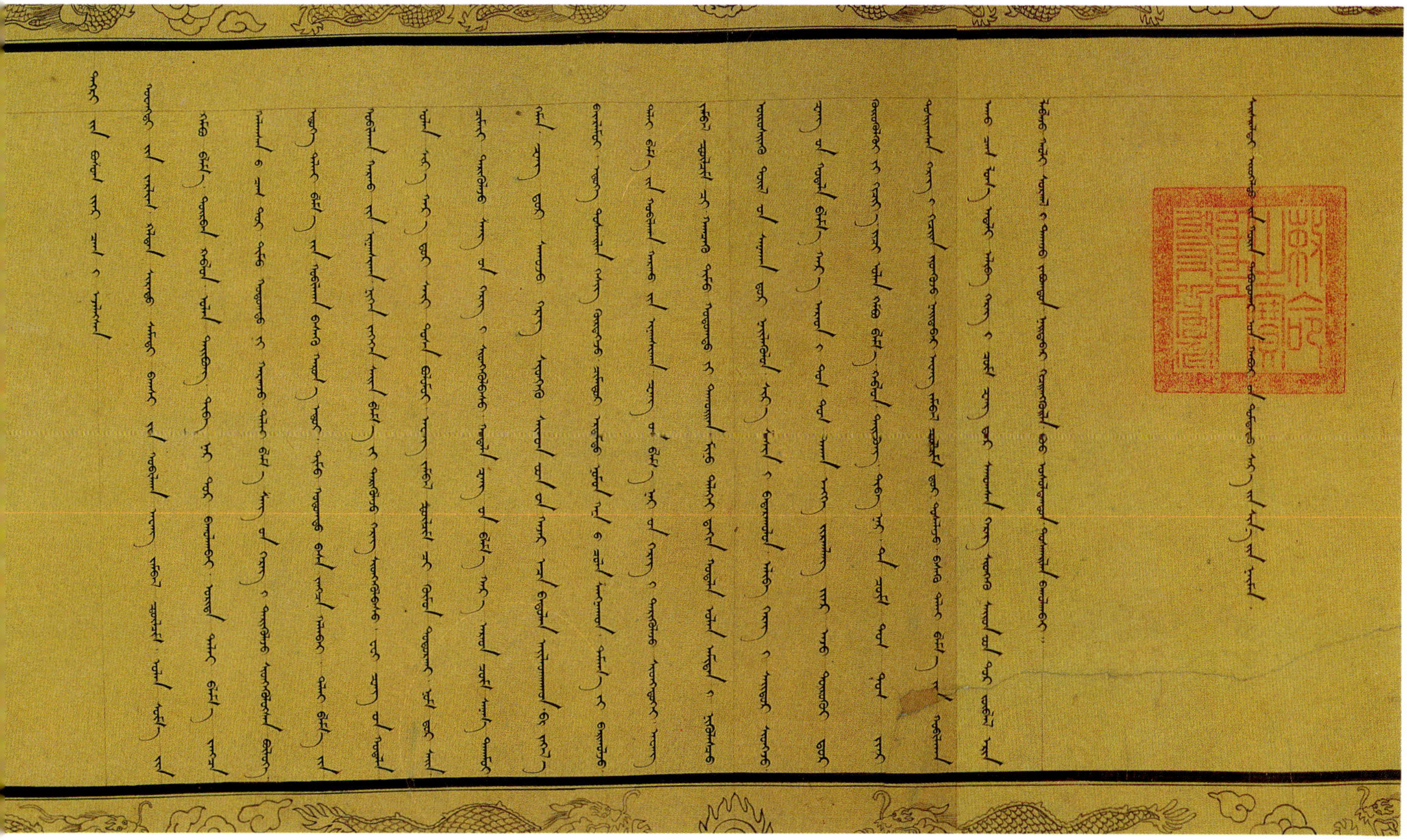

57 - 2

57 - 3

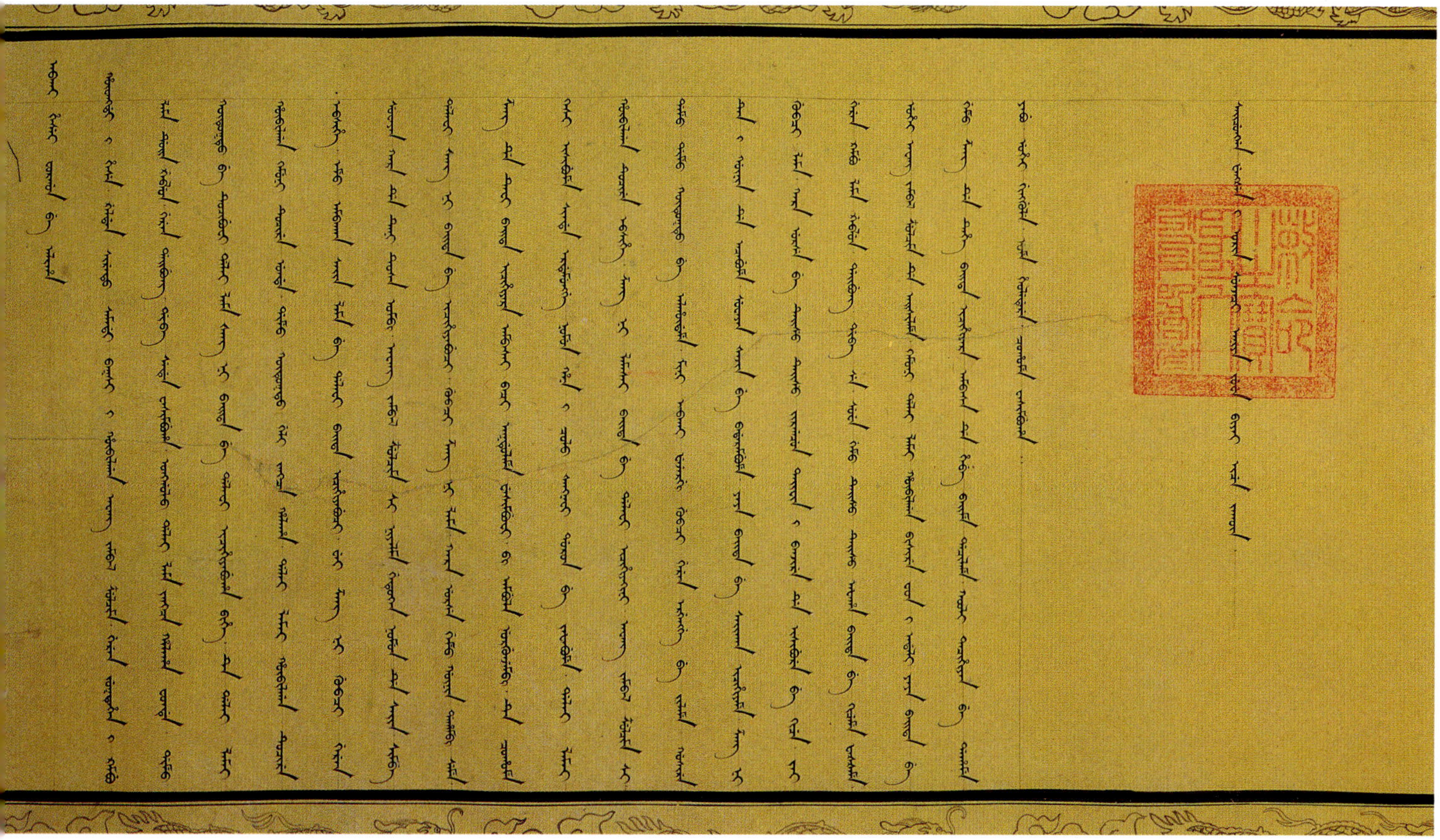

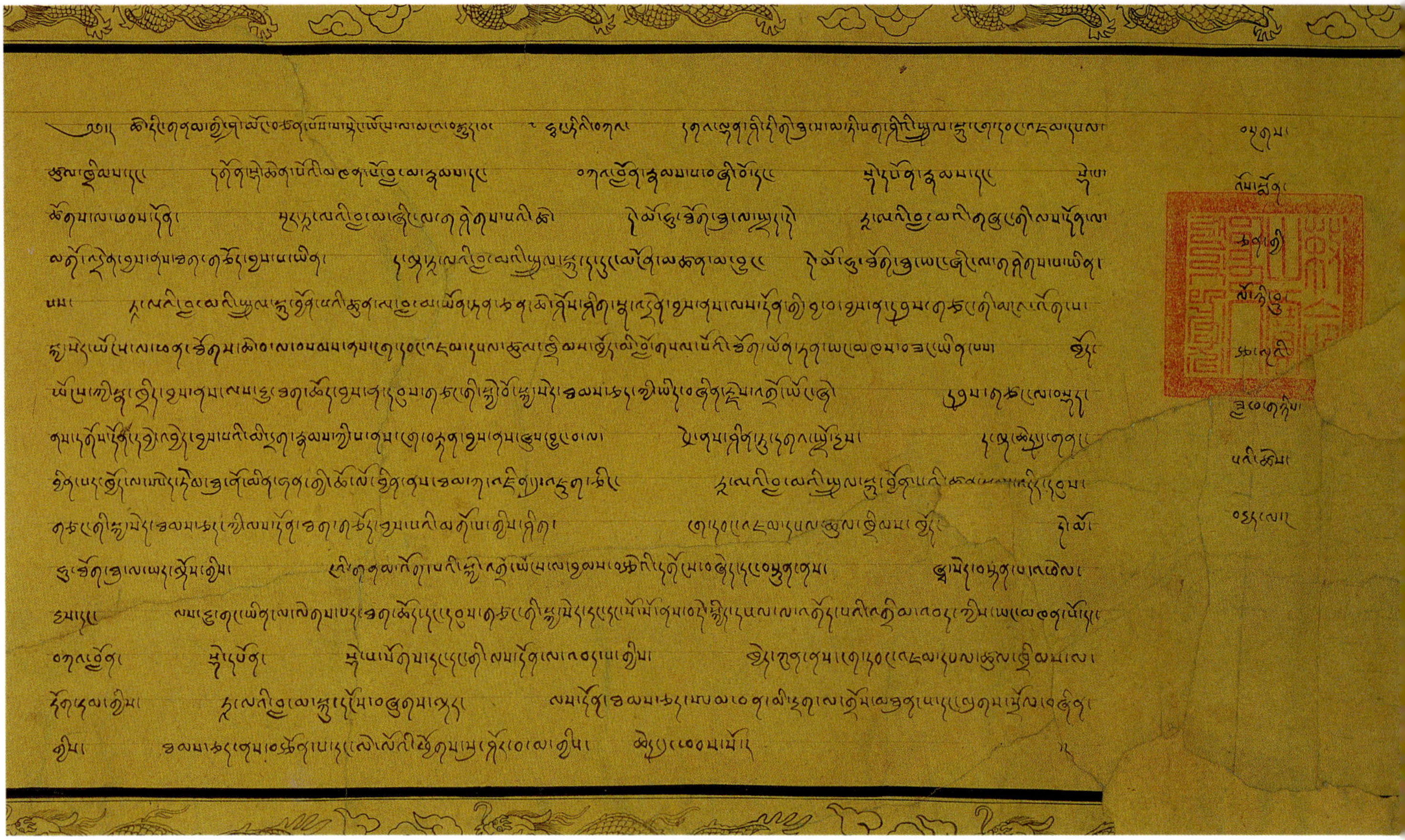

57 - 4

# གོང་མ་སྲིད་གསལ་གྱིས་ཏཱ་ལའི་བླ་མ་ཞིང་བཏེགས་རྗེས་གནས་སྐབས་སྲིད་སྐྱོང་བསྐོ་དགོས་སྐོར་ངག་དབང་འཇམ་དཔལ་ཚུལ་ཁྲིམས་ལ་བསྩལ་པའི་བཀའ་ལུང་།

# 道光皇帝爲達賴喇嘛圓寂暫需攝政事給阿旺强白楚臣的敕諭

# Emperor Daoguang's Decree to Ungwang Jampal Tshulkhrim on the Need for an Interim Regent Following the Demise of the Dalai Lama

166 × 100

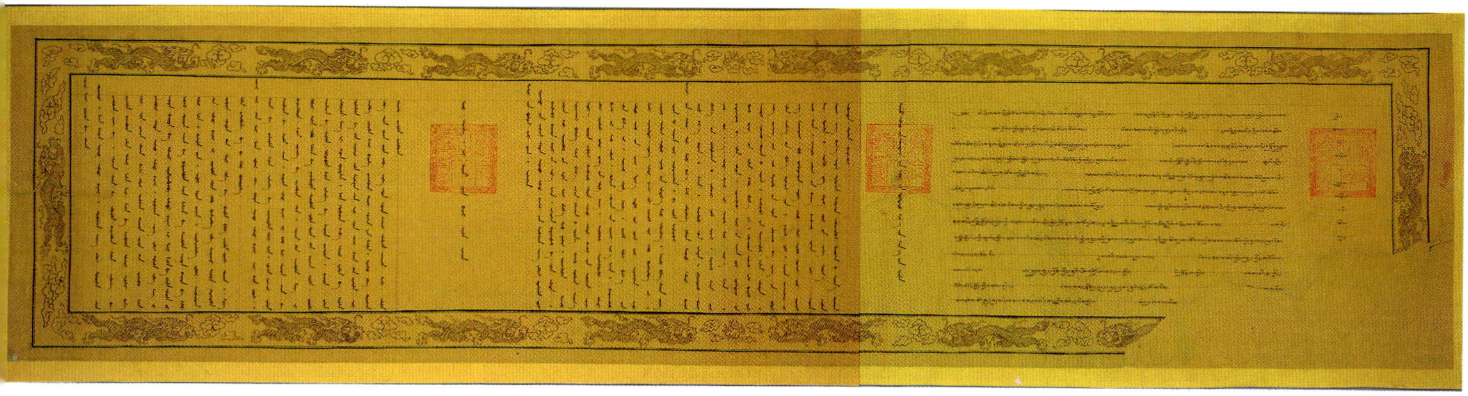

58 - 1

བོད་རང་སྐྱོང་ལྗོངས་ཡིག་ཚགས་ཁང་དུ་ཉར་ཚགས་བྱས་ཡོད།

奉天承運皇帝詔曰：

諭噶爾丹錫勒圖薩瑪第巴克什之呼畢勒罕阿旺强白楚臣。爲弘揚西地黄教、俾衆生安居樂業事，達賴喇嘛欽遵朕旨，始終效力。達賴喇嘛圓寂之後，呼畢勒罕尚未出時，前曾降諭著噶爾丹錫勒圖薩瑪第巴克什之呼畢勒罕阿旺强白楚臣爲首辦理衛藏所有事務。薩瑪第巴克什爾接朕旨以來，弘揚黄教，教導衆喇嘛，凡事均如達賴喇嘛在時一樣，清楚辦理，殊堪嘉獎。今薩瑪第巴克什爾特遣使堪布貢嘎强巴等，敬獻丹書克，乘便恭請朕安，進獻禮物，忠誠進表，朕均鑒察之。仰蒙皇天恩佑，朕體甚安康。噶爾丹錫勒圖薩瑪第巴克什爾親尊佛法，導引衆生，按照達賴喇嘛所傳，勤習經藝，善哉。薩瑪第巴克什爾惟仰副朕崇奉黄教、普度衆生之至意，訓導全藏衆堪布喇嘛，勤習經典，宣揚佛教，爲衆生安居樂業而祈禱；又爲盼達賴喇嘛之呼畢勒罕盡快出，率藏地衆寺喇嘛等，勤奮誦經，勿得怠惰。今爾使返回，乘便問候爾好，隨敕賞賜三十兩重銀茶桶一個、各色大緞十二匹、大小哈達各七條携往，至時祇領。特諭。

道光二年（公元1822年）二月初八

西藏自治區檔案館藏

His Majesty the Emperor, who reigns by the mandate of Heaven, decrees:

These are the instructions to Gavldan Shirigethu Samatipagshivi Ungwang Jampal Tshulkhrim concerning the promotion of the Yellow Sect of Lamaism in Tibet for the peace and happiness of all living beings. The Dalai Lama has always served in accordance with my wish. Between his demise and the appearance of his reincarnation, I issued a decree naming Gavldan Shirigethu Samatipagshivi Ungwang Jampal Tshulkhrim to head the administration of affairs in Tibet. Since receiving my decree, Samatipagshivi has been promoting the Yellow Sect of Lamaism and guiding the lamas, making sure that everything goes as smoothly as if the Dalai Lama were still alive, for which you deserve to be commended. Today Samatipagshivi has sent an envoy, Khanpo Kungav Byampa, to respectfully present a *danshuke* to me, taking the opportunity to pay respects, present gifts and submit a petition to me, all of which I have inspected. By the grace of Heaven, I am in good health. You, Gavldan Shirigethu Samatipagshivi, have been personally honouring the Buddhist doctrines, giving guidance to all living beings and working hard to study the Buddhist writings in accordance with the Dalai Lama's instructions. To live up to my earnest wish for the promotion of the Yellow Sect of Lamaism and the well–being of all living beings, you, Samatipagshivi, should instruct all the Khanpo lamas in Tibet to study the Buddhist classics, expound Buddhism and pray for peace for all living beings and lead all the lamas in Tibet in chanting the scriptures to bring about the appearance of the child Dalai Lama as quickly as possible, sparing no effort in this regard. With your envoy I send you my greetings and present you with a 30–*liang* silver container for tea leaves, 12 rolls of assorted satin, and seven large and seven small *hatas*, which he is carrying back with him. This is the end of the instructions.

The 8th day of the 2nd month of the 2nd year of Daoguang (1822)

Preserved by the Archives of the Tibet Autonomous Region.

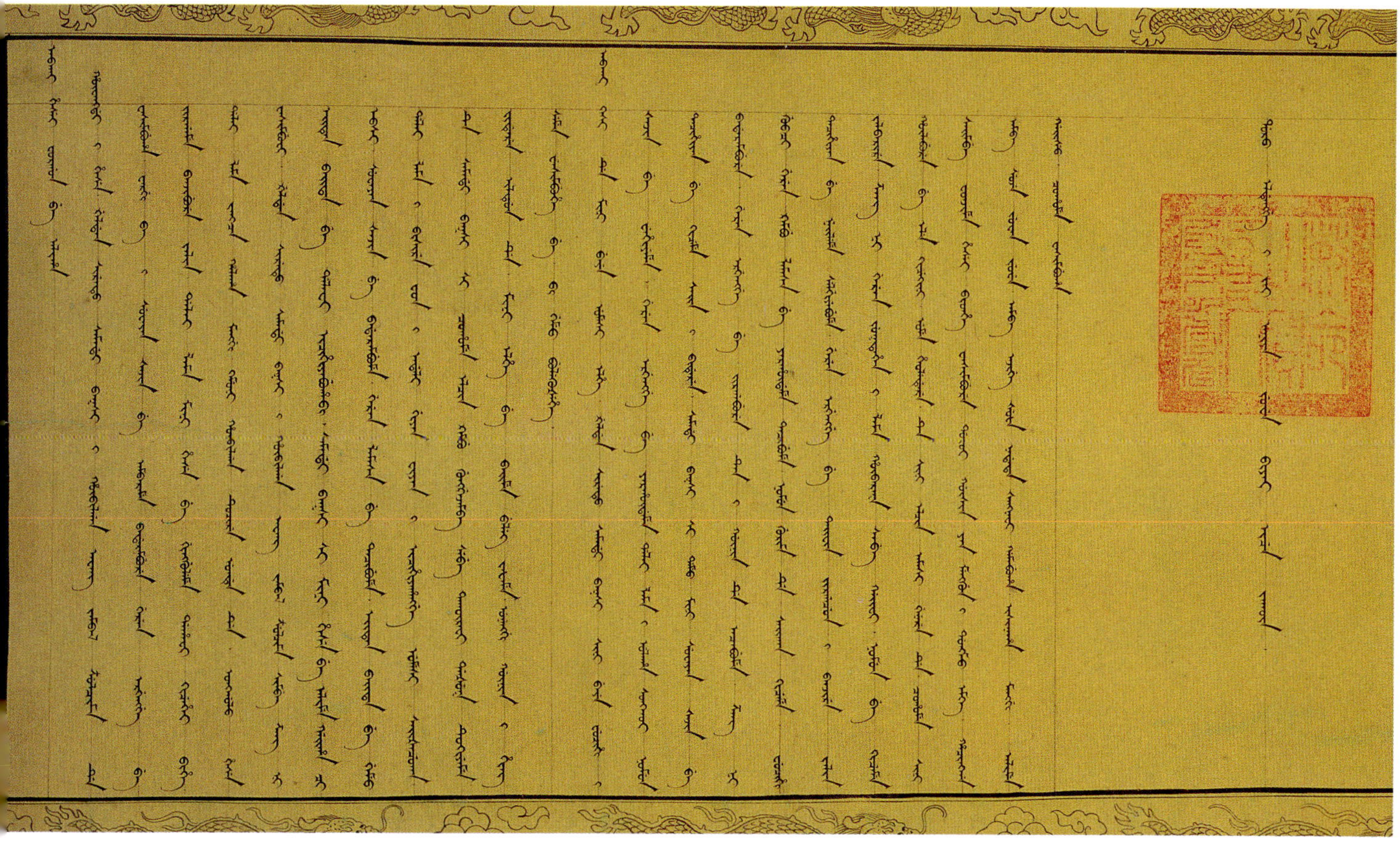

58 - 2

58 - 3

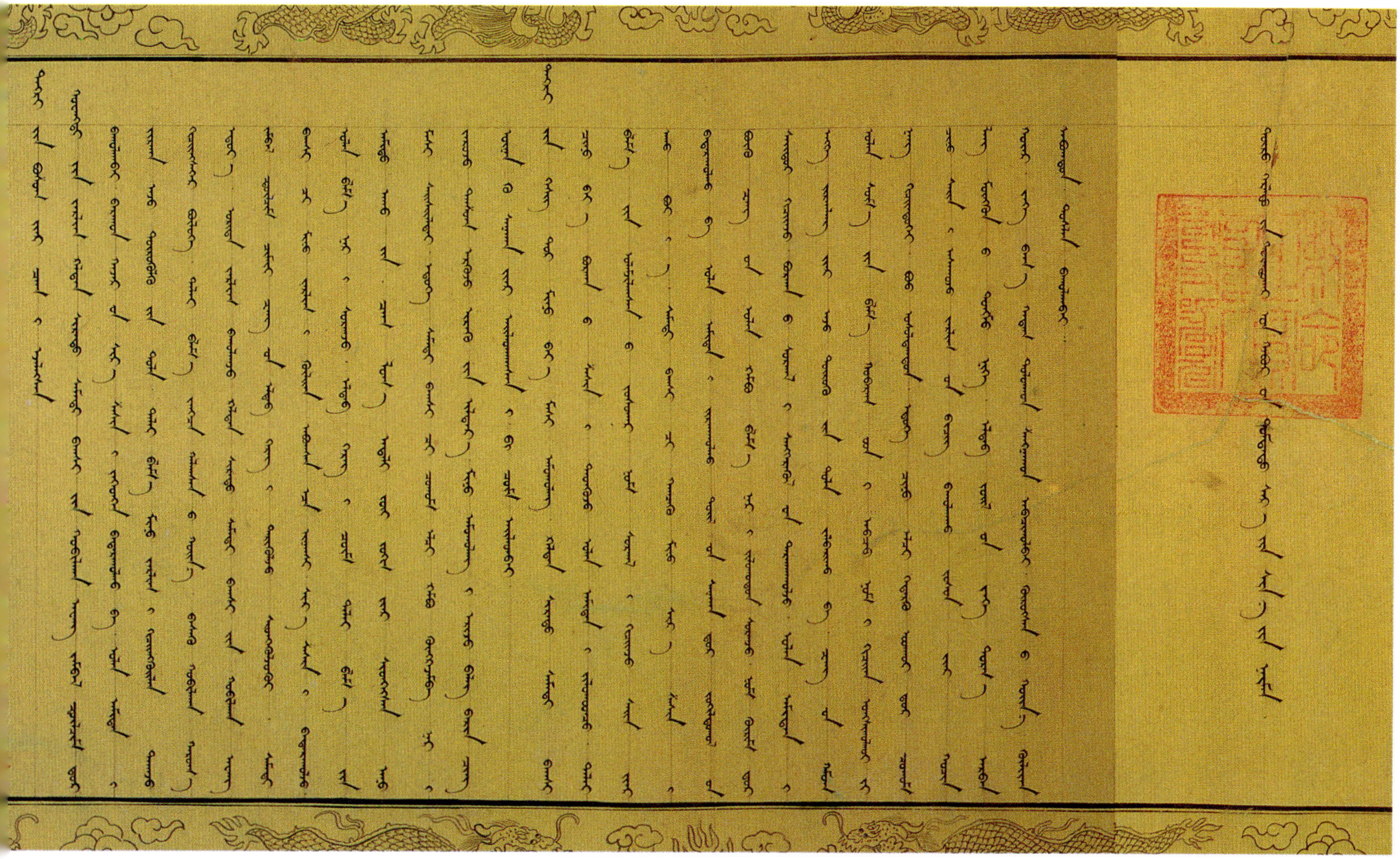

༄༅། །ཞེ་དེ། །གནམ་ནས་ཀྱི་ཁྲི་ཡོ། །བཙན་པོ་ཡི་མ་རྟེ། །ཡོ་ཁྲ་ལ་ལ་ཏ། །འཇམ་དབྱངས་ལ་འདྲེན་རྫུ་ཧྲིའི་བཀག། །གནམ་ལུགས་གྲི་རི་གི་སྐྱེ་མ་ལ་རྟེ་འཇིག་ཀྱི་སྐྱ་ལ་རྒྱ། ཁོ་བ་འཁྲུང་ལ་བས་ལྗོངས་ལ་ཞིབ་མ་ལ་ཁའ།

པ། ཀུན་ཆེ་མ་ཀྱི་ཀླུ་པོ་དང་ཀྱི་འདུ་ཀ་པ་ཆེ། ཞི་དང་ཏ་ཞི་ལ་བ། །ཤེས་པ་རྩེག་ལ་གོ་ཀྱི་ཏ་ཐུ་བ་རི་ཀྱིང་། ནཱ་ལ་རི་ཐུ་ལམ་པོ་ཀྱི་བ་ཀ་ཏ་བ་ཆེས།

ལུ་ཚོགས་བཅེས་ཀྱི་རྡོ། ལ་ནཱ་ལ་རི་ཐུ་ལ་ཆེ། ལ་གཟིགས་པ་བཀའི་རྗེ་པ་ཤེས་པ། །སྐྱ་ལ་རྒྱ་ལ་ཁྲོ་ག་བ་ལ་ལ་ཐུ་ཁམ། །ཁྲ་ཞེ་བཀག་ཡབ་སྐྱེ། གནམ་ལུགས་གྲི་རི་གི་སྐྱེ་མ་ལ་རྟེ་འཇིག་ཀྱི་སྐྱ་ལ།

རྒྱ། ཁོ་བ་འཁྲུང་ལ་བས་ལྗོངས་ལ་ཞིབ་མ་གྱོ། ལ། ཐུ་པ་ག་ཙེ་ཁི། གོ་པ་ཀྲི་ཐེ་ཀྲིང་། ལུག་པ་ཡིན་པ་ས། པ་ལ་རྟེ་འཇིག་ཀྱི་ཀྱོ། ཁྲོ་ཀྱི་བཀག། ལིན་ཐུ་པ་ཡིན་པ། སྐུ་པེ་ང་ཀྱི།

འདྲ་ག་ཏ་ཞི་ལ་ཆེ། ཁེ་ཏ་ཀྱི་ཚོགས་ཀྱི་སྲི་ག་ཉེ་ང་། གཙུག་ཡ། གོ་མ་ཐེ་ག། ཁ་ཏ། ཟླ་ལམ་ཙི། སྡར་ཀྱི་ཐུ་ལ་རྒྱ། ཁ་འཆུག་མ་སྟེ་ལ་བཅེས་ག་པ་ལ་ཟབ་ལ་ལོ། ཐུ་པ་པ་ཞེ།

ཤེས་ཀུ་བསྡུས་པ་དང་ཏོས། ། ལས་པ་ལ་རྟེ་འཇིག་ཀྱོ། ལི་རྣ་ལ་འཆག་པོ་ཀྱི། ག་བ་ཐུ་ས་པ་ལ་རྣ་ལ་མ་ཅི་ལ་ཁྲོ་པ་ཤ་པ་འདྲ་འཇུག་མ་ཏ་ཐུ་ལ་བཏི་ཟོ།

ཏཚ་ལ་ཀྱེ་དྭེ་ཀ་ཞུ་ལ་ཆེ། བཅེ་པ་ལ་པ་ཀྱི་ཀྱུ་ཐུ་བ་ལ་ཁྲ་ཤ་མ་ཟླ་ལ་མ་ཚེ་བོ་ཐུ། །གཉིས་ཀྱི་ལྡུ་ཏི་བཀག་རྟེ་ཀ་ལ་འདྲེ་ཀ་ཤ་ཁྲ་ཀྱི་རྒྱ་ལ་ཚ་ལ་མ་ཏེ་ཀ་སྐུ་ཅེ་བཞ་ལ།

ཤ་ཡ་ལ་རྟེ་འཇིག་ཀྱོ། ཁ་ཞུ་ཡ་པ་ཀྱི་བཏ་ག་པ་ཏ་ཞི་ལ་ཆེ། ཀྱི་ཏ་ཀྱི། ནཱ་ལ་མ་ལ་གོ་ཏ་རྟེ་ཀ། ནཱ་ལ་རི་ཐུ་ལ་ཏི་ལེ་ག་མ་སྟེ་ལ་བཅེས་སྐྱེ་ག་ཉེ་ང་ལ་བ་ཚོགས་པ་བཟ། པ་ལ་རྟེ།

བཀྲི་ཀྱོ་པོ་ཀྱི་ཀླུ་པེ་ང་ཀྱི་བཏ་ག་པ་ཏ་ཞི་ལ་ཆེ། པེ་ལམ་ཙ་ག་ལ་གོ་ཀྱི་ཏ་ཐུ་བ་ཏི། ལྔ་ག་མ། འདྲ་ཀ་ཤ་མ། ཀ་ཏི་ཐུ་ལེ་ཀ་ཀ་ཡོ་ག་མ་ཏ་རྟེ་ཀ་ཟབ་པ་ཤ་མ་ཡོ་མ་ཀྱི་ཐུ་བ་འཇུག་དེ་ལ།

ལེ་ག་མ་པ་ང་ལ་ཙོག་ཙི། །རྡ་ལ་བཏི་བཏ་ག་པ་ཟླ་མ་པ། པེ་ལམ་ཙ་ག་ལ་གོ་ཀྱི་ཏ་ཐུ་འཇིག་ར་ག་མཚོ་ལ་བ།

ཡག་མ་པོ་འདྲ་ལ། ཡ། སྐྱ་ལ་སྒུ་ར་ཏེ་ཀ་ཞི་ཟླ་ཀྱི་རྡི་མ་ཏ་ཀྱོ་ལ་ཏ་ཐུ་པ་ཀྱི་ས། ལོ་སྤྲེ་ད་ལ་ཀྱི་ས། ། ལ་ས་ལ་ལི་རྟ་ཁྱི་ད།

ལོག་ག་རོ། ཅེ་ཀྱི་ཏ་ཚ་ལ་ཏེ། བཀ་ཀ་ཏ་བ་རྟེ་ཀྱི་ཟླ་ལ་ཟླ་ཐུ་ལ་ཀྱི་ལྷོ་ལོ་གཙེག ཀ་གཉིས།

ཟ་བདག་མ་ཤི་ལུ་ཤ་ཀ་དེ་བཙམ་ག་ཏ་བ་མ་རྫོ་ག་ཞི་བ་ཡོ་ལེ་ཤ་ཀྱི་ས། ཡོ་ལ་ཁ་བ་པ་ཡིན།

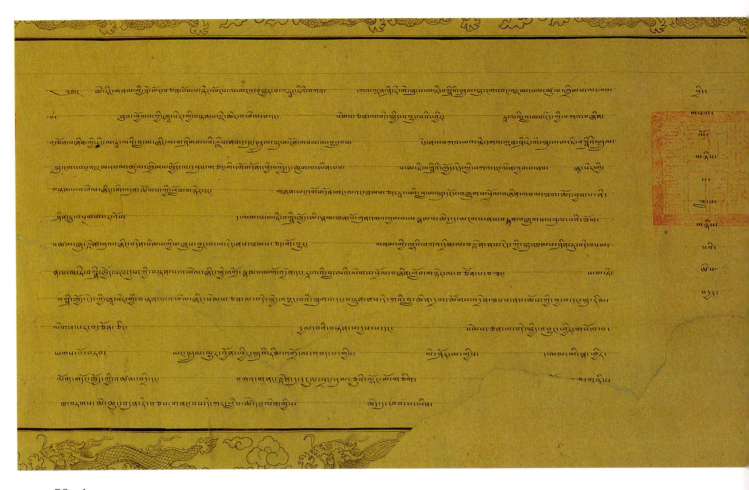

སྤྲི།
གསལ།
ལོ།
གཉིས།
པ།
ཟླ་བ།
གཉིས།
པའི།
ཡིས།
བྱུ།

# གོང་མ་སྡིད་གསལ་གྱིས་ལེགས་སྐྱེས་ཕུལ་བར་གསོལ་རས་གནང་བའི་དོན་དུ་ཏཱ་ལའི་བླ་མར་བསྩལ་བའི་བཀའ་ལུང་།

# 道光皇帝爲貢尚事給達賴喇嘛的敕諭

# Emperor Daoguang's Decree to the Dalai Lama on Presenting Him with Gifts

156×67

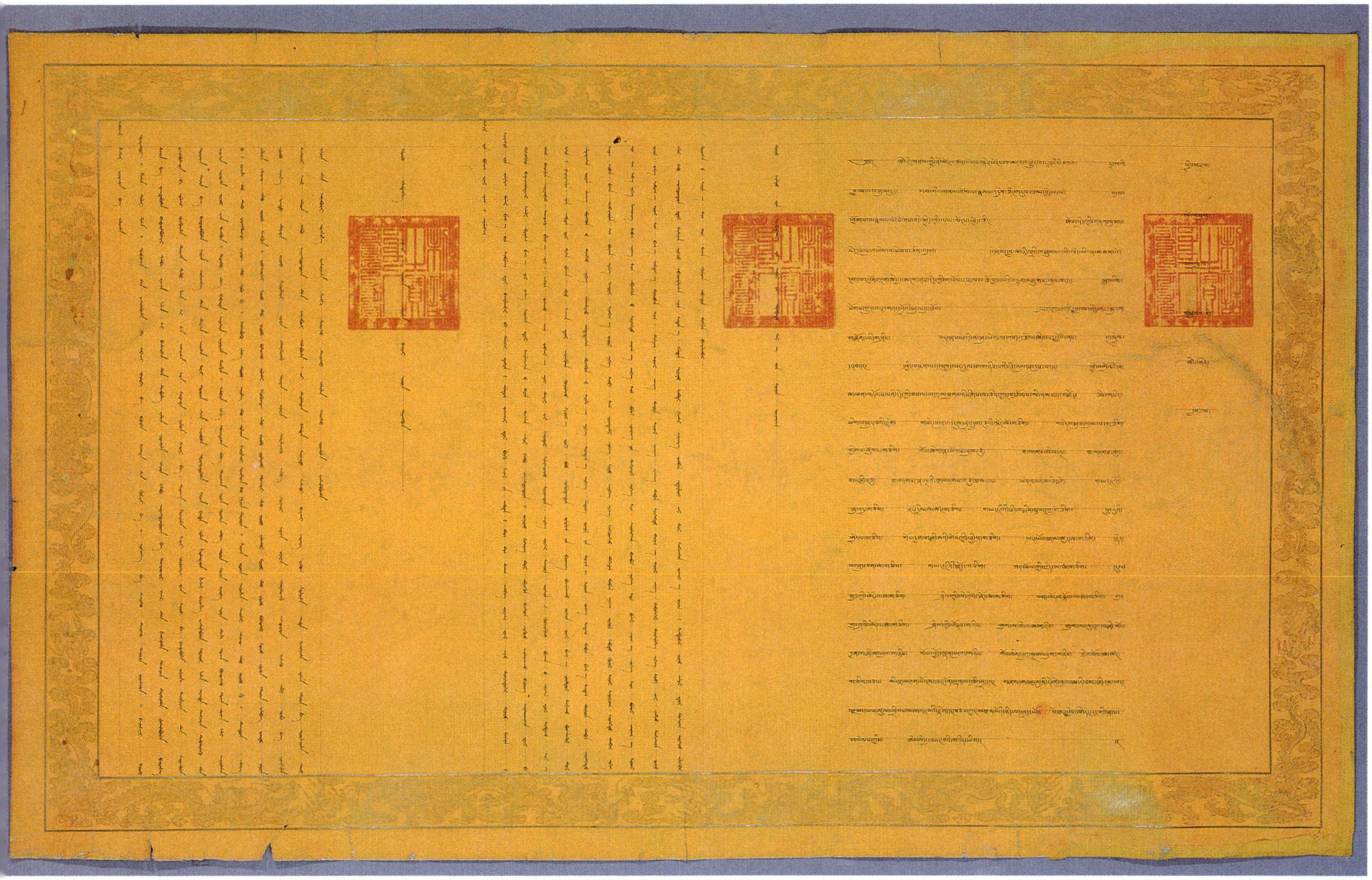

59 - 1

བོད་རང་སྐྱོང་ལྗོངས་ཡིག་ཚགས་ཁང་དུ་ཉར་ཚགས་བྱས་ཡོད།

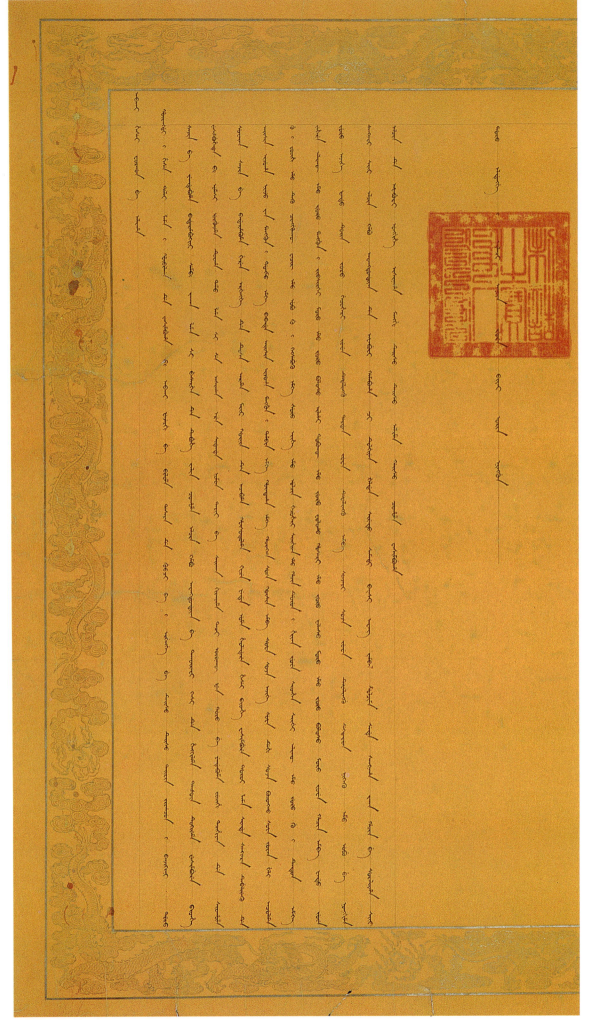

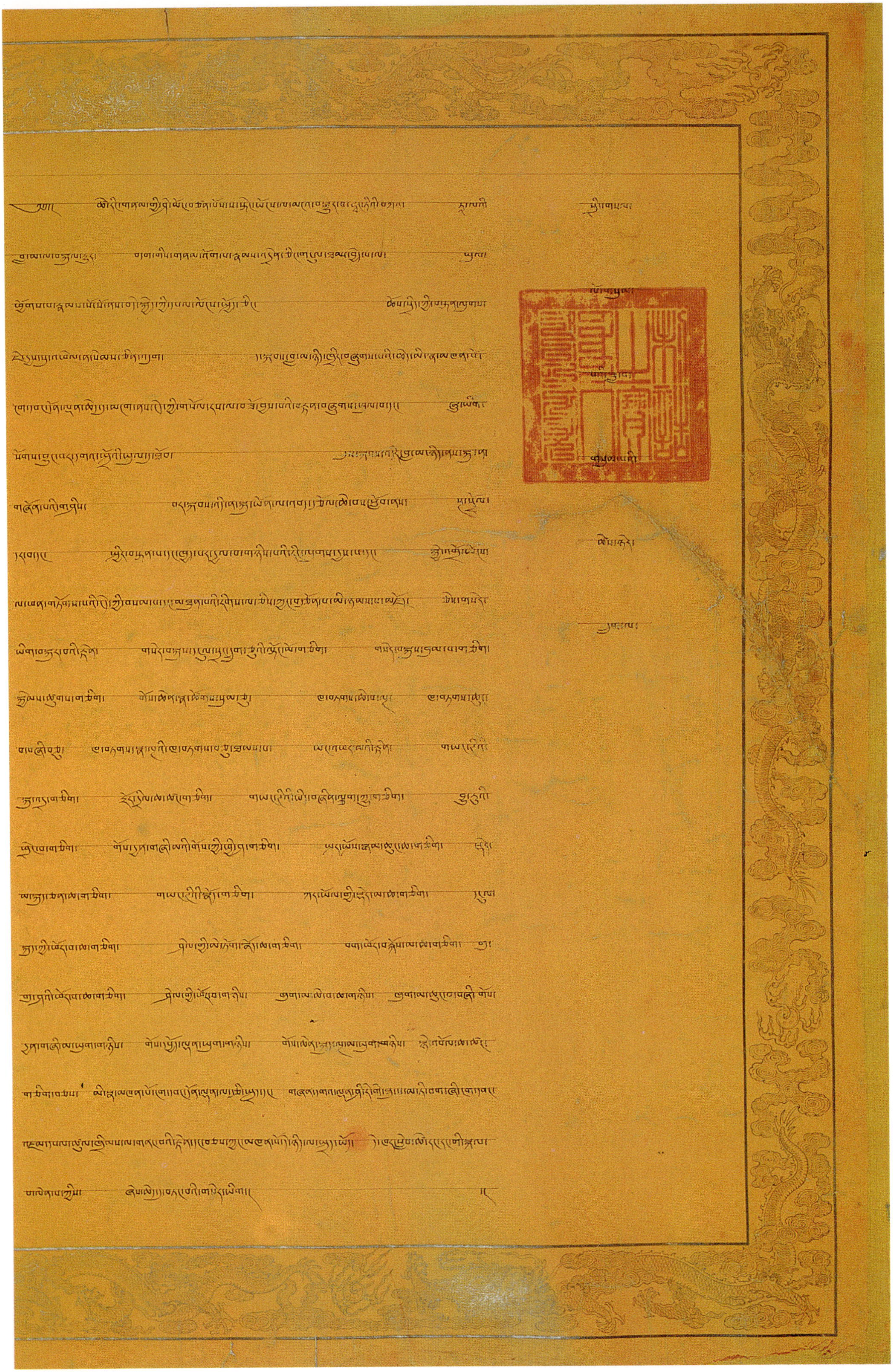

奉天承運皇帝詔曰：

諭達賴喇嘛之呼畢勒罕。朕撫馭天下，率土之民，各安生業，推興政教。適才喇嘛爾爲坐床事特遣使者堪布阿旺頓典叩恩，敬獻丹書克，恭進奏表，朕欣閱之。惟喇嘛爾年少，此間須勤習經咒，務興舊道，專注佛訓，弘揚黄教，造福衆生，勤奮盡力，仰體朕意，勿得怠惰。隨敕賞賜爾鍍金六十兩重銀茶桶一個、鍍金銀瓶一個、大酒盅一隻、各色綢緞三十匹、大哈達五條、小哈達四十條、五色哈達十條。又另增賞玉佛一尊、鈴杵一套、玉如意一支、珊瑚念珠一串、蟒袍一件、香餅二匣、絲盤一對、玉器一件、瓷盤一對、銀造碗一對、玻璃花瓶一對、雕花盒一對、珐琅碗一對、玻璃碗二隻、大荷包二雙、小荷包四雙、蟒緞二匹、妝緞二匹、五絲緞二匹、靠褥一對。交付爾使者堪布阿旺頓典携往以外，賞賜噶爾丹錫勒圖薩瑪第巴克什阿旺强白楚臣等什物一併交付爾使携回。至時各自祗領。特諭。

道光三年（公元1823年）二月二十六日

西藏自治區檔案館藏

His Majesty the Emperor, who reigns by the mandate of Heaven, decrees:

These are the instructions for the child Dalai Lama. I rule the Empire allowing people throughout the country to live in peace, improve the political system and promote religion. You have just sent an envoy, Khanpo Ngwang Donldan, to express your deep gratitude for your enthronement, present a *danshuke* and submit a petition. I was pleased on reading your petition. You are still young and should work diligently to study the scriptures, promote the traditional way, follow Buddha's teachings, expound the Yellow Sect of Lamaism, see to the well- being of all living beings and work tirelessly to live up to my expectations. With this decree I am presenting you with a 60 - *liang* gold-plated silver container for tea leaves, a gold-plated silver vase, a large goblet, 30 rolls of assorted silk, five large and 40 small *hatas* and 10 five-colour *hatas,* in addition to a jade figure of Buddha, a set of bells and sticks, a jade *ruyi,* a chaplet of coral beads, a python-patterned robe, two boxes of fragrant cakes, a pair of cloisonne trays, a jade piece, a pair of porcelain plates, a pair of silver bowls, a pair of glass vases, a pair of carved boxes, a pair of enamelware bowls, two glass bowls, two pairs of large pouches, four pairs of small pouches, two rolls of python-patterned satin, two rolls of *zhuang* satin, two rolls of *wusi* satin and a pair of padded mattresses, all with your envoy Khanpo Ngwang Donldan to bring back to you. Your envoy is also carrying presents for Gavldan Shirigethu Samatipagshivi Ungwang Jampal Tshulkhrim. When they arrive, each person should receive these gifts with respect. This is the end of the instructions.

The 26th day of the 2nd month of the 3rd year of Daoguang (1823)

Preserved by the Archives of the Tibet Autonomous Region.

# བོད་བཞུགས་ཨམ་བན་ཧུའི་ཤན་སོགས་ཀྱིས་ར་སྒྲེང་དགོན་པའི་ཏཱ་བླ་མ་ཁ་སྐོང་བྱེད་རྒྱུའི་སྐོར་ནོ་མིན་ཧན་ལ་བཏང་བའི་ཡི་གེ

# 駐藏大臣惠顯等爲熱振寺大喇嘛補缺事咨諾門汗文

# Communication of Resident Minister in Tibet Hui Xian to Nominhan Regarding the Filling Up of a Vacancy Left by the Death of a Grand Lama in Ragreng Monastery

66.7 × 41.2

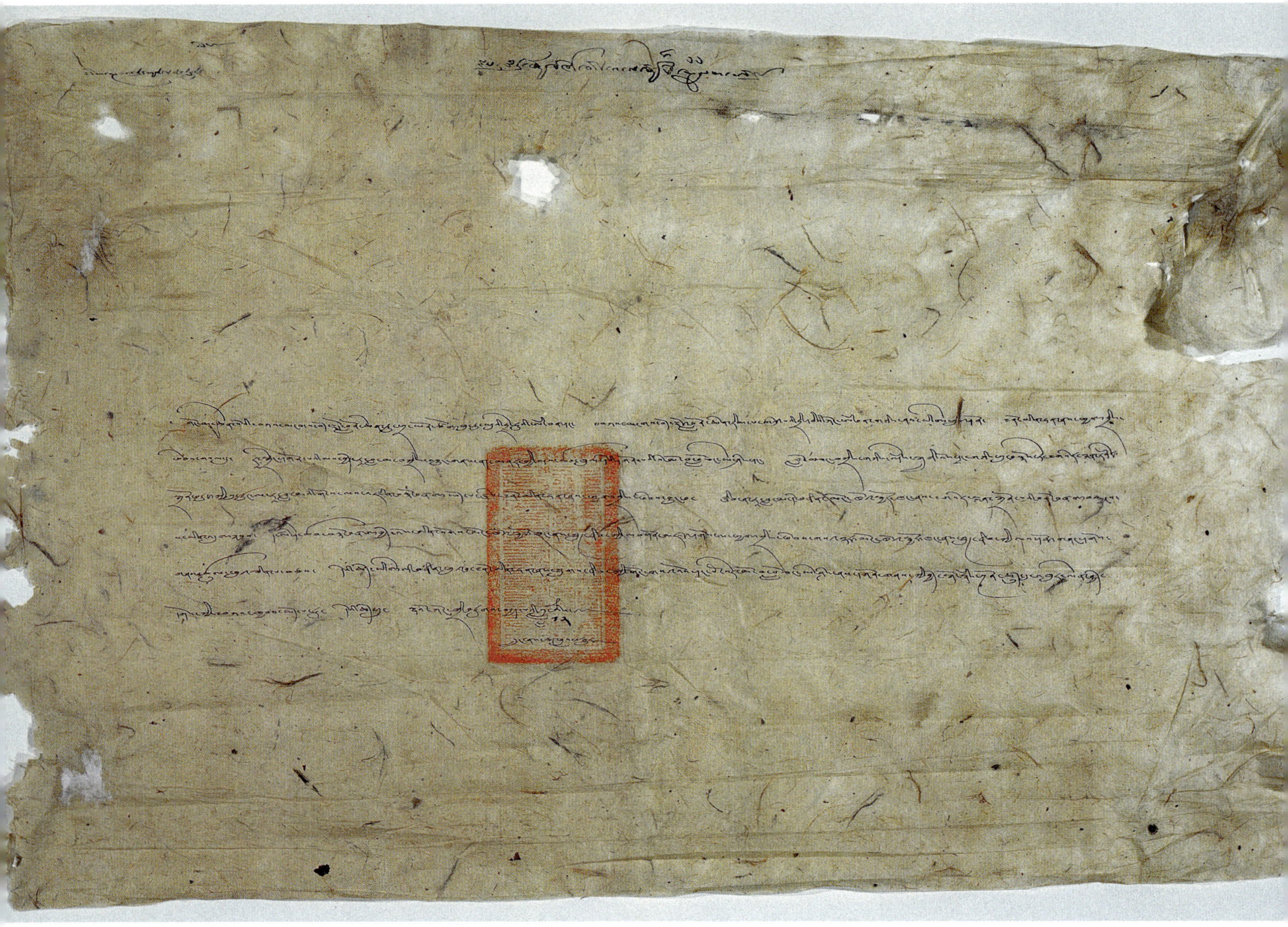

བོད་རང་སྐྱོང་ལྗོངས་ཡིག་ཚགས་ཁང་དུ་ཉར་ཚགས་བྱས་ཡོད།

欽差駐藏大臣都察院左副都御史惠顯、駐藏幫辦大臣三等侍衛廣慶咨行掌辦商上事務之諾門汗：

據諾門汗來文内開：熱振寺執事大喇嘛扎西瓊乃因卒出缺，擬由當地寺廟高僧洛桑益西、洛桑扎西二人分别列爲正選和備選，其中適宜者補缺等因。案查，大喇嘛應由理藩院擬選，故此事須報理藩院定奪。又據諾門汗來文内開：已呈報理藩院等因。

請諾門汗頒發委任狀，將洛桑益西擬正，暫主持寺廟一切活動。特呈。

道光八年（公元1828年）四月十二日

藏曆土鼠年四月十一日

西藏自治區檔案館藏

Hui Xian, Resident Minister in Tibet by Imperial Order and Vice Director of the Supervisory Office, along with Guang Qing, Deputy Resident Minister in Tibet and 3rd Ranking Imperial Bodyguard, send the following communication to Nominhan, who is in charge of local Tibetan affairs:

Nominhan's communication states that "the eminent priests Blozang Yeshes and Blozang Krashis, who come from local monasteries, have been proposed as the main and alternate candidates respectively to fill the vacancy brought about by the death of the Grand Lama Krashis Byungnas, abbot of Ragreng Monastery, to be chosen on the basis of the candidates' strengths, weaknesses, etc." It has previously been stipulated that the selection of the Grand Lama falls within the province of the Minority Nationality Administration Office, so the matter must be referred to that office for final decision. Nominhan's communication also states that "this matter has been reported to the Minority Nationality Administration Office, etc."

Nominhan is requested to issue the appointment order confirming Blozang Yeshes as the main candidate to temporarily preside over all activities in the monastery.

The 12th day of the 4th month of the 8th year of Daoguang (1828)

The 11th day of the 4th month of the Year of the Earth Rat, Tibetan Calendar

Preserved by the Archives of the Tibet Autonomous Region.

## 61

གོང་མ་ཏྲིད་གསལ་གྱིས་མི་སྣ་བཏང་སྟེ་གསེར་བུམ་དཀྲུགས་པ་དང་གསེར་ཁྲི་མངའ་གསོལ་སྐོར་དུ་ཡབ་ཞི་བླ་མའི་ཡང་སྲིད་ལ་བསྩལ་བའི་བཀའ་ལུང་།

# 道光皇帝爲派員掣簽坐床事給達賴喇嘛靈童的敕諭

# Emperor Daoguang's Decree to the Holy Child Dalai Lama Concerning the Sending of Officials to Draw Lots and Officiate at the Enthronement Ceremony

180×102

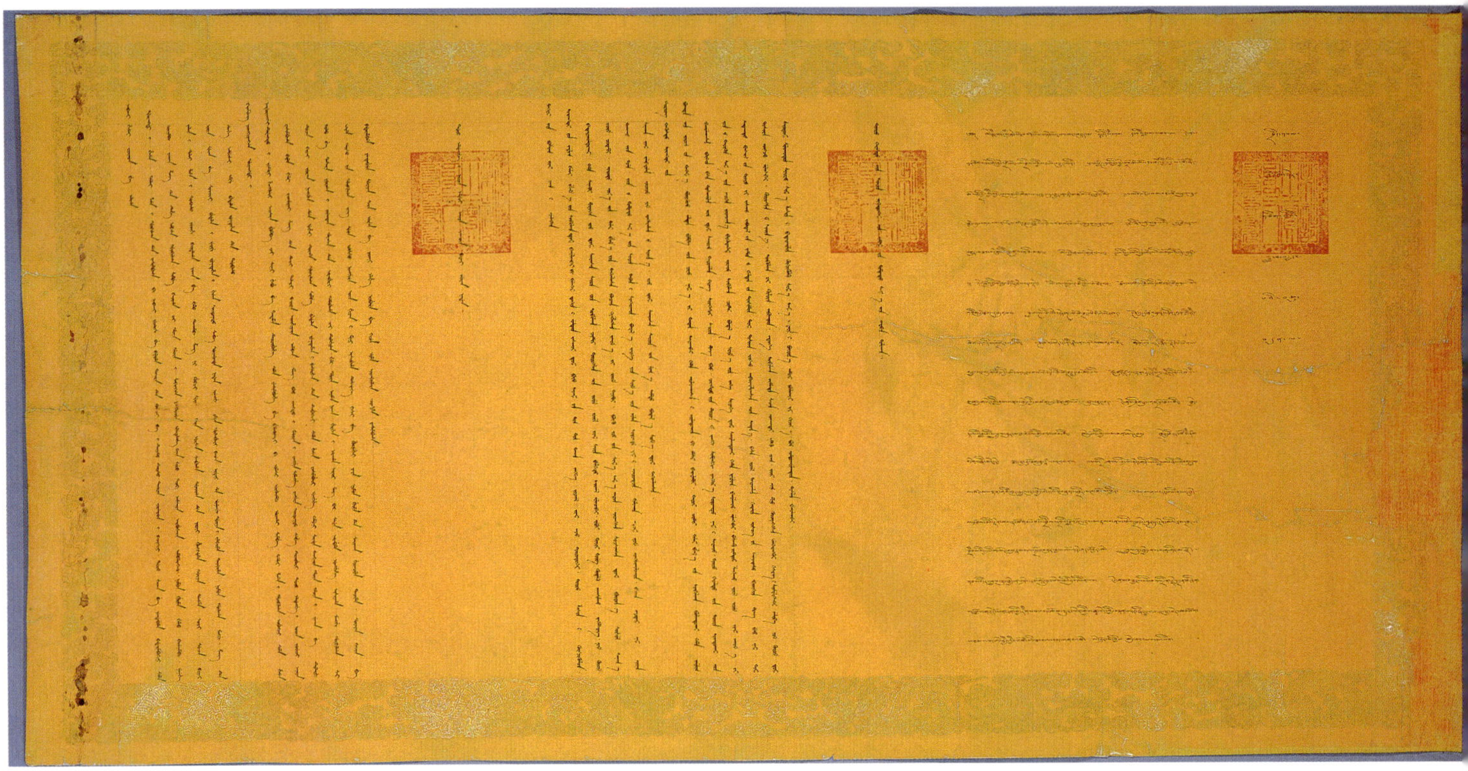

61 - 1

བོད་རང་སྐྱོང་ལྗོངས་ཡིག་ཚགས་ཁང་དུ་ཉར་ཚགས་བྱས་ཡོད།

奉天承運皇帝詔曰：

論達賴喇嘛之呼畢勒罕。朕撫馭天下，惟期率土之民，各安生業，推興政教。頃據駐藏大臣奏稱：呼畢勒罕爾自降生以來，均有吉祥佳兆，容貌端莊，舉止大方，熟諳經典，能辨識前世達賴喇嘛所供佛尊用物，全藏僧俗之所見所聞，皆傾心悅服，故擇於五月二十五日，著布達拉宮之衆呼圖克圖預先誦經七日，班禪額爾德尼等虔誠祝禱誦經之後，與駐藏大臣一同於布達拉宮供奉之高宗純皇帝聖像前叩拜，由金奔巴瓶內掣出爾名等情。朕覽奏，甚爲愉悅，即降諭著爾作爲達賴喇嘛之呼畢勒罕，又降諭特遣駐藏首席辦事大臣孟保、成都副都統席孟格、章嘉呼圖克圖等於道光二十二年四月十六日共同看視，著呼畢勒罕爾於布達拉宮坐床等因咨文。仍將賞爾諸項什物交付理藩院司員携往以外，又逐項繕寫漢字清單，交付孟保等帶往，至時呼畢勒罕爾祇領之。今呼畢勒罕正值聰明長進之時，理宜感戴朕施鴻恩，專心學習所有經典，弘揚黄教，俾僧俗衆人安居，勿得怠惰。特諭。

道光二十一年（公元1841年）八月十七日

西藏自治區檔案館藏

His Majesty the Emperor, who reigns by the mandate of Heaven, decrees:

These are the instructions to the child Dalai Lama. I rule the Empire allowing the people all over the land to live in peace, improve the political situation and promote religion. The Resident Minister in Tibet has just sent a petition to the throne as follows: "Since the birth of the child Dalai Lama auspicious signs have appeared. He has a dignified appearance and a calm manner, is familiar with the scriptures and can recognize the articles with which the Dalai Lama of the last incarnation worshipped Buddha. All the monks and lay people in Tibet have heard of all this and are completely convinced. On the 25th day of the 5th month, therefore," continues the petition, "the Living Buddhas from the Potala Palace were ordered to chant the scriptures for seven days. After piously praying and chanting the scriptures, the Panchen Erdeni prostrated himself with the Resident Minister in Tibet before the sacred portrait of His Majesty Emperor Gaozong enshrined in the Potala Palace and drew a lot inscribed with your name from the gold vase, etc." I was very pleased on reading the petition, and have issued a decree making you the next Dalai Lama. I have also issued an edict sending Meng Bao, Chief Resident Minister in Tibet, Xi Mengge, Vice Military Commander of Chengdu, and Living Buddha Lcangkya to officiate at your enthronement ceremony in the Potala Palace on the 16th day of the 4th month of the 22nd year of Daoguang. While the articles presented to you are being carried by officials from the Minority Nationality Administration Office, the itemized list, which is written in the Han language, is being carried by Meng Bao. You are to accept them respectfully when they arrive. You, the child Dalai Lama, are still growing physically and intellectually and should therefore conscientiously devote yourself to the study of all the Buddhist classics and promote the Yellow Sect to show your appreciation for my gracious magnanimity, so that all the monks and lay people may live in peace, working tirelessly for these aims. This is the end of the instructions.

The 17th day of the 8th month of the 21st year of Daoguang (1841)

Preserved by the Archives of the Tibet Autonomous Region.

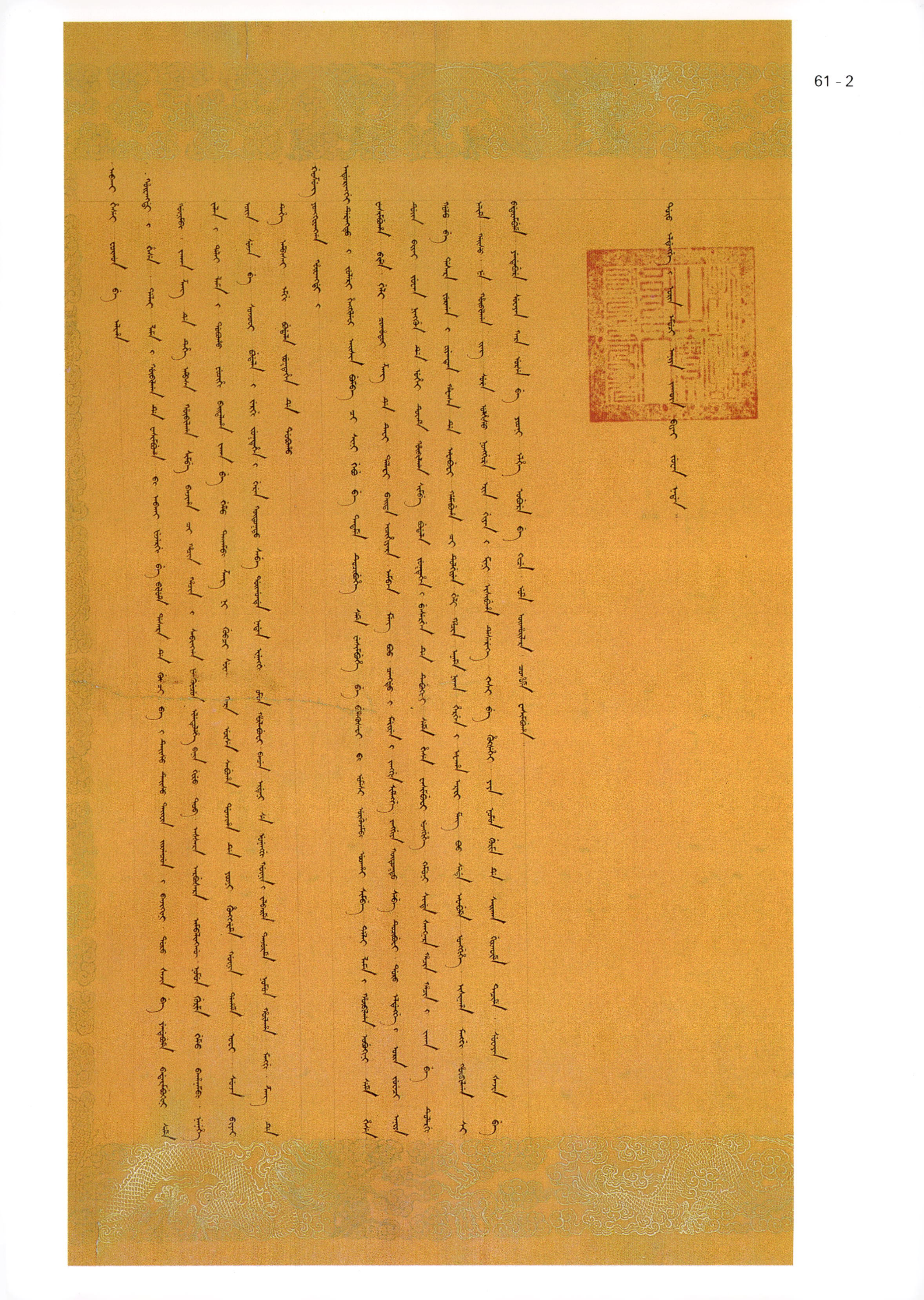

[illegible]

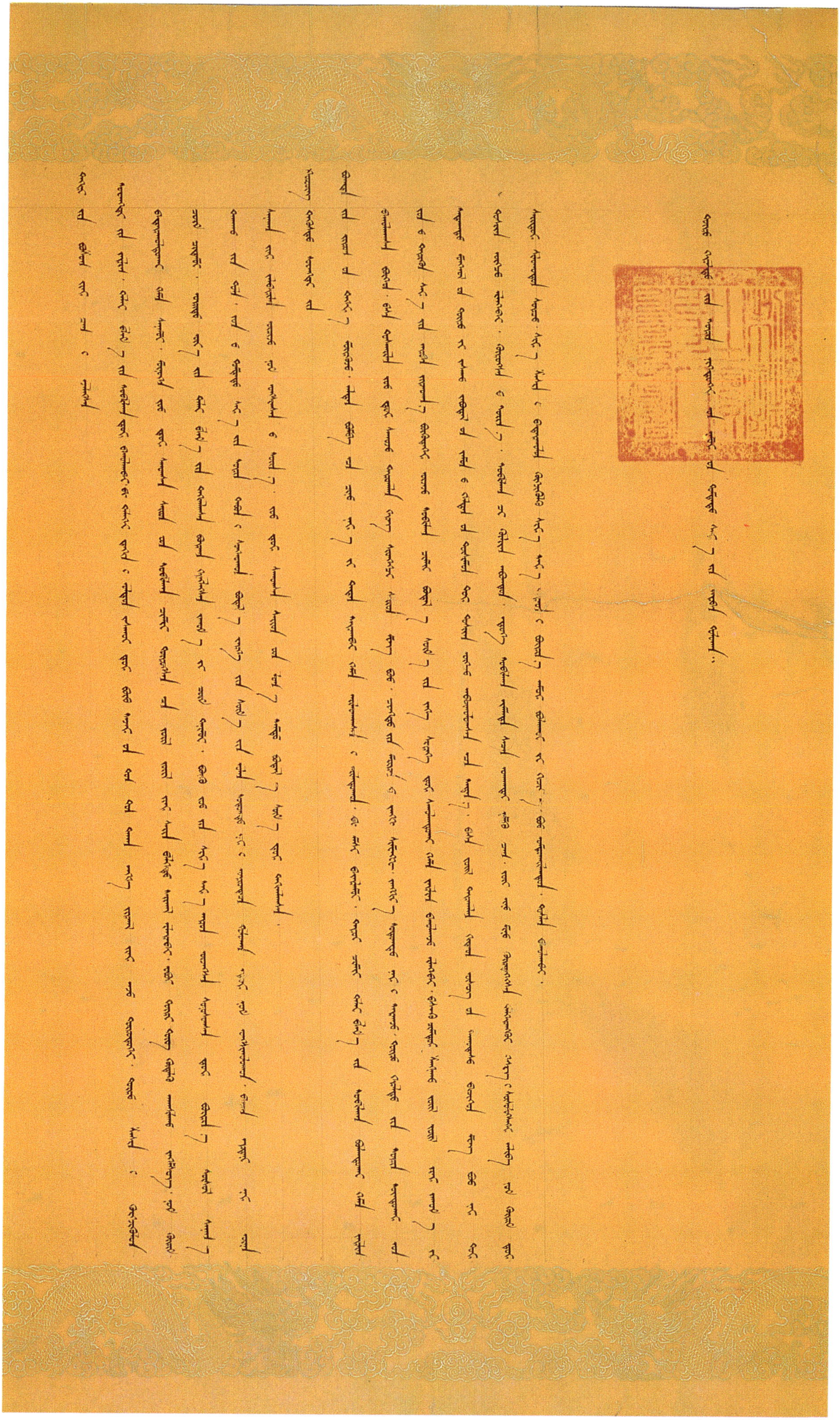

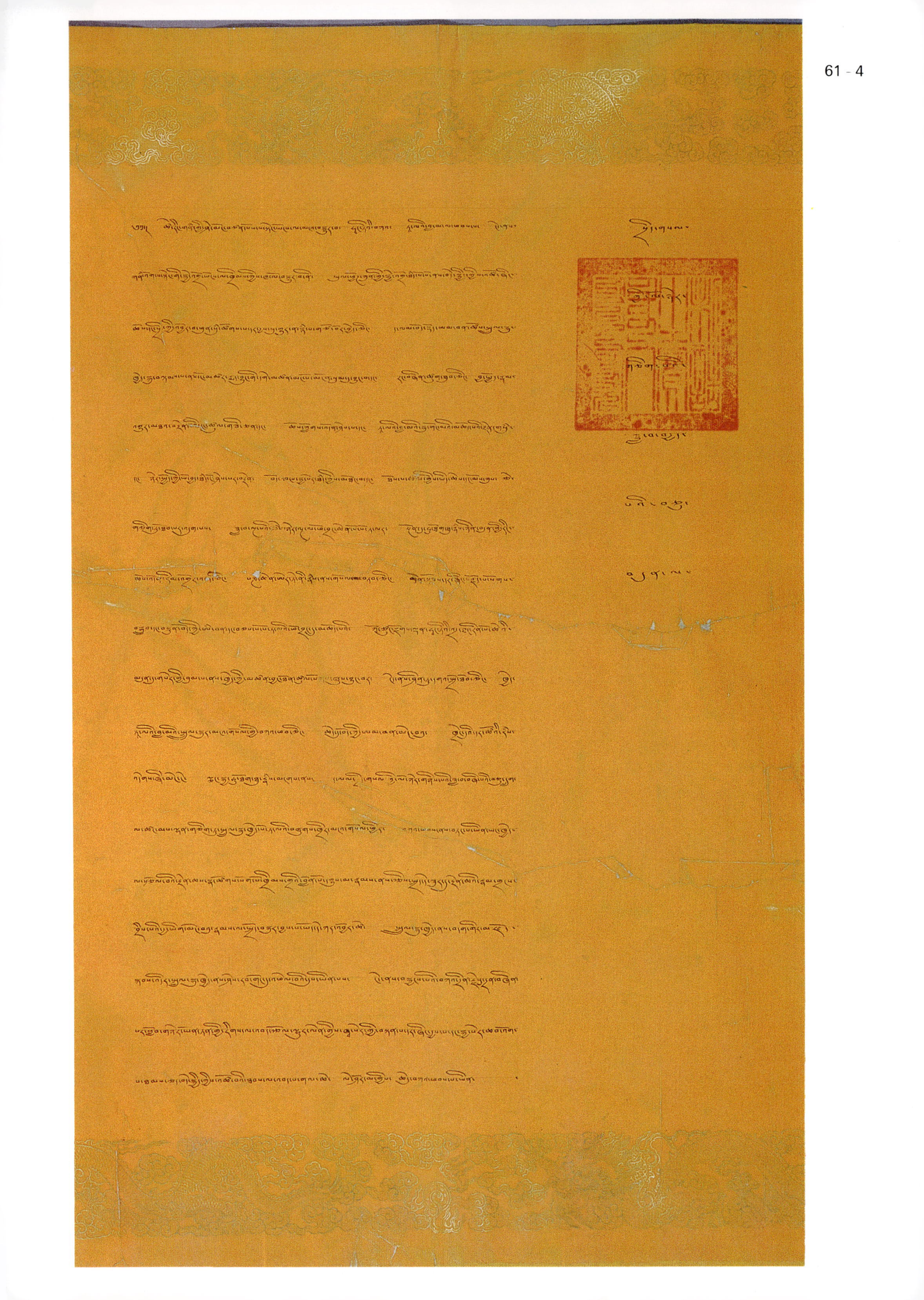

[illegible]
[illegible]
[illegible]
[illegible]
[illegible]
[illegible]
[illegible]
[illegible]
[illegible]
[illegible]
[illegible]
[illegible]
[illegible]
[illegible]
[illegible]
[illegible]
[illegible]
[illegible]

[illegible]
[illegible]
[illegible]
[illegible]
[illegible]
[illegible]

# ལྷ་སར་སྡོད་པའི་དམག་སྣར་གྱི་ཤུ་སྤྱིས་ནས་བཀའ་བློན་དང་མདའ་དཔོན་སོགས་ནུས་ཤུགས་བརྟོན་མཁན་གྱི་དཔོན་རིགས་འོས་སྦྱོར་བྱེད་རྒྱུའི་སྙར་གྱི་ཞུ་ཡིག
# 駐防拉薩營守備保舉噶倫、代本等效力官員折
# Petition from the Garrison Commander of Lhasa Recommending Men to Serve as Government Ministers, *Dapons* and Other Posts

བོད་རང་སྐྱོང་ལྗོངས་ཡིག་ཚགས་ཁང་དུ་ཉར་ཚགས་བྱས་ཡོད།

［內容提要：道光二十二年（公元1842年）八月駐防拉薩漢藏營守備具折保舉前往拉森之噶倫、代本、如本、宗本、甲本等官員。復經皇帝頒諭，分别予以提升官職、封爵襲蔭、賞賜頂戴花翎，以表彰勇敢效力者。］

西藏自治區檔案館藏

[Summary: In the 8th month of the 22nd year of Daoguang (1842), the commander of the Han–Tibetan battalion garrisoning Lhasa submitted a petition recommending men to serve as government ministers, *dapons, rupons, dzongpons* and *gyapons* who were to set out for Lasing. His Majesty the Emperor then issued a decree giving them promotions, conferring on them titles which were to be inherited by their descendants, and granting them the honour of wearing peacock feathers in recognition of their brave service.]

Preserved by the Archives of the Tibet Autonomous Region.

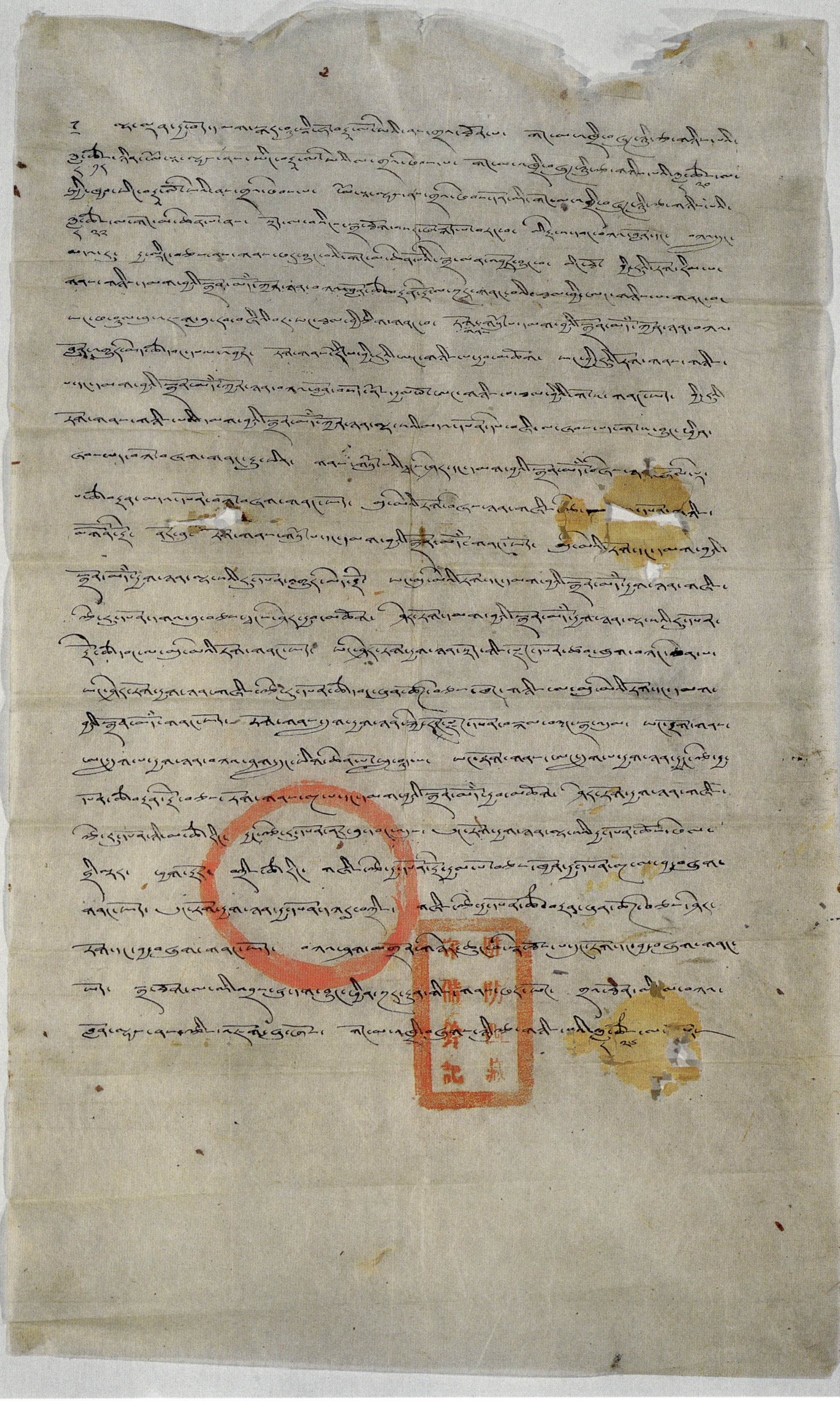

# གོང་མ་ཀུན་ཁྱབ་འཕེལ་རྒྱས་ཀྱིས་ཏཱ་ལའི་བླ་མའི་ཡང་སྲིད་སྐུ་ན་ཕྲ་སྐབས་གནས་སྐབས་རིང་སྲིད་སྐྱོང་བསྐོ་དགོས་སྐོར་རྭ་སྒྲེང་བླ་མར་བསྩལ་བའི་བཀའ་ལུང་།

# 咸豐皇帝爲達賴喇嘛靈童年少暫需攝政事給熱振活佛的敕諭

# Emperor Xianfeng's Decree to Living Buddha Rasgreng Concerning the Need for a Provisional Regent Pending the Maturation of the Holy Child Dalai Lama

279 × 64

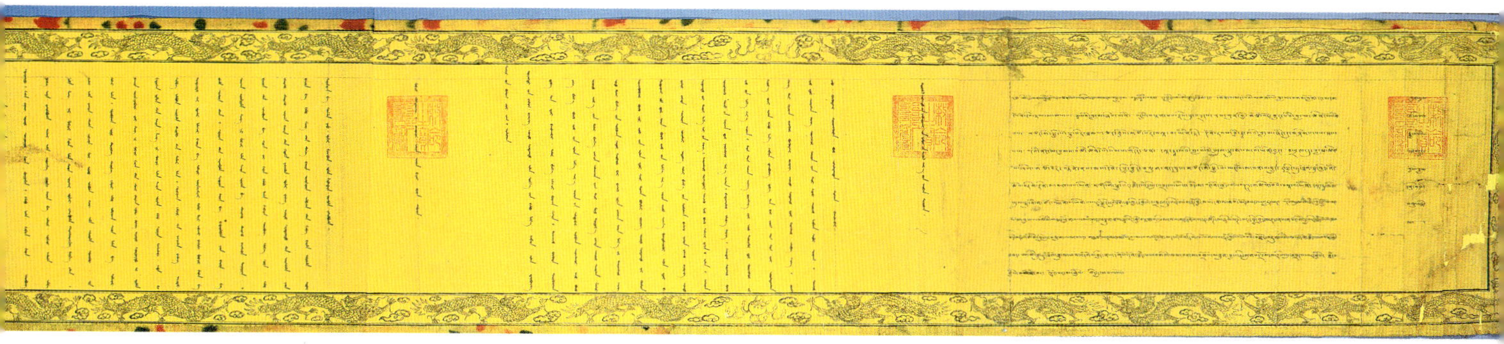

63－1

བོད་རང་སྐྱོང་ལྗོངས་ཡིག་ཚགས་ཁང་དུ་ཉར་ཚགས་བྱས་ཡོད།

奉天承運皇帝詔曰：

諭熱振阿齊圖呼圖克圖及衆寺之堪布喇嘛、噶倫、衆代本第巴等。達賴喇嘛乃總管釋教之大喇嘛，藏地僧俗衆人所尊奉瞻仰。前世達賴喇嘛圓寂之時，朕心惻然，甚是憐憫。今達賴喇嘛之呼畢勒罕雖已出，若仍由一賢良大喇嘛爲首辦事，則於衛藏全境衆民方有裨益，熱振阿齊圖呼圖克圖爾人誠實賢良，藏地僧俗衆民皆心悦誠服，朕深爲贊許。今達賴喇嘛之呼畢勒罕尚屬年少，熱振阿齊圖呼圖克圖爾即爲首辦理喇嘛事務，以仰副朕仁恤天下衆民之至意，弘揚黄教，妥善辦理諸事，俾藏地僧俗各享安居之福。再，衆堪布、喇嘛、噶倫、代本、第巴等均須盡心效力本職，共同輔佐熱振阿齊圖呼圖克圖，凡事均須與駐藏辦事大臣商定。照章行事，共勉勿怠。特諭。

咸豐八年（公元1858年）九月十四日

西藏自治區檔案館藏

His Majesty the Emperor, who reigns by the mandate of Heaven, decrees:

These are the instructions to Living Buddha Rasgreng Achithu and the Khanpo lamas,

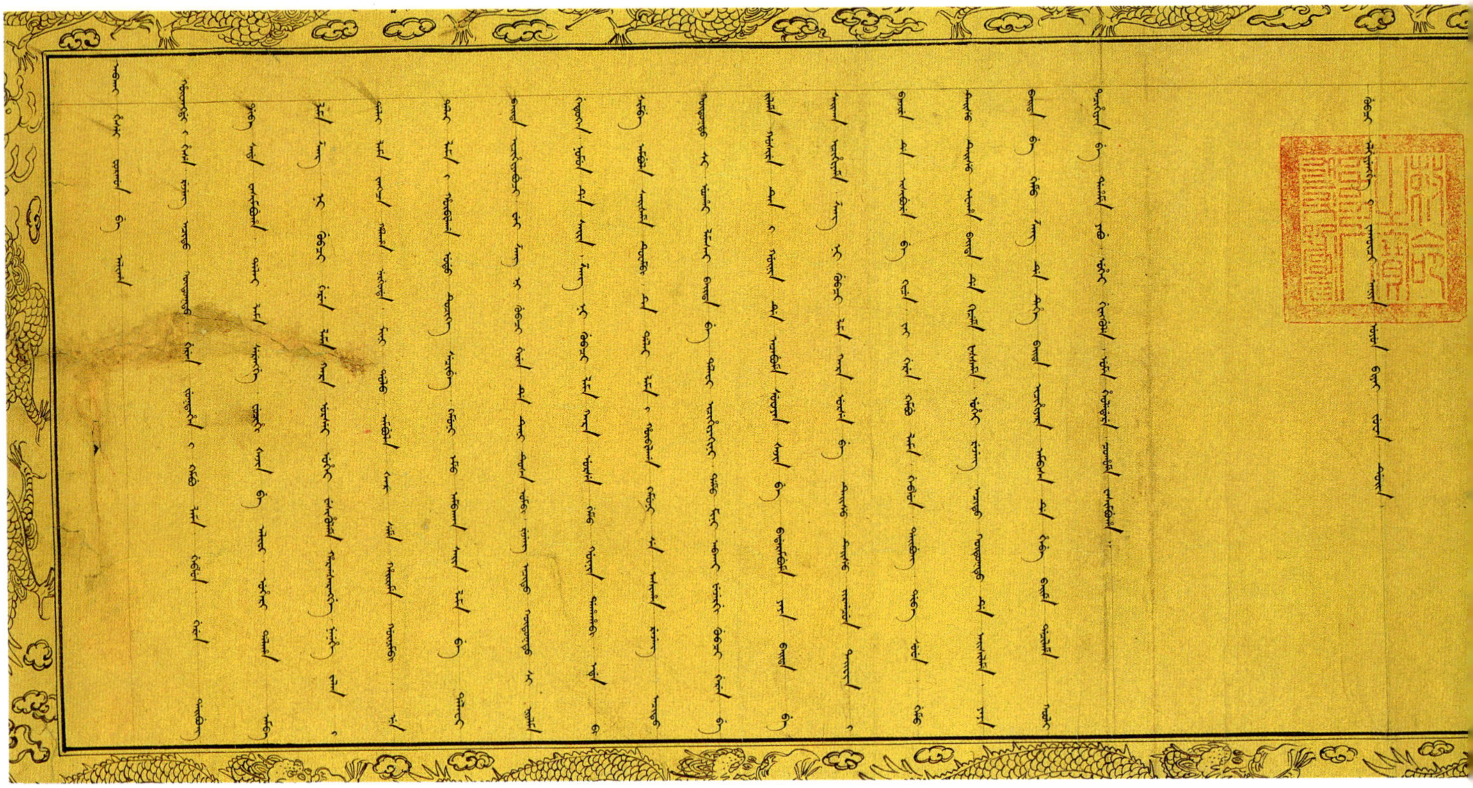

63 - 2

63 - 3

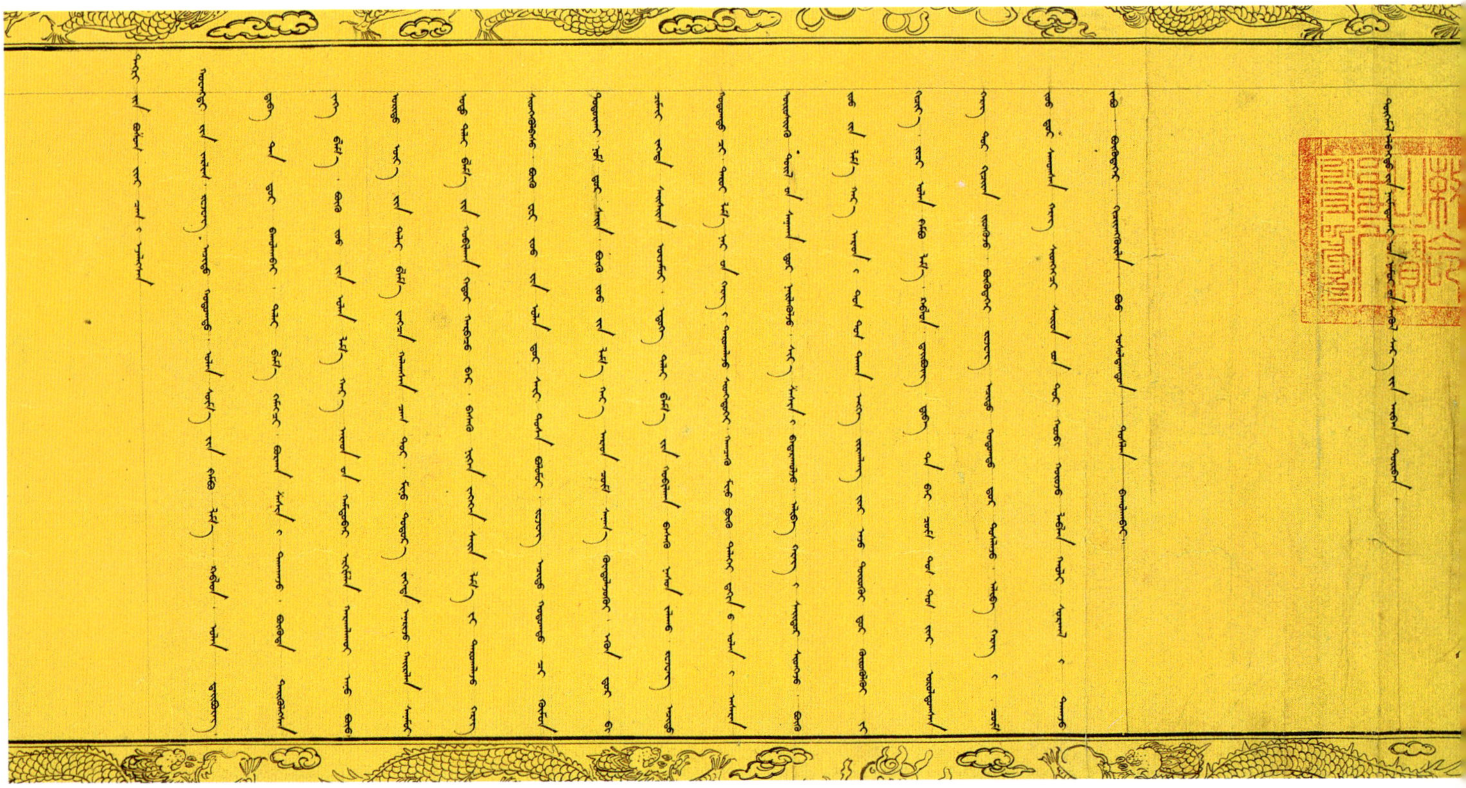

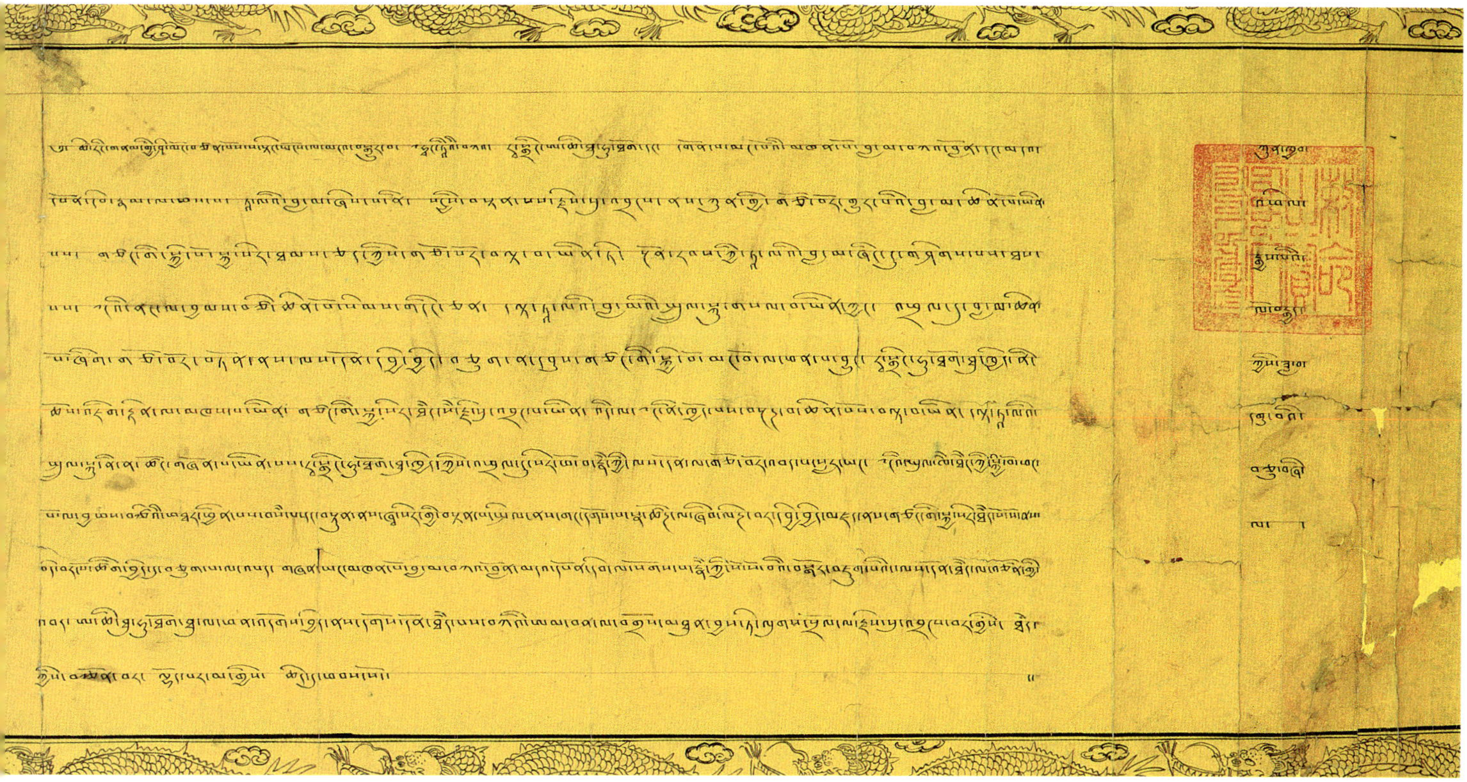

63-4

government ministers, *dapons* and *dibas* of the monasteries. As the Grand Lama who administers all Buddhist affairs, the Dalai Lama is revered and worshipped by the monks and lay people throughout Tibet. When the Dalai Lama of the last incarnation passed away, I was filled with grief and compassion. Although the Holy Child who is to succeed him has now made his appearance, an able and virtuous grand lama heading the administration will prove beneficial to the people all over Tibet. You, Living Buddha Rasgreng Achithu, being honest and upstanding and respected by all in Tibet, have my heartfelt approval. Since the child Dalai Lama is still young, you, Living Buddha Rasgreng Achithu, are hereby appointed to take charge of Lamaist affairs to fulfil my earnest wish to show compassion to all the people. You should promote the Yellow Sect of Lamaism and handle all matters properly so that the monks and lay people in Tibet may enjoy the happiness of living in peace. Furthermore, all Khanpos, lamas, government ministers, *dapons* and *dibas* should devote themselves wholeheartedly to their work and cooperate in assisting Living Buddha Rasgreng Achithu. You should consult the Resident Ministers in Tibet on all matters and act in accordance with regulations, working tirelessly to achieve these aims. This is the end of the instructions.

The 14th day of the 9th month of the 8th year of Xianfeng (1858)

Preserved by the Archives of the Tibet Autonomous Region.

# གོང་མ་ཀུན་ཁྱབ་འཕེལ་རྒྱས་ཀྱིས་གསེར་ཁྲིར་མངའ་གསོལ་སྐོར་ཏཱ་ལའི་བླ་མར་བསྩལ་པའི་བཀའ་ལུང་།

# 咸豐皇帝爲坐床事給達賴喇嘛靈童的敕諭

# Emperor Xianfeng's Decree to the Holy Child Dalai Lama Regarding His Enthronement

180 × 103

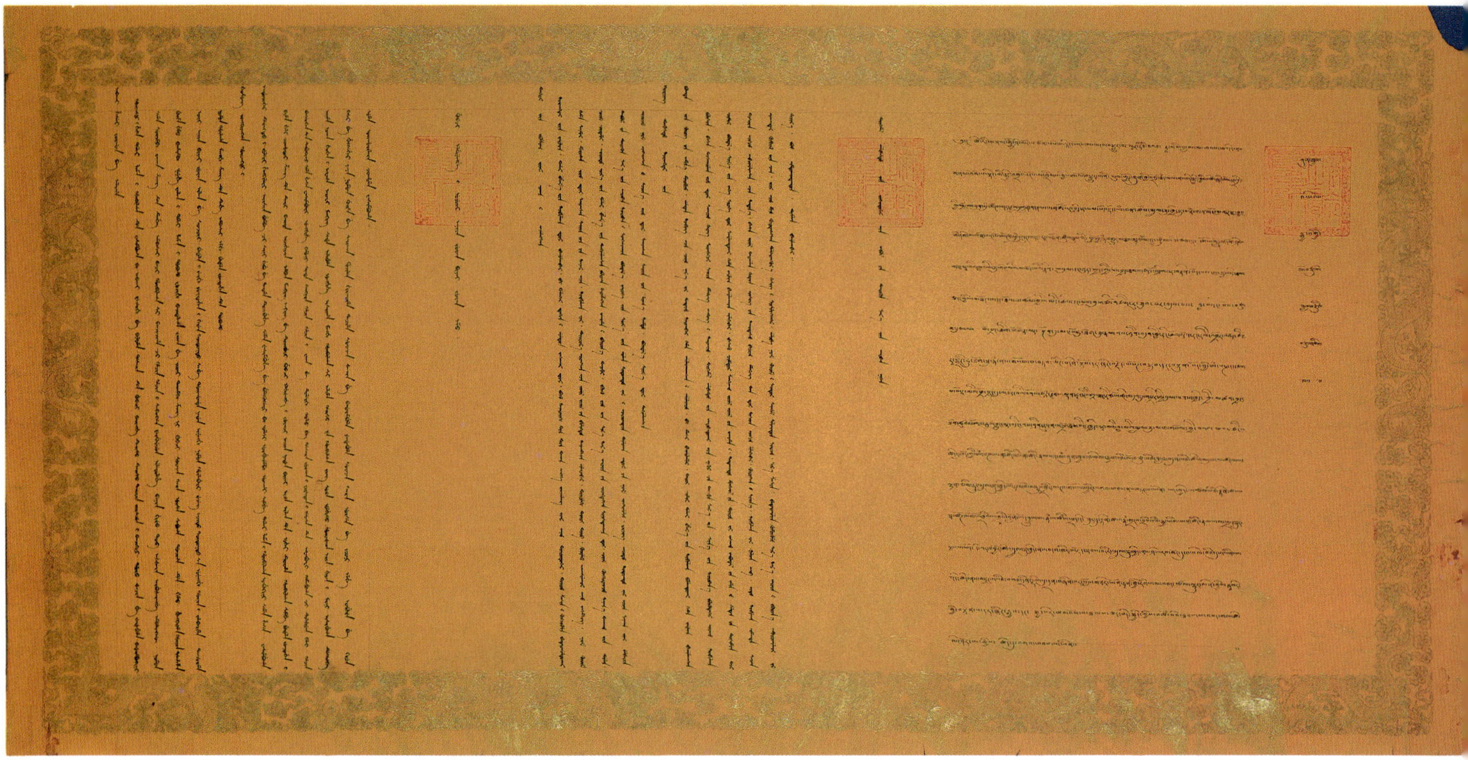

64 - 1

བོད་རང་སྐྱོང་ལྗོངས་ཡིག་ཚགས་ཁང་དུ་ཉར་ཚགས་བྱས་ཡོད།

奉天承運皇帝詔曰：

諭達賴喇嘛之呼畢勒罕。朕統馭天下，惟期率土之民，各享安居之福，推興政教。頃據駐藏大臣奏稱：呼畢勒罕爾降生以來，均有吉祥佳兆，性貌端莊，舉止大方，熟諳經典，能辨識前世達賴喇嘛所供佛尊用器，衛藏僧俗衆人之所見所聞，皆傾心歸順，故擇正月十三日，令布達拉宮衆呼圖克圖預先誦經七日，熱振呼圖克圖等虔誠祝禱誦經之後，與駐藏大臣一同於布達拉宮高宗純皇帝聖像之前掣籤，由金奔巴瓶掣出爾名等情。朕覽奏，甚爲嘉悦，即降諭令爾爲達賴喇嘛之呼畢勒罕。且又降諭特遣駐藏辦事大臣滿慶、恩慶令呼畢勒罕爾於布達拉宮坐床等因咨文。將賞爾之諸項物件交付理藩院司員携往以外，並逐項繕寫漢字清單咨呈滿慶，抵達之後呼畢勒罕爾衹領之。今呼畢勒罕正值聽慧長進之時，理宜感戴朕施鴻恩，專心學習所有經典，弘揚黄教，俾僧俗衆人均獲安康太平，勿得怠惰。特諭。

咸豐十年(公元1860年)十月十一日

西藏自治區檔案館藏

His Majesty the Emperor, who reigns by the mandate of Heaven, decrees:

These are the instructions to the child Dalai Lama. I rule the Empire so that people throughout the land may enjoy the happiness of living in peace, improve the political situation and promote religion. The Resident Ministers in Tibet have just sent a petition to the throne as follows. "Since the child Dalai Lama's birth there have been many suspicious signs. He has a dignified appearance and an easy manner, is well acquainted with the Buddhist classics, and can recognize the articles with which the Dalai Lama of the last incarnation worshipped Buddha. All the monks and lay people in Tibet have learned of all this and are completely convinced. It was decided," continues the petition, "that on the 13th day of the 1st month, the Living Buddhas of the Potala Palace were to chant the scriptures for seven days. Then, having piously offered prayer and chanted the scriptures, Living Buddha Rasgreng Achithu, together with the Resident Ministers in Tibet, drew the lot inscribed with the child Dalai Lama's name from the gold vase in front of the sacred portrait of His Imperial Majesty Emperor Gaozong enshrined in the Potala Palace, etc." I was very pleased on reading the petition and have issued a decree making you the next Dalai Lama. I have also issued an edict sending Resident Ministers Man Qing and En Qing to officiate at your enthronement ceremony in the Potala Palace. The presents awarded to you are being forwarded by officials of the Minority Nationality Administration Office, while the itemized list written in Han characters is being carried by Man Qing. You are to accept them respectfully when they arrive. You are still growing physically and intellectually and should devote yourself to the study of all the Buddhist classics and promote the Yellow Sect of Lamaism to show your appreciation of my magnanimity so that the monks and lay people may live in peace, working tirelessly for these aims. This is the end of the instructions.

The 11th day of the 10th month of the 10th year of Xianfeng (1860)

Preserved by the Archives of the Tibet Autonomous Region.

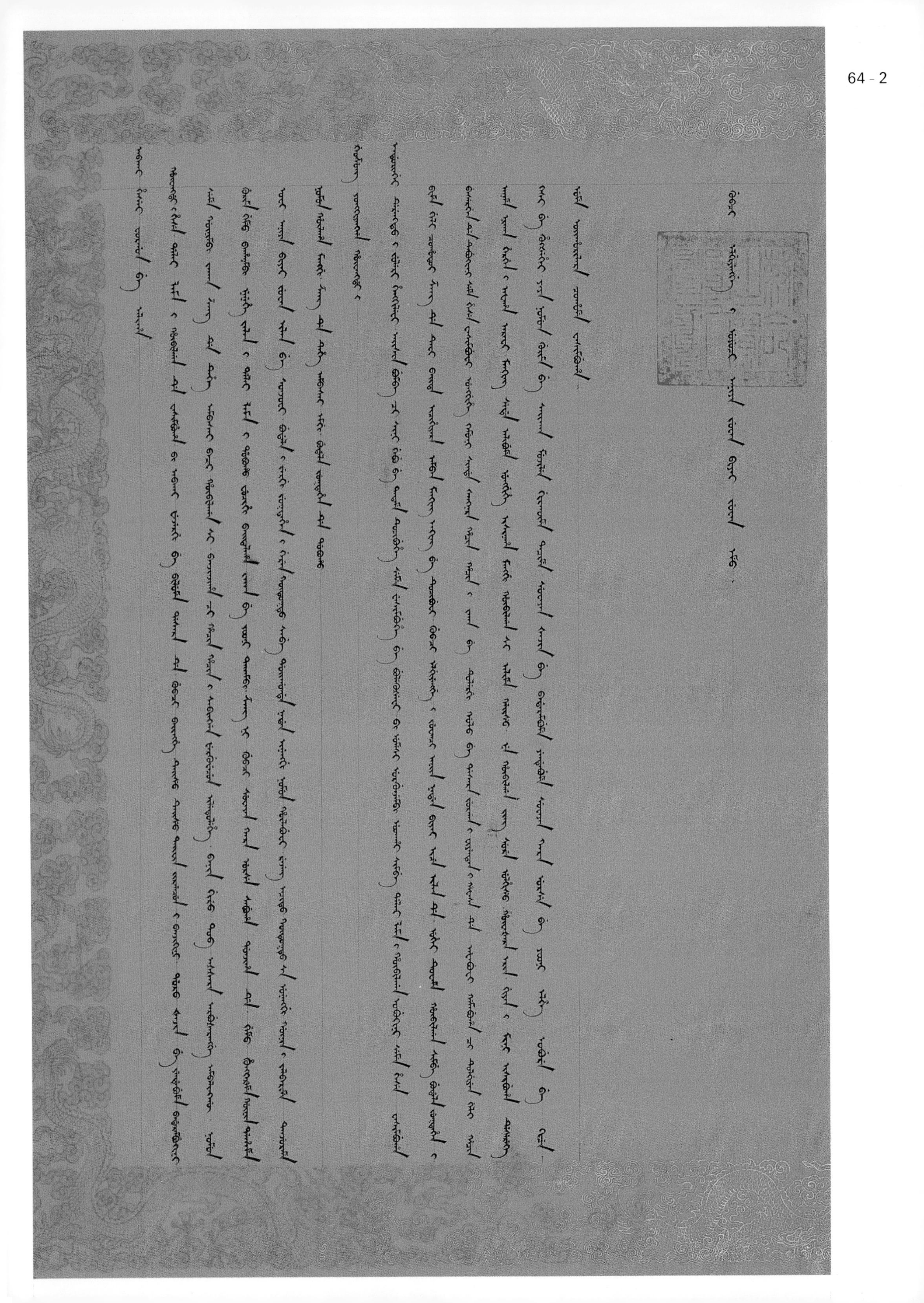

[illegible]
[illegible]
[illegible]
[illegible]
[illegible]
[illegible]
[illegible]
[illegible]
[illegible]
[illegible]
[illegible]
[illegible]
[illegible]
[illegible]
[illegible]
[illegible]

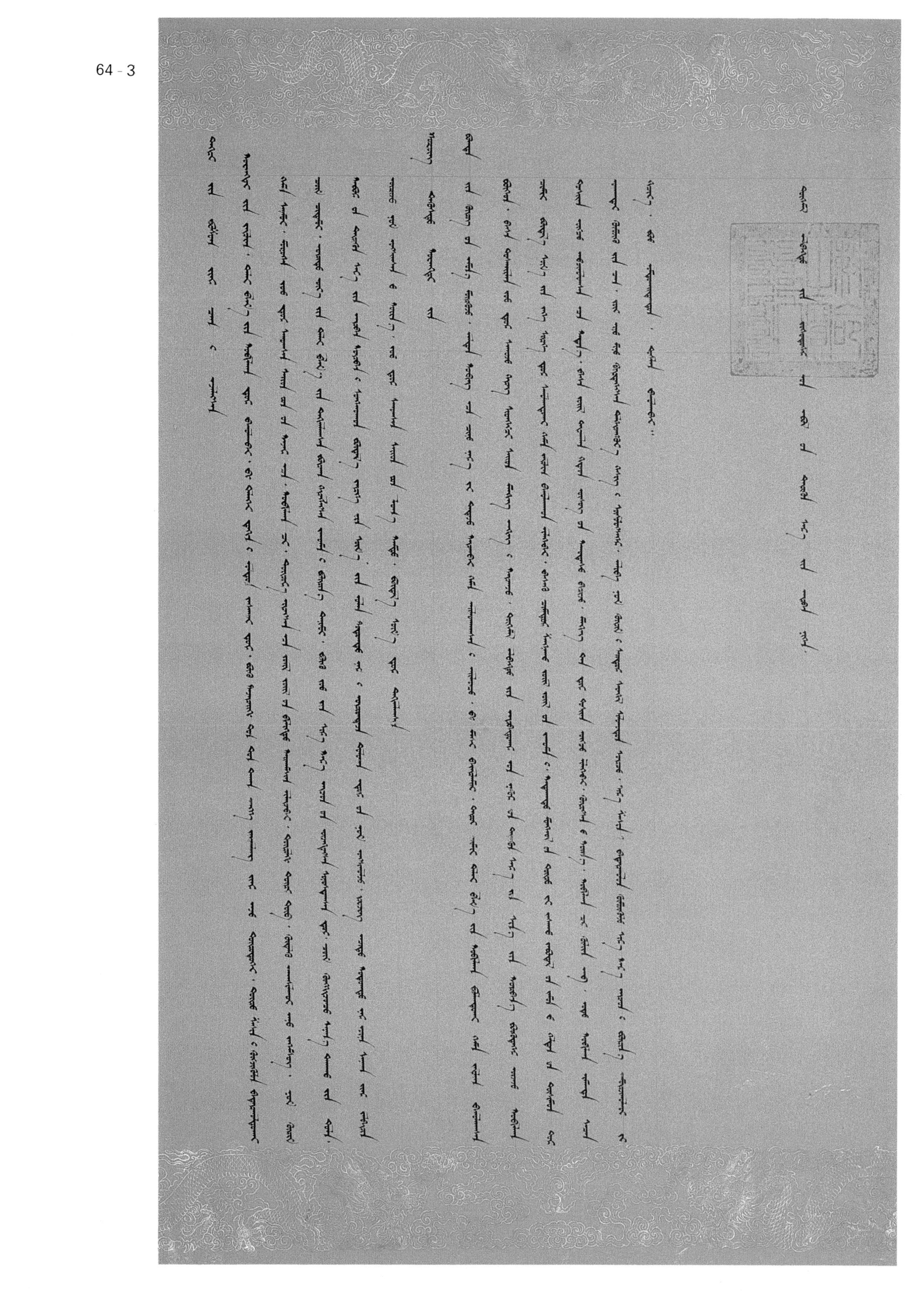

[illegible]

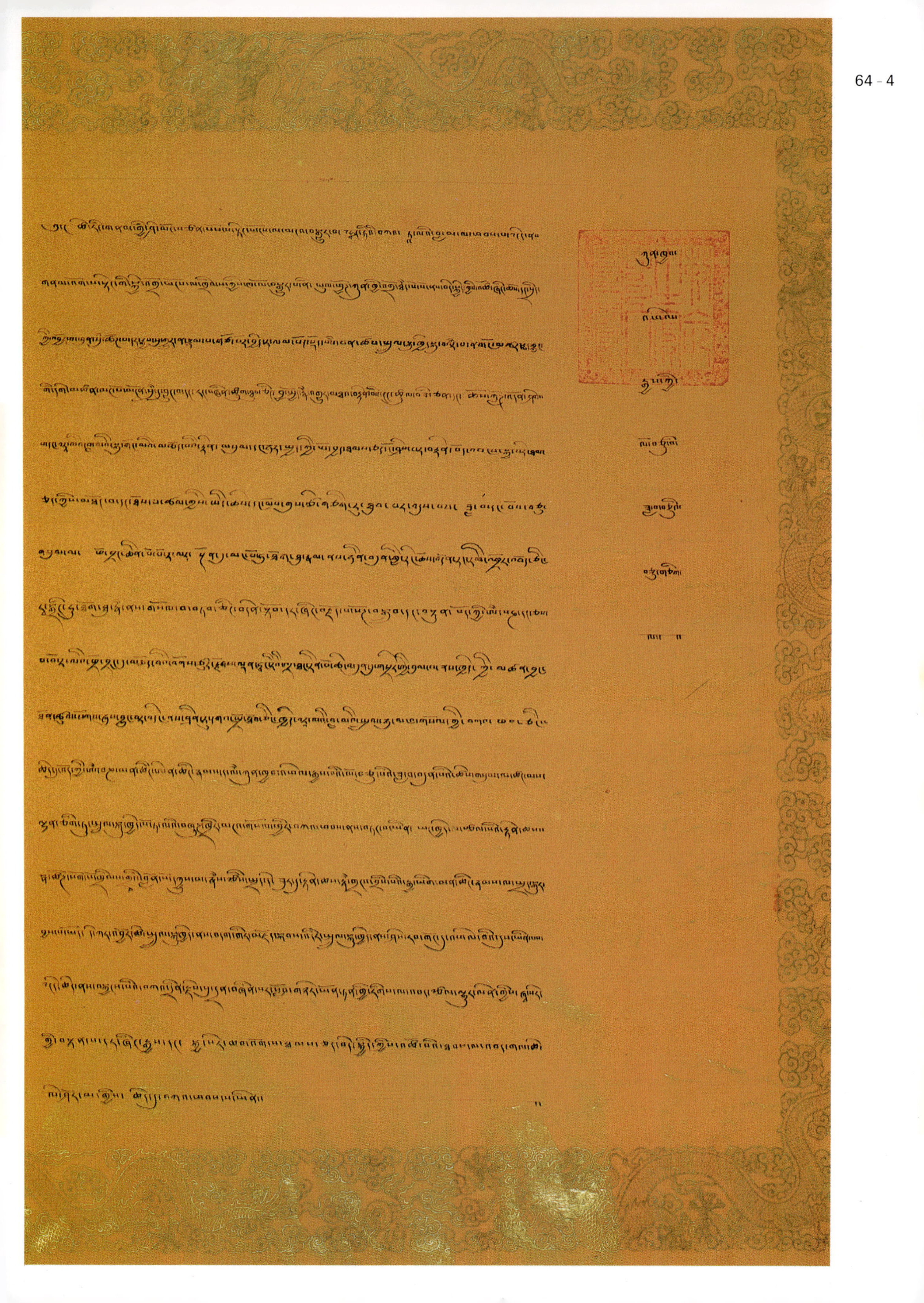

[illegible]

# རྗེ་དྲུང་ཧོ་ཐོག་ཐུ་དང་བཀའ་བློན་ཐུན་མོང་ནས་བོད་ཀྱི་དཔོན་རིགས་ཁ་སྐོང་བྱེད་རྒྱུའི་སྐོར་བོད་བཞུགས་ཨམ་བན་ལ་བཏང་བའི་ཡི་གེ།

# 濟隆呼圖克圖及諸噶倫爲補缺事咨駐藏大臣文

# Communication from Living Buddha Rjedrung and the Government Ministers to the Resident Ministers in Tibet Regarding the Filling of Vacancies by Tibetan Staff

61.7 × 49.5

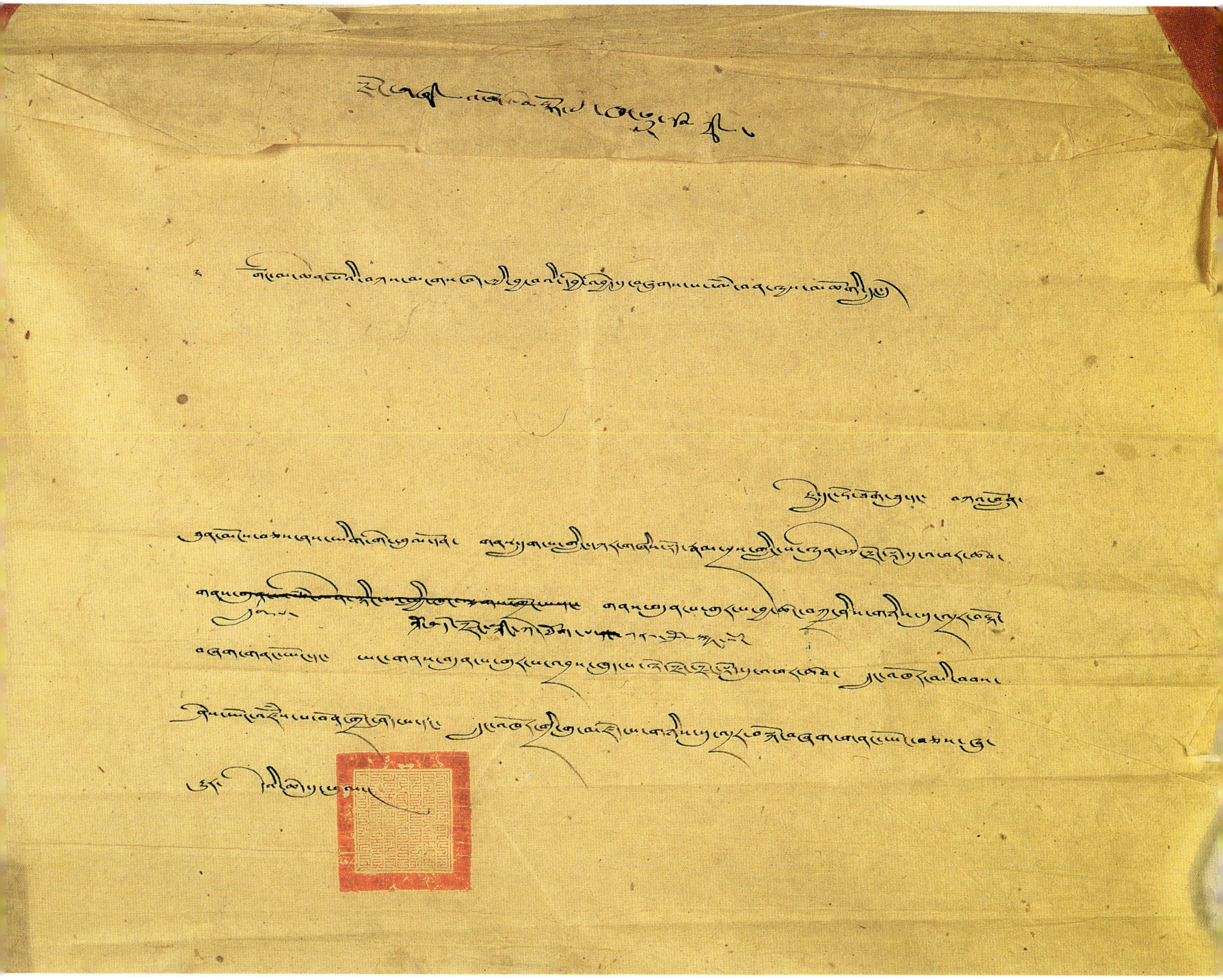

བོད་རང་སྐྱོང་ལྗོངས་ཡིག་ཚགས་ཁང་དུ་ཉར་ཚགས་བྱས་ཡོད།

濟隆呼圖克圖及諸噶倫咨行欽差駐藏諸大臣。

因六品官林噶溪堆朗塞林巴提升爲隆子宗本，由六品官雪朵宗寧噶妥巴或七品官古爾巴加倉扎西二名之中選補其缺，又，古爾巴哲濆巴提升爲洛宗宗堆，由德高學深之奔仲雪巴或仲科哲古佐巴二名之中選補其缺。

特此呈報。

西藏自治區檔案館藏

This is the communication from Living Buddha Rjedrung and the government ministers to the Resident Ministers in Tibet:

The vacancy created by the promotion of 6th rank officer Lingka Zhisdod Namsras Lingpa to *dzongpon* of Lhunze County should be filled by 6th rank officer Nyingka Thogpa of Shomdo or 7th rank officer Gurpa Byatshang Krashis. The vacancy created by the promotion of Gurpa Braskhudpa to *zongtui* of Lho County should be filled by either the learned and prestigious Bongrong Shodpa or Drungkhor Grigud Sodpa.

This is the end of the special communication.

Preserved by the Archives of the Tibet Autonomous Region.

# གོང་མ་ཀོང་ཞུ་ནས་གསེར་ཁྲི་མངའ་གསོལ་སྐོར་དུ་ལའི་བླ་མའི་ཡང་སྲིད་ལ་བསྩལ་པའི་བཀའ་ལུང་།

# 光緒皇帝爲坐床事給達賴喇嘛靈童的敕諭

# Emperor Guangxu's Decree to the Holy Child Dalai Lama Regarding His Enthronement

174×100

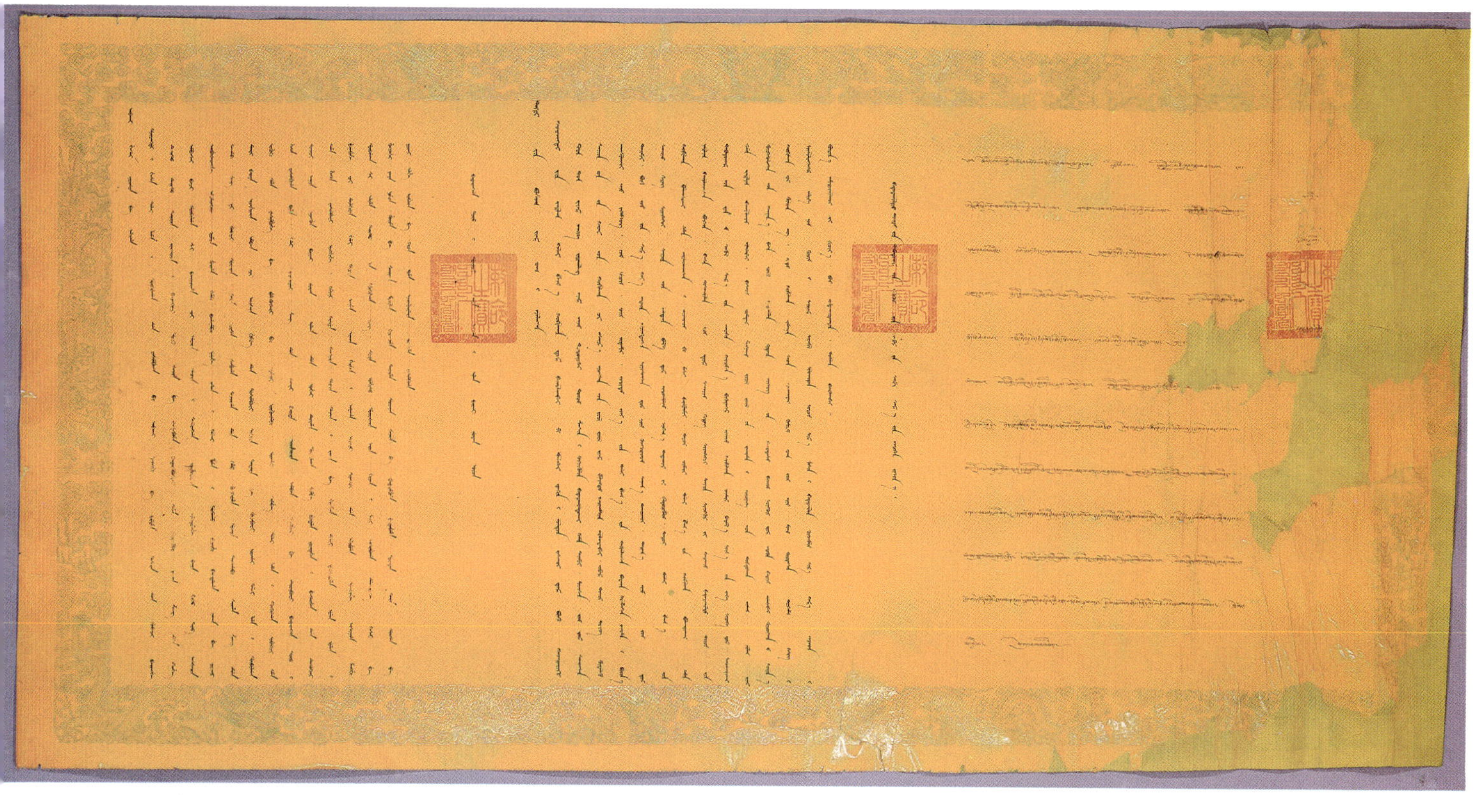

66 - 1

བོད་རང་སྐྱོང་ལྗོངས་ཡིག་ཚགས་ཁང་དུ་ཉར་ཚགས་བྱས་ཡོད།

奉天承運皇帝詔曰：

諭達賴喇嘛之呼畢勒罕。朕撫馭天下，惟期率土之民，各享安居之福，推興政教。頃據駐藏辦事大臣處奏稱：呼畢勒罕爾自降生以來，均有吉祥佳兆，性貌端莊，舉止大方，諳習經典，能辨認前世達賴喇嘛所供佛尊用器，衛藏僧俗衆人之所見所聞，皆傾心歸順，繼由駐藏辦事大臣將爾名繕入金奔巴瓶內，免予掣簽，即作爲達賴喇嘛之呼畢勒罕等情。朕覽奏，深感嘉悅，即降諭令爾作爲達賴喇嘛之呼畢勒罕，又降諭特遣駐藏辦事大臣松溎於光緒五年六月十三日共同看視，着呼畢勒罕爾於布達拉宮坐床等因咨文。仍將賞爾之諸項物品由驛飛遞解送以外，並逐項繕寫漢字清單咨呈松溎。抵達之後呼畢勒罕爾祇領之。今呼畢勒罕正值聰明長進之時，理宜感戴朕施鴻恩，專心勤習經卷，弘揚黃教，俾僧俗衆人安居，勿得懈怠。特諭。

光緒五年(公元1879年)閏三月十九日

西藏自治區檔案館藏

His Majesty the Emperor, who reigns by the mandate of Heaven, decrees:

These are the instructions for the child Dalai Lama. I rule the Empire allowing the people in the country to enjoy the happiness of living in peace, improve the political situation and promote religion. The Office of the Resident Ministers in Tibet has recently sent a petition to the throne as follows."Since the birth of the child Dalai Lama there have been many auspicious signs. He has a dignified appearance and an easy manner, is well acquainted with the Buddhist classics and can recognize the articles with which the Dalai Lama of the last incarnation worshipped Buddha. All the monks and lay people in Tibet have learned of all this and are completely convinced. The Resident Ministers thereupon wrote his name on a lot and put it in the gold vase, giving him the status of the next incarnation of Dalai Lama without going through the procedure of drawing lots." I was very pleased on reading the petition and have issued a decree naming you the next incarnation of the Dalai Lama. I have also issued an edict sending Song Gui, Resident Minister in Tibet, to officiate over your enthronement ceremony in the Potala Palace on the 13th day of the 6th month of the 5th year of Guangxu. The articles awarded to you are being delivered post-haste by couriers, while an itemized list in Han characters is being carried by Song Gui. You are to respectfully accept them when they arrive. You are still growing physically and intellectually and should apply yourself to the study of Buddhist classics and promote the Yellow Sect of Lamaism to show appreciation for my magnanimity so that the monks and lay people may live in peace, working tirelessly towards these aims. This is the end of the instructions.

The 19th day of the 3rd month (leap month) of the 5th year of Guangxu (1879)

Preserved by the Archives of the Tibet Autonomous Region.

敕命之寶

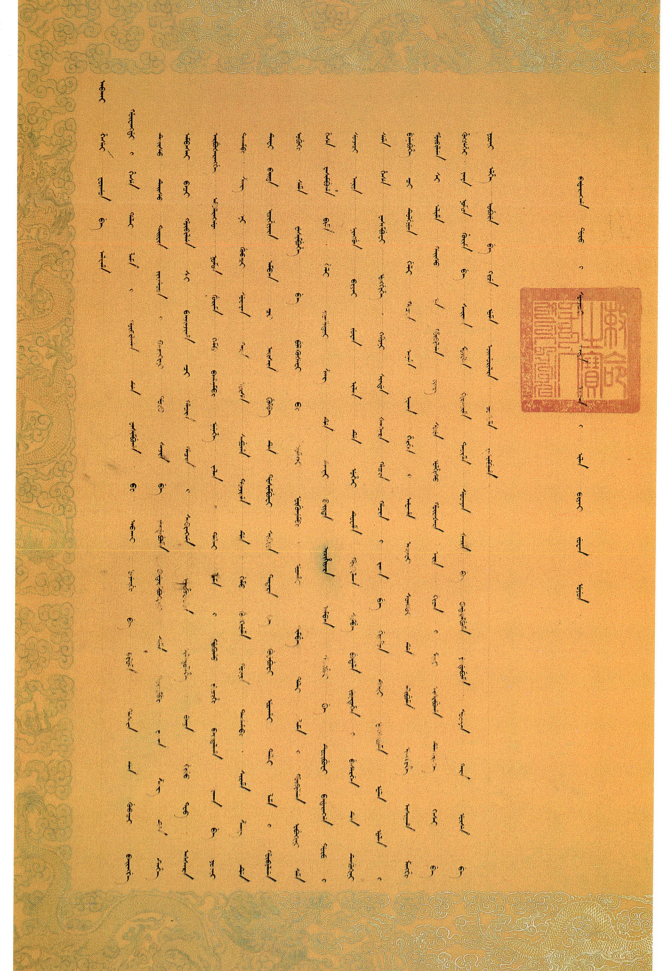

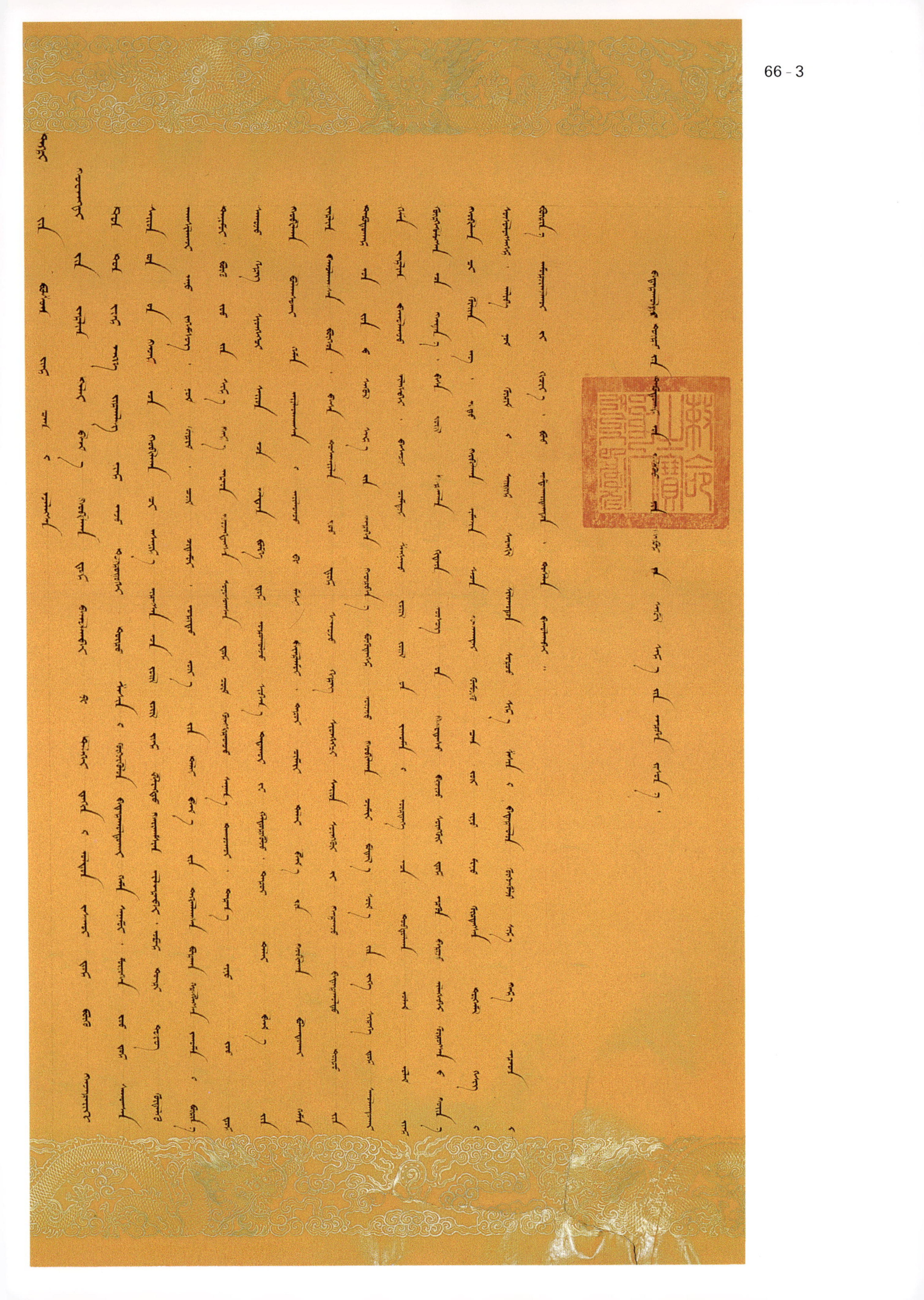

敕命之寶

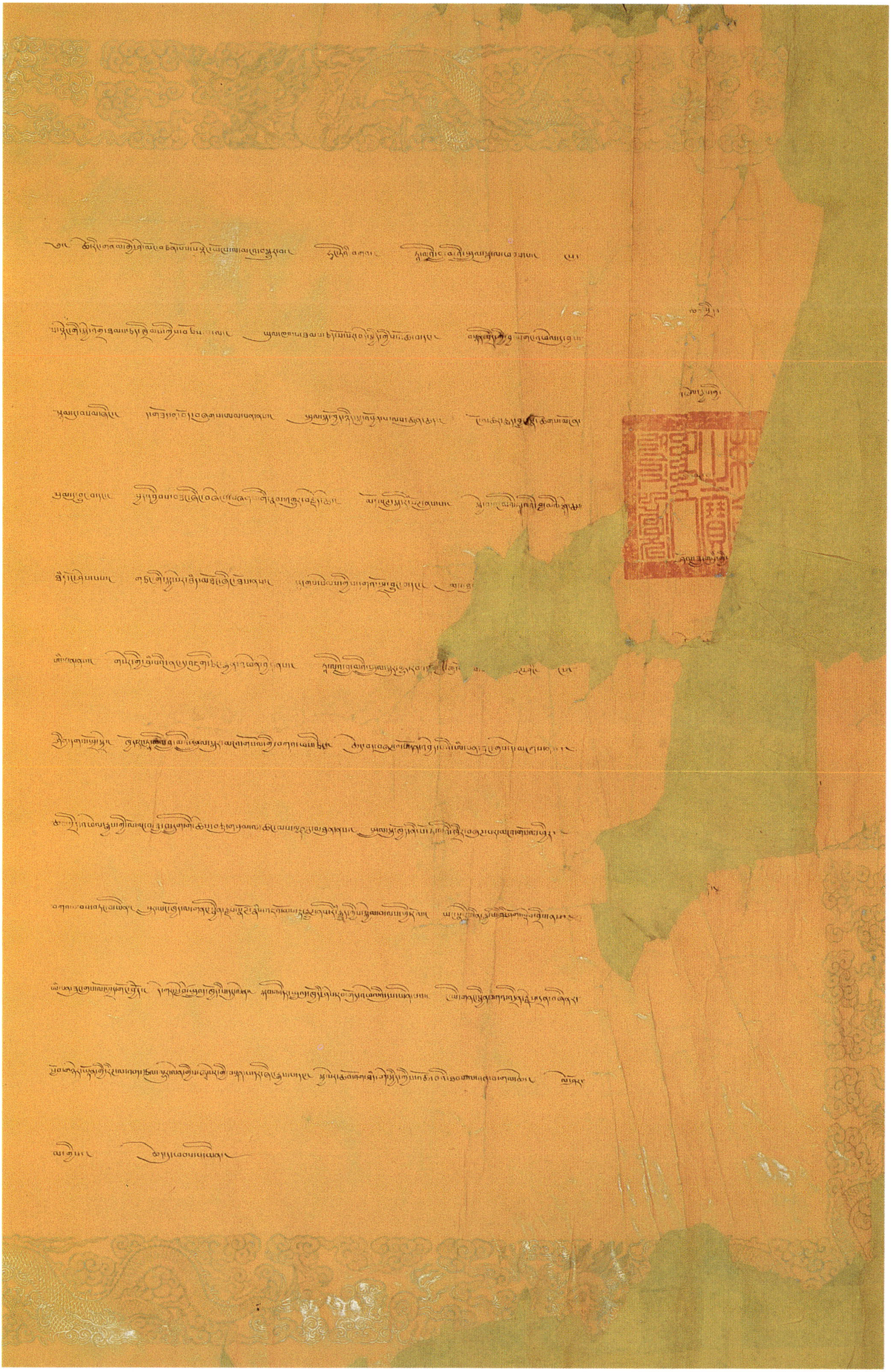

**67**

# བོད་བཞུགས་ཨམ་བན་ཧྲེན་ཐེ་ནས་དཔོན་རིགས་ཁ་སྐོང་དང་ལས་གནས་སྤོ་རྒྱུའི་སྐོར་དེ་མོ་ཧོ་ཐོག་ཐུ་ལ་བཏང་བའི་ཡི་གེ
# 駐藏大臣升泰爲官員調補事咨第穆呼圖克圖文
# Communication from Sheng Tai, Resident Minister in Tibet, to Living Buddha Demo Regarding the Promotion or Transfer of Tibetan Staff

71 × 59, 35 × 18

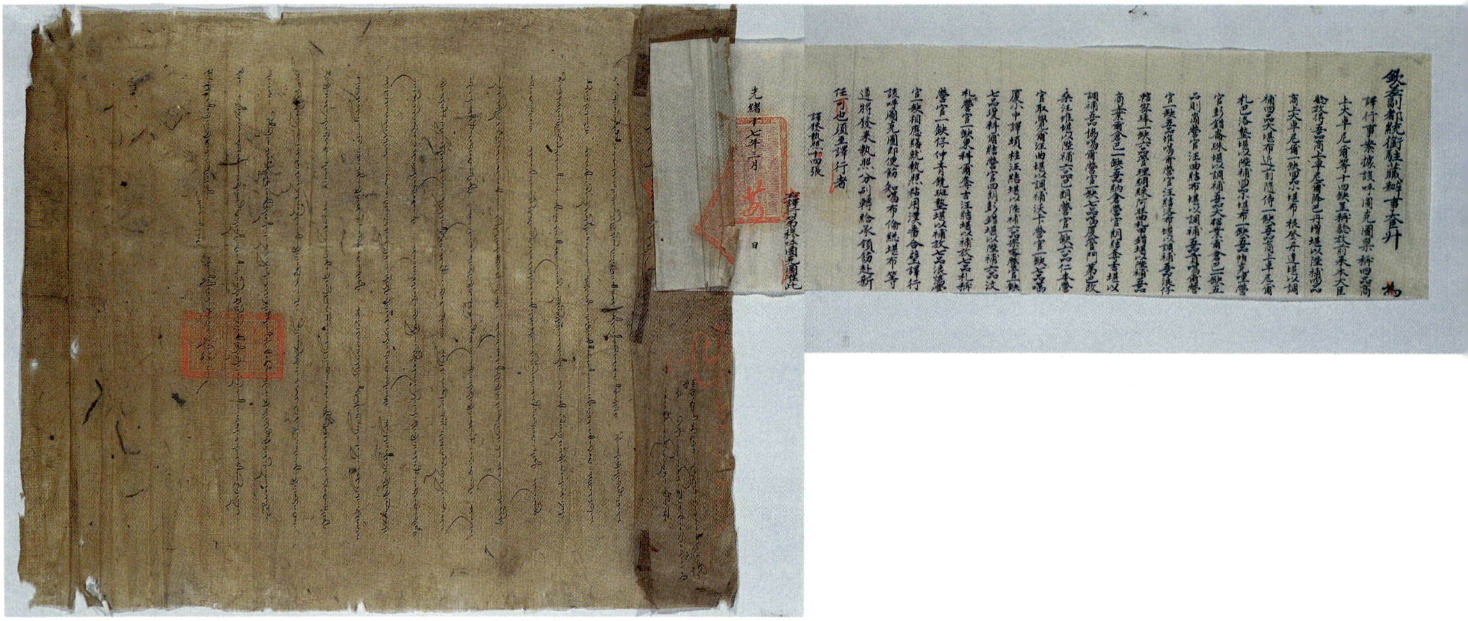

67 - 1

བོད་རང་སྐྱོང་ལྗོངས་ཡིག་ཚགས་ཁང་དུ་ཉར་ཚགས་བྱས་ཡོད།

西藏自治區檔案館藏

Vice Commander Sheng, Resident Minister in Tibet by Imperial Order, issues the following communication:

The Living Buddha's communication has listed the names of 14 candidates for approval to fill vacancies of 4th–ranking senior *zhuoni'er* and below. The Resident Minister has examined the list and decided that 5th–ranking *zhuoni'er* Yampa Tandsin can be promoted to 4th–ranking senior *zhuoni'er*, 4th–ranking junior Khanpo Gedun Tandar can be transferred to assume the duties of 4th–ranking senior Khanpo attendant, 5th–ranking *zhuoni'er* Krapa Lopa can be promoted to 4th–ranking junior Khanpo, 5th–ranking Pagri military camp

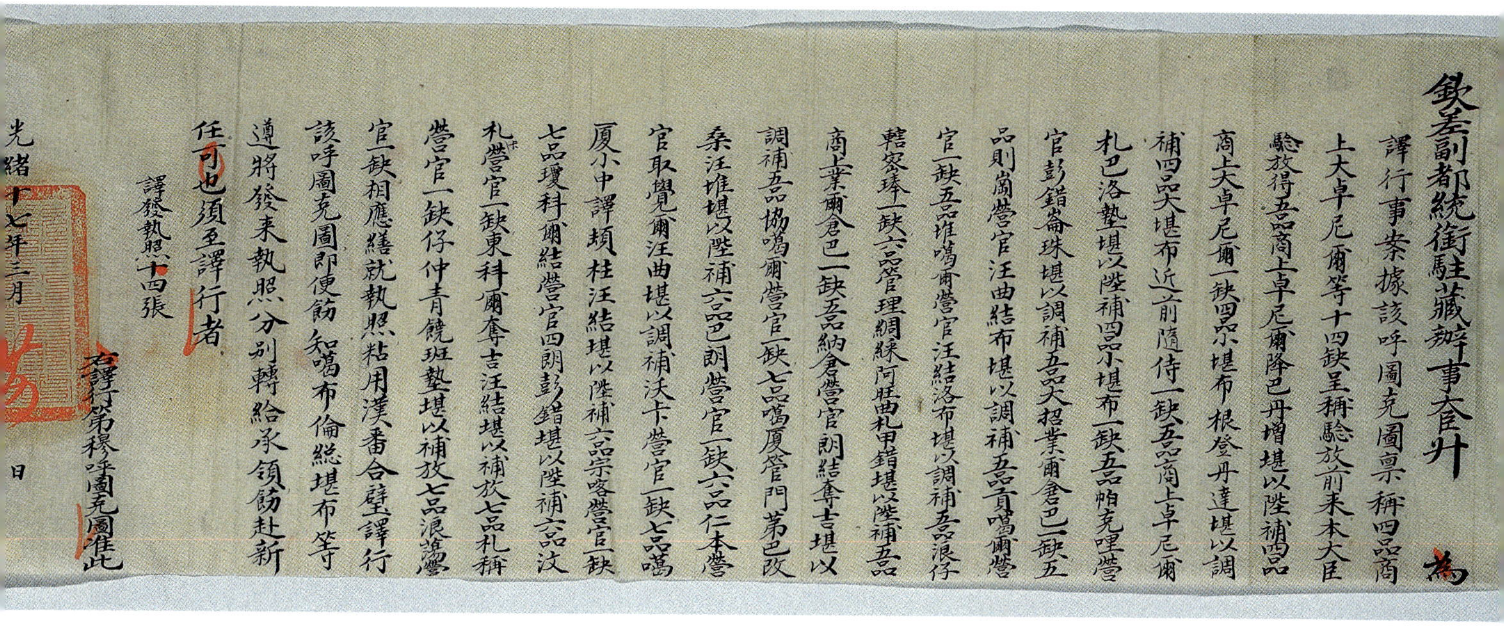
欽差副都統銜駐藏辦事大臣升 為
譯行事案據該呼圖克圖稟稱四品商
上大卓尼爾等十四缺呈稱驗放前來本大臣
驗放得五品商上卓尼爾降巴丹增堪以陞補四品
商上大卓尼爾一缺四品小堪布根登丹達堪以調
補四品大堪布近前隨侍一缺五品商上卓尼爾
札巴洛墊堪以陞補四品小堪布一缺五品帕克哩營
官彭錯崙珠堪以調補五品大招業爾倉巴一缺五
品則崗營官汪曲結布堪以調補五品貢噶爾營
官一缺五品堆噶爾營官汪結洛布堪以調補五品浪仔
轄密琫一缺六品管理綢緞阿旺曲札甲錯堪以陞補五品
商上業爾倉巴一缺五品納倉營官朗結奪吉堪以
調補五品協噶爾營官一缺七品噶廈管門第巴孜
桑汪堆堪以陞補六品巴朗營官一缺六品仁本營
官取覺爾汪曲堪以調補沃卡營官一缺七品噶
廈小中譯頓柱汪結堪以陞補六品宗喀營官一缺
七品瓊科爾結營官四朗彭錯堪以陞補六品汶
札營官一缺東科爾奪吉汪結堪以補放七品札稱
營官一缺仔仲青饒班墊堪以補放七品浪蕩營
官一缺相應繕就執照粘用漢番合璧譯行
該呼圖克圖即便飭知噶布倫總堪布等
遵將發來執照分別轉給承領飭赴新
任可也須至譯行者
譯發執照十四張
右譯行第穆呼圖克圖准此
光緒十七年三月 日

67-2

commander Phuntshog Lhungrub can be transferred to assume the duties of 5th–ranking senior *tsenyer tshangpa*, 5th–ranking Zegang military camp commander Wangphyug Gyalpo can be transferred to assume the duties of 5th–ranking Gonggar military camp commander, 5th– ranking Doigar military camp commander Wangchen Norbu can be transferred to assume the duties of 5th–ranking *langzixiami*, 6th– ranking official in charge of silk, Ngagwang Chosgrag Gyamtsho, can be promoted to 5th–ranking *yertshangpa*, 5th–ranking Nagtshang military camp commander Namgyalr Dorje can be transferred to serve as 5th ranking Xegar military camp commander, 7th–ranking *Kashak* gate–keeper *dipa* Kalzang Wangphyug can be promoted to Chanpinbailang military camp commander, 6th–ranking Rinbung military camp commander Chosbyor Wangphyug can be transferred to serve as Volgav military camp commander, 7th–ranking *Kashak* Drungchung Dongrub Wanggyas can be promoted to 6th–ranking Zongga military camp commander, 7th–ranking Chongke'erjie military camp commander Suolang Phuntshog can be promoted to 6th–ranking Wenzaka military camp commander, Drungkhor Dorje Wanggyas can be appointed as 7th–ranking Zaqing military camp commander, and Tsisdrung Khenrab Paldan can be appointed as 7th–ranking Langtang military camp commander. Corresponding letters of appointment have been written in both the Han and Tibetan languages and are now being sent to the Living Buddha who shall pass them on to the government ministers and Khanpos for distribution to the above–mentioned persons along with orders to set out for their new posts.

Fourteen letters of appointment are to be delivered.

Approved by Living Buddha Demo. The 24th day of the 3rd month of the 17th year of Guangxu (1891)

Preserved by the Archives of the Tibet Autonomous Region.

光绪十七年三月 日

[illegible]

[illegible]

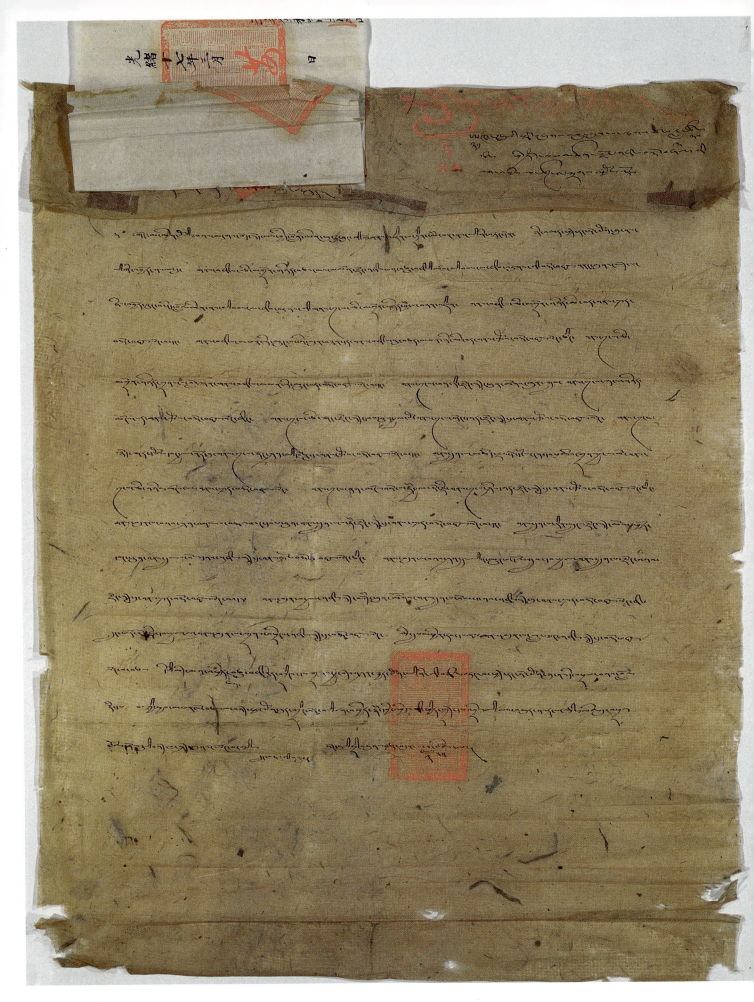

# བོད་བཞུགས་ཨན་བན་ཧྲིན་ཐེ་དང་དེ་མོ་ཧོ་ཐོག་ཐུ་ནས་དངུལ་ལོར་འགྲོ་རྒྱུག་སྐོར་བཀྲམས་པའི་རྩ་ཚིག
# 駐藏大臣升泰、第穆呼圖克圖爲曉諭銀錢流通事佈告
# Notice Issued by Resident Minister Sheng Tai and Living Buddha Demo Concerning the Circulation of Silver Coins

134 × 60

བོད་རང་སྐྱོང་ལྗོངས་ཡིག་ཚགས་ཁང་དུ་ཉར་ཚགས་བྱས་ཡོད།

西藏自治區檔案館藏

Vice Commander Sheng, Resident Minister in Tibet by Imperial Order, and Living Buddha Demo, Assistant in the Administration of District Affairs, hereby issue the following important notice:

We all know that silver coins have been in circulation in Tibet for many years, but recently some bad elements have been arbitrarily deciding on the percentage of silver in the coins, whether old or new, shiny or worn, thus creating money circulation problems. This may well give rise to quarrels and conflicts, running counter to the purpose of issuing money, which is for the convenience of the people. Therefore, it has been decided to put samples of silver coins on display, along with the following instructions. This is to inform all Han and Tibetan soldiers and civilians in Upper and Lower Tibet, plus the guild hall members, merchants and monks from the three major monasteries, plus all Kanbas, Mongolians, Gurkhas and Bhutanese that henceforth all types of silver coins, old or new, shiny or worn, as shown in the displays, are to be kept in circulation, without discrimination. Dealing in coins made of copper, iron, tin or lead is forbidden. Whoever is found by local Han or Tibetan officials to be illegally selling or using such coins shall be penalized severely and expeditiously in public. Cutting off the rim of a one half dollar coin is forbidden. Whoever is found violating this rule shall be punished severely without leniency. We, the Minister and the Living Buddha, are impartial and trustworthy. Do not step outside the law or you will regret it later. Abide strictly by these instructions. This is the end of the instructions.

[Numeral for the day is missing in theoriginal document] the fourth day of the 5th month of the 17th year of Guangxu (1891)

To be put up at the market of Gyangze. Do not deface these instructions in any way.

Preserved by the Archives of the Tibet Autonomous Region.

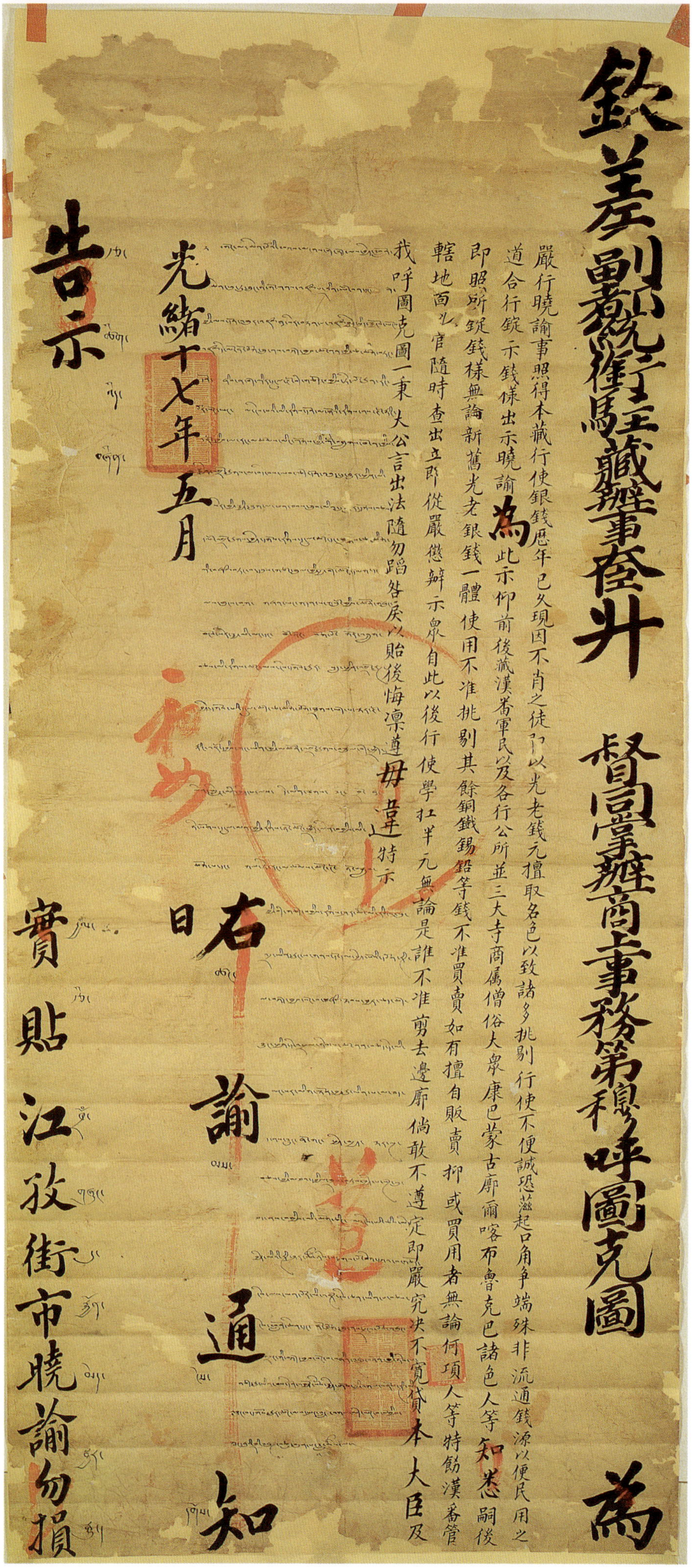

欽差副都統銜駐藏辦事大臣升 為

督同掌辦商上事務第穆呼圖克圖

嚴行曉諭事照得本藏行使銀錢歷年已久現因不肖之徒即以光老錢元擅取名色以致諸多挑剔行使不便誠恐滋起口角爭端殊非流通錢源以便民用之道合行鋟示錢樣出示曉諭 為此示仰前後藏漢番軍民以及各行公所並三大寺商屬僧俗大衆康巴蒙古廓爾喀布魯克巴諸色人等知悉嗣後即照所鋟錢樣無論新舊光老銀錢一體使用不准挑剔其餘銅鐵錫鉛等錢不准買賣如有擅自販賣抑或買用者無論何項人等特飭漢番管轄地面之官隨時查出立即從嚴懲辦示衆自此以後行使學扛半元無論是誰不准剪去邊廓倘敢不遵定即嚴究決不寬貸本大臣及我呼圖克圖一秉大公言出法隨勿蹈咎戾以貽後悔凜遵毋違特示

右諭通知

光緒十七年五月 日

告示

實貼江孜街市曉諭勿損

# བོད་བཞུགས་ཨམ་བན་ཀྲང་དབྱིན་ཐང་སོགས་ཀྱིས་བོད་དུ་ལམ་གཏེར་སོགས་ལས་ཁུངས་འཛུགས་རྒྱུའི་སྐོར་བཀྲམས་པའི་བསྐོ་བཞག་གི་ཡི་གེ

# 駐藏大臣張蔭棠等爲新設路礦等局發布委任令書

# Appointment Orders Issued by Resident Minister Zhang Yintang in Connection with Establishment of the Bureau of Highways and Mines and Other Bureaus

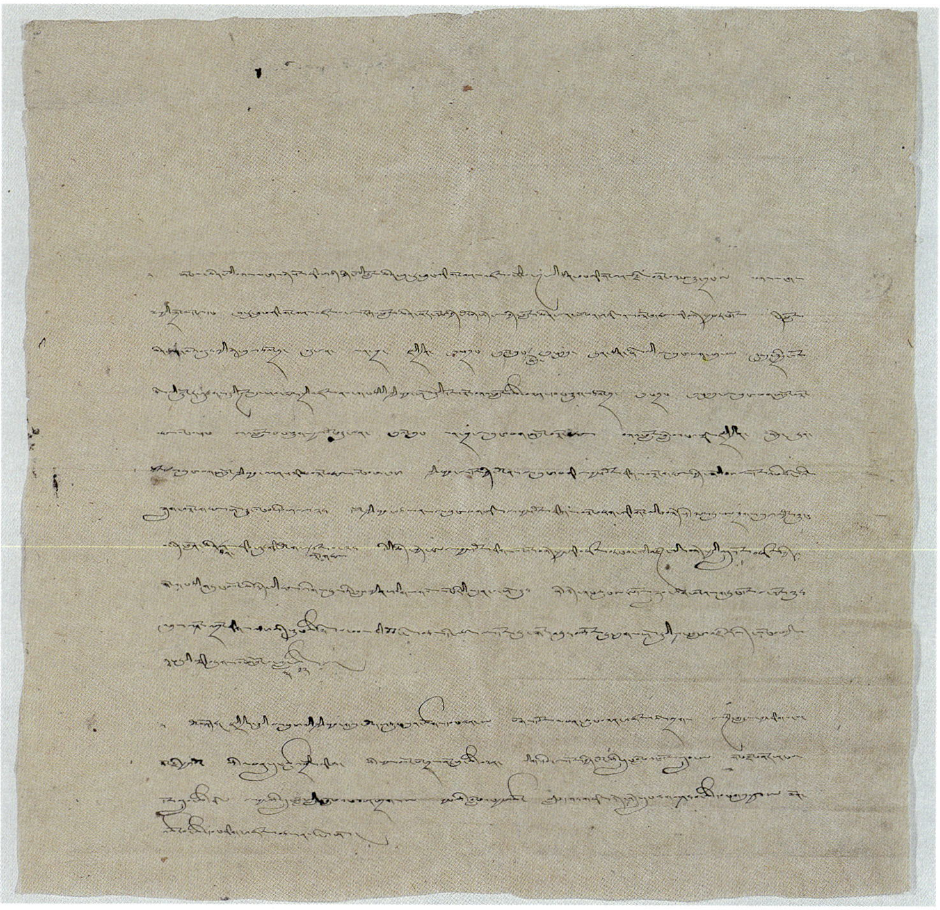

བོད་རང་སྐྱོང་ལྗོངས་ཡིག་ཚགས་ཁང་དུ་ཉར་ཚགས་བྱས་ཡོད།

經本二大臣詳議，決定在西藏設置糾察、督練、監茶、財政、工商、路礦、學務、農務、巡警並另建植物院，任噶丹池巴爲九局統領基巧、任噶倫 · 才旦旺久爲糾察、工商、農務三局之掌管，任噶倫 · 旺久杰布爲督練、路礦、監茶三局之掌管，任噶倫 · 洛桑成來爲財政、學務、巡警三局之掌管。九局職員由統領基巧提名選任。二大臣適才按時接到統領基巧的咨文和九局職員的選任名册後，經本二大臣詳議同意任命。各職員須將“委任令”的條款作爲座右銘來遵行，並耿耿於公務，力求褒獎。倘若查出對公務敷衍了事，假公濟私，必將革職法辦，爲此所有職員保證對工作盡職盡責。

光緒三十三年(公元1907年)三月十二日

著財政局掌管玉托·平措旺旦和糧餉官堪窮·丹增曲扎，助理拉亞加日巴·多吉杰布、孜堪仲·楚成尼瑪、孜恰桑頗色·洛布次旦，檔案員孜仲·洛桑頓珠，貢噶宗堆若朗巴·頓珠次仁，職員羅林·洛桑扎巴、降澤·洛桑加措、林噶溪堆雪仲·賈夏瓦·才旺玉加、曼措瓦·才旺仁增一體知曉。

西藏自治區檔案館藏

After thoroughly discussing the matter, we, the Resident Minister and Deputy Resident Minister in Tibet, have decided on the establishment in Tibet of nine bureaus to administer the public order, training of the army, salt and tea, finance, industry and commerce, highways and mines, education, agriculture, and the police, as well as the construction of a botanical garden. Gavldang Khripa is being appointed general director of the nine bureaus; Kaloon Tshetan Wangphyug, director of the Bureau of Public Order, Bureau of Industry and Commerce, and Bureau of Agriculture; Kaloon Wangphyug Gyalpo, director of the Bureau for Army Training, Bureau of Highways and Mines, and Bureau of Salt and Tea; and Kaloon Blozang Phrinlas, director of the Bureau of Finance, Bureau of Education and Bureau of Police. The staffs of the bureaus are to be nominated for selection by the general director. We, the Resident Minister and Deputy Resident Minister in Tibet, have just received a communication from the general director, containing the list of candidates for selection. After a thorough discussion, we agreed on his recommendations for appointment. All staff members should abide by the articles contained in the "appointment order" as their maxims to work by, wholeheartedly working for the public good to do their best to draw praise and respect. Those to be found only doing their work perfunctorily or using their public office for private gain will be removed from office and punished according to law; therefore, all staff members should make sure they fulfil their duties conscientiously.

The 12th day of the 3rd month of the 33rd year of Guangxu (1907)

This document is to be brought to the attention of the director of the Bureau of Finance, Yuthog Phuntshog Wangldan; the officer in charge of rations, Khanchung Tandsin Chosgrag and their assistants Glayabya Rigpa Rdorje Gyalpo, Tsekhandrung Tshulkhrim Nyima and Tsephyag Samphosras Norbu Tshetan; and archivists Tsedrung Blozang Dongrub, and Nornangpa Dongrub Tshering, in addition to other staff members, including Blogling Blozang Nyangrag, Byangtse Blozang Gyatsho, Shoddrung Cagsharba Tshewang Yugyal and Montshoba Tshewang Rigdsin.

Preserved by the Archives of the Tibet Autonomous Region.

# བོད་བཞུགས་ཨམ་བན་ལེན་ཡུས་ནས་ཚྭ་ཁྲལ་བསྡུ་རྒྱུའི་སྐོར་བཀྲམས་པའི་རྩ་ཚིག
# 駐藏大臣聯豫爲征收監税事發布告示
# Notice Issued by the Resident Minister in Tibet Lian Yu Regarding the Levying of the Salt Tax

134 × 60

བོད་རང་སྐྱོང་ལྗོངས་ཡིག་ཚགས་ཁང་དུ་ཉར་ཚགས་བྱས་ཡོད།

西藏日喀則地區檔案館藏

Vice Commander Lian, Wearer of Peacock Feathers by Imperial Order, Assistant Minister by Proxy and Resident Minister in Tibet, issues the following notice:

It should be noted that though there are hundreds of things that need to be done in Tibet, the drilling of the troops is especially important. Since carrying out these many enterprises demands heavy expenditures, it is essential to raise funds locally to cover these operating expenses. Salt is a necessity of life and a gift of nature found in great abundance in Tibet. Hitherto, merchants have been freely trading in salt, keeping all the profits for themselves, without paying any tax. Now the situation has changed and we need to collect salt tax in order to provide funding for drilling the army. The district government has requested permission to establish a bureau for levying the tax, together with the regulations and tax bills for approval. After conducting a thorough investigation I, the Resident Minister, have found the report in keeping with precedent. This should be put into effect immediately. Furthermore, the tax rate that has been suggested, one dollar of Tibetan money per 60 kg load, is modest and should not be too hard on the merchants, who can raise the price to cover the tax, a case of robbing Peter to pay Paul. While the money seems to come from the merchants, it is ultimately the consumers who pay. It will do no harm to the businessmen and will help to provide funding for the soldiers′ pay. Therefore, these instructions are to be spread among the merchants and all other people. Henceforth, all salt dealers, both Han and Tibetan, must report to the outpost for inspection and pay the tax according to the regulations, after which they shall be issued bills allowing them to sell the salt. Any violator of these regulations will be considered an unlawful dealer whose goods shall be subject to confiscation, so strictly abide by these instructions. This is the end of the instructions.

The 22nd day of the 9th month of the 33rd year of Guangxu (1907)

Preserved by the Xigaze Prefectural Archives of Tibet.

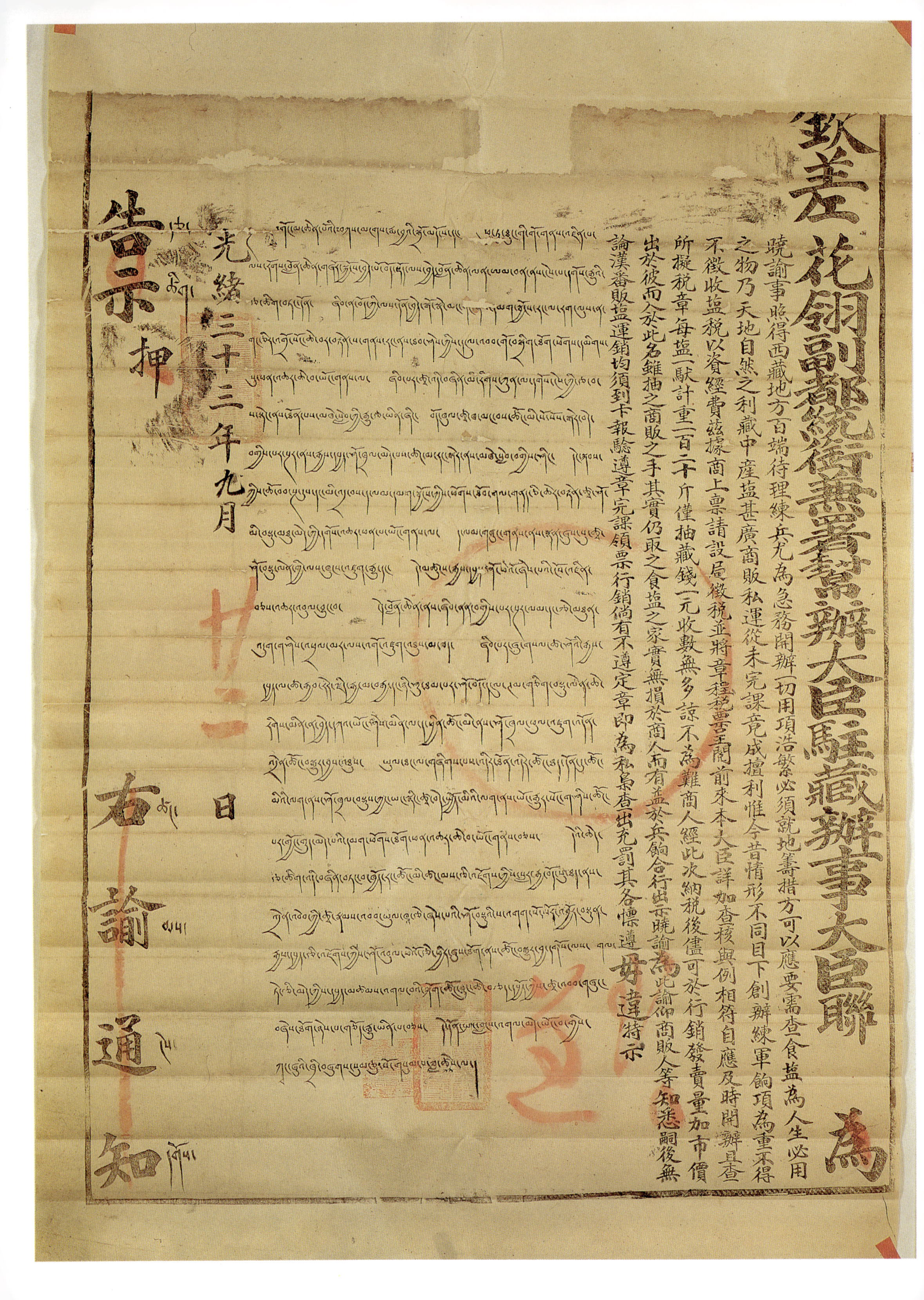

欽差花翎副都統銜兼署幫辦大臣駐藏辦事大臣聯　為

曉諭事照得西藏地方百端待理練兵尤為急務開辦一切用項浩繁必須就地籌措方可以應要需查食鹽為人生必用之物乃天地自然之利藏中產鹽甚廣商販私運從未完課竟成擅利惟今昔情形不同目下創辦練軍餉項為重不得不徵收鹽稅以資經費茲據商上稟請設局徵稅並將章程呈閱前來本大臣詳加查核與例相符自應及時開辦查所擬稅章每鹽一馱計重一百二十斤僅抽藏錢一元收數無多諒不為難商人經此次納稅後儘可於行銷發賣量加市價出於彼而入於此名雖抽之商販之手其實仍取之食鹽之家實無損於商人而有益於兵餉合行出示曉諭為此諭仰商販人等知悉嗣後無論漢番販鹽運銷均須到卡報驗遵章完課領票行銷倘有不遵定章即為私梟查出充罰其各懍遵毋違特示

[illegible]

光緒三十三年九月　　日

告示　押

右諭通知

[illegible]

# གོང་མ་ཡུང་ཅིན་ནས་ཏཱ་ལའི་བླ་མ་སྐུ་ཕྲེང་བདུན་པར་བསྩལ་བའི་གསེར་གྱི་ཐམ་ཀ།
# 雍正皇帝頒給七世達賴喇嘛之金印
# Gold Seal Awarded by Emperor Yongzheng to the 7th Dalai Lama

71－1

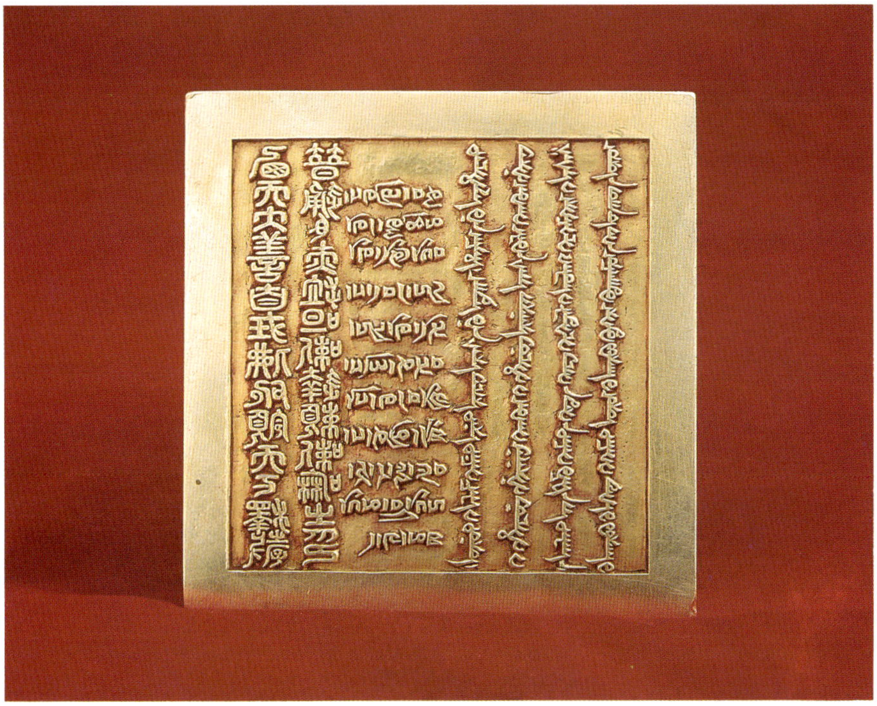

71－2

71－3

རྒྱ་གསེར་མཐའི་རིང་ཚད་ལི་སྨི་༡༡.༤

བོད་རང་སྐྱོང་ལྗོངས་རིག་དངོས་དོ་དམ་ཨུ་ཡོན་ལྷན་ཁང་དུ་ཉར་ཚགས་བྱས་ཡོད།

西天大善自在佛所領天下釋教普通瓦赤拉呾喇達賴喇嘛之印。

金質，邊長11.4厘米

西藏自治區文物管理委員會藏

An 1.4 cm. by 11.4 cm. gold seal.

Preserved by the Historical Relics Administration of the Tibet Autonomous Region.

# གོང་མ་ཆན་ལུང་གིས་ཏཱ་ལའི་བླ་མ་སྐུ་ཕྲེང་བརྒྱད་པ་ལ་བསྩལ་བའི་ཆོ་ལོ་དང་གཡང་ཏིའི་འཇའ་ས།
# 乾隆皇帝册封八世達賴喇嘛之玉册
# Jade Certificate Presented to the 8th Dalai Lama by Emperor Qianlong

72－1

བོད་རང་སྐྱོང་ལྗོངས་རིག་དངོས་དོ་དམ་ཨུ་ཡོན་ལྷན་ཁང་དུ་ཉར་ཚགས་བྱས་ཡོད།

西藏自治區文物管理委員會藏

Preserved by the Historical Relics Administration of the Tibet Autonomous Region.

༄༅། །ཚེ་རིང་གནམ་ཀྱི་ཤེ་མོང་གཙོན་པོས་སྐྱོང་ཡོངས་
ལ་ཨཨཨ་སྒྲུང་བ། རྒྱང་ནི་ཉི་བཀའ། ཆབ་སྲིད་བརྒྱུད་ལྷུག་གི་བར
ཕྱི་ནང་ཐམས་ཅད་བདེ་སྐྱིད་དང་སྐྱོ་འགྲོ་མ་ལུས་པ་ལ་ཁྲིམས
ཀྱིས་ཁ་ལོ་སྒྱུར་ནས་རྗེ་བཙུན་ཙོང་ཁ་པ་ཆེན་པོའི་ལུ་སེ
ཀྱི་ཀ་ཐུན་པ་རིན་པོ་ཆེ་ཆེ་རབ་དར་བ་དང་ཆོས་ལུགས་སེ
དུ་འཕེལ་ཞིང་རྒྱས་པར་གྱུར། ཏཱ་ལའི་བླ་མ་ཕྱིད་ནི་རྒྱ
བཙོང་ཁ་པའི་ཐུགས་སྲས་ཀྱི་གཙོ་བོ་ཡིན་ཞིང་། དགེ་འདུན
ཐུབ་ཀྱི་སྐུ་རབས་བརྒྱུད་པའི་སྤྲུལ་སྐུ་ཡིན། ཡེ་ཤེས་དང་ཡོན་ཏན
མ་ལུས་པ་སྐུ་ཚེ་དུ་མའི་སྔོན་རོལ་ནས་ཡོངས་སུ་རྫོགས་ཤིང་། ལུང
པའི་བསམ་པ་རྣམ་པར་དག་པ་རབ་ཏུ་བརྟན་ཞིང་། མཐའ་དབུས
ཀྱི་སྐྱེ་འགྲོ་ཐམས་ཅད་ཀྱི་མགོན་སྐྱབས་སུ་མཛད། སྔོན་ཡང་མང
རྒྱལ་པོ་ཤེ་ཡི་པ་དང་ས་བག་ཆེའི་སྐབས་སུ། རྒྱལ་དབང་ལྔ
ཏཱ་ལའི་བླ་མ། རྒྱལ་ཁབ་ཆེན་པོ་ཡ་སྤྲང་ཏུ། གོང་མ་དང་འཕྲད
ནས་བདག་རྐྱེན་ཆེན་པོ་སྦྱལ་བ་ནས་བཟུང་། དབང་སྐྱེ་རབས
མཆེད་ཞིབ་རོ་དུ། ཆབ་སྲིད་ཀྱི་གསོལ་རས་མ་ལུས་པ་སྙིང་ནས
སེམས་རྩེ་གཅིག་པར། བྱམས་བརྩེའི་ཆེན་པོས་རྗེས་སུ
འཛིན་ནས་ལྕེ་སེར་གྱི་བསྟན་པ་རྒྱ་ཆེར་དར་བ་བྱས། ཏཱ་ལའི
བླ་མ་ཕྱིད་ནི་ལྕེ་སེར་གྱི་བསྟན་པའི་བདག་པོ་བླ་མ་ཆེན་པོ
ཡིན་ཅིང་། སྐུ་ཚེ་མང་པོར། ས་སྟེང་གི་སྐྱེ་འགྲོ་མཐའ
དག་མཆོན་མཐོ་དང་ངེས་ལེགས་ལ་འགོད་པ་སོགས་ངོ་མཚར་བའི
རྣམ་འཕྲུལ་ལེགས་པར་འགྲོ་གསལ་པར་མཛད་པ་ནས་ངེས
པར་ཆབ་སྲིད་ཀྱི་བསོད་ནམས་ཆེན་པོ་དང་དགའ་སྟོན་གྱི
འཕྲིན་ལས་ཡིན་ནོ། བླ་མ་ཕྱིད་ཀྱི་ཡོན་ཏན་ཡོངས་སུ
རྫོགས་ཤིང་། སངས་རྒྱས་ཀྱི་བསྟན་པ་རིན་པོ་ཆེ་ཕྱོགས
དུས་ཀུན་ཏུ་དར་ཞིང་རྒྱས་པར་མཛད་པ་ལ། ངང་
འཕེལ་ནས་ད་ལྟ་མ། ཕྱིད་དུ་འཕགས་པའི་བདག

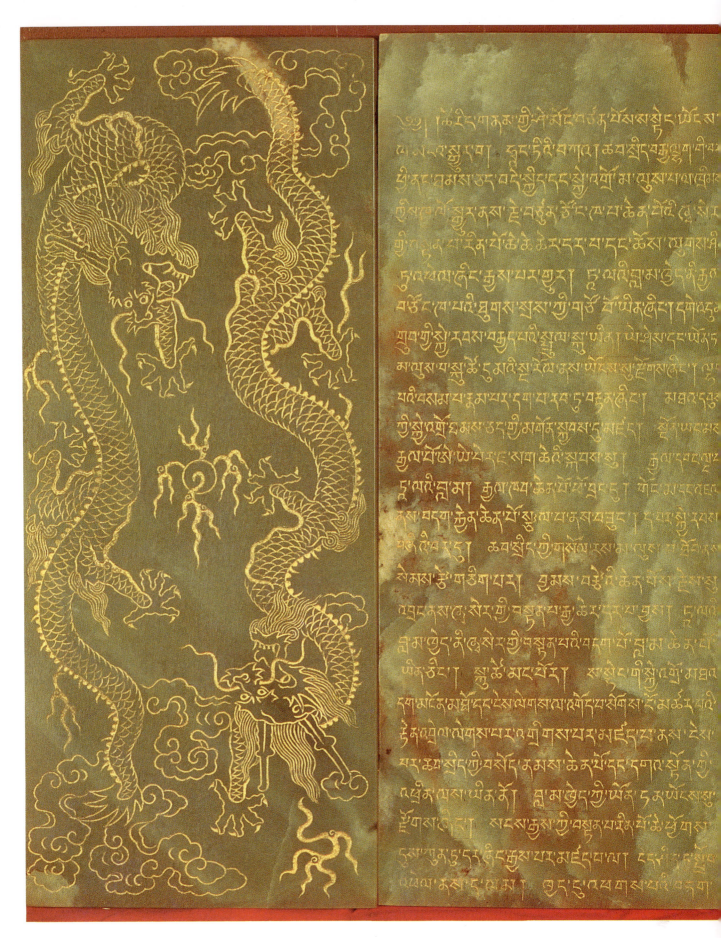

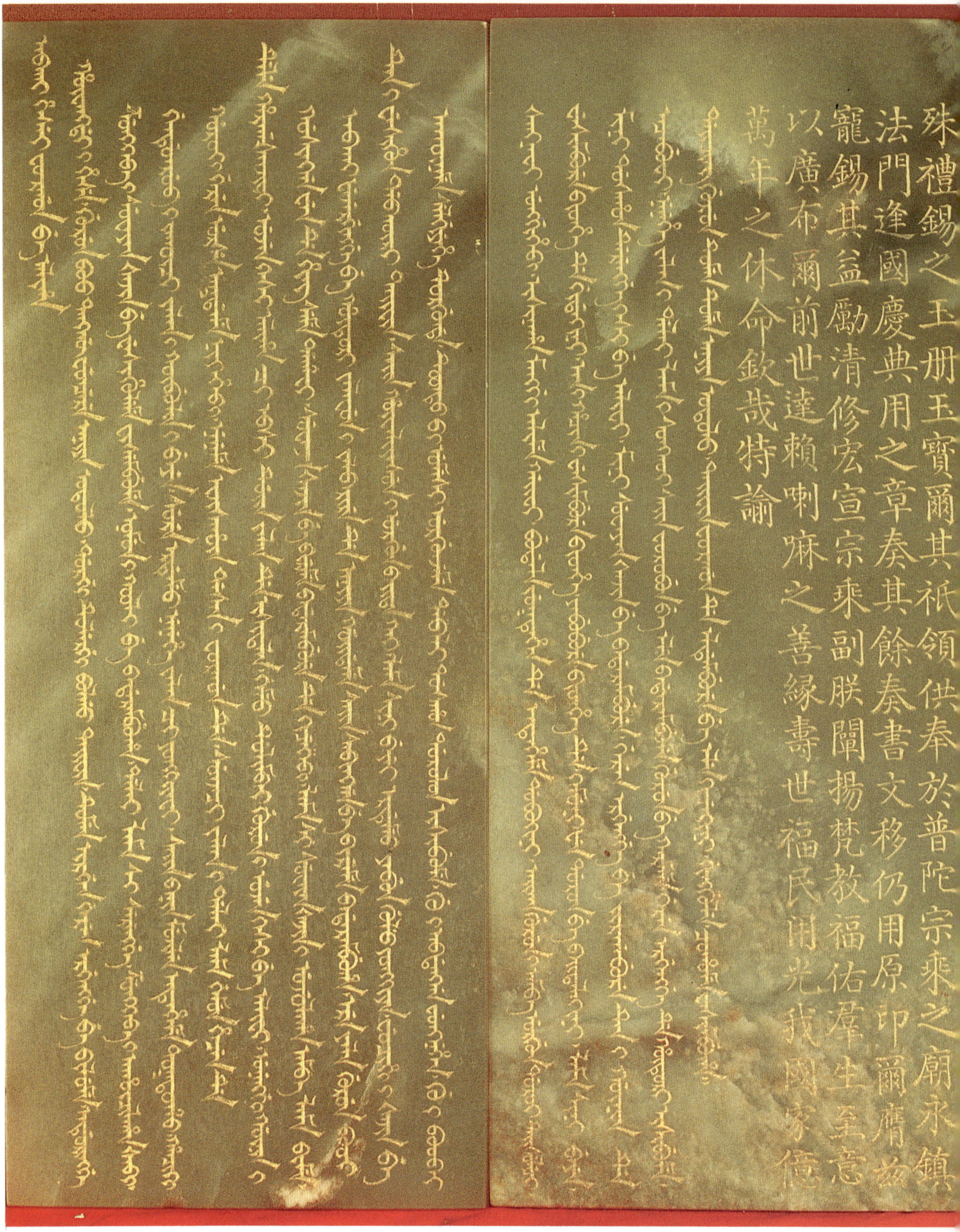
殊禮錫之玉册玉寶爾其祇領供奉於普陀宗乘之廟永鎮
法門逢國慶典用之章奏其餘奏書文移仍用原印爾膺茲
寵錫其益勵清修宏宣宗乘副朕闡揚梵教福佑羣生至意
以廣布爾前世達賴喇嘛之善緣壽世福民用光我國家億
萬年之休命欽哉特諭

72－3

奉
天承運
皇帝制曰國家海宇清宴民物敉寧撫育中外振興黃教自宗
喀巴崇闡宗風宣揚律爾達賴喇嘛乃宗喀巴之法嗣根
敦嗜布八轉世身也夙慧圓成性身常住十方供奉華夏皈
依先是順治年間五轉世達賴喇嘛來京瞻
覲恩禮崇隆自茲四世咸傾心依向廣布教乘寵渥有加焉爾達
賴喇嘛教演禪宗誠殷嗥祝普天福壽永世吉祥誠國家道
洽

# གོང་མ་ལྷ་སྐྱོང་གིས་པོ་བྲང་པོ་ཏ་ལར་བསྩལ་བའི་ཕྱག་བྲིས་ཕྱག་བསྟར་མའི་པན་ཡིག
# 乾隆皇帝賜予布達拉宮之御筆匾文
# Plaque with Inscription by Emperor Qianlong Presented to the Potala Palace

315×137

བོད་རང་སྐྱོང་ལྗོངས་ཡིག་ཚགས་ཁང་དུ་ཉར་ཚགས་བྱས་ཡོད།

西藏自治區檔案館藏

Preserved by the Archives of the Tibet Autonomous Region.

# གོང་མ་སྲིད་གསལ་གྱིས་ཏཱ་ལའི་བླ་མ་སྐུ་ཕྲེང་བཅུ་གཅིག་པ་ལ་བསྩལ་པའི་ཚོ་ལོ་དང་གསེར་གྱི་འཛའ་ས།

# 道光皇帝册封十一世達賴喇嘛之金册

# Golden Certificate Presented to the 11th Dalai Lama by Emperor Daoguang

23.2 × 9.9

74 - 1

བོད་རང་སྐྱོང་ལྗོངས་རིག་དངོས་དོ་དམ་ཨུ་ཡོན་ལྷན་ཁང་དུ་ཉར་ཚགས་བྱས་ཡོད།

西藏自治區文物管理委員會藏

Preserved by the Archives of the Tibet Autonomous Region.

敕封第十一輩達賴喇嘛文册

74 - 2

74 - 3

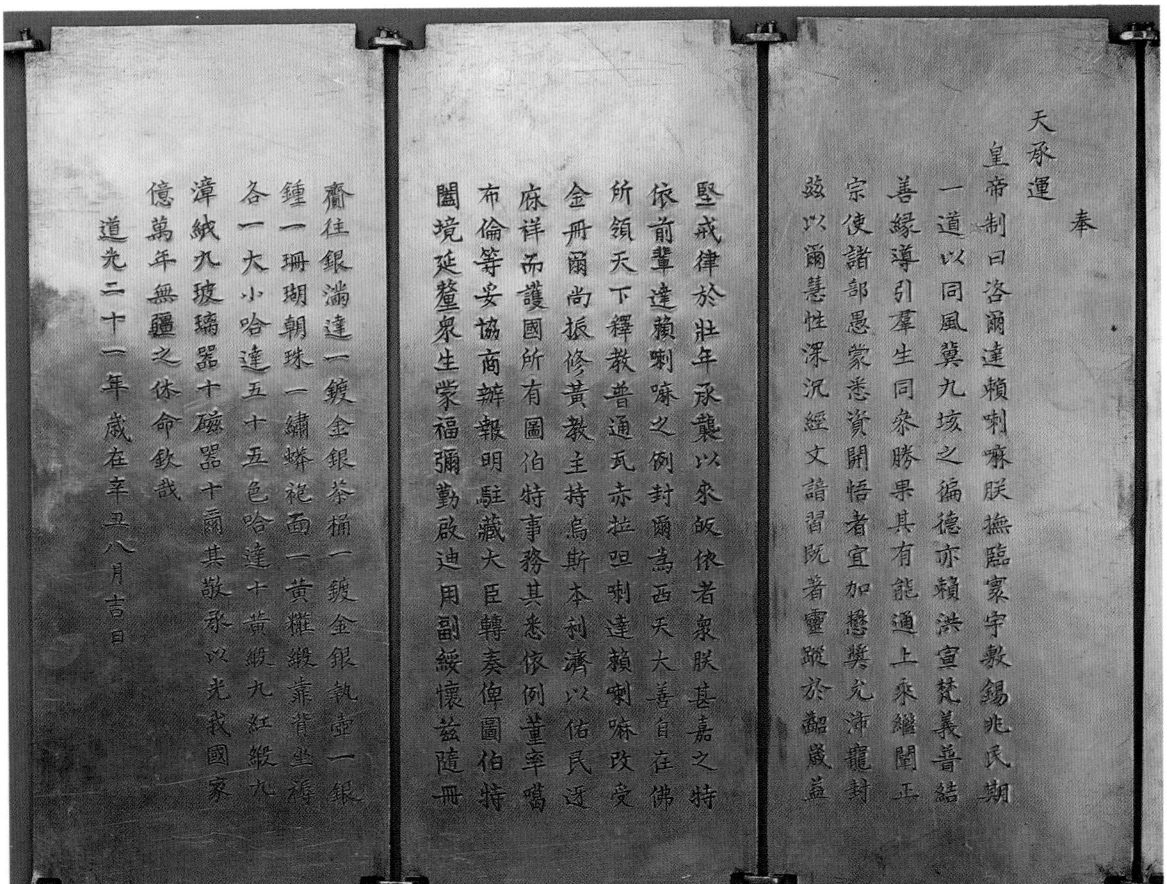
奉
天承運
皇帝制曰咨爾達賴喇嘛朕撫臨寰宇敷錫兆民期
一道以同風奠九垓之徧德亦賴洪宣梵義普結
善緣導引羣生同參勝果其有能通上乘繼闡正
宗使諸部愚蒙悉資開悟者宜加懋奬允沛龍封
茲以爾慧性深沉經文諳習既著靈蹤於齠歲益
堅戒律於壯年承襲以來皈依者衆朕甚嘉之特
依前輩達賴喇嘛之例封爾為西天大善自在佛
所領天下釋教普通瓦赤拉怛喇達賴喇嘛改受
金冊爾尚振修黃教主持烏斯本剎濟以佑民逕
麻詳而護國所有圖伯特事務其悉依例董率噶
布倫等妥協商辦報明駐藏大臣轉奏俾圖伯特
闔境延釐衆生蒙福彌勤啟迪用副綏懷茲隨冊
賚住銀滿達一鍍金銀茶桶一鍍金銀執壺一銀
鍾一珊瑚朝珠一繡蟒袍面一黃糚緞靠背坐褥
各一大小哈達五十五色哈達十黃緞九紅緞九
漳絨九玻璃器十磁器十爾其敬承以光我國家
億萬年無疆之休命欽哉
道光二十一年歲在辛丑八月吉日

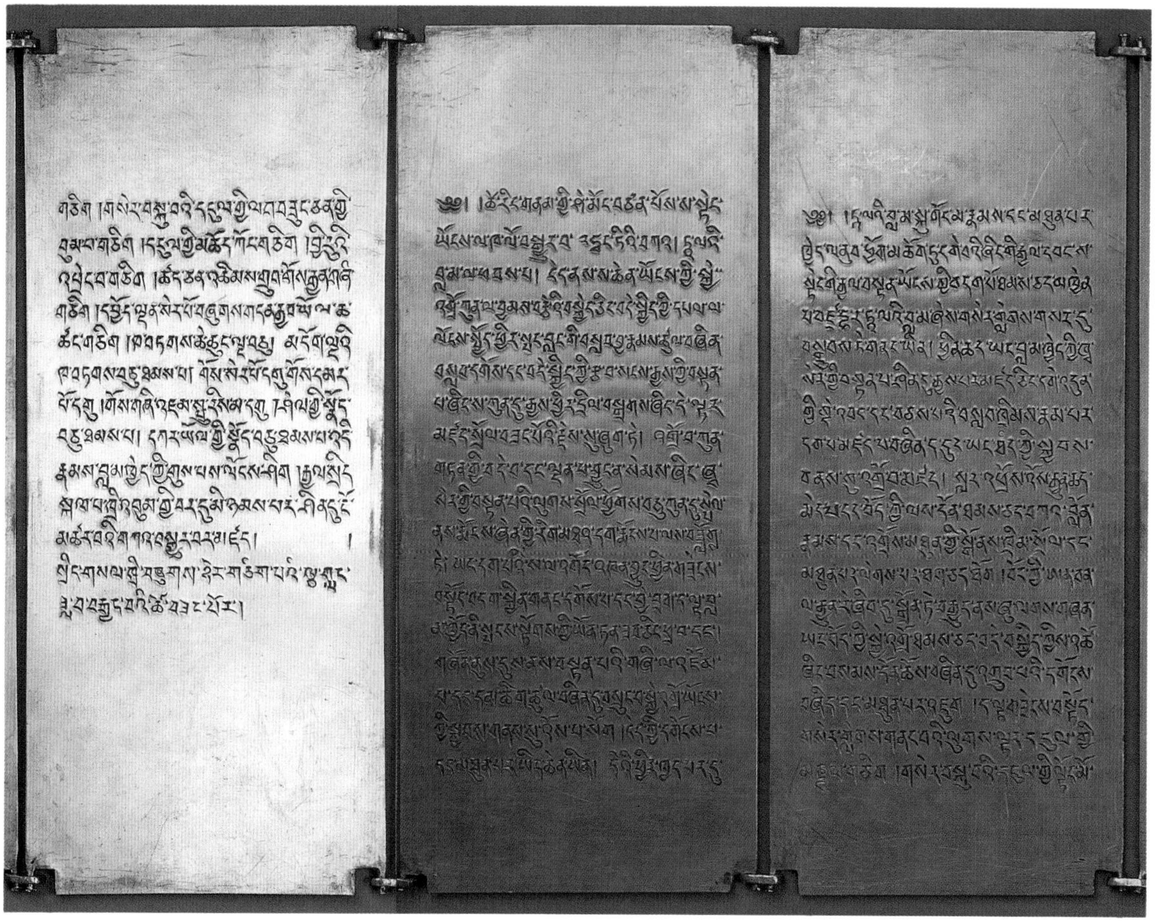

74 - 4

74 - 5

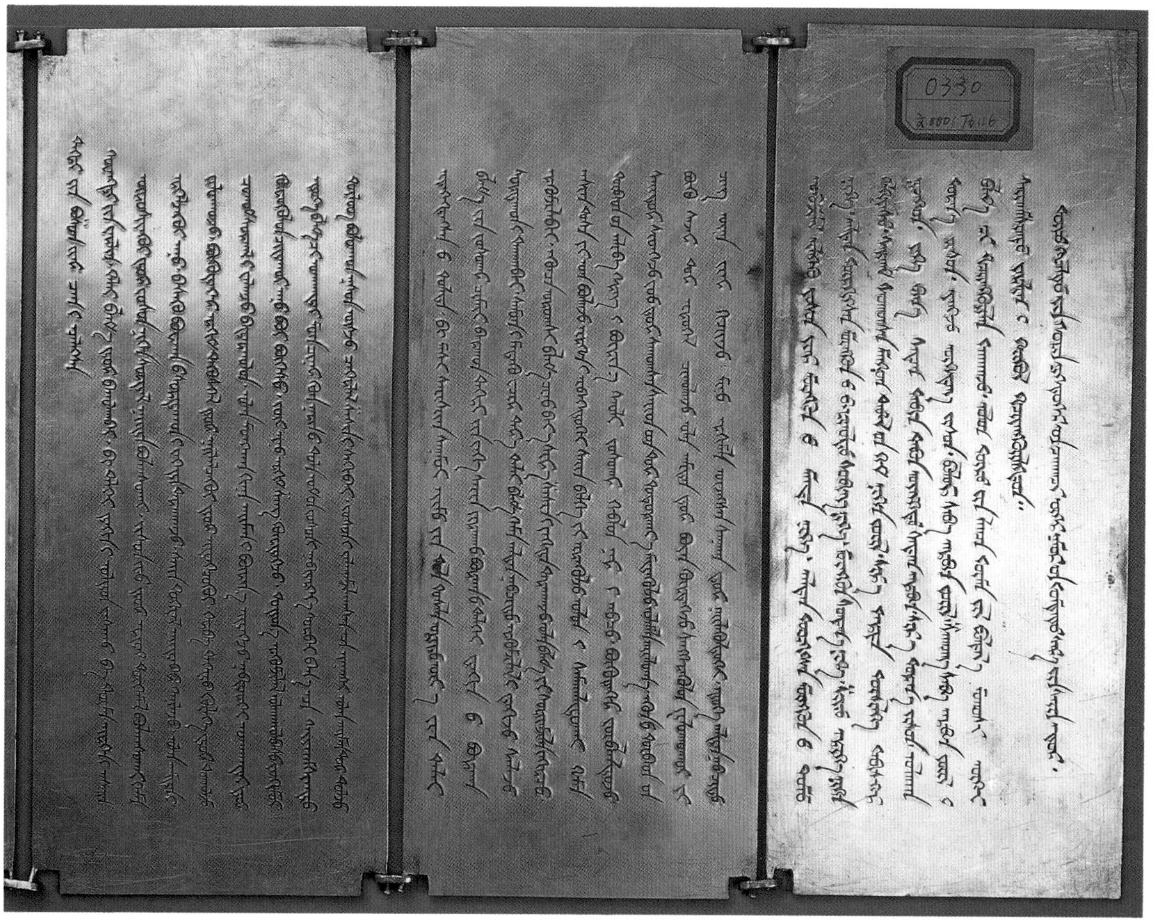

## གོང་མ་སྲིད་གསལ་གྱིས་སྨིན་གྲོལ་གླིང་ལ་བསྩལ་བའི་ཕྱག་བྲིས་ཕྱག་བསྐར་མའི་པན་ཡིག

## 道光皇帝賜予門珠林寺之御筆匾文

## Plaque with Inscription by Emperor Daoguang Presented to the Mingrolling Monastery

227 × 74

བོད་རང་སྐྱོང་ལྗོངས་ཡིག་ཚགས་ཁང་དུ་ཉར་ཚགས་བྱས་ཡོད།

西藏自治區檔案館藏

Preserved by the Historical Relics Administration of the Tibet Autonomous Region.

# གོང་མ་ཐུང་ཀྲི་ནས་བཀྲ་ཤིས་ལྷུན་པོ་དགོན་པར་བསྩལ་པའི་ཕྱག་བྲིས་ཕྱག་བསྐུར་མའི་པན་ཡིག
# 同治皇帝賜予札什倫布寺之御筆匾文
# Plaque with Inscription by Emperor Tongzhi Presented to the Tashilhunpo Monastery

98 × 58

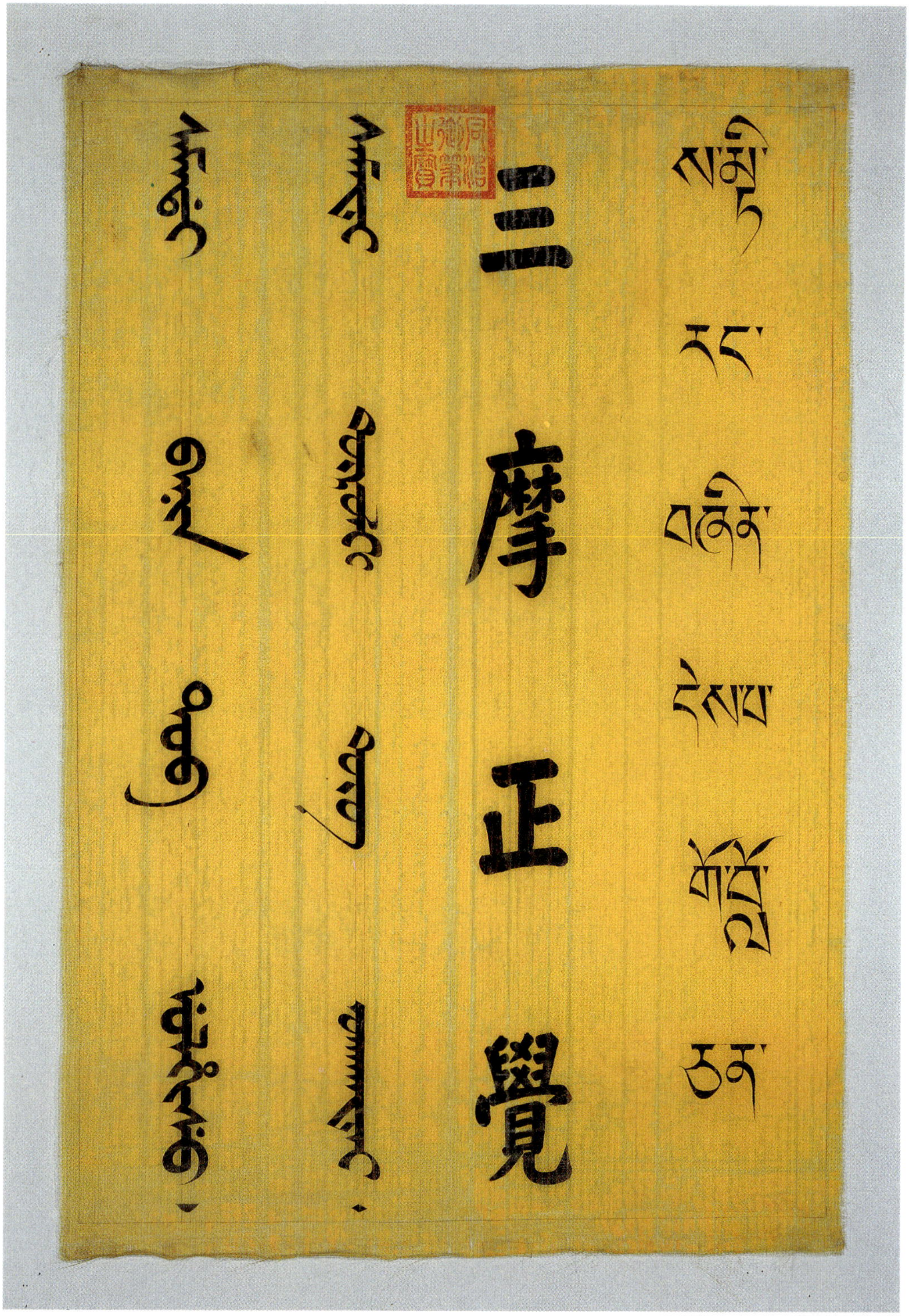


བོད་རང་སྐྱོང་ལྗོངས་ཡིག་ཚགས་ཁང་དུ་ཉར་ཚགས་བྱས་ཡོད།

西藏自治區檔案館藏

Preserved by the Archives of the Tibet Autonomous Region

རྒྱལ་ཡུམ་ཚེ་ཤིས་ཐའེ་ཧུས་ཏཱ་ལའི་བླ་མ་སྐུ་ཕྲེང་བཅུ་གསུམ་པར་བསྩལ་པའི་ཕྱག་བྲིས་
ཕྱག་བསྐྲར་མའི་རི་མོ།

# 慈禧太后賜予十三世達賴喇嘛之親筆畫

# Painting by Empress Dowager Cixi Presented to the 13th Dalai Lama

155×53

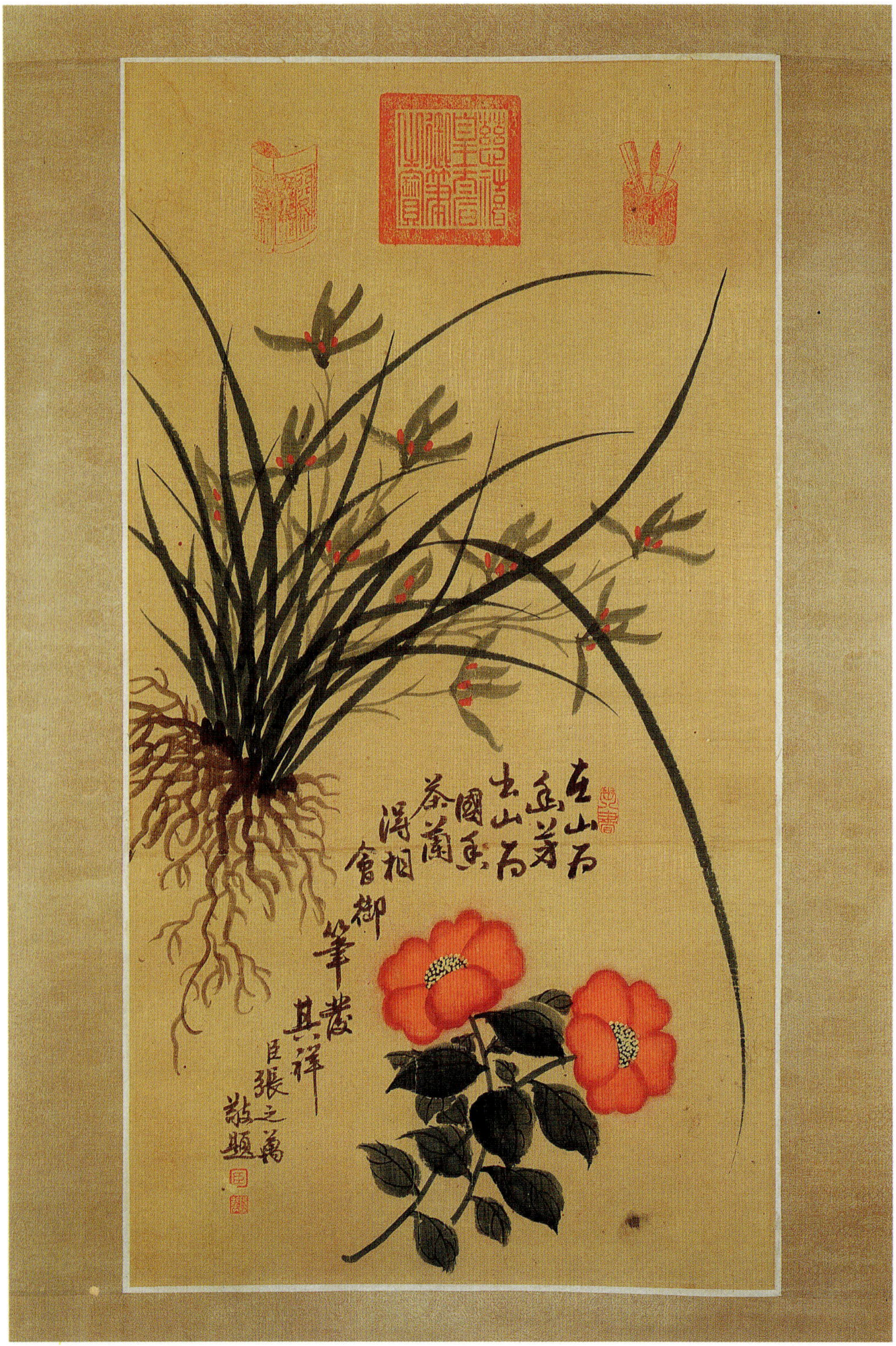

བོད་རང་སྐྱོང་ལྗོངས་ཡིག་ཚགས་ཁང་
དུ་ཉར་ཚགས་བྱས་ཡོད།

西藏自治區檔案館藏

Preserved by the Archives of the Tibet Autonomous Region.

# གོང་མ་ཀོང་ཞུའི་འདྲ་པར།
# 光緒皇帝畫像
# Portrait of Emperor Guangxu

80 × 40

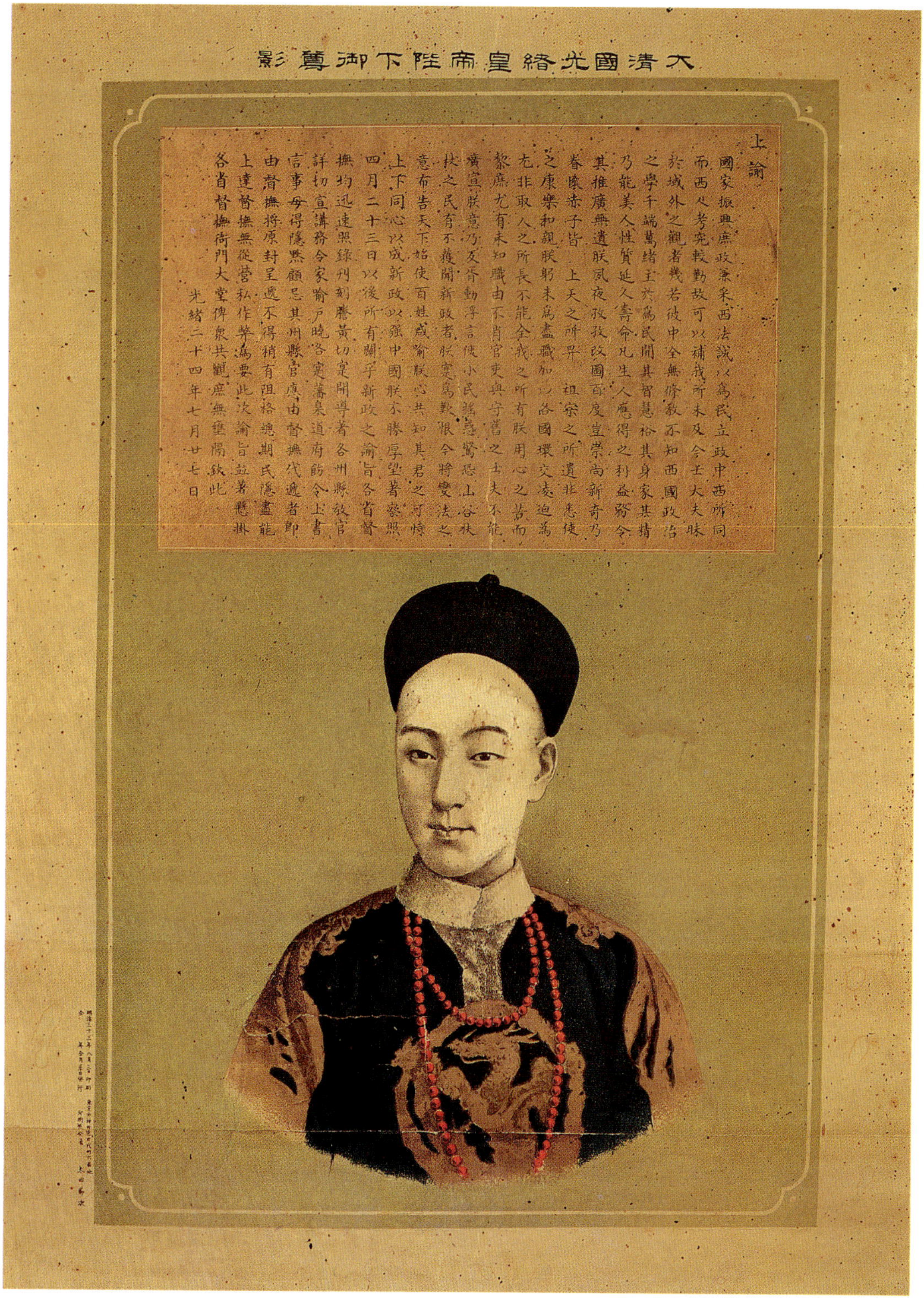


བོད་རང་སྐྱོང་ལྗོངས་ཡིག་ཚགས་ཁང་དུ་ཉར་ཚགས་བྱས་ཡོད།

西藏自治區檔案館藏

Preserved by the Archives of the Tibet Autonomous Region.

# རྒྱལ་ཡུམ་ཚི་ཞིས་ཐའི་ཧྲུས་ཀྱི་འདྲ་པར།
# 慈禧太后畫像
# Portrait of Empress Dowager Cixi

80 × 40

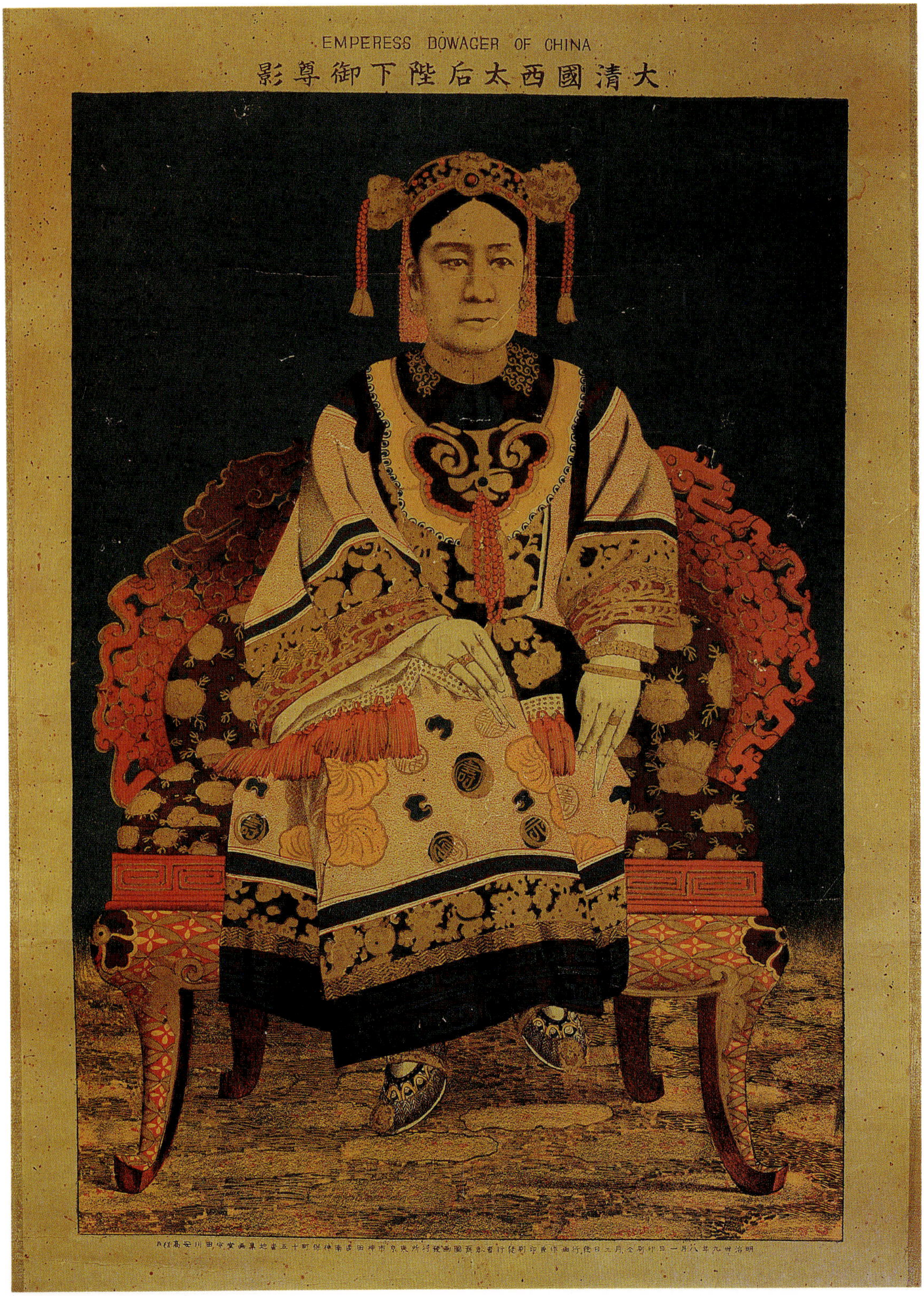


བོད་རང་སྐྱོང་ལྗོངས་ཡིག་ཚགས་ཁང་དུ་ཉར་ཚགས་བྱས་ཡོད།

西藏自治區檔案館藏

Preserved by the Archives of the Tibet Autonomous Region.

# མིང་གོའི་སྐབས་ཀྱི་ཡིག་ཚགས།

མིང་གོའི་སྐབས་ཅང་ཅེ་ཧྲེས་ཏཱ་ལའི་བླ་མར་བཏང་བའི་ཕྱག་བྲིས་ཕྱག་བསྟར་མ། མིང་གོ་སྲིད་གཞུང་གི་ཆོ་ལོ་དང་བཀའ་རྒྱ། པཎ་ཆེན་སྐུ་ཕྲེང་དགུ་པའི་ཞལ་ཆེམས། ཝུ་ཀྲུང་ཞིན་གྱི་ཏར་ཡིག རྒྱལ་དམངས་ཚོགས་ཆེན་གྱི་འཐུས་མིའི་ལག་ཁྱེར་དང་འདྲ་པར་སོགས་ནི་ཆིང་རྒྱལ་རབས་རྗེས་ཀྲུང་དབྱང་སྲིད་གཞུང་ནས་བོད་ས་གནས་ལ་མུ་མཐུད་དབང་བསྒྱུར་བྱས་པའི་ལོ་རྒྱུས་ཀྱི་དཔང་རྟགས་ཞིག་རེད།

# 民國檔案

民國時期，蔣介石給達賴喇嘛的親筆信、國民政府的册文和命令、九世班禪遺囑、吳忠信的電文、國民大會代表證書和照片等，是清以後西藏地方仍處在中央政府統轄之下的歷史見證。

# Archives from the Period of the Republic of China

These items, including Chiang Kai-shek's letter to the Dalai Lama, documents and decrees of the National Government, the will of the 9th Panchen, a telegram sent by Wu Zhongxin, credentials issued to a National Assembly delegate and various photos, prove beyond any doubt that the Tibetan area remained under the jurisdiction of the Central Government of China after the Qing Dynasty.

# མིང་གོའི་གནས་སྐབས་ཀྱི་ཙུང་ཐུང་ཆེན་པོས་བོད་སོག་གཅིག་སྒྱུར་ཆབ་སྲིད་ལེགས་བཅོས་ལྷན་ཚོགས་བཙུགས་པར་ཆོག་མཆན་བཀོད་པའི་དོན་དུ་བསྒྲལ་པའི་བཀའ།

# 臨時大總統爲批准成立蒙藏統一政治改良會事發布的命令

# Decree from the Provisional President of the Republic of China Granting Approval for the Establishment of the Mongolian and Tibetan Committee for Unified Political Reform

447 × 25.7

གནས་སྐབས་ཙུང་ཐུང་ཆེན་པོའི་བཀའ།

ཏཱ་ལའི་བླ་མ་དང་། པཎ་ཆེན་ཨེར་ཏེ་ནི། རྗེ་བཙུན་དམ་པ་ཧོ་ཐོག་ཐུ་རྣམ་པ་གསུམ་པོ་བོད་སོག་སོ་སོར་བཞུགས་ནས་དགེ་ལུགས་པའི་བསྟན་པའི་བདག་པོར་གྱུར་པ་དང་། སྐུ་ཐོག་རིམ་བྱོན་ནས་སུ་སུས་བརྒྱུད་འཛིན་གནང་བར་ཀུན་གྱིས་དད་པ་ཚད་མེད་སྐྱེས། བདག་ཅག་གི་བོད་སོག་མི་དམངས་རྣམས་ནས་ཐར་སྒྲོལ་གཞིར་བཟུང་གིས་ནུབ་བྱང་གི་མཐའ་ཁོངས་སྲུང་བ་དང་བག་ཕེབས་དང་བློ་ཁ་ནང་དུ་ཕྱོགས་བཞིན་ཡོད་པ་རེད། ཉེ་བའི་ལོ་ཤས་ནང་མཐའ་མཚམས་ཀྱི་དཔོན་ཆེན་ནས་བྱ་ཐབས་མི་ལེགས་པའི་མགོ་གཏོན་མི་ཤུང་བ་བྱས་ཡོད། ཐ་ན་དཔོན་ཆེན་གཅིག་གིས་རྒྱ་འཕྲོག་བསླད་འདོགས་ཀྱིས་བཤུ་གཞོག་བཏང་བའི་རྐྱེན་གྱིས་ཀུན་གྱི་ཞེན་པ་ལོག་བྱུང་བས་མི་སེམས་ཕྱིར་དུ་སོང་བའི་གནས་ཚུལ་དེ་དག་བསམ་དུས་ཁོང་ཁྲོ་འགོག་མེད་དུ་བྱུང་། ད་ལྟ་ཆབ་སྲིད་སྒྲིག་གཞི་སྤྱི་མཐུན་ལ་བཟོ་བཅོས་བྱས་ཏེ་མི་རིགས་ཆེན་པོ་རྣམ་ལྔ་ཚང་མ་འདྲ་མཉམ་དུ་བསྒྱུར་ཡོད། ཙུང་ཐུང་ཆེན་པོ་ངས་བློ་བརྟན་འགྱུར་མེད་ཀྱིས་སྔར་གྱི་ལམ་ལུགས་སྙིང་པའི་སྲིད་ངན་བྱ་ངན་རྣམས་བཀག་འགོག་དང་སྒྱུར་བཅོས་གཏོང་རྒྱུའི་དམ་བཅའ་བཞག་ཡོད་པ་དང་། ལྷག་པར་དུ་ཞིབ་དཔྱད་བྱས་ནས་བོད་སོག་ས་ཁུལ་གྱི་གནས་ཚུལ་དངོས་དང་བསྟུན་ཏེ་བདེ་འཇགས་ཡོང་རྒྱུར་སྲུང་སྐྱོབ་བྱེད་རྒྱུ་ཡིན། ད་ལྟ་ནན་ཅིང་དུ་བཞུགས་པའི་ཇ་སག་བླ་མ་སོགས་ཀྱིས་བོད་སོག་གཅིག་སྒྱུར་ཆབ་སྲིད་ལེགས་བཅོས་ལྷན་ཚོགས་སྒྲིག་འཛུགས་བྱེད་རྒྱུའི་རེ་འདུན་ཞུས་པ་དེར་ཞིབ་དཔྱད་བྱེད་དུས་དེའི་དམིགས་ཡུལ་ནི་མི་རིགས་རྣམ་ལྔ་འདྲ་མཉམ་ཡིན་པ་དྲིལ་བསྒྲགས་བྱེད་རྒྱུ་དང་། བདག་ཅག་གི་བོད་སོག་མི་ཡི་ཐོབ་ཐང་ཞུ་བ་བཅས་ཡིན་པས་ཐོན་དུ་ལྷན་ཚོགས་འཛུགས་རྒྱུའི་ཆོག་མཆན་སྤྲོད་རྒྱུ་ཡིན། དེ་སྔོན་ཕྱི་ནང་གི་སོག་པོའི་ཇ་སག་དང་མོན་ཆི་སོ་སོ་དང་བོད་ས་ཁུལ་བཅས་ལ་སྔར་ནས་སྡུག་བསྔལ་གྱིས་མནར་བའི་གནས་ཚུལ་ཡོད་པ་དེ་དག་བརྟག་དཔྱད་གསལ་པོ་བྱས་ཏེ་རིམ་བཞིན་མེད་པ་བཟོ་རྒྱུ་མ་ཟད། ཤང་ཀུང་། ཧོ་ཐོག་ཐུ། བླ་མ་སོགས་ནས་ཀྱང་ཀྲུང་དབྱང་གི་ཆབ་སྲིད་དང་ས་གནས་ཁག་གི་དར་རྒྱས་གཏོང་དགོས་རྒྱུ་དང་སྒྱུར་བཅོས་གཏོང་རྒྱུའི་ལས་དོན་ཐད་ཕྱོགས་སོ་སོའི་མཐོང་ཚུལ་རྣམས་སྐབས་འཕྲལ་སྙན་སེང་ཞུས་ཏེ་ལེགས་ཆ་ཕེད་སྤྲོད་གཏོང་རྒྱུའི་རེ་བ་ཡོད། བོད་སོག་མི་དམངས་རྣམས་ཀྱི་སྤྱི་དབང་དང་སྒེར་དབང་ཚང་མ་ངེས་པར་དུ་ནང་ཁུལ་དང་འདྲ་མཉམ་ཡོང་བ་བྱས་ཏེ་མཐུན་མོང་གི་བདེ་སྐྱིད་ལ་ལོངས་སུ་སྤྱོད་རྒྱུའི་རེ་བ་དང་བཅས་བཀའ་འདི་བསྒྲལ་ཏོ། །

ཀྲུང་གོའི་ལོ་དང་པོ (སྤྱི་ལོ་༡༩༡༣) ཟླ་བ་གསུམ་པའི་ཚེས་ཉེར་ལྔ་ཉིན་ཏེ་ཆུ་བྱི་ལོ་ཟླ་བ་གཉིས་པའི་ཚེས་བདུན་ཉིན་ཙུང་ཐུང་ཆེན་པོ་ནས་ཐམ་ཀ་བརྒྱབ།

བོད་རང་སྐྱོང་ལྗོངས་ཡིག་ཚགས་ཁང་དུ་ཉར་ཚགས་བྱས་ཡོད།

80－1

西藏自治區檔案館藏

Decree from the Provisional President:

The Dalai Lama and the Panchen Erdeni, and Living Buddha Jetsun Dampa, who reside in Tibet and Mongolia respectively, are leaders of the Yellow Sect of Lamaism. This leadership has long been handed down from generation to generation, and these men are firm in their beliefs. All the Mongolian and Tibetan peoples have followed tradition, defended the country on the northern and western borders and supported the central areas. However, recent governors in bordering areas have administered the areas poorly, often oppressing the local people, and sometimes even cruelly exploiting the people. Bad conduct such as this naturally arouses resentment among all sectors of society, causing people to lose their faith in these officials, which saddens me. The political system has been changed to that of a republic and the five major nationalities are now all equal. As the President, I will firmly and resolutely work to do away with all such wrongdoing. The Mongolian and Tibetan authorities must be attentive to the people's feelings and maintain social order. The Dsasag Lama and others in

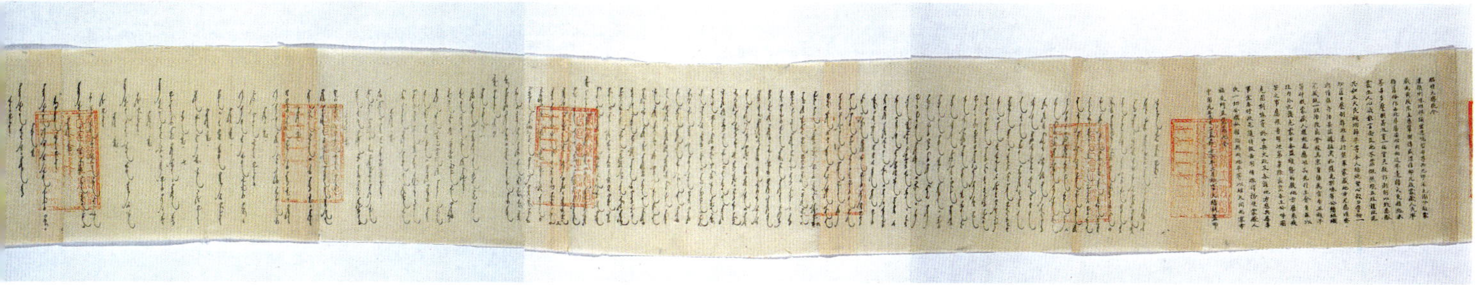

the capital have asked for permission to establish the Mongolian and Tibetan Committee for Unified Political Reform, with the aim of promulgating the concept of equality among the five major nationalities and guaranteeing the civil rights of the Mongolian and Tibetan peoples and I am approving the establishment of this committee. Hereafter, in all the leagues and banners of Inner and Outer Mongolia and Tibet, all complaints should be investigated and the wrongs should be put to right. I hope that the nobility, Living Buddhas and lamas will submit their views concerning the administration of the Central Government or those concerning new undertakings to be initiated and reform to be carried out in the different localities. Their reports should be sent in promptly so that action can be taken. This is to make both the public and private rights of Mongolian and Tibetan peoples the same as those enjoyed by people in other areas, to bring about a great unity of all peoples and happiness for all. This is my ardent hope.

March 25, 1912, the first year of the Republic of China

(The seal of the President)

Preserved by the Archives of the Tibet Autonomous Region.

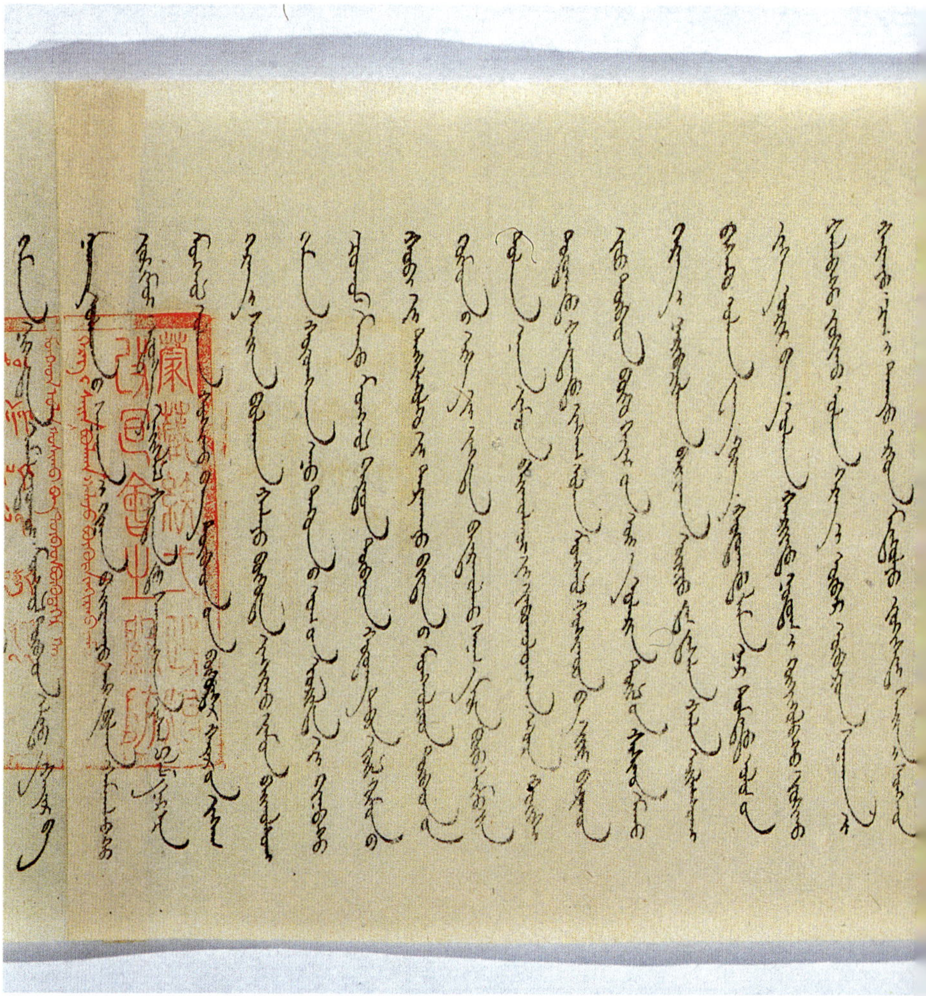

80-3

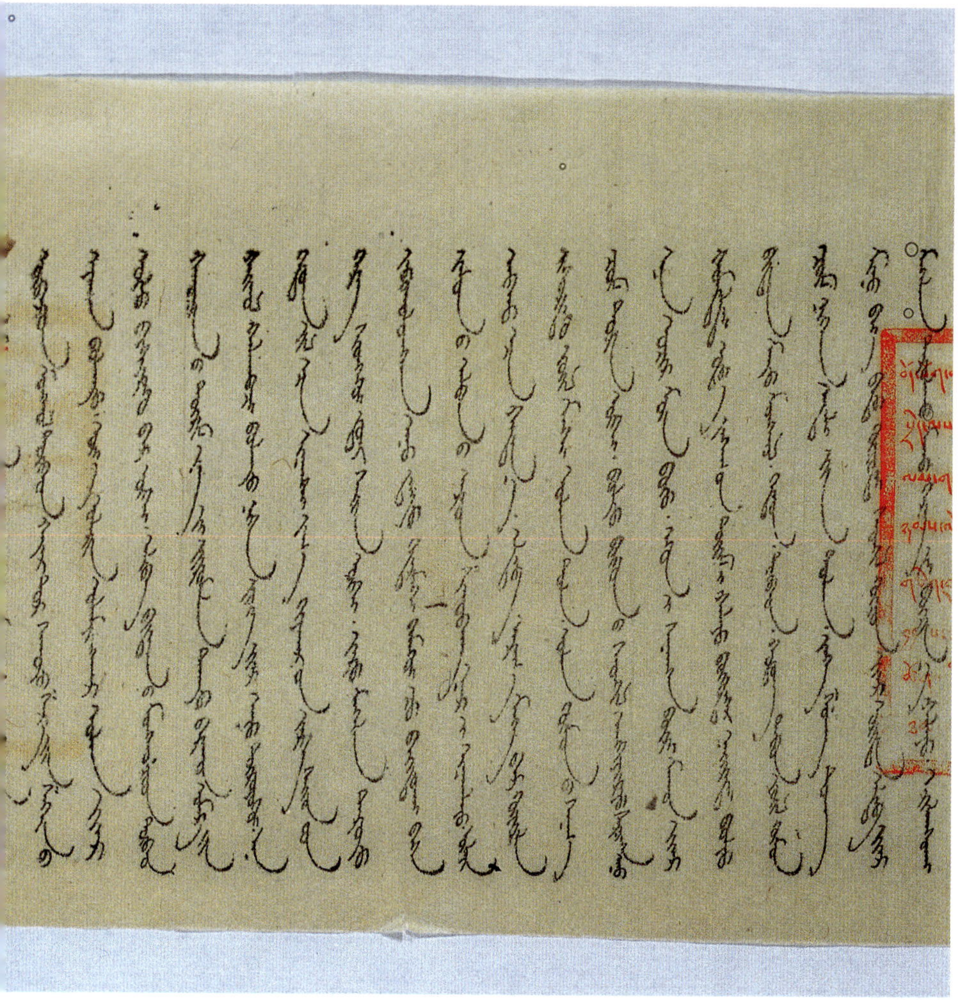

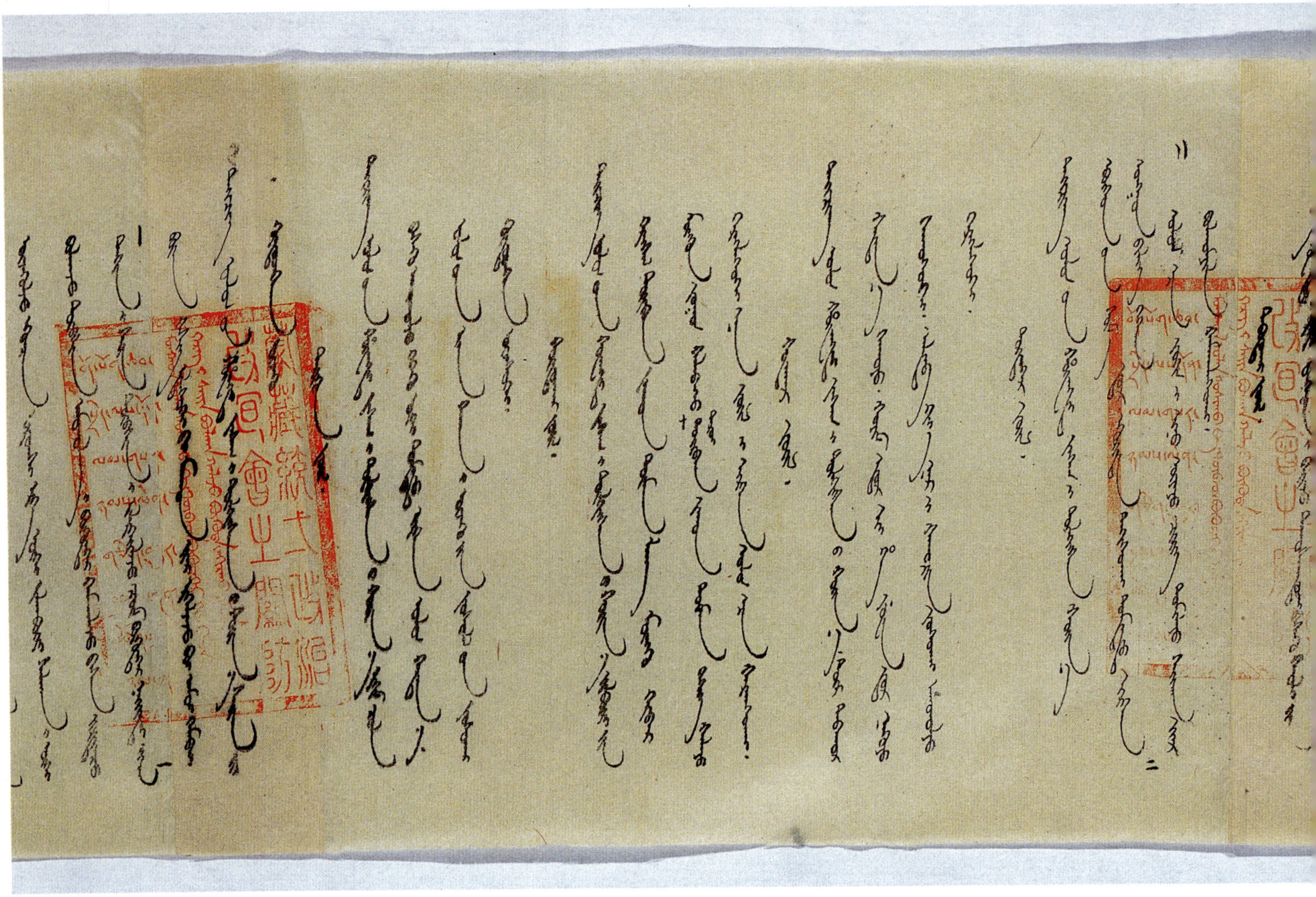

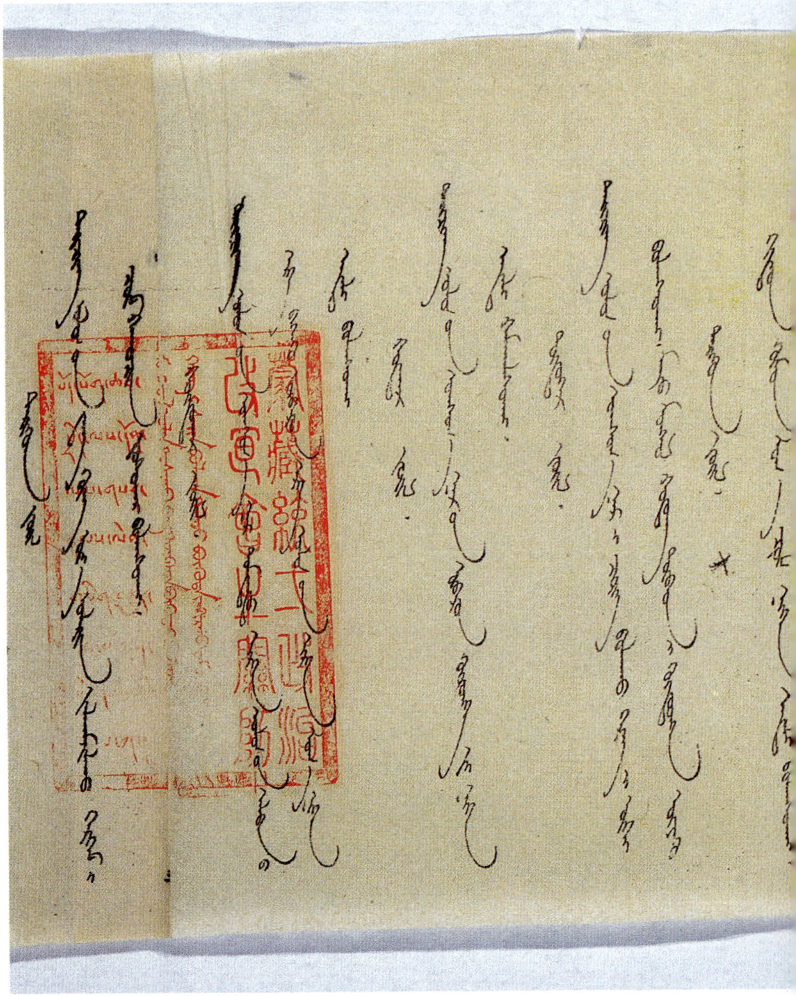

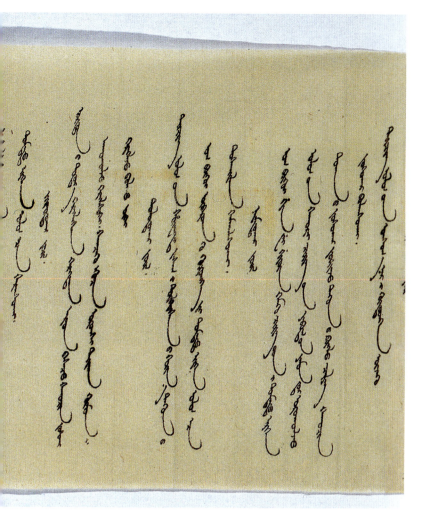

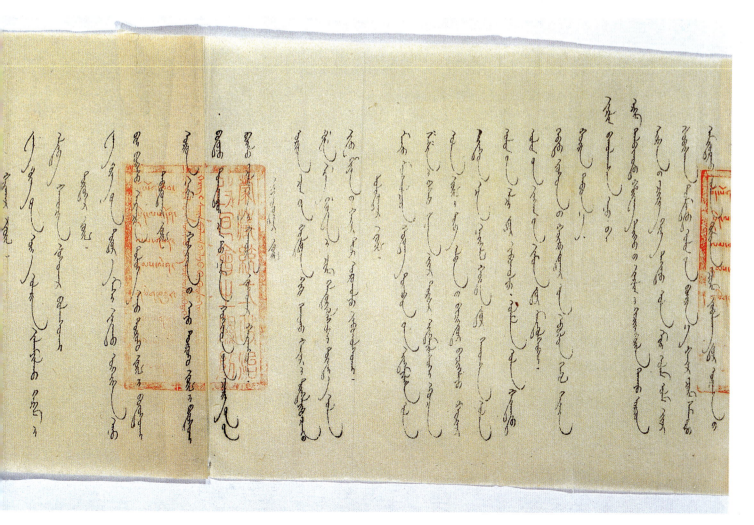

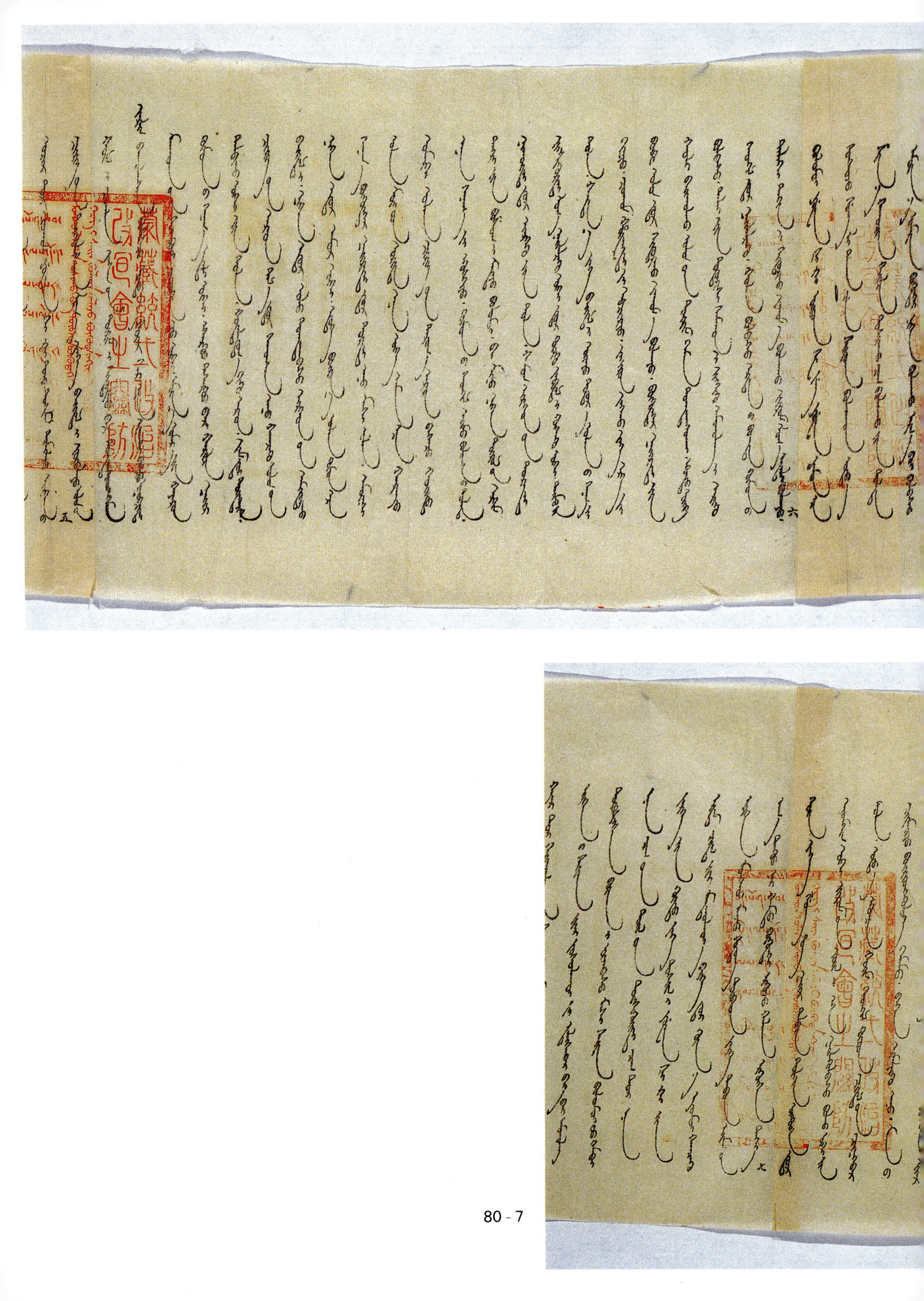

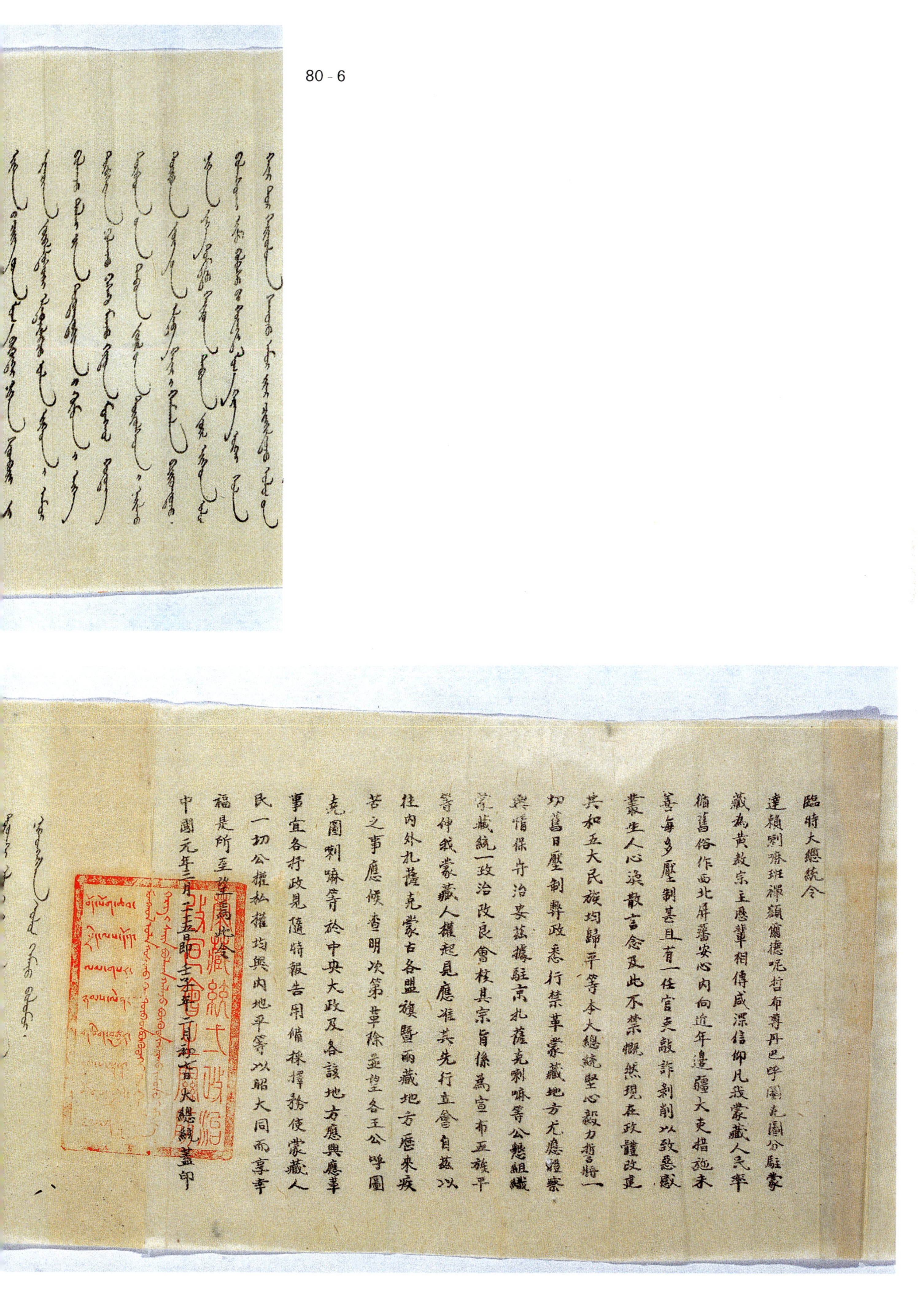

臨時大總統令

達賴喇嘛班禪額爾德呢哲布尊丹巴呼圖克圖分駐蒙
藏為黃教宗主歷輩相傳咸深信仰凡我蒙藏人民率
循舊俗作西北屏藩安心內向近年邊疆大吏措施未
善每多壓制甚且有一任官吏敲詐剝削以致惡感
叢生人心渙散言念及此不禁慨然現在政體改建
共和五大民族均歸平等本大總統堅心毅力掃除一
切舊日壓制弊政悉行禁革蒙藏地方尤應體察
輿情保守治安茲據駐京札薩克喇嘛等公懇組織
蒙藏統一政治改良會核其宗旨係為宣布五族平
等俾我蒙藏人權起見應准其先行立會自茲以
往內外札薩克蒙古各盟旗暨兩藏地方歷來疾
苦之事應候查明次第革除並望各王公呼圖
克圖喇嘛等於中央大政及各該地方應興應革
事宜各抒政見隨時報告用備採擇務使蒙藏人
民一切公權私權均與內地平等以昭大同而享幸
福是所至盼此令
中國元年三月二十五日即壬子年二月初八日大總統蓋印

# ཅང་ཀྲུང་ཀྲིན་གྱིས་ཏཱ་ལའི་བླ་མ་ལ་ཕུལ་བའི་འཕྲིན་ཡིག
# 蔣中正給達賴喇嘛的信
# Letter from Chiang Chung–cheng (Chiang Kai–shek) to the Dalai Lama

36 × 26.2

༄༅། །དབུ་བླ་ཆེན་མོ་ཏཱ་ལའི་བླ་མ་མཆོག་གི་ཆོས་ཁྲིའི་དྲུང་དུ།

ཉེ་ལམ་བཀུད་ཧྲིའི་དམག་སར་འབྱུས་མི་དཀོན་ངོས་འཕྲད་ཐོག་བཀའ་ཡིག་རིན་པོ་ཆེ་གནང་བྱུང་ཞིང་དབུ་བླ་མཆོག་གིས་ཀྲུང་དབྱང་ལ་ཐུགས་ཁ་ཕྱོགས་པའི་ལྷག་བསམ་དང་གུས་པར་ཐུགས་བརྩེ་འདོར་མེད་ཀྱི་གནས་ལུགས་ཞུས་གནང་བ་དང་སྤྲུགས་མཐལ་དར། སྐུ་དཔར། གསེར་གྱི་ཞལ་དཀར། ཏྲུམ་གདན་བཅས་རྫ་ཆེའི་དངོས་རིགས་གསོལ་རས་བསྩལ་བྱུང་བ་གུས་ཞབས་ཆེན་པོས་ཞུས་པ་དང་དགའ་སྤྲོ་དཔག་མེད་བྱུང་། སྔོན་དུས་ནས་རྒྱ་བོད་ཁྱིམ་གཅིག་ཡིན་ལུས་ཐོག་བར་སྐབས་དུས་འགྱུར་དབང་གིས་ཕན་ཚུན་ཕྲུག་ཁྲིས་འབྲུལ་རྒྱུ་སོགས་ཧ་ཅང་ཉུང་ངུར་སོང་འདུག་ན། ད་ཆ་ཀྲུང་ཀྲིན་ངོས་ནས་ཙུང་ལིའི་ཞལ་ཆེམས་ལྟར་རྒྱལ་ནང་མི་རིགས་ཚང་མར་ཕན་ཚུན་འདྲ་མཉམ་གྱི་ཐོབ་ཐང་སྤྲོད་པ་མ་ཟད། ལྷག་པར་དུ་བོད་འབངས་རྣམས་ལ་རོགས་སྐྱོར་བྱ་རྒྱུའི་ཆེད་སེམས་ཡོད་ལུགས་སྔ་ལོ་དཀོན་མཁན་པོ་བོད་དུ་བསྐྱོད་སྐབས་དེ་དོན་ནང་སྙན་ཞུ་རྒྱུར་མངགས་གཏམ་བྱས་པ་ལྟར་སྙན་སྔོངས་ལེགས་ཞུས་གནང་བར་བརྟེན་དཀོན་མཁན་པོ་སོགས་རྒྱལ་སར་མངགས་ནས་བོད་དོན་གྲོས་མོལ་གནང་བ་དང་། ཀྲུང་དབྱང་ནས་བརྟོན་པའི་དོན་ཚན་བརྒྱད་ལ་གང་ཙམ་ཞིག་གི་བཀའ་ལན་གནང་བྱུང་བའི་ཐོག་ནས་བདེན་དོན་ཟབ་རྟོགས་དང་ཁྱིམ་རྒྱུད་ཡུལ་ཁམས་ལ་བྱམས་སྐྱོང་གནང་བ་མཐོང་བས་དགའ་ཚོར་ཆེན་པོ་བསམ་གྱིས་མི་ཁྱབ་པ་བྱུང་། བོད་སོག་ལས་ཁུངས་ཀྱི་སྤྱི་ཁྱབ་རྣ་ཡུ་ཡོན་ཀྲང་ལ་འགན་དཀྲི་བཙོས་ཏེ་འབྱུས་མི་དཀོན་སོགས་དང་ལྷག་བསམ་ཐོལ་མེད་ཀྱིས་གྲོས་མོལ་ཞིབ་ཕྲ་གནང་སྟེ་བར་སྐབས་སུ་བྱུང་བའི་འཁོན་སེམས་སེལ་བ་དང་སྔོན་དུས་ཀྱི་མཐུན་ལམ་སླར་གསོ་ཡོང་རྒྱུའི་འདུན་པ་ཡོད་པ་དེ་དོན་དབུ་བླ་མཆོག་ནས་ཀྱང་འབྱུས་མི་དཀོན་སོགས་ལ་བཀའ་མངགས་གནང་སྟེ་ཁྲིན་ཡོངས་ལ་གཟིགས་རྟོགས་ཀྱིས་རྣ་ཡུ་ཡོན་ཀྲང་དང་ཞི་བའི་སྒོ་ནས་དོན་གཅོད་གནང་སྟེ་ཕྱོགས་ཡོངས་ནས་ལེགས་སྒྲུབ་ཞུ་རྒྱུའི་འདུན་པ་ཡོད། བོད་ཀྱི་བདག་དབང་ཉིན་རེ་བཞིན་སྲ་བརྟན་ཡོང་བ་དང་། སངས་རྒྱས་ཀྱི་བསྟན་པ་རིན་པོ་ཆེའི་བྱ་བ་སྤར་ལས་ལྷག་པའི་སྒོ་ནས་དར་རྒྱས་གཏོང་བ། བོད་ལྗོངས་སུ་བདེ་སྐྱིད་སྨྲུན་པའམ་མེས་རྒྱལ་ལ་སྲུང་སྐྱོབ་གནང་བ་བཅས་ནི་དབུ་བླ་ཉིད་དང་གུས་པ་ཀྲུང་ཀྲིན་བཅས་མི་སྣེར་ཁོ་ནའི་གཟི་བརྗིད་ཙམ་དུ་སྨྲས་པ་ག་ལ་ཆོག དམག་སའི་འཁྲུག་རྗོད་ཡོད་པ་དེ་དག་རིང་མིན་མཇུག་སྒྲིལ་བྱ་རྒྱུ་དང་། ལོག་སྤྱོད་པ་ཚང་མ་གད་རྒྱབ་པ་བཞིན་གཙང་བཟོས་ཐོག་ཁྲིན་ཡོངས་ཀྱི་བརྟན་ལྷིང་སྐད་ཅིག་ཙམ་གྱི་རིང་ལ་བཟོ་ཐུབ། སྐུ་ཉིད་ཀྱི་བསོད་ནམས་དཔལ་གྱིས་སྐྱོང་བའི་འོག་ཀྲུང་ཀྲིན་ངོས་ཀྱི་ལུས་འཚོ་སྟར་བཞིན་བདེ་ཐང་ཡོད་པས་གོང་ས་མཆོག་ལ་སླར་ཡང་ཐུགས་རྗེ་ཆེ་ཞུ་རྒྱུ་དང་སྐུ་ཁམས་གསལ་བཞིན་མཛད་འཕྲིན་རྒྱས་པ་ཡོང་བའི་གསོལ་བ་སྨོན་ལམ་ཞུ་སྨྲས་བཅས།

ཀྲུང་ཀྲིན་ནས་ཕུལ།

བོད་རང་སྐྱོང་ལྗོངས་ཡིག་ཚགས་ཁང་དུ་ཉར་ཚགས་བྱས་ཡོད།

西藏自治區檔案館藏

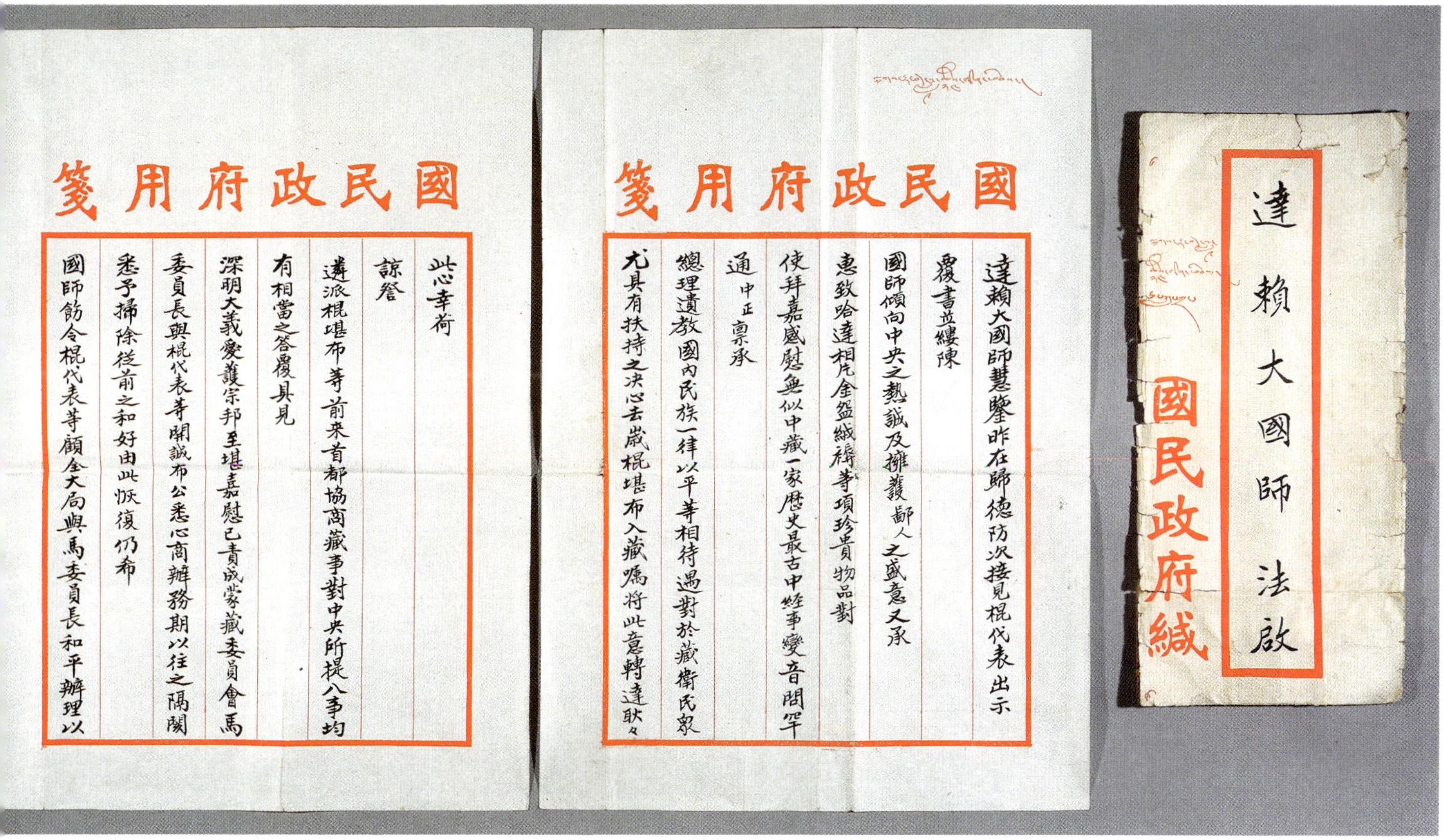
達賴大國師法啟
國民政府緘

國民政府用箋
達賴大國師慧鑒昨在歸德防次接見棍代表出示
覆書並縷陳
國師傾向中央之熱誠及擁護鄙人之盛意又承
惠致哈達相片金盆絨褥等項珍貴物品對
使拜嘉感慰無似中藏一家歷史最古中經事變音問罕
通中正稟承
總理遺教國內民族一律以平等相待遇對於藏衛民衆
尤具有扶持之決心去歲棍堪布入藏囑將此意轉達耿耿

國民政府用箋
此心幸荷
諒詧
遴派棍堪布等前來首都協商藏事對中央所提八事均
有相當之答覆具見
深明大義愛護宗邦至堪嘉慰已責成蒙藏委員會馬
委員長與棍代表等開誠布公悉心商辦務期以往之隔閡
悉予掃除從前之和好由此恢復仍希
國師飭令棍代表等顧全大局與馬委員長和平辦理以

81－1

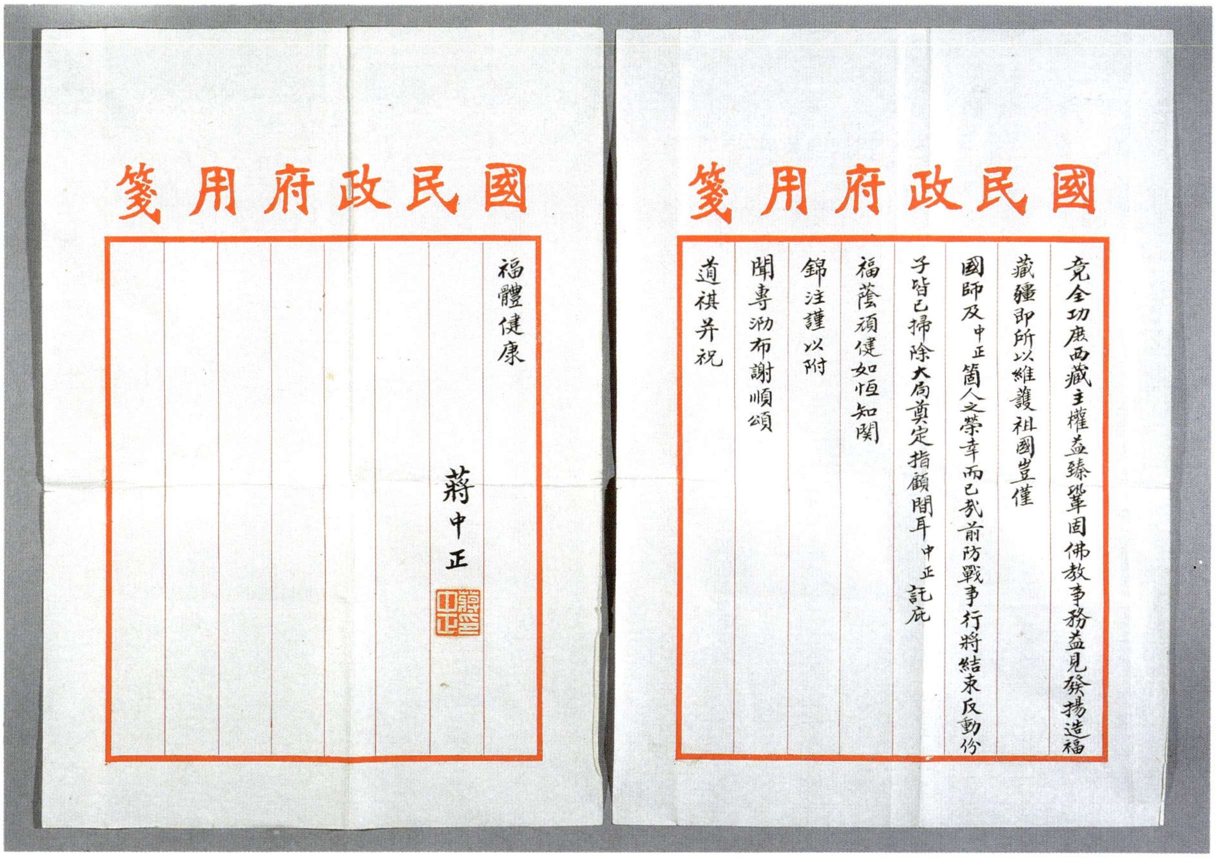
國民政府用箋
竟全功庶西藏主權益臻鞏固佛教事務益見發揚造福
藏疆即所以維護祖國豈僅
國師及中正箇人之榮幸而已哉前防戰事行將結束反動份
子皆已掃除大局奠定指顧間耳中正託庇
福蔭頑健如恒知關
錦注謹以附
聞專泐布謝順頌
道祺并祝

國民政府用箋
福體健康
蔣中正

81－2

To the Great State Tutor Dalai,

When I met with your representative Mr. Khon in the garrison area of Guid yesterday, he delivered your letter of reply clearly pledging your earnest support for the Central Government and myself. He also delivered the hatas, photographs, gold bowls, down quilts and other precious gifts and conveyed your best wishes, all of which moved me greatly and I cannot thank you enough. The Han people and Tibetan people are part of the same family with a long history, though contact between our two peoples has decreased lately due to certain difficulties. I am following the way of Prime Minister Sun Yat–sen by treating every nationality in the country the same; in particular I am supporting the Tibetan people. When Khon Khanpo prepared to return to Tibet last year, I asked him to convey this message to you, and I sincerely hope that you will be able to thoroughly understand it. Khon Khanpo was selected to come to the capital at this time to discuss Tibetan affairs with us and to bring your replies to the proposals made by the Central Government, showing your farsightedness and love for the country, which pleases me greatly. I have instructed Mr Ma, Chairman of the Committee for Mongolian and Tibetan Affairs, to sincerely and honestly work together with your representative Khon Khanpo to eliminate the past estrangement and revive our friendship. I still hope that you will instruct your representative Khon Khanpo to take the interests of the whole into account and cooperate with Chairman Ma for a peaceful settlement of the problems. Consolidating Tibetan sovereignty and promoting Buddhism will not only reflect well on yourself and myself but also bring happiness to all the people in Tibet and help to safeguard the Motherland. The war on the front is about to end, the reactionaries have been annihilated and the situation will soon be back to normal. I have been in good health. In gratitude to you for the concern you have shown for me, I am writing to you to express my heartfelt thanks and best wishes, and to wish you good health.

Chiang Chung–cheng

Preserved by the Archives of the Tibet Autonomous Region.

# གོ་མིང་སྲིད་གཞུང་གིས་ཏཱ་ལའི་བླ་མར་བསྟུལ་བའི་ཆེ་ཡོ།
# 國民政府追封達賴喇嘛的册文
# Decree Commending the Dalai Lama from the National Government

23.9 × 8.7

བོད་རང་སྐྱོང་ལྗོངས་ཡིག་ཚགས་ཁང་དུ་ཉར་ཚགས་བྱས་ཡོད།

西藏自治區文物管理委員會藏

His great career started in the snowy mountains and his teaching of Buddhism astounds the whole world like the roar of a lion. In the Ruoshui River a sacred soul related to Grdhrakuta was born. The Dalai Lama has taken charge of and protected the orthodox religion. He has supported and assisted China. He has spread benevolence and disseminated Buddhism in Tibet. The title of "the Great Master of Enlightenment, Benevolence, Perfection and Awareness Who Protects the Nation" has been granted posthumously to him. The wonderful teaching of Buddhism is spreading far and wide and constantly renewed like the Ih Ju Monastery and the law of Buddhism will remain for ever like the towering Anavta Mountain. This decree officially commends his merits.

February 12, the 22nd year of the Republic of China (1933)

Preserved by the Historical Relics Administration of the Tibet Autonomous Region.

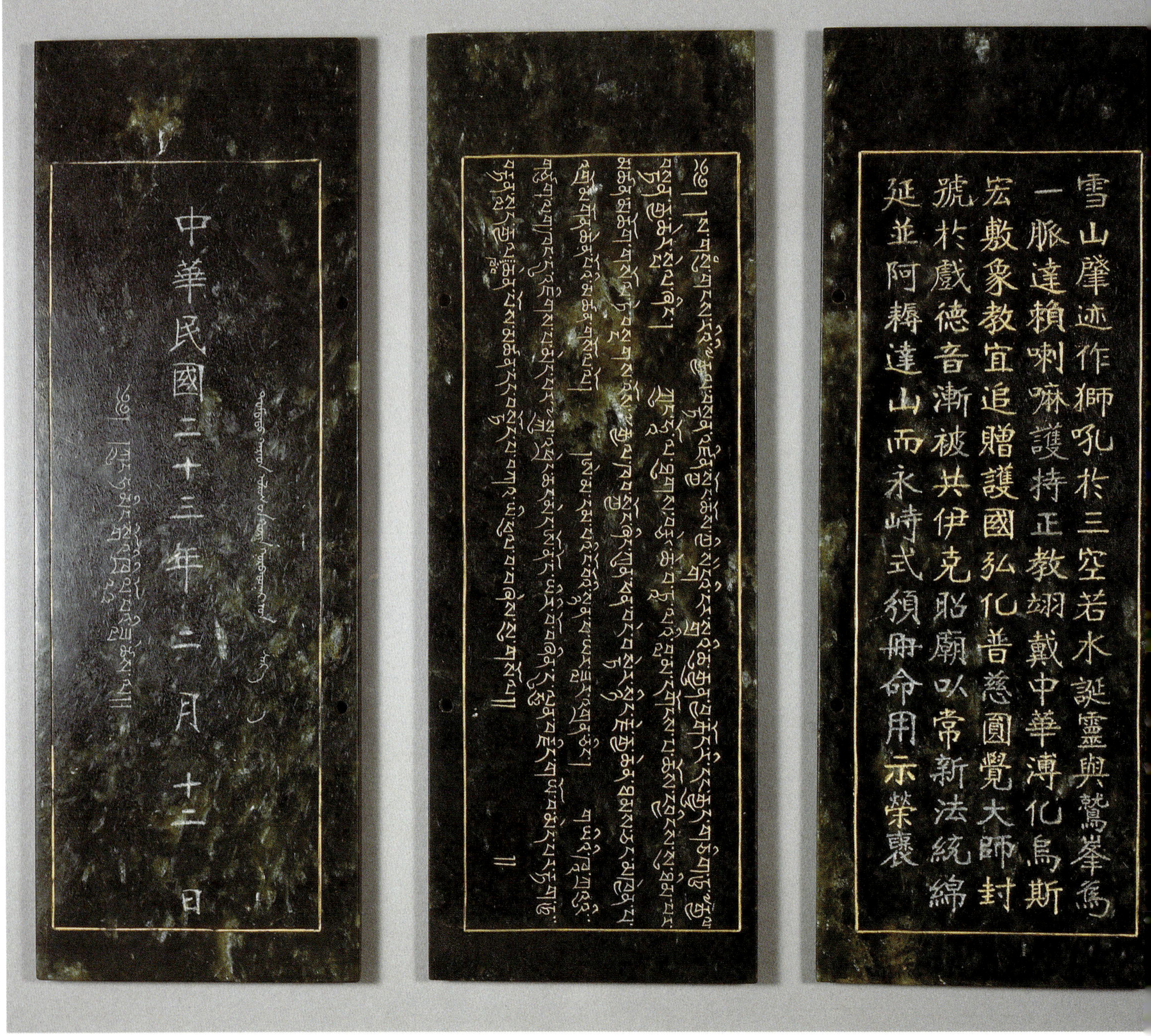
雪山肇迹作獅吼於三空若水誕靈與鷲峯爲
一脈達賴喇嘛護持正教翊戴中華溥化烏斯
宏敷象教宜追贈護國弘化普慈圓覺大師封
號於戲德音漸被共伊克昭廟以常新法統綿
延並阿耨達山而永峙式須冊命用示榮褒
中華民國三十三年二月十二日

82 - 1

82-2

གོ་མིང་སྲིད་གཞུང་གིས་པཎ་ཆེན་ཨེར་ཏི་ནི་ལ་མཚན་སྙན་གསོལ་བའི་དོན་དུ་བསྐུལ་པའི་བཀའ།

國民政府爲授予班禪額爾德尼名號事頒發的命令

The National Government Decree Granting Title to the Panchen Erdeni

28.2 × 20.2

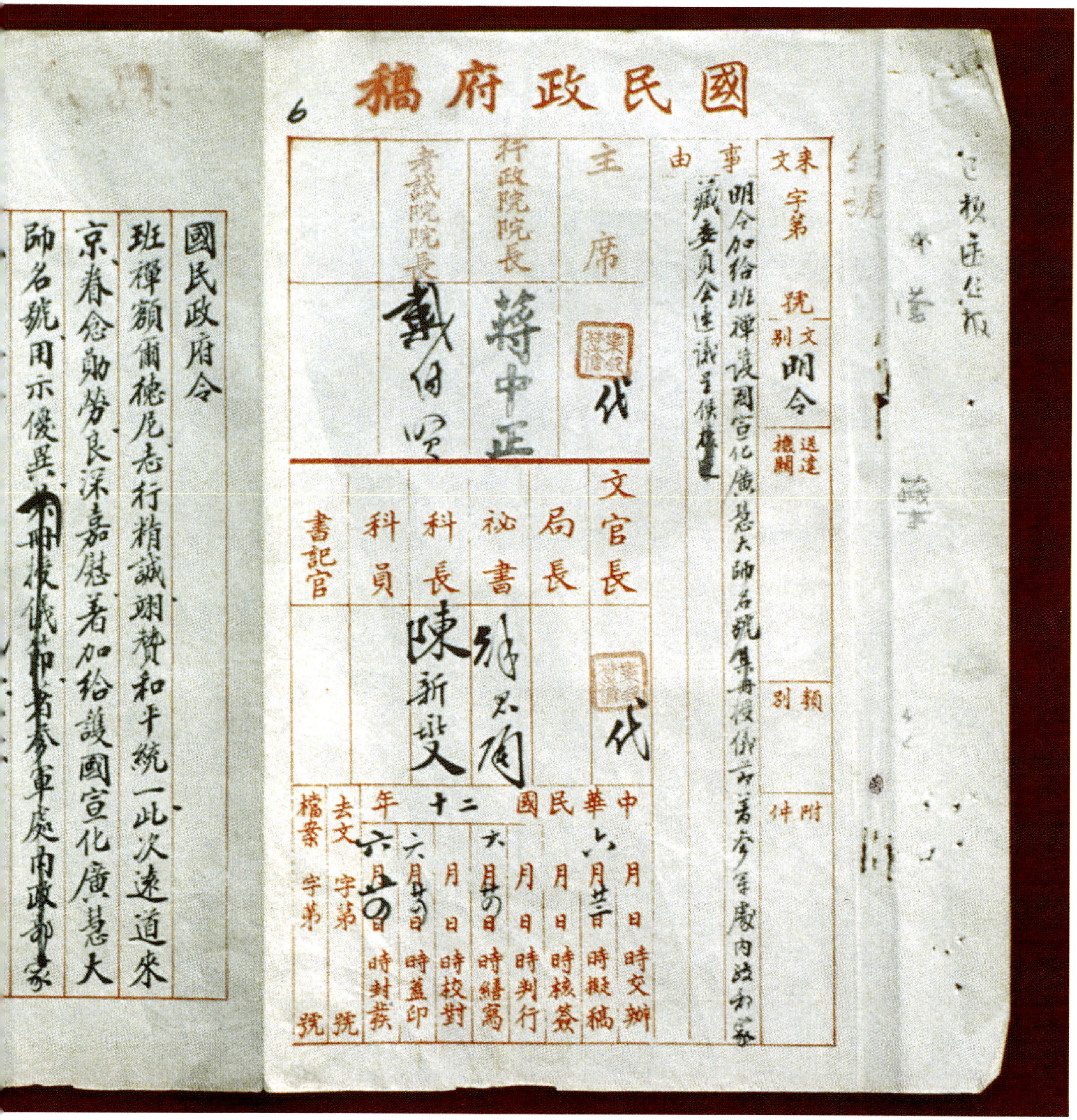

# 國民政府稿

| 來文 | 字第　號 |
|---|---|
| 文別 | 明令 |
| 送達機關 | |
| 類別 | |
| 附件 | |

事由：明令加給班禪護國宣化廣慧大師名號集冊授儀并著參軍處內政部蒙藏委員會遵議呈候核定

| 主席 | 行政院院長 | 考試院院長 |
|---|---|---|
| 代 | 蔣中正 | 戴傳賢 |

| 文官長 | 局長 | 秘書 | 科長 | 科員 | 書記官 |
|---|---|---|---|---|---|
| 代 | | 張丕介 | 陳新燮 | | |

中華民國二十年

六月　日　時交辦
六月廿三日　時擬稿
月　日　時核簽
月　日　時判行
六月廿四日　時繕寫
月　日　時校對
六月廿四日　時蓋印
六月廿四日　時封發

去文　字第　號
檔案　字第　號

國民政府令

班禪額爾德尼志行精誠翊贊和平統一此次遠道來京眷念勛勞良深嘉慰著加給護國宣化廣慧大師名號用示優異其冊授儀節著參軍處內政部蒙藏委員會

གོང་མིང་སྲིད་གཞུང་གི་བཀའ།

པཎ་ཆེན་ཨེར་ཏི་ནི་གང་ཉིད་སྙིང་སྟོབས་དང་མཛད་སྤྱོད་རྣམ་པར་དག་པ་དང་། ཞི་བདེ་གཅིག་གྱུར་ལ་ཡིད་མཐུན་གྱིས་ད་ཐེངས་ཐག་རིང་ནས་ནན་ཅིང་དུ་ཕེབས་པར་ངེད་ནས་ཁྱེད་ཀྱི་མཛད་རྗེས་ཆེད་པོ་ཡིད་དུ་འཁོར་བཞིན་སེམས་གཏིང་ནས་ཁྱེད་ལ་གཟིགས་བསྟོད་དང་འཚམ་འདྲི་ཞུ་བ་དང་རྒྱལ་ཁབ་སྐྱོང་ཞིང་དམ་ཆོས་རྒྱ་ཆེར་སྤེལ་བའི་སྐྱེ་རྒུའི་འདྲེན་མཆོག་དགེ་རྒན་ཆེན་མོ་ཞེས་པའི་མཚན་གསོལ་ཏེ་དམིགས་གསལ་གྱི་གཟིགས་སྐྱོང་བྱས་པའི་བཀའ་འདི་བསྒྲལ་ཏོ། །

ཀྲུང་ཧྭ་མིང་གོའི་ལོ་ཉི་ཤུ་པ (སྤྱི་ལོ་༡༩༣༡) ཟླ་བ་དྲུག་པའི་ཚེས་ཉེར་བཞི་ཉིན།

ཀྲུང་གོའི་ལོ་རྒྱུས་ཡིག་ཚགས་ཁང་ཨང་གཉིས་པར་ཉར་ཚགས་བྱས་ཡོད།

中國第二歷史檔案館藏

The National Government decrees:

The Panchen Erdini has been firm and loyal in his support for the peaceful reunification of the country. It was a long trip for him to come to the capital, representing a meritorious and moving deed. The title of "the Great Master Who Protects the Country and Spreads Enlightenment with His Great Intelligence" is hereby granted to him in recognition of his merit.

June 24, the 20th year of the Republic of China (1931)

Preserved by China No. 2 Historical Archives.

# ཀོ་མིང་སྲིད་གཞུང་གིས་པཎ་ཆེན་ཨེར་ཏི་ནི་ལ་གཟེངས་བསྟོད་གནང་བའི་བཀའ།
# 國民政府頒給班禪額爾德尼的褒獎令
# Citation to Be Given to the Panchen Erdeni from the National Government

28.2 × 20.2

ཀོ་མིང་སྲིད་གཞུང་གི་བཀའ།

རྒྱལ་ཁབ་སྐྱོང་ཞིང་དམ་ཆོས་རྒྱ་ཆེར་སྤེལ་བའི་སྐྱེ་རྒུའི་འདྲེན་མཆོག་དགེ་རྒན་ཆེན་མོ་ནུབ་ཕྱོགས་མཐའ་ཁུལ་གྱི་འགྲོ་བ་འདུལ་མཁན་པཎ་ཆེན་ཨེར་ཏི་ནི་མཆོག་ནི། ཏང་གོ་ལ་ཐུགས་སེམས་དཀར་བ་དང་། ཤུགས་ཆེན་པོས་འཐེན་ལས་དར་རྒྱས་གཏོང་བ། དེ་སྔོན་འགྲོ་བ་འདུལ་བའི་འགན་འཁུར་ཏེ་ཚ་གྲང་གི་དཀའ་ངལ་ལ་མ་འཛེམས་པར་མཐའ་མཚམས་ཀྱི་ཡུལ་གྲུར་ཕེབས་ནས་ཀྲུང་དབྱང་གི་དགོངས་འདུན་དྲིལ་བསྒྲགས་བྱས་པ་དང་། སོག་རིགས་རྣམས་ཀྱི་ལྷག་བསམ་ལ་བསྐུལ་མ་བཏང་བ་བཅས་ཀྱི་སྙན་གྲགས་ཀུན་ཏུ་ཁྱབ་པས་ཡུལ་གྲུ་རྣམས་ཀྱི་བར་ལ་མཐུན་ལམ་ཡག་པོ་ཆགས་ཡོད། དེང་གི་ཆ་ལའང་རྒྱལ་ཁབ་ཀྱི་དཀའ་ངལ་ད་དུང་སེལ་ཐུབ་མེད་པ་དང་། མཐའ་མཚམས་སུ་འཁྲུགས་ཟིང་མང་པོ་ཡོད་པར་ནུས་ཤུགས་གང་ཡོད་བཏོན་ནས་ཉེན་ཁ་དང་དོགས་པ་སེལ་བར་བྱས་ཏེ། མཐའ་མཚམས་ཀྱི་གནས་ཚུལ་སྙིང་འཇགས་སུ་གཏོང་དགོས། ཉིད་ཀྱི་མཛད་རྗེས་ཆེན་པོ་ཡིད་ལ་འཁོར་བཞིན་གཞན་ལས་ལྷག་པའི་བསྟགས་བརྗོད་དང་འཚམས་འདྲི་ཞུ་དགོས་པ་ཡིན་པས་དེའི་ཆེད་དུ་དམིགས་བསལ་གྱི་མཛད་རྗེས་ཆེན་པོར་གཟེངས་བསྟོད་བྱེད་རྒྱུའི་བཀའ་འདི་བསྒྲལ་ཏོ། །

ཀྲུང་ཧྭ་མིང་གོའི་ལོ་ཉེར་གཉིས་པ (སྤྱི་ལོ་༡༩༣༣) ཟླ་བ་བཅུ་པའི་ཚེས་བཅོ་བརྒྱད་ཉིན།

ཀྲུང་གོའི་ལོ་རྒྱུས་ཡིག་ཚགས་ཁང་ཨང་གཉིས་པར་ཉར་ཚགས་བྱས་ཡོད།

中國第二歷史檔案館藏

The National Government decrees:

The Panchen Erdeni, the Great Master Who Protects the Country and Spreads Enlightenment with His Great Intelligence and the Envoy Who Spreads Enlightenment on the Western Frontier, has been loyal to the Party and the nation. He has braved heat and cold, and defied hardship and illness to fulfil his task to enlighten the western frontier areas. He carried out the policies of the Central Government and encouraged loyalty among the Mongolian people. His message has been heard far and wide and all areas are now on friendly terms with one another. Recently, there were some incidents in the border area, but our envoy remained firm and was able to resolve this dangerous situation. His remarkable deeds are therefore being acknowledged.

October 18, the 22nd year of the Republic of China (1933)

Preserved by China No. 2 Historical Archives.

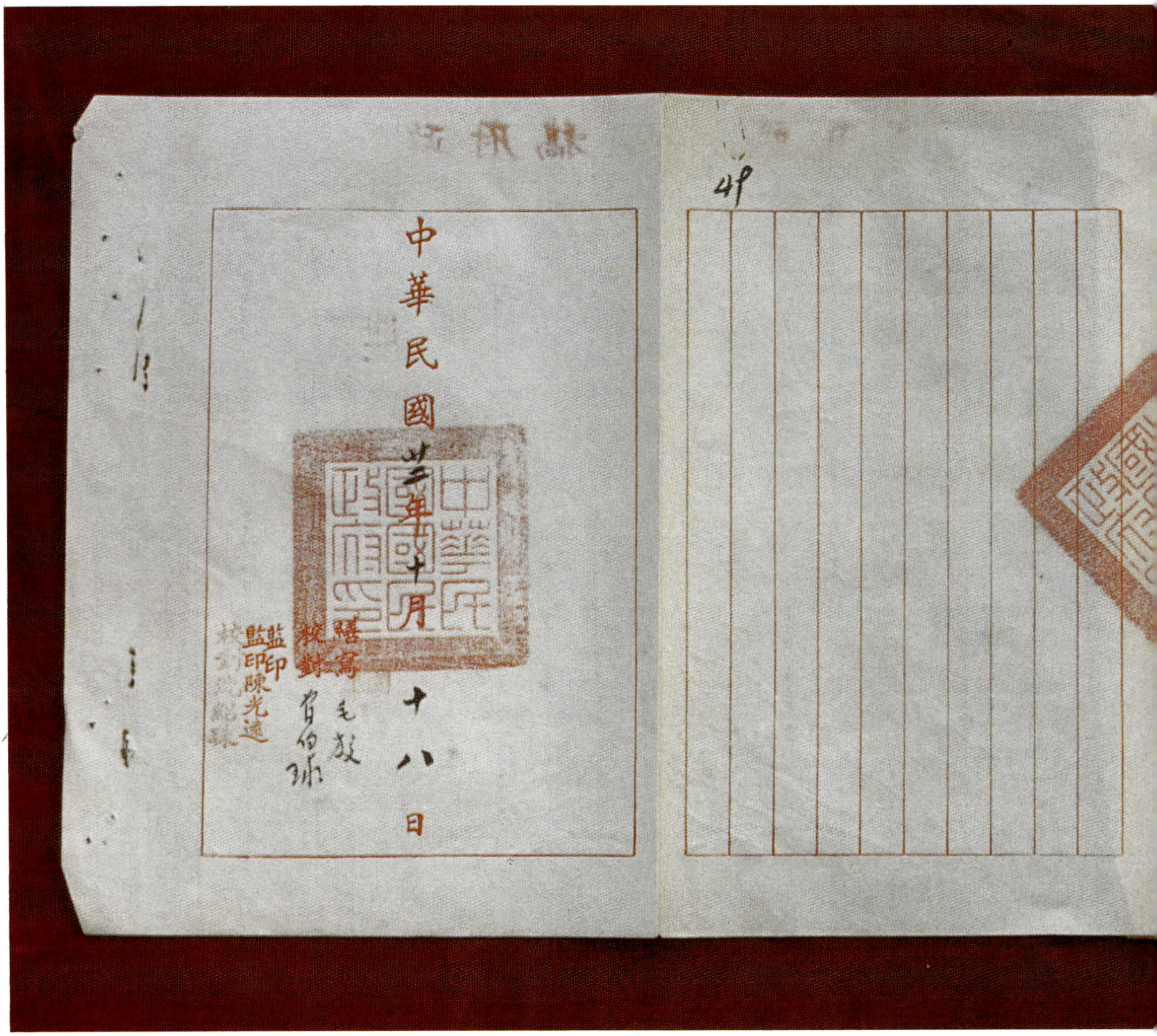
中華民國廿三年十月十八日
繕寫
校對
監印
監印陳光遠
41

最速件

# 國民政府稿

48

已抄登公報

文 字第5132號

文別：令

事由：明令褒獎班禪額爾德尼

主席：林森　十二、十六

行政院院長：汪兆銘

文官長：魏懷

局長：[illegible]

秘書：黎承福

科長：陳新燮

中華民國二十二年

| 交辦 | 擬稿 | 核簽 | 判行 | 繕寫 | 校對 | 蓋印 | 封發 |
| --- | --- | --- | --- | --- | --- | --- | --- |
| 月日時 | 十二月十五日時 | 月日時 | 月日時 | 十二月十八日時 | 十二月十八日時 | 十二月十八日時 | 月日時 |

去文 字第 號

檔案 字第 號

附件

國民政府令

護國宣化廣慧大師西陲宣化使班禪額爾德尼、宣化邊陲、寒暑屢遷、不辭勞瘁、

顧力振宗風、忠黨愛國、膺使命、艱教邊陲、成績昭著、

上以闡揚中央之意志、下以激發蒙族之忠忱、用能德音廣被、

兩歷歲寒、外馳驅、備嘗艱險、中經國難、尤能

訪閱督勵、頃者國難未已、疆場多故、該使力

鎮危疑、維繫邊局、眷懷勞勛、嘉慰良深、特予明

令褒獎、以彰殊績、此令

# ཧྲང་མའོ་སུང་གིས་ཏཱ་ལའི་བླ་མའི་ཡང་སྲིད་འཚོལ་རྒྱུའི་དོན་དུ་ར་སྒྲེང་སོགས་ལ་བཏང་བའི་དྲར།

# 黄慕松爲尋訪達賴喇嘛靈童事給熱振等人的電函

# Huang Musong's Telegram to Ragreng and Others Concerning the Matter of Searching for the Holy Child Dalai Lama

28.2×20.2

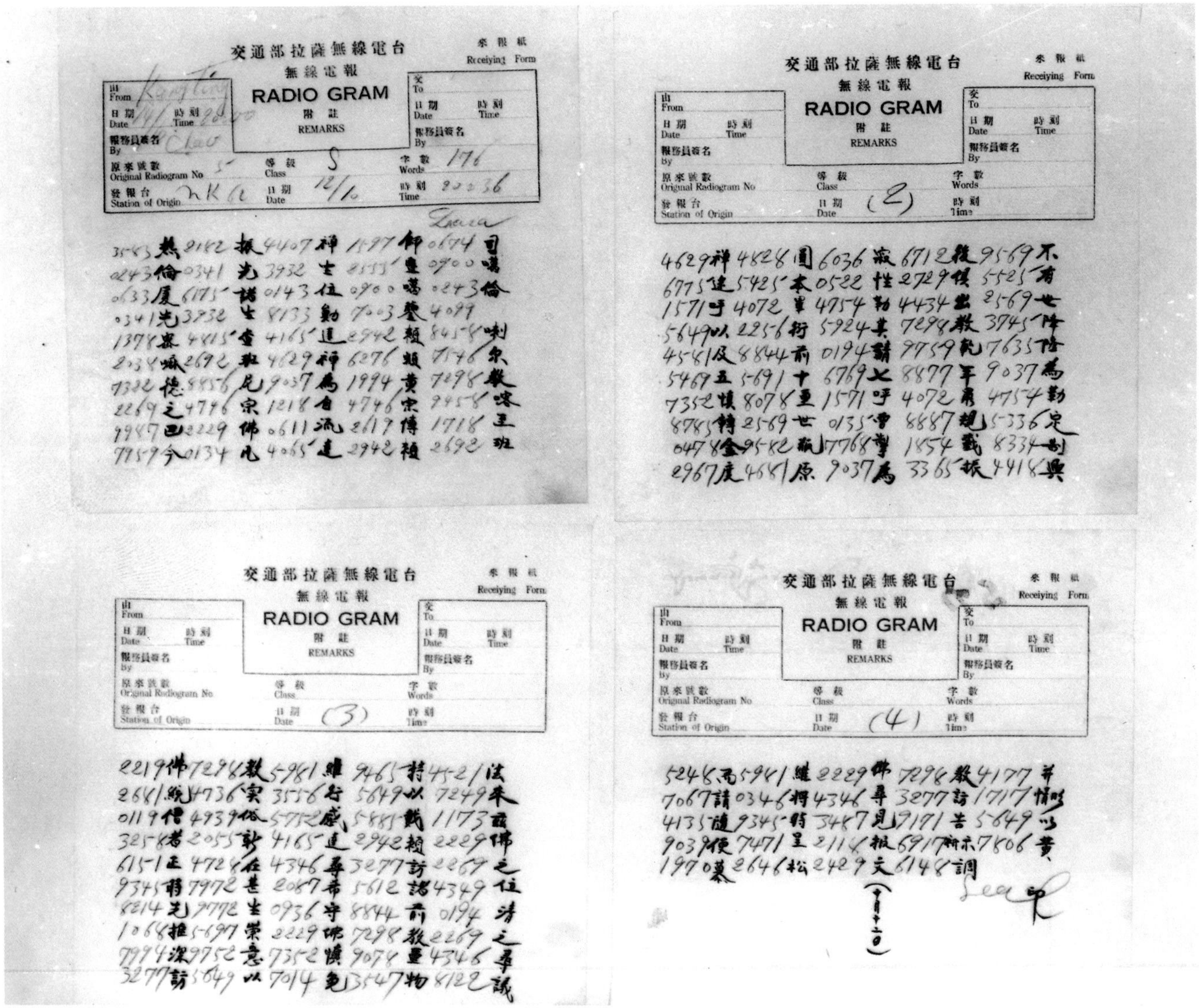

བསམ་གཏན་གྱི་སློབ་དཔོན་ར་སྒྲེང་དང་།  སྐུ་ཞབས་སྲིད་བློན།  བཀའ་ཤག  སྐུ་ཞབས་བཀའ་བློན་ལྷན་རྒྱས་ཀྱི་དྲུང་དུ།

གསང་བའི་ཞིབ་འཇུག་བྱས་པ་ལྟར་ན།  ཏཱ་ལའི་བླ་མ་དང་པཎ་ཆེན་ཨེར་ཏི་ནི་རྣམ་གཉིས་ནི་དགེ་ལུགས་པའི་བསྟན་པའི་བདག་པོ་ཡིན་ལ།  རྒྱལ་བ་ཙོང་ཁ་པ་ནས་བཟུང་རིམ་པར་བརྒྱུད་དེ་ད་ལྟའི་བར་དུ་ཏཱ་ལའི་དང་པཎ་ཆེན་ཡིན་ཕྱིན་ཞིང་བརྗེས་བརྗེས་རང་བཞིན་འཁྲུལ་བྲལ་གྱི་ཡང་སྲིད་འཁྲུངས་རྒྱུ་ཡོད་པར་བརྟེན་ནས་བསྐལ་བ་ཇི་སྲིད་བར་དུ་དམ་ཆོས་རྒྱུན་འཛིན་བྱེད་ཀྱིན་ཡོད།  དེ་སྔ་མཉྫུ་ཤྲཱི་སྐྱོང་ཁྲི་བཞུགས་ང་བདུན་ལོར།  ཡང་སྲིད་ངོས་འཛིན་ནན་ཏན་བྱེད་པའི་ཆེད་དུ་གསེར་བུམ་དཀྲུག་རྒྱུའི་ལམ་ལུགས་གཏན་འཁེལ་བྱས་ཡོད་པ་དེའི་དགོངས་དོན་ནི་སངས་རྒྱས་ཀྱི་བསྟན་པ་དར་རྒྱས་ཡོང་བ་དང་ཆོས་ཀྱི་ལམ་སྲོལ་རྒྱུན་འཛིན་བྱེད་རྒྱུའི་ཆེད་དུ་ཡིན་པས།  ལག་བསྟར་བྱས་རྗེས་སེར་སྐྱ་དམངས་ཀྱི་འདོད་བློར་འབབ་པ་རེད།  ད་ཆ་ཏཱ་ལའི་བླ་མའི་ཡང་སྲིད་འཚོལ་བཞིན་པའི་སྐབས་འདིར་སྐུ་ཞབས་རྣམ་པ་ཚོར་དེ་སྔ་མཉྫུས་སངས་རྒྱས་བསྟན་པར་དད་གུས་དང་དར་རྒྱས་བཏང་བའི་དགོངས་པ་ཟབ་མོ་གཞིར་བཟུང་སྟེ་ནན་ཏན་གྱིས་བཙལ་ནས་མི་ཁ་མི་ཟུག་པ་དང་སངས་རྒྱས་བསྟན་པ་སྲུང་བ་བཅས་ཀྱི་རེ་འདུན་ཞུ་རྒྱུ་མ་ཟད།  གོང་དུ་སྙན་སེང་ཞུལ་ནས་བཀའ་ལན་ཞུ་རྒྱུའི་ཆེད་དུ་ཡང་སྲིད་བཙལ་བའི་གནས་ཚུལ་སྐབས་འཕྲལ་དུ་སྙན་ཞུ་ཡོད་པ་བཅས།  ཧོང་མའོ་སུང་གིས་ཕྲིས་ཏེ་ཐམ་ཀ་བརྒྱབ།

ཀྲུང་ཧྭ་མིང་གོའི་ལོ་ཉེར་བཞི་པ (སྤྱི་ལོ་༡༩༣༥) ཟླ་བ་བཅུ་པའི་ཚེས་བཅུ་གཉིས་ཉིན།

ཀྲུང་གོའི་ལོ་རྒྱུས་ཡིག་ཚགས་ཁང་ཨང་གཉིས་པར་ཉར་ཚགས་བྱས་ཡོད།

中國第二歷史檔案館藏

The Venerated Buddhist Master Ragreng, and the Respected Chief Executive and Ministers of the Tibetan Government,

Careful investigation has shown that the Dalai Lama and the Panchen Erdeni are the highest lamas of the Yellow Sect of Lamaism, which has been handed down from the Tsongkhapa Buddha. The Dalai and the Panchen in all reincarnations keep the same nature and when the Holy Child enters the world, he will continue to respect the Buddhist doctrines. The system of drawing lots from a gold vase was formulated in the Qing Dynasty in the 57th year of Emperor Qianlong's reign for the discreet handling of the reincarnation of the Holy Child in the promotion of Buddhism and preservation of its doctrines. Both monks and laymen have been very pleased with the system since its implementation. The search is now underway for the new Dalai Lama and we hope that you will observe the regulations made in the Qing Dynasty, which greatly honoured Buddhism, and be very careful in your search for the new Dalai, in order to avoid later criticism and safeguard Buddhism. Keep me informed at all times of your progress in looking for the new Dalai so that I can report this to the higher authorities and ask for instructions.

Yours sincerely,

Huang Musong (seal)

October 12, the 24th year of the Republic of China (1935)

Preserved by China No. 2 Historical Archives.

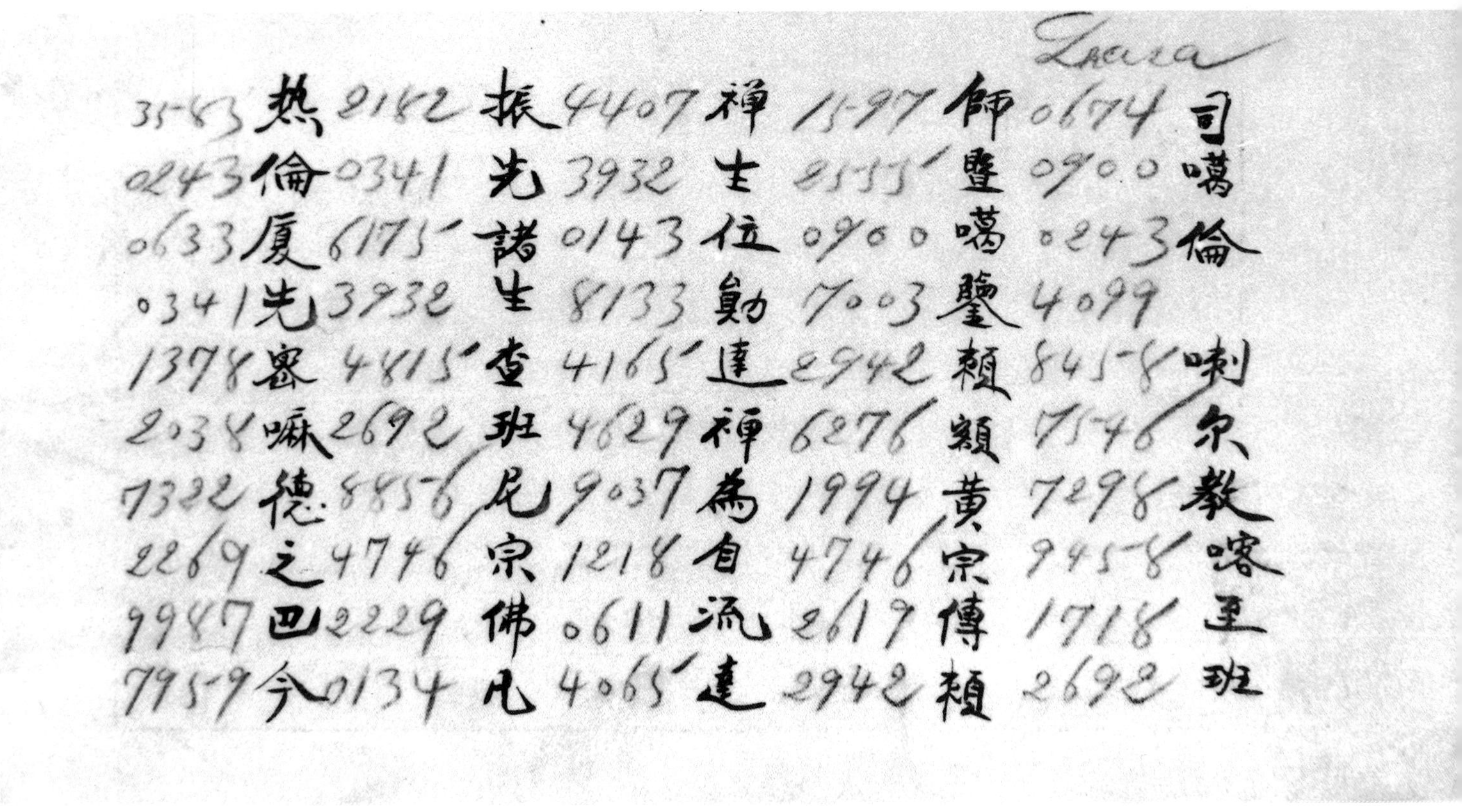


| | | | | | | | | | |
|---|---|---|---|---|---|---|---|---|---|
| 3583 | 熱 | 2182 | 振 | 4407 | 禪 | 1597 | 師 | 0674 | 司 |
| 0243 | 倫 | 0341 | 先 | 3932 | 生 | 2555 | 豐 | 0900 | 噶 |
| 0633 | 厦 | 6175 | 諸 | 0143 | 位 | 0900 | 噶 | 0243 | 倫 |
| 0341 | 先 | 3932 | 生 | 8133 | 勳 | 7003 | 鑾 | 4099 | |
| 1378 | 塞 | 4815 | 查 | 4165 | 達 | 2942 | 賴 | 8458 | 喇 |
| 2038 | 嘛 | 2692 | 班 | 4629 | 禪 | 6276 | 額 | 7546 | 爾 |
| 7322 | 德 | 8856 | 尼 | 9037 | 為 | 1994 | 黃 | 7298 | 教 |
| 2269 | 之 | 4746 | 宗 | 1218 | 自 | 4746 | 宗 | 9458 | 喀 |
| 9987 | 回 | 2229 | 佛 | 0611 | 流 | 2617 | 傳 | 1718 | 里 |
| 7759 | 今 | 0134 | 凡 | 4065 | 達 | 2942 | 賴 | 2692 | 班 |

85－2

85－3

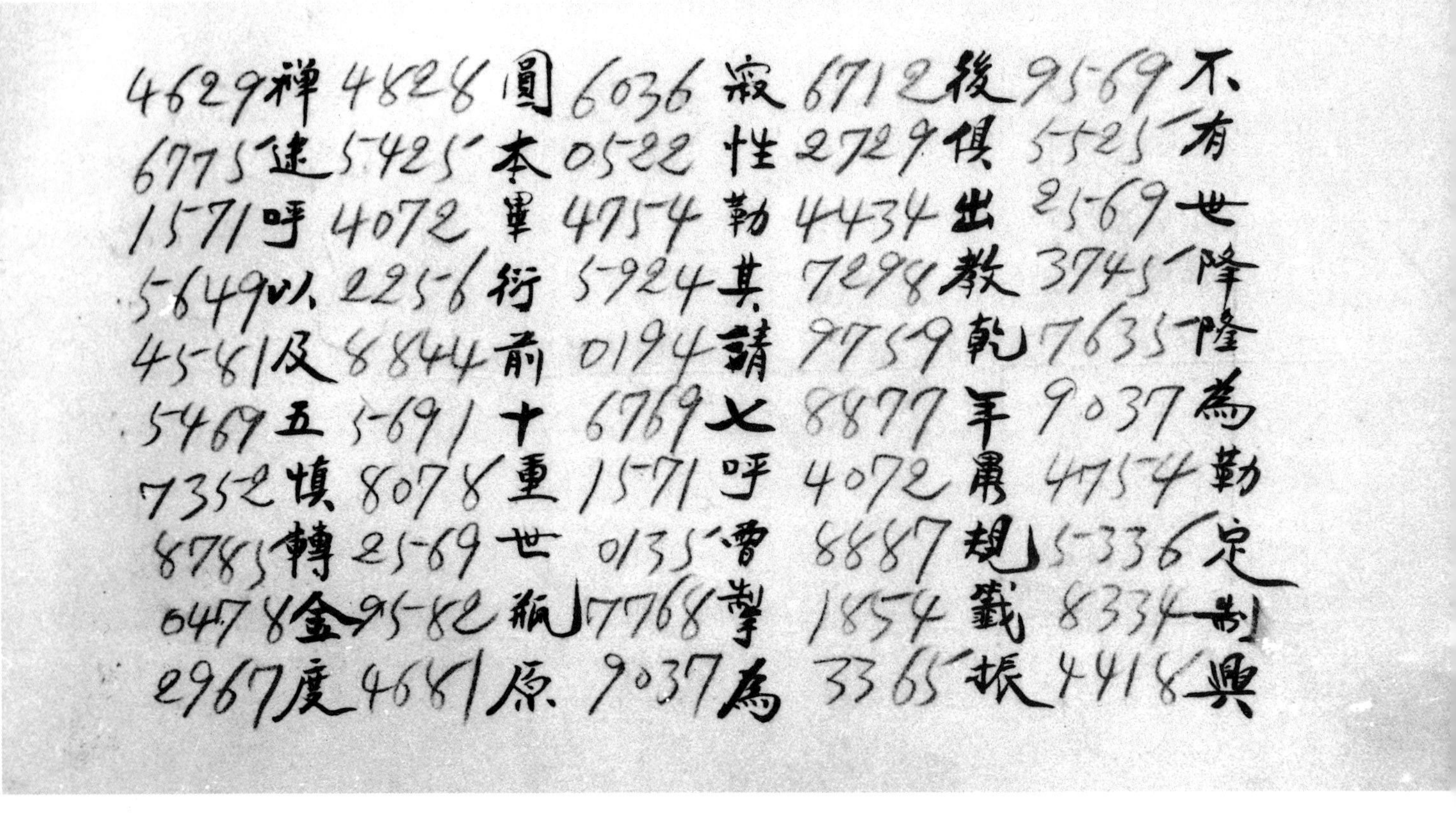

| | | | | | | | | | |
|---|---|---|---|---|---|---|---|---|---|
| 4629 | 禪 | 4828 | 圓 | 6036 | 寂 | 6712 | 後 | 9569 | 不 |
| 6775 | 逮 | 5425 | 本 | 0522 | 性 | 2729 | 俱 | 5525 | 有 |
| 1571 | 呼 | 4072 | 畢 | 4754 | 勒 | 4434 | 出 | 2569 | 世 |
| 5649 | 以 | 2256 | 衍 | 5924 | 其 | 7298 | 教 | 3745 | 降 |
| 4581 | 及 | 8844 | 前 | 0194 | 請 | 7759 | 乾 | 7635 | 隆 |
| 5461 | 五 | 5691 | 十 | 6769 | 七 | 8877 | 年 | 9037 | 為 |
| 7352 | 慎 | 8078 | 重 | 1571 | 呼 | 4072 | 畢 | 4754 | 勒 |
| 8785 | 轉 | 2569 | 世 | 0135 | 曾 | 8887 | 規 | 5336 | 定 |
| 0478 | 金 | 9582 | 瓶 | 7768 | 掣 | 1854 | 籤 | 8334 | 制 |
| 2967 | 度 | 4681 | 原 | 9037 | 為 | 3365 | 振 | 4418 | 興 |

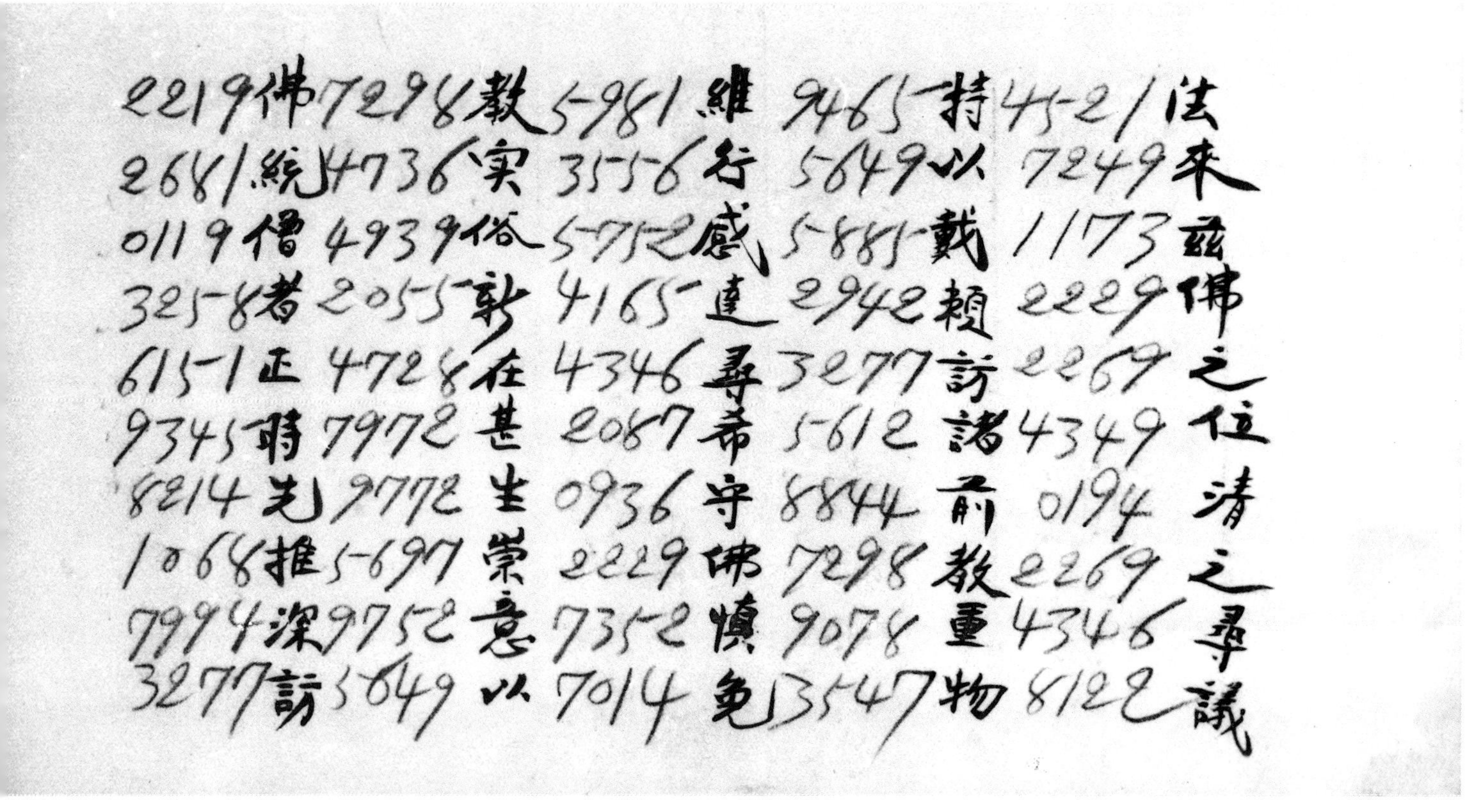
2219佛7298教5981維9465持4521法
2681統4736实3556行5649以7249来
0119僧4939俗5712感5885戴1173兹
3258者2055新4165達2942賴2229佛
6151正4728在4346尋3277訪2267之
9345時7972甚2087帝5612諾4349位
8214先9772生0936守8844前0194清
1068推5697崇2229佛7298教2267之
7994深9752意7352慎9078重4346尋
3277訪5649以7014免3547物8122議

85－4

85－5

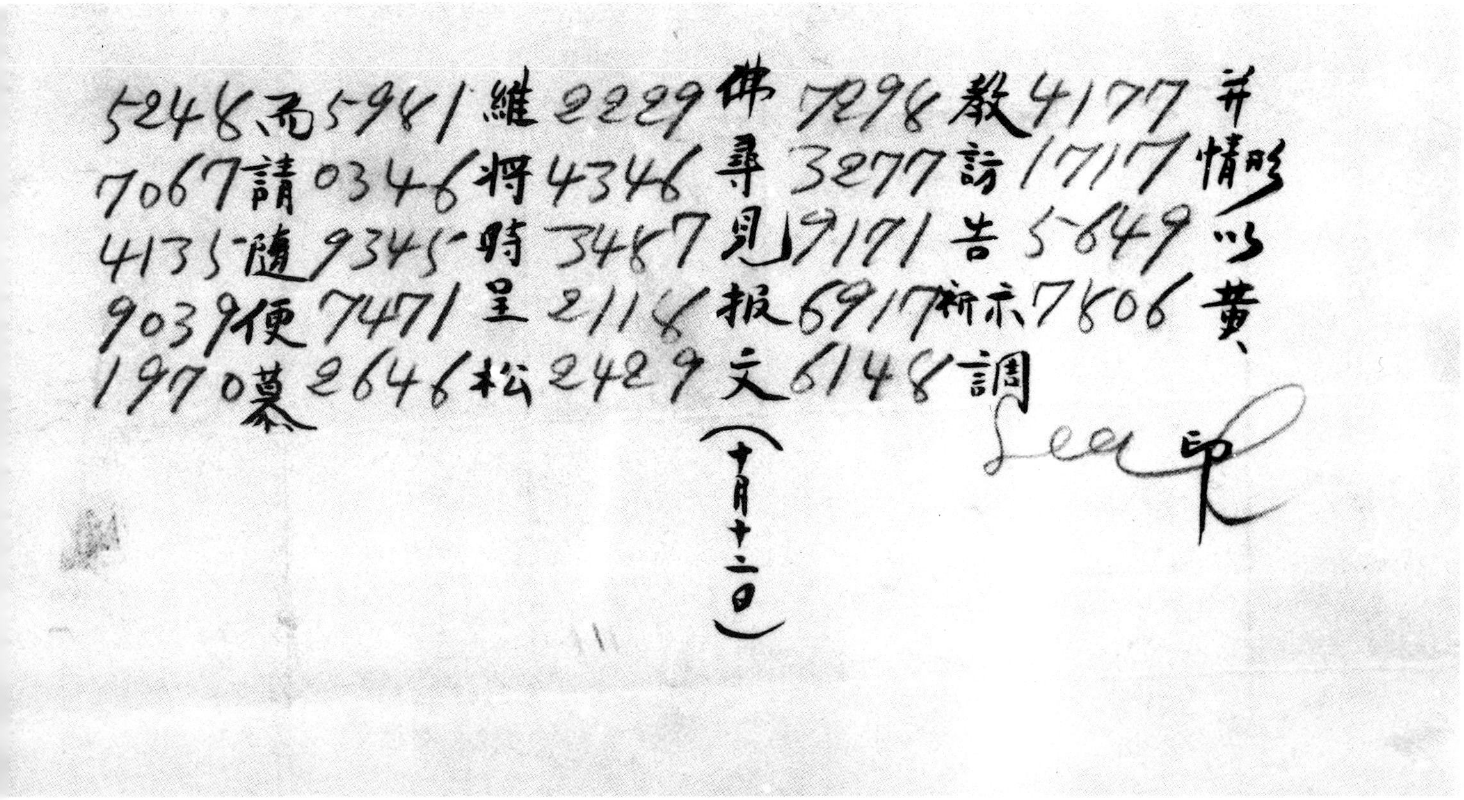
5248而5981維2229佛7298教4177并
7067請0346將4346尋3277訪1717情形
4135隨9345時3487見9171告5649以
9039便7471呈2118报6917祈示7806黄、
1970慕2646松2429文6148調

Lee印

（十月十二日）

# པཎ་ཆེན་ཨེར་ཏི་ནི་སྐུ་ཕྲེང་དགུ་པའི་ཞལ་ཆེམས།
# 九世班禪額爾德尼遺囑
# The 9th Panchen Erdeni's Will

20.1 × 20

བོད་སོག་ཨུ་ཡོན་ལྷན་ཁང་གི་ཨུ་ཡོན་ཀྲུང་མཆོག་གི་དྲུང་དུ།

པཎ་ཆེན་རིན་པོ་ཆེའི་ཞལ་ཆེམས་ཀྱི་བསྒྱུར་ཡིག་སྙན་ལམ་དུ་འབུལ་རྒྱུ་ནི་འདི་ལྟ་སྟེ། པཎ་ཆེན་གྱི་ཞལ་ཆེམས་ནི་ཀྲུང་དབྱང་ལ་བརྩི་འཇོག་དང་བསྟན་པ་དར་རྒྱས། མི་རིགས་ལྔའི་མཐུན་སྒྲིལ་ལ་སྐུལ་འདེད། རྒྱལ་ཁབ་དར་རྒྱས་འོང་བར་སྲུང་སྐྱོབ་བྱ་རྒྱུ་བཅས་ནི་རང་ཉིད་ཀྱི་ཚོགས་གང་པོའི་འདུན་པ་ཆེ་ཤོས་ཡིན། ཉེ་བའི་ལོ་བཅོ་ལྔའི་རིང་ལ་ནང་ལོག་གི་ས་ཕྱོགས་གང་སར་བསྐྱོད་སྐབས་ཀྲུང་དབྱང་ནས་གཟིགས་སྐྱོང་ཆེན་པོ་གནང་བ་དེའི་ཐོག་ནས་ཀྲུང་དབྱང་གིས་དངོས་འབྲེལ་སངས་རྒྱས་བསྟན་པར་དད་གུས་གནང་བ་དང་བོད་རིགས་ལ་འདྲ་མཉམ་གནང་བ་བཅས་མཐོང་ཐུབ་པས་ངའི་བློ་ཐེ་བདེ་ར་སོང་བ་དང་སེམས་ཐེ་བརྟན་དུ་ཕྱིན་སོང་། ད་ལན་ནུབ་ཕྱོགས་མཐའ་མཚམས་སུ་འགྲོ་བ་འདུལ་བར་མངགས་ཏེ་བོད་ཀྱི་ས་ཆར་ལོག་རྩིས་བྱས་ཀྱང་། བསམ་དོན་གྲུབ་མ་ཐུབ་པར་ལམ་བར་དུ་ཚེ་ལས་འདས་པར་བརྟེན། ད་ལྟ་དོན་དག་ཁ་ཤས་ཞུ་རྒྱུ་ཡོད་པ་དེ་དག་ཡི་གེ་ནང་འཁོད་པ་གཤམ་གསལ། གཙང་གི་སྲིད་དོན་དེ་སྔ་ནས་བློ་བཟང་རྒྱལ་མཚན་ཛ་སག་བླ་མར་བསྐོས་ནས་འགྲོ་བ་འདུལ་བའི་ལས་འགན་ཡོད་ཚད་ཀྱང་གནས་སྐབས་ཙམ་ལ་ཁོང་གིས་ཆབ་བྱས་ནས་འཁུར་རྒྱུ། ལས་གནས་ཐོག་ཏུ་མ་འབྱོར་གོང་ལ་ཐམ་ཀ་གཉེར་སྐྱེས་བླ་མར་རེ་ཞིག་རྩིས་སྤྲོད་བྱ་རྒྱུ་དང་སྦྲགས། ནང་མ་སྒང་དང་བོད་ལ་ཕྱིར་ལོག་ཇུས་བཀོད་ཨུ་ཡོན་དྲུག་ནས་མཉམ་དུ་འགན་འཁུར་དགོས་པའི་སྐོར་ཀྲུང་དབྱང་ལ་སྙན་སེང་ཞུས་ནས་ཐག་གཅོད་ཀྱི་བཀའ་སྩལ་དགོས། ནང་མ་སྒང་གི་གོ་མཚོན་ནང་ནས་སྐུ་སྲུང་ཏུ་ཁག་དང་སྐུ་འཁོར་གྱི་རང་སྲུང་གི་ཆེད་དུ་ཉར་བ་རྣམས་ཕུད། དེ་ཕྱིངས་རྒྱལ་ཁབ་ཀྱི་དཀའ་ངལ་སེལ་བའི་ཆེད་དུ་ཀྲུང་དབྱང་ལ་ཕུལ་ནས་ཡང་སྲིད་འཁྲུངས་རྗེས་ཕྱིར་སྤྲོད་རོགས་ཞུ། གཞན་ཡང་པཎ་ཆེན་སྐུ་ཕྲེང་རིམ་བྱོན་ནས་ཡོངས་སུ་སྤྱོད་པའི་དབང་ཆ་རྣམས་མགྱོགས་པར་སླར་གསོ་བྱེད་ཐུབ་པའི་བྱ་ཐབས་སྲེལ་དགོས། བོད་ཀྱི་སེར་སྐྱ་དཔོན་འབངས་རྣམས་ནས་ཀྲུང་དབྱང་གི་མི་རིགས་རྣམ་ལྔ་རྒྱལ་འཛུགས་ཀྱི་སྲིད་དོན་གཞིར་བཟུང་གིས་རྒྱ་བོད་མཐུན་ལམ་ཡོང་རྒྱུར་འབད་བརྩོན་བྱེད་དགོས། ལྷག་པར་དུ་ཛ་སག་བླ་མ་དང་མཁན་པོ་རྣམས་ཀྱིས་ངའི་བསམ་དོན་རྒྱུན་འཁྱོངས་གང་ལེགས་བྱས་ཏེ་ཁ་ཆེམས་འདི་དོན་ཐོག་ཏུ་འབེབས་པར་སྐུལ་ལྕག་གཏོང་དགོས།

ཐག་རིང་ནས་ཐུགས་འཁུར་གནང་གིན་ཡོད་པ་ཤེས་ཏེ་ཏར་འདི་ཆེད་དུ་ཕུལ། ནུབ་ཕྱོགས་མཐའ་ཁུལ་དུ་འགྲོ་བ་འདུལ་མཁན་གྱི་སྤྱི་ཁང་གི་དྲུང་ཡིག་ཁང་ནས་གུས་པས་ཕུལ། ཆོས་ལྔ་ལ་ཐམ་ཀ་བརྒྱབ།

ཀྲུང་ཧྭ་མིང་གོའི་ལོ་ཉེར་དྲུག་པ(སྤྱི་ལོ་༡༩༣༧)ཟླ་བ་བཅུ་གཉིས་པའི་ཚེས་བདུན་ཉིན།

ཀྲུང་གོའི་ལོ་རྒྱུས་ཡིག་ཚགས་ཁང་ཨང་གཉིས་པར་ཉར་ཚགས་བྱས་ཡོད།

中國第二歷史檔案館藏

Chairman Wu of the Committee for Mongolian and Tibetan Affairs,

Following is a translation of Master Panchen's will:

It has been my life–long aspiration to support the Central Government, propagate Buddhism, support the union of the five major nationalities and maintain the country's prosperity. Over the last fifteen years I toured the central areas, where the treatment I received from the Central Government clearly showed that the government respects Buddhism and provides equal treatment for the Tibetan people. This pleased me greatly and strengthened my determination. Recently, I was instructed to spread Buddhism and teach the canons in the western border area. Though I had planned to return to Tibet, I shall not be able to fulfil my task because I shall soon pass away. These are my arrangements for handling various matters. Government affairs in Lower Tibet are to be entrusted to Lozang Gyaltshan as the Dsasag Lama as well as the responsibility to propagate Buddhism and teach the canons. The seal is to remain in Blama Denggyas' hands until Lozang Gyaltshan takes up his position. My duties are to be temporarily carried out by the six members of the Khanpolija (*Tr.* the highest administrative organ under the Panchen) and the Return–to–Tibet Planning Committee with all decisions subject to the approval of the Central Government. All firearms in my office, except for those of the guards and those that the attendants use for self–defence, are to be presented to the Central Government to help the country deal with its difficulties and returned to me in the next reincarnation. The rights accorded to the Panchen in previous generations should be restored soon. Finally, I hope the Tibetan people, both officials and civilians, and both followers of Lamaism and laymen, in accordance with the spirit of the five–nationality policy promulgated by the Central Government, will endeavor to cement the friendship between the Tibetan and Han peoples. Dsasag Lama and the Khanpos are to take over my unfinished missions and carry them to completion.

I would like to express my gratitude for all the concern shown for me by others.

The Secretariat of the Office of the Envoy for the Dissemination of Buddhism and the Teaching of the Canons in the Western Border Area. [seal, 5th of December]

December 7, the 26th year of the Republic of China (1937)

Preserved by China No. 2 Historical Archives.

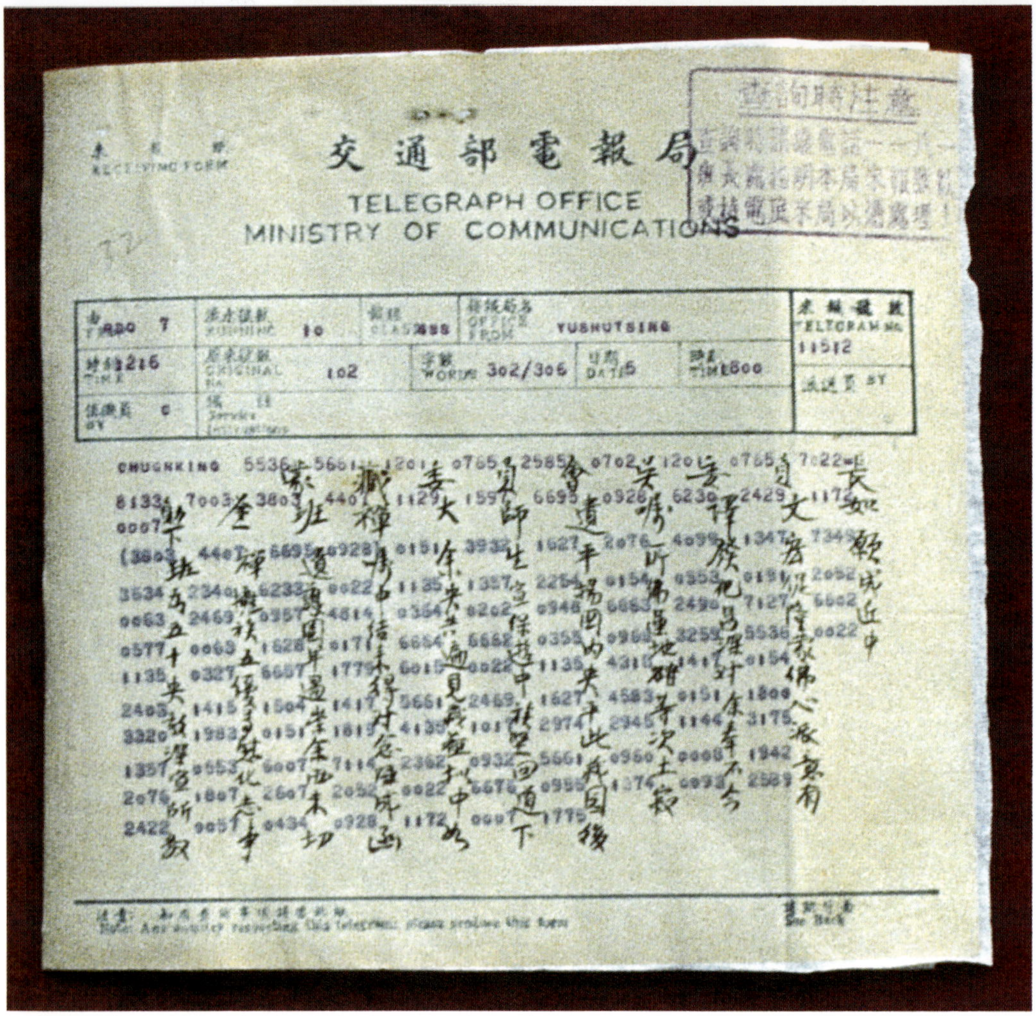

交通部電報局
TELEGRAPH OFFICE
MINISTRY OF COMMUNICATIONS

查詢時注意

| 由 FROM 7 | 流水號數 RUNNING 10 | 類別 CLASS | 發報局名 OFFICE FROM YUSHUTSING | 來報號數 TELEGRAM No. 11512 |
|---|---|---|---|---|
| 時刻 TIME 216 | 原來號數 ORIGINAL No. 102 | 字數 WORDS 302/306 | 日期 DATE 5 | 時刻 TIME 1800 |
| 值機員 BY C | 說明 Service Instructions | | | 派送員 BY |

CHUNGKING 5536 5661 1201 0765 2585 0702 1201 0765 7022

86 - 1

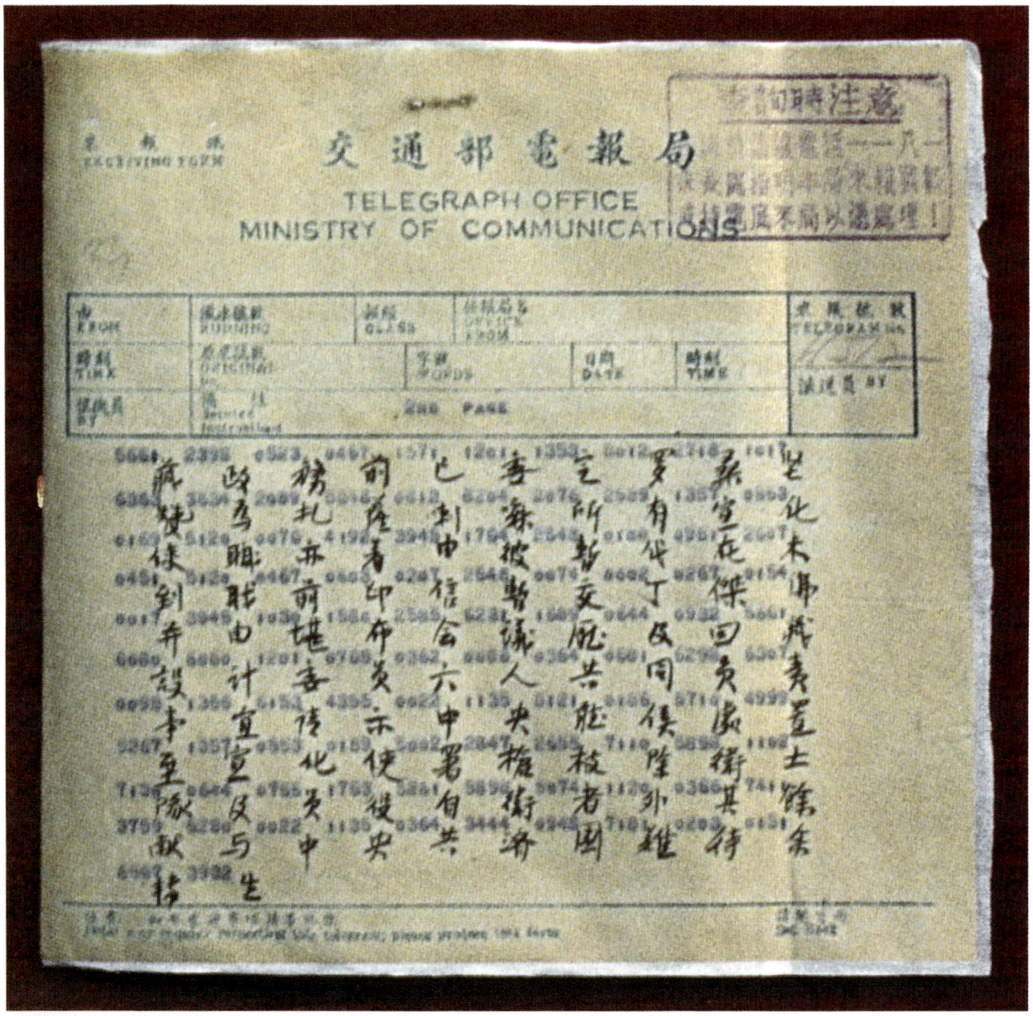

交通部電報局
TELEGRAPH OFFICE
MINISTRY OF COMMUNICATIONS

查詢時注意

| 由 FROM | 流水號數 RUNNING | 類別 CLASS | 發報局名 OFFICE FROM | 來報號數 TELEGRAM No. |
|---|---|---|---|---|
| 時刻 TIME | 原來號數 ORIGINAL No. | 字數 WORDS | 日期 DATE | 時刻 TIME |
| 值機員 BY | 說明 Service Instructions | 2ND PAGE | | 派送員 BY |

86 - 2

86－3

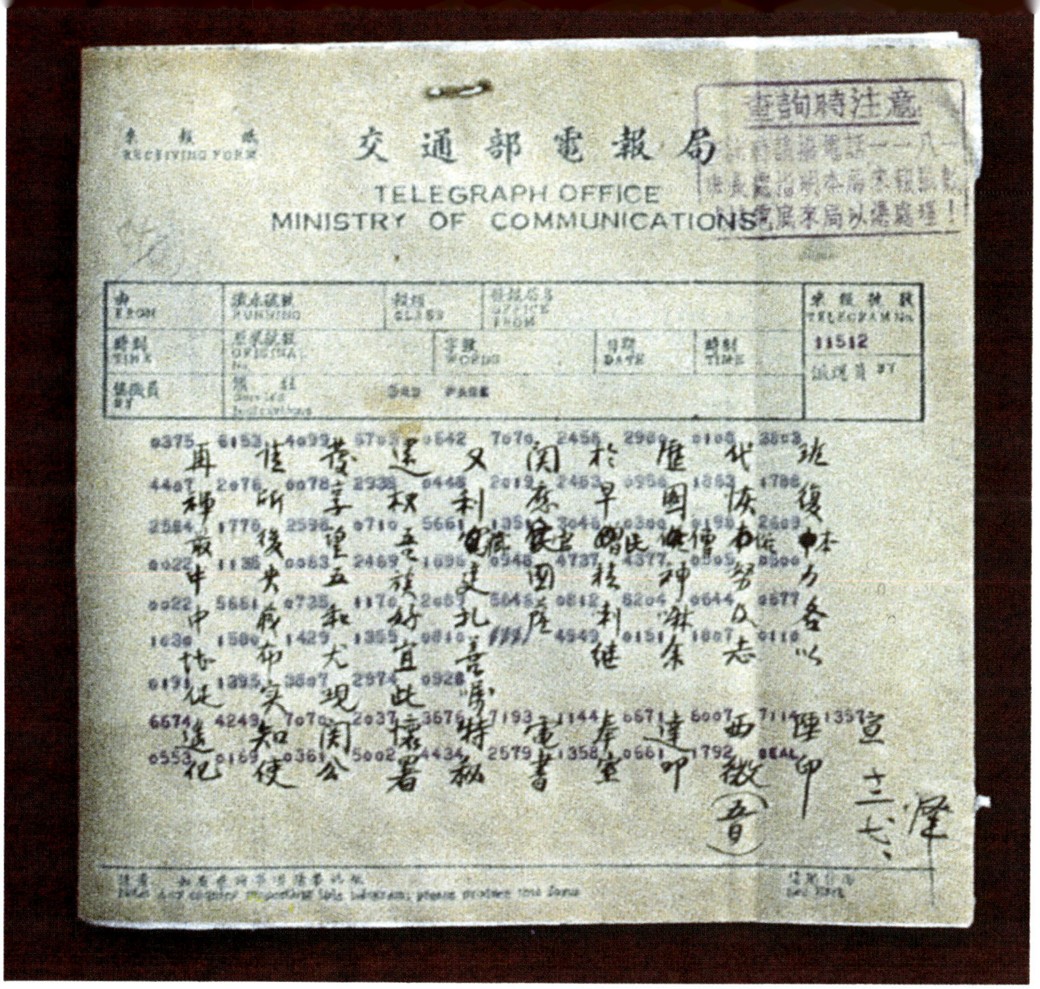

查詢時注意

交通部電報局

TELEGRAPH OFFICE

MINISTRY OF COMMUNICATIONS

來報紙

RECEIVING FORM

| 由 FROM | 流水號數 RUNNING | 報類 CLASS | 發報局名 OFFICE FROM | | 來報號數 TELEGRAM No. |
|---|---|---|---|---|---|
| 時刻 TIME | 原來號數 ORIGINAL No. | 字數 WORDS | 日期 DATE | 時刻 TIME | 11512 |
| 送報員 BY | 第 頁 | 3RD PAGE | | | 抄錄員 BY |

再佳誉逯又阅於雁代班

神所享权利庶早国恢復

[illegible]

中央五族建国精神努力

中藏和好礼庶利渊及各

協布尤宜喜继承志以

促实现此愿

逯知阅怀特电奉达西陲宣

化使公署秘书室叩微印

十二、十七

86－4

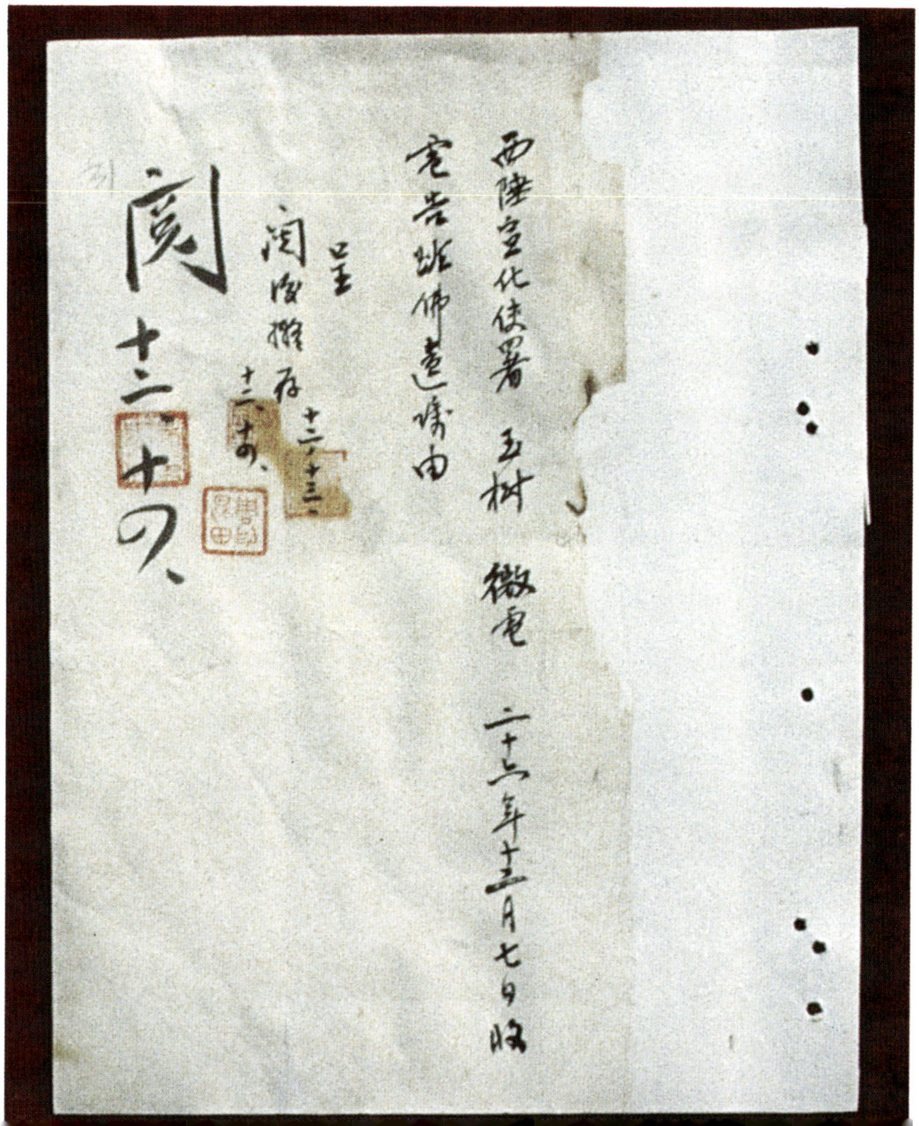

西陲宣化使署 玉树 微电

电告班佛逝世情由

二十六年十二月七日收

呈

阅后掷存

十二、十三

十二、十四

阅

十二、十八

ཀོ་མིང་སྲིད་གཞུང་གིས་ཝུ་ཀྲུང་ཤིན་ཆེད་དུ་མངགས་ནས་རྭ་སྒྲེང་དང་མཉམ་དུ་ཏཱ་ལའི་བླ་མ་འཁྲུངས་པའི་ལས་དོན་གྱི་གཙོ་འགན་འཁུར་དགོས་སྐོར་བསྒྲལ་པའི་བཀའ།

國民政府特派吳忠信會同熱振主持達賴喇嘛轉世事宜令

Decree from the National Government Dispatching Wu Zhongxin to Join Ragreng in Presiding Over the Reincarnation of the 14th Dalai Lama

28.2 × 20.2

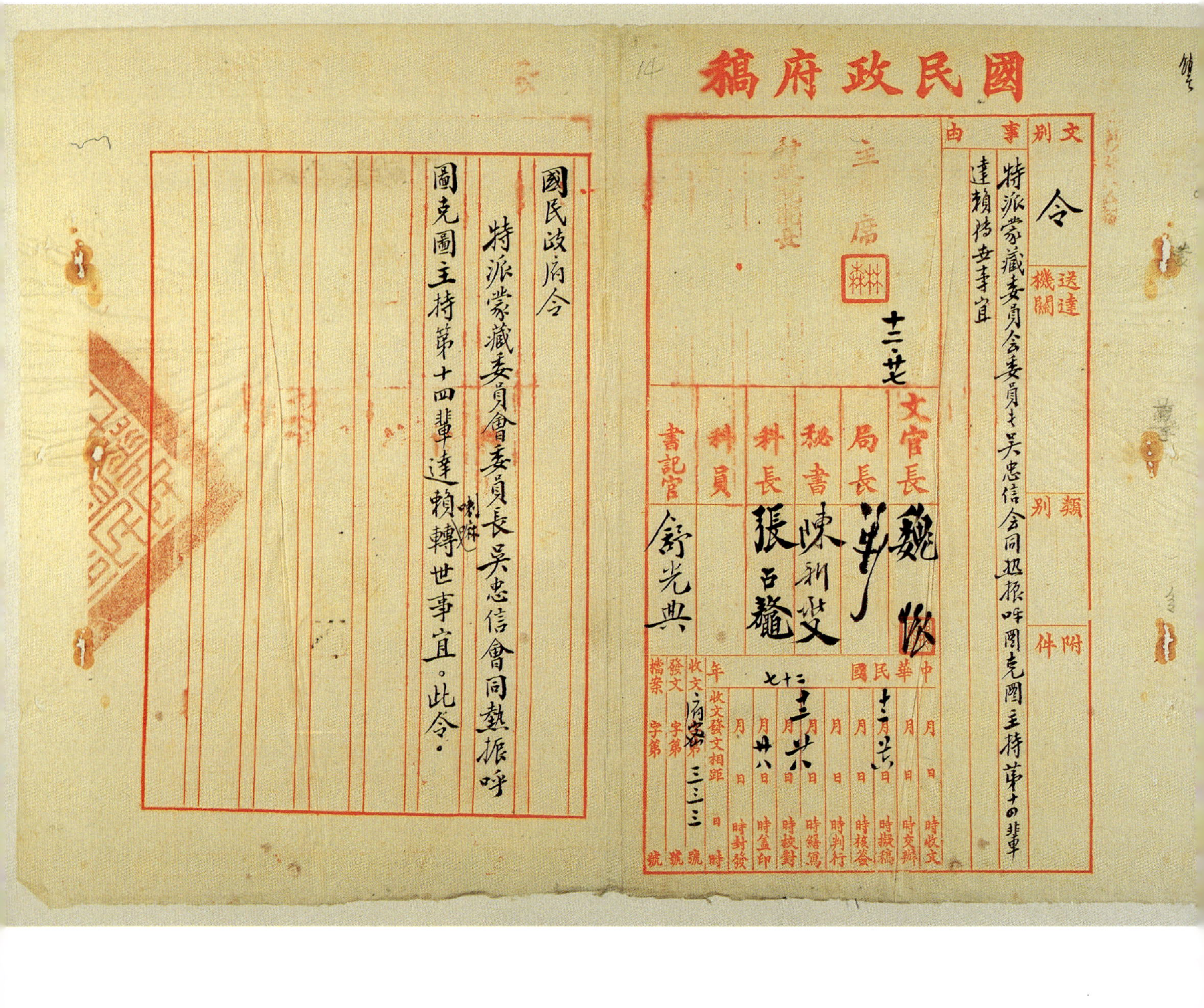

གོ་མིང་སྲིད་གཞུང་གི་བཀའ།

བོད་སོག་ཨུ་ཡོན་ལྷན་ཁང་གི་ཨུ་ཡོན་ཀྲང་ཝུ་ཀྲུང་ཞིན་ཆེད་མངགས་ཀྱིས་རྭ་སྒྲེང་ཧོ་ཐོག་ཐུ་དང་མཉམ་དུ་ཏཱ་ལའི་བླ་མ་སྐུ་ཕྲེང་བཅུ་བཞི་པ་འཁྲུངས་པའི་ལས་དོན་གྱི་གཙོ་འགན་འཁུར་རྒྱུའི་བཀའ་འདི་བསྒྲལ།

ཀྲུང་ཧྭ་མིང་གོའི་ལོ་ཉེར་བདུན་པ (སྤྱི་ལོ་༡༩༣༨) ཟླ་བ་བཅུ་གཉིས་པའི་ཚེས་ཉེར་བརྒྱད་ཉིན།

ཀྲུང་གོའི་ལོ་རྒྱུས་ཡིག་ཚགས་ཁང་ཨང་གཉིས་པར་ཉར་ཚགས་བྱས་ཡོད།

中國第二歷史檔案館藏

Decree from the National Government:

Wu Zhongxin, Chairman of the Commitee for Mongolian and Tibetan Affairs, is being specially sent to join Living Buddha Ragreng in presiding over the reincarnation of the 14th Dalai Lama.

December 28, the 27th year of the Republic of China (1938)

Preserved by China No. 2 Historical Archives.

# གོ་མིང་སྲིད་གཞུང་གིས་ཝུ་ཀྲུང་ཞིན་ཆེད་དུ་མངགས་ཏེ་ར་སྒྲེང་དང་མཉམ་དུ་ཏཱ་ལའི་བླ་མ་འཁྲུངས་པའི་ལས་དོན་གྱི་གཙོ་འགན་འཁུར་དགོས་སྐོར་སྲིད་འཛིན་ཁང་ལ་བསྐུལ་པའི་བཀའ།

# 國民政府爲特派吳忠信會同熱振主持達賴喇嘛轉世事致行政院指令

# Decree of the National Government to the Executive Yuan on the Dispatch of Wu Zhongxin to Preside Over the Reincarnation of the Dalai Lama Together with Ragreng

28.2 × 20.2

སྲིད་འཛིན་ཁང་ལ་བཀའ་བསྐུལ་བ།

ལོ་ཉེར་བདུན་པའི་ཟླ་བ་བཅུ་གཉིས་པའི་ཚེས་ཉེར་བཞི་ཉིན་ཕུལ་བའི་དབྱུ་ཡིག་ཨང་༡༠༦༦༤པ་ལས། རང་ཁང་གི་ཚོགས་འདུས་བོད་སོག་ཨུ་ཡོན་ལྷན་ཁང་གི་ཨུ་ཡོན་ཀྲང་ཝུ་ཀྲུང་ཞིན་ཆེད་དུ་བཏང་ནས་ར་སྒྲེང་ཧོ་ཐོག་ཐུ་དང་མཉམ་དུ་ཏཱ་ལའི་བླ་མ་སྐུ་ཕྲེང་བཅུ་བཞི་པ་འཁྲུངས་པའི་ལས་དོན་གྱི་གཙོ་འགན་འཁུར་རྒྱུར་གྲོས་ཐག་བཅད་དོན་དུ་ཆེད་མངགས་ཚོག་པའི་བཀའ་གསལ་པོ་སྩོལ་འཚལ་ཞེས་པའི་ཞུ་ཡིག་ལག་འབྱོར་བྱུང་བ་དང་། ཆེད་དུ་མངགས་པའི་བཀའ་གསལ་པོ་བཏང་ཚར་བས་ཁྱོད་ཚོ་ནས་ངེས་དགོས་པའི་བཀའ་འདི་བསྐུལ།

ཀྲུང་ཧྭ་མིང་གོའི་ལོ་ཉེར་བདུན་པ(སྤྱི་ལོ་༡༩༣༨)ཟླ་བ་བཅུ་གཉིས་པའི་ཚེས་ཉེར་བརྒྱད་ཉིན།

ཀྲུང་གོའི་ལོ་རྒྱུས་ཡིག་ཚགས་ཁང་ཨང་གཉིས་པར་ཉར་ཚགས་བྱས་ཡོད།

中國第二歷史檔案館藏

Decree to the Executive Yuan

Ref: Your report (Chongqing Document No. 10664) dated December 24 of the 27th year

It was decided at the meeting of the Executive Yuan to dispatch Wu Zhongxin, Chairman of the Committee for Mongolian and Tibetan Affairs, for the mission of presiding over the reincarnation of the 14th Dalai Lama together with Living Buddha Ragreng.

We have received your report and we have already dispatched Mr. Wu for this mission by special decree.

December 28, the 27th year of the Republic of China (1938)

Preserved by China No. 2 Historical Archives.

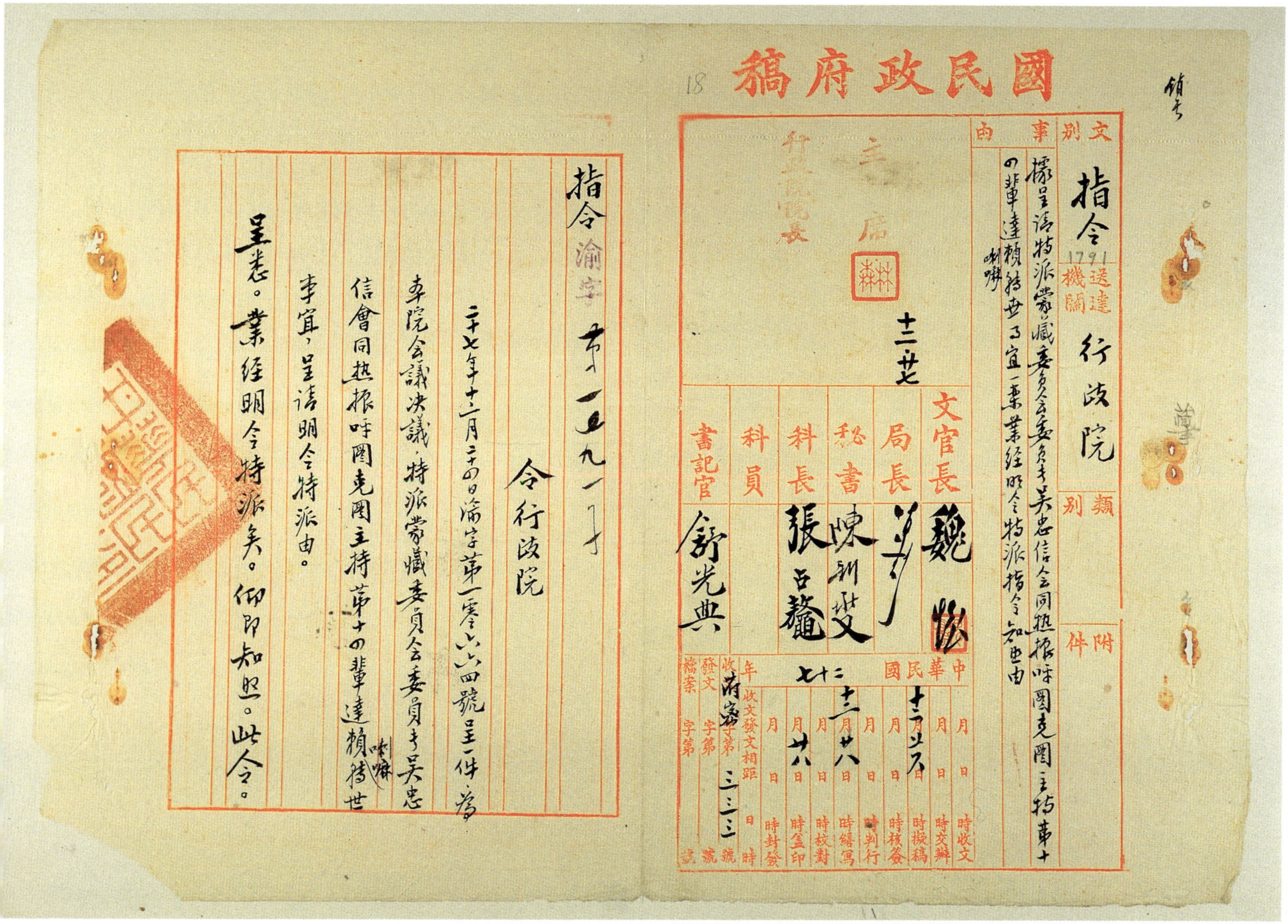

國民政府稿

| 文別 | 指令 |
| --- | --- |
| 送達機關 | 行政院 |
| 事由 | 據呈請特派蒙藏委員会委員吴忠信会同热振呼圖克圖主持第十四辈達賴轉世事宜一案，業經明令特派，指令知照由 |

主席 林（印） 十二.廿七

行政院院長

| 文官長 | 局長 | 秘書 | 科長 | 科員 | 書記官 |
| --- | --- | --- | --- | --- | --- |
| 魏懷 | | 陳訓畬 | 張占鼇 | | 舒光典 |

中華民國二十七年　收文 十二月廿六日　十二月廿八日　廿八日

收文府密字第三三三三號

指令渝字第一五九一一号

令行政院

二十七年十二月二十四日渝字第一零六六四號呈一件，為本院会議決議，特派蒙藏委員会委員吴忠信會同热振呼圖克圖主持第十四辈達賴轉世事宜，呈請明令特派由。

呈悉。業經明令特派矣。仰即知照。此令。

88－1

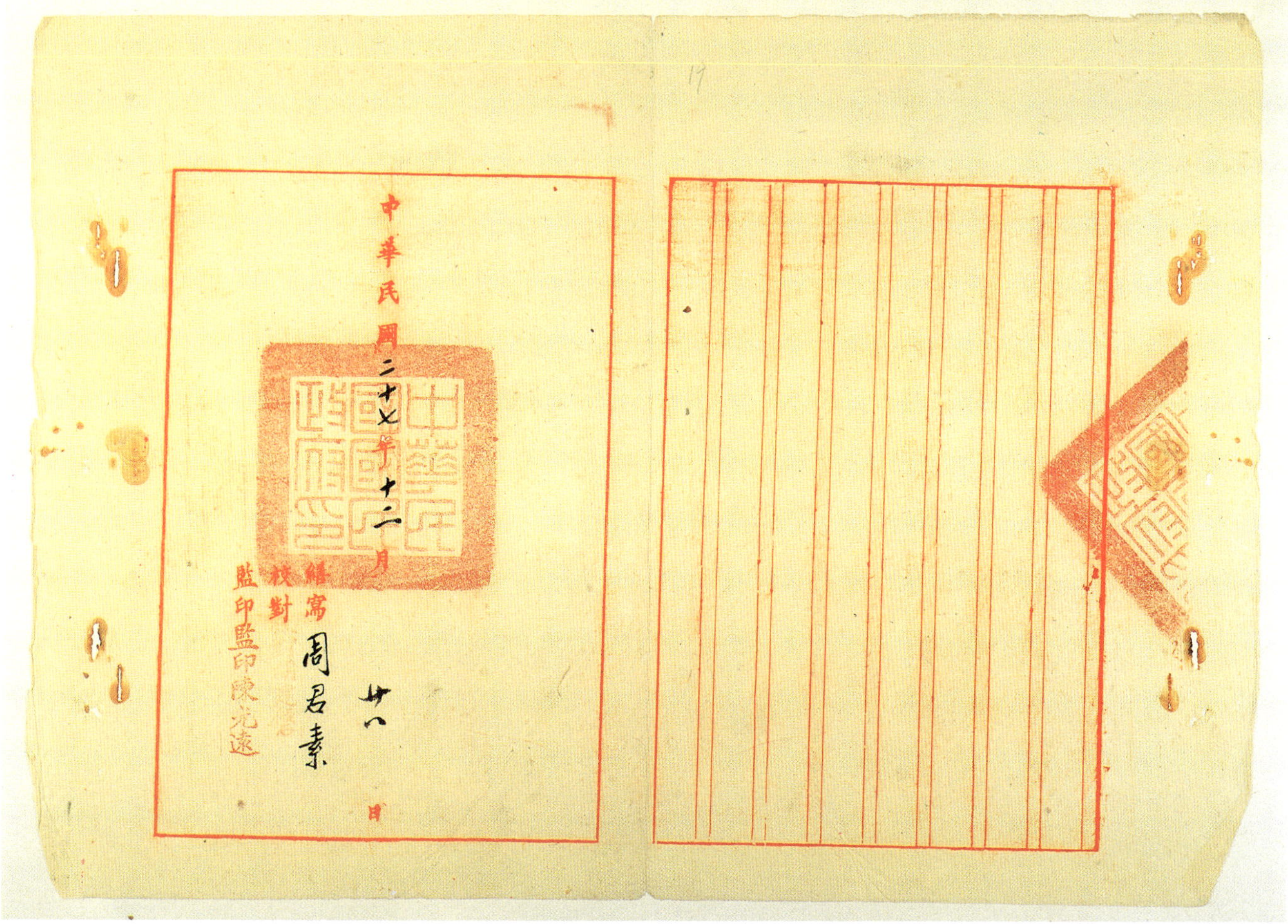

中華民國二十七年十二月廿八日

繕寫　周君素
校對
監印　監印陳光遠

88－2

## གོ་མིང་སྲིད་གཞུང་གིས་ལྷ་མོ་དོན་གྲུབ་མཆོག་ཏཱ་ལའི་བླ་མ་སྐུ་ཕྲེང་བཅུ་བཞི་པར་ངོས་འཛིན་བྱུང་བའི་དོན་དུ་བཏང་བའི་བཀའ།

## 國民政府就認定拉木登珠爲第十四世達賴喇嘛事發布的命令命令

## The Decree of the National Government Confirming Lhamo Dongrub as the 14th Dalai Lama

28.2 × 20.2

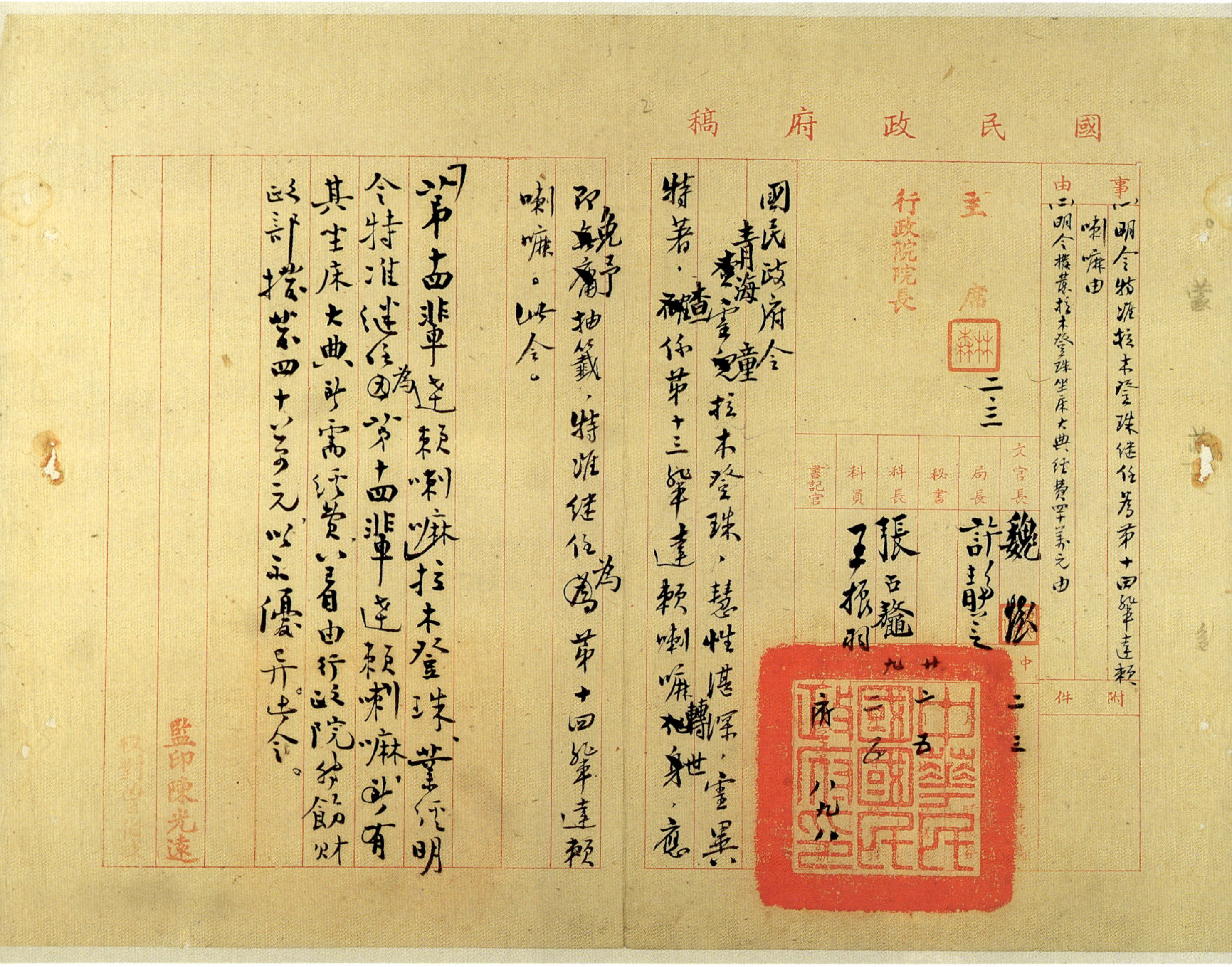

གོ་མིང་སྲིད་གཞུང་གི་བཀའ།

མཚོ་སྔོན་ནས་འཁྲུངས་པའི་ཡང་སྲིད་ལྷ་མོ་དོན་གྲུབ་མཆོག་ནི། ཤེས་རབ་ཟབ་མོ་ལྡན་ཞིང་བློ་རིག་ཁྱད་པར་དུ་འཕགས་པ་ཞིག་ཡིན་པ་ཁྱིད་རང་ཏཱ་ལའི་བླ་མ་བཅུ་གསུམ་པའི་ཡང་སྲིད་ཡིན་པར་ཞིབ་འཇུག་བཏང་ཟིན་པས། གསེར་བུམ་དཀྲུགས་མི་དགོས་པར་བྱས་ཏེ་ཏཱ་ལའི་བླ་མ་སྐུ་ཕྲེང་བཅུ་བཞི་པར་དམིགས་བསལ་གྱི་བསྐོ་བཞག་ཆོག་མཆན་བཀོད་པའི་བཀའ་འདི་བསྒྲལ།

"ཏཱ་ལའི་བླ་མ་སྐུ་ཕྲེང་བཅུ་བཞི་པ" ལྷ་མོ་དོན་གྲུབ་མཆོག་ལ་བཀའ་གསལ་པོས་ཏཱ་ལའི་བླ་མ་སྐུ་ཕྲེང་བཅུ་བཞི་པར་ཆེད་དུ་བསྐོ་བཞག་ཡོད་པ་ཁོང་གསེར་ཁྲི་མངའ་གསོལ་གྱི་འགྲོ་སྣོའི་གྲོན་དངུལ་ཚང་མ་སྲིད་འཛིན་ཁང་གིས་ནོར་སྲིད་ཕྱུའུ་ནས་སྐོར་འབུམ་ཕྲག་བཞི་སྤྲོད་དུ་བཅུག་སྟེ། དམིགས་བསལ་གྱི་ཐུགས་འཁུར་བྱས་པ་མཚོན་བྱེད་ཀྱི་བཀའ་འདི་བསྒྲལ་ཏོ། །

ཀྲུང་ཧྭ་མིང་གོའི་ལོ་ཉེར་དགུ་པ（སྤྱི་ལོ་༡༩༤༠）ཟླ་བ་གཉིས་པའི་ཚེས་གསུམ་ཉིན།

ཀྲུང་གོའི་ལོ་རྒྱུས་ཡིག་ཚགས་ཁང་ཨང་གཉིས་པར་ཉར་ཚགས་བྱས་ཡོད།

中國第二歷史檔案館藏

The National Government decrees:

The Holy Child Lhamo Dongrub from Qinghai is profoundly intelligent and an extraordinary person. Now that the 13th incarnation of the Dalai Lama is no longer with us, the drawing of the lots is to be done away with and special approval is granted for you to become the 14th Dalai Lama.

The Ministry of Finance, in line with instructions from the Executive Yuan, is allotting 400,000 yuan to you to cover the expense of the enthronement ceremony.

February 3, 1940

Preserved by China No. 2 Historical Archives.

ཏཻ་ཁྲིན་ཞན་གྱིས་ལྷ་མོ་དོན་གྲུབ་ཏཱ་ལའི་བླ་མ་སྐུ་ཕྲེང་བཅུ་བཞི་པར་ངོས་འཛིན་བྱུང་བའི་དོན་དུ་ར་སྒྲེང་ལ་བཏང་བའི་རྟེན་འབྲེལ་ཞུ་བའི་དཔར།

# 戴傳賢爲祝賀拉木登珠被認定爲第十四世達賴喇嘛事致熱振電

# Dai Chuanxian′s Telegram to Ragreng Congratulating Lhamo Dongrub on His Being Confirmed as the 14th Dalai Lama

28.2 × 20.2

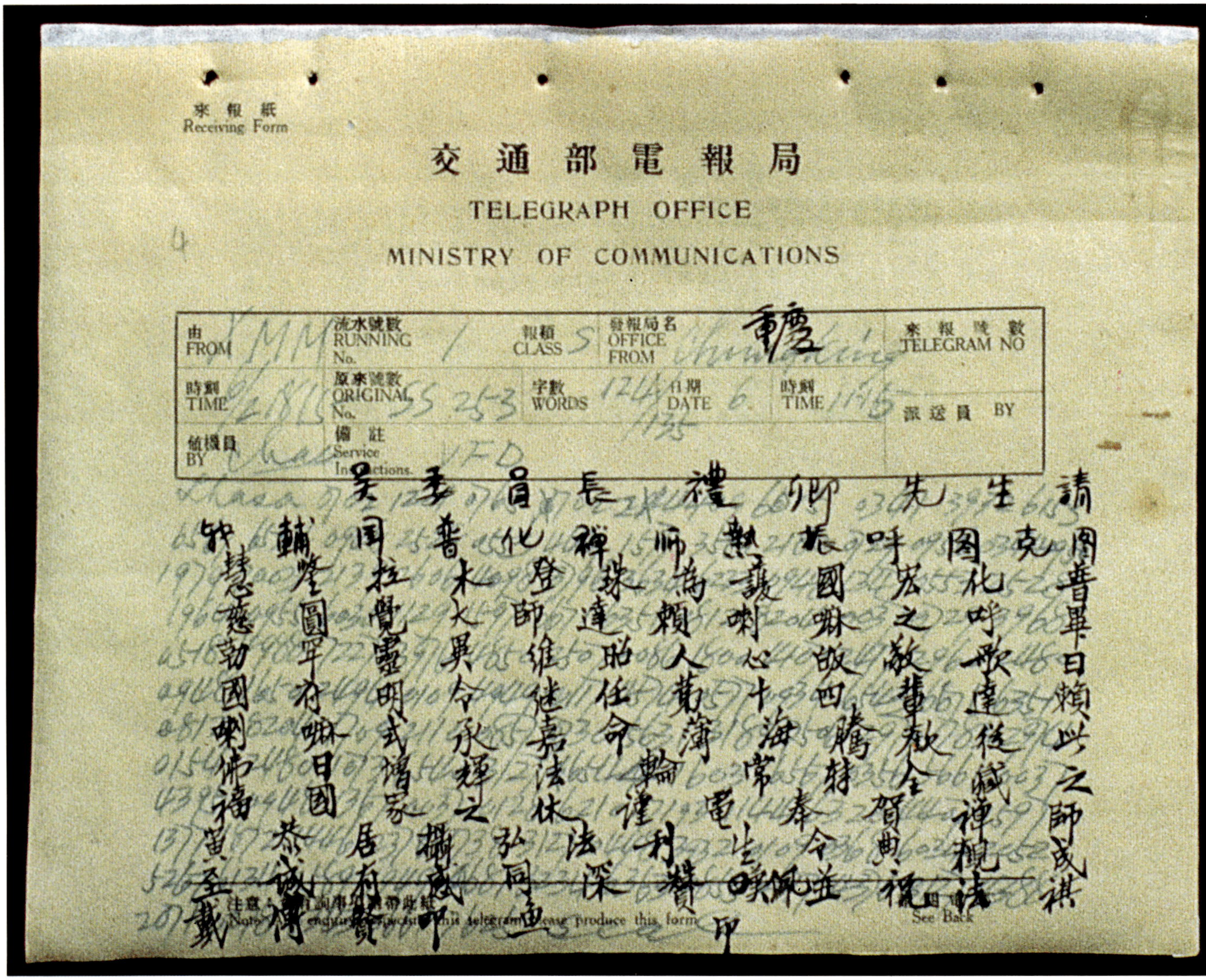

來報紙
Receiving Form

交通部電報局
TELEGRAPH OFFICE
MINISTRY OF COMMUNICATIONS

由 FROM | 流水號數 RUNNING No. | 報類 CLASS | 發報局名 OFFICE FROM | 來報號數 TELEGRAM NO
時刻 TIME | 原來號數 ORIGINAL No. | 字數 WORDS | 日期 DATE | 時刻 TIME | 派送員 BY
値機員 BY | 備註 Service Instructions.

吳委員長禮卿先生

注意：如有查詢事項，須帶此紙
Note: Any enquiry respecting this telegram please produce this form
See Back

90－1

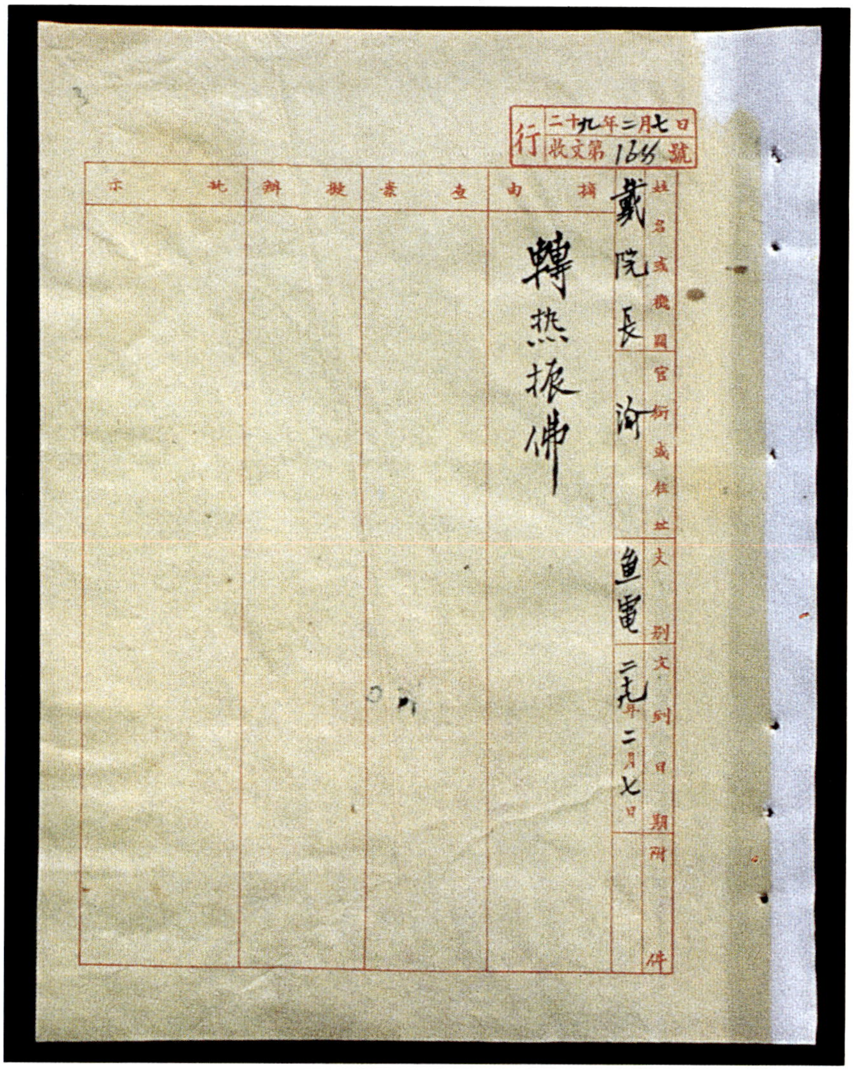

行 二十九年二月七日
收文第1644號

| 姓名或機關官銜或住址 | 文別 | 文到日期 | 附件 |
| --- | --- | --- | --- |
| 戴院長 洽 | 魚電 | 二九年二月七日 | |

| 摘由 | 擬辦 | 批示 |
| --- | --- | --- |
| 轉熱振佛 | | |

ལྷ་སར། ཕྲུ་ཤུ་ཡོན་ཀྲང་ལི་ཆེན་སྐུ་ཞབས་ལགས་རྒྱུད་ནས་རྒྱལ་ཁབ་རོགས་བྱེད་འགྲོ་བ་ཀུན་འདུལ་བསམ་གཏན་གྱི་སློབ་དཔོན་ར་སྒྲེང་ཧོ་ཐོག་ཐུ་ཡི་ཆོས་ཀྱི་མདུན་སར།

ལྷ་མོ་དོན་གྲུབ་མཆོག་ནི་རྒྱལ་ཁབ་སྐྱོང་ཞིང་སྙིང་རྗེ་རྒྱ་ཆེན་ཀུན་ལ་ཕན་སྡེར་ཐམས་ཅད་མཁྱེན་པ་འགྲོ་མགོན་ཆེན་མོ་ཏཱ་ལའི་བླ་མའི་ཡང་སྲིད་ཡིན་ལ། བློ་རིག་རབ་ཏུ་གསལ་བ་དང་སྐྱེ་རྒྱུའི་སྐབས་གནས་སུ་ཕྱུར་པ་ཞིག་ཡིན་པས། གོ་མིང་སྲིད་གཞུང་ནས་ཆོས་ལྔ་ཉིན་ཏཱ་ལའི་བླ་མ་སྐུ་ཕྲེང་བཅུ་བཞི་པ་རྒྱུད་འཛིན་བྱེད་དུ་བཅུག་པའི་བཀའ་གསལ་པོ་བསྒྲལ་པས་ས་ཕྱོགས་ཀུན་ཏུ་དགའ་སྤྲོའི་རྣམ་པ་ཁེངས་པ་ནས་བཟུང་། སངས་རྒྱས་ཀྱི་ཉི་མའི་འོད་ཟེར་ཇི་ཆེར་འཕྲོ་ཞིང་ཆོས་ཀྱི་འཁོར་ལོ་རྟག་ཏུ་བསྐོར་བར་འགྱུར་བ་འདི་ནི་བོད་ཡོངས་ཀྱི་བདེ་སྐྱིད་ཡིན་ལ། རྒྱལ་ཁབ་ཀྱི་བསོད་ནམས་ཀྱང་ཡིན་པར་བརྟེན། རྟེན་འབྲེལ་ཞུ་བའི་གློག་འཕྲིན་འདི་ཕྲུལ། བསམ་གཏན་གྱི་སློབ་དཔོན་ཉིད་ནས་དད་གུས་ཆེན་པོའི་ངང་སྲིད་སྐྱོང་གི་ལས་དོན་བསྒྲུབས་པ་དང་སངས་རྒྱས་ཀྱི་ཆོས་རྒྱ་ཆེར་སྤེལ་བ། འགྲོ་ལ་ཕན་བཏགས་པ། ཁྲིམས་ལུགས་སྲུང་བའི་བྱས་རྗེས་གཟིངས་སུ་ཐོན་ཡོད་པས། སྙིང་ཐག་པ་ནས་དགའ་བའི་བཀུར་བསྟི་དང་བསྟོད་བསྔགས་ཞུ་རྒྱུ་མ་ཟད། ཁྱེད་ལ་བཀྲ་ཤིས་བདེ་ལེགས་ཞུ། །ཏེ་ཁྲིན་ཞན་ནས་གུས་ཕྱག་བཅས་ཆོས་དྲུག་ཉིན། ཐམ་ག་བརྒྱབ།

ཀྲུང་ཧྭ་མིང་གོའི་ལོ་ཉེར་དགུ་པ(སྤྱི་ལོ་༡༩༤༠)ཟླ་བ་གཉིས་པའི་ཆོས་དྲུག་ཉིན། ཐམ་ག་བརྒྱབ།

ཀྲུང་གོའི་ལོ་རྒྱུས་ཡིག་ཚགས་ཁང་ཨང་གཉིས་པར་ཉར་ཚགས་བྱས་ཡོད།

中國第二歷史檔案館藏

Lhasa, February 6, the 29th year of the Republic of China (1940)

To: Living Buddha Ragreng, the Great Master Who Assists in State Affairs and Disseminates Buddhism

c/o Chairman Wu Liqing

Lhamo Dongrub is the Holy Child of the Dalai Lama, the Great Master of Infinite Wisdom Who Protects the Country, Disseminates Buddhism and Spreads Benevolence. His well–known wisdom and moral integrity have won the respect and worship of the people. As decreed by the National Government on the 5th, he is to become the 14th Dalai Lama. Since receiving the auspicious decree, the whole region has been in a holiday mood. Hereafter, the spirit of Buddhism shall shine brighter than ever before and the Buddhist doctrines shall continue to pass from generation to generation. It is truly a double blessing for Tibet as well as the whole country. We hereby offer our sincere congratulations. With Master Yin Gong as the regent, both the religion and the people will benefit. We deeply appreciate the success and religious piety of the grand ceremony and convey our best wishes for Buddhism.

Sincerely yours,

Dai Chuanxian (seal)

Preserved by China No. 2 Historical Archives.

## ལྷོ་ཀྲུང་ཤིན་གྱིས་ཏཱ་ལའི་བླ་མ་གསེར་ཁྲིར་མངའ་གསོལ་སྐོར་གོ་མིང་སྲིད་གཞུང་གི་ཀྲུའུ་ཞི་སོགས་ལ་བཏང་བའི་ཏར།

## 吴忠信爲報達賴喇嘛坐床事致國民政府主席等電

## Wu Zhongxin's Telegram on the Enthronement Ceremony of the 14th Dalai Lama to the President of the National Government and the President of the Executive Yuan

28.2 × 20.2

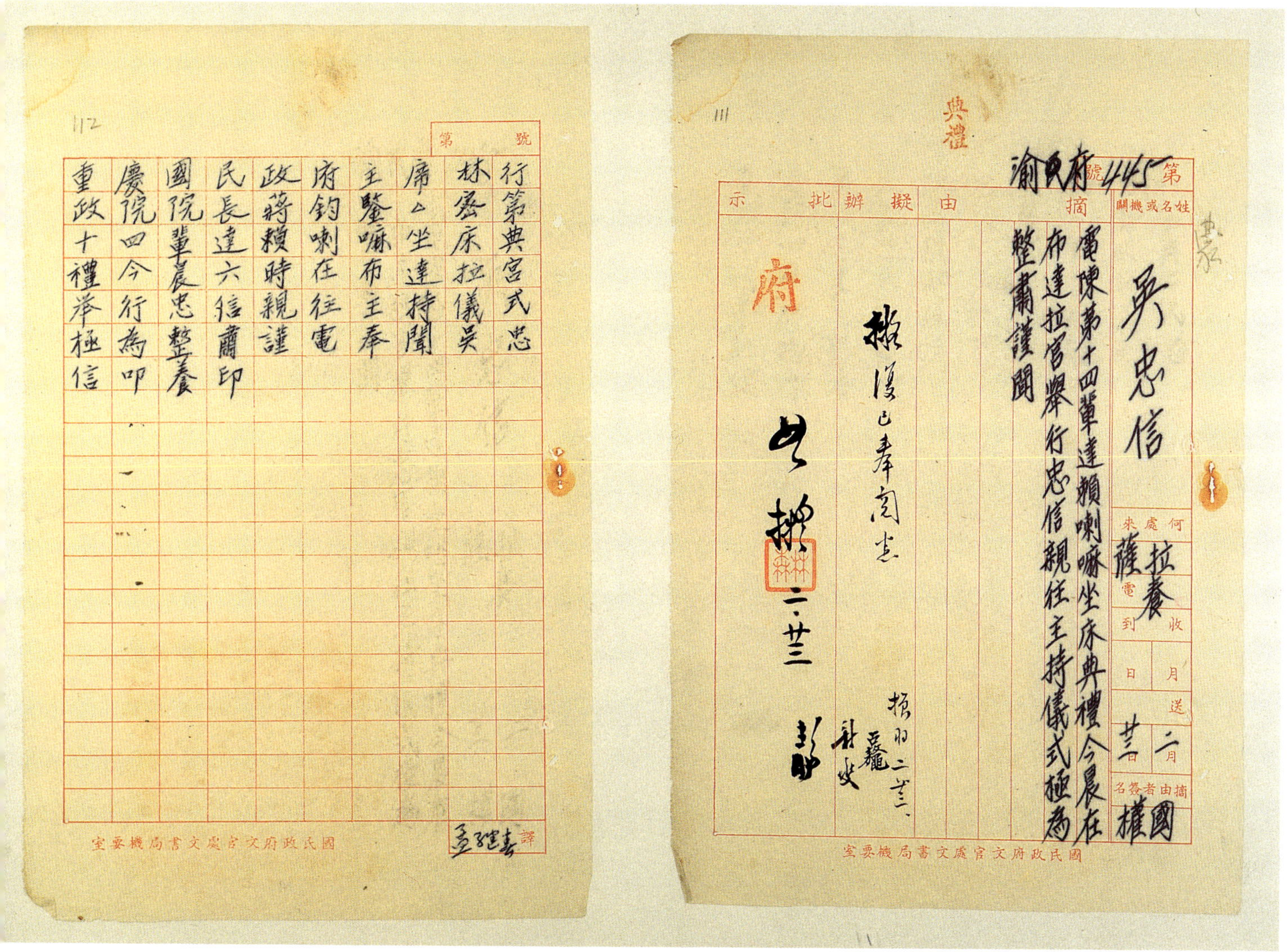
第 號
重慶國民政府主席林行
政院院長蔣鈞鑒ム密第
十四輩達賴喇嘛坐床典
禮今晨六時在布達拉宮
举行忠信親往主持儀式
極為整肅謹電奉聞吳忠
信叩養印
國民政府文官處文書局機要室

姓名或機關：吳忠信
摘由：電陳第十四輩達賴喇嘛坐床典禮今晨在布達拉宮舉行忠信親往主持儀式極為整肅謹聞
何處來：薩拉養電
收到：二月廿三日
第445號 渝民府
典禮
府
國民政府文官處文書局機要室

ཁྲུང་ཆིན་དུ། གོ་མིང་སྲིད་གཞུང་གི་ཀྲུའུ་ཞི་ལིན་དང་། སྲིད་འཛིན་ཁང་གི་ཡོན་ཀྲང་ཅང་མཆོག་གི་ཞབས་དྲུང་དུ།

གསང་བ། ཏཱ་ལའི་བླ་མ་སྐུ་ཕྲེང་བཅུ་བཞི་པ་གསེར་ཁྲི་མངའ་གསོལ་བའི་མཛད་སྒོ་དེ་རིང་ཞོགས་པའི་ཆུ་ཚོད་དྲུག་པ་ལ་ཕོ་བྲང་པོ་ཏ་ལར་སྲེལ། ཀྲུང་ཤིན་རང་ཉིད་དངོས་སུ་སོང་ནས་མཛད་སྒོའི་གཙོ་འགན་འཁུར་བ་ཡིན། མཛད་སྒོ་ནི་ཤིན་ཏུ་གཟབ་ནན་ཞིག་རེད། འདིར་གུས་པས་ཏར་ཡིག་བརྒྱུད་ནས་སྙན་སེང་ཞུ་བ་ཡིན། ཝུ་ཀྲུང་ཤིན་གྱིས་གུས་ཕྱག་བཅས་ཚེས་ཉེར་གཉིས་ཉིན་ཐམ་ཀ་བརྒྱབ།

ཀྲུང་ཧྭ་མིང་གོའི་ལོ་ཉེར་དགུ་པ (སྤྱི་ལོ་༡༩༤༠) ཟླ་བ་གཉིས་པའི་ཚེས་ཉེར་གཉིས་ཉིན།

ཀྲུང་གོའི་ལོ་རྒྱུས་ཡིག་ཚགས་ཁང་ཨང་གཉིས་པར་ཉར་ཚགས་བྱས་ཡོད།

中國第二歷史檔案館藏

Chongqing, February 22, the 29th year of the Republic of China (1940)

To: Mr Lin, President of the National Government and Mr Jiang, President of the Executive Yuan

Confidential. The Enthronement Ceremony of the 14th Dalai Lama was held at 6:00 A.M. today at the Potala Palace. Zhongxin presided over the solemn ceremony.

Sincerely yours,

Wu Zhongxin (seal)

Preserved by China No. 2 Historical Archives.

# ལྷ་མོ་དོན་གྲུབ་མཆོག་ནས་རང་ཉིད་ཏཱ་ལའི་བླ་མ་སྐུ་ཕྲེང་བཅུ་བཞི་པར་ངོས་འཛིན་བྱས་པར་གོ་མིང་སྲིད་གཞུང་ལ་བཏང་བའི་འཕྲིན་ལན།

# 拉木登珠就其被認定爲第十四世達賴喇嘛事致國民政府的覆函

# Reply to the National Government from Lhamo Dongrub Regarding His Being Confirmed as the 14th Dalai Lama

28.2 × 20.2

གྲུང་གོའི་ལོ་རྒྱུས་ཡིག་ཚགས་ཁང་ཨང་གཉིས་པར་ཉར་ཚགས་བྱས་ཡོད།

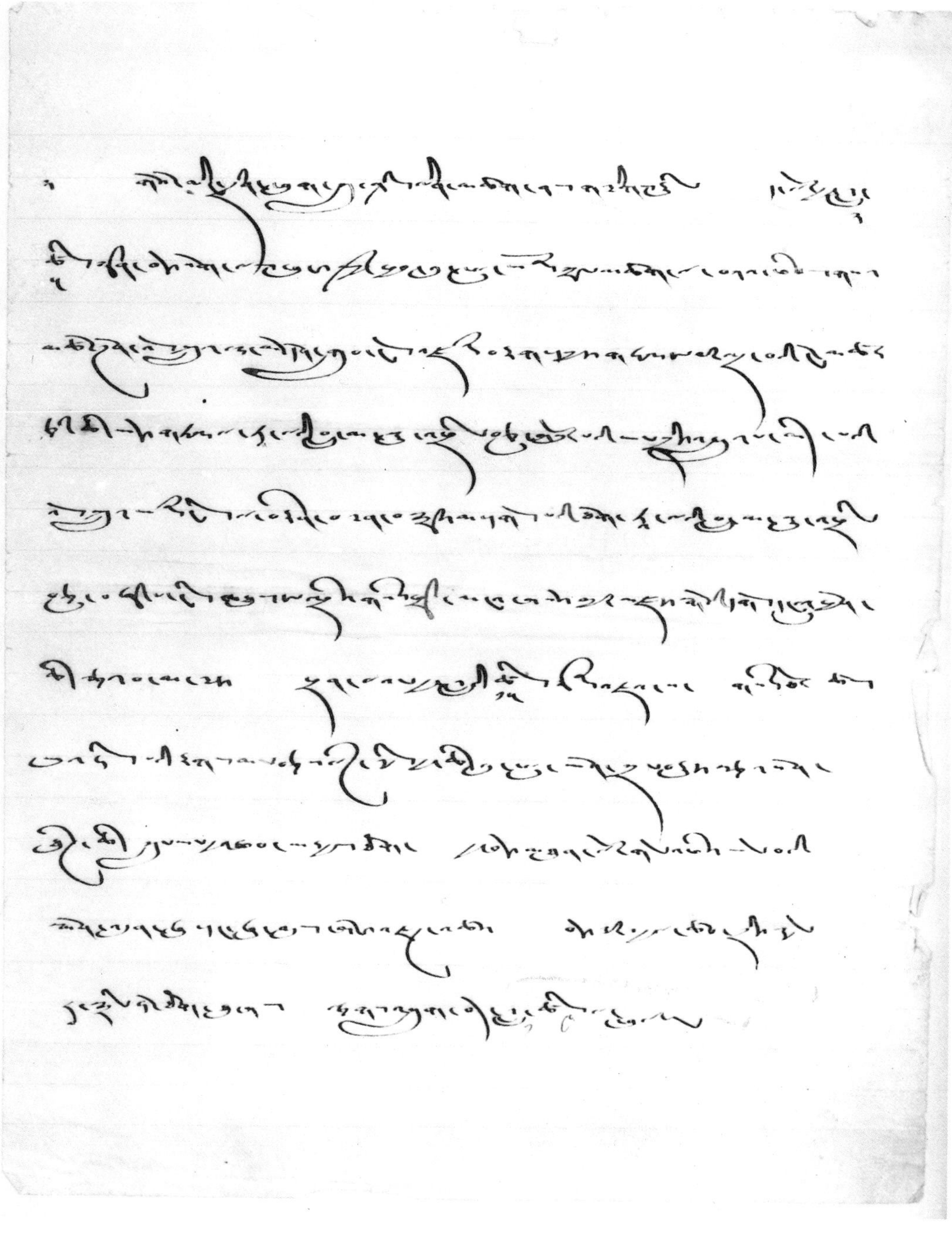

92－1

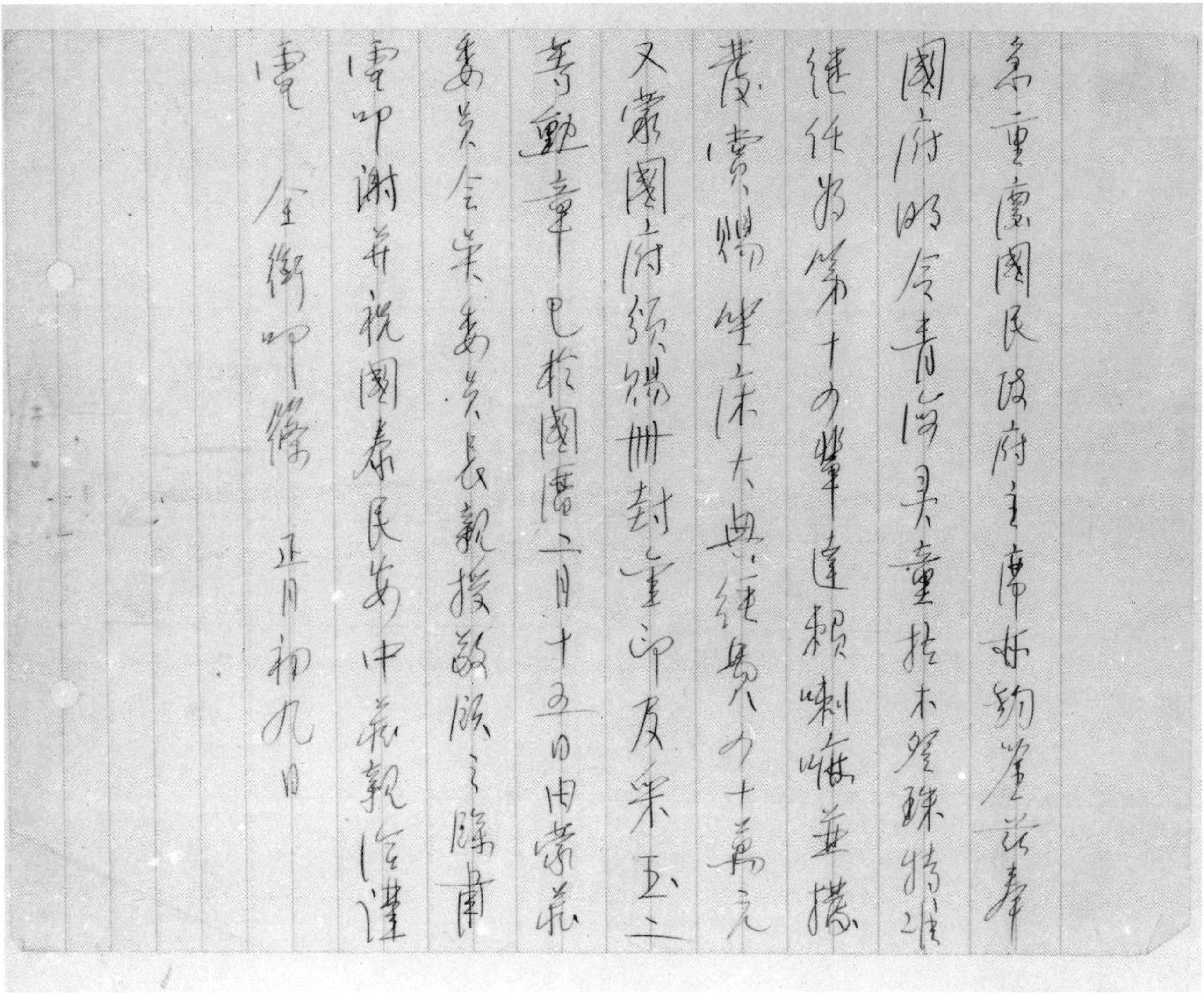
急重慶國民政府主席林鈞鑒蒙
國府明令青海靈童拉木登珠特准
繼任為第十四輩達賴喇嘛並撥
發慶賀坐床大典經費四十萬元
又蒙國府頒賜冊封金印及采玉二
等勳章已於國曆二月十五日由蒙藏
委員會吳委員長親授敬領之餘肅
電叩謝並祝國泰民安中藏親密謹
電　全銜叩佳　正月初九日

中國第二歷史檔案館藏

Urgent

President Lin of the Chongqing National Government,

I wish to express my humble thanks to you for the instructions issued by the National Government approving Lhamo Dongrub, the Holy Child from Qinghai, to become the 14th Dalai Lama, for the grant of 400,000 yuan to cover the expense of holding the enthronement ceremony, for the gold seal and for the Class II medal conferred on me by Chairman Wu of the Committee for Mongolian and Tibetan Affairs on February 15 of the national calendar.

In addition to expressing my gratitude, I also would like to express my desire to see our country prosper and our people able to live in peace, with the Han and Tibetan peoples maintaining friendly relations.

With best wishes,

The 9th day of the first month

Preserved by China No. 2 Historical Archives.

ཐུབ་བསྟན་བཟང་པོ་ལ་བསྩལ་བའི་གོ་མིང་ཚོགས་ཆེན་གྱི་འཐུས་མིའི་ལག་ཁྱེར།

向土丹桑布頒發的國民大會代表證書

National Assembly Delegate Credentials Issued to Thubtan Zangpo

37 × 31

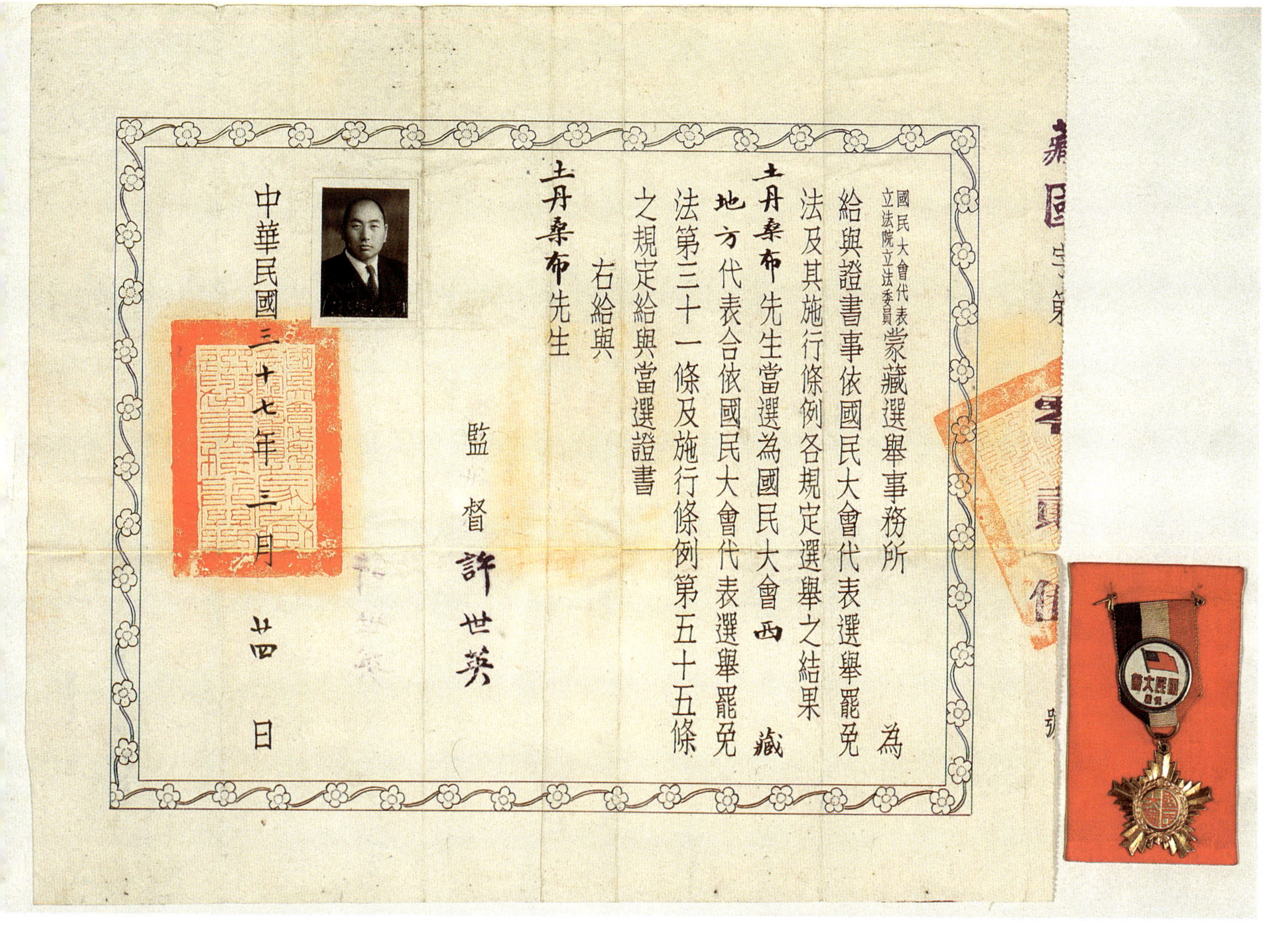

國民大會代表
立法院立法委員
蒙藏選舉事務所　為
給與證書事依國民大會代表選舉罷免
法及其施行條例各規定選舉之結果
土丹桑布先生當選為國民大會西藏
地方代表合依國民大會代表選舉罷免
法第三十一條及施行條例第五十五條
之規定給與當選證書
右給與
土丹桑布先生
監督　許世英
中華民國三十七年三月廿四日

གོ་མིང་ཚོགས་ཆེན་གྱི་འཐུས་མི་དང་ཁྲིམས་བཟོ་ཁང་གི་ཁྲིམས་བཟོ་ཨུ་ཡོན་བོད་སོག་འདེམས་བསྐོའི་ལས་དོན་ཁང་ལ།

ལག་ཁྱེར་སྟེར་བའི་དོན་དུ་གོ་མིང་ཚོགས་ཆེན་གྱི་འཐུས་མིའི་འདེམས་བསྐོའི་གོ་གནས་བསྐོ་འཛིན་གྱི་ཁྲིམས་ཡིག་དང་དེའི་ལག་བསྟར་གྱི་དོན་ཚན་ཁག་གི་གཏན་འབེབས་ལྟར་འདེམས་བསྐོ་བྱས་འབྲས་ལ། སྐུ་ཞབས་ཐུབ་བསྟན་བཟང་པོ་གོ་མིང་ཚོགས་ཆེན་གྱི་བོད་ས་གནས་ཀྱི་འཐུས་མིར་འདེམས་བསྐོ་བྱས། དེ་ནི་གོ་མིང་ཚོགས་ཆེན་གྱི་འཐུས་མི་འདེམས་བསྐོའི་གོ་གནས་བསྐོ་འཛིན་རྩ་ཁྲིམས་དོན་ཚན་སོ་གཅིག་པ་དང་དེའི་ལག་བསྟར་གྱི་དོན་ཚན་ང་ལྔ་པའི་"གཏན་འབེབས་དང་མཐུན་པས་ལག་ཁྱེར་སྐུ་ཞབས་ཐུབ་བསྟན་བཟང་པོར་སྤྲད་པ་ཡིན་ནོ། །

ལྟ་ཞིབ་པ། ཤུས་ཧྲི་དབྱིང་ནས།

ཀྲུང་ཧྭ་མིང་གོའི་ལོ་སོ་བདུན་པ (སྤྱི་ལོ་༡༩༤༨) ཟླ་བ་གསུམ་པའི་ཚེས་ཉེར་བཞི་ཉིན།

བོད་རང་སྐྱོང་ལྗོངས་ཡིག་ཚགས་ཁང་དུ་ཉར་ཚགས་བྱས་ཡོད།

西藏自治區檔案館藏

The Mongolian and Tibetan Electoral Affairs Office of the National Assembly Delegates and Legislative Yuan Members,

This is to certify that, as a result of the election held in accordance with the laws and regulations concerning election and recall of National Assembly delegates, Mr Thubtan Zangpo has been elected to represent the area of Tibet in the National Assembly. These credentials are issued to Mr Thubtan Zangpo in line with Article 31 of the Law Concerning Election and Recall of National Assembly Delegates and Article 55 of the related enforcement regulations.

Xu Shiying, Supervisor

March 24, the 37th year of the Republic of China (1948)

Preserved by the Archives of the Tibet Autonomous Region.

# བོད་སོག་ཨུ་ཡོན་ལྷན་ཁང་གིས་པཎ་ཆེན་ཨེར་ཏི་ནིའི་ཡང་སྲིད་གསེར་ཁྲིར་མངའ་གསོལ་བྱེད་རྒྱུའི་སྐོར་བཀའ་ཤག་ལ་བཏང་བའི་ཏར།
# 蒙藏委員會爲班禪靈童坐床事給噶厦公所的電函
# Telegram from the Committee for Mongolian and Tibetan Affairs (CMTA) to the Kashak Concerning the Enthronement Ceremony for the Holy Child Panchen

32×23, 36.2×26.5

བོད་རང་སྐྱོང་ལྗོངས་ཡིག་ཚགས་ཁང་དུ་ཉར་ཚགས་བྱས་ཡོད།

西藏自治區檔案館藏

From Mr Xu, Chairman, Committee for Mongolian and Tibetan Affairs,

To the *Kashak* (the local government of Tibet),

The telegram of July 22, 1948 from all the monks and laymen of the Tashilhunpo Monastery in Lower Tibet has been received. The succession and reincarnation of the Panchen are extremely important to the religious and political future of Tibet. The Central Government, which has the responsibility of maintaining Buddhism in Tibet, realizes that unless this matter is handled by the Central Government in the established way, people will not have faith in it, and even the slightest indiscretion will cause sharp disputes. That would certainly be unfortunate for the Tibetan people. Please fix a date for the lot–drawing ceremony as soon as possible in accordance with our telegram of January 29, the 36th year of the Republic of China (1947) and promptly inform the Central Government of the date, so that the Government can appoint an official of high rank to preside alongside the religious leaders in Tibet over the lot–drawing and enthronement ceremonies. The Central Government can also send someone to lead officials from Lower Tibet when they go to meet and escort the chosen Holy Child to Tibet. From Xu Shiying, Chairman of the Committee for Mongolian and Tibetan Affairs. Also cabled to you is a translation of this telegram.

To the *Kashak* (the local government of Tibet).

A translated copy is enclosed.

Relayed by Chen Xizhang,

Deputy Director and Acting

Director of the CMTA Office in Tibet

Preserved by the Archives of the Tibet Autonomous Region.

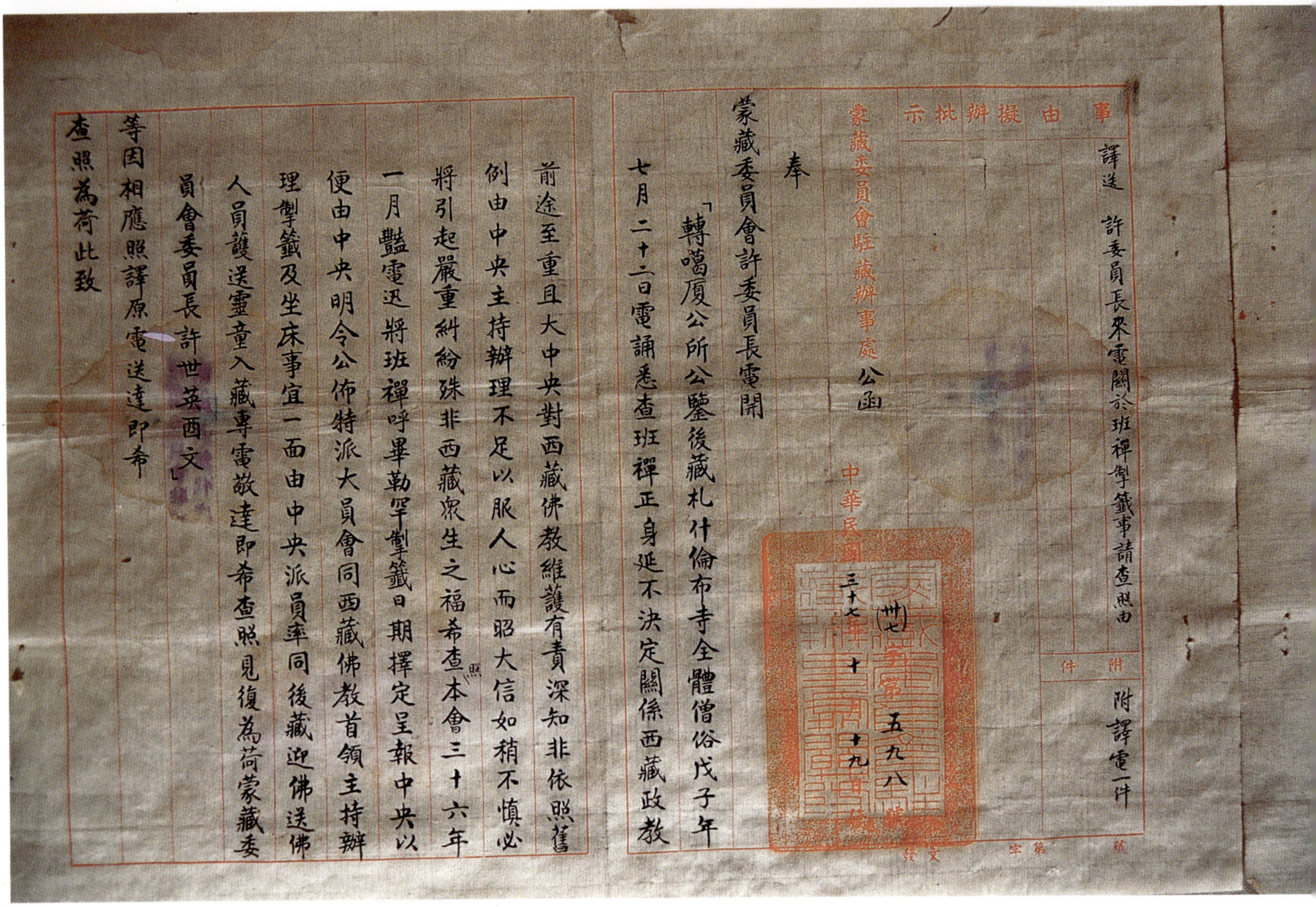

事由　擬辦　批示

譯送　許委員長來電關於班禪掣籤事請查照由

附件　附譯電一件

蒙藏委員會駐藏辦事處公函

中華民國三十七年十一月十九日　(卅七)藏字第五九八號

奉

蒙藏委員會許委員長電開

「轉噶廈公所公鑒後藏札什倫布寺全體僧俗戊子年七月二十二日電誦悉查班禪正身延不決定關係西藏政教前途至重且大中央對西藏佛教維護有責深知非依照舊例由中央主持辦理不足以服人心而昭大信如稍不慎必將引起嚴重糾紛殊非西藏衆生之福希查照本會三十六年一月豔電迅將班禪呼畢勒罕掣籤日期擇定呈報中央以便由中央明令公佈特派大員會同西藏佛教首領主持辦理掣籤及坐床事宜一面由中央派員率同後藏迎佛送佛人員護送靈童入藏專電敬達即希查照見復為荷蒙藏委員會委員長許世英酉文」

等因相應照譯原電送達即希

查照為荷此致

94 - 1

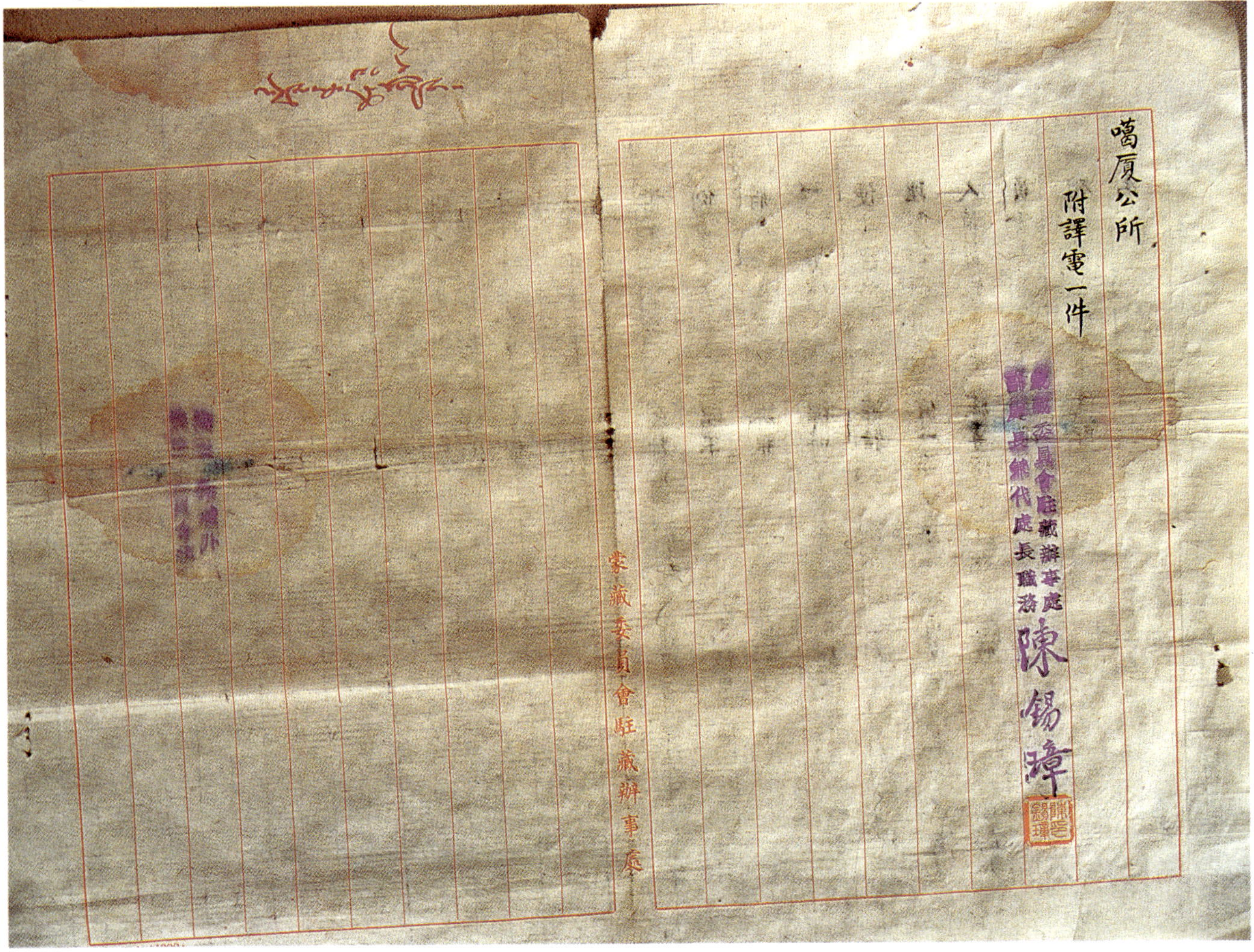

噶廈公所

附譯電一件

蒙藏委員會駐藏辦事處

副處長兼代處長職務陳錫璋

蒙藏委員會駐藏辦事處

94 - 2

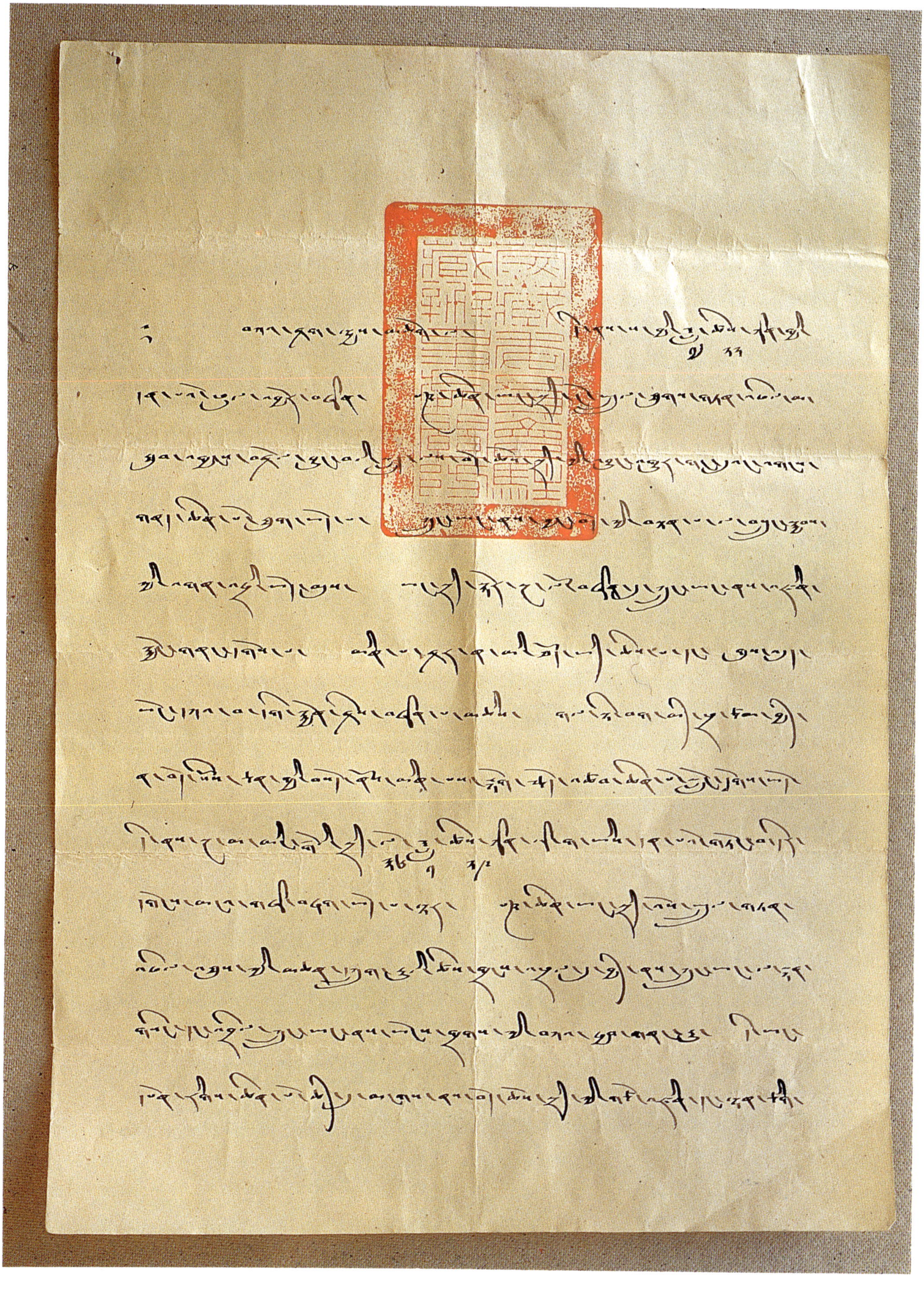

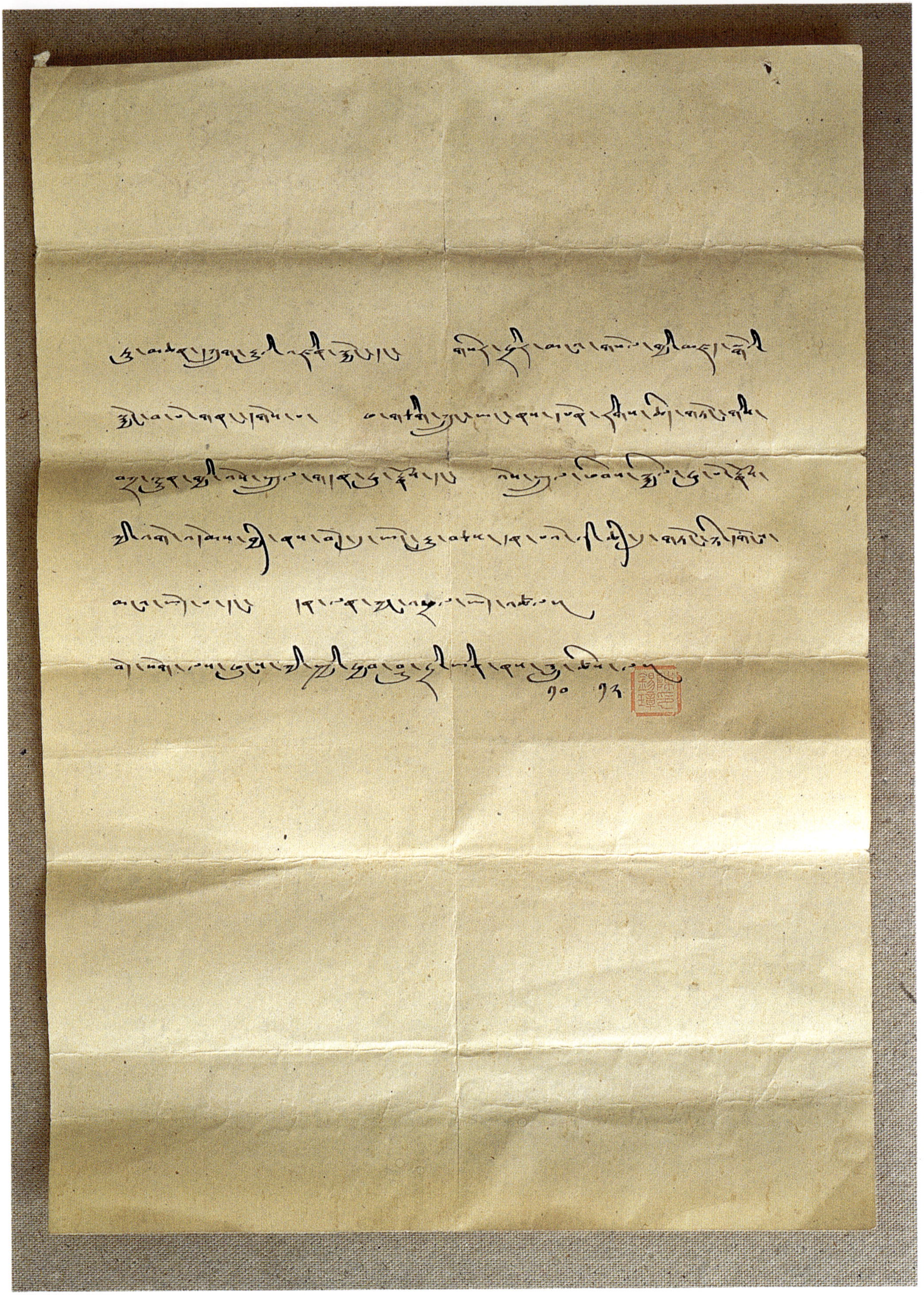

94 - 4

# ཙུང་ཐུང་ཁང་གིས་པཎ་ཆེན་ཨེར་ཏི་ནི་སྐུ་ཕྲེང་བཅུ་པས་ཕུལ་བའི་ཐུགས་རྗེ་ཆེ་ཞུས་པའི་ཏར་སྐོར་བོད་སོག་ཨུ་ཡོན་ལྷན་ཁང་ལ་བཏང་བའི་ཡི་གེ

# 總統府爲抄送十世班禪致謝電事給蒙藏委員會的箋函(附抄件)

# Letter from the Presidential Palace to the Committee for Mongolian and Tibetan Affairs Concerning Copying the 10th Panchen Erdeni's Telegram of Thanks

28.2 × 20.2

ཙུང་ཐུང་ལས་ཚབ་ཀྱིས་ཐེ་ལིང་པཎ་ཆེན་ཨེར་ཏི་ནི་སྐུ་ཕྲེང་བཅུ་པ་ནས་ཆོས་བཅུ་གཅིག་ཉིན་བཏང་བའི་ཏར་ཞིག་སྤྲོད་བྱུང་བའི་ནང་དོན་ནི་འཚམ་རྟགས་གནང་བར་ཐུགས་རྗེ་ཆེ་ཞུས་པ་དང་། ཀྲུང་དབྱང་ལ་བློ་ཁ་ཕྱོགས་པ་སོགས་བཀོད་ཡོད། ཡང་ཁོང་གིས་ཏར་ལན་བཏང་ནས་བསྐུལ་མ་གཏོང་དགོས་ཞེས་དང་། སྲིད་འཛིན་ཁང་དང་བོད་སོག་ལྷན་ཁང་ལ་བཤུས་འབུལ་ཕྱོས་ཞེས་བཀའ་གནང་བྱུང་བས་འདིར་ཕར་ཚུར་བཏང་བའི་ཏར་ཡིག་ཁག་ནས་འདྲ་མཚུངས་རེ་ཙེ་བཤུས་བྱས་ཏེ། བོད་སོག་ཨུ་ཡོན་ལྷན་ཁང་ལ་ཕུལ་བར་ཞིབ་དཔྱད་གནང་འཚལ་ལོ། །

ཙུང་ཐུང་ཁང་གི་ཙུས་གཉིས་པ་ནས།

ཀྲུང་ཧྭ་མིང་གོའི་ལོ་སོ་བརྒྱད་པ (སྤྱི་ལོ་༡༩༤༩) ཟླ་བ་བརྒྱད་པའི་ཚེས་བཅོ་བརྒྱད་ཉིན།

ནང་གསེས། བཤུས་མ་དང་པོ།

ཆེས་ཛ་དྲག ཀོང་ཀྲའུ། ཙུང་ཐུང་ལས་ཚབ་ལི་མཆོག་གི་ཞབས་དྲུང་དུ།

པཎ་ཆེན་བདག་གི་སྐྱེ་བའི་ཕྲེང་བར་རྒྱལ་ཁབ་ཀྱི་ཐུགས་རྗེ་དང་དམིགས་བསལ་གྱི་གཟིགས་སྐྱོང་བླ་མེད་ཐོབ་ཀྱིན་ཡོད་པ་དང་། ཐེངས་འདིར་ཡང་ཙུང་ཐུང་ལས་ཚབ་ལི་མཆོག་ནས་པཎ་ཆེན་སྐུ་ཕྲེང་དགུ་པའི་ཆོས་བརྒྱུད་རྒྱུན་འཛིན་ཆོག་པའི་དམིགས་བསལ་གྱི་བཀའ་གསལ་པོ་བསྩལ་པ་མ་ཟད། ཀོན་ཧྲི་ཡུས་དང་ཀྲ་ཧྲུ་ཧྲང་གཉིས་ཆེད་མངགས་པོ་ཉ་རྣན་གཞོན་བྱས་ནས་མངགས་རྫོངས་ཀྱིས་མཚོ་སྔོན་དུ་ཕེབས་ཏེ་གསེར་ཁྲིར་མངའ་གསོལ་གྱི་མཛད་སྒོའི་གཙོ་འགན་འཁུར་བ་དང་རྩ་ཆེ་བའི་གནང་སྐྱེས་བཟང་པོ་གསོལ་རས་སུ་བསྩལ་པ་དེ་དག་གུས་པས་དང་ལེན་ཞུས་པ་དང་སེམས་འགུལ་ཆེན་པོ་ཡང་ཐོབ་བྱུང་། ཟླ་བ་བརྒྱད་པའི་ཚེས་བཅུ་ཉིན་སྐུ་འབུམ་དགོན་དུ་གསེར་ཁྲིར་མངའ་གསོལ་གྱི་མཛད་སྒོ་སྒྲིལ། འབྱུང་འགྱུར་བློ་གཅིག་སེམས་གཅིག་གིས་པཎ་ཆེན་སྐུ་ཕྲེང་རིམ་བྱོན་གྱིས་ཐོག་མཐའ་བར་གསུམ་དུ་ཀྲུང་དབྱང་ལ་བློ་ཁ་ཕྱོགས་པ་དང་། འགྲོ་ཀུན་སྐྱབས་འོག་ལས་མི་འདོར་བའི་དགོངས་འདུན་ལ་བརྩི་སྲུང་ཞུས་ཏེ་འབད་བརྩོན་ཆེན་པོས་ལས་འགན་གང་ལེགས་བསྒྲུབ་ནས་གཟིགས་སྐྱོང་གུས་བཀུར་དང་ཐུགས་འཁྲུར་བླ་མེད་གནང་བར་བཀའ་དྲིན་འཇལ་རྒྱུའི་རེ་སྨྲུག་བྱ་རྒྱུ། ཏར་འདི་ཕུལ་ནས་ཐུགས་རྗེ་ཆེ་ཞུ་རྒྱུ་དང་། གུས་བཏུད་དང་བཅས་གང་ཉིད་སྐུ་ཁམས་བདེ་ཐང་ཡོང་བའི་སྨོན་འདུན་ཞུའོ། །

པཎ་ཆེན་ཨེར་ཏི་ནི་སྐུ་ཕྲེང་བཅུ་པས་ཆོས་བཅུ་གཅིག་ཉིན་གུས་ཕྱག་དང་བཅས་ཐམ་ཀ་བརྒྱབ།

ནང་གསེས། བཤུས་མ་གཉིས་པ།

ཐེ་ལིང་། པཎ་ཆེན་ཨེར་ཏི་ནིའི་ཆོས་ཀྱི་མདུན་སར།

གསང་བ། ཆོས་བཅུ་གཅིག་ཉིན་གྱི་ཏར་ལ་བལྟས་ཟིན་པས་ནང་དོན་ཞིབ་རྟོགས་བྱུང་། གསེར་ཁྲིར་མངའ་གསོལ་མཛད་སྒོ་ཆེན་པོ་ལེགས་པར་བསྒྲུབས་ཟིན་པས་དགའ་སྤྲོ་དང་སེམས་གསོ་ཚད་ལས་འདས་པ་བྱུང་། དམ་ཆོས་རྒྱ་ཆེར་སྤེལ་བ་དང་། ཚུལ་ཁྲིམས་སྲུང་བ། ཆོས་ལུགས་ཀྱིས་སྲིད་དོན་ལ་རོགས་སྐྱོར་བྱེད་རྒྱུ་བཅས་ཀྱི་རེ་འདུན་ཞུ། བཀའ་དྲིན་ཆེ།

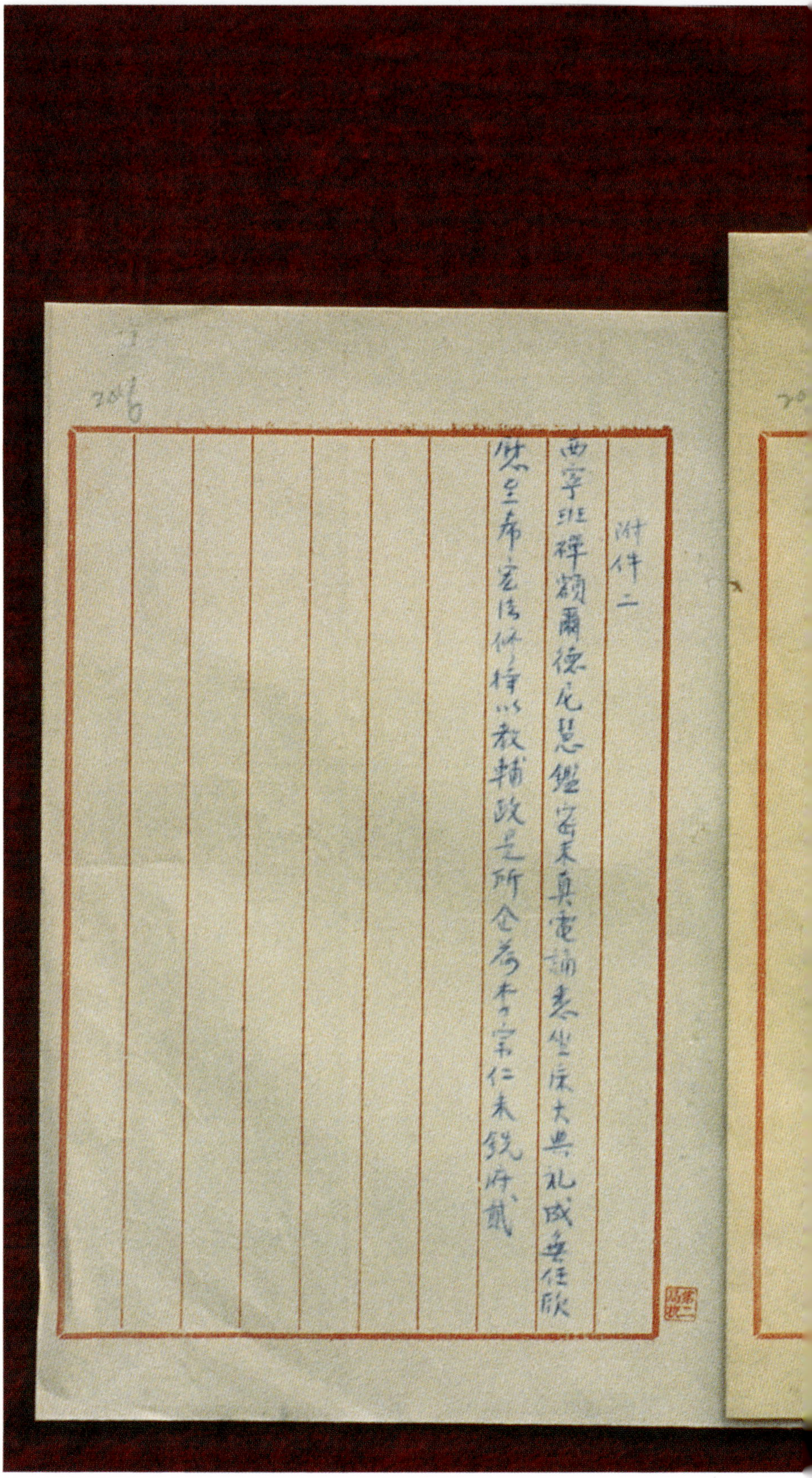
附件二

西寧班禪額爾德尼慧鑒密未真電誦悉坐床大典禮成無任欣慰至布宣德化俾以教輔政是所企盼李宗仁未銑府戴

ལི་ཙུང་རེན་ནས་ཆོས་བཅུ་དྲུག་ཉིན། རྒྱ་གཉིས་པ་ནས།
ཀུང་གོའི་ལོ་རྒྱུས་ཡིག་ཚགས་ཁང་ཨང་གཉིས་པར་ཉར་ཚགས་བྱས་ཡོད།

中國第二歷史檔案館藏

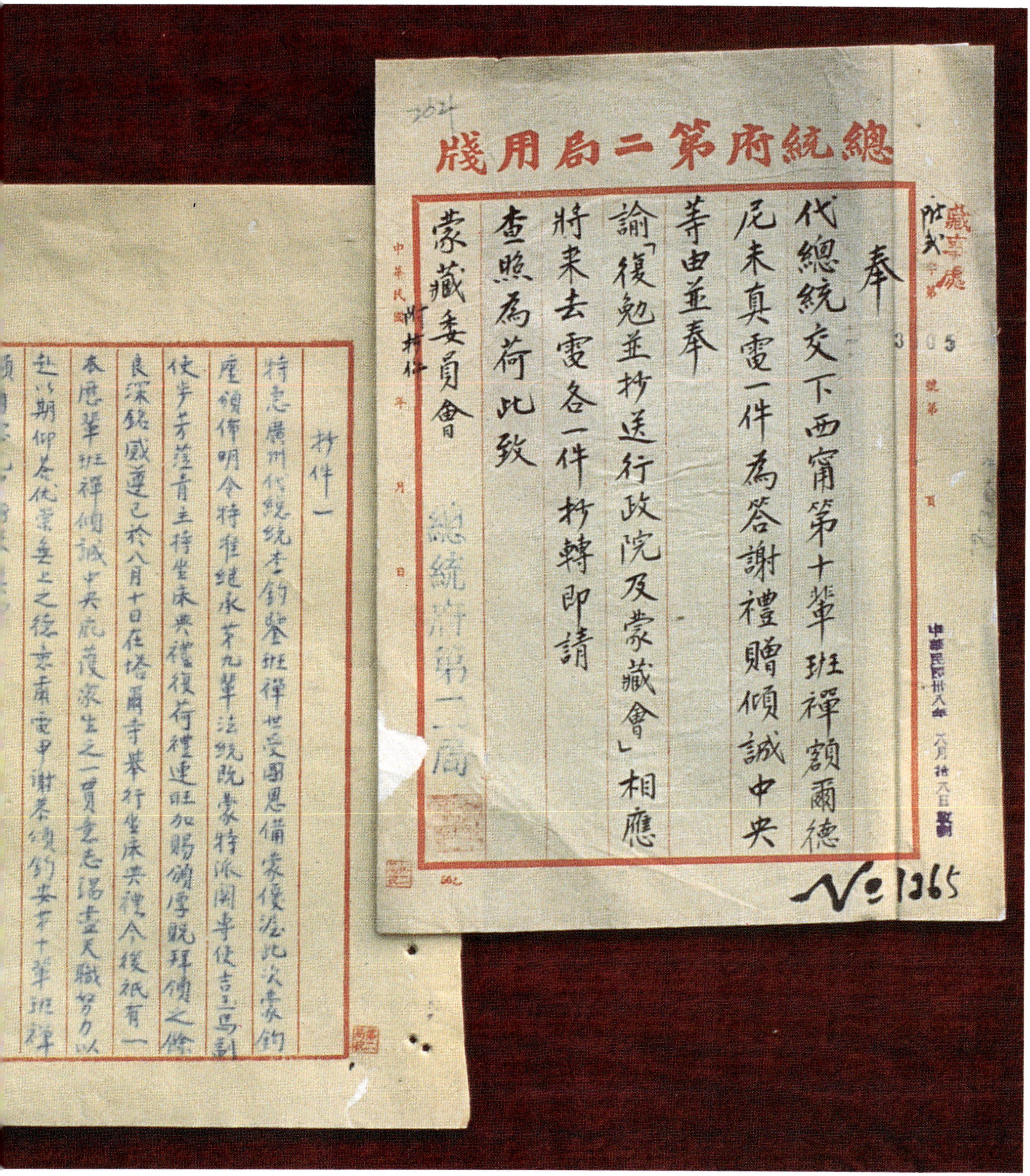
總統府第二局用箋

奉
代總統交下西甯第十輩班禪額爾德
尼未真電一件為答謝禮贈傾誠中央
等由並奉
諭「復勉並抄送行政院及蒙藏會」相應
將來去電各一件抄轉即請
查照為荷此致
蒙藏委員會
附抄件
總統府第二局

No 1265

抄件一
特急廣州代總統李鈞鑒班禪世受國恩備承優渥此次蒙鈞
座頒佈明令特准繼承第九輩法統既蒙特派關專使吉玉馬副
使步芳蒞青主持坐床典禮復荷禮運旺加賜頒厚貺拜領之餘
良深銘感遵已於八月十日在塔爾寺舉行坐床典禮今後祇有一
本歷輩班禪傾誠中央底護國家生之一貫意志竭盡天職努力以
赴以期仰答优崇垂上之德意肅電申謝恭頌鈞安第十輩班禪

Date: August 18, the 38th year of the Republic of China (1949)

To: The Committee for Mongolian and Tibetan Affairs

The Acting President has handed us a telegram dated August 11 from the 10th Panchen Erdeni in Xining expressing thanks for the presents he received and his loyalty to the Central

Government. The Acting President has requested us to write a reply of encouragement and send duplicate copies to the Executive Yuan and the Committee for Mongolian and Tibetan Affairs. Accordingly, we enclose a copy of the telegram the Acting President received and the telegram he sent in reply. Please check them.

Second Bureau of the Presidential Palace

Encl. Duplicate 1

Extra Urgent

Canton

Date: August 11 (38th year)

To: Acting President Li

Every reincarnation of the Panchen has received favourable treatment from the country. Once again I have been honoured by your official decree concerning my succession to the 9th Panchen. I am indebted to you for sending special envoy Guan Jiyu and deputy envoy Ma Bufang to Qinghai to preside over the enthronement ceremony and for your generous presents. In accordance with your decree, we held the enthronement ceremony in Ta′er Monastery on August 10. I shall follow the tradition of my predecessors by being loyal to the Central Government and protecting all living beings, fulfil my holy mission and do my utmost to repay your kindness. Once again I wish to express my heartfelt gratitude.

Best wishes.

Yours sincerely,

The 10th Panchen Erdeni (seal)

Encl. Duplicate 2

Xining

Date: August 16

To: The Panchen Erdeni

Confidential. I have read your telegram dated August 11 and am very glad to hear about the success of the enthronement ceremony. I sincerely hope that you will propagate the Buddhist doctrine and work at self–perfection so that the religion will benefit government affairs.

Li Zongren

Second Bureau of the Presidential Palace

Preserved by China No. 2 Historical Archives.

# རྒྱལ་ཁབ་རོགས་བྱེད་འགྲོ་བ་ཀུན་འདུལ་བསམ་གཏན་གྱི་སློབ་དཔོན་ར་སྒྲེང་ཧོ་ཐོག་ཐུའི་ཐམ་ཀ

# 輔國普化禪師熱振呼圖克圖之印

# The Seal of Living Buddha Ragreng, the Great Master Who Assists in State Affairs and Disseminates Buddhism.

96 - 1

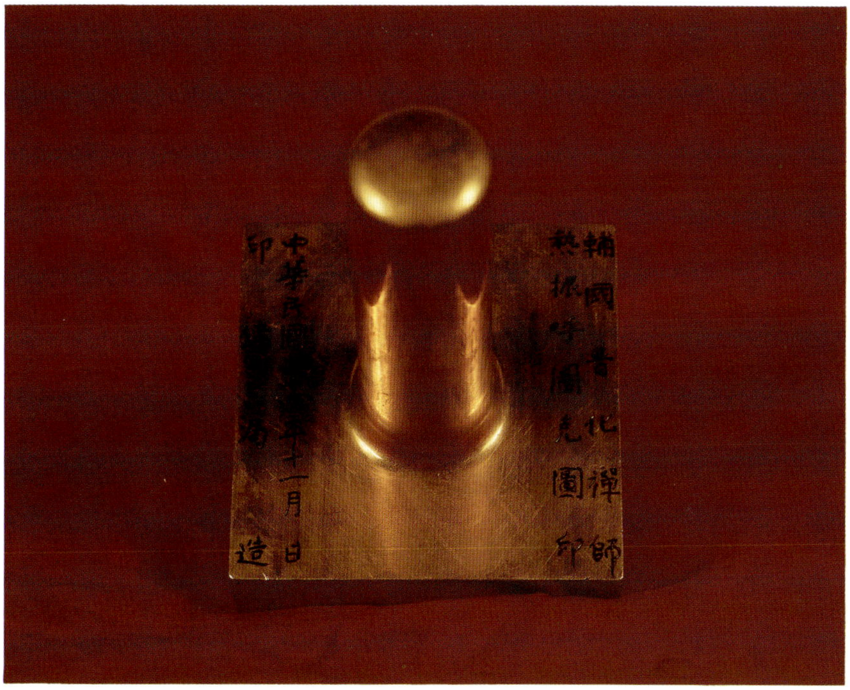

96 - 2

96 - 3

ཀྲུང་ཧྭ་མིང་གོ་ལོ་ཉེར་བཞི་ཟླ་བ་བཅུ་གཅིག་ལ་ཐམ་བཟོ་ཁང་གིས་བཟོས།

མཐའི་རིང་ཚད་ལི་སྨིས་༨.༨

བོད་རང་སྐྱོང་ལྗོངས་རིག་དངོས་དོ་དམ་ཨུ་ཡོན་ལྷན་ཁང་དུ་ཉར་ཚགས་བྱས་ཡོད།

中華民國二十四年十一月印鑄局造。

銅質，邊長8.8厘米。

西藏自治區文物管理委員會藏

Made by The Seal Administration in November, the 24th year of the Republic of China (1935)

An 8.8 cm. by 8.8 cm. copper seal.

Preserved by the Historical Relics Administration of the Tibet Autonomous Region.

# ཀྲུང་ཧྭ་མི་དམངས་སྤྱི་མཐུན་རྒྱལ་ཁབ་ཀྱི་ཡིག་ཚགས།

«བོད་ཞི་བས་བཅིངས་འགྲོལ་བྱུང་ཐབས་སྐོར་གྱི་གྲོས་མཐུན་དོན་ཚན་བཅུ་བདུན»་དང་། ཀྲུང་གོའི་ཏང་སྲིད་འགོ་ཁྲིད་ཀྱི་ཕྱག་བྲིས་ཕྱག་བསྐུར་མ། སྲིད་གཞུང་གི་ཙ་ཚིག ཏཱ་ལའི་བླ་མས་ལེགས་རྩོམ་གནང་བའི་ཤེས་ཚིག་སོགས་ནས་ཀྲུང་གོའི་བོད་འདི་ཉིད་ཇི་ལྟར་བྱས་ཏེ་གུང་ཁྲན་ཏང་གི་འགོ་ཁྲིད་འོག་ཞི་བའི་བཅིངས་འགྲོལ་ཐོབ་པ་དང་སྤྱི་ཚོགས་གསར་པར་བསྐྱོད་འགོ་ཚུགས་པའི་ལོ་རྒྱུས་ཀྱི་བརྒྱུད་རིམ་གཏིང་ཟབ་པ་ཞིག་མཚོན་པར་བྱས་ཡོད།

# 中華人民共和國檔案

《西藏和平解放十七條協議》、中國黨政領導人的親筆信、官方佈告、達賴喇嘛寫的讚文等，深刻反映了西藏在中國共產黨的領導下獲得和平解放並開始進入新社會的歷史過程。

# Archives from the Period Following the Founding of the People's Republic of China

The archives include the 17–Article Agreement on the Peaceful Liberation of Tibet, personal letters by Chinese Party and government leaders, official notices and an ode to Chairman Mao written by the Dalai Lama. These documents reflect the historical process whereby Tibet, under the leadership of the Communist Party of China, was peacefully liberated, after which it evolved into a new society.

# ཏཱ་ལའི་བླ་མས་ཞི་བའི་གྲོས་མོལ་བྱེད་རྒྱུའི་སྐོར་སྲིད་སྐྱོང་ལས་ཚབ་ལ་བསྩལ་བའི་བཀའ།

# 達賴喇嘛爲和談事給代理攝政的令稿

# Instructions Concerning the Peace Talks Issued by the Dalai Lama to the Acting Regents

93.5 × 67.3

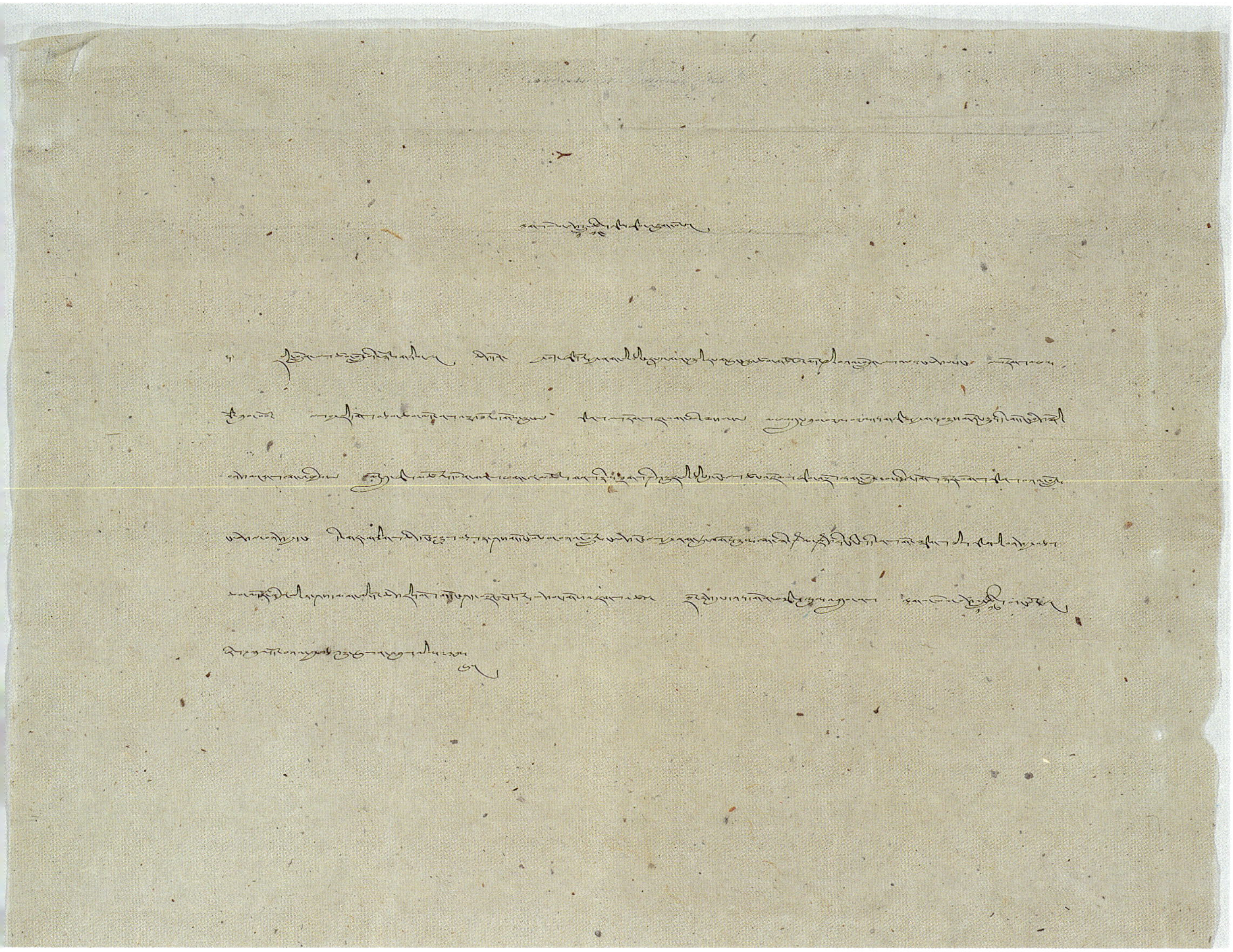

བོད་རང་སྐྱོང་ལྗོངས་ཡིག་ཚགས་ཁང་དུ་ཉར་ཚགས་བྱས་ཡོད།

代理攝政洛、第二位：

藏漢和談將在北京舉行。我政府首席代表多麥總管阿沛、助手堪仁·土桑及隨員應速從昌都啟程。此地將選派助手札薩克凱墨、堪仲土丹旦達，隨帶“和談提要”和贈給毛主席等領導的禮品，途經印度前往北京。全體代表和隨員到北京後充分商議的和談提要、給噶倫阿沛的指令書、爲你們閱讀的抄件已派驛使送交。噶倫阿沛及全體代表在北京所需一切經費和物品，由你們籌辦，連同發給阿沛的指令書，選派若干精幹的驛使火速護送昌都，切記。

上亞東東嘎扎西倫珠寺，藏曆鐵兔年(公元1951年)元月十六日頒賜，鈐蓋內宮印的指令。

西藏自治區檔案館藏

To Acting Regents Blo and Bde,

The Tibetan–Han peace talks are to be held in Beijing. The chief delegate of our government, Mdosmad Manager Ngapoi, his assistant Khanrin Thubzang and their entourage are to leave immediately from Qamdo. Assistants Dsasag Khemad and Khandrung Thubtan Tandar will leave here for Beijing via India, bringing with them "Key Points Concerning the Peace Talks" plus gifts for Chairman Mao and other leaders. These notes on the talks are to be discussed by all after you arrive in Beijing. The instructions to Ngapoi and the copies for you to read have been sent by our messenger. You are to arrange for the money and other things Kaloon Ngapoi and all the other delegates will need in Beijing, and as soon as they are ready send them together with the instructions for Ngapoi to Qamdo by capable messengers.

Issued from the Krashislhungrubgon Monastery in Dungkar, Grotod on the 16th day of the first month of the Year of the Iron Rabbit in the Tibetan calendar [seal of the Inner Palace] (1951)

Preserved by the Archives of the Tibet Autonomous Region.

# ཀྲུང་ཧྭ་མི་དམངས་སྤྱི་མཐུན་རྒྱལ་ཁབ་ཆབ་མདོ་ས་ཁུལ་མི་དམངས་བཅིངས་འགྲོལ་ཨུ་ཡོན་ལྷན་ཁང་གི་ཙ་ཚིག

# 中華人民共和國昌都地區人民解放委員會佈告

# Notice from the People's Liberation Committee of Qamdo Prefecture of the People's Republic of China

114 × 72

བོད་རང་སྐྱོང་ལྗོངས་ཡིག་ཚགས་ཁང་དུ་ཉར་ཚགས་བྱས་ཡོད།

西藏自治區檔案館藏

No. [missing in the original document]

In accordance with the cabled order from the Southwest Military and Administrative Commission of the People's Republic of China, since Qamdo Prefecture has been liberated, the People's Liberation Committee of Qamdo Prefecture has been duly established in order to protect the life and property of the entire population, to implement the policy of religious freedom, protect the lamaseries, and maintain public security and establish revolutionary order. The committee is charged with the responsibility of supervising military and administrative matters and coordinating relations between the People's Liberation Army and the local areas. A total of 35 persons, including Wang Qimei, Krashis Namgyal, Vodzer Gyaltshan, Gao Heng, Xia Zhongyuan, Khargo Prulku, Lozang Gyaltshan, Pamdav Rabgav, Pamdav Rdorje, Hui Yiran, Chen Jingbo, Tersras Chimed, Tshogosras, Horkhangsras, Ngapoi, Rjedrung, Ngagwang Gyaltshan, Living Buddha Lodan Shesrab, Lozang Namgyal, Lozang Konchog, Phuntshog Wanggyal, Li Anzhai, Yu Shiyu, Living Buddha Vphagspalha Lozang Lungtog, Shesrab Sengge, Living Buddha Zhibalha, Wu Zhong, Yin Fatang, Kalzang Wangdus, Byampa Vodgan, Tsheyang Palmo, Chen Zizhi, Zhou Jiading, Vogme Sodnam and Song Song, have been appointed to form the committee, with Wang Qimei as chairman and Living Buddha Vphagspalha Lozang Lungtog, Ngapoi, Living Buddha Lodan Shesrab, Pamdav Rdorje, Phuntshog Wanggyal, Hui Yiran, Tsheyang Palmo and Kalzang Wangdus as vice–chairmen. Ten positions on the committee have been reserved for the following areas, with one representative each: Zay Shomdo, Govjo, Lhorongdsong, Tshawarong and Tshakha, with two each for Bomi and the Thirty–nine Tribes. Acting on this order, the committee was inaugurated on January 1 and Wang Qimei and his committee assumed office on the same day to serve the Tibetan people in accordance with the policies concerning nationality affairs issued by the Central People's Government of the People's Republic of China, and notices released by the Southwest Military and Administrative Commission, the Southwest Military Area of the Chinese People's Liberation Army and its Tibet Front Headquarters. This matter is to be made public knowledge.

Chairman Wang Qimei

Vice Chairmen Living Buddha Vphagspalha Lozang Lungtog, Ngapoi, Living Buddha Lodan Shesrab, Pamdav Rdorje, Phuntshog Wanggyal, Hui Yiran, Tsheyang Palmo and Kalzang Wangdus

January [Numeral for the day is missing in the original document], 1951

Preserved by the Archives of the Tibet Autonomous Region.

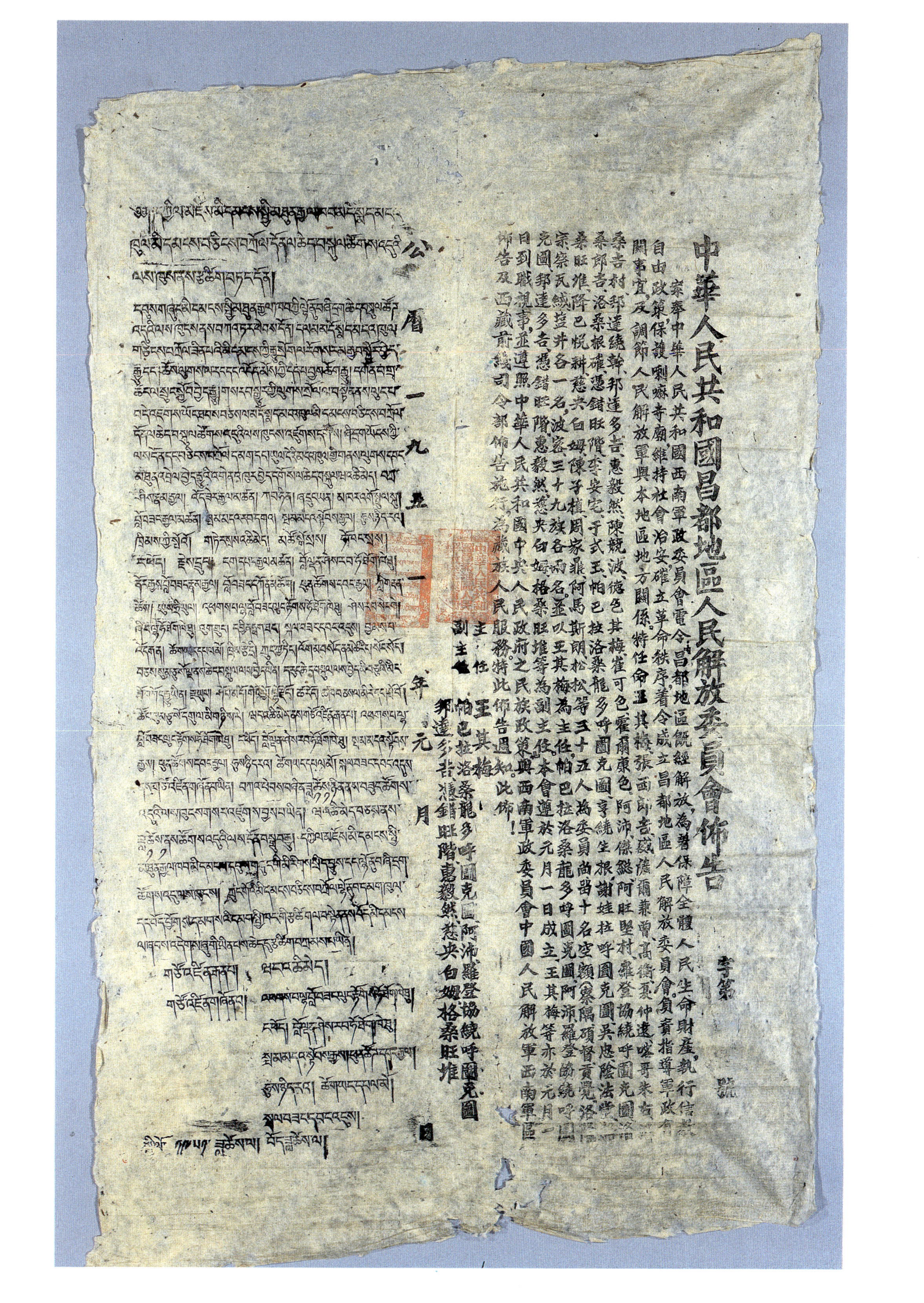

# 中華人民共和國昌都地區人民解放委員會佈告

字第　號

案奉中華人民共和國西南軍政委員會電令：昌都地區既經解放，為着保障全體人民生命財產，執行信教自由政策，保護喇嘛寺廟，維持社會治安，確立革命秩序，着令成立昌都地區人民解放委員會，負責指導軍政各關事宜，及調節人民解放軍與本地區地方關係。特任命王其梅、張西郎、吉嶺薩爾兼曾、高衛夏、仲達、喀哥來古、[illegible]桑吉村、邦達繞幹、邦達多吉、惠毅然、陳競波、德色、其梅崔可色、霍爾康色、阿沛、傑總阿旺堅村、羅登協繞呼圖克圖、[illegible]桑郎吉、洛桑根確、憑錯旺階、李安宅、于式玉、帕巴拉洛桑龍多呼圖克圖、享繞生根、謝娃拉呼圖克圖、吳忠、陰法唐、[illegible]桑旺堆、降巴悅耕、慈央白姆、陳子植、周家鼎、阿馬斯朗松松等三十五人為委員，尚留十名空額（察隅碩督、貢覺、洛[illegible]宗察瓦絨、盐井各一名，波密三十九族各兩名。並以王其梅為主任，帕巴拉洛桑龍多呼圖克圖、阿沛、羅登協繞呼圖克圖、邦達多吉、憑錯旺階、惠毅然、慈央白姆、格桑旺堆等為副主任。本會遵於元月一日成立，王其梅等亦於元月一日到職視事，並遵照中華人民共和國中央人民政府之民族政策，與西南軍政委員會中國人民解放軍西南軍區佈告及西藏前線司令部佈告施行，為藏族人民服務。特此佈告週知。此佈！

主　任　王其梅

副主任　帕巴拉洛桑龍多呼圖克圖
阿沛羅登協繞呼圖克圖
邦達多吉
憑錯旺階
惠毅然
慈央白姆
格桑旺堆

公曆一九五一年元月　日

[illegible]

# ལྷོ་ནུབ་དམག་སྲིད་ཨུ་ཡོན་ལྷན་ཁང་དང་ཀྲུང་གོ་མི་དམངས་བཅིངས་འགྲོལ་དམག་ལྷོ་ནུབ་དམག་ཁུལ་ཁང་གི་ཙ་ཚིག
# 西南軍政委員會、中國人民解放軍西南軍區佈告
# Proclamation of the Southwest Military and Administrative Commission and the Southwest Military Area of the Chinese People′s Liberation Army

109.3 × 86

བོད་རང་སྐྱོང་ལྗོངས་ཡིག་ཚགས་ཁང་དུ་ཉར་ཚགས་བྱས་ཡོད།

西藏自治區檔案館藏

No. [missing in the original document]

Deeply concerned about the Tibetan people who have long suffered from the oppression of British and American imperialism and the reactionary Chiang Kai–shek government, Chairman Mao Zedong of our Central People′s Government and Commander–in–Chief Zhu De of the People′s Liberation Army have instructed our army units to move into Tibet in order to help the Tibetan people rid themselves of this oppression once and for all. All our Tibetan people, religious or secular, should unite as one and fully assist the People′s Liberation Army in expelling the imperialist forces of aggression, thereby bringing about regional national autonomy in Tibet, establishing a relationship of fraternity and mutual help with the people of all other nationalities in the country and working together to build a new Tibet and a new China.

After moving into Tibet, the People′s Liberation Army will protect the lives and property of all the Tibetan people, both religious and secular, guarantee their freedom of religious be-

# 西南軍政委員會
# 中國人民解放軍西南軍區 佈告

字第　　號

我中央人民政府毛澤東主席和人民解放軍朱德總司令，深切關懷西藏人民長期遭受英美帝國主義及蔣介石反動政府的壓迫，特令本軍開入西藏，幫助西藏人民永遠擺脫此種壓迫。我西藏全體僧俗人民，應即團結一致，給人民解放軍以充分的援助，以便驅逐帝國主義侵畧勢力，實現西藏民族的區域自治，並與國內其他各民族建立像兄弟一樣的友愛互助關係，共同建設新中國和新西藏。

人民解放軍入藏之後，保護西藏全體僧俗人民的生命財產；保障西藏人民之宗教信仰自由；保護一切喇嘛寺廟；幫助西藏人民發展教育和農、牧、工、商各業，改善人民生活。對於西藏現行政治制度及軍事制度，不予變更，西藏現有軍隊成為中華人民共和國國防武裝之一部份。各級僧俗官員頭人等照常供職。一切有關西藏各項改革事宜，完全根據西藏人民意志由西藏人民及西藏領導人員採取協商方式解決。過去親帝國主義與親國民黨之官吏，一經事實證明與帝國主義及國民黨脫離關係，不進行破壞和反抗，仍可一律繼續任職，不究既往。

人民解放軍紀律嚴明，忠實執行中央人民政府上述各項政策，尊重西藏人民宗教信仰和風俗習慣；說話和氣，買賣公平，不妄取民間一針一線；借用傢具，均經物主同意，如有損毀，決按市價賠償；僱用人畜差役，均付相當代價，不拉伕，不捉牲畜。人民解放軍為中國各族人民的軍隊，全心全意為人民服務，望我西藏農、牧、工、商全體人民，一律安居樂業，切勿輕信謠言，自相驚擾。切切此佈！

西南軍政委員會主席　劉伯承

中國人民解放軍西南軍區司令員　賀龍

政治委員　鄧小平

公曆一九五〇年　　月　　日

༄༅། །ལྷོ་ནུབ་དམག་སྲིད་ཨུ་ཡོན་ལྷན་ཁང་དང་། ཀྲུང་གོ་མི་སེར་བཅིང་འགྲོལ་དམག

དཔུང་ལྷོ་ནུབ་དམག་གི་ས་གནས་ལས་ཁུངས་སྤྱན་སྔོན་ནས་རྩ་ཆེ་གསང་དོན།།

དཔལ་ཀྲུང་གཡང་མི་སེར་སྲིད་གཞུང་ཀྲུ་ཞི་མའོ་ཙེ་ཏུང་དང་མི་སེར་བཅིང་འགྲོལ་དམག་དཔུང་ཙུང་སི་ལིང་ཀྲུ་ཏེ་ལྷན་རྒྱས་གཉིས་ནས་བོད་ཀྱི་མི་སེར་ཡུན་རིང་དུ་དབྱིན་ཇི་དང་ཨ་མེ་རི་ཀ་གཉིས་ཀྱི་བཙན་དབང་རྒྱལ་ཁབ་ཀྱི་ལུགས་དང་ཅང་ཀེ་ཧྲེའི་སྲིད་གཞུང་ལོག་སྤྱོད་པ་བཅས་ཀྱི་བཙན་པོ་གཡུལ་ངོན་བཟོད་ཐབས་དང་བྲལ་བ་རྣམས་ཐུགས་དགོངས་ཟབ་མོར་མངའ་བ་བཞིན་དུ་བོད་ཀྱི་མི་སེར་རྣམས་ད་ནས་བཟུང་སྡུག་བསྔལ་གྱིས་བཅིང་བ་ལས་ཀུན་ནས་བཀྲོལ་བའི་རོགས་རམ་ལ་ངའི་དམག་དཔུང་བོད་ལ་ཆེད་གཏོང་བྱས་པ་ཡིན་པས། ང་རེའི་བོད་ཀྱི་མི་སེར་སྐུ་སེར་མེད་པ་ཐམས་ཅད་ནས་མྱུར་དུ་སེམས་གཅིག་འདྲིལ་གྱི་སྒོ་ནས་མི་སེར་བཅིང་འགྲོལ་དམག་དཔུང་ལ་རང་གི་ནུས་པ་བཞིན་དུ་རོགས་རམ་བྱེད་ཅིང་བཙན་དབང་རྒྱལ་ཁབ་ལུགས་ཀྱི་སྣོན་འཛུལ་གྱི་བཙན་ཤུགས་མཐའ་འསྐྲོད་དུ་གཏོང་ཐུབ་བོད་ཀྱི་མི་རིགས་རྣམས་ཀྱི་ས་ཁུལ་རང་སྐྱོང་ཡོང་བའི་ཐབས་ལམ་ལག་ལེན་དུ་ཐེབས་ངེས་མ་ཟད། རང་རེའི་རྒྱལ་ཁབ་ནང་གི་མི་རིགས་གཞན་དག་དང་སྤུན་འབྲེལ་ལྟ་བུའི་རྩེ་གདུང་བྱམས་སེམས་དང་གཅིག་ལ་གཅིག་རམ་གྱིས་འབྲེལ་བ་བཟུང་ནས་ཐུན་མོང་དུ་ཀྲུང་གོ་གསར་པ་དང་བོད་ལྗོངས་གསར་པ་ཞིག་འཛུགས་དགོས་སོ། མི་སེར་བཅིང་འགྲོལ་དམག་དཔུང་བོད་དུ་སླེབ་ནས་བོད་ལྗོངས་སྐུ་སེར་མེད་པ་མི་སེར་སྤྱིང་གི་སྲོག་ལུས་དབང་ཐང་དང་བོད་མི་རྣམས་ཀྱི་ཆོས་ལ་དད་པ་རང་མོས་ལྟར་བྱེད་པའི་དགོན་སྐྱབས་ཡོད་པ་དང་། དགོན་ཁག་གཙུག་ལག་ཁང་ལ་སོགས་ཐམས་ཅད་ལ་སྲུང་སྐྱོང་བྱེད་པ་མ་ཟད། བོད་ཀྱི་མི་སེར་ལ་བསླབ་བྱ་དང་སོ་ནམས་དང་། འབྲོག་ལས་དང་། བཟོ་ལས་དང་། ཚོང་རིགས་བཅས་ཀྱི་གོང་འཕེལ་ནས་དར་རྒྱས་ཡོང་བར་མགོ་འདྲེན་གྱི་སྒོ་ནས་མི་སེར་གྱི་འཚོ་བ་བཅས་གོང་འཕེལ་དུ་སྐྱུར་རྒྱུ་དང་། བོད་རང་ལ་ཡོད་པའི་ཆབ་སྲིད་དང་དམག་ལས་ཀྱི་ལམ་ལུགས་རྣམས་སྒྱུར་བཅོས་མི་གཏོང་སྔར་བོད་ཀྱི་དམག་དཔུང་ཡོད་པ་དེ་མི་སེར་སྤྱི་མཐུན་རྒྱལ་ཁབ་ཀྱི་མཐའ་མཚམས་སྲུང་བའི་དྲག་ཤུགས་ཀྱི་གྲངས་ཤིག་ཏུ་སྒྱུར་རྒྱུ་དང་། སྐུ་སེར་གྱི་དཔོན་རིགས་མགོ་པ་བཅས་སྔར་བཞིན་དུ་རང་འཁྱག་སྡོད་ཆོག བོད་ལ་བཟོ་སྒྱུར་གྱི་བྱ་བ་གང་ཕྱིན་ནས་བོད་ཀྱི་མི་སེར་དང་མགོ་བྱེད་རྣམས་བཀའ་མོལ་གྱི་ཐོག་ནས་མི་སེར་སྤྱིའི་བློ་ཕྱོགས་ལ་བརྟེན་ནས་བརྒྱུད་སྟེགས་ཚད་རྒྱུ་དང་། སྔོན་དུས་བཙན་དབང་རྒྱལ་ཁབ་ཀྱི་ལུགས་དང་གོ་མིན་ཏང་བཅས་ལ་བློ་ཉེ་བའི་དཔོན་རིགས་རྣམས་བཙན་དབང་རྒྱལ་ཁབ་ཀྱི་ལུགས་དང་གོ་མིན་ཏང་བཅས་ནས་འབྲེལ་ཐག་ཆོད་པའི་རྟགས་མཚན་མངོན་དུ་སྟོན་རྒྱུ་ཡོད་ཙེ་ང་ཚོ་ལ་གནོད་པ་དང་ངོ་རྒོལ་བྱེད་མཁན་མིན་ཚེ་སྔར་ཡང་སྔར་བཞིན་གྱི་གོ་སར་གནས་ཆོག་པ་མ་ཟད། སྔར་གྱི་ཉེས་པ་རྣམས་ལ་ཡང་རྩད་གཅོད་མེད་དོ།།

མི་སེར་བཅིང་འགྲོལ་དམག་དཔུང་ནི་བཅས་པའི་ཁྲིམས་དམ་པོར་སྲུང་ཞིང་ཀྲུང་གཡང་མི་སེར་སྲིད་གཞུང་ནས་བཀའ་གནང་བའི་སྲིད་ཇུས་རྣམས་ངེས་པར་དུ་ལག་ལེན་སྒྲུབ་མཁན་ཡིན་པས། བོད་ཀྱི་མི་སེར་ཆོས་ལ་དད་པ་བྱེད་པ་དང་ཡུལ་སྲོལ་དང་ཡུལ་གྱི་གོམས་པའི་གཤིས་ཁ་བཅས་ལ་རྩིས་འཛོག་བྱེད་ཅིང་གཏམ་འཇམ་པོར་བཤད། ཉོ་ཚོང་དྲང་པོར་བྱེད། མི་སེར་གྱི་དངོས་པོ་ནོར་མེད་དུ་ཁབ་དང་སྐུད་པ་ཙམ་ཡང་མི་ལེན། ཅ་ལག་གཡར་དགོས་ན་བདག་པོ་ལ་གཡར་པོ་ཞུ། གལ་སྲིད་ཅ་ལག་ལ་བཅག་གྲུག་ཤོར་ན་ཡུལ་གྱི་ཐོང་གོང་ལྟར་དུ་སྤྲོད་པར་རྒྱུ། མི་སེར་ལ་ལས་ཀ་བཀོལ་བ་དང་མི་སེར་གྱི་རྟ་ཁལ་གླ་བ་རྣམས་ལ་གླ་རྒྱ་ཇི་འབབ་བཞིན་སྤྲོད་པ་མ་གཏོགས་མི་སྟབ་རྟ་ཁལ་སྟབ་ཁལ་སུ་ཐུབ་བཅས་དེ་མི་ཆོག མི་སེར་བཅིང་འགྲོལ་དམག་དཔུང་ནི་ཀྲུང་གོའི་མི་རིགས་ཐམས་ཅད་ཀྱི་མི་སེར་གྱི་དམག་དཔུང་ཡིན་པ་དང་། སེམས་ཐག་པ་ནས་མི་སེར་ལ་ཞབས་ཞུ་ཡིན་པས་བོད་ཀྱི་སོ་ནམས་པ་འབྲོག་པ། བཟོ་པ། ཚོང་པ་མི་སེར་རྣམས་ནས་རང་གི་བྱ་བར་དོན་དུ་གཉེར་ཏེ་བདེ་བར་གནས་པ་མ་གཏོགས་གཏམ་འཆུར་ལ་ཞུན་ནས་རང་གིས་རང་ལ་མགོ་འཁྱོག་དང་སེམས་འཁྲུགས་མེད་པར་གལ་ཆེ་བས་ཀུན་གྱི་ཡིད་ལ་ངེས་པར་བཀྲིས་ཞིག།  ། །

ལྷོ་ནུབ་དམག་སྲིད་ཨུ་ཡོན་ཀྲུས་ཀྲུ་ཞིས་ལིའུ་པེ་ཁྲིང་དང་ཀྲུང་གོ་མི་སེར་བཅིང་འགྲོལ་དམག་དཔུང་གི་ལྷོ་ནུབ་དམག་གི་ས་གནས་ལས་ཁུངས་སི་ལིང་ཡོན་ཧོ་ལུང་དང་ཆབ་སྲིད་ཀྱི་ཨུ་ཡོན་ཏེང་ཞའོ་ཕིན་བཅས་ནས་བཏང་བའི་རྩ་ཆེག།  ། །

སྤྱི་ལོ་༡༩༥ ཟླ་བ་པའི་ཚེས་བཟང་པོ་ལགས།  །

lief, protect all the lamaseries and help the Tibetan people develop their education, agriculture, animal husbandry, and industry and trade in order to improve their standard of living. The current political and military systems in Tibet are not to be changed. The present Tibetan troops will become part of the national defence forces of the People's Republic of China. Religious and secular officials at all levels as well as tribal chiefs will hold office as usual. All matters of reform in Tibet will be resolved by the Tibetan people and the leading personnel in Tibet through consultation and in exact accordance with the Tibetan people's wishes. Officials who were formerly pro– imperialist and pro–Kuomintang may still hold office provided that the facts show that they have broken off relations with the imperialists and the Kuomintang and are not involved in sabotage and resistance. Their past misdeeds can be forgiven.

The People's Liberation Army is highly disciplined. It faithfully follows the above–mentioned policies of the Central People's Government and respects the religious belief of the Tibetan people and their customs and habits. The PLA men speak politely, conduct their buying and selling activities fairly and are not allowed to take even a single needle or a piece of thread from the people. In the event that furniture needs to be borrowed, the consent of the owners must be obtained. If damage occurs, compensation is to be made at market prices. Hired manual labour and the use of livestock are to be paid for appropriately. Press–ganging of men and seizure of livestock shall not be practised. The People's Liberation Army is the army of the people of all nationalities in China, serving the people heart and soul. It is hoped that the entire Tibetan people, whether engaged in agriculture, animal husbandry, industry or trade, will live and work in peace and will not give credence to rumours or raise false alarms. This proclamation is hereby issued in all sincerity and earnestness.

Liu Bocheng

Chairman of the Southwest Military and Administrative Commission

He Long

Commander of the Southwest Military Area of the Chinese People's Liberation Army

Deng Xiaoping

Political Commissar of the Southwest Military Area of the Chinese People's Liberation Army

195 [Finally numeral of year, as well as month and day, not given in the original document]

Preserved by the Archives of the Tibet Autonomous Region.

**100**

# ཀྲུང་དབྱང་མི་དམངས་སྲིད་གཞུང་དང་བོད་ཀྱི་ས་གནས་སྲིད་གཞུང་གཉིས་བོད་ཞི་བས་བཅིངས་འགྲོལ་འབྱུང་ཐབས་སྐོར་གྱི་གྲོས་མཐུན།

# 中央人民政府和西藏地方政府關於和平解放西藏辦法的協議

# The Agreement Between the Central People's Government and the Local Government of Tibet on Measures for the Peaceful Liberation of Tibet

474 × 35.7, 522.5 × 35.7

100 - 1

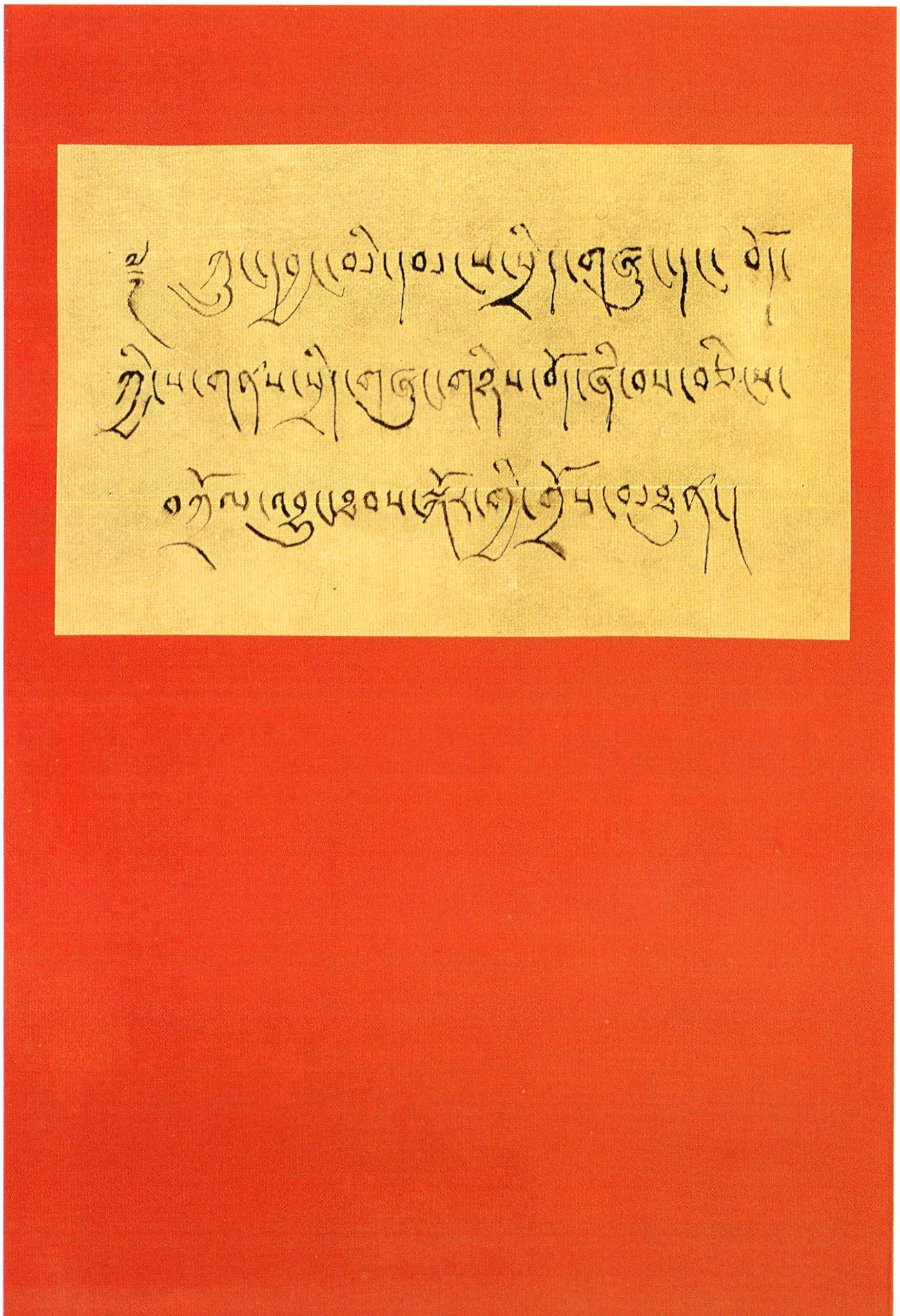

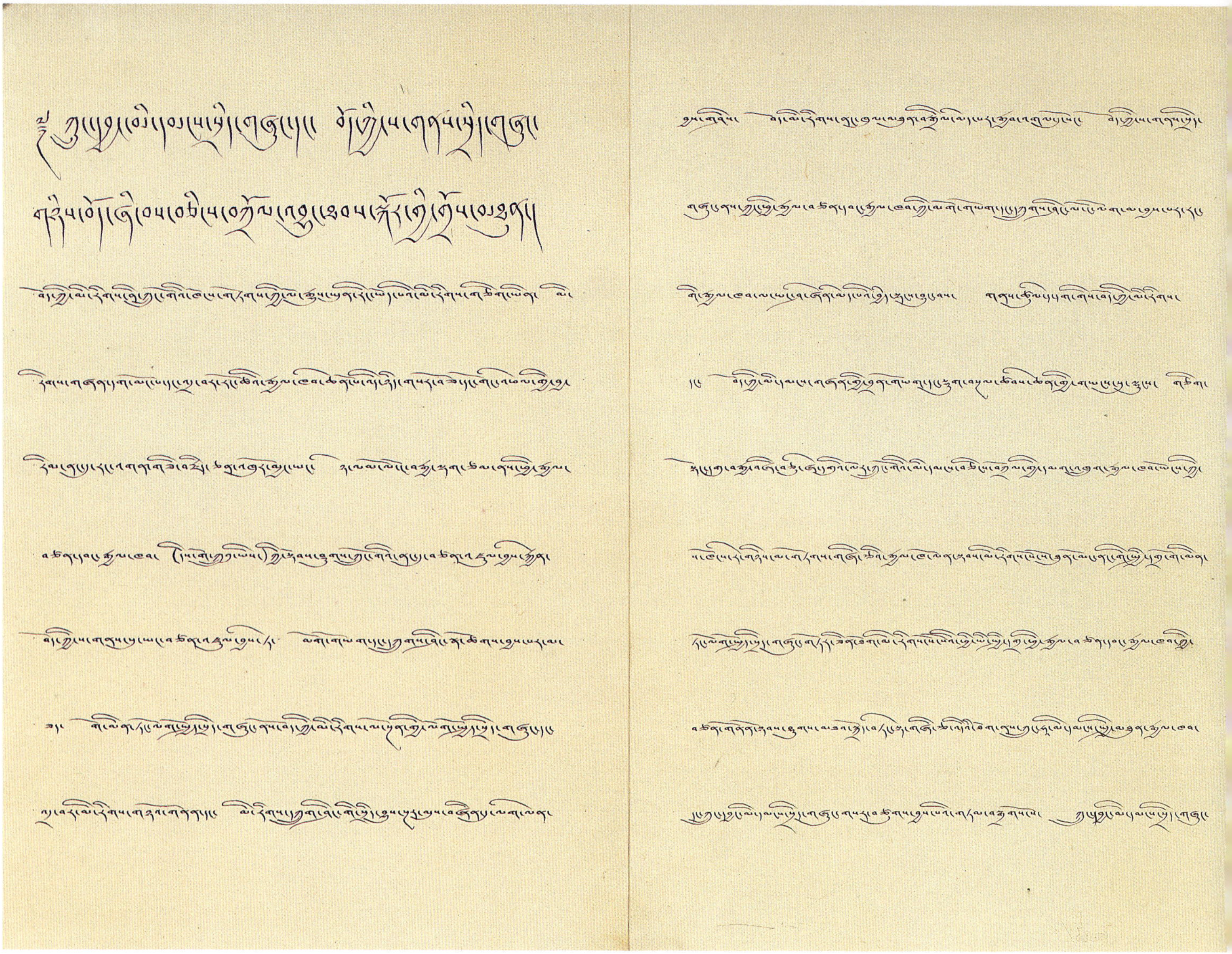

100 - 2

བོད་རང་སྐྱོང་ལྗོངས་ཡིག་ཚགས་ཁང་དུ་ཉར་ཚགས་བྱས་ཡོད།

西藏自治區檔案館藏

The Tibetan nationality is one of the nationalities with a long history within the boundaries of China and, like many other nationalities, it has performed its glorious duty in the creation and development of our great motherland. Over the last hundred years or more, however, imperialist forces penetrated into China, and consequently also penetrated into the Tibetan region, carrying out all kinds of acts of deception and sowing discord by various means. Like the previous reactionary governments, the reactionary Kuomintang government continued to carry out a policy of national oppression and sowing dissension among the nationalities, causing divisions and disunity among the Tibetan people. The local government of

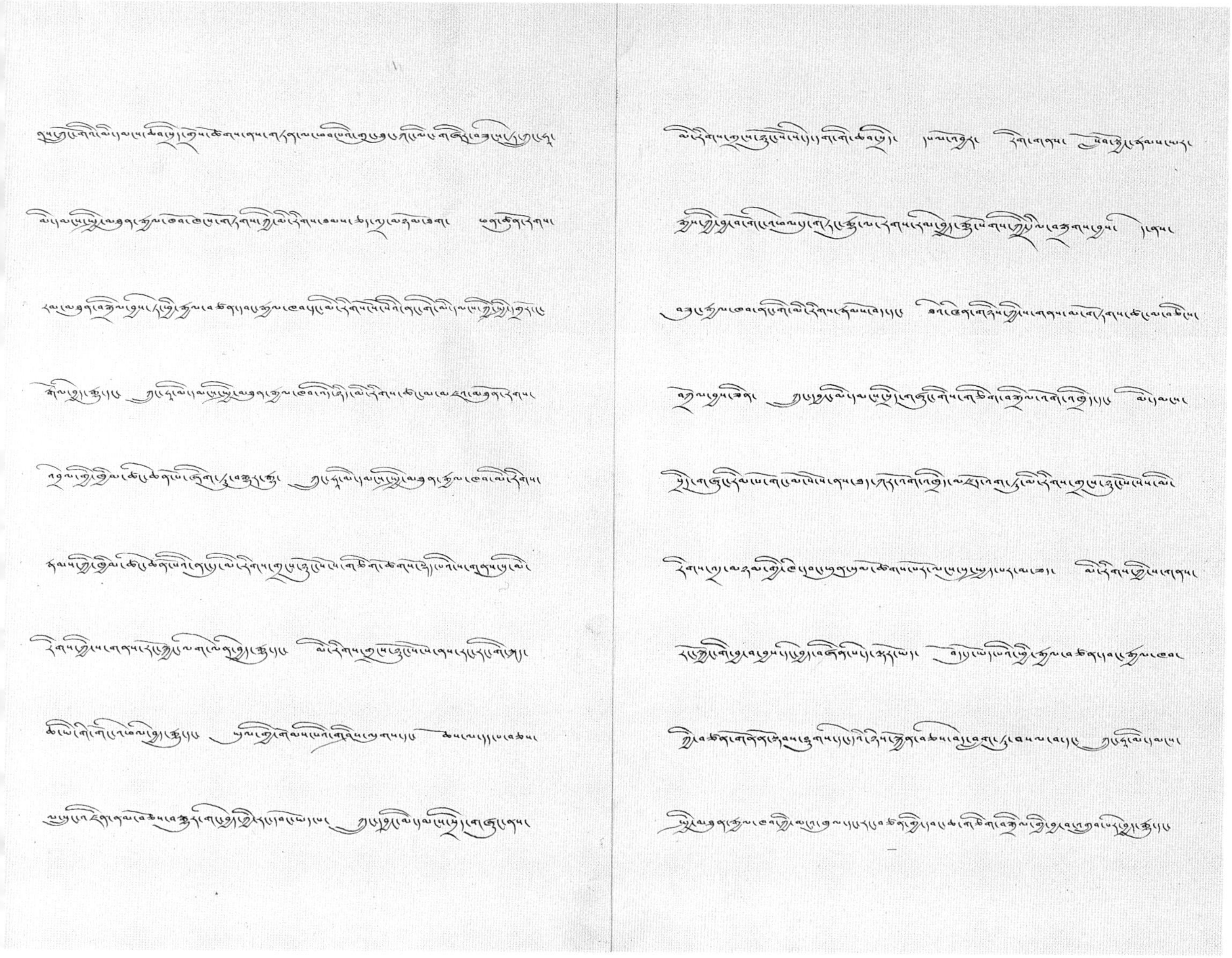



Tibet did not oppose the imperialist acts of practising deception and sowing discord, and adopted an unpatriotic attitude towards our great motherland. Under such conditions, the Tibetan nationality and people were subjected to the worst enslavement and suffering.

In 1949, victory was basically achieved on a nation- wide scale in the Chinese People's War of Liberation. The common internal enemy of all the nationalities – the reactionary Kuomintang government – was overthrown and the common external enemy of all the nationalities – the imperialist forces of aggression – was driven out. It was on this basis that the founding of the People's Republic of China and of the Central People's Government was proclaimed. In accordance with the Common Programme adopted by the Chinese People's Political Consultative Conference, the Central People's Government declared that all the nationalities within the boundaries of the People's Republic of China are equal, and that they shall establish unity and mutual aid and oppose imperialism and their own public enemies, so that the People's Republic of China will become one large fraternal and cooperative family, com-

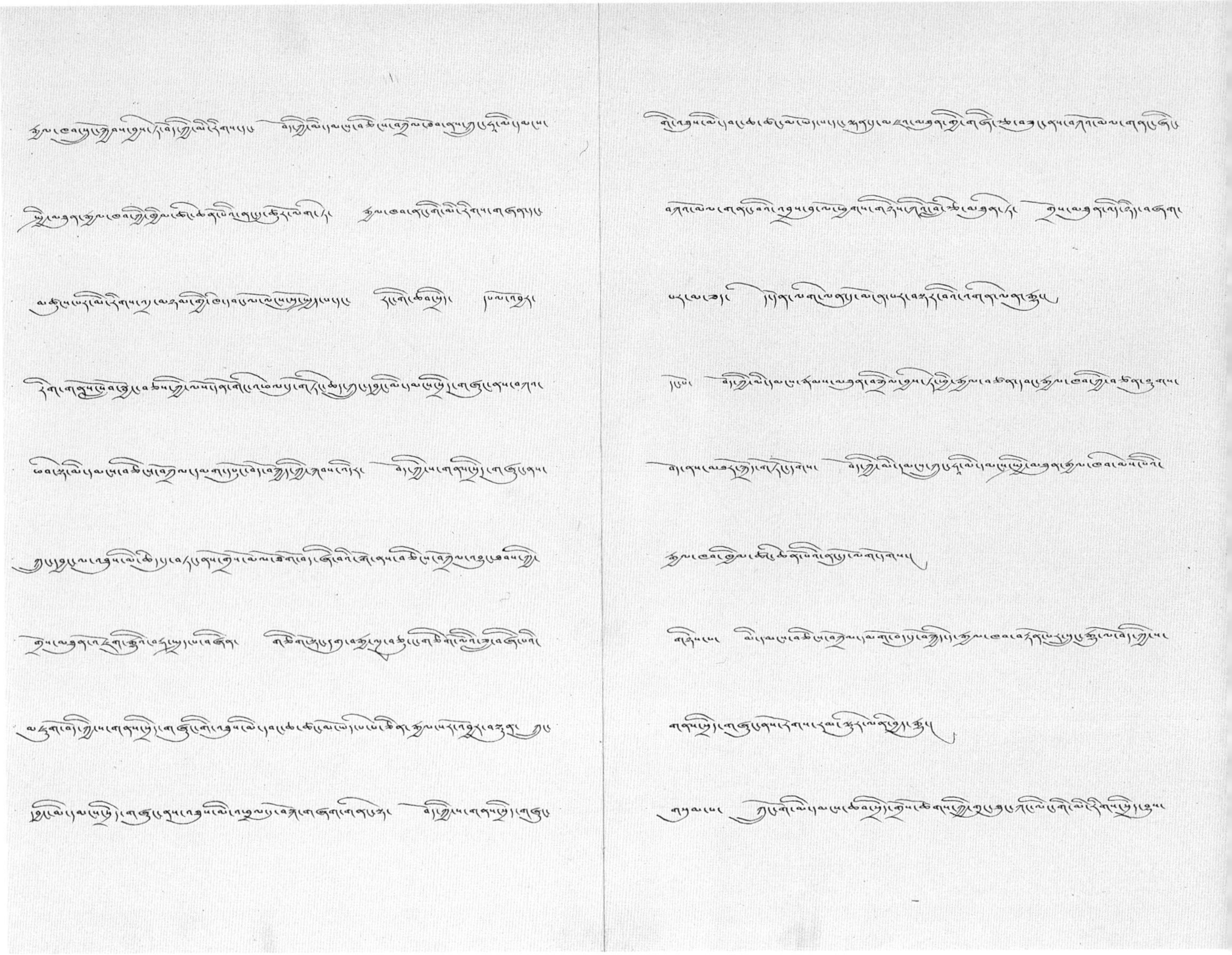

100 - 4

posed of all its nationalities. Furthermore, within this large family of all the nationalities of the People's Republic of China, national regional autonomy shall be exercised in areas where people of the national minorities live in compact communities, and all the national minorities shall be free to develop their spoken and written languages and to preserve or reform their customs, habits and religious beliefs with the assistance of the Central People's Government extended to all the national minorities to develop their political, economic, cultural and educational undertakings. Since then, all the nationalities within the country, with the exception of those in the areas of Tibet and Taiwan, have been liberated. Under the unified leadership of the Central People's Government and the direct leadership of all the higher levels of the people's government, all the national minorities are fully enjoying the right of national equality and have established, or are establishing, national regional autonomy.

In order to successfully eliminate the influence of the imperialist forces of aggression in Tibet, accomplish the reunification of the territory and sovereignty of the People's Republic

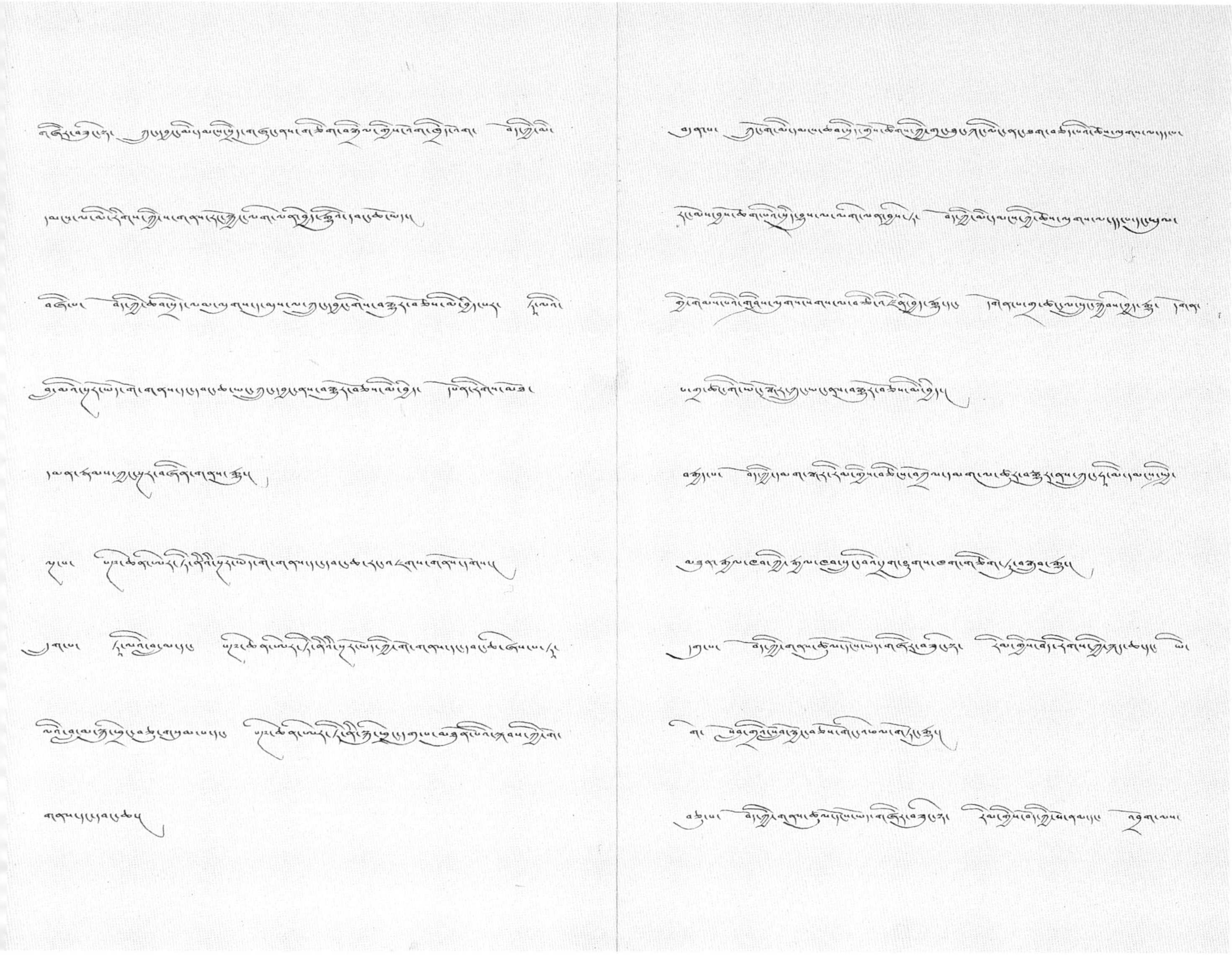

100－5

of China and maintain national defence and in order for the Tibetan nationality and people to be liberated and return to the large family of the People's Republic of China to enjoy the same rights of national equality as all the other nationalities in the country and develop their political, economic, cultural and educational undertakings, the Central People's Government, when it ordered the People's Liberation Army to march into Tibet, notified the local government of Tibet to send delegates to the central authorities to conduct talks for the conclusion of an agreement on measures for the peaceful liberation of Tibet.

In the latter part of April 1951, the delegates with the full authority of the local government of Tibet arrived in Beijing. The Central People's Government immediately appointed delegates with full authority to conduct talks on a friendly basis with the delegates with the full authority of the local government of Tibet. As a result of these talks, both parties agreed to conclude this agreement and guarantee that it will be put into effect.

1. The Tibetan people shall unite to drive the imperialist forces of aggression out of Tibet

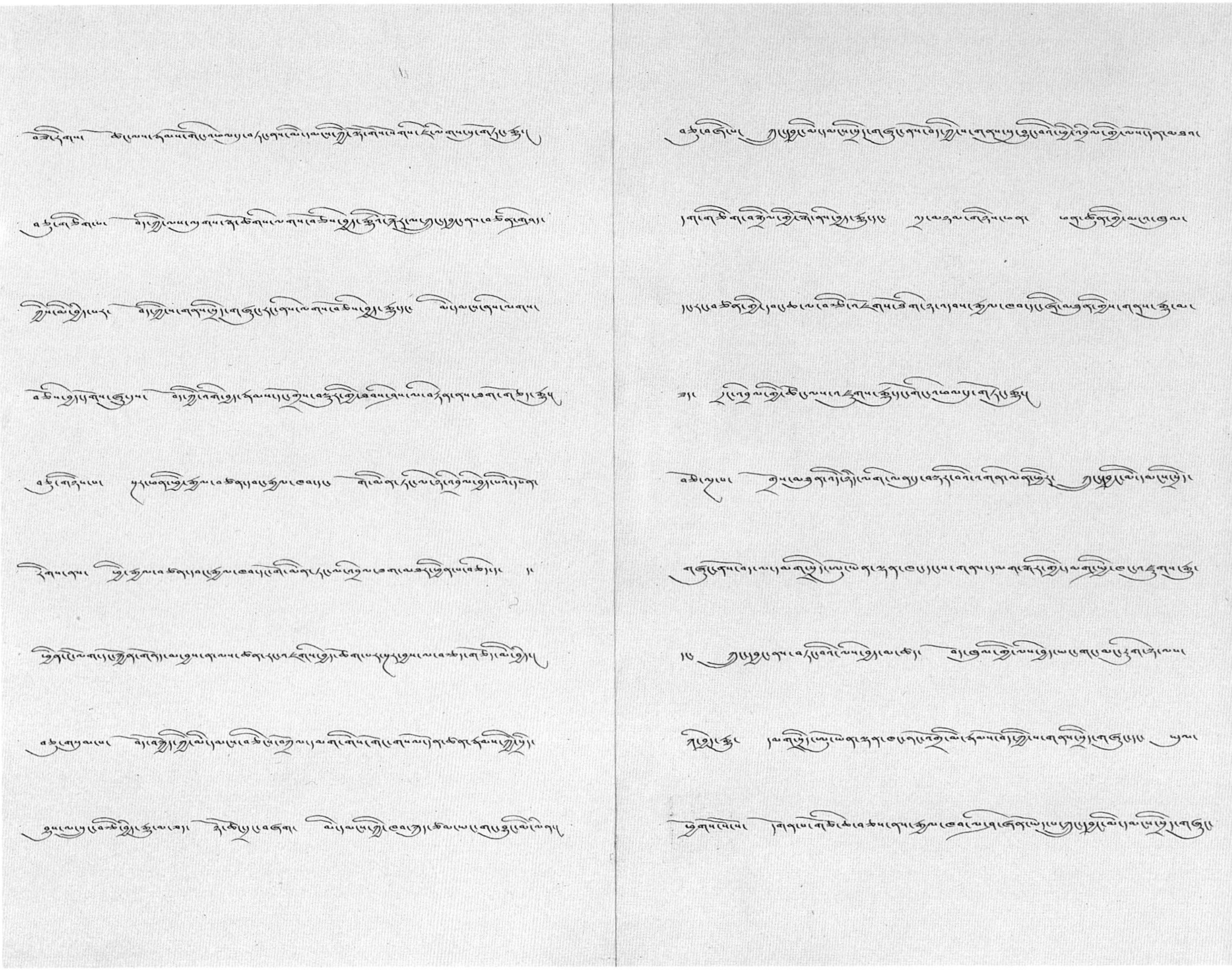

100 - 6

and the Tibetan people shall return to the large family of the motherland—the People's Republic of China.

2. The local government of Tibet shall actively assist the People's Liberation Army to enter Tibet and consolidate the national defence.

3. In accordance with the policy towards nationalities laid down in the Common Programme of the Chinese People's Political Consultative Conference, the Tibetan people have the right to exercise national regional autonomy under the unified leadership of the Central People's Government.

4. The central authorities will not alter the existing political system in Tibet. The central authorities also will not alter the established status, functions and powers of the Dalai Lama. The officials of all ranks shall hold office as usual.

5. The established status, functions and powers of the Panchen Erdeni shall be maintained.

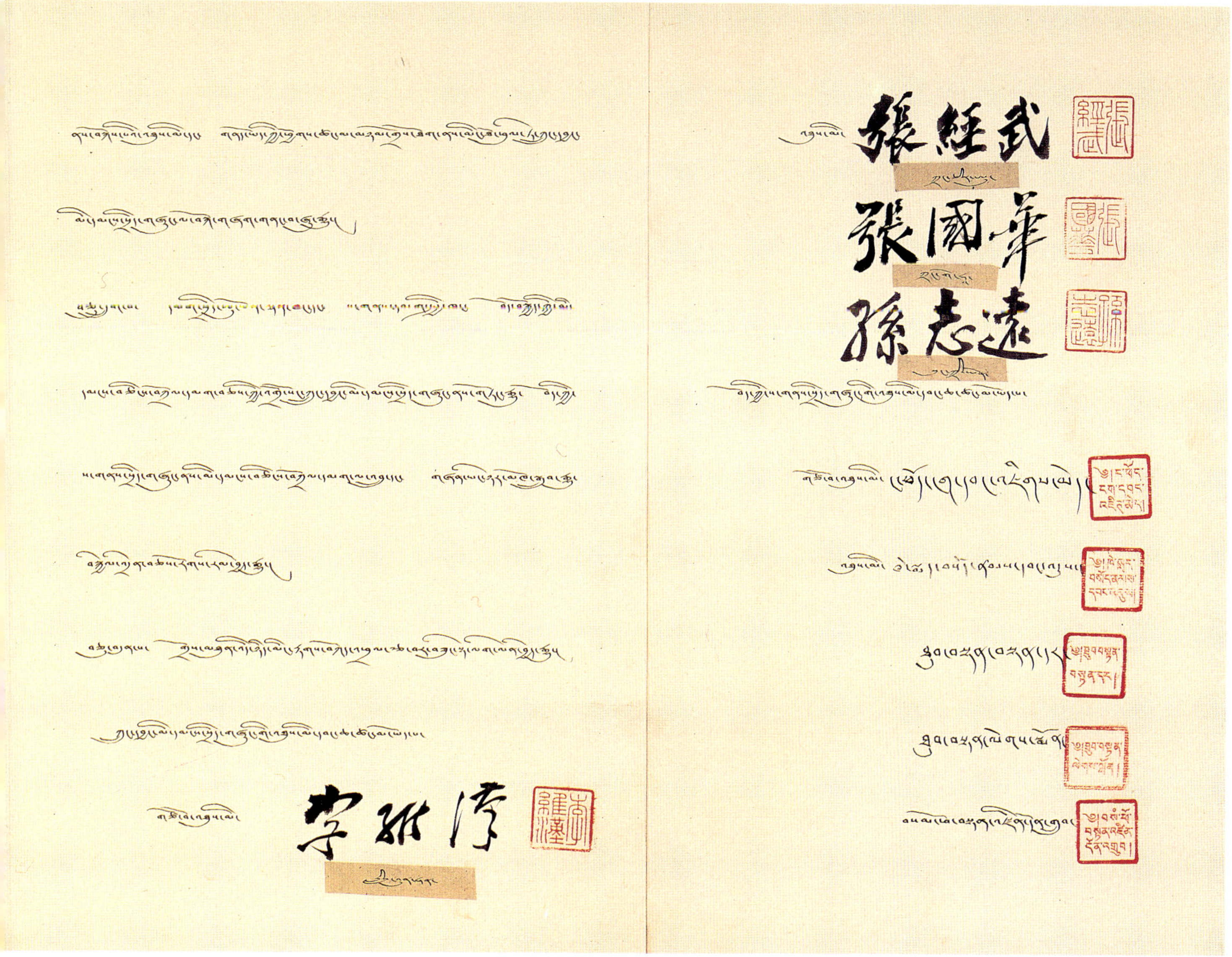




6. By the established status, functions and powers of the Dalai Lama and of the Panchen Erdeni are meant the status, functions and powers of the 13th Dalai Lama and of the 9th Panchen Erdeni when they maintained amicable relations with each other.

7. The policy of freedom of religious belief laid down in the Common Programme of the Chinese People's Political Consultative Conference shall be executed. The religious beliefs, customs and habits of the Tibetan people shall be respected, and the lamaseries shall be protected. The central authorities will not effect any change in the income of the monasteries.

8. The Tibetan troops shall be reorganized by stages into the People's Liberation Army and become a part of the national defence forces of the People's Republic of China.

9. The spoken and written languages and school education of the Tibetan nationality shall be developed step by step in accordance with the specific conditions in Tibet.

10. Tibetan agriculture, animal husbandry, industry and commerce shall be developed step by step, and the people's livelihood shall be improved step by step in accordance with the

100-8

specific conditions in Tibet.

11. In matters related to various reforms in Tibet, there will be no compulsion on the part of the central authorities. The local government of Tibet should carry out reforms of its own accord, and when the people raise demands for reform, they shall be settled by means of consultation with the leading personnel of Tibet.

12. As long as former pro–imperialist and pro–Kuomintang officials resolutely sever relations with the imperialists and the Kuomintang and do not engage in sabotage or resistance, they may continue to hold office irrespective of their past.

13. The People's Liberation Army entering Tibet shall abide by all the above–mentioned policies and shall also be fair in all buying and selling activities and shall not arbitrarily take even a single needle or a piece of thread from the people.

14. The Central People's Government shall handle all external affairs of the area of Tibet on a centralized basis. There will be peaceful co–existence with neighbouring countries and

100-9

fair commercial and trading relations will be established and developed on the basis of equality, mutual benefit and mutual respect for territorial sovereignty.

15. In order to ensure the implementation of this agreement, the Central People's Government shall set up a military and administrative commission and a military area command in Tibet, and, apart from the personnel sent there by the Central People's Government, shall employ as many local Tibetan personnel as possible in the work.

Local Tibetan personnel taking part in the military and administrative commission may include patriotic personages from the local government of Tibet, all districts and leading monasteries; the name-list shall be drawn up after consultation between the representatives

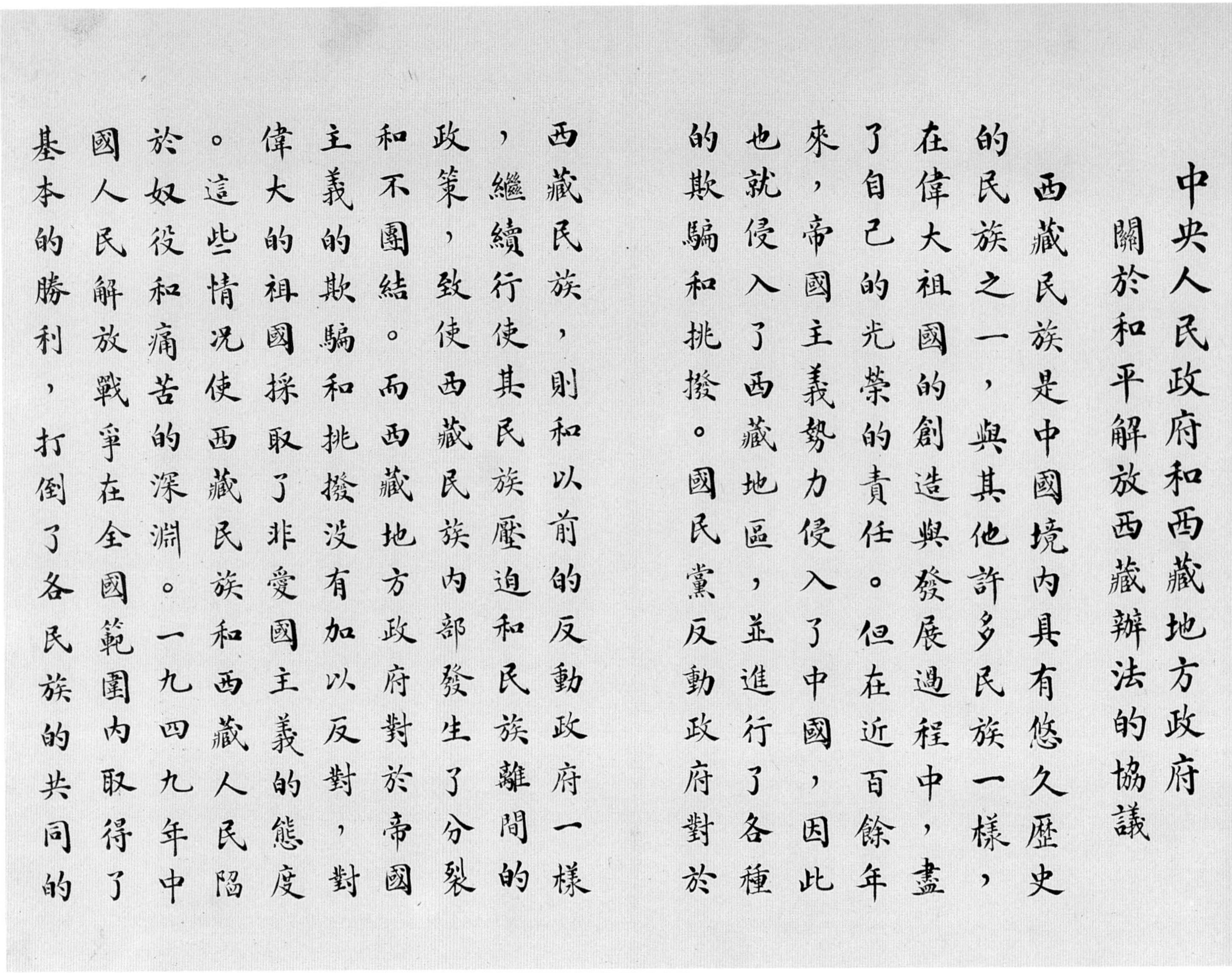

中央人民政府和西藏地方政府
關於和平解放西藏辦法的協議

西藏民族是中國境內具有悠久歷史的民族之一，與其他許多民族一樣，在偉大祖國的創造與發展過程中，盡了自己的光榮的責任。但在近百餘年來，帝國主義勢力侵入了中國，因此也就侵入了西藏地區，並進行了各種的欺騙和挑撥。國民黨反動政府對於西藏民族，則和以前的反動政府一樣，繼續行使其民族壓迫和民族離間的政策，致使西藏民族內部發生了分裂和不團結。西藏地方政府對於帝國主義的欺騙和挑撥沒有加以反對，對偉大的祖國採取了非愛國主義的態度。這些情況使西藏民族和西藏人民陷於奴役和痛苦的深淵。一九四九年中國人民解放戰爭在全國範圍內取得了基本的勝利，打倒了各民族的共同的

100 - 10

designated by the Central People's Government and all quarters concerned, and shall be submitted to the Central People's Government for appointment.

16. Funds needed by the military and administrative commission, the military area command and the People's Liberation Army entering Tibet shall be provided by the Central People's Government. The local government of Tibet will assist the People's Liberation Army in the purchase and transport of food, fodder and other daily necessities.

17. This agreement shall come into force immediately after signatures and seals are affixed to it.

Signed and sealed by:

Delegates with the full authority of the Central People's Government:

Chief Delegate:

Li Weihan

Delegates:

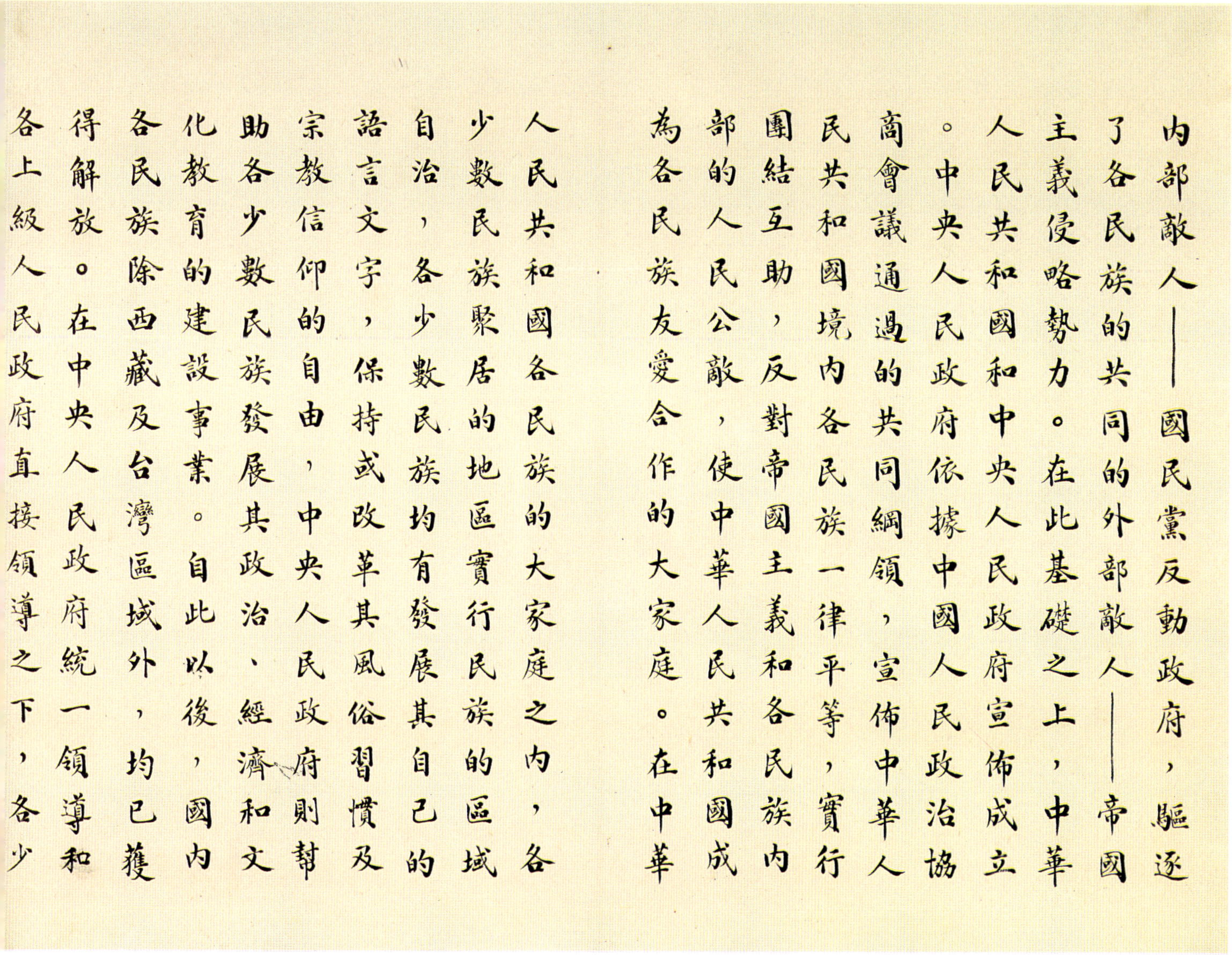
内部敵人——國民黨反動政府，驅逐了各民族的共同的外部敵人——帝國主義侵略勢力。在此基礎之上，中華人民共和國中央人民政府宣佈成立。中央人民政府依據中國人民政治協商會議通過的共同綱領，宣佈中華人民共和國境內各民族一律平等，實行團結互助，反對帝國主義和各民族內部的人民公敵，使中華人民共和國成為各民族友愛合作的大家庭。在中華人民共和國各民族的大家庭之內，各少數民族聚居的地區實行民族的區域自治，各少數民族均有發展其自己的語言文字，保持或改革其風俗習慣及宗教信仰的自由，中央人民政府則幫助各少數民族發展其政治、經濟和文化教育的建設事業。自此以後，國內各民族除西藏及台灣區域外，均已獲得解放。在中央人民政府統一領導和各上級人民政府直接領導之下，各少

100 - 11

Zhang Jingwu

Zhang Guohua

Sun Zhiyuan

Delegates with the full authority of the local government of Tibet:

Chief Delegate:

Ngapoi Ngawang Jigmi

Delegates:

Khemad Sodnam Wangdus

Thubtan Tandar

Thubtan Legmon

Bsampho Tandsin Dongrub

May 23, 1951 Beijing

Preserved by the Archives of the Tibet Autonomous Region.

數民族均已充分享受民族平等的權利，並已經實行或正在實行民族的區域自治。為了順利地清除帝國主義侵略勢力在西藏的影響，完成中華人民共和國領土和主權的統一，保衛國防，使西藏民族和西藏人民獲得解放，回到中華人民共和國的大家庭中來，與國內其他各民族享受同樣的民族平等的權利，發展其政治、經濟、文化教育事業，中央人民政府於命令人民解放軍進軍西藏之際，通知西藏地方政府派遣代表來中央舉行談判，以便訂立和平解放西藏辦法的協議。一九五一年四月下旬西藏地方政府的全權代表到達北京。中央人民政府當即指派全權代表和西藏地方政府的全權代表於友好的基礎上舉行了談判。談判結果，雙方同意成立本協議，並保證其付諸實行。

一、西藏人民團結起來，驅逐帝國



主義侵略勢力出西藏，西藏人民回到中華人民共和國祖國大家庭中來。

二、西藏地方政府積極協助人民解放軍進入西藏，鞏固國防。

三、根據中國人民政治協商會議共同綱領的民族政策，在中央人民政府統一領導之下，西藏人民有實行民族區域自治的權利。

四、對於西藏的現行政治制度，中央不予變更。達賴喇嘛的固有地位及職權，中央亦不予變更。各級官員照常供職。

五、班禪額爾德尼的固有地位及職權，應予維持。

六、達賴喇嘛和班禪額爾德尼的固有地位及職權，係指十三世達賴喇嘛與九世班禪額爾德尼彼此和好相處時的地位及職權。

100－14

七、實行中國人民政治協商會議共同綱領規定的宗教信仰自由的政策，尊重西藏人民的宗教信仰和風俗習慣，保護喇嘛寺廟。寺廟的收入，中央不予變更。

八、西藏軍隊逐步改編為人民解放軍，成為中華人民共和國國防武裝的一部分。

九、依據西藏的實際情況，逐步發展西藏民族的語言、文字和學校教育。

十、依據西藏的實際情況，逐步發展西藏的農牧工商業，改善人民生活。

十一、有關西藏的各項改革事宜，中央不加強迫。西藏地方政府應自動進行改革，人民提出改革要求時，得採取與西藏領導人員協商的方法解決之。

100－15

十二、過去親帝國主義和親國民黨的官員，只要堅決脫離與帝國主義和國民黨的關係，不進行破壞和反抗，仍可繼續供職，不究既往。

十三、進入西藏的人民解放軍遵守上列各項政策，同時買賣公平，不妄取人民一針一線。

十四、中央人民政府統一處理西藏地區的一切涉外事宜，並在平等、互利和互相尊重領土主權的基礎上，與鄰邦和平相處，建立和發展公平的通商貿易關係。

十五、為保證本協議之執行，中央人民政府在西藏設立軍政委員會和軍區司令部，除中央人民政府派去的人員外，儘量吸收西藏地方人員參加工作。參加軍政委員會的西藏地方人

員，得包括西藏地方政府及各
地區、各主要寺廟的愛國分子
，由中央人民政府指定的代表
與有關各方面協商提出名單，
報請中央人民政府任命。

十六、軍政委員會、軍區司令部及入
藏人民解放軍所需經費，由中
央人民政府供給。西藏地方政
府應協助人民解放軍購買和運
輸糧秣及其他日用品。

十七、本協議於簽字蓋章後立即生效
。

中央人民政府全權代表

首席代表 李維漢

代表 張經武 張國華 孫志遠



西藏地方政府全權代表

首席代表

代表

一九五一年 五月 二十三日 於北京

# ཏཱ་ལའི་བླ་མ་སྐུ་ཕྲེང་བཅུ་བཞི་པས་གྲོས་མཐུན་བྱུང་བར་བརྩི་བཀུར་ཞུ་བའི་དོན་དུ་ཀྲུའུ་ཞི་མའོ་ཙེ་ཏུང་ལ་ཕུལ་བའི་ཏར།
# 第十四世達賴喇嘛爲擁護協議事致毛澤東主席電
# The 14th Dalai Lama's Cables to Chairman Mao Zedong Expressing Support for the Agreement

29.8 × 20.9

ཀྲུང་དབྱང་ཡིག་ཚགས་ཁང་དུ་ཉར་ཚགས་བྱས་ཡོད།

中央檔案館藏

The Central People's Government,

Following is the translation of two cables sent by the Dalai Lama to Chairman Mao:

(1) Chairman Mao of the Central People's Government,

This year the local government of Tibet sent five delegates with full authority headed by Kaloon Ngapoi to Beijing in late April 1951 to conduct peace talks with delegates with full authority appointed by the Central People's Government. On the basis of friendship, delegates on both sides concluded the Agreement on Measures for the Peaceful Liberation of Tibet on May 23, 1951. The local government of Tibet as well as the Tibetan monks and laymen unanimously support this agreement, and under the leadership of Chairman Mao and the Central People's Government, will actively assist the People's Liberation Army in Tibet to consolidate national defence, drive imperialist influences out of Tibet and safeguard the unification of the territory and the sovereignty of the motherland. I hereby send this cable to inform you of this.

Preserved by the Central Archives.

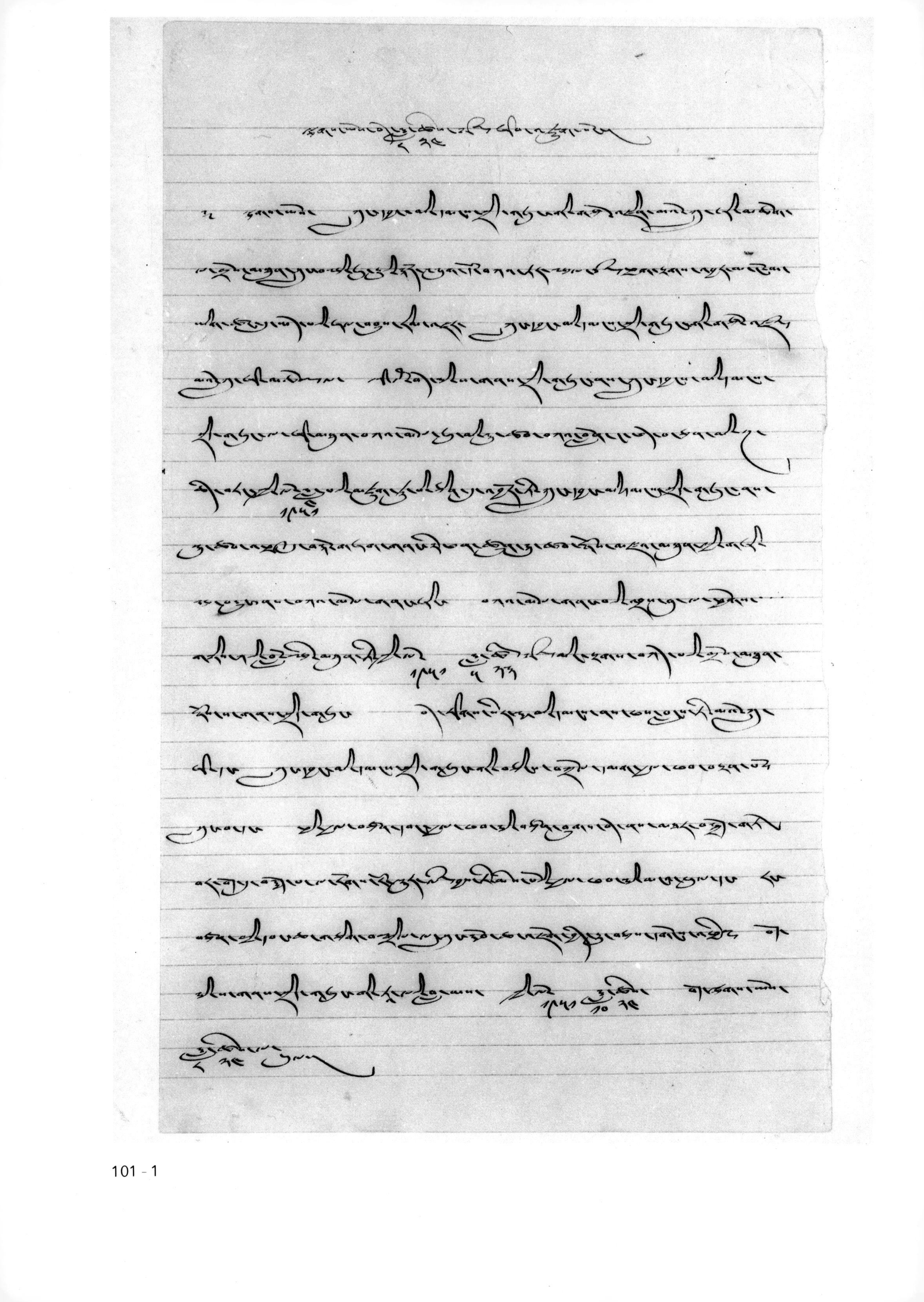

主席閱　　　　主席已閱

等級 AAAA　　拉薩 台來　A 西 No. 55

軍聯A西 No. 176　　政情 類　　195 1, 10, 24

附註 抄 ABCDF、陳黎、聶、統戰、民委、總情、軍聯

達賴向毛主席
致電擁護執行協議

中央：

茲將達賴喇嘛給毛主席的兩份電報譯轉如下：

(甲)中央人民政府毛主席：

今年西藏地方政府特派全權代表噶倫阿沛等五人於一九五一年四月底抵達北京，與中央人民政府指定的全權代表進行和談。雙方代表在友好基礎上已于一九五一年五月二十三日簽訂了關於和平解放西藏辦法的協議。西藏地方政府及藏族僧俗人民一致擁護，并在毛主席及中央人民政府領導下積極協助人民解放軍進藏部隊鞏固國防，驅逐帝國主義勢力出西藏，保護祖國領土主權的統一，謹電奉聞。

# ཀྲུའུ་ཞི་མའོ་ཙེ་ཏུང་ནས་ཏཱ་ལའི་བླ་མར་བཏང་བའི་ཏར་ལན།
# 毛澤東主席給達賴喇嘛的覆電
# Chairman Mao Zedong's Reply Cable to the Dalai Lama

33 × 24

སྐུ་ཞབས་ཏཱ་ལའི་བླ་མ་མཆོག་ལ།

ཁྱེད་ཀྱིས་ཕྱི་ལོ་ཆིག་སྟོང་དགུ་བརྒྱ་ང་གཅིག་ལོའི་ཟླ་བ་བཅུ་པའི་ཚེས་ཉེར་བཞི་ཉིན་བཏང་བའི་ཏར་ཡིག་ལག་སོན་བྱུང་། ཁྱེད་ཀྱིས་བོད་ཞི་བས་བཅིངས་གྲོལ་བྱུང་ཐབས་སྐོར་གྱི་གྲོས་དོན་ལག་བསྟར་བྱ་རྒྱུའི་ཐད་ལ་འབད་བརྩོན་གནང་བར་ངས་ཐུགས་རྗེ་ཆེ་ཞུ་རྒྱུ་དང་ཆབས་ཅིག་སྙིང་ཐག་པ་ནས་རྟེན་འབྲེལ་ཞུ། །

མའོ་ཙེ་ཏུང་ནས།

༡༩༥༡ལོའི་ཟླ་༡༠ཚེས་༢༦ཉིན།

བོད་རང་སྐྱོང་ལྗོངས་ཡིག་ཚགས་ཁང་དུ་ཉར་ཚགས་བྱས་ཡོད།

西藏自治區檔案館藏

Mr. Dalai Lama,

I have received your cable dated October 24, 1951. I wish to express my thanks for your efforts in the implementation of the Agreement on the Peaceful Liberation of Tibet and extend my heartfelt congratulations to you.

Mao Zedong

October 26, 1951

Preserved by the Archives of the Tibet Autonomous Region.

1951.10.26

中央人民政府發電紙

發往 张经武

等級 AAAA 毛主席致達賴喇嘛覆電

附註 366 號 88

摘由

「達賴喇嘛先生：

你於一九五一年十月二十四日的來電，已經收到了。我感谢你对实行和平解放西藏协议的努力，並致衷心的祝贺。

毛泽东

一九五一年十月二十六日」

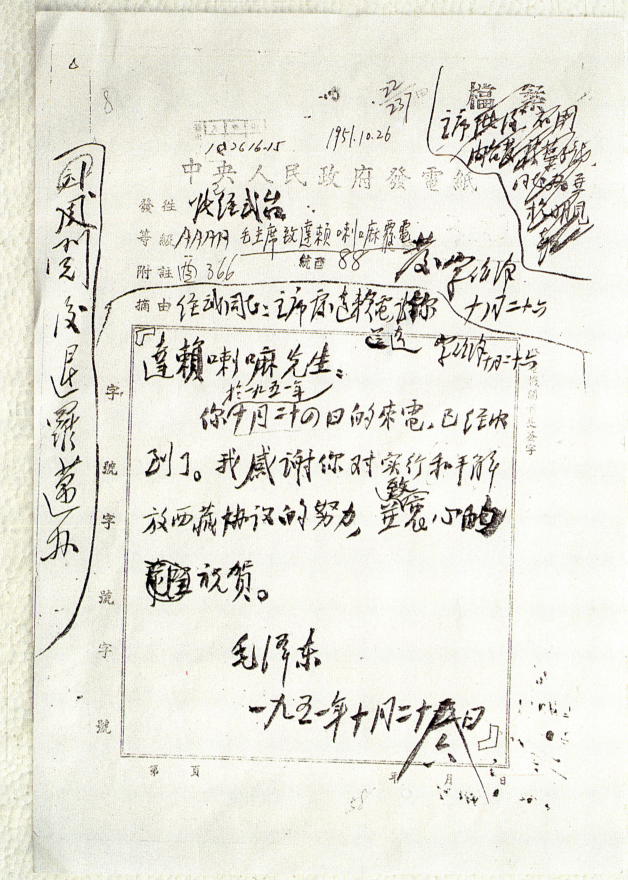

第 頁 年 月 日

# ཀྲུའུ་ཞི་མའོ་ཙེ་ཏུང་ནས་ཏཱ་ལའི་བླ་མ་ལ་བཏང་བའི་འཕྲིན་ཡིག
# 毛澤東主席給達賴喇嘛的信
# Chairman Mao Zedong's Letter to the Dalai Lama

33 × 24, 58.5 × 44

བོད་རང་སྐྱོང་ལྗོངས་ཡིག་ཚགས་ཁང་དུ་ཉར་ཚགས་བྱས་ཡོད།

西藏自治區檔案館藏

Dear Dalai Lama,

I was pleased to receive your letter dated July 6, 1955. I often think of you and the happy time we spent when you were in Beijing. When shall I be able to see you again? Probably in three years, if you come here to attend the Second National People's Congress. I appreciate your many actions since your return to Tibet. The Preparatory Committee of the Tibet Autonomous Region will soon be established and the people of all nationalities will be happy about it. Tibet is making progress. Of course we should not be impatient; as long as there is some progress each year, it will be good. I hope you will take good care of your health. The situation here is satisfactory. We have made some mistakes which are now being criticized and rectified. China is a large country, but she is still not prosperous or strong. We hope that with the combined efforts of the people of all nationalities and following the completion of several five–year plans, China can become prosperous and strong. Tibet has a promising future and I hope you will do your best to bring it about. I was pleased to see the Tibetan flowers you sent me with your letter and I am presenting you with some tea in return. I hope you can write to me often about any topic whatever. Please ask Comrade Zhang Guohua about any other matters. I have just told Zhang Guohua to learn from you in real earnest.

Best wishes for your health and happiness.

Mao Zedong

November 24, 1955

Preserved by the Archives of the Tibet Autonomous Region.

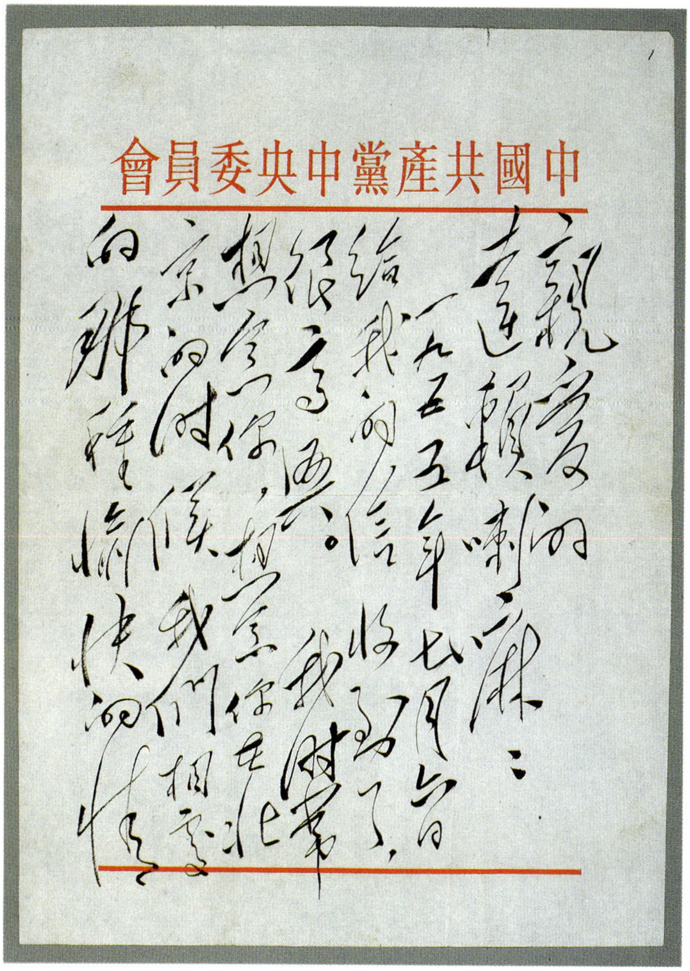

中國共產黨中央委員會

亲爱的达赖喇嘛：

一九五五年七月六日给我的信收到了，很高兴。我时常想念你，想念你在北京的时候，我们相处的那种愉快的情

103－1

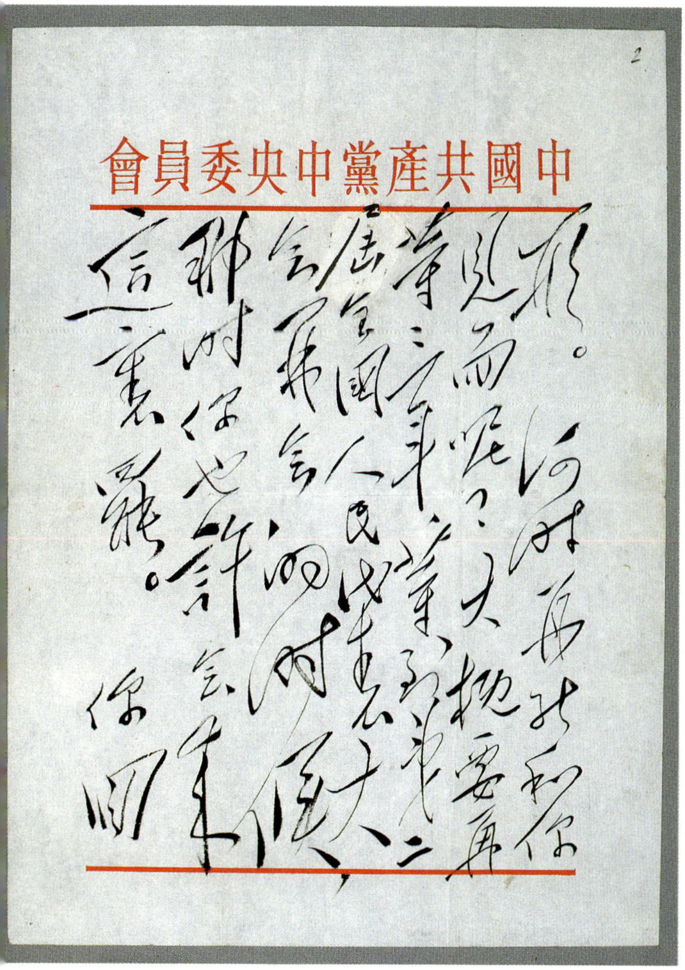

中國共產黨中央委員會

形。何时再和你见面呢？大概要再等二三年，等到二届全国人民代表大会开会的时候，那时你也许会来京罢。你回

103－2

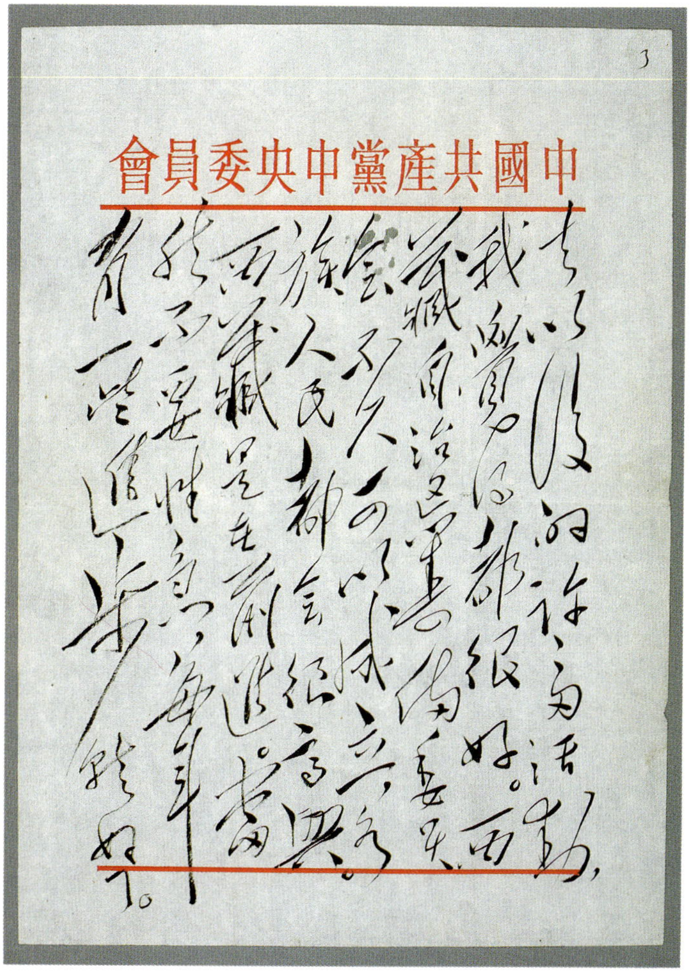

中國共產黨中央委員會

去以后的活动，我觉得都很好。西藏自治区筹备委员会成立以后，藏族人民都会很高兴。西藏是在前进当中，我不要性急，每年有一些进步，就好了。

103－3

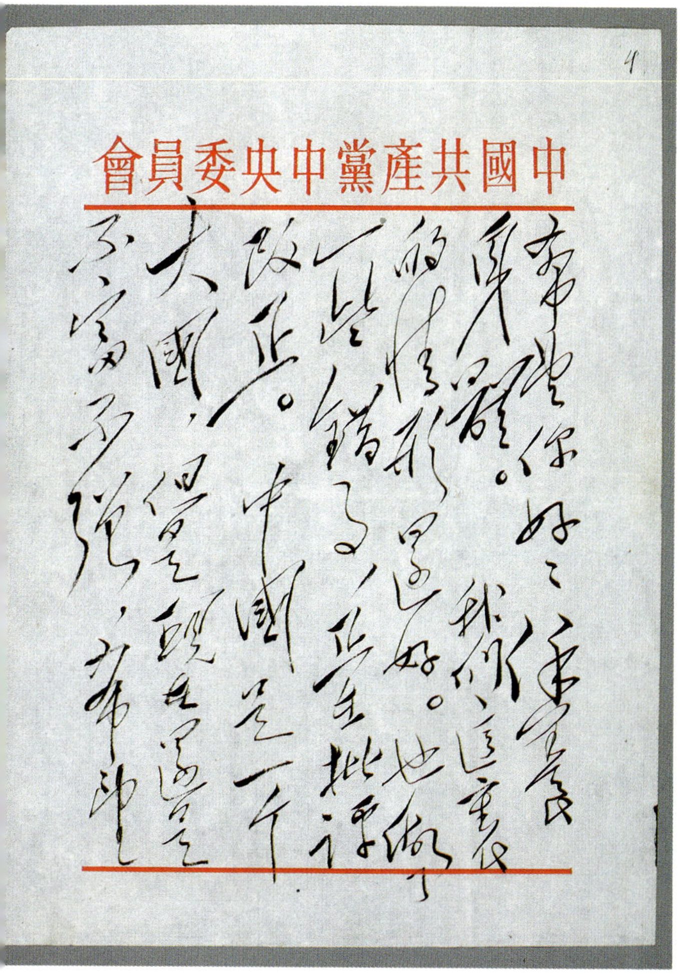

中國共產黨中央委員會

希望你好好保重身体。我们这里的情形也还好。也有一些错误，正在批评改正。中国是一个大国，但是现在还是不富不强，希

103－4

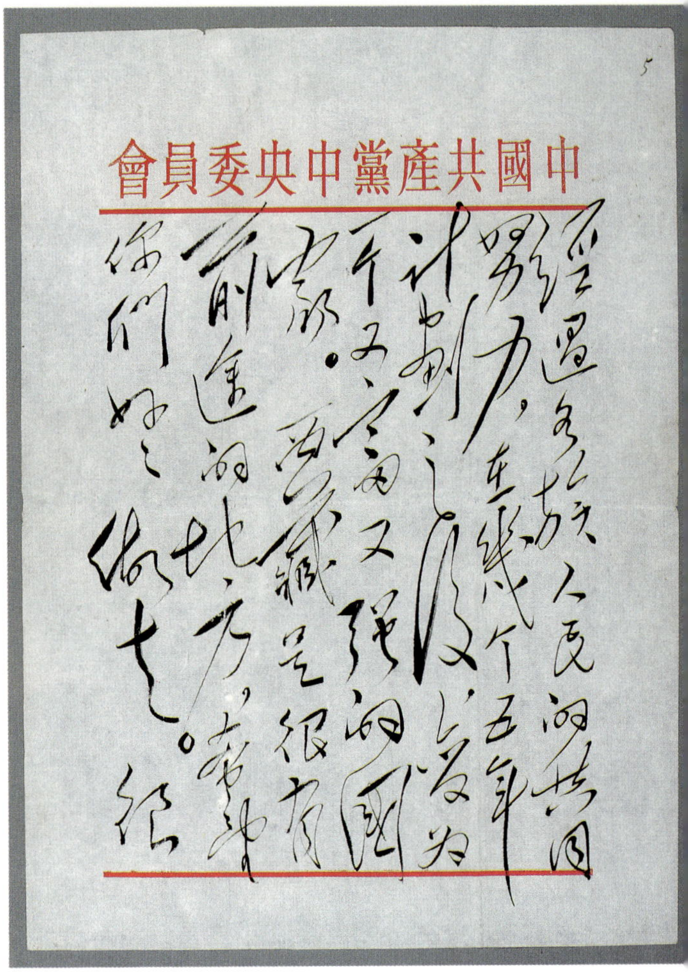
中國共產黨中央委員會

经过各族人民的共同努力，在几个五年计划之后，必为一个富强的国家。西藏是很有前途的地方，希望你们好好做去。给

103 - 5

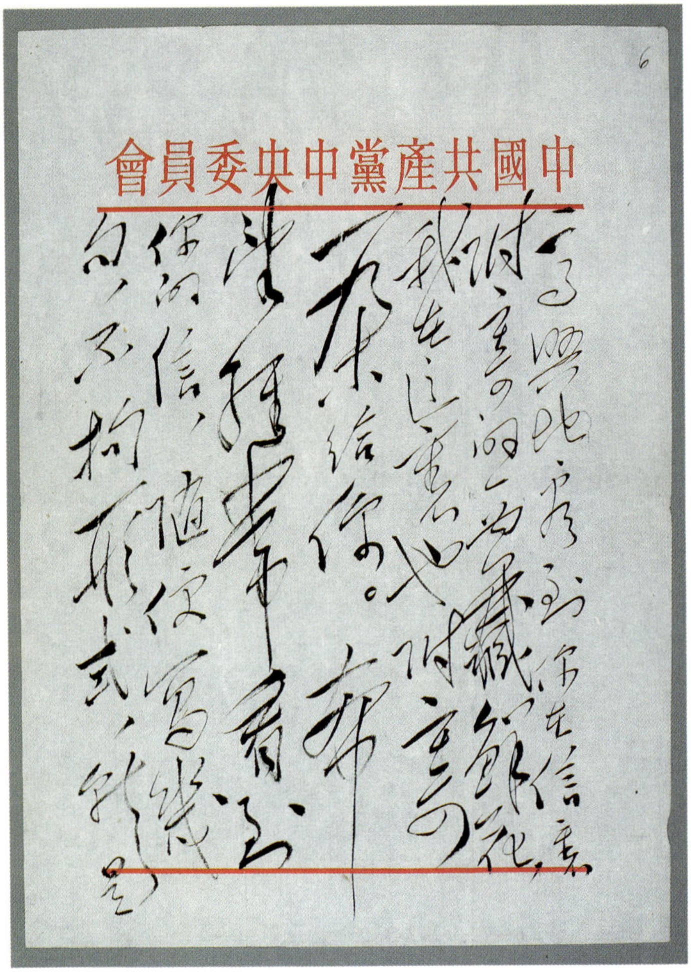
中國共產黨中央委員會

[illegible]照片，已由你处信来，对我的[illegible]，藏铜佛，我在这里也[illegible]以[illegible]东西给你。请经常来信。你的信，随便你写几句，不拘形式，就是

103 - 6

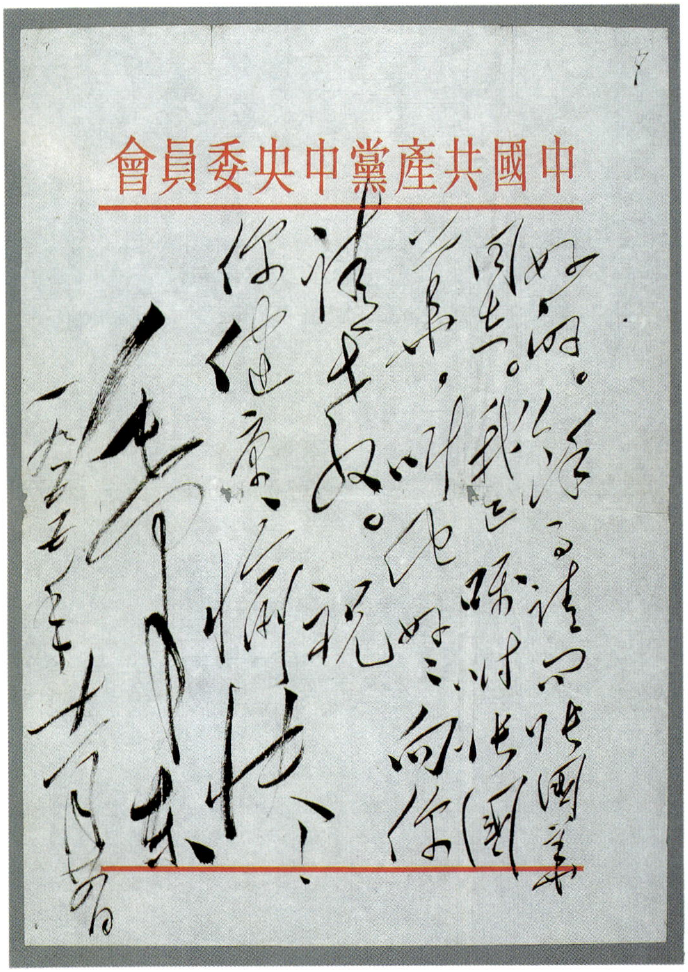
中國共產黨中央委員會

好的。今后请只[illegible]国华同志。我已嘱咐张国常来，以后好好向你请教。祝你健康愉快！

毛泽东

一九五五年十一月[illegible]日

103 - 7

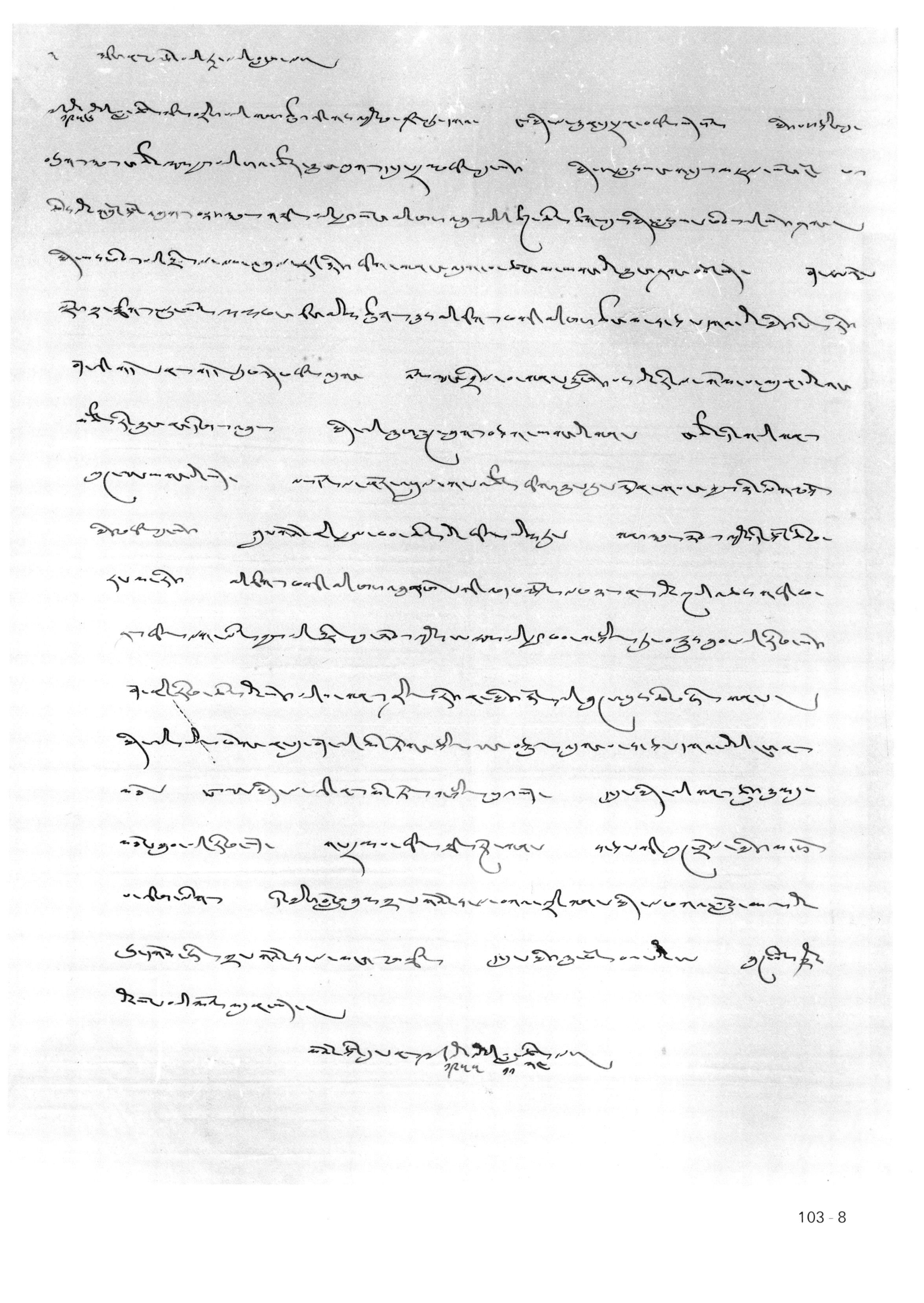

 [illegible]

[illegible] ༡༨༥༥ [illegible]

[illegible]

[illegible]

[illegible]

[illegible]

[illegible]

[illegible]

[illegible]

[illegible]

[illegible]

[illegible]

[illegible]

[illegible]

[illegible]

[illegible]

[illegible]

[illegible]

[illegible]

[illegible]

[illegible]

༡༨༥༥ ༡༡ ༢༨

# ཀྲུང་ལི་ཀྲུའུ་ཨེན་ལའི་ནས་ཏཱ་ལའི་བླ་མ་ལ་བཏང་བའི་འཕྲིན་ཡིག
# 周恩來總理給達賴喇嘛的信
# Premier Zhou Enlai's Letter to the Dalai Lama

26×18

བོད་རང་སྐྱོང་ལྗོངས་ཡིག་ཚགས་ཁང་དུ་ཉར་ཚགས་བྱས་ཡོད།

西藏自治區檔案館藏

104－1

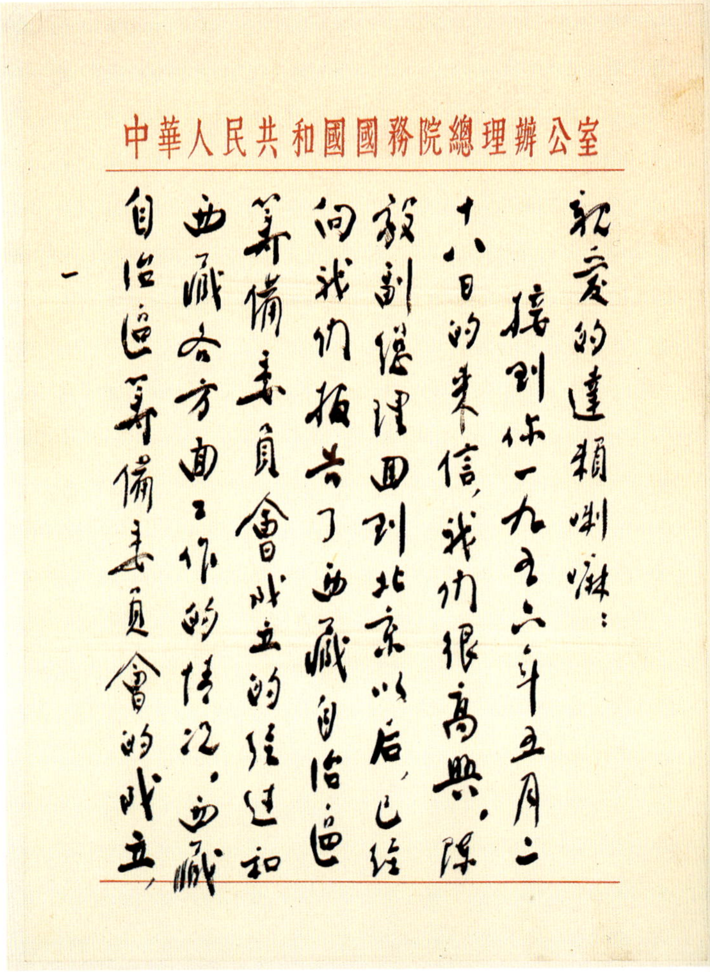
中華人民共和國國務院總理辦公室

親愛的達賴喇嘛：

接到你一九五六年五月二十八日的來信，我們很高興。保發副總理回到北京以后，已經向我們報告了西藏自治區籌備委員會成立的經過和西藏各方面工作的情況。西藏自治區籌備委員會的成立，

一

104－2

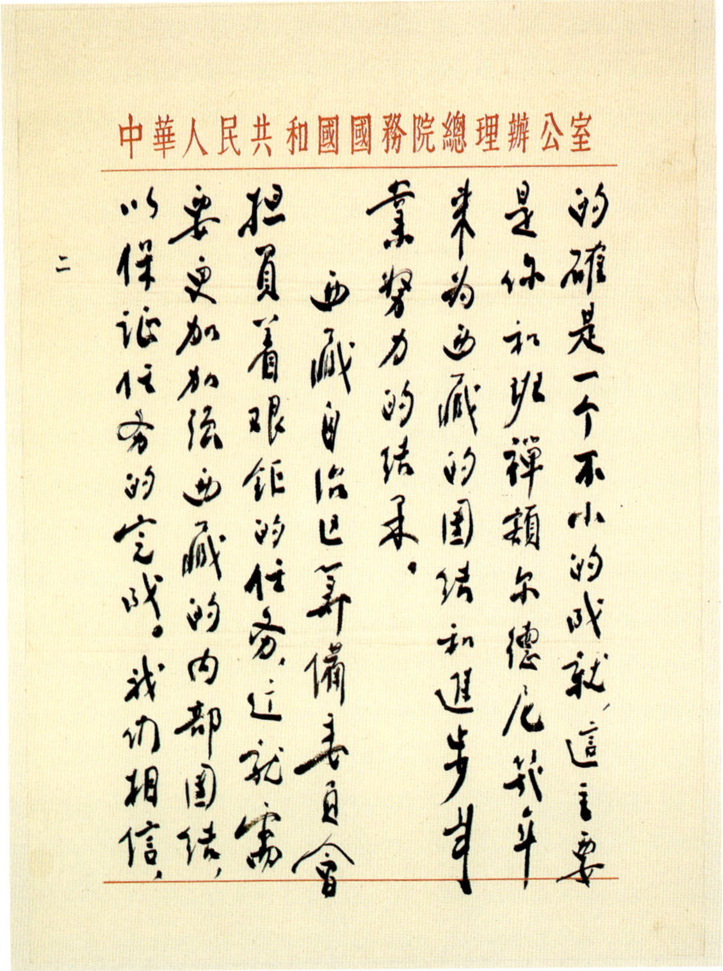
中華人民共和國國務院總理辦公室

的確是一个不小的成就，這主要是你和班禪額爾德尼幾年來為西藏的团结和進步事業努力的結果。

西藏自治區籌備委員會担負着艰鉅的任务，它就需要更加加強西藏的內部团结，以保証任务的完成。我们相信，

二

中華人民共和國國務院總理辦公室

三

在今後的工作中，如能多多為西藏各階層人民的利益着想，西藏自治區籌備委員會就更能夠得到西藏人民的擁護。而這些為人民謀利益的事，也不能求之過急，要有准備地一步一步去做。如果你在工作中遇到困难，請你隨時

104－3

中華人民共和國國務院總理辦公室

四

寫信或者打電報來同我們商量。中央人民政府將會給你一切幫助。

你的姐姐堯西·澤仁卓瑪向我提到，由于你們的一些家屬在國外的活動，你常常感到不安。我當然能夠了解你的心情，但是我覺得沒有必要感到不

104－4

中華人民共和國國務院總理辦公室

五

安，因為你的情况和他們的情况完全不同。你是了解中央的民族政策的，你也親眼看到了祖國各地正在蒸蒸日上地進行着的社會主義建設。自從西藏和平解放以來，不論是在中央和西藏地方的关係方面，或者是在西藏的內部團結方面，你

104－5

中華人民共和國國務院總理辦公室

六

都表現出是有遠見的，並且作了積極的努力。因此，中央和毛主席都完全信任你。

至于你在國外的一些家屬，據我們知道，美、英帝國主義分子的確想利用他們來破壞西藏的團結進步事業。現在，美、英帝國主義分子正以噶倫

104－6

中華人民共和國國務院總理辦公室

七

堡作为他们的特务组织的中心，
不断地在策划各种破坏活动。
这是应该引起我们的注意和
警惕的。但是，另一方面，你也不
必急于动你的这些家属回国。
他们对于祖国各民族的团结和
西藏近几年来所取得的进
步，还有怀疑，因而对于回国问



中華人民共和國國務院總理辦公室

八

题目前是会犹豫的。因此，你可
以先同他们经常通信，告诉他
们关于中央的政策和西藏的真
实情况。如果他们有经济上的困
难，你也可设法接济他们。目前，
主要是开导他们，并且使他们
从祖国和家属方面得到温暖；
如果急于动他们回来，反而会



中華人民共和國國務院總理辦公室

九

得不到结果。
最近，印度和尼泊尔都曾经
邀请你去访问。我们同意你所
作的答复，那就是，在原则上不
排除将来去访问的可能性，但
是，由于西藏自治区在筹备期
间工作重要，现在不能去。我们
觉得，暂时这样答复是比较



中華人民共和國國務院總理辦公室

十

好的，因为，一方面，西藏自治区
筹备委员会的工作的确需要
你主持，另一方面，也应该适当
地估计到美、英帝国主义分
子的破坏活动。因此，关于你出
国访问的问题，我们应该采取
慎重的和有准备的步骤。
西藏和内地之间的航空线

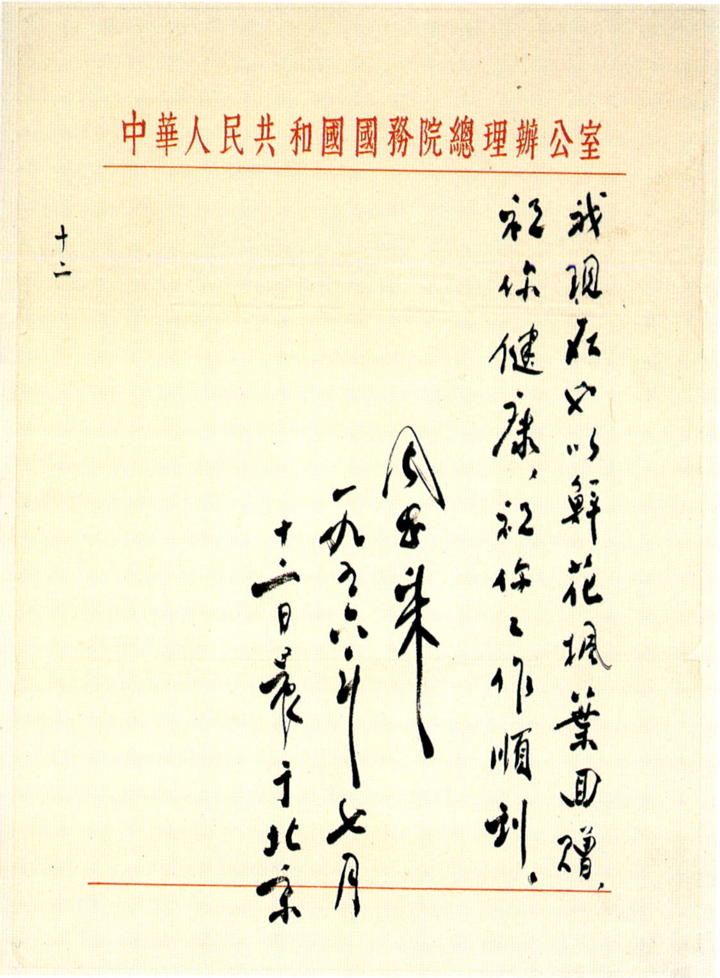

中華人民共和國國務院總理辦公室

十二

我现在以鲜花枫叶回赠，
祝你健康，祝你工作顺利，

周恩来

一九五六年七月
十二日晨于北京

104 - 12

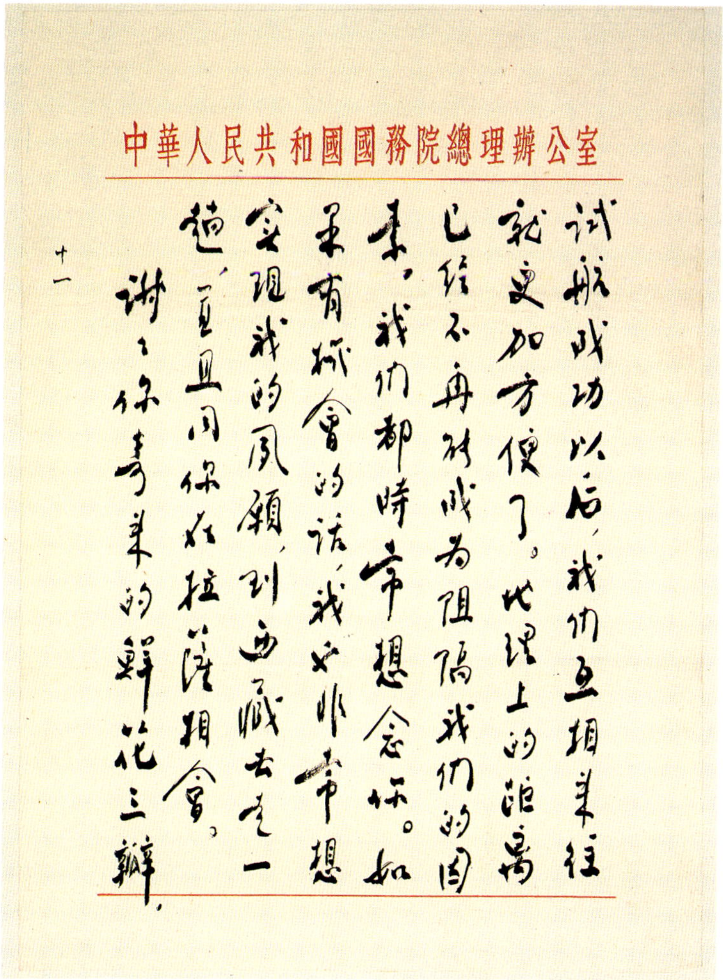

中華人民共和國國務院總理辦公室

十一

试航成功以后，我们互相来往
就更加方便了。地理上的距离
已经不再成为阻隔我们的因
素，我们都时常想念你。如
果有机会的话，我也非常想
实现我的夙愿，到西藏去走一
趟，并且同你在拉萨相会，
谢谢你寄来的鲜花三瓣，

104 - 11

104 - 13

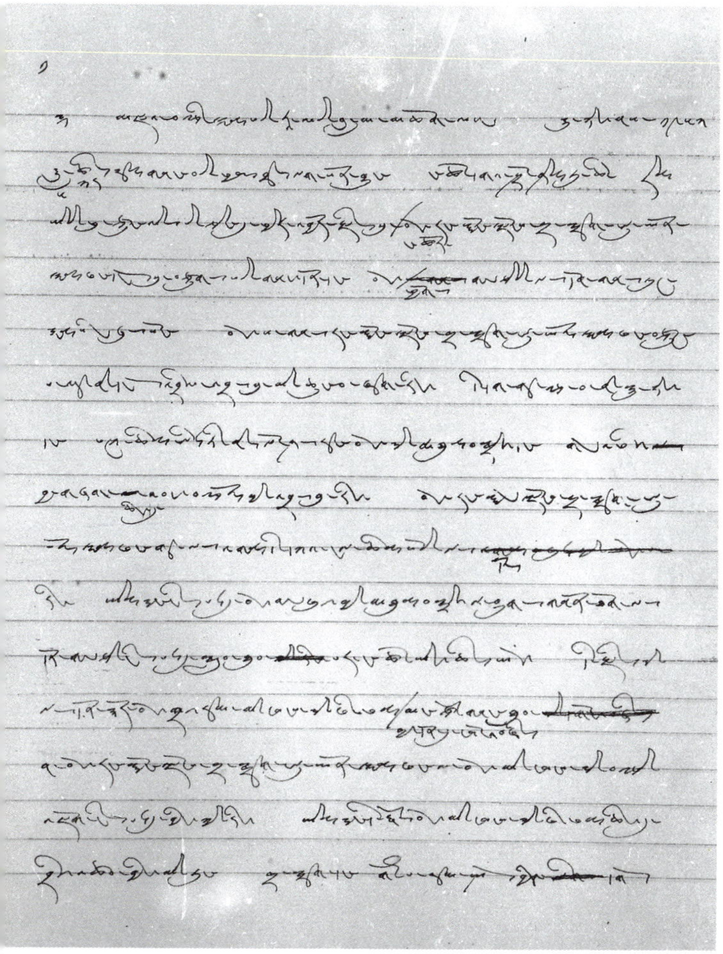

104 - 14

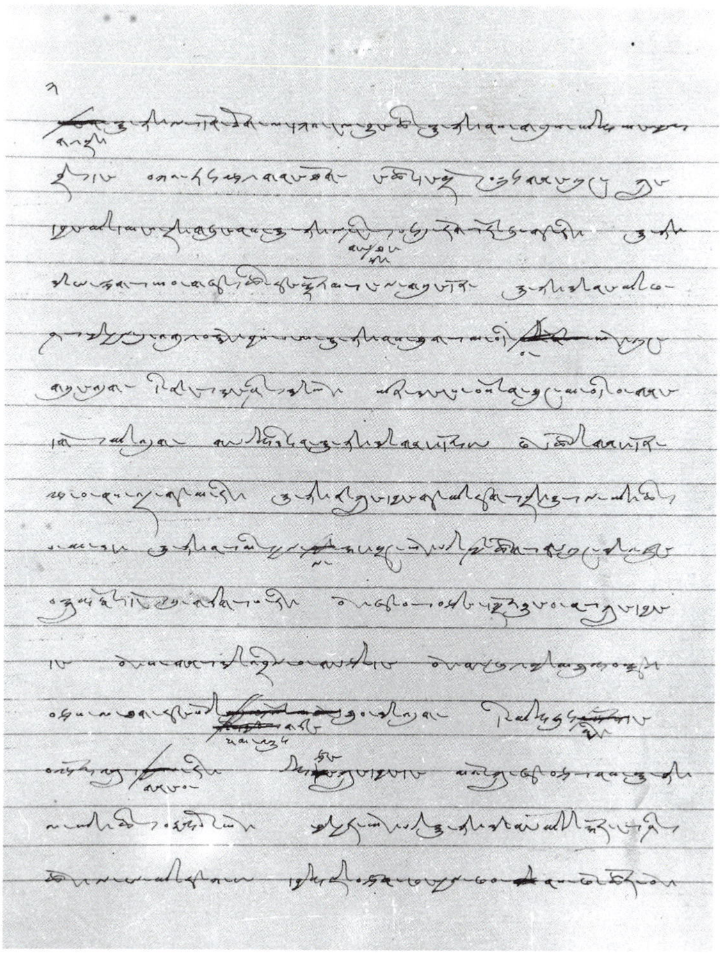

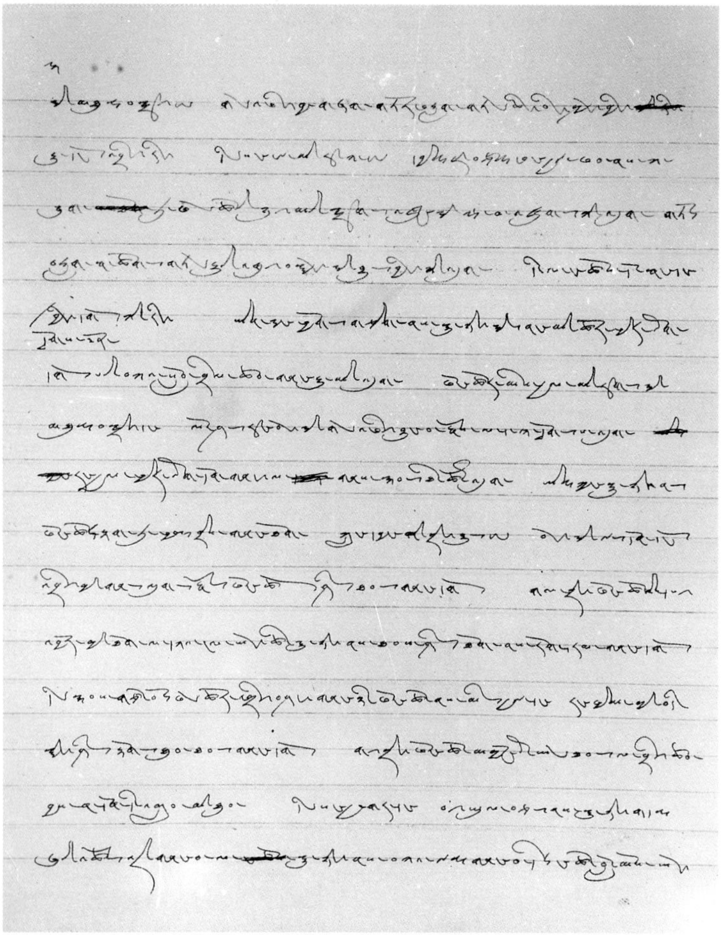

104 - 15

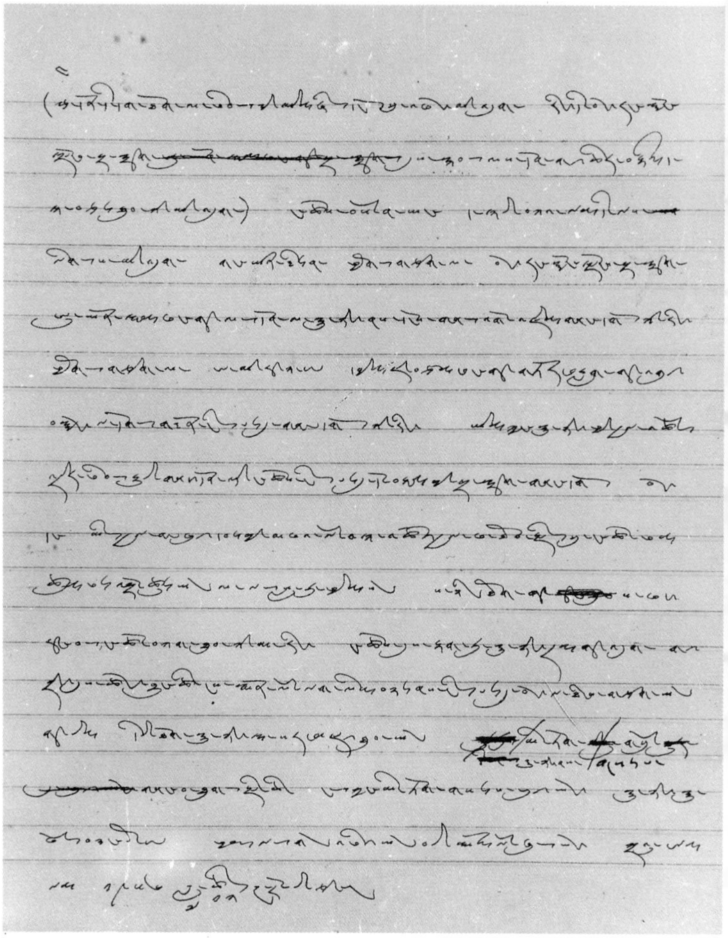

104 - 16

Dear Dalai Lama,

We were pleased to receive your letter dated May 28, 1956. After he returned to Beijing, Vice–Premier Chen Yi reported to us about the establishment of the Preparatory Committee of the Tibet Autonomous Region and the progress of the work on various fronts in Tibet. The establishment of the Committee is indeed a great achievement, which is mainly the result of years of effort on the part of yourself and the Panchen Erdeni in working toward achieving unity and progress in Tibet.

The Preparatory Committee has a mammoth and difficult task, requiring the strengthening of the internal unity of Tibet to guarantee its fulfilment. We are confident that the Committee will gain even more support from the Tibetan people if it can demonstrate that it is fully taking into consideration the interests of the Tibetan people of all social strata in its future work. Of course we should not rush too hastily into such endeavours, even though they benefit the people. We must proceed step by step according to a prepared plan. If you come across any difficulties in your work, please write or cable us at any time and the Central People's Government will offer you all the help it can.

Your elder sister Yabzhis Tshering Grolma mentioned to me that you are often upset because of the activities of your relatives abroad. I can well understand your feeling. However, I do not think you should be perturbed since you and they are in entirely different situations. You understand the nationality policies of the Central Government and you have seen the mighty socialist construction now being carried out throughout the country. Ever since the peaceful liberation of Tibet, you have taken a far–sighted stand and played an active role both in the relationship between the Central Government and Tibet and the internal unity of Tibet. Consequently, the Central Government and Chairman Mao fully trust you.

As to the matter of your relatives living abroad, according to our information, American and British imperialists have indeed tried to use them to harm the cause of unity and progress in Tibet. With Kalimpong as the centre of their spy organizations, American and British imperialists are constantly plotting various disruptive activities. This merits our attention and should put us on our guard. Nevertheless, on the other hand, you need not be anxious about persuading your relatives to return to China. As they are suspicious about the unity of all the nationalities of our homeland and the progress Tibet has made in the past several years, they are naturally hesitant about coming back. Therefore you may first of all write to them often, informing them of the policies of the Central Government and the true situation in Tibet. If they have financial problems you can also assist them. At present your main task is to try to make them see what is right and wrong and let them feel the warmth of family and homeland. Nothing will be gained if you are impatient in attempting to persuade them to return.

Recently both India and Nepal extended invitations to you to visit them. I still agree with your reply, which was that in principle, you would not rule out the possibility of a future visit, but that since you have important work to do during the establishment of the Tibet Autonomous Region, you could not make such a visit at this time. I still think that such a response is best for the time being because, on the one hand, there is a real need for you to preside over the work of the Preparatory Committee of the Tibet Autonomous Region and, on the other hand, we must give due consideration to the attempts at sabotage on the part of the American and British imperialists. Therefore, we should take cautious and calculated steps with regard to your visit abroad. After trial flights between Tibet and the rest of China have been carried out successfully, it will be more convenient for us to visit each other. The geographic distance will no longer be an obstacle between us. You are often in our thoughts. I would also very much like to fulfil my long–standing wish to go to Tibet and meet with you in Lhasa if I get the chance.

Thank you for the three fresh flowers you sent me. I am sending some flowers and maple leaves in return. I wish you good health and success in your work.

Zhou Enlai

July 12, 1956 Beijing

Preserved by the Archives of the Tibet Autonomous Region.

# ཨུ་ཡོན་ཀྲང་ལིའུ་ཧྲོའོ་ཆི་ནས་ཏཱ་ལའི་བླ་མ་ལ་བཏང་བའི་འཕྲིན་ཡིག

# 劉少奇委員長給達賴喇嘛的信

# Chairman Liu Shaoqi's Letter to the Dalai Lama

21.6 × 18

སྙིང་ནས་བརྩེ་བའི་ཏཱ་ལའི་བླ་མ་མཆོག་ལ།

ཁྱེད་ཀྱིས་ཟླ་བ་ལྔ་པའི་ཚེས་ཉེར་བརྒྱད་ཉིན་བཏང་བའི་འཕྲིན་ཡིག་འབྱོར་བྱུང་། ཁྱེད་ཀྱིས་འཚམ་འདྲི་གནང་བ་ལ་ཐུགས་རྗེ་ཆེ་ཞུ། ཉེ་ཆར་བདག་གི་ལུས་ཕུང་ཧ་ཅང་བདེ། ཐུགས་ཁྲལ་མི་གནང་བ་ཞུ།

ཙུང་ལི་གཞོན་པ་ཁྲིན་དབྱི་བོད་ལྗོངས་ནས་ཕྱིར་ལོག་རྗེས་སུ། བོད་ལྗོངས་ཀྱི་ལས་ཀའི་གནས་ཚུལ་ཀུང་དབྱང་ལ་སྙན་སེང་ཞུས་བྱུང་། བོད་རང་སྐྱོང་ལྗོངས་གྲ་སྒྲིག་ཨུ་ཡོན་ལྷན་ཁང་བཙུགས་པའི་ཚོགས་ཆེན་དེ། ཁྱེད་ཀྱི་འགོ་ཁྲིད་དང་པཎ་ཆེན་ཨེར་དེ་ནི་སོགས་རམ་མཛད་པའི་འོག་ཏུ་ལེགས་པར་ཚོགས་ཐུབ་པ་བྱུང་བ་དེ་ང་ཚོས་ཉན་རྗེས་སུ་ཚང་མ་ཧ་ཅང་དགའ་པོ་བྱུང་།

རང་སྐྱོང་ལྗོངས་གྲ་སྒྲིག་ཨུ་ཡོན་ལྷན་ཁང་བཙུགས་པའི་ཚོགས་འདུའི་ཐོག་བོད་ལྗོངས་ཀྱི་དེང་ཕྱིན་གྱི་ལས་ཀ་ལ་གྲོས་མོལ་དང་གོ་བསྡུར་བྱས་པ་མ་ཟད། ཆོད་དོན་ཡང་བཞག་ཡོད་པས་བོད་ལྗོངས་མི་རིགས་ཀྱི་དར་རྒྱས་དང་སྔོན་ཐོན་བྱེད་རྒྱུ་ལ་ཕྱར་ལས་ཕན་པ་ཡོད་པའི་ཆ་རྐྱེན་གསར་སྤྲུན་བྱས་ཡོད་པ་རེད། ཁྱེད་ནས་ཆ་རྐྱེན་འདི་དག་བེད་སྤྱོད་བཏང་སྔེ་ཕྱར་ལས་ལྷག་པའི་ལས་ཀ་ཡག་པོ་ཞིག་སྒྲུབ་རྒྱུའི་རེ་བ་ཞུ། འོན་ཀྱང་གནས་ཚུལ་འདི་འདྲའི་འོག་ལ་ཡང་སྔར་བཞིན་ཕྱོགས་སོ་སོའི་མི་སྣ་ལ་མཐུན་སྒྲིལ་གཅིག་གྱུར་བྱེད་པར་དོ་སྣང་བྱས་ནས། སྒྲུབ་དགོས་པའི་བྱ་བ་རྣམས་ཁོང་ཚོ་དང་གྲོས་མོལ་བྱས་ཏེ། ཁོང་ཚོའི་མོས་མཐུན་དང་རྒྱབ་སྐྱོར་ཐོབ་པར་བྱེད་རྒྱུ། སྤྱི་ཚོགས་བསྒྱུར་བཅོས་བྱེད་པར་བོད་ལྗོངས་ཀྱི་བྱེ་བྲག་གི་གནས་ཚུལ་གཞིར་བཟུང་ནས་གོམ་པ་རེ་རེ་བཞིན་དུ་བསྒྲུབ་དགོས་པ་ལས། བྲེལ་འཚུབ་བྱེད་མི་ཉན། དེང་ཕྱིན་གྱི་དུས་སྐབས་ཤིག་གི་ལས་ཀའི་ནང་དུ། ཁྱེད་ཀྱིས་སྔར་ལས་ལྷག་པའི་གྲུབ་འབྲས་ཤིག་སྒྲུབ་ཐུབ་པར་ང་ཚོར་ཡིད་ཆེས་ཡོད། འདིའི་རིང་ལ་ང་ཚོས་རོགས་རམ་བྱེད་དགོས་ས་ཡོད་ན་ང་ཚོས་ཁྱེད་ལ་སྟོབས་ཤུགས་ཅི་ཡོད་ཀྱིས་རོགས་གང་ཐུབ་ཞུ་རྒྱུ་ཡིན།

སྐབས་དང་པོའི་རྒྱལ་ཡོངས་མི་དམངས་འཐུས་མི་ཚོགས་ཆེན་ཐེངས་གསུམ་པའི་ཚོགས་འདུ་ཧ་ཅང་ཡག་པོ་འཚོགས་ཐུབ་པ་བྱུང་བ་རེད། འཐུས་མི་མང་པོ་ཞིག་གིས་ཁ་ཞེ་གཉིས་མེད་ཀྱིས་རྒྱལ་ཁབ་ཀྱི་ལས་ཀ་ལ་སྐྱོན་བརྗོད་དང་གྲོས་འགོ་བཏོན་པ་རེད། བསམ་འཆར་འདི་དག་ནི་རྒྱལ་ཁབ་ལས་ཁུངས་ཀྱི་ལས་ཀ་དང་ལྷག་པར་དུ་འགོ་ཁྲིད་ཀྱི་ལས་ཀ་ལེགས་བཅོས་སུ་གཏོང་རྒྱུ་ལ་ཕན་པ་ཧ་ཅང་ཆེན་པོ་ཡོད། ཁྱེད་དུས་ཏག་ཏུ་པེ་ཅིན་དུ་བཞུགས་ནས་རྒྱུན་ལས་ཨུ་ཡོན་ལྷན་ཁང་གི་ལས་ཀར་འགོ་ཁྲིད་བྱེད་མི་ཐུབ་སྟབས། ཁྱེད་ཀྱིས་དུས་རྒྱུན་པར་འཕྲིན་ཡིག་བཏང་ནས་རྒྱུན་ལས་ཨུ་ཡོན་ལྷན་ཁང་གི་ལས་ཀར་བསམ་འཆར་འདོན་རྒྱུའི་རེ་བ་ཞུ།

ཉེ་ལམ་ཁྱེད་ཀྱི་སྐུ་གཟུགས་ཧ་ཅང་བདེ་བར་ཡོད་དམ། སྐུ་གཟུགས་ལ་གཅེས་སྲུས་ཡག་པོ་གནང་རྒྱུའི་རེ་བ་ཞུ།

ལིའུ་ཧྲོའོ་ཆི་ནས།

༡༩༥༦ལོའི་ཟླ་༨ཚེས་༣༠ཉིན།

བོད་རང་སྐྱོང་ལྗོངས་ཡིག་ཚགས་ཁང་དུ་ཉར་ཚགས་བྱས་ཡོད།

全國人民代表大會常務委員會

親愛的達賴喇嘛：

你五月二十八日的来信收到了。谢谢你的问候。近来我的身体很好，请释念。

陈毅付总理从西藏回来后向中央汇报了西藏的工作情况，西藏自治区筹备委员会的成立大会在你的领导和班禅额尔德尼的协助下

105－1

全國人民代表大會常務委員會

开得很成功，我们听了都非常高兴。

在自治区筹备委员会成立的会议上，对西藏今后的工作进行了协商和讨论，并且作出了决议，为西藏民族的发展和进步创造了更有利的条件。希望你能利用这些条件更好地进行工作。但是，就是在这种情况下，也仍然要

105－2

全國人民代表大會常務委員會

注意和各方面的人士团结一致，要作的事，多和他们商量，以便取得他们的同意和支持。社会改革要根据西藏的具体情况，一步一步地去做，而不要操之过急。我们相信在今后一个时期的工作中，你将作出更大的成绩，在这中间，有什么需要我们帮助

105－3

全國人民代表大會常務委員會

的地方，我们当尽力协助你。

第一届全国人民代表大会第三次会议开的很好，很多代表坦率地对国家工作提出了批評和建议，这些意见对于改进国家机关的工作，特别是领导工作有很大好处。因为你不能经常住在北京领导常委会的工作，希望你能够常来信，对常委

105－4

105-5

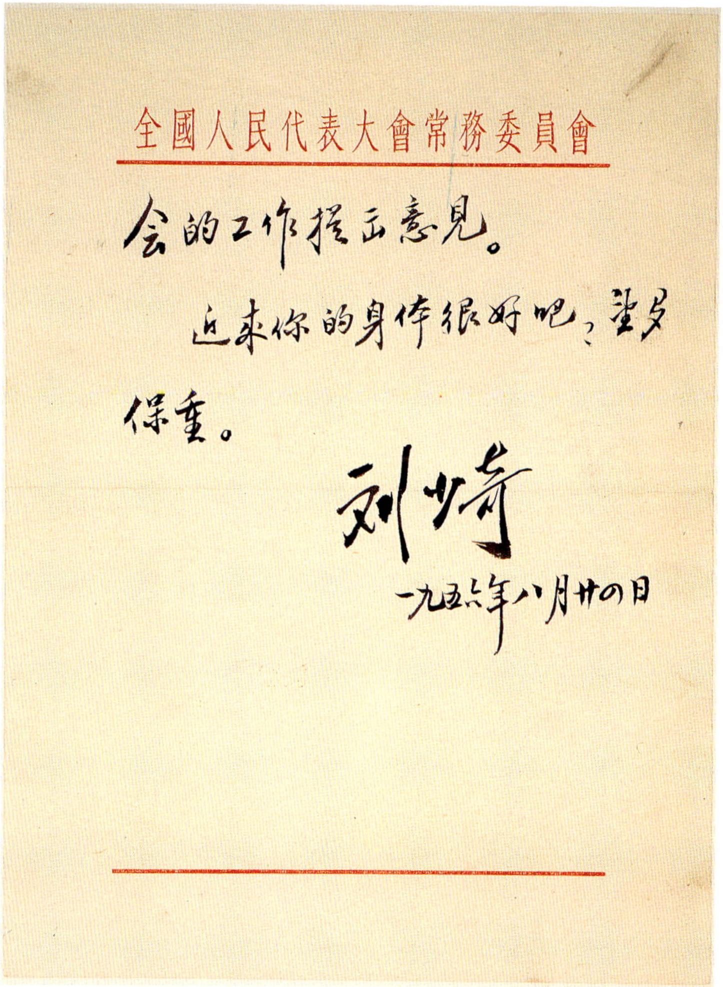

全國人民代表大會常務委員會

会的工作提出意見。

近来你的身体很好吧，望多保重。

刘少奇

一九五六年八月廿四日

西藏自治區檔案館藏

Dear Dalai Lama,

I have received your letter dated May 28. Thank you for your concern. I am in good health, so please set your mind at ease.

Vice-Premier Chen Yi reported to the Central Government on the situation in Tibet on his return from there. We were all glad to hear that the inaugural meeting of the Preparatory Committee of the Tibet Autonomous Region, under your leadership and with the assistance of the Panchen Erdeni, was a great success.

At the inaugural meeting, consultations and discussions were held on the future work in Tibet and a resolution was adopted, creating even more favourable conditions for the development and progress of the Tibetan nationality. I hope they can help you to do a better job. Even so, attention should also be paid to unity with people from all sectors of society. They must be consulted on work to be done so as to win their agreement and support. Social reform must be carried out step by step according to the specific conditions in Tibet and action with undue haste should be avoided. We are confident that you will attain even greater achievements in your work in the days ahead. During this time we are ready to offer you any help you need.

The Third Session of the First National People's Congress has been very successful. Many deputies offered open-minded criticism and suggestions on the work of the state, which will be of great benefit to the state organs, particularly to the work of leadership. As you are unable to come to stay in Beijing to lead the work of the Standing Committee, I hope you can write often, giving your ideas on its work.

I hope you are in good health these days. Please take care.

Liu Shaoqi

August 24, 1956

Preserved by the Archives of the Tibet Autonomous Region.

# ཀྲུའུ་ཞི་གཞོན་པ་ཀྲུའུ་ཏེ་ནས་ཏཱ་ལའི་བླ་མ་ལ་བཏང་བའི་འཕྲིན་ཡིག
# 朱德副主席給達賴喇嘛的信
# Vice–Chairman Zhu De′s Letter to the Dalai Lama

32 × 24

སྙིང་ནས་བརྩེ་བའི་ཏཱ་ལའི་བླ་མ་མཆོག་ལ།

ང་ཚོས་དགའ་སྤྲོ་ཆེན་པོའི་ངང་ནས་ཁྱེད་ཀྱིས་༡༩༥༨ལོའི་ཟླ་བ་ལྔ་པའི་ཚེས་ཉེར་བརྒྱད་ཉིན་བཏང་བའི་འཕྲིན་ཡིག་དེ་བཀླགས་པ་མ་ཟད། དགའ་སྤྲོ་ཆེན་པོའི་ངང་ནས་ཙུང་ལི་གཞོན་པ་ཁྲིན་དབྱིས་ཞུས་པའི་བོད་ལྗོངས་ཀྱི་ཕྱོགས་སོ་སོའི་ལས་ཀའི་གྲུབ་འབྲས་ཀྱི་སྙན་ཞུ་ཡང་ཉན་པ་ཡིན། ལོ་འགའི་རིང་ལ། ཁྱེད་དང་པཎ་ཆེན་ཨེར་ཏི་ནིས་འགོ་ཁྲིད་གནང་བའི་འོག་ཏུ། བོད་ས་གནས་སྲིད་གཞུང་དང་པཎ་ཆེན་བླ་བྲང་བར་གྱི་མཐུན་སྒྲིལ་ལ་ཤུགས་བསྣོན་ཆེན་པོ་ཐེབས་པ་དང་། བོད་ལྗོངས་ཀྱི་ཕྱོགས་སོ་སོའི་ལས་ཀ་ཚང་མར་གྲུབ་འབྲས་ཏ་ཅང་ཆེན་པོ་ཐོབ་ཡོད་པ་དེར་ཀྲུང་དབྱང་དང་མའོ་ཀྲུའུ་ཞི་ནས་ཤེས་རྟོགས་གསལ་པོ་བྱུང་ཡོད།

བོད་རང་སྐྱོང་ལྗོངས་གྲ་སྒྲིག་ཨུ་ཡོན་ལྷན་ཁང་བཙུགས་པ་དེ་ནི། དེང་ཕྱིན་བོད་ལྗོངས་ཀྱི་ཕྱོགས་སོ་སོའི་ལས་ཀ་གོམ་གང་མདུན་སྤོས་ཀྱིས་འཕེལ་རྒྱས་འགྲོ་བར་སྔར་ལས་ལྷག་པའི་སྲ་བརྟན་གྱི་རྨང་གཞི་བཏིང་བ་རེད། དེང་ཕྱིན་གྱི་ལས་ཀའི་ཁྲིད་དུ་གལ་ཏེ་གོམ་གང་མདུན་སྤོས་ཀྱིས་ཕྱོགས་སོ་སོའི་མཐུན་སྒྲིལ་གྱི་ལས་ཀ་སྒྲུབ་ཐུབ་པ་དང་། སྔར་ལས་ལྷག་པའི་སྒོ་ནས་ཀྲུང་དབྱང་མི་དམངས་སྲིད་གཞུང་གི་སྲིད་ཇུས་ཁག་དང་བོད་ལྗོངས་ས་ཁུལ་གྱི་ཆེ་བྲག་གི་ཁྱད་ཆོས་ཟུང་འབྲེལ་བྱས་ཏེ་གྲ་སྒྲིག་ཡོད་པ་དང་གོ་རིམ་ཡོད་པའི་སྒོ་ནས་བསྒྲུབ་ཐུབ་པར་གྱུར་ཚེ། དེང་ཕྱིན་བོད་ལྗོངས་ཀྱི་ཕྱོགས་སོ་སོའི་ལས་ཀ་དར་སྤེལ་དུ་གཏོང་རྒྱུར་སྔར་ལས་ལྷག་པའི་བདེ་བླག་འབྱུང་བ་དང་། གྲུབ་འབྲས་ཀྱང་སྔར་ལས་ཆེ་བ་ཞིག་ཐོབ་ཐུབ་རྒྱུར་ང་ཚོར་ཡིད་ཆེས་ཡོད།

ལས་ཀ་དང་སློབ་གཉེར་ཐད་ལ་ཏ་ཅང་སྐུ་མཉེལ་པོ་བྱུང་སྐབས། ཁྱེད་ཀྱི་སྐུ་གཟུགས་བདེ་ཐང་ལ་གནོད་པ་ཐེབས་ཡོད་ཟེར་བ་ཐོས་པས། ང་ཚོས་ཤིན་ཏུ་སེམས་འཁུར་བྱེད་ཀྱིན་ཡོད། དོན་དངོས་ཀྱི་སྟེང་དུ་བོད་རང་སྐྱོང་ལྗོངས་གྲ་སྒྲིག་ཨུ་ཡོན་ལྷན་ཁང་བཙུགས་རྗེས་སུ་ཁྱེད་ཀྱིས་འཁུར་བའི་བྱ་བའི་ལས་འགན་ནི་སྔར་ལས་ལྗི་བར་གྱུར་བ་དང་། ཁྱེད་ཀྱིས་ལས་ཀའི་ཐོག་གྲུབ་འབྲས་དང་ལྡན་པའི་འབད་བརྩོན་གནང་ཡོད་པ་དེ་དག་ང་ཚོས་ཤེས་རྟོགས་བྱེད་ཐུབ་ཀྱི་ཡོད། འོན་ཀྱང་རྒྱུན་རིང་པོའི་ཁེ་ཕན་ལ་བསམ་བློ་བཏང་སྟེ། ཁྱེད་ཀྱིས་ལས་ཀ་དང་སློབ་གཉེར་ཚད་ལས་འདས་པ་བྱས་ནས་སྐུ་གཟུགས་བདེ་ཐང་ལ་ངལ་དུབ་ཀྱི་གནོད་པ་མི་འབྱུང་བའི་རེ་བ་ཞུ། འདི་ལྟར་བྱས་ཚེ་གཞི་ནས་ཡུན་རིང་པོའི་ཁེ་ཕན་དང་མཐུན་ཐུབ་ཀྱི་རེད། ང་ཚོ་ཚང་མ་གཟུགས་པོ་ཏ་ཅང་བདེ་པོ་ཡིན་པས་ཁྱེད་ཀྱིས་ཐུགས་འཁུར་གནང་བ་ལ་ཐུགས་རྗེ་ཆེ་ཞུ།

མའོ་ཀྲུའུ་ཞིའི་སྐུ་ཁམས་ཀྱང་ཏ་ཅང་བདེ་པོ་ཡིན། ཁོང་དང་ཀྲུང་དབྱང་གི་འགན་འཁུར་བློ་མཐུན་ཚང་མས་ཁྱེད་ལ་ཐུགས་འཁུར་ཆེན་པོ་བྱེད་ཀྱིན་ཡོད།

ཁྱེད་ཀྱི་ལས་ཀ་བདེ་བླག་ཏུ་འགྲུབ་པའི་སྨོན་འདུན་ཞུ་རྒྱུ་དང་། ཁྱེད་ཀྱི་སྐུ་གཟུགས་བདེ་ཐང་ཡོང་བའི་སྨོན་འདུན་ཞུའོ། །

ཀྲུའུ་ཏེ་ནས།

༡༩༥༨ལོའི་ཟླ་བ་བརྒྱད་པའི་ཚེས་བཅོ་ལྔ་ཉིན་པེ་ཅིན་ནས།

བོད་རང་སྐྱོང་ལྗོངས་ཡིག་ཚགས་ཁང་དུ་ཉར་ཚགས་བྱས་ཡོད།

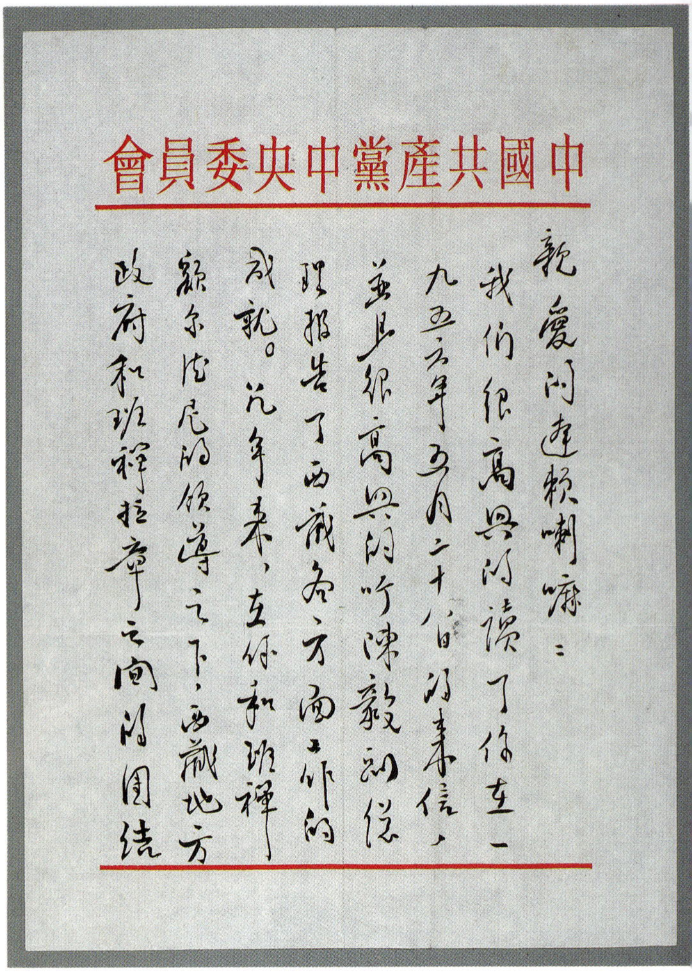

中國共產黨中央委員會

親愛的達賴喇嘛：

我們很高興的讀了你在一九五五年五月二十日的來信，並且很高興的聽陳毅同志報告了西藏各方面工作的成就。幾年來，在你和班禪額尔德尼的領導之下，西藏地方政府和班禪拉章之間的團結

106 - 1

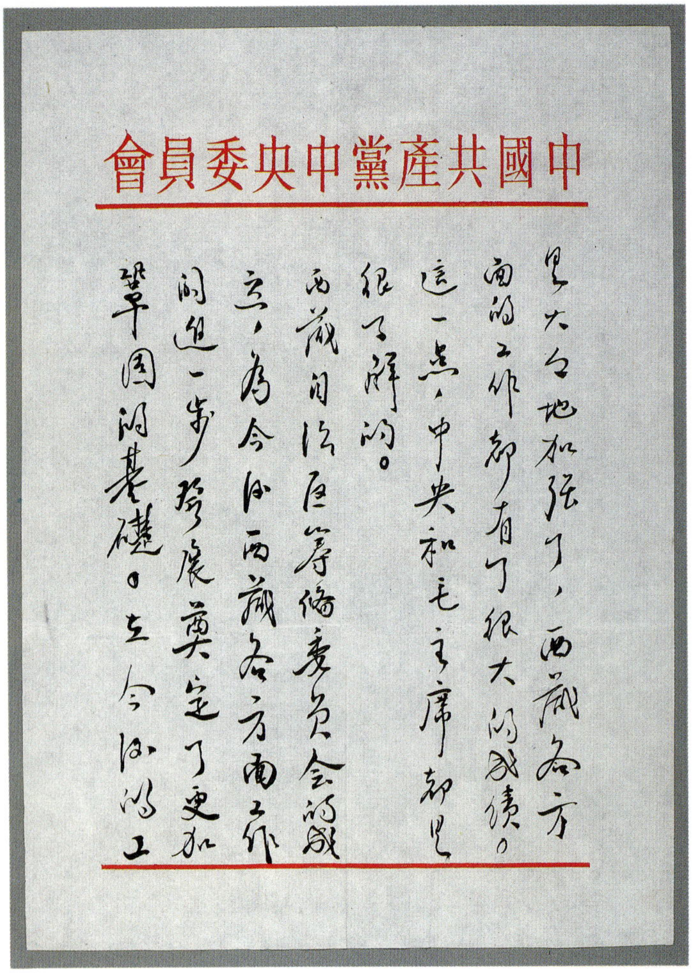

中國共產黨中央委員會

是大大地加強了，西藏各方面的工作都有了很大的成績。這一點，中央和毛主席都是很了解的。

西藏自治區籌備委員會的成立，為今後西藏各方面工作向進一步發展奠定了更加牢固的基礎。在今後的工

106 - 2

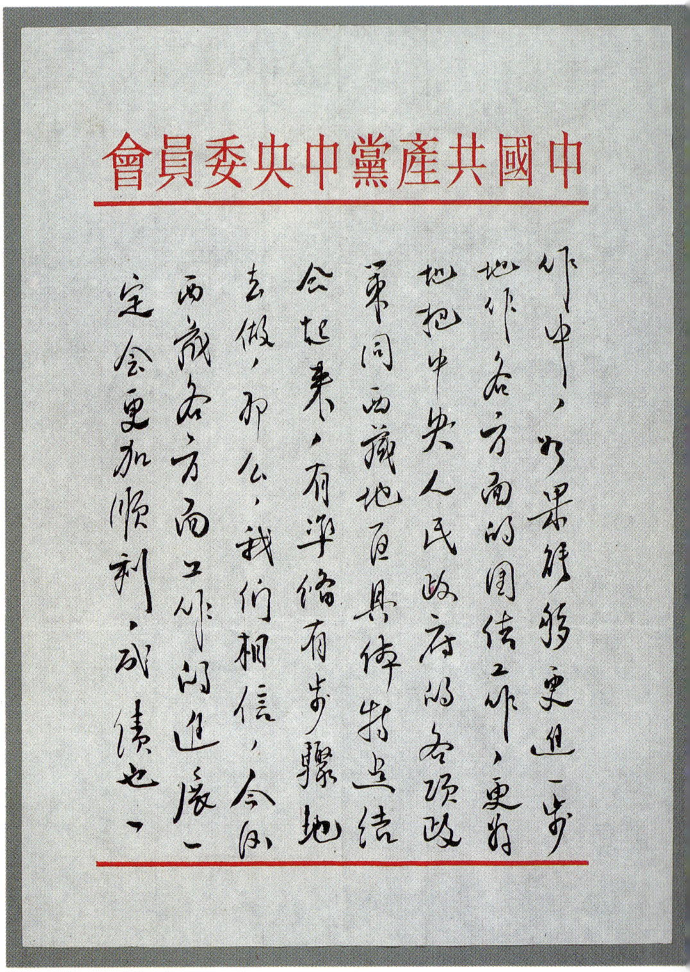

中國共產黨中央委員會

作中，如果能夠更進一步地作好各方面的團結工作，更好地把中央人民政府的各項政策同西藏地區具体特點結合起來，有準備有步驟地去做，那么，我們相信，今後西藏各方面工作的進展一定會更加順利，成績也一

106 - 3

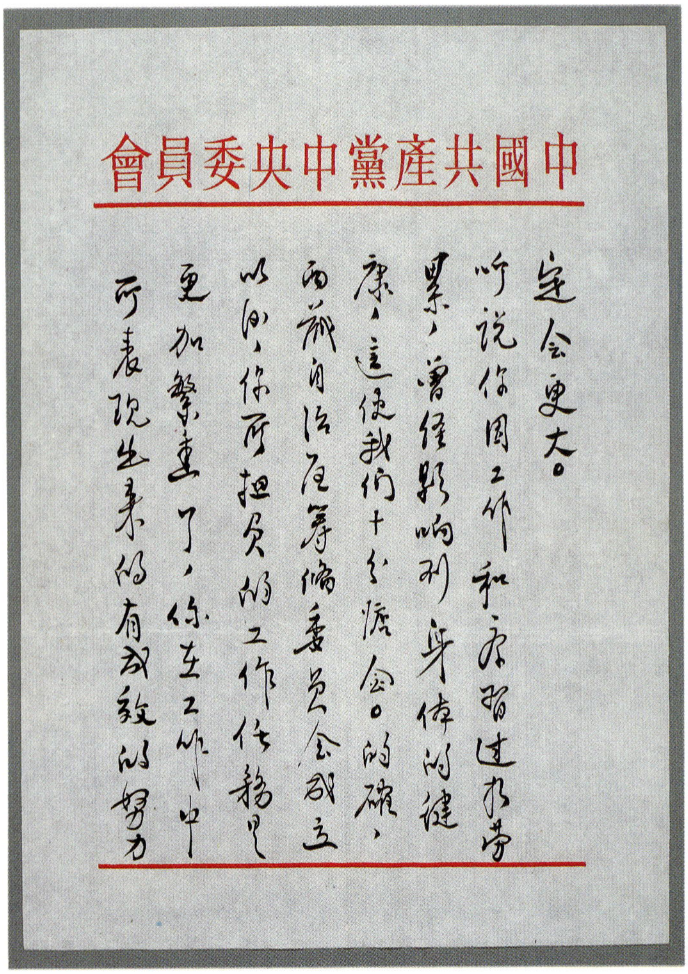

中國共產黨中央委員會

定會更大。

聽說你因工作和學習過於勞累，曾經影响到身体的健康，這使我們十分懸念。的確，西藏自治區籌備委員會成立以后，你所担负的工作任務是更加繁重了，你在工作中所表現出來的有成效的努力

106 - 4

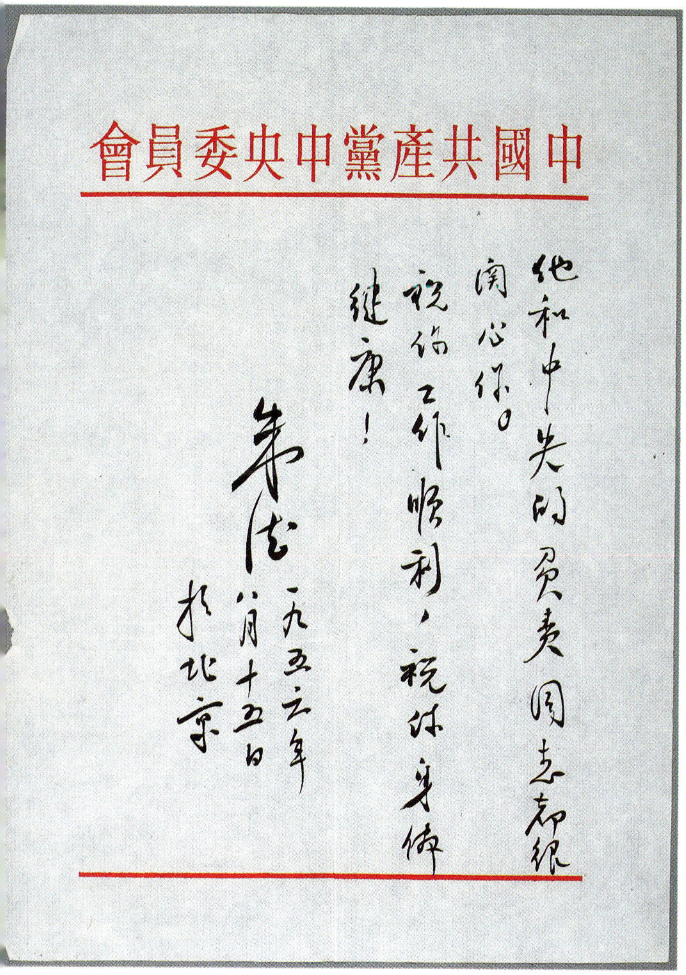
中國共產黨中央委員會

他和中央的負責同志都很
關心你。
祝你工作順利，祝你身体
健康！
朱德
一九五六年八月十五日
於北京

106－6

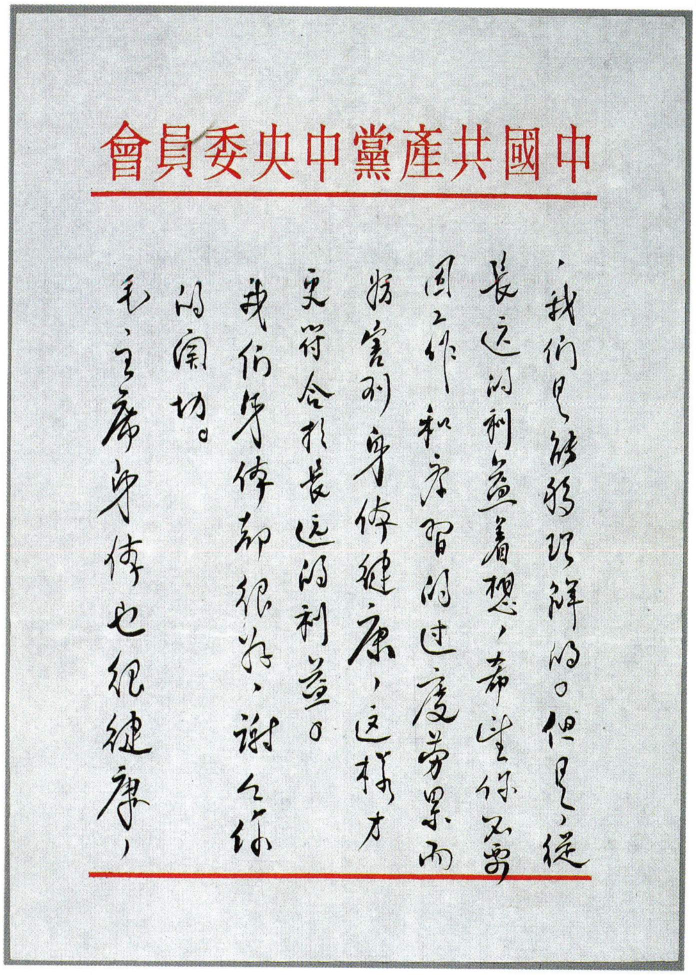
中國共產黨中央委員會

，我們只能將理解的。但只要從
長遠的利益着想，希望你不要
因工作和個人習慣過度勞累而
妨害到身体健康，這樣才
更符合於長遠的利益。
我們身体都很好，謝謝你
的關切。
毛主席身体也很健康，

106－5

西藏自治區檔案館藏

Dear Dalai Lama,

We were pleased to receive your letter dated May 28, 1956 and to hear the report by Vice–Premier Chen Yi on various achievements in Tibet. Over the past several years, under the leadership of yourself and the Panchen Erdeni, the unity between the Tibetan local government and Panchenblabrang has been greatly strengthened and substantial achievements have been made in various undertakings in Tibet. The Central Government and Chairman Mao are aware of this.

The establishment of the Preparatory Committee of the Tibet Autonomous Region has laid a more solid foundation for future development in Tibet. We are confident that the work in various fields in Tibet will go even more smoothly and be more fruitful if we can do more to unite every sector and better coordinate policies of the Central People's Government and the specific characteristics of the Tibetan region on a step–by–step basis.

We have heard that your health has been affected by overwork and study. We are very concerned about this. Indeed, since the establishment of the Committee, you have been shouldering heavier tasks and your hard work has paid off, which we can understand well. However, for the sake of the long–term interests, we advise you not to let work and study affect your health.

We are well and appreciate your concern.

Chairman Mao is also in good health. He and the other leaders of the Central Government are concerned about you.

Wishing you success in your work and good health.

Zhu De

August 15, 1956 Beijing

Preserved by the Archives of the Tibet Autonomous Region.

# ཏཱ་ལའི་བླ་མ་སྐུ་ཕྲེང་བཅུ་བཞི་པས་ཀྲུའུ་ཞི་མའོ་ཙེ་ཏུང་ལ་བསྟོད་པའི་སྙན་ཚིག
# 第十四世達賴喇嘛頌揚毛澤東主席的讚文
# Ode to Chairman Mao Zedong, by the 14th Dalai Lama

—— Prayer for Chairman Mao's Longevity and Happiness

77 × 34.9, 29.8 × 20.9

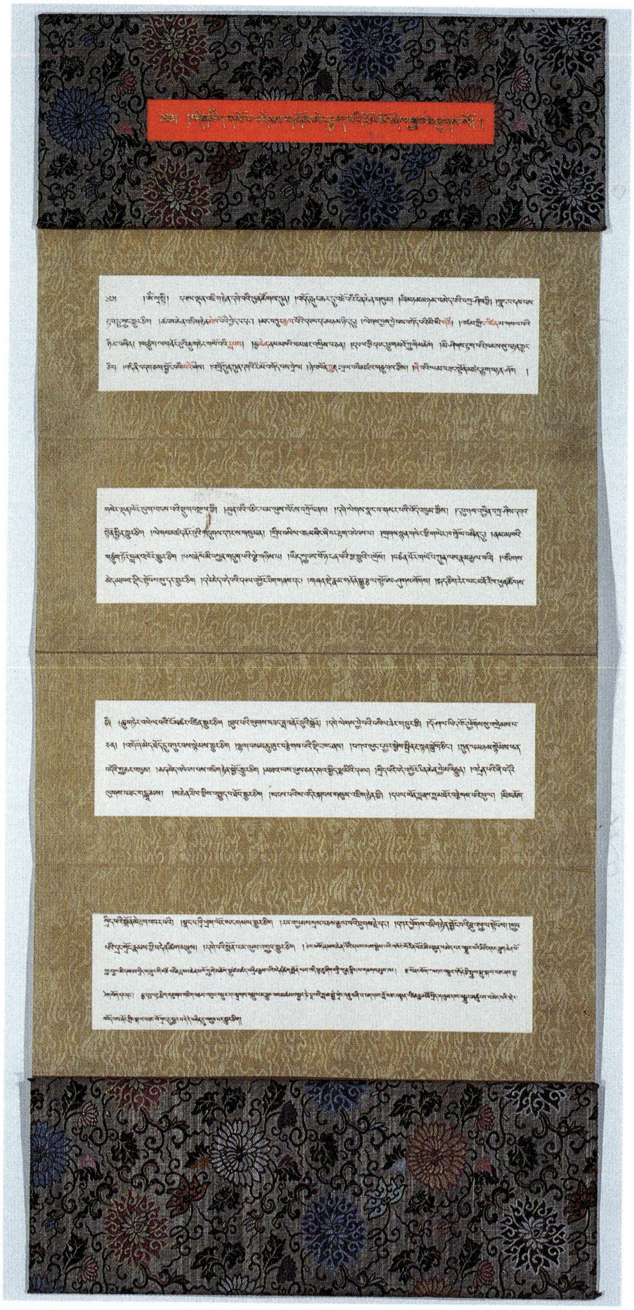

107 - 1

བོད་རང་སྐྱོང་ལྗོངས་ཡིག་ཚགས་ཁང་དུ་ཉར་ཚགས་བྱས་ཡོད།

༄༅། །ཨོཾ་སྭསྟི། དཔལ་ལྡན་འཇིག་རྟེན་དགེ་བའི་ཕུན་ཚོགས་ཀུན། །འདོད་རྒུར་ཆར་དུ་འཇོ་བའི་རིན་ཆེན་གསུམ། །ཡི་མཉམ་མཉམ་པ་མེད་པའི་བཀྲ་ཤིས་ཀྱི། །སྣང་བ་དམ་པས
དག་ཏུ་སྤུང་གྱུར་ཅིག །ཆོས་ཆེན་འཇིག་རྟེན་ཡེས་པོའི་ཕྱེད་པ་དང་། །མང་བཀུར་རྒྱལ་པོའི་དཔལ་དང་མཉམ་ཉིད་དུ། །ལེགས་བྱས་བྱེ་བས་བཀོད་པའི་མི་ཡི་གཙོ། །འཛམ་གླིང་འཛིན་མ་གསལ་བའི
ཉི་མ་བཞིན། །གཙུག་ལག་ཨོར་ཕུའི་རྒྱུ་གཏེར་གསོ་བའི་སྟབས། །རྒྱ་ཆེན་ནམ་མཁའི་ཕ་མཐར་འགྲེམ་པ་ཅན། །དཔལ་གྱི་དབང་ཕྱུག་མགོན་ཀུ་ཞི་མཆོག །མི་ཤིགས་རྟག་པའི་ཁམས་སུ་བརྟན་གྱུར
ཅིག །འདི་ནི་བདག་ཅག་སྐྱོང་བའི་མགོན་ཞེས། །འགྲོ་ཀུན་ཀུན་གྱི་རེ་མོ་འགོད་པས་བྱེལ། །ཉེ་གནས་ཀུ་ཧཱུཾ༔ ཕྱག་བའི་མཛད་བ་གཙུག་གས་ཀྱིས། །ཞི་བའི་ལམ་བཟང་སྟོན་མཛད་རྟག་བརྟན་ཤོག །

གསེར་ལྡན་ལོར་ཡུག་ཡངས་པའི་སྡུག་བསྔལ་གྱི། །ཕྱུན་པའི་བཅིང་བམ་ལུས་ཡོངས་བཀྲོལ་ནས། །དགེ་ལེགས་སྣང་བ་གསར་པའི་འོད་འབུམ་གྱིས། །དཔུངས་འབྱིན་བཀྲ་ཤིས་དཔལ
རྟེན་འབྱིན་གྱུར་ཅིག །ལེགས་མཛད་དོན་ཕུའི་གཏོགས་དཀར་ས་གསུམ་ན། །ཀྲིམ་བསིལ་འཇམ་ཞིང་ཞི་བར་རྟག་འབེབས་པ། །ཀུགས་སྐྱན་གསེར་གྱི་གཡེར་ཁ་གྲོལ་བཞིན་དུ། །ནམ་མཁའི
གཙུག་ཏོར་ལྡན་པའི་གྱུར་ཅིག །ཡས་ཆོས་ལ་མི་བསྒྱུར་གདུག་པའི་ལྟེ་གཉིས་པ། །ཡིད་སྤྱངས་ཡོ་ཉེ་དན་པའི་ཀྱ་ཕྱིའི་འགྲོས། །མཚན་པོར་གཡོ་བ་ཀུན་ལས་རྣམ་རྒྱལ་བའི། །འཛིགས
མེད་མཁའ་ལྡིང་སྟོབས་སུ་དར་གྱུར་ཅིག །དེ་མེད་བདེ་བའི་དཔལ་འབྱོར་རིག་གནས་དང་། །གཞན་ནི་རྣམ་གཞོན་ལྷ་རྒྱལ་སྟོབས་ཕྱུགས་སོགས། །སྐྱིད་ཅིག་རེར་ཡང་མཐོ་རིས་ཕུན་ཚོགས

ཀྱི། །རྒྱ་གཏེར་འཕེལ་བའི་དོ་མཚར་འཛིན་གྱུར་ཅིག །ཐུབ་པའི་ལུགས་བཟང་བློ་བཙོར་ཕུའི་སྒྲོན། །དགེ་ལེགས་བྱེ་བའི་བསིལ་ཟེར་གཏེར་ཀུར་གྱི། །དོ་ཁལ་ཡིད་འོད་ཕྱོགས་སུ་འགྲེམས་པ
ཅན། །འགོག་མེད་ཐོད་དུ་བཀུར་བས་སྐྱེམས་གྱུར་ཅིག །ཕྱག་བསམ་རྒྱ་ཆུར་བརྩེགས་པའི་གླིང་ཁང་ནས། །བཀའ་ལུང་དཔྱར་སྒྲིས་སྤྲིན་དཀར་སྔུན་གླུ་གཏིང་། །ཀུན་ལ་མཉམ་སྙོམས་པན
བདེའི་ཀུ་ཆར་འབེབས། །ཆད་མེད་འཕེལ་བས་འཇིག་རྟེན་སྐྱོང་གྱུར་ཅིག །མཐའ་ཡས་ལུས་ཅན་དགའ་སྐྱིད་ལྷ་མིའི་དཔལ། །སྲིད་པའི་བདེ་འབྱོར་རིན་ཆེན་བྱེ་མའི་རྒྱུན། །འདྲེན་པའི་ཞི་བདེའི
ལུགས་བཟང་གཉྫ་མས། །ས་ཆེན་རོལ་གྱིས་འཁྱུད་པ་ཐོབ་གྱུར་ཅིག །ཡངས་པའི་ཞིང་འདིར་སྐབས་གསུམ་འཇིག་རྟེན་གྱི། །དཔལ་ཡོན་བླུན་བླ་མཐོར་བརྩེགས་པའི་ཕུལ། །མི་མཆོག

སྲིད་པའི་སྒྲོན་མེ་རྟག་འབར་བའི། །སྣང་བ་ཁྲི་ཕྲག་ལོར་ཡང་གསལ་གྱུར་ཅིག །རབ་འབྱམས་སྲུས་བཅས་རྒྱལ་བའི་ཐུགས་རྗེ་དང་། །དཀར་ཕྱོགས་འཇིག་རྟེན་སྐྱོང་བའི་ལྷ་ཡི་སྟོབས། །ཀུན
བའི་དུར་སྲིད་རྣམས་ཀྱི་བདེན་ཚིག་མཐུས། །དགེ་བའི་སྨོན་པམ་ལུས་འགྲུབ་གྱུར་ཅིག ། ཅེས་བསོད་ནམས་ཆེན་པོའི་དཔལ་ལས་སྐྱེས་པའི་གཡོར་ལོ་ཉི་ཤུ་ཆེ་མི་མཐུན་པ་མེད་པར་བསྒྱུར་བའི་མིའི་དབང་ཕྱུག་ཆེན་པོ
གུང་དབྱང་མི་དམངས་སྲིད་གཞུང་གི་གཙོ་འཛིན་ཏ་ཕམས་ཆེན་མའོ་ཀུ་ཞི་མཆོག་ལྷ་ཚེ་མཛད་འཕྲིན་རྒྱས་པའི་བདེན་ཚིག་སྨོན་ལམ་འདི་ལྟ་བུ་ཞིག་འབྲི་འདུན་སྙིང་ལ་གཅགས་མུས་ཁར། སྔ་ལོ་ནང་སོག་ བཀའ་འགྱུར་དཀོན་ཕྱི་ཕྱུལ་སྐྱ་སྐལ་བཟང་ནས་ལྷ
རིག་སོག་དང་དང་། རྒྱ་དཔལ་ཏ་ཧྲིག་གཟུགས་གཅིག་བཅས་འབུལ་བསྐུར་དང་སྨྲགས་བསྐུལ་མ་བྱུང་བས་མཚམས་སྦྱར་ཏེ་ཏཱ་ལའི་བླ་མ་སྐྱེ་ཕྲེང་བཅུ་བཞི་པ་བཀའ་དྲིན་བློ་བཟང་བསྟན་འཛིན་རྒྱ་མཚོ་སྲིད་གསུམ་དབང་བསྒྱུར་མཉམ་མེད་པའི་སྡེ་
བཀོད་པས་ཚོར་གྱིས་སྐལ་བཟང་ཡོ་ཕྲང་དུ་སྨྲར་བ་དེ་དེ་བཞིན་དུ་འགྲུབ་པར་གྱུར་ཅིག།

毛主席頌

——實語祈禱無壞常樂讚文——

第十四世達賴喇嘛造

世間最勝諸圓滿，如意降賜三寶尊，雖等無等衆吉祥，殊勝光明常照護。

能降給世界一切幸福的佛法僧三寶啊！

請用無可比擬的吉祥光輝永不間斷的照耀保護我們！

（譯者註：第一段按照藏文詩一般的習慣是祈禱三寶的保護，下面才是讚頌毛主席的正文）

等同大梵世界祖，衆敬國王諸德業，俱胝福感大領袖，普照大地如日昇。

毛主席啊！您的光榮和事業有如創造世界的大梵天和衆敬國王！

積聚了無量數的福氣才產生了這樣的領袖，好像大地上有了照耀一切的太陽！

（譯者註：衆敬國王是印度傳說中最古的國王。）

聖典寶珠如海潮，充滿廣大虛空際，功德自在毛主席，常界不壞願久住。

您的著作珍貴如寶珠，豐富有力如同海潮一直達到天空的邊際。

榮譽無比的毛主席啊！願您萬壽無疆！

保護吾人如慈母，衆生隨躍繪其像，離諸怨敵、親愛心，示和平道願久住。

人們都把您當做保護自己的慈母，極其興奮的把您的相貌描繪下來。願您永遠駐在世間，給我們指示和平的道路！

廣大地上諸疾苦，黑暗，拘練皆解放，頭旋億者新光明，吉祥勝會普安慰。

大地雖然遼闊，但是黑暗和痛苦的枷鎖壓得人喘不出氣來，是您用新的光芒破除了黑暗，解放了枷鎖，人們才能透過氣來盡情的歡會。

妙聚白傘蓋三地，常衛清涼和平樂，美麗金鈴徧鳴響，恆旋轉於虛空頂。

您的和平事業猶如摩尼白傘，清涼的覆蓋着天上，地下，人間。

您的聲譽猶如傘上的金鈴，永遠鳴響，永遠在天空的頂上旋轉。

凶暴怨敵如毒蛇，擾亂惡使彎曲行，戰勝帝國諸蠢動，無畏大鵬力增盛。

我們的敵人——殘暴的帝國主義者，有如毒蛇，它是惡魔的使者，蠕蠕地蠢動，您是馴服毒蛇的無畏大鵬，願您的威力永遠不斷的增長。

無比富樂諸明處，及伏他軍工藝等，希有天趣諸盛事，剎那增盛如大海。

使人民繁榮富强和摧伏敵人武裝力量的文化及工業建設，如同大海一般，每一剎那都向上發展，發展得如天國一樣的充足圓滿。

能仁教軌月珠炬，放照億萬清涼光，分布虎蓋香瓔珞，頂戴無遮可矜持。

釋迦牟尼的善良的宗教好像月明珠的燈放射着萬道清涼的光輝，又像放龍腦香的珠鬘，現在我們能毫無障礙地頂戴着它，這是多麼值得驕傲的啊！

增上意樂雲幄中，宣示教旨如雷鳴，降澍平等利樂雨，願無間斷澤世間。

您的意願比如雲聚，號召比如雷鳴，從這裏面不斷地降着無私地潤澤世界的甘霖。

和平軌如殑伽女，導無邊衆歡喜事，人天富樂寶沙流，願繞祇席此大地。

恆河能把寶沙沖徧得充滿大地，和平正義能引來無邊衆生的喜悅。

願此寬廣大地上，如天界徧轉增盛，偉大世燭恆熾然，經歷萬歲常光顯。

願人間逐步變得如天堂般的幸福！

願世界的火炬偉大的領袖千秋萬歲永遠熾然！

（譯者註：頌的正文到此完了，下面一段是對這個頌文本身如願實現的祈禱）

諸佛菩薩慈悲力，白品護世神通力，成就大仙諦語力，令此善願皆圓滿。

願佛菩薩的慈悲、護法神的神通，成就大仙的真實語這三種力量使這一切善良的願望都能實現！

祖國偉大領袖中央人民政府毛主席，廣大微妙福德所生之轉輪聖王也。余久已著願撰文讚頌以祈禱長壽無疆，事業宏廣。適有內蒙甘珠寺格桑活佛於去歲遠道寄禮囑撰，恰符私願。因寫此篇以贈之。

十四世達賴喇嘛阿旺羅桑丹增嘉措書於羅布林卡福宮。

西藏自治區檔案館、中央檔案館藏

The triad of the Buddha, the Dharma and the Sangha – the
Triratna which bestows happiness on the world,
Please protect us and let us bathe in your unparalleled,
auspicious and everlasting brilliant glow!

Chairman Mao, your honour and deeds are equal to those of Brahma
who created the world, and those of the King of Universal Respect.
Only a mass of boundless fortune could produce such a leader,
one who shines upon the world like the sun.

Your works are as valued as pearls, abundant and powerful like
the tides of the sea extending to the horizon.
O, incomparably honourable Chairman Mao, may you live for ever!

People look on you as a loving mother and enthusiastically draw your picture.
May you remain in this world for ever to guide us down a road of eternal peace!

Though the earth is vast, people struggled for breath
in their bondage of darkness and pain.
With a new radiance you have dispelled the darkness and broken
the bondage, and people can now breathe freely and enjoy life.

Your campaign of peace is like Mani's white umbrella which
shields the heavens, the earth and the people with pleasant coolness.
Your fame is like the constant tinkling of a golden bell on the
umbrella that for ever swings from the ceiling of the sky.

Our enemy – cruel imperialism – is like a wriggling poisonous
snake, an envoy from the devil.
You are a fearless roc that overcomes it.
May your might continue to increase for ever!

Culture and industry, which bring happiness and prosperity to
the people and destroy the enemy's armed forces, are like a
wide sea swelling at every moment.
They will be as perfect as the Kingdom of Heaven.

Sakyamuni's religion of goodwill is like the clear and cool
radiance of the infinite rays from the bright pearly moon.
It is also like a pouch of borneo camphor incense which we can
now carry on our heads without restriction. This is truly something to be proud of!

Your will is like a mass of clouds and your call is like the sound of thunder.
A sweet rain constantly emanates from them to unselfishly refresh the world.

As the Ganges is able to fill the land with its flood of precious sand,
Peace and justice is able to bring happiness to all living beings.

May this world become a place as full of content as the Paradise!
May the great leader, a torch for the world, shine for ever!

May the benevolence of Buddha, the supernatural power of
Dharmapala and the true words of the God of Success make
all my fine wishes come true!

Chairman Mao of the Central People's Government, the great leader of the motherland, is the embodiment of magnanimity, kindness, happiness and virtue. I have long wanted to write an ode to wish you a long life and magnificent career. Last year, Living Buddha Kalzang from Gangrub Monastery, Inner Mongolia, wrote me a letter, asking me to write such an ode, which had already been my intention. Therefore, I have written this piece.

Ngagwang Lozhang Tandsin Gyatsho, the 14th Dalai Lama, in Norling Kalzhang Palace.

Preserved by the Archives of the Tibet Autonomous Region and the Central Archives.

# མཇུག་བྱང་།

དེབ་འདིར་རྩ་ཆེ་བའི་བོད་ལྗོངས་ལོ་རྒྱུས་ཡིག་ཚགས་དང་ཐམ་ག་སོགས་རིག་དངོས་༡༠༧བསྡུས་བཀོད་བྱས་ཤིང་། བོད་ཡིག་དང་། ཧོར་ཡིག་གསར་པ། རྒྱ་ཡིག མཆུའི་ཡི་གེ སོག་ཡིག་བཅས་ཕྱོགས་གཅིག་ཏུ་བཀོད་ཡོད། ཐེངས་དང་པོར་ཁྲབ་བསྒྲགས་བྱས་པའི་གྲངས་༨༨ཡོད་པ་ལས་གྲངས་༨༡བོད་རང་སྐྱོང་ལྗོངས་ཡིག་ཚགས་ཁང་ནས་མགོ་འདོན་བྱས་པ། གྲངས་༥བོད་ལྗོངས་གཞིས་རྩེ་ས་ཁུལ་ཡིག་ཚགས་ཁང་སོགས་ནས་མགོ་འདོན་བྱས་ཡོད། འདི་ནི་ཀྲུང་དབྱང་ཆབ་སྲིད་ཚུས་ཀྱི་ཨུ་ཡོན། རྒྱལ་དོན་ཨུ་ཡོན་བློ་མཐུན་ལི་ཐེ་དབྱིང་སྐུ་ངོ་མས་མཛའ་བརྩེའི་ཐུགས་འཁུར་གནང་བའི་འོག་བོད་རང་སྐྱོང་ལྗོངས་ཡིག་ཚགས་ཁང་ནས་དངོས་སུ་སྒྲིག་འཛུགས་བྱས་ཏེ་བསྒྲུབས་པ་ཞིག་ཡིན། དེའི་རིང་རྒྱལ་ཁབ་ནོར་སྲིད་སྤྱི་ཁག་དང་། ཀྲུང་དབྱང་ཡིག་ཚགས་ཁང་། ཀྲུང་དབྱང་རྩོམ་སྒྲུར་ཁང་། རྒྱལ་ཁབ་ཡིག་ཚགས་ཚུས། རྒྱལ་ཁབ་རིག་དངོས་ཚུས། གསར་འགྱུར་དཔེ་སྐྲུན་ཧྲུའུ། ཀྲུང་གོ་སྤྱི་ཚོགས་ཚན་རིག་ཁང་གི་མི་རིགས་ཞིབ་འཇུག་སོའོ། ཀྲུང་གོ་ལོ་རྒྱུས་ཡིག་ཚགས་ཁང་ཨང་དང་པོ། ཀྲུང་གོ་ལོ་རྒྱུས་ཡིག་ཚགས་ཁང་ཨང་གཉིས་པ། ཀྲུང་གོ་འདྲ་པར་ཡིག་ཚགས་ཁང་། བོད་ལྗོངས་གཞིས་རྩེ་ས་ཁུལ། བོད་ལྗོངས་སྨད་ཁ་ས་ཁུལ། བོད་རང་སྐྱོང་ལྗོངས་རིག་དངོས་དོ་དམ་ཨུ་ཡོན་ལྷན་ཁང་སོགས་ཀྱིས་སྤྱི་སེམས་འཁོལ་བའི་རོགས་རམ་གནང་བ་དང་། བོད་རང་སྐྱོང་ལྗོངས་ཀྱི་ཧྲུའུ་ཅི་ཁྲིན་ཁྲུས་ཡོན། ཀྲུའུ་རིན་རག་ཧྲིས། ཀྲུའུ་ཞི་རྒྱལ་མཚན་ནོར་བུ། ཧྲུའུ་ཅི་གཞོན་པ་བསྟན་འཛིན། རྒྱུན་ལས་ཨུ་ཡོན་ཁྲིན་ཏན་ཁྲང་། དྲུང་ཡིག་ཆེན་མོ་ལི་ཧྲི་གོ་དང་ལྗོངས་དཔལ་འབྱོར་ཞིབ་འཇུག་ཁང་གི་ཀྲུའུ་རིན་ཤའོ་ཧྲོད་ཡོན་སོགས་ཀྱིས་ཐུགས་འཁུར་རྒྱབ་སྐྱོར་གནང་བ། གྲགས་ཅན་བོད་རིག་པ་མཁས་དབང་དུང་དཀར་བློ་བཟང་འཕྲིན་ལས་དང་། ཧོར་ཁང་བསོད་ནམས་དཔལ་འབར། ཁྲི་རུ་ཚེ་དབང་རྣམ་རྒྱལ་སོགས་ཀྱིས་གང་ཅིའི་བཀའ་སློབ་གནང་ཡོད།

དེབ་འདིའི་སྤྱི་ཁྲབ་རྩོམ་སྒྲིག་པ་བོད་རང་སྐྱོང་ལྗོངས་ཡིག་ཚགས་ཁང་གི་ཀོན་ཀྲང་མཁྱེན་ལྡན་མ་སྒྲོལ་དཀར་སོགས་ནས་དེབ་ཧྲིལ་པོའི་འཆར་གཞི་ཧྲུས་འགོད། རྒྱ་ཆ་འདེམས་སྒྲུག བོད་རྒྱ་ཡི་གེ་ཞུ་དག་སོགས་ལས་དོན་ཁག་གི་ལས་འགན་བཞེས་པ་དང་། དགེ་རྒན་ཆེན་མོ་ཛ་གུ་ན་སུ་ཐུ་ནས་ཡོན་རྒྱལ་རབས་སྐབས་ཀྱི་ཧོར་ཡིག་གསར་པའི་སོག་སྐད་ཀྱི་རྒྱལ་པོའི་ལུང་སོགས་རྒྱ་ཡིག་ཏུ་བསྒྱུར་པའི་ལས་འགན་བཞེས་པ། ཞིབ་འཇུག་པ་ཆེན་མོ་འོད་ཟེར་ནས་ཡོན་རྒྱལ་རབས་སྐབས་ཀྱི་བོད་ཡིག་གི་ཏི་ཤྲིའི་གཏམ་སོགས་རྒྱ་ཡིག་ཏུ་བསྒྱུར་པ་དང་ཧོར་ཡིག་གསར་པའི་སོག་སྐད་ཀྱི་རྒྱལ་པོའི་ལུང་སོགས་རྒྱ་ཡིག་ཏུ་བསྒྱུར་པའི་བསྒྱུར་ཡིག་རྣམས་བོད་ཡིག་ཏུ་བསྒྱུར་པ་སོགས་ཀྱི་ལས་འགན་བཞེས་པ། དགེ་རྒན་ཆེན་མོ་བློ་གྲོས་རྒྱ་མཚོ་ནས་ཡོན་རྒྱལ་རབས་རྗེས་ཀྱི་བོད་རྒྱ་ཡིག་ཚགས་ཁག་ཅིག་བོད་

ཡིག་ནས་རྒྱ་ཡིག་ཏུ་བསྒྱུར་པ་དང་རྒྱ་ཡིག་ནས་བོད་ཡིག་ཏུ་བསྒྱུར་པ་སོགས་ཀྱི་ལས་འགན་བཞེས་པ། ཞིབ་འཇུག་པ་ཆེན་མོ་ཆུས་ཧྥེའུ་ཧྲེང་ནས་ཆིང་རྒྱལ་རབས་སྐབས་ཀྱི་མན་ཇུའི་ཡི་གེའི་བཀའ་ལུང་རྒྱ་ཡིག་ཏུ་བསྒྱུར་པ་སོགས་ཀྱི་ལས་འགན་བཞེས་པ། སྒྱུར་ཞུས་པ་ཆེན་མོ་ཚུའི་ སི་ཁྲུན་དང་། སྒྱུར་ཞུས་པ་ཆེན་མོ་ཀྲང་ཙུང་ཀྲི་སོགས་ནས་རྒྱ་ཡིག་གི་ཟིན་བྲིས་རྣམས་དབྱིན་ཡིག་ཏུ་བསྒྱུར་བའི་ལས་འགན་བཞེས་པ། སྒྱུར་ཞུས་པ་ཆེན་མོ་ཞུས་ མེ་ཅང་ནས་དབྱིན་ཡིག་ཏུ་བསྒྱུར་པའི་བསྒྱུར་ཡིག་ལ་ཞུ་དག་བཏང་བའི་ལས་འགན་བཞེས་པ། ཞིབ་འཇུག་པ་གཞོན་པ་ཞུས་ལྷུན་ལེང་དང་། ཀྲུའུ་རིན་ལག་རྩལ་དགེ་རྒན་ལེའུ་ཅི་ཧྲོ། པར་རྒྱག་དགེ་རྒན་སྲུན་ཀྲི་ཁྲང་། སྲས་མོ་སྲུང་ལི་སོགས་ནས་ཡིག་ཚགས་མ་ཡིག་པར་རྒྱག་བརྟན་ལེན་གྱི་ལས་འགན་བཞེས་པ་བཅས་རེད། དེབ་འདིའི་བརྟག་ཞིབ་དང་། རྒྱ་ཆ་འདེམས་སྒྲུག པར་རྒྱག ཡིག་སྒྱུར། རྩོམ་སྒྲིག ཞུ་དག་སོགས་ཀྱི་ལས་དོན་ནང་བཞུགས་མཁན་གྲས་སུ་ད་དུང་ཞིབ་འཇུག་པ་གཞོན་པ་ར་སྒྲེང་ཡེ་ཤེས་ཚུལ་ཁྲིམས་དང་། ལི་གོ་ཆིང་། བྱམས་པ་དཔལ་འབྱོར། ངག་དབང་ཆོས་དར། ཚེ་རིང་རྒྱལ་པོ། བློ་བཟང་རྒྱལ་མཚན་དང་། སྐུ་ཞབས་བསོད་ནམས་དགེ་ལེགས། བློ་བཟང་རྣམ་རྒྱལ། དབང་འདུས། ཡེ་ཤུབ། ལྷག་པ་ཚེ་རིང་། མགོན་པོ་ཚེ་བརྟན། ཕང་ཡའོ་ཉན་སོགས་ཡོད།

མདོར་བསྡུས་ན། གལ་ཏེ་མང་ཚོགས་ཀྱི་བློ་གྲོས་སྟོབས་ཤུགས་དང་གོང་རིམ་འབྲེལ་ཡོད་སྡེ་ཁག་གི་རྒྱབ་སྐྱོར་དང་ཁ་བྲལ་བ་ཡིན་ན། དེབ་འདིའི་རྩོམ་སྒྲིག་དང་། ཟིན་བྲིས་བཀོད་དེ་དཔེ་སྐྲུན་བྱ་རྒྱུ་ནི་བློ་ཡུལ་ལས་འདས་པ་ཞིག་ཡིན་སྐབས། འདིར་ཡི་གེར་འཁོད་ཡོད་པ་དང་འཁོད་མེད་པའི་དེབ་འདིའི་ལས་དོན་ཁག་ལ་ཐུགས་འཁུར་དང་རྒྱབ་སྐྱོར་གནང་མྱོང་བའི་མི་ཡོད་དགུ་རྣམས་ལ་སྙིང་ཐག་པ་ནས་ཐུགས་རྗེ་ཆེ་ཞུ་རྒྱུ་མ་ཟད། སྔོན་ཚུད་ནས་དེབ་འདིའི་མི་རིགས་མི་འདྲ་བ་དང་། རྒྱལ་ཁོངས་མི་འདྲ་བའི་གྲོགས་པོའམ་ཀློག་པ་པོ་རྣམས་ལ་བཀྲ་ཤིས་བདེ་ལེགས་ཞུའོ། །

སྒྲིག་པ་པོས་སྤྱི་ལོ་༡༩༨༩ལོའི་ཟླ་བ་༡༠པར་ལྷ་ས་ནས།

# 後　記

本書共收載寶貴的西藏歷史檔案及印章等文物107件，匯藏文、八思巴文、漢文、滿文、蒙文爲一體；首次公布的檔案文獻66份，其中61份由西藏自治區檔案館提供，5份由日喀則地區檔案館等提供。本書作爲一項艱巨的系統工程，是在中央政治局委員、國務委員李鐵映同志親自關懷下，由西藏自治區檔案館具體組織完成的。期間，得到了國家財政部門、中央檔案館、中央編譯局、國家檔案局、國家文物局、新聞出版署、中國社會科學院民族研究所、中國第一歷史檔案館、中國第二歷史檔案館、中國照片檔案館、西藏日喀則地區、西藏山南地區、西藏自治區文物管理委員會等熱情協助；得到了西藏自治區陳奎元書記、熱地主任、江村羅布主席、旦增副書記、陳漢昌常委、李立國秘書長和區經濟研究中心蕭懷遠主任等關心支持；得到了著名藏學家東嘎·洛桑赤列、霍康·索南邊巴、楚如·次旺南杰等多方指教。

本書總編、西藏自治區檔案館館長卓嘎女士等承擔了全書規劃設計、材料選擇、藏漢文字審校等多項任務；照那斯圖教授承擔了將元代八思巴文蒙古語聖旨等譯成漢文的任務；唯賽研究館員承擔了將元代藏文法旨等譯成漢文和將元代八思巴文聖旨等漢文譯文譯成藏文等任務；洛珠加措教授承擔了將元代以後部分藏、漢文檔案譯成漢文、藏文等任務；屈六生研究館員承擔了將清代滿文詔書譯成漢文等任務；崔思淦譯審、張宗熾譯審等承擔了將漢文書稿譯成英文的任務；徐梅江譯審承擔了英文譯文審校任務；徐文亮副研究館員、劉自和主任技師、孫之常攝影師和宋麗小姐等承擔了檔案原件的翻拍任務。參加本書調研、選材、拍照、翻譯、審校等工作的還有副研究館員熱振·益西楚臣、李國清、强巴班覺、阿旺曲達、慈仁杰布、洛桑更參及索朗格來、洛桑南杰、旺堆、依蘇、拉巴次仁、貢布次旦、王耀年先生等。

總而言之，如果離開了群體的智慧和力量以及上級有關部門的支持，本書的編纂、脱稿和出版是不可想象的。故借此，向見於文字或未見於文字的曾關心和支持過本書各項工作的所有的人們表示衷心感謝。并預祝本書的不同民族、不同國籍的讀者朋友吉祥如意。

編者1994年10月於拉薩

# POSTSCRIPT

This book is a collection of 107 photoprints of precious Tibetan historical archives, seals and other cultural relics, presented in Tibetan, Phags-pa Mongolian, Chinese, Manchu and Mongolian languages. Sixty-six archives are being made public for the first time. Among them, 61 archives are provided by the Archives of the Tibet Autonomous Region. and 5 are provided by the Xigaze Prefectural Archives of Tibet and others. This arduous task of systems engineering has been accomplished with the kindly care of Comrade Li Tieying, Member of the Political Bureau of the Central Committee of the Communist Party of China and State Councillor and under the concrete organization of the Archives of the Tibet Autonomous Region. We have obtained enthusiastic help from the financial department of the state, the Central Archives, the Central Translation Bureau, the State Archives Bureau, the State Bureau of Cultural Relics, the Press and Publication Administration of China, the Institute of Nationality Studies under the Chinese Academy of Social Sciences, China No.1 Historical Archives Museum, China No.2 Historical Archives Museum, China Photographic Archives Museum, Xigaze Prefecture of Tibet, Shannan Prefecture of Tibet, and the Historical Relics Administration of the Tibet Autonomous Region. We have received care and support of Chen Kuiyuan, Secretary of the Party Committee of the Tibet Autonomous Region; Ragdis, Chairman of the Standing Committee of the Regional People's Congress; Gyltshan Norbu, Chairman of the Regional People's Government; Tandzin, Deputy Secretary of the Regional Party Committee; Chen Hanchang, member of the Standing Committee of the Regional Party Committee; Li Liguo, Secretary-general of the Regional Party Committee; and Xiao Huaiyuan, Director of the Regional Economic Research Centre. We have also got a great deal of advice from such noted Tibetan scholars as Dungkar Lozang Phrinlas, Horkhang Sodnam Palpa and Khroru Tshewang Namgyal.

Ms Sgrolkar, the chief editor of this book and Director of the Archives of the Tibet Autonomous Region, and others are in charge of the planning, designing, selection of materials and examination and collation of the Tibetan and Chinese texts. Professor Jaguna Suthu translated imperial edicts and other documents of the Yuan Dynasty from classical Mongolian (Phags–pa script) into Chinese; Professor of Archives Science Vodzer translated Tibetan documents of the Yuan Dynasty into Chinese and Chinese translations of imperial edicts of the Yuan Dynasty in Phags–pa script into Tibetan; Professor Logros Gyatsho translated some of the Tibetan and Chinese archives dated after the Yuan Dynasty into Chinese and Tibetan; Professor of Archives Science Qu Liusheng translated documents of the Qing Dynasty from Manchu into Chinese; Professor of Translation Cui Sigan, Professor of Translation Zhang Zongchi and others translated the Chinese scripts into English; Professor of Translation Xu Meijiang went over all the English translations; Associate Professor of Archives Science Xu Wenliang, Senior Technician Liu Zihe, Photographer Sun Zhichang and Miss Song Li reproduced the original archives. Also taking part in the investigation and survey, selection of materials, photography, translation, editing, examination and collation were Associate Professor of Archives Science Ragreng Yeshes Tshalkhrim, Mr Li Guoqing, Mr Byampa Palbyor, Mr Ngagwang Chosdar, Mr Tshering Gyalpo, Mr Lozang Gyaltshan, Mr Sodnam Geleg, Mr Lozang Namgyal, Mr Wangdus, Mr Yesub, Mr Lhagpa Tshering, Mr Gonpo Tshetan and Mr Wang Yaonian.

In short, without the collective wisdom and teamwork and the support of the departments concerned, the compilation, completion and publication of this book would have been unthinkable. We would like to express our heartfelt thanks to all those who have been concerned about and supported the production of this book no matter their names have been mentioned or not in this postscript. Good luck and happiness to our readers of different nationalities around the globe!

The Editor, Lhasa, October 1994

མདུན་ཤོག་གི་ཡི་གེ་འབྲི་མཁན།　　ང་ཕོད་ངག་དབང་འཇིགས་མེད།
　　རྒྱལ་མཚན་ནོར་བུ།
མདུན་ཤོག་གི་འཆར་འགོད་མཁན།　　ཁྲིའུ་ཏེ་ཧུའུ།
རྩོམ་སྒྲིག་འགན་འཁུར་པ།　　ཧོང་ཝུན་ཁུན།
　　ལིའུ་ཞའོ་ཏའེ།
པར་སྐྲུན་འགན་འཁུར་པ།　　ལིའུ་ཅིང་ཧྲེང་།

封面題字　阿沛・阿旺晉美
　　江村羅布
封面設計　仇德虎
責任編輯　黄文昆
　　劉小黛
責任印製　劉京生

Inscriptions on the cover　Ngapoi Ngawang Jigmi
　　Gyltshan Norbu
Cover design　Qiu Dehu
Editors in charge　Huang Wenkun
　　Liu Xiaodai
Printing supervisor　Liu Jingsheng

（京）新登字056號

西藏歷史檔案薈粹

西藏自治區檔案館編

*

文物出版社出版發行

蛇口以琳彩印製版有限公司製版
中國環球（蛇口）印務有限公司印刷

1995年9月第一版　1995年9月第一次印刷
889×1194　1/16　印張：26
ISBN 7—5010—0876—0/K·376（精　裝）
ISBN 7—5010—0879—5/K·378（特精裝）